# The Pentateuch

## THE COMPLETE PORTRAIT
## OF THE MESSIAH

Volume 1

Other volumes in The Complete Portrait of the Messiah series

Volume 1: *The Pentateuch*
Volume 2: *The Gospels*
Volume 3: *The Historical Books*
Volume 4: *Acts*
Volume 5: *The Wisdom Books*
Volume 6: *Paul's Letters*
Volume 7: *The Major Prophets*
Volume 8: *General Letters*
Volume 9: *The Minor Prophets*
Volume 10: *Revelation*

Also available from Time to Revive and Laura Kim Martin

*reviveDAILY: A Devotional Journey from Genesis to Revelation, Year 1*
*reviveDAILY: A Devotional Journey from Genesis to Revelation, Year 2*

# The Pentateuch

## THE COMPLETE PORTRAIT
## OF THE MESSIAH

Volume 1

Kyle Lance Martin

Time to Revive and reviveSCHOOL

time to
revive
Richardson, Texas

*The Pentateuch*

Published in conjunction with
Iron Stream Media
100 Missionary Ridge
Birmingham, AL 35242
IronStreamMedia.com

Copyright © 2022 by Time to Revive

Library of Congress Control Number: 2022939215

978-1-63204-094-7 (hardback)
978-1-63204-095-4 (ebook)

1 2 3 4 5—25 24 23 22 21

# DEDICATION

Greetings friends and colaborers of the Lord Jesus Christ!

I am writing to you with an excitement that is beyond words. For I would like to dedicate this book to individuals like yourselves whose desire to grow closer to Jesus and go deeper in the Word of God brings such JOY to my heart. And my prayer for each one of you is that the Holy Spirit will reveal more of Himself to you in this in-depth time of studying the Word of God daily. Jesus said, "Blessed are those who hunger and thirst for righteousness, for they will be satisfied" (Matthew 5:6 NASB). So as you embark on this journey of studying each book of the Bible, may you experience a freshness and a fulfillment that can only come from the Spirit of God. You will have days that you won't want to wake up early and read. There will be moments when life throws you a situation that delays your personal devotional time with Him. But please press in and allow the Holy Spirit to strengthen your every step. This will allow you to exercise your faith muscles and walk out what you are learning in this. From my experience, obedience will bring education to life!

It will be quite a strenuous commitment, yet it's a part of an intentional strategy to equip the saints for His return. And your participation with revive-SCHOOL is a unique part of this preparation.

May the Lord receive all the glory, honor, and fame in this pursuit of righteousness.

Praying,
Dr. Kyle Lance Martin

# CONTENTS

**WEEK 13**

**WEEK 14**

**WEEK 15**

**WEEK 16**

# reviveSCHOOL History and Introduction

In January of 2015, our ministry, Time to Revive, was invited from our home base in Richardson, Texas, to Goshen, Indiana, to help equip the local church to learn how to go out and share the gospel in their community. We called it reviveINDIANA. During this frigid first trip in January, our intention was to help facilitate a week of prayer and outreach as a form of training, which we hoped would lead to an intentional week of outreach later that year. Little did we know that God had other plans.

The week of prayer and outreach started with about 450 people from various churches in the community and, to our surprise, quickly swelled to over 3,000. And by the end of that first week, the Holy Spirit confirmed to a group of us, including local pastors, that the Time to Revive team should stay for 52 straight days! Imagine the phone calls we had to make to our spouses telling them we were going to stay a "little" longer.

Over the course of these seven weeks, the local church witnessed God move in mighty ways, and each person involved could tell you miraculous testimonies of how they witnessed, firsthand, how God was moving. The 52 days culminated on March 4 of that year where an estimated 10,000 people showed up to brave the cold temperatures and go out and share the love of Jesus Christ.

All the while, word of this was spreading throughout the state, and it led to the Time to Revive team being invited to seven different cities in Indiana over the course of the next seven months. We continued to witness the local body of believers in these various communities encouraged and equipped to continue to take out their faith and share with others. The gospel wasn't intended to stay only in the church building. Jesus commissioned each one of us to go and make disciples in our own Jerusalem, Judea, and Samaria and to the ends of the earth. Back in Goshen, the local body continued to go out regularly after those initial 52 days while keeping track of the days since that first amazing week. A couple of years later in 2017, the local believers invited our team to celebrate their 1,000th day of outreach in their community. It was during that time when a local man shared with us a dream he had, which led us to start a two-year Bible study in the community. Similar to the Apostle Paul as he taught 12 disciples in Ephesus to study the Word of God on a daily basis, Time to Revive's desire was to also provide in-depth teaching that would focus on where the Messiah is found in every book of the Bible from Genesis to Revelation. We knew this would deepen their commitment to sharing the gospel as well as deepen their relationship with the Lord and with those whom they were discipling.

But when some became hardened and would not believe, slandering the Way in front of the crowd, he withdrew from them and met separately with the disciples, conducting discussions every day in the lecture hall of Tyrannus. —Acts 19:9

This local Bible study started with 12 men who signed up and committed to study the Word of God in a barn on a county road in Goshen, Indiana. And on January 1, 2018, we launched reviveSCHOOL with 54 men in this initial group. They studied the Scriptures daily, using the online resources, then gathered in the barn to discuss them in person. Each student studied the Bible daily using these resources:

• a Scripture reading plan to stay on track,
• a 29-minute teaching video (by Kyle Lance Martin, Indiana pastors, and TTR teachers),
• a devotion (written by Laura Kim Martin),
• reading guide questions to help facilitate discussion and critical thinking,
• lesson plans to summarize the daily teaching, and
• a painting of each book of the Bible by Mindi Oaten.

Upon the completion of the two-year study in the Word, Time to Revive celebrated over 200 students who had joined reviveSCHOOL with a graduation ceremony in January 2020. Plans were made for these individuals to take the Word and launch reviveSCHOOL groups not only in the United States but also throughout various nations. However, with worldwide travel restrictions due to the COVID-19 pandemic, this travel didn't happen. Thankfully, God had another plan, His plan was "above and beyond" all that Time to Revive could ask or think of (Ephesians 3:20–21).

With all the reviveSCHOOL materials already available online, the Holy Spirit spread the word to pastors and leaders of nations all throughout the world. Believers were hungry for biblically sound teaching and resources to grow closer to the Lord. As exemplified in Acts 19 with Paul and the disciples, and all the people of Asia, the Word of God through reviveSCHOOL truly spread—from a barn in Indiana to the nations.

And this went on for two years, so that all the inhabitants of Asia, both Jews and Greeks, heard the message about the Lord. —Acts 19:10

By God's grace, reviveSCHOOL has become an outlet for individuals to gain fresh insight into the Messiah all throughout the Scriptures, as well as to develop an understanding of the role of Israel from a biblical perspective.

I am humbled and honored that you would select reviveSCHOOL for your learning. When we started with 12 guys in a Bible study, we had no idea that revive-SCHOOL would be as far reaching as it has become. Our team would delight in knowing that you are studying the Word of God and using the resources with reviveSCHOOL. We pray that through these resources you will grow closer to the Lord and that you are inspired to walk out the plans that God has for your life by exposing others to the love of Christ.

To God be the glory!
Dr. Kyle Lance Martin

For further information about how to sign up for this two-year study in the Word of God or if you would like to launch a reviveSCHOOL group in your community, state/province, or country, please go online to www.reviveSCHOOL.org.

# How to Use This Bible Study Series

The Complete Portrait of the Messiah Bible study series contains multiple components for each lesson. These components work together to provide an in-depth study of how Jesus is revealed throughout the whole of Scripture. Below is a description of each component and how you can use each one to maximize your study experience.

## Teaching Notes & Video Lessons
The teaching notes summarize the main points of each video lesson and include a QR code to access the video teaching. If you have access to the internet via your phone or tablet, you can scan the QR code to watch the video lesson.

## The Daily Word Devotional
Dig deeper into personal application for each lesson through "The Daily Word" devotion. This day-by-day devotion encourages you with thoughts for application and further Scripture readings.

## Reading Guide Questions
These questions will guide you into a more detailed exploration of each lesson's content. Examine the concepts of the daily Scripture readings in more detail.

## The Bible Art Collection
This Bible study series is augmented by a one-of-a-kind, especially inspired series of original artwork created by artist Mindi Oaten. These 66 acrylic paintings creatively depict the revelation of Christ in each book of the Bible. Viewing each of these original art pieces will inspire and further enrich your understanding of Jesus throughout all of the Scriptures. These can be found at https://www.mindioaten.com/pages/mindi-oaten-art-bible-art-collection or https://www.reviveschool.org/

# About the Cover

*Genesis*
"The Promised Seed"

Artist Notes: Mindi Oaten

*In the beginning God created the heavens and the earth.* —Genesis 1:1

In Genesis, the first book of the Bible, we see the beginning of the *Seed*.\* Yet, I chose to focus on the Garden and the fall of man to begin this painting series. We entered God's plan in the Garden, walking with Him in the cool of the day. Then something went terribly wrong as man yielded to temptation, choosing to sin, which separated us from God. Mankind was expelled from the Garden and so began our life's journey apart from communion with God. Despite this disobedience, God had a plan to return us to that place of intimacy through Jesus Christ, the Promised *Seed* to come. Jesus, the *Seed*, was there in the beginning.

## The Apples

*The woman said to the serpent, "We may eat the fruit from the trees in the garden. But about the fruit of the tree in the middle of the garden, God said, 'You must not eat it or touch it, or you will die.'"*

*"No! You will not die," the serpent said to the woman. "In fact, God knows that when you eat it your eyes will be opened and you will be like God, knowing good and evil." Then the woman saw that the tree was good for food and delightful to look at, and that it was desirable for obtaining wisdom. So she took some of its fruit and ate it; she also gave some to her husband, who was with her, and he ate it. Then the eyes of both of them were opened, and they knew they were naked; so they sewed fig leaves together and made loincloths for themselves.* —Genesis 3:2–7

Not really thinking about it, I chose to paint two apples, one whole and one bitten. Prophetically, the whole apple represents first love, relationship, and union, whereas the bitten apple represents division and the nature of sin. In Scripture, the number two is symbolic of union. God designed union when He created us to have an intimate relationship with Him in the Garden of Eden. The relational and physical union created between a man and a woman symbolizes the spiritual union of Christ and His bride, the Church. The number two can also represent separation or division, as well as good and evil. In Genesis, Adam and Eve were forced to leave the Garden, separating us from intimacy with God when they chose to eat the forbidden fruit. Here, division entered the world. By going deeper, we see the "first" Adam brought separation and division into the world, while the "second" Adam, Jesus Christ the Messiah, reestablished intimate union by bringing us back into a right relationship with God through redemption and eternal life. The number two is used with prophetic representation throughout the Scriptures. Even the entirety of God's testimony is divided into two sections, the Old and the New Testament.

## The Garden Below

*So the LORD God sent him away from the garden of Eden to work the ground from which he was taken. He drove man out and stationed the cherubim and the flaming, whirling sword east of the garden of Eden to guard the way to the tree of life.* —Genesis 3:23–24

As I was praying about what to paint, God showed me a picture of the Garden below the surface. He spoke to me about the Garden still being with us; it's just not in plain sight. There's been a separation, but it's still accessible through Christ, the Promised *Seed*. In the painting, the flowers below the surface represent this separation from God after Eve and Adam ate of the fruit from the tree of life. Walking with the Lord gives us daily access to the Garden until Jesus returns, establishing His kingdom, a new heaven and new earth. As a symbol that He is always with us, God instructed me to paint an aspect of the Garden in each painting of the Bible.

## The Seed and New Sprout: Hope

*I will put hostility between you and the woman,*
*and between your seed and her seed.*
*He will strike your head,*
*and you will strike his heel.*
—Genesis 3:15

I painted a seed that fell into soil from the core of the apple. Spiritually, the seed represents Christ. As a physical seed is planted in the woman to bear a child, God's plan for redemption is the *Seed* that will come through chosen generations. This *Seed*, the Messiah, was foretold in Isaiah 7:14: "Therefore, the Lord himself will give you a sign. Behold, the virgin shall conceive and bear a son, and shall call his name Immanuel" (ESV).

*In reviveSCHOOL, the theme name for Jesus in Genesis is *Seed*.

# Lesson 1: Genesis 1—3
*Seed*: The *Seed* of the Woman Is Jesus!

## Teaching Notes

### Intro

Over the course of 730 days, we're going to give you a picture of what Christ looks like in all 66 books of the Bible. We're not going to go over everything in the Scriptures . . . it's too much. We're going to focus on where we see the Messiah in these passages. It will be like a puzzle. What I'm after is that you actually get the picture, one piece at a time, of who the Messiah really is. How does all the stuff in the Old Testament point to Christ in the New Testament? You've got the pre-incarnate Christ (when Jesus showed up in the Old Testament), the type and antitypes (such as when Jesus is compared to the light), and the foreshadowed Christ (such as Adam in Genesis, the first Adam, who was a foreshadow of the second Adam—Jesus).

We want to focus in on the image of Jesus throughout the Scriptures. For each book, we're going to give you one word. And at the end of the study, you're going to have 66 words that paint a picture of the Messiah throughout the entire Bible.

### Teaching

For the entire book of Genesis, as we focus on Jesus, we're going to see Him as the *Seed*. When the fall of man took place, God still had an answer. It is the *Seed*, Christ.

*Genesis 1—3*: In Genesis 1, the details of the seven days of creation are given. In Genesis 2, both man and woman are created. In Genesis 3, we'll take the discussion a little deeper. After the woman had eaten from the fruit of the tree and given it to the man to eat, "So the Lord God asked the woman, 'What is this you have done?'" (v. 13). And she blamed the serpent (v. 14).

God cursed the serpent. Some people believe that before the curse, snakes had arms and legs.[1] Whether God took away arms and legs or a voice or not, the

---

[1] See the interesting discussion "Did the Serpent Originally Have Legs" by Bodie Hodge, Answers in Genesis, January 26, 2010, https://answersingenesis.org/genesis/garden-of-eden/did-the-serpent-originally-have-legs/.

serpent was forced to move on its belly and eat dust all the days of its life. Then God moved on to curse the others who followed the seed of the serpent (v. 15). God created enmity, which means a state of feeling actively opposed and hostile toward someone or something, between the woman and the serpent. There is always strife—it doesn't stop!

Why? Why was there hostility? Because the woman and the man had taken a bite of the fruit that God told them not to. Because they disobeyed God, there's going to be hostility. Hostility would therefore exist between the serpent and the woman, and between the *Seed* of the woman and the seed of the serpent. The *Seed* of the woman will strike the serpent's head, and the serpent will strike His heel. There's going to be a battle between Satan and the *Seed* of the woman, who is Jesus. There's always going to be a battle.

*Ephesians 6:10-14*: "Finally, be strengthened by the Lord and by His vast strength. Put on the full armor of God so that you can stand against the tactics of the Devil" (vv. 10-11). The whole goal of Satan was to deceive the woman and attack everything Jesus stands for. "For our battle is not against flesh and blood, but against the rulers, against the authorities, against the world powers of this darkness, against the spiritual forces of evil in the heavens. This is why you must take up the full armor of God" (vv. 12–14). As we go through this school, when you understand that every day is a battle, you've already won half of it. So, what does this mean, the whole idea that the *Seed* of the woman will crush the serpent?

*Hebrews 2:14*: "Now since the children have flesh and blood in common, Jesus also shared in these, so that through His death He might destroy the one holding the power of death—that is, the Devil." Jesus totally trumped Satan by dying on the cross. Even though the battle began with a bite of fruit in the garden, God had already put in the *Seed*, Christ, for His answer!

*Romans 16:20a*: "The God of peace will soon crush Satan under your feet." In this battle that is raging, eventually Jesus will defeat Satan and—boom—it will be over. But we're not there yet. Even though Jesus died, was buried, and rose again, it isn't until Jesus comes back again that Satan will be ultimately finished. Right now, he functions as god of this air. The question is, "Will we give in to the seed of the serpent, or will we function in the *Seed*, Christ?"

*Galatians 3:19*: This verse talks about the *Seed*. Why was the Law—Genesis, Exodus, Leviticus, Numbers, Deuteronomy—given? Because of Adam and Eve's sin, we needed the Law. It's the parameters that we need to function within. Pastor Tony Evans describes the Law as a football field. God sets the parameters. He creates the boundaries of the field. But we have the free will. The Law was given until the *Seed* would come. So, has the *Seed* come? Or are we still waiting?

In Paul's context, Jesus had already come, so we're not under the Law anymore. Since He's come, the Law is no longer our driving force. So how do we know the *Seed* was Jesus?

*Galatians 3:16*: The "*Seed* of the Woman" is Jesus! When we believe in the death, burial, and Resurrection of Jesus, we have the *Seed*, Christ. I have to tell you, that's the only way we get through life. When you have the *Seed*, Christ, you can overcome the seed of the serpent anytime. In fact, when you have the *Seed*, Christ, you've already won!

*1 Corinthians 15:56-57*: Paul explained how the seed of the serpent, death, no longer has a sting. Now the sting of death is sin, the power of sin is Law. But thanks be to God who gives the victory through Jesus Christ. He is our *Seed*!

# Closing

The *Seed* that is deposited in Genesis 3:15 will become our thread all the way through Genesis. We want to talk about Christ in the Scriptures so that we can overcome the temptation and the sin that was set in place because of the seed of the serpent with Adam and Eve. John Walvoord, the late president of Dallas Theological Seminary, said: "A ray of light is provided in the Adamic Covenant because God promised a Redeemer that would come." That Redeemer is the *Seed*, Christ, in Genesis 3:15.

## The Daily Word

Every day is a battle between the two seeds—Satan and Jesus. How does this battle between Satan and Jesus affect your walk with Christ today? The enemy comes to steal, kill, and destroy.

As you walk with Jesus through the everyday battles, remember the victory belongs to the Lord Jesus; He is our God of peace.

**The LORD God said, "Since man has become like one of Us, knowing good and evil." —Genesis 3:22**

Further Scripture: John 10:10; Ephesians 6:10–11; 1 Corinthians 15:54–57

# Questions

1. What was Jesus' role in creation? (John 1:1, 3; Colossians 1:16)

2. How is "light" in creation (Genesis 1:3) a foreshadowing of Christ? (Psalm 27:1; John 1:5-10; 8:12; 2 Corinthians 4:6)

3. How is Christ the second Adam? (Romans 5:14–19; 1 Corinthians 15:45–47)

4. What/Who is the "seed" in Genesis 3:15? (Galatians 3:16,19; 4:4; Hebrews 2:14)

5. In Genesis 3:21, what did God cover Adam and Eve's nakedness with? How does this foreshadow Christ? (Leviticus 17:11; Hebrews 9:22; 10:1–18)

6. What did the Holy Spirit highlight to you in Genesis 1—3 through the reading or the teaching?

# Lesson 2: Genesis 4—6
## *Seed*: The Gift of the Firstborn

## Teaching Notes

### Review

Yesterday, in Genesis 1—3, we saw Jesus in Genesis as the *Seed*. Genesis 3:15 states, "I will put hostility between you and the woman, and between your seed and her *Seed*. He will strike your head, and you will strike his heel." The first Messianic prophecy was found in the fall of man.

### Teaching

For the entire book of Genesis, as we focus on Jesus, we're going to see Him as the *Seed*. When the fall of man took place, God still had an answer. It is the *Seed*.

*Genesis 4:1–2*: Eve conceived and gave birth to Cain. Some of us get stuck in sin, and we don't move forward; but Adam and Eve knew there was hope, so they moved forward and had a child. Eve gave birth to a second son, Abel, who became a shepherd of the flock. Cain cultivated the land; he became a farmer. Since names are important in Scripture, we should note that "Cain" means to acquire or to possess. A literal English translation would be "got." "Abel" can be translated as "breath," meaning short-lived.

*Genesis 4:3–4*: In Genesis 3:15, we first noted two different seeds. In this passage, there are two different types of seeds functioning here. Cain as a farmer presented *some* of the land's produce as an offering to the Lord, but he held back. Abel on his part gave the firstborn. He did not hold back. God saw the heart behind what they presented; He saw their motives. In his offering, Cain personified Isaiah 29:13: "The Lord said: Because these people approach Me with their mouths to honor Me with lip-service—yet their hearts are far from Me, and their worship consists of man-made rules learned by rote." Cain asked, "What can I get by with?" So you have the seed of the serpent functioning with Cain. He was reproducing that spiritual enmity with God. And in Abel, you see the *Seed* of the woman (the Messiah), the love of God.

This is constantly the tension we have to go against: Do we want to function as a seed of the woman, knowing we have the *Seed*, Christ? Or do we function as the seed of the serpent, always trying to go against God and get away with whatever we can?

In Scripture, the firstborn is important. Exodus 34:19 says, "The firstborn male from every womb belongs to Me, including all your male livestock, the firstborn of cattle or sheep." Deuteronomy 12:6 says, "You are to bring there your burnt offerings and sacrifices, your tenths and personal contributions, your vow offerings and freewill offerings, and the firstborn of your herds and flocks." You are supposed to give the best to the Lord, not what you can get away with.

Abel was willing to give everything he could to his Father because he realized it was an offering to the Lord. Your life is not yours if you have the *Seed*, Christ, in you. Yet for some reason we think that each day we can choose whether we live for ourselves or the Lord. Walter Kaiser Jr. said, "God always inspects the giver and the worshiper before He inspects the gift, service, or worship."[1] I want us to have pure motives as we do everything in the reviveSCHOOL. When we do that, God will honor that!

*1 Corinthians 15:20:* "But now Christ has been raised from the dead, the first-fruits of those who have fallen asleep." Abel was presenting a foreshadowing of Christ as he offered the firstfruits.

*1 Corinthians 15:21–22:* "For since death came through a man, the resurrection of the dead also comes through a man. For as in Adam all die, so also in Christ all will be made alive." When you function in the spirit of the seed of the serpent, you die; but when you function in the spirit of the *Seed*, Christ, you live!

*1 Corinthians 15:23–25:* "But each in his own order: Christ, the firstfruits; afterward, at His coming, those who belong to Christ. Then comes the end, when He hands over the kingdom to God the Father, when He abolishes all rule and all authority and power. For He must reign until He puts all His enemies under His feet." It starts with the firstfruits.

*1 Corinthians 15:26–29:* "The last enemy to be abolished is death. For God has put everything under [Jesus'] feet. But then it says 'everything' is put under [Jesus] it is obvious that [God] who puts everything under [Jesus] is the exception. And everything is subject to Christ, then the Son Himself will also be subject to [God]

---

[1] Walter C. Kaiser Jr. et al., *Hard Sayings of the Bible* (Downers Grove, IL: InterVarsity, 1996), 101.

who subjected everything to [Jesus], so that God may be all in all." It starts with Christ as the *Seed*. When we consider the picture of Abel, then Christ, all of a sudden, is the first fruit.

*Genesis 4:5–7*: God didn't have regard for Cain and his offering. But God effectively told Cain, "If you do what is right, you will be accepted" (v. 7). Here's what I love about how God works. Even though Cain messed up, God gave him a second chance! If you do what is right, you will be accepted. God gave Cain a way out. All we have to do is humble ourselves and admit we are wrong. According to Isaiah 66:2, "My hand made all these things, and so they all came into being. This is the LORD's declaration. I will look favorably on this kind of person: one who is humble, submissive in spirit, and trembles at My word." God accepts those who are humble and submissive in spirit.

Cain murdered his brother because he functioned in the seed of the serpent. Proverbs 28:13 states: "The one who conceals his sins will not prosper, but whoever confesses and renounces them will find mercy." Praise the Lord for second chances (James 4:8)! Seasons of refreshing come from the presence of the Lord (Acts 3:19). Do you know how that happens? It happens through the firstfruits. God sent Jesus Christ as our firstfruits. And how is He the firstfruits? Because He is the *Seed* that we know was the answer to overcome all of this.

## Closing

It wasn't about what Cain gave; it was about his heart condition. Cain was still giving something, but he was thinking more about himself. Jude 1:11–13 warns, "Woe to them! For they have traveled in the way of Cain . . . these are the ones who are like dangerous reefs at your love feasts . . . nurturing only themselves without fear. They are like waterless clouds carried along by winds; trees in late autumn—fruitless, twice dead, pulled out by the roots," These are the ones who are dangerous . . . they are fruitless.

We have to start being careful of people in the Church. If we want to change culture, we can't be about ourselves. We have to be about Him! We have to bring the *best* to the table. The whole book of Jude is about warning people that it's not going to get better. We have to contend for the faith. According to 1 John 3:11–13, "For this is the message you have heard from the beginning: We should love one another, unlike Cain, who was of the evil one and murdered his brother. And why did he murder him? Because his works were evil, and his brother's works were righteous. Do not be surprised, brothers, if the world hates you." We should love one another, unlike Cain, who was of the evil one.

When you have the *Seed*, Christ, you have love for God and love for others. When you have the seed of the serpent, like Cain, you think of yourself.

Don't be surprised if the world hates you. What I really believe is happening is that as the Lord is coming, if you function in righteousness and bring the first-fruits, the world will hate you. If you bring the firstfruits, which is Christ, to the table, then you've got nothing to lose because your life isn't yours anyway.

Abel brought his best. It was a foreshadowing of Christ being the best. Don't bring the leftovers. It's an interesting picture in Genesis 1—6: the seed and the firstfruits all point to Christ.

## The Daily Word

The Lord calls believers to check their hearts. Ask yourself, "Am I walking with a seed of Cain, having evil motives, or am I walking with a seed of Abel, having righteous motives?" The Lord longs for you to live with a pure heart. Then you will see Him. May you hold nothing back from the Lord so you may see all God has for you!

**The Lord had regard for Abel and his offering, but He did not have regard for Cain and his offering. —Genesis 4:4–5**

Further Scripture: Psalm 26:2; Psalm 51:10; Matthew 5:8

## Questions

1. In Genesis 4:3–4, what is the difference between Cain and Abel's offerings to the Lord? Knowing that the Lord looks at the heart (Isaiah 29:13), what would an offering like Abel's look like in your life?

2. In Genesis 4:1–12, how is Abel and his offering a foreshadowing of Christ? (Hebrews 11:4; 1 Corinthians 15:20, 23)

3. Whose seed does Cain carry, and whose seed does Abel carry? (1 John 3:12; Jude 11–13)

4. The Lord gave Cain a second chance in Genesis 4:6 and kept him from death in Genesis 4:13–15. What does this reveal about God's character?

5. In what ways does Jesus' blood surpass that of Abel's? (Hebrews 12:24; Ephesians 5:2)

6. What did the Holy Spirit highlight to you in Genesis 4—6 through the reading or the teaching?

# Lesson 3: Genesis 7—9
*Seed*: God's Judgment and Redemption: The Flood

## Teaching Notes

### Intro

In Genesis 1—3, we saw the first mention of the *Seed*, the Messiah, with Genesis 3:15 assuring us we have hope in the *Seed*, Christ. Genesis 4—6 recorded the account of Cain the farmer and his brother, Abel the rancher. Cain committed the first murder when he slew his brother, and sin continued to affect humanity.

### Teaching

We will study Genesis 7—9. Ongoing sin had gotten so bad that in Genesis 7, God was ready to destroy the whole world.

*Genesis 7:13*: "On that same day Noah along with his sons Shem, Ham, and Japheth, Noah's wife, and his three sons' wives entered the ark with him." This is probably one of the most significant moments in all of history. Eight people entered the ark. These eight lived, and everyone else died. In Genesis 8, the flood recedes, and in Genesis 8:16, God spoke to Noah: "Come out of the ark." How cool is this: the *Seed*, Christ, continued through one of these eight people. How do we know? Because in Genesis 3:15, we have the promise that the lineage will continue, that the *Seed*, the Messiah, will crush the head of Satan.

*Genesis 8:21*: "When the Lord smelled the pleasing aroma, He said to Himself, 'I will never again curse the ground because of man, even though man's inclination is evil from his youth. And I will never again strike down every living thing as I have done." At this point, God said He would never again bring about a massive flood and destroy everyone. It's a beautiful picture and we'll get into this with the covenant. I want to focus specifically on Genesis 9:1–29 for the remainder of this lesson.

*Genesis 9:1*: "God blessed Noah and his sons and said to them, 'Be fruitful and multiply and fill the earth.'" This is a common phrase we hear from God in Genesis. In Genesis 1:28, we've already heard this. God told Adam and Eve,

"Be fruitful, multiply, fill the earth, and subdue it." In Genesis 8:17, God said to Noah, "Bring out all the living creatures that are with you . . . and they will spread over the earth and be fruitful and multiply on the earth." In Genesis 9:7, God told Noah and his sons: "But you, be fruitful and multiply; spread out over the earth and multiply on it." All of humanity had been destroyed except eight people, so God was saying he needed them to multiply.

*Genesis 9:2–4*: "The fear and terror of you will be in every living creature on the earth." The animals were put under the authority of man. This was a first: God gave meat to humanity for eating. "However, you must not eat meat with its life-blood in it" (v. 4). This command was meant to instill respect for the sacredness of life. Leviticus 17:11 explained, "For the life of a creature is in the blood." This is a foreshadowing of Christ and what's to come. I love this picture because it points to Christ in the New Testament on the cross. His blood is the lifeline for all of us! Blood is a symbol of life.

*Genesis 9:5* This verse is an explanation of why God gave these rules and regulations. He was starting all over with these eight people. This was a picture of capital punishment. God wants us to value life. Tom Constable said that it's important for us to value life because there are seven layers to a person: (1) spiritual; (2) personal; (3) moral; (4) relational; (5) rational; (6) emotional; and (7) creative.[1] All these things are entailed in life. So when you take someone's life, you're taking the image of God and crushing it. Author Elmer Gray wrote: "A person extinguishes a revelation of God when he or she murders somebody."[2] This was the first time God established a divine structure for government. In Romans 13:4, Paul explained that government is God's source for bringing good; government is God's servant.

*Genesis 9:6*: "For God made man in His image." This is why it's so important! Remember those seven things we talked about? Those are all a reflection of God!

*Genesis 9:7*: "But you, be fruitful and multiply." Nancy Pearcey explained: "'Be fruitful and multiply,' means to develop the *social* world: build families, churches, schools, cities, governments, laws . . . 'subdue the earth' means to harness the *natural* world: plant crops, build bridges, design computers, compose music . . .

---

[1] Thomas L. Constable, *Thomas Constable's Notes on the Bible: Volume 1: Genesis-Deuteronomy* (Hurst, TX: Tyndale Seminary Press, 2010).

[2] Elmer L. Gray, "Capital Punishment in the Ancient Near East," *Biblical Illustrator* 13:1 (Fall 1986): 65–67; quoted in Thomas L. Constable, *Expository Notes of Dr. Thomas Constable: Genesis*, 152, https://planobiblechapel.org/tcon/notes/pdf/genesis.pdf.

to create culture, build civilizations."[3] The problem is that we have let those who don't have the *Seed*, Christ, take over and determine culture. We were the ones God intended to build culture. But we're letting the seed of the serpent take over.

*Genesis 9:8–11*: This is the Noahic Covenant, for Noah and all of his descendants. God covers everything . . . a covenant for all living things! The Hebrew word for rainbow is *qeset*, which means "battle bow." God was saying the battle was over. God would no longer destroy by a flood. But what's happened is that some individuals in America have taken this rainbow, this sign of God's promise not to destroy us, as permission to do whatever they want, and they are abusing God's mercy to the point that they don't care anymore.

*Genesis 9:12–17*: The rainbow is a blessing for us. It is a reminder to us even today of God's promise.

*Genesis 9:18*: Ham was the youngest son (recorded in Genesis 9:24). He was the father of Canaan. There's discussion about which son was the oldest, Shem or Japheth. Noah was a cultivator of the vineyard. Noah got drunk and, while by himself, was uncovered, naked, in the tent.

*Genesis 9:22–25*: Ham saw Noah naked and told Shem and Japheth. Then Shem and Japheth walked backwards and placed the cloak over their father (they couldn't see their father naked). We don't know for sure what Ham did, but it certainly seems it was more than just seeing his father naked because of what we see in verses 24–25. There's discussion (among scholars) that there must have been some sort of sexual perversion that took place.

Ham was the father of Canaan, and he was cursed to be the lowest of the slaves to his brothers. This was the first time that man cursed man. Prophetically, this was fulfilled. The descendants of Ham became slaves/forced labor for Solomon in 1 Kings 9:20–21. Rahab was a Canaanite and the only one who was an exception to this curse because she helped Joshua and Caleb, the two Jericho spies. Genesis 10:6–10 provided the list of Ham's four sons: Cush, Egypt, Put, and Canaan. They functioned in godless and worldly power. The Canaanites were not good people, and we see the seed of the serpent functioning in Ham's life. The Philistines, the Assyrians, and the Babylonians also came from the lineage of Ham (Psalm 105:23).

---

[3] Nancy Pearcey, *Total Truth: Liberating Christianity from Its Cultural Captivity* (Wheaton, IL: Crossway Books, 2004), 47.

*Genesis 9:26*: Next, Noah spoke into Shem: "Praise the Lord, the God of Shem, Canaan will be his slave." Shem was the ancestor of all of the sons of Eber (Genesis 10:21). "Shem" actually meant "name." Eber was the original root word for Hebrew. The first Hebrew identified in the Bible was Abraham! Shem carried on the lineage of the *Seed*, the Messiah.

*Genesis 9:27*: Canaan was a slave to Shem and Japheth. These verses say that Japheth would dwell in the tents of Shem. Japheth had seven sons. If Japheth shared in the tents of Shem, what do you think that means? Yes, they lived together. Japheth produced the Indo-European peoples. Do you know what this really means? The Gentiles! If Shem was the father of the Hebrews (the Jews, the Semites), and Japheth was the father of the Gentiles, then this meant the Gentiles would dwell in the tents of the Jews. Canaanites carry the seed of the serpent— they do not walk with the Lord.

Although this isn't dogmatic, it's an incredible picture. In Acts 15:7, the gospel was shared with the Gentiles. Gentiles were given the opportunity to be a part of what was originally intended for the tent of Shem. Romans 15:16 records just one of the times when Paul stated his calling to take the gospel to the Gentiles. God knew what He was doing, even after the flood. God's plan for the Gentiles was even apparent in Noah's blessing to his three sons (Galatians 2:2). Over and over, the Gentiles were given an opportunity to hear and respond to the gospel. The Gentiles were given a chance because Noah blessed Japheth. Noah blessed Shem. And Noah cursed Ham.

## Closing

Luke 3:23–38 records the lineage of Christ back to Adam . . . what started from Adam to Seth . . . to Noah to Shem . . . to Christ. Because of Noah blessing his son Shem, the *Seed*, Christ, continued. The *Seed* of the woman continued to fight against the seed of the serpent. And somewhere in this, Japheth was grafted into the tent of Shem. All because a father blessed and cursed his sons.

## The Daily Word

Even back in the days when the Lord wiped out the entire earth with a flood, the Lord thought of you and desired to reach you with the gospel. Therefore He preserved Noah and his family so the *Seed* could continue.

There may be moments when you feel as though your current situation has no purpose, but trust that the Lord had a plan for you, even before the beginning of time: a plan for the *Seed*, Christ, to penetrate your life so you could know and receive His love. The Lord even gave us a rainbow to remind us of the promise of His everlasting love between Him and His people.

I am bringing a flood—floodwaters on the earth to destroy every creature under heaven with the breath of life in it. Everything on earth will die. But I will establish My covenant with you, and you will enter the ark with your sons, your wife, and your sons' wives. —Genesis 6:17–18

Further Scripture: Genesis 9:16; Psalm 139:13–14; Jeremiah 29:11

## Questions

1. According to Genesis 7:13, how many people escaped the flood, and why were they able to escape? How does this paint a picture of who will escape the "coming flood"—the coming of the Son of Man? (2 Peter 2:5; 3:5–7)

2. In what ways were the days of Noah similar and different from the coming of the Son of Man? (Matthew 24:36–39; Luke 17:26–27)

3. How does the ark and flood foreshadow salvation and baptism? (1 Peter 3:20–21)

4. What is the Noahic covenant, and what did God choose as the symbol for this covenant? (Genesis 9:8–17)

5. Noah's curse to one of his sons in Genesis 9:25 was the first man-to-man curse. Which son did he curse? Why? (Genesis 9:18–25)

6. Noah blessed two of his sons in Genesis 9:26–27. In Luke 3:36, one of Noah's blessed sons is listed in the genealogy of Jesus. Which son is listed? How does this tell us in which one of Noah's sons the *Seed* of the woman, Christ, resided?

7. What did the Holy Spirit highlight to you in Genesis 7—9 through the reading or the teaching?

# Lesson 4: Genesis 10—12
*Seed*: God's Promises to Abraham

## Teaching Notes

### Review

When Adam and Eve ate the fruit, sin entered the world. The *Seed*, Christ, was promised in Genesis 3:15, meaning we have hope because Jesus will come and crush Satan. In Genesis 4—6, through the story of Cain and Abel, the *Seed* of the woman and the seed of the serpent continued to battle. In Genesis 7—9, God chose Noah's family to survive the flood. Afterward, God told them to be fruitful and multiply. But Ham, who became the father of Canaan, went wrong, creating division in the family. Noah cursed Ham but blessed Shem, who was in the lineage of Abram.

### Teaching

*Genesis 11:27–29*: Following the record of Shem's lineage (v. 10), Terah fathered Abram, Nahor, and Haran. So Abram, as one of Terah's three sons, was in the lineage of Shem (v. 27). Haran died in his native land while his father, Terah, was still alive (v. 28). Abram's wife was Sarai. Nahor's wife was Milcah, the daughter of Haran (Nahor married his niece). Before his death, Haran had three children: Milcah, Iscah, and Lot. In verse 29, Abram married his half-sister, Sarai, daughter of Terah by another wife (Genesis 20:12).

*Genesis 11:30*: Sarai was barren. Now this was important because the *Seed* had been passed down from Adam to Seth to Noah to Shem to Terah (Luke 3:23–38). Interestingly, this whole family worshiped the moon god. The name Terah could literally mean "moon." These people didn't have a background in the Lord.

*Genesis 11:31*: Terah took Lot, Abram, and Sarai and headed to the land of Canaan. But on the way there, they settled in Haran instead. They didn't even make it to their goal. Have you ever been called to something and stopped before you got there? I think the church is hearing constantly from the Holy Spirit, but when we're asked to do something, we'd rather stop in our "Harans" because it's more comfortable. It feels more right to be comfortable in Haran rather than to do something radical. But God knew there was something special with the young man Abram, whose family worshipped a moon god. For some reason, God elected Abram for a special call in his life. God has a special plan for your future! You have to be OK with the fact that He's chosen you to do this. That's a part of the *Seed*.

God chose Abram to carry out the *Seed* that began in Genesis 3:15. God knew Abram was a man of faith. Hebrews 11 is known as the Heroes of Faith. In this chapter, most heroes got one verse. Moses got six verses. But Abram got 12 verses; he truly is the Father of Faith. Abram became the father of three religions: Judaism, Islam, and Christianity.

*Genesis 12*: In this chapter, we're going to learn about faith and that despite our flaws, God can use us. As a matter of fact, we're going to see that Abram messed up at times. Second Timothy 2:13 is the reminder, "If we are faithless, He remains faithful, for He cannot deny Himself." God will bring His plan to fruition, even if we're faithless.

*Genesis 12:1–3*: How does this little nugget of treasure in Genesis 12:1–3 paint a picture of the Messiah? After Abram's father Terah died, God told Abram to leave his father's house and go to the land God would show him. In Genesis 11, Terah originally headed for the land of Canaan; maybe that was part of Abram's calling. But they stopped short. When Terah died, Abram was released, and God called him to go. Verse 2 records God's promise to Abram to make his name great. Abram, who possibly grew up worshipping the moon god, suddenly heard from God! In verse 3, God promised that the people on earth would be blessed through Abram. Remember the *Seed*? The *Seed* went from Shem all the way to Terah, and then it continued to Abram.

One man, Abram, would see seven things radically lived out—maybe in his lifetime or maybe after. You will be given *land*. God promised Abram in Genesis 12:7: "I will give this land to your offspring." That land was Canaan, where the descendants of Ham, the cursed son, lived. There would be hostility when Abram went into this land (Hebrews 11:8–10; Genesis 12:1–3).

Abram built an altar there to the Lord who had appeared to him (v. 7). I believe this was the pre-incarnate Lord Jesus Christ who appeared to Abram before He was born in Bethlehem. How do we know that this was the pre-incarnate Christ? It can't be 100 percent proven, but in Genesis 17 and Genesis 18, Jesus showed up to Abraham. Every time Abram encountered Him, the relationship grew.

Exodus 33:21 says, "You cannot see My face, for no one can see Me and live." This verse refers to God the Father (Exodus 33:12-23; John 1:18). I believe that over and over in the Old Testament, God the Son showed up. We can't prove it for sure, but in John 8:56, Jesus said, "Your father Abraham was overjoyed that he would see My day; he saw it and rejoiced."

You will become a *great nation*. Abram's wife was barren, but God promised to make him into a great nation. Hebrews 11:12 explains: "Therefore from one man—in fact, from one as good as dead—came offspring as numerous as the stars of heaven and as innumerable as the grains of sand by the seashore."

Your *name will be great*. Look at Genesis 23:6. Eventually, you know what happened? Abram was buried amongst the kings.

You will be *blessed*. God promised Abram His favor for his lifetime. Psalm 30:5: "For His anger lasts only a moment, but His favor, a lifetime." Abram was a friend of God. Three different times, Abraham was called a friend of God (2 Chronicles 20:7; Isaiah 41:8; James 2:23). For every single one of you who has the *Seed*, Christ, in you, you are a friend of God! This blessing came because Abram was obedient.

*Genesis 22:17–18*: "I will indeed bless you . . . because you have obeyed My command." That's the challenge in the church today! You want to be blessed? Be obedient.

You will *be a blessing*. People interacted with Abram, and they were blessed because of it. Psalm 1:3 states: "He is like a tree planted beside streams of water that bears its fruit in season and whose leaf does not wither. Whatever he does prospers." I think this was a picture of Abram. The fruit from Abram was a blessing to *others*. Our fruit is a blessing to *others*.

*Bless those who bless you and curse those who treat you with contempt*. Pharaoh took Sarai as his wife, and his whole household was cursed. Abimilech took Sarai as his wife, and the same thing happened to him (Genesis 20). Don't mess with Abram and his people!

Every time the American presidency has made a decision against Israel, something bad has happened to America. For example, as depicted in the movie *The Perfect Storm*, as soon as President Bush made a decision about how to work with Israel and the settlements in the land, the perfect storm came and actually took out his vacation home in Kennebunkport, Maine. Every time we've decided to take land away from Israel or made a decision against Israel, something bad has come to America and/or its leaders. Genesis 12:3 is still relevant today! Please don't compromise the land and the people of Israel!

*All peoples will be blessed*. Abram received the *Seed*. The *Seed* went from Shem, eventually to Terah, and then to Abram. Remember, the people of Japheth were blessed through Shem and would "dwell in the tents of Shem" (Genesis 9:27). They would be grafted in and blessed through Abram. Ultimately, this blessing comes through one person: All the peoples of the earth will be blessed through the Messiah (Galatians 3:16–19a).

# Closing

The promise in Genesis 12:1–3 eventually points to Christ . . . all because of Abram's faith, despite his flaws, our Messiah came to earth. And whether you believe it or not, that very *Seed*, possibly Christ Himself, came and spoke that very promise to Abram! It happened because Abram overcame his fear and went by faith. C. S. Lewis said, "If I find in myself a desire which no experience in this world can satisfy, the most probable explanation is that I was made for another world."[1]

Abram continued to go to where God called him, and God continued to unfold the promise. I believe Abram 100 percent knew he was meant for another place. Scripture tells us so in Hebrews 11:8–10. And because of that, all of us— Jews and Gentiles—have the opportunity to be blessed through the Messiah, Jesus Christ.

## The Daily Word

The Lord blessed Abram to carry the *Seed*, Christ, even though at the time it didn't make sense because Abram's wife Sarai was barren. The Lord promised to make Abram a great nation, and Abram walked the promise of God out in faith.

You may ask yourself: "How am I going to walk out my calling?" The Word of the Lord says to not fear and that you are called by name. No matter what you pass through, the Lord will be with you. Walk out your calling, knowing with confidence that the Lord is with you!

**I will make you into a great nation, I will bless you, I will make your name great, and you will be a blessing. —Genesis 12:2**

Further Scripture: Isaiah 43:1–2; Isaiah 41:10; Hebrews 11:8

# Questions

1. Terah, Abram, Sarai, Lot, and Haran were headed to Canaan, but they ended up settling in Haran. Why do you think the family stopped in Haran instead of continuing to Canaan? What got them back on track? (Genesis 11:31; 12:4–5)
2. How was the Lord's call of Abram in Genesis 12:1–3 and Abram's response a foreshadowing of Christ? (John 6:38; Philippians 2:5–8; Hebrews 11:8)

---

[1] C. S. Lewis, *Mere Christianity*, rev. and amp. ed. (New York: Harper & Brothers, 1952; renewed 1980), 136–37.

3. What did God promise to Abraham in Genesis 12:3? How does this reveal the gospel (righteousness through faith)? In what ways are we still partaking in this promise? (Galatians 3:7–9)

4. Which one of Terah's children carried the *Seed*, Christ: Nahor, Abram, or Haran? How did Genesis 12:3,7 reveal the *Seed*, Christ? (Matthew 1:1; Galatians 3:16–19; Acts 7:5; Hebrews 11:12) Note: At this time, Abram and Sarai did not have physical offspring.

5. Who spoke to Abram in Genesis 12:7? Do you believe this was the pre-incarnate Christ? Why or why not? (Genesis 17:1; John 8:56)

6. Although Abram was the "Father of Faith," he still missed the mark. What did Abram do in Genesis 12:10–20? Did God still use him? How is this an encouragement to you? (2 Timothy 2:13)

7. What did the Holy Spirit highlight to you in Genesis 10—12 through the reading or the teaching?

# Lesson 5: Genesis 13—15
## *Seed*: The Promise of Offspring

## Teaching Notes

### Review

The *Seed*, Christ, was passed down through Abram who had been promised all these things. God had spoken it to him, but nothing had happened yet. In Genesis 13, Abram and Lot had acquired so many possessions that they had to split up and go different directions. In Genesis 14, Abram came to the rescue of Lot, who had been captured. Melchizedek, the "priest to God Most High" (Genesis 14:18), met with Abram. Jesus, on the road to Emmaus, explained to the disciples all that the Scriptures said about Him (Luke 24:27), and this could be one of the things He would have talked about. Melchizedek was a type of Christ—not Christ but a picture of Him. Nowhere else in the Old Testament is there someone who was both a king and a priest. And that is exactly who Jesus Christ is—He is both the Priest and the King.

### Teaching

*Genesis 15:1*: "After these events . . ." To understand this phrase, look back at the events in Genesis 14. Abram heard that Lot had been taken prisoner, so Abram assembled 318 trained men. He led them in pursuit to Dan, attacked, and then pursued them as far as Hobah, north of Damascus (v. 15). Abram brought Lot, his goods, and his family back home. After Abram returned from defeating Chedorlaomer and the three kings (v. 17), Melchizedek blessed Abram, and Abram gave Melchizedek "a tenth of everything" (vv. 19–20). This is one of the verses that supports the concept of the tithe—or giving ten percent to God.

The word of the Lord came to Abram in a vision. "Do not be afraid." After you go through battles, you usually feel confident. But Abram lived in a state of fear of the kings' retaliation. Isn't it amazing how God knows our hearts so much and speaks right to us? God wants us to know, "I'm with you, but you have to walk this out!" God is our shield and our great reward. I think when God said, "Your reward will be very great," He was turning the corner and would now begin to fulfill the seven promises to Abram.

*Genesis 15:2*: Abram responded: "Lord God, what can You give me, since I am childless?" For some reason, Abram responded with doubt. Abram didn't necessarily believe God's promise that those seven things would come true. Maybe he was thinking about the possibility of military retaliation and what would happen since he didn't have an heir but only had Eliezer, his servant. Here, this man of faith still doubted even though he had encountered God. He was like a surging sea (James 1:6). We cannot function in faith and doubt at the same time. Abram had heard the promise, but in the moment, he saw nothing—no heir and no son.

*Genesis 15:3*: Abram pointed out that since he had no offspring, one of his slaves would be his heir. Practically, if there were no children in the household, the slave became the heir. The *Seed* would then have come through Eliezer.

*Genesis 15:4*: But God responded that Abram's heir would come from his own body. The *Seed*, Christ, physically came from Abram's body. God used human beings by faith to continue His *Seed*. Look back at Genesis 12:7. God promised the land to Abram's "offspring." "Offspring" here means "seed"—Abram's own children. Abram had allowed fear to get in the way. I believe this, again, is the pre-incarnate Christ (Genesis 13:15–16). Over and over, in Genesis 12, 13, and 15, God's message was, "Abram, you're going to have offspring!"

*Genesis 15:5*: "He took him outside and said, 'Look at the sky and count the stars, if you are able to count them.' Then He said to him, 'Your offspring will be that numerous.'" I love the visual. God is so practical. Sometimes I pray through how I want to leave a legacy in my life here on earth. How do I want my kids to perceive who I am? I don't want to be just the fun dad. I want to be known as the guy that my kids say, "My dad functioned by faith." When you walk by faith and believe the things that God has spoken into your life, I believe God will honor that.

*Genesis 15:6*: "Abram believed the Lord, and He credited it to him as righteousness." Tom Constable, among others, said this "righteousness" means Abram trusted the Lord, established himself in the Lord, or he confirmed himself in the Lord.[1] Most commentators say that this righteousness is based on God and not Abram. This righteousness had nothing to do with works. It was because Abram *believed* God. How do we know? Scripture confirms it. Hebrews 11:8 states, "By faith Abraham, when he was called, obeyed and went out to a place he was going to receive as an inheritance" Abram believed God. Romans 4:11 says Abram was

---

[1] Thomas Constable, *Expository Notes of Dr. Thomas Constable: Genesis*, 237, https://planobiblechapel.org/tcon/notes/pdf/genesis.pdf.

the father of all who believed, not based on what he did, but simply because he believed. The only way our righteousness is credited is because we believe. There was something deposited in Abram, and this seed started to grow a little bit stronger, and he started to believe God.

*Genesis 15:7*: "I am Yahweh who brought you from Ur of the Chaldeans to give you this land to possess."

*Genesis 15:8*: But Abram asked for some proof from God! It was much like Gideon, who asked for the fleece to be wet when the ground was dry, and then dry when the ground was wet. He asked, "Lord, would you confirm this?"

*Genesis 15:9–11*: God told Abram to bring a three-year-old cow, goat, and ram, a turtledove, and a young pigeon. God gave Abram the instructions. Abram cut all these animals in half except the birds.

*Genesis 15:12–15*: This is considered the second component of Abram's vision. Great terror and darkness descended on Abram. God told Abram, "Your offspring will be foreigners in a land that does not belong to them; they will be enslaved and oppressed 400 years." In Genesis 12:1–3, God gave a general promise to Abram. In Genesis 15:5–6, it became more specific. God said Abram's offspring would not get the land for 400 years. Abram, who was promised the *Seed*, Christ, would be a blessing to so many people, was even told how he was going to die. It went from a general prophecy over his life to a specific word.

*Genesis 15:16*: "In the fourth generation they will return here, for the iniquity of the Amorites has not yet reached its full measure." Why 400 years? It was all about timing. God gave the Amorites time to continue in their sin. And let's look at this from another angle. Not only did the Amorites need time, Abram needed time for his offspring to grow, to become as the stars in the sky, to become as many as the sand on the shore. The children of Abram wouldn't be numerous enough to possess the land. Abram's offspring needed time to be fruitful and multiply. In our culture, we're such a microwave society that we want to "take the land" right now. But the bigger picture of the Lord needs time, so the seed doesn't always have to happen right away. Calling attention to a planting of a seed deposited in the ground, I want to point out that the seed doesn't just shoot up right away. It has to have time to germinate. And the promise of God over Abram needed time to germinate.

*Genesis 15:17*: The Lord made a covenant with Abram with no conditions based on Abram. Has God brought this to fruition yet today and given the entire land to the Israelites? Not all of it. In 1948, they were given only some of the land back. I get excited because the Old Testament is not done yet. Israel is not done yet. God's covenant with Abram is not done and hasn't been completely fulfilled.

## Closing

Bob Deffinbaugh, who writes for Bible.org, says, "Faith is seldom strengthened by success but by believing God in the midst of delays and difficulties."[2] Abram didn't see a whole lot of what God promised him, and yet he still walked by faith. God needed the people of Israel to be strong. It is in delay and difficulties that our faith is strengthened. And all I know is that it started all the way back in Genesis when God set this all in motion with the *Seed*. Roman 8:31–39 reminds us, "If God is for us, who can be against us?"

## The Daily Word

Abram's calling did not make logical sense to him. However, Abram turned to God for clarity, and the Lord gave Abram specifics on his calling. Abram believed God and walked by faith.

The Lord has called you to your own path. To walk by faith is to fear God more than man, to trust God in every circumstance. Today, walk by faith, just as Abram did, while carrying the *Seed*, Christ. Take one step at a time, and the Lord will direct your path.

**He took him outside and said, "Look at the sky and count the stars, if you are able to count them." Then He said to him, "Your offspring will be that numerous." Abram believed the LORD, and He credited it to him as righteousness. —Genesis 15:5–6**

Further Scripture: Proverbs 3:5–6; 2 Corinthians 5:7; Hebrews 11:1
The Promise of Offspring

## Questions

1. In Genesis 13:1–18, why did Abram and Lot separate? What land did each of them end up occupying, and why was this significant? (Genesis 14:1–12)
2. Who was Melchizedek in Genesis 14:18–20? How did he reveal Christ? Do you believe he could have been pre-incarnate Christ? (Psalm 110:4; Hebrews 5:6; 6:20; 7:1–21)

---

[2] Bob Deffinbaugh, "The Focal Point of Abram's Faith (Genesis 15:1-21)," Bible.org, May 12, 2004, https://bible.org/seriespage/16-focal-point-abram-s-faith-genesis-151-21.

3. Based on the conversation between Abram and the Lord in Genesis 15:1–11, was Abram's heart positioned in faith or fear/doubt? (James 1:6; Hebrews 11:6)

4. In Genesis 15:6, why did the Lord credit righteousness to Abram? How did this reveal the gospel—righteousness through faith not works? (Romans 4:3–5; 4:11–13; Galatians 3:5–6; Hebrews 11:8; James 2:23)

5. Why did it take 400 years for Abram's offspring to receive the land promised in Genesis 15:12–21? Has the promise to Abram been brought to fruition today?

6. What did the Holy Spirit highlight to you in Genesis 13—15 through the reading or the teaching?

# Lesson 6: Genesis 16—17
*Seed*: God Provided the Offspring

## Teaching Notes

### Review

God told Abraham that his offspring would first be strangers in a land that does not belong to them (Genesis 15:13). How many of us as believers feel as though we're strangers? Hebrews 11:9–10 says that by faith Abram lived as a foreigner in the land of promise. In 1 Peter 2:11, believers are described as strangers and temporary residents who are called to abstain from pleasures that tempt. There's a constant temptation to go back to the things of the flesh. God told Abram that his reward was coming. But Abraham was confronted with the option to make it happen on his own.

### Teaching

*Genesis 16:2*: Sarai told Abram to have a child by her servant, Hagar. Abram swayed to the seed of the serpent and decided they should try to make happen what God had promised.

*Genesis 16:7–10*: Appearing to Hagar, "Then the Angel of the Lord said to her." Many people believe this Angel of the Lord could be the pre-incarnate Christ again. Remember, we know Christ was present physically before He was born in Bethlehem. In Genesis 1, Jesus was the Creator. He was a part of creation (John 1:1, 10).

*Genesis 16:11–12*: Again, to Hager in verses 11–12: "Then the Angel of the Lord said to her: You have conceived and will have a son. You will name him Ishmael, for the Lord has heard your cry of affliction. This man will be like a wild donkey. His hand will be against everyone, and everyone's hand will be against him; he will live at odds with all his brothers." This is what happens when you don't wait on God. Ishmael would be like a wild donkey. While Abram and Sarai's intent was right—they just wanted to see this promise from God come to fruition—they shouldn't have tried to make it happen in their own timing. You can't make things happen in your own timing. You have to wait on the Lord. So, all because of Sarai's insecurity and Abram's impatience and doubt, we have a serious problem in society still today with the Ishmaels—the wild donkeys who fight against everyone. All because Abram didn't wait.

*Genesis 16:16*: When you force the hand of God, major problems happen. Remember what God told Abram in Genesis 15:1. Just when we begin to question God's hand, He speaks into us: "Don't be afraid. Your reward *will* be great. Just wait on My timing."

*Genesis 17:1*: "When Abram was 99 years old, the LORD appeared to him, saying, 'I am God Almighty. Live in My presence and be blameless.'" We know Ishmael was born, and then Genesis 17 takes place some 12 to 13 years later. Abram was 99. The phrase, "I am God Almighty," is the translation for *El Shaddai*, which meant "(1) The Powerful, Strong One . . . and (2) The One Who Suffices."[1] Waltke quoted Wenham: "Shaddai evokes the idea that God is able to make the barren fertile and to fulfill His promises."[2] God can do whatever He needs to do. God told Abram, "Live in My presence and be blameless" (1 Kings 9:4–5; 2 Kings 20:3).

*Genesis 17:2*: "I will establish My covenant between Me and you, and I will multiply you greatly." In Genesis 12, 13, 15, 17 and even into 18, God reminded Abram over and over, "I'm going to do what I told you I would; I just need you to hang in there." When you walk by faith, you need these gentle reminders constantly. God promised to establish His covenant and multiply Abraham, which sounded much like promises God made to Abram in Genesis 12:1–3.

*Genesis 17:3*: "Then Abram fell facedown and God spoke with him." Abram fell facedown in humility. Leviticus 9 and Joshua 5 recorded other times when people fell facedown in the presence of the Lord. Robert E. Coleman was a man who mentored me and every time I was around that man, he would fall on his face when he prayed. Genesis 17 contains five divine speeches where God spoke into Abraham in five different situations. Verses 1–2 described one, and then verses 4–8 described another.

*Genesis 17:4*: "You will become the father of many nations." This was the same promise from God recorded in Genesis 12:1–3.

---

[1] Bruce K. Waltke, *Genesis: A Commentary* (Grand Rapids: Zondervan, 2001), 259.

[2] Waltke, 259.

*Genesis 17:5*: "Your name will no longer be Abram, but your name will be Abraham." God changed Abram's name to Abraham, which meant "father of many." In Genesis 12, God's promise to Abram was general. In Genesis 15, it was specific, and now in Genesis 17, it became personal. As it continued to grow and build, it pointed to the Messiah. The father of many nations implied the *Seed*, Christ, would come through Abraham. In Galatians 3:16–19, Paul wrote, "Now the promises were spoken to Abraham and to his seed. He does not say 'and to seeds,' as though referring to many but referring to one, and to your seed, who is Christ . . . God granted it to Abraham through the promise." When Abram became Abraham, he knew he was getting closer to what God was calling him to do.

*Genesis 17:6*: In verse 6, God tells Abraham, "I will make you extremely fruitful and will make nations and kings come from you" (Genesis 1:29; Genesis 9). The word "everlasting" described an everlasting covenant that was established through a man whose father worshipped the moon god. He carried the seed that points to the Messiah. The Messiah would come through Abraham all because he was chosen by God and he walked by faith (v. 7). God promised Abraham the land of Canaan as an "eternal possession." God's everlasting covenant will *never* stop. It will be *forever*. That's a pretty crazy prophecy that the seed of Abraham pointed to the Messiah (v. 8). God launched into another divine speech here. He kept going and continued to hammer in all He wanted to take place through Abraham and his offspring (v. 9).

*Genesis 17:10–13*: In Genesis 12, 15, and 17, over and over again God said Abraham was the man who would carry the *Seed*, Christ, who would lead us to an everlasting covenant—the *Seed* being the Messiah. At this time, God instituted circumcision as the sign of this covenant. "Every one of your males must be circumcised" (v. 10). Anyone who was connected to Abraham was commanded to be circumcised. Abraham was old, verse 1 said he was 99. Circumcision was not normal, especially at this age. God instituted something new. Today, Christians are not commanded to be circumcised (under the new covenant), but many do. According to Constable, God had a purpose for this: First, it was a frequent reminder to every male of God's promises involving the seed. Second, it was a symbol—cutting off the flesh. Do I want to function in the flesh or in the *Seed* being Christ? Third, it resulted in a greater cleanliness of life. It resulted in freedom from the effects of sin.[3] At that time, every adult

---

[3] Thomas L. Constable, *Expository Notes of Dr. Thomas Constable: Genesis*, 259, https://planobiblechapel.org/tcon/notes/pdf/genesis.pdf.

male was circumcised, and then from that point forward, every male born into the family of Abraham was circumcised.

*Genesis 17:14*: Any man who was not circumcised was cut off from God's covenant.

*Genesis 17:15*: This was the beginning of another of God's divine speeches. God changed Abraham's wife's name from Sarai to Sarah, a change from "my princess" to "the royal princess" (v. 15). "I will bless her; indeed, I will give you a son by her. I will bless her, and she will produce nations; kings and peoples will come from her" (v. 16). This was the same woman who gave Hagar to her husband. God gave her a second chance. Kings of people would come from her, His name is Jesus! Christ came from Sarah.

*Genesis 17:17—18*: Abraham fell facedown. This time it probably wasn't in humility. It was probably to cover up his laughter. Abraham laughed and questioned God (like God couldn't see him laughing). "If only Ishmael were acceptable to You!" Can you believe Abraham said that to God? How long had he been waiting for the heir?

*Genesis 17:19—22*: Verses 19–21 comprise God's fifth and final divine speech in Genesis 17. He didn't say, "I'm done with you Abraham!" Instead, God confirmed His promise. Scripture then transitions from the seed of Abraham to the seed of Isaac. And it will happen next year.

## Closing

The *Seed*, first mentioned in Genesis 3:15, the *Seed* that was going to crush Satan, the *Seed* that came into Abel and went into Noah, and then to his son Shem, and from Shem to Abraham, was now promised to go to Isaac. It's all building, and it was never easy. This whole process is never ever easy. It's called walking by faith.

And I don't want to miss this: Ishmael was the chosen son of the Islamic faith. Isaac was the chosen son of Judaism and Christianity. Hence the wild donkey, Ishmael (Islam) constantly fights against Jews and Christians. The seed of the serpent and the *Seed* of the woman . . . the enmity continues, even in Genesis 17.

## The Daily Word

God was a personal God to Abram and gave him a new name, Abraham. The Lord *knows* you and calls you by name. When He calls you to something, He will make a way. He will give you all you need, specifically for *you*. How does the Lord reveal to you personally He is with you? May the Lord open your eyes to see what He sees and encourage you to keep walking in faith.

**Your name will no longer be Abram, but your name will be Abraham, for I will make you the father of many nations. I will make you extremely fruitful and will make nations and kings come from you. —Genesis 17:5–6**

Further Scripture: Deuteronomy 20:4; Psalm 139:1–6; Hebrews 13:20–21

## Questions

1.  In Genesis 16, Abram and Sarai were confronted with the option to make God's promises happen. What choice did they make, and what were the results of that choice? How can you relate this to your life?

2.  Do you believe the angel who appeared to Hagar could have been pre-incarnate Christ? How would you explain Genesis 16:13–14?

3.  In Genesis 17:1–2, what conditions did God set for the covenant with Abraham? Were they attainable? (Leviticus 19:2; 1 Kings 9:4–5; Matthew 5:48)

4.  What did the names "Abram" and "Abraham" mean? Why were the name changes for Abram and Sarai significant? (Ephesians 3:15)

5.  In Genesis 17:16–19, God promised Abraham a son by Sarah and said to name him Isaac. In which of Abraham's sons would the *Seed*, Christ, reside? (Matthew 1:2)

6.  What was the sign of the Abrahamic covenant, and why did God choose to implement it? (Genesis 17:9–14)

7.  What did the Holy Spirit highlight to you in Genesis 16—17 through the reading or the teaching?

# Lesson 7: Genesis 18
## *Seed*: Abraham's Divine Visitors

## Teaching Notes

### Review

Acts 19:9–10 reveals that Paul "met separately with the disciples, conducting discussions every day . . . for two years." If Paul could do this daily, and we have the same Holy Spirit, we can do this! Remember, the goal of reviveSCHOOL is not to consume what we're learning but to share it. The whole intent is to apply this and live this out. We need to be telling these stories! We need to point others to the only *Seed*, Jesus Christ, who can truly change lives.

In Genesis 1—17, my prayer has been that you see that this *Seed* has been literally interwoven throughout it. Matthew 5:17 says, "Jesus said, 'Don't assume that I came to destroy the Law or the Prophets. I did not come to destroy but to fulfill.'" In this entire study, we will see the fulfillment of the Messiah. Matthew 5:18 says: "For I assure you: Until heaven and earth pass away, not the smallest letter or one stroke of a letter will pass from the Law until all things are accomplished." Until all the things that God promised in Genesis 12:1–3 come to fruition, Christ isn't coming back. Romans 9:10–11 assures us that God's not done with the people of Israel, His chosen people. He wants to use them to point people to the Messiah. Never forget—Jesus is Jewish.

### Teaching

*Genesis 18:1–2*: "Then the LORD appeared to Abraham at the oaks of Mamre while he was sitting in the entrance of his tent during the heat of the day." Who were these three guys who approached Abraham? From verse 3 on, there was a whole conversation between them. In Genesis 16, we talked about whether it was the pre-incarnate Christ who interacted with Hagar. Could this really have been Jesus before He was born? While I can't prove this *was* Jesus, I think we can show there is a really good chance that it was. In Scripture, "theophany" is a term used to denote an appearance of God. Likewise, the term "Christophany" denotes an appearance of Christ. Let's look at three reasons why this might be an appearance of Christ:

29

"No one has ever seen God," but Jesus "has revealed Him" (John 1:18). Jesus later said, "The Father who sent Me has Himself testified about Me. You have not heard His voice at any time, and you haven't seen His form" (John 5:37). If no one has seen God, then who was this person who appeared in human form to Abraham?

Jesus existed before all things (Colossians 1:16-17). Jesus was with God in the beginning (John 1:1–3,14). Jesus was part of creating everything. He is the glue who holds all things together (Colossians 1:17b). In John 8:58, Jesus said, "Before Abraham was, I am." Consider also Genesis 1:26: "Then God said, 'Let Us make man.'" "Us" could be God, Jesus, and the Holy Spirit (the Spirit hovered over the waters in Genesis 1:2).

Jesus "is the image of the invisible God, the firstborn over all creation" (Colossians 1:15). This goes back to Cain and Abel. Jesus is the firstborn, the firstfruits. In John 14:9, Jesus said to Philip, "Have I been among you all this time without your knowing Me, Philip? The one who has seen Me has seen the Father." Every time you see Christ, you see the Father. In 2 Corinthians 4:4, Paul said Christ is the image of God.

Throughout the Old Testament, if no one saw God, whom did they see? If Jesus is the image of the invisible God, and He was there from the very beginning, Jesus could have been the pre-incarnate Christ. Walter Kaiser did a study of the 214 times the Hebrew term for "angel" was used in the Old Testament. He found that theologians considered about one-third of those occurrences to be a Christophany, a time when Christ appeared in the Old Testament.[1] What does pre-incarnate mean? In Genesis 18, the visitor actually ate with Abraham. Jesus' words in John 5:39 really puts all of this into perspective. Jesus said the Scriptures (Old Testament) testify about Him.

*Genesis 18:2*: Notice that Abraham ran to these men he had never met and bowed down. Would Abraham have done that if it wasn't the pre-incarnate Christ? Then again, maybe he *had* already seen this person in Genesis 12 or in Genesis 16 when the Lord appeared to Abraham. Maybe he did recognize it was the Lord he had seen before! Keith Krell, in an article written for www.bible.org, said Abraham always used speed (v. 2—ran, v. 6—hurried, v. 7—ran) as he rushed, three different times, to respond to these visitors. Why? Because he knew he was in the presence of someone really special.[2]

---

[1] Walter C. Kaiser Jr., "Jesus in the Old Testament," Gordon Conwell Theological Seminary, August 9, 2011, http://www.gordonconwell.edu/resources/Jesus-in-the-Old-Testament.cfm.

[2] Keith Krell, "A Divine Encounter (Genesis 18:1-15)"; available from https://bible.org/seriespage/22-divine-encounter-genesis-181-15.

*Genesis 18:3–5*: The phrase "My lord" is a bad translation. The Hebrew language indicates that this should be a capital L for Lord, implying God. Abraham said, "My Lord, if I have found favor in your sight" (v. 3). You don't use this phrase unless you are in the presence of someone of high rank, and Abraham knew he was. Abraham just wanted them to rest and be strengthened (vv. 4–5).

*Genesis 18:6–8*: Remember those three words that described how Abraham used speed to respond to these men? Abraham was giving his best! The measurement of fine flour was almost 30 quarts of flour. He was having a party for just three people. Most commentators would say the whole tender choice calf could guarantee at least 100 pounds. Abraham had 30 quarts of flour for bread, 100 pounds of meat, and curds and milk. He gave his very best for these three men!

Remember Abraham had 318 men in his house who had to be circumcised (Genesis 14:14). Yet, Abraham did everything himself. He saw that serving these men was so important, he did everything as he served these men, selecting his best, and running all over the place. I believe one of these men was the pre-incarnate Christ and the other two were angels. I think this is an awesome picture of Jesus being the image of the invisible God in Genesis 18. He's the One who existed in the very beginning, before all things. And Abraham ran out to Him and bowed down and said, "My Lord, let me serve you!"

*Genesis 18:9*: Remember, in this culture, they didn't always welcome the women. Then, He reiterated the promise that Abraham would have a son. And He gave the specific details.

*Genesis 18:11–12*: Sarah had already heard this promise multiple times, so why did she laugh? She was well past the age of childbearing.

*Genesis 18:13–14*: If you believed this was the pre-incarnate Christ, wouldn't it have been awesome to hear Him say this? "Is anything impossible for the Lord?" Over and over and over, the prophets talked about this. In Jeremiah 32:17: "Oh, Lord God! You Yourself made the heavens and earth by Your great power and with Your outstretched arm. Nothing is too difficult for You!" Again, in Jeremiah 32:27: "Look, I am Yahweh, the God of all flesh. Is anything too difficult for Me?" In Mark 10:27, Jesus said to the disciples: "With men it is impossible, but not with God, because all things are possible with God." I believe Jesus showed up with two angels and spoke life into Abraham and Sarah and said it was happening. "The *Seed*, Christ, has been promised to you; it's going to happen." In Luke 1:37, the angel told Mary: "For nothing will be impossible with God." This was in reference to Mary's virgin conception of

Jesus! You know why this is cool? Because "the *Seed* of the woman" that was prophesied in Genesis 3:15 appeared here in Genesis 18.

*Genesis 18:15*: Sarah laughed because she was afraid. Despite Sarah's laughter and doubt and fear and lying, God remained faithful. In 2 Timothy 2:13, Paul wrote: "If we are faithless, He remains faithful, for He cannot deny Himself." Despite our faithlessness, God will remain faithful. And what He has started, He will always finish. He promised Abraham and Sarah that He would be back a year from then.

## Closing

I'm excited to dig in next week because in Genesis 21, the Angel of the Lord came back. He honored His promise to Abraham and came back a year later. From the *Seed* of the woman to the *Seed* of Abraham, the story continued to the *Seed* of Isaac.

## The Daily Word

Nothing is too difficult for the Lord. Yet Sarah laughed at God for calling her to have a child in the midst of her barrenness. For Sarah to carry the *Seed*, Jesus, the impossible had to happen, and the Lord had to open her womb. But Sarah laughed.

Do you laugh when God calls you to the impossible? God says to trust in Him. Pour out your heart to the Lord, and trust God to do the impossible.

Is anything impossible for the LORD? —Genesis 18:14

Further Scripture: Psalm 62:8; Jeremiah 32:17; Luke 1:37–38

## Questions

1. What are the meanings of *theophany* and *Christophany*? How do these tie into the possibility that Christ appeared in the Old Testament? (John 1:1–3; 1:18; 5:37; 8:58; 14:9; Colossians 1:15–17; Genesis 1:26)
2. Do you believe Abraham's interactions in Genesis 18 were with the pre-incarnate Christ? Why or why not? Who were the "three men"?
3. What were the three instances in Genesis 18:1–15 where Abraham acted with urgency? Why were they significant? (Genesis 14:14)
4. What was Sarah's reaction to overhearing the news about bearing a child in Genesis 18:9–15? Faith or fear/doubt? (Hebrews 11:11)

5. What truth did you find about the character of the Lord in Genesis 18:14? (Jeremiah 32:17; Matthew 19:26; Mark 10:27; 14:36; Luke 1:37)

6. What did the Holy Spirit highlight to you in Genesis 18 through the reading or the teaching?

# Lesson 8: Genesis 19

*Seed*: Problems with Being in the World

## Teaching Notes

### Review

Genesis 18 gave the backdrop for the events of Genesis 19. God had just spoken to Abraham and Sarah and promised them a son, but Abraham and Sarah laughed. The three visitors were two angels and the pre-incarnate Christ who came to Abraham and looked over Sodom (Genesis 18:16). "Then the Lord said, 'Should I hide what I am about to do from Abraham?'" (v. 17). Again, in verse 19, God promises that Abraham would become a great and powerful nation. God protected Abraham and his seed and his family because ultimately that would lead to Christ. The sin of Sodom and Gomorrah was immense (v. 20). The remainder of Genesis 18 is Abraham's negotiations with God to save the city.

### Teaching

Genesis 19 may be one of the most extreme chapters in Scripture. What can be worse than Sodom and Gomorrah? One occasion may be when Jesus cursed the three cities in Matthew 11:20–24 because they did not repent of their sin. There's nothing politically correct in this lesson. We're just going to look at the Word of God. When we fall into sin and temptation, it leads to this, and it isn't good.

*Genesis 19:1*: Were these the same two angels that were just with Abraham? It would make sense. Abraham was sitting at the opening of the tent (literally at "the gate") when the angels came, showing that he still functioned as a foreigner in the land. Lot sat at the gate of Sodom and had become entrenched in the city. Warren Wiersbe said this was a sign of authority, maybe even as an elder or a lawyer.[1] Abraham viewed his home as the heavenly city, not of this world. Lot viewed his home as the earthly city of Sodom. Wiersbe said Abraham was a friend of God and not this world, whereas Lot was a friend of this world[2] (James 2:23; 4:4).

---

[1] Warren Wiersbe, *The Bible Exposition Commentary: Genesis–Deuteronomy* (Colorado Springs: David C. Cook, 2001), 93.

[2] Wiersbe, 93.

Based on how they lived their lives, Abraham was a friend of God, and Lot was an enemy of God. Lot was spared because of his relationship with Abraham and not because of anything he did. People associated with Abraham were blessed.

*Genesis 19:2*: Lot didn't show much hospitality. Lot knew things weren't good in Sodom, so he offered them a place to stay but didn't seem to go out of his way to welcome them as Abraham had (Hebrews 13:2).

*Genesis 19:3–4*: Lot prepared a feast and baked unleavened bread for the men. That evening, "the men of the city of Sodom, both young and old, the whole population, surrounded the house." Based on what is known, the "whole population" of young and old men are estimated at 600 to 1,200 men. Remember, Abraham had a tent, but Lot had a home. This wasn't originally the case for Lot. Along the journey, Lot made Sodom his home (Genesis 13:10–12).

*Genesis 19:5*: The men of Sodom wanted to have sexual relations with the men who were guests in Lot's home. There are over 20 references to Sodom and Gomorrah outside of Genesis 19 (Leviticus 18:22; 20:13; Isaiah 3:9; Jude 1:7). Understand that what happened in Sodom and Gomorrah was not good. It was detestable. So, God said He would destroy this place (Jeremiah 23:14; Ezekiel 16:49–50; Matthew 10:14–15; 11:23–24). The more we open up the doors and say it's tolerable or that people are born like this, then we ignore that it's sin. I think that's why America is getting closer and closer to destruction.

*Genesis 19:6–8*: Lot went outside because he knew the men of Sodom, but he was also courageous (v. 6). Lot knew the distinction between good and evil. In 2 Peter 2:6–8, we're told that God rescued "righteous Lot, distressed by the unrestrained behavior of the immoral." Lot, a righteous man, lived amongst these evil things and was tormented by what he saw. Does anyone else have a red flag here? He offered his two daughters to the men of Sodom instead of the men who were his guests. Maybe Lot knew something we don't know . . . maybe he thought if they did something to his daughters, he could punish them? Deuteronomy 22:23–24 prescribed death by stoning to a man who had sex with a virgin engaged to another. But this was Mosaic Law, which hadn't been implemented yet, so this is a weak argument.

*Genesis 19:9–14*: Suddenly the men of Sodom called Lot a foreigner (v. 9). Bruce Waltke said it was like their eyes were dazzled and they were deceived; they couldn't tell which way was which.[3] It's interesting that God cared for Lot's fam-

---

[3] Bruce Waltke, *Genesis: A Commentary* (Grand Rapids: Zondervan, 2001).

ily, just like He did for Noah's family. Look at how Lot's sons-in-law responded. They thought Lot was crying wolf. Lot had no credibility with his family (v. 14). Wiersbe said that after Lot left Abraham, his character deteriorated. But once again God came in and spared him.[4]

*Genesis 19:15–20*: Lot's sons-in-law did not go with him. In Genesis 18:24, Abraham had prayed, "Will you really sweep it away?" The sweeping away was coming. Lot hesitated. He didn't have that depth of trust in the Lord. He'd put his roots down. Bruce Waltke said that Lot found more security in the evil city than he did in leaving the city with God and going into the unknown.[5] Even though Lot hesitated, God spared him (v. 16). This was the theme—the sweeping was coming. Run! Don't look back (v. 17)! Lot was still constantly debating and arguing. Fear had overtaken Lot. He was completely functioning in fear (vv. 18–20).

*Genesis 19:21–25:* The small town was named Zoar, which means "insignificant." The historian Josephus said, "God sent a thunderbolt to set the city on fire."[6] K. A. Mathews said: "This heaven's rain cannot be explained solely as a natural phenomenon such as an earthquake; it was exceptional, never again repeated. . . . The twin calamities of Noah and Lot illustrate Jesus' teaching on the suddenness of the coming of the Son of Man."[7] The point was that the suddenness of this destruction. At any given time, Christ can return.

*Genesis 19:26–28*: Lot's wife looked back for her safety and security. She was turned into a pillar of salt. Compare this with Psalm 107:34: God turns a "fruitful land into salty wasteland, because of the wickedness of its inhabitants." Salt implies no fruit (salty wasteland). When you look back, you're missing out on what God has for you in the future (Luke 9:62; 17:31–33). If you want to live your life in such a way, being comfortable at the gate, destruction is coming. Remember this was where Abraham had looked over the town and negotiated with Christ earlier in Genesis 19.

*Genesis 19:29*: Lot was connected to the *Seed*, because of Abraham, and God spared Lot. God showed us this destruction so we can see how He has spared us from that same demise. I don't think we really realize what hell is like. I don't

---

[4] Wiersbe, 94.

[5] Waltke.

[6] Josephus, *Antiquities of the Jews*, 1:11:4; quoted in Thomas L. Constable, *Expository Notes of Dr. Thomas Constable: Genesis*, 273, https://planobiblechapel.org/tcon/notes/pdf/genesis.pdf.

[7] K. A. Mathews, *New American Commentary: Genesis 11:27-50:26* (Nashville: Broadman & Holman, 2005), 241.

think we realize that if we are apart from the *Seed*, Christ, destruction is coming to you and me. Until we put our trust in the *Seed*, hands to the plow, not looking back, destruction is coming. We must put our trust in Christ, who was the *Seed* of Abraham.

## Closing:

Please don't be conformed to the world. Romans 12:2 says, "Don't be conformed to this age, but be transformed by the renewing of your mind so that you may discern what is the good, pleasing, and perfect will of God." Abraham was able to discern this. Lot had a hard time.

Titus 3:5 says, "He saved us not by the works of righteousness that we had done, but according to His mercy, through the washing of regeneration and renewal by the Holy Spirit." It has nothing to do with what we have done and has everything to do with His mercy. We are at a point where we need to plead for His mercy. And my prayer is that you will see that mercy can come because of the *Seed* who is Christ.

## The Daily Word

As the people of Sodom and Gomorrah gave in to their lusts, they acted in the flesh and did not depend on God. The Lord saved Lot but destroyed an entire city. In many ways, our generation, like Sodom and Gomorrah, continues to give in to temptation and live in the flesh, not depending fully on the Lord. Thankfully, Jesus saved each one of us because of His grace and mercy through His death, burial, resurrection, and His gift of the Holy Spirit.

Today, give thanks for the grace and mercy of the Lord. Ask yourself, *Am I living in a way that is pleasing to Christ, or am I giving in to temptations and my flesh?* May this be a generation that seeks His face.

**So it was, when God destroyed the cities of the plain, He remembered Abraham and brought Lot out of the middle of the upheaval when He demolished the cities where Lot had lived. —Genesis 19:29**

Further Scripture: Psalm 24:3–6; Titus 3:3, 5–7

## Questions

1.  Why did both Abraham and Lot show hospitality to the strangers (angels)? Do you think they knew they were angels? (Genesis 18:6–8; Hebrews 13:2)

2. In what ways did Lot steadily compromise with sin leading up to Genesis 19? How can you relate this to your actions? (Genesis 13:10–12; 14:12)

3. What sin did the men of Sodom desire to commit in Genesis 19:4–9? According to the verses listed, what did God think about it? (Genesis 2:24; Leviticus 18:22; 1 Corinthians 6:9–11; Romans 1:26–28; Jude 1:7)

4. Sodom was destined for judgment. Why do you think Lot and his family were saved from the judgment in Genesis 19:16? Why was Lot considered righteous? (Genesis 19:29; 12:1–4; Deuteronomy 7:8; 2 Peter 2:7–9)

5. Why do you think Lot's wife looked back in Genesis 19:26? What can you learn from it? (Luke 9:62; 17:31–33)

6. What did the Holy Spirit highlight to you in Genesis 19 through the reading or the teaching?

# Lesson 9: Genesis 20—21
*Seed*: The Birth of Isaac

## Teaching Notes

### Intro

In Genesis 1—19, we have discussed how the *Seed*, Christ, is carried as a theme throughout the book of Genesis. The *Seed* came through Abraham. Genesis 20 and 21 continues the theme of how God spared Abraham because he carried the *Seed*.

In Genesis 20, Abraham travelled to the Negev and told a half-lie to Abimelech—that Sarah was his sister. So Abimelech took her as a wife, and then Abimelech was about to die. But God came to Abimelech, and so he returned Sarah with loads of blessings and silver. And then because he made everything right, God healed Abimelech's wife, and she was able to bear children. All this happened because of God's hand of protection on Abraham because of the blessing that would come from him. Genesis 21 is the repeat of how God blessed Abraham, and we are a product of this blessing.

### Teaching

*Genesis 21:1–5*: Verse 1 records: "The LORD . . . did for Sarah what He had promised." Remember when God showed up the last time? In Genesis 17:15–16, He promised that Sarah would produce nations and kings of peoples. In Genesis 18:14, God promised that in a year, she would have a son. Which brings us to Genesis 21:1—the year God promised. God had done what He said He would do. We can trust that God is constantly faithful to what He says. In verse 2, Sarah's role now increased. Have you ever had a prophetic word spoken over your life, and then after some time, you saw it come to fulfillment? This is what happened with Sarah. "Sarah became pregnant and bore a son to Abraham in his old age, at the appointed time God had told him" (v. 2). It's like when Jesus stood up in Nazareth and read the scroll of Isaiah and said now it is fulfilled. "At the appointed time"—it's all in God's timing. Remember what happened with Hagar and Ishmael? But now was the time.

Let's review Genesis 12:1–3. What happened in Genesis 21 was because of Genesis 12. This was the fulfillment of a portion of Genesis 12. Follow God's promises given in Genesis 17:7; Genesis 13:15–16; Genesis 15:4; and Genesis 17:19. Over and over and over, God kept His promise! What happened in Genesis 21:2? The everlasting covenant took off! Hebrews 11:8–9 confirmed that Isaac was a coheir to the promise that was given in Genesis 12. And that's what we're going to see unfold today.

In verse 3, Abraham named his son Isaac. Why? Because God told Abraham to name him Isaac (Genesis 17:19). Isn't it cool when God speaks to us, and then we get to respond and do what He says? The question is, are we listening to Him? But as we've seen, Abraham wasn't perfect. If God could use Abraham, He can use us too. We just have to be willing. In verse 4, when Isaac was eight days old, Abraham circumcised him in obedience to God's command (Genesis 17:9–12). Abraham was obedient.

"Abraham was 100 years old when his son Isaac was born to him" (v. 5). God rewards patience. Even though Abraham went wrong with Hagar, God was still faithful. Abraham and Sarah waited 25 years to see the fulfillment of God's promise. Hebrews 6:12 says to "be imitators of those who inherit the promises through faith and perseverance." We want the blessings, but we're not willing to persevere in the faith. James 1:3 promises that "the testing of your faith produces endurance." We want to believe, but will we endure?

Warren Wiersbe said, "Trusting God's promises not only gives you a blessing at the end, but it also gives you a blessing while you're waiting."[1] Romans 4:17 revealed this was such a radical fulfillment of God's promise! Abraham even considered himself as good as dead!

*Genesis 21:6–7*: "Isaac" means laughter. Constable said Isaac was a source of joy to his parents as fulfillment of the promised seed.[2] God is a God of miracles. Through these events, we can see a living link from Adam and Eve to Noah to Abraham and Sarah to Isaac (v. 7).

*Genesis 21:8–10*: Three years old was the typical age for weaning. When Isaac turned three, Abraham threw a great feast (v. 8). Sarah saw Ishmael mocking Isaac. To mock means to ridicule. Sarah saw Ishmael as a threat to Isaac. Back in Genesis 19:14, when the sons-in-law didn't believe Lot, this was the same image. Later, in Judges 16:25, when the Philistines wanted Samson to entertain them, they wanted to make a mockery of him. Ishmael carried the seed of the serpent. The Muslims are descendants of Ishmael. But the *Seed* of the woman went to Isaac. Isaac carried the *Seed*, Christ. Ishmael would not be a coheir with Isaac

---

[1] Warren Wiersbe, *The Bible Exposition Commentary: Genesis–Deuteronomy* (Colorado Springs: David C. Cook, 2001), 99.

[2] Thomas L. Constable, *Expository Notes of Dr. Thomas Constable: Genesis*, 282; https://planobiblechapel.org/tcon/notes/pdf/genesis.pdf.

(v. 10). According to the "laws of Lipit-Ishtar," if a slave bears children, and the father then grants freedom to her and her children, the children of the slave shall not divide the estate with children of their former master.[3]

*Genesis 21:11–13*: "Now this was a very difficult thing for Abraham because of his son" (v. 11). Difficult means distressed, grievous, shaking. Abraham knew Ishmael was born of the flesh, whereas Isaac was born of the Spirit. This truth became more and more prominent as the seed unfolded. Notice this weird pattern that the firstborn was rejected in favor of the second born: Cain and *Abel*, Ishmael and *Isaac*, Esau and *Jacob*, Manasseh and *Ephraim*.

Verse 12 explains that it came down to divine choice. God chose Abraham and then Isaac. Hagar was the mother of Ishmael. Sarah was the mother of Isaac. The child with Hagar resulted from Abraham and Sarah's coercion to force the fulfillment of the promises on their own. With Sarah and Abraham, there was freedom and there was waiting.

In verse 13, God said He would still bless Ishmael, even though Ishmael was not part of His plan. The problem comes when we aren't patient and do it our own way instead of God's. Because Hagar and Abraham did not wait, we have Islam today. Really because Sarah said, "I can't wait." So now we have this tension. We have tension because of someone else's sin. Please don't forget that your sin will always impact someone else.

*Genesis 21:14–16*: Before sending Hagar and Ishmael away, Abraham provided them with bread and waterskins for the journey. The skins would have contained about three gallons or 24 pounds of water. Once it was gone, Hagar left Ishmael under a bush. Bruce Waltke said Hagar basically abandoned her child.[4]

*Genesis 21:17–21*: God heard their cries (v. 17). God still wants to redeem everyone. God promised to make Ishmael a great nation. God took care of this people group (v. 18). He provided sustenance. God opened the eyes of Hagar and provided a well. Even though they were rejected, He saw them and cared for them. This sounds to me like the woman at the well. In John 4, Jesus met the Samaritan woman at the well. Though others did not value her, Jesus knew this person still mattered. He promised her living water. Even if you're functioning in the seed of the serpent, Jesus still offers the water of life. John 7:37–39, Jesus said: "If *anyone* is thirsty, he should come to Me and drink! The one who believes in Me, as the Scripture has said, will have streams of living water flow from deep within him."

---

[3] Constable, 283.

[4] Bruce Waltke, *Genesis: A Commentary* (Grand Rapids: Zondervan, 2001), n. p.

# Closing

Those who believe in the *Seed*, Christ, will receive the Spirit. This *Seed* that came through Abraham is available to everyone. Wiersbe said, "Hagar is certainly a picture of the needy multitudes in the world today: wandering, weary, thirsty, blind, and giving up in despair."[5] God cares for everybody. He cares for the Hagars and the Sarahs. What Jesus promised through the pre-incarnate Christ . . . He did. Sarah became a mom, and Isaac was the chosen one. My prayer is that you see God's hand was obviously on Isaac, but the message of hope is available for all.

## The Daily Word

This story unfolded out of two mothers' hearts: Sarah for Isaac and Hagar for Ishmael. Sarah sought the Lord and was filled with joy and laughter at the birth of her promised son Isaac. Hagar despaired because she had to let go of her son and trust the Lord with his future. Yet even in her despair, she sought the Lord for help.

The Lord sees what you are pondering in your heart. May the Lord bless you today as you walk in the hope we have in the Messiah. Delight yourself in the Lord, trust in His time and in His way, and He will give you the desires of your heart.

**But God said to Abraham, "Do not be concerned about the boy and your slave. Whatever Sarah says to you, listen to her, because your offspring will be traced through Isaac. But I will also make a nation of the slave's son because he is your offspring." —Genesis 21:12–13**

Further Scripture: Psalm 20:4; Psalm 37:3–5; Acts 15:8

## Questions

1. In Genesis 20:2, Abraham repeated the same lie he had told previously (Genesis 12:11–13). How can you keep from falling back into past sin?

2. Despite Abraham's sin, God was still faithful to keep His promises. How do you see God's faithfulness in Genesis 20:3–6? Why does God keep us from sin at times, but other times, He doesn't? (Genesis 12:15–17; 39:9; 1 Samuel 25:26,34; Acts 5:3)

3. In Genesis 21, how was Isaac a picture of Jesus? (Genesis 18:13–14; 21:2; Luke 1:34–37; 2:10-11; Galatians 4:4)

---

[5] Wiersbe, 102.

4. Which of Abraham's sons carried the *Seed*, Christ: Isaac or Ishmael? Do you think Islam originated with Ishmael? Why or why not? (Genesis 21:9–10)

5. In Genesis 21:19, God opened Hagar's eyes to see His love and His compassion for her and Ishmael. What did this show about God's character even though Isaac was the chosen one and not Ishmael? (John 4:10–14; 7:37–39)

6. What did the Holy Spirit highlight to you in Genesis 20—21 through the reading or the teaching?

# Lesson 10: Genesis 22
## *Seed*: God's Command to Sacrifice Isaac

## Teaching Notes

### Intro

Our goal for the book of Genesis is to emphasize one word—seed. Throughout Genesis, the seed of the serpent and the *Seed* of the woman—the Messiah—were constantly in tension. In Genesis 21:34, Abraham lived as a foreigner. He never had a home but was constantly on the move, walking by faith.

### Teaching

*Genesis 22:1*: God tested Abraham. After all the things Abraham had been through, Abraham was so in tune with God that his immediate response was "Here I am." Unlike Samuel and Eli, Abraham knew God was speaking to him. Testing is not a temptation. Satan tempted Adam and Eve. Will God ever tempt us with sin? No. Temptation comes from a desire within. A test or trial comes from the Lord with a specific purpose to fulfill. God wants to refine us. Abraham had given up more than anyone at this point. Dr. Tom Constable gave six instances when Abraham was tested and gave up something, then God gave him abundantly more in return:[1]

- Abraham left his homeland, but God gave him a new one.
- Abraham left his extended family, and then God gave him a bigger one.
- Abraham gave Lot the best land, but God gave him more.
- Abraham rejected the reward from an earthly king, and then God gave him greater riches.
- Abraham sent Ishmael away, but God still blessed Ishmael and made him the father of nations.
- And because Abraham was willing to give up his son Isaac, God spared Isaac and used him to give Abraham nations.

---

[1] Thomas L. Constable, *Expository Notes of Dr. Thomas Constable: Genesis*, 297, https://planobiblechapel.org/tcon/notes/pdf/genesis.pdf.

Many of us want the results, but we don't want to go through the testing. Constable said that when you go through a sacrifice or time of testing, it will always lead to more of the Lord.[2]

*Genesis 22:2*: "Moriah" means where the Lord provides or the Lord appears. This is the same place where David built an altar, where Solomon built his temple, and possibly where Christ died. This land of Moriah was where God appeared and God provided repeatedly . . . to David, to Solomon, and to Christ. The question is, will we walk by faith to get to that point?

*Genesis 22:3*: One day God told Abraham to sacrifice his one and only son with Sarah, Isaac. Then, "early the next morning" Abraham obeyed. There was no hesitation and no debate. Hebrews 11:19 says Abraham had radical faith. He believed it was going to be OK; he believed God could bring Isaac back from the dead (even though he'd never seen that before). Wiersbe said, "In one sense, it's a compliment when God gives us a test because it shows He wants to promote us in the school of faith."[3]

*Genesis 22:4*: "On the third day Abraham looked up and saw the place in the distance." For three days, Abraham knew he was going to kill his son. There was plenty of time for him to turn around and go back home. I believe God gave Abraham ample time to question whether he was really called to do this. Abraham didn't resist; he embraced faith.

*Genesis 22:5*: With confidence, Abraham told the servants who had accompanied him on the journey, "The boy and I will return." Abraham believed *both* he and his son would come back. Josephus, a Roman-Jewish historian, said Isaac was probably 25 years old, while most other theologians say he was likely 15 to 16 years old. Regardless, Isaac was old enough to be fully aware of what was happening. Wiersbe said, "Abraham believed God and obeyed him when he didn't know *where* (Hebrews 11:8), when he didn't know *when* (Hebrews 11:9–10), when he didn't know *how* it would unfold (Hebrews 11:11), and when he didn't know *why* (Hebrews 11:17)."[4] Part of the test is not knowing the answers . . . the where, when, how, and why.

---

[2] Constable, 298.

[3] Warren W. Wiersbe, *The Bible Exposition Commentary: Genesis–Deuteronomy* (Colorado Springs: David C. Cook, 2001), 104.

[4] Wiersbe, 105.

*Genesis 22:6–9*: Just as Isaac carried the wood and the knife for his sacrifice (v. 6), I think of Christ carrying the cross, the weapon that would be used to kill Him. "God Himself will provide the lamb for the burnt offering" (v. 8). The land of Moriah means where God provides (vv. 7–8). Hamilton said, "If Abraham displays faith that obeys, then Isaac displays faith that cooperates. If Isaac was strong and big enough to carry the wood for his sacrifice, maybe he was strong enough to resist or subdue his father."[5] Even if Isaac could have resisted, he chose not to. Abraham's faith was beginning to show up in his son Isaac. When you walk in faith, you will impact other people.

*Genesis 22:10–11*: A sacrifice was a slaughter (v. 10). There was a sense of urgency when God spoke to Abraham: "Abraham, Abraham!" Just as Abraham responded to God with, "Here I am," so did other faithful followers of God. God intervened at critical points in each of these men's walk of faith. In Genesis 46:1–2, when God called, "Jacob, Jacob," Jacob responded, "Here I am." In Exodus 3:4, when God called, "Moses, Moses," Moses responded, "Here I am." In 1 Samuel 3:10, when God called, "Samuel, Samuel," Samuel responded, "Speak, for your servant is listening." In Acts 9:4, Saul heard a voice saying, "Saul, Saul."

*Genesis 22:12*: As Abraham raised the knife to kill his son in obedience to God, the Angel of the Lord stopped him and said, "Do not lay a hand on the boy. . . . For now I know that you fear God." Waltke described Abraham's obedience as an "Obedience which does not protect even what is most precious but trusts God with the future."[6] When obedience is radical, it means not holding on to anything anymore. Faith was no longer just words to Abraham; it was full on action. James 2:21–22 described Abraham's faith: "You see that faith was active together with his works, and by works, faith was perfected." It's one thing to say you believe in God, and it's another thing to walk it out.

*Genesis 22:13–14*: "Abraham looked up and saw a ram caught in the thicket by its horns." Jehovah Jireh is the name for God used here, and it means "The Lord will provide." Over and over, this mountain of the Lord, Mt. Moriah, has been referenced in the Psalms (24:3; 48:1; 99:9; 133:3) and in Isaiah (2:2–3; 30:29). This was the mountain of the Lord where God showed up! God always shows up in time of need. We, too, can trust that God will show up when we need him (Hebrews 4:16).

---

[5] Victor P. Hamilton, *The Book of Genesis: Chapters 18–50*, The New International Commentary on the Old Testament (Grand Rapids: Eerdmans, 1995), 110; quoted in Constable, 293.

[6] Bruce Waltke, *Genesis: A Commentary* (Grand Rapids: Zondervan, 2001), 308.

*Genesis 22:15–18*: "'By Myself I have sworn,' this is the Lord's declaration: 'Because you have done this thing and have not withheld your only son, I will indeed bless you . . . your offspring will possess the gates of their enemies.'" Remember that Abraham was spared when Sodom and Gomorrah were destroyed, and even Lot, who sat in the gates of Sodom, was spared because of Abraham. Because of Abraham's sacrifice and obedience, God promised He was going to do it . . . He was going to give Abraham more. Isaac was a picture of Christ offered as a sacrifice. In John 1:29, John the Baptist said, "Here is the Lamb of God, who takes away the sin of the world." Because Abraham was obedient, the seed continued and ultimately led to Jesus.

## Closing

The seed continues even now. Dr. Tom Constable said there were four types of seed:[7]

- natural seed—any physical descendants of Abraham (Isaac and Ishmael)
- natural/spiritual seed—believing physical descendants of Abraham (Isaac)
- spiritual seed—nonphysical, believing descendants (believing Gentiles)
- ultimate *Seed*—Christ Himself (Galatians 3:16)

There are layers to this "seed" theme that we're tracing. The crazy thing is that Abraham was willing to give up all of this to obey God. No matter where we go . . . when, how, why . . . we're just supposed to walk by faith. When you face a test, if it doesn't contradict the Word of God, then walk it out. God just might want to fulfill something . . . through you.

## The Daily Word

The Lord gave Abraham instructions to sacrifice his son Isaac. As difficult as the task was for Abraham, and as much as it did not make sense to kill his seed-bearer, Abraham said, "Here I am, Lord," and obeyed the Lord. However, as Abraham walked out the test, the Lord provided a ram to sacrifice, saving Isaac.

Today, the Lord may be calling you into a season of testing that does not make sense from your perspective. Keep an eternal perspective, one that deepens and strengthens your faith, so that you will lack nothing and reflect more and more of Jesus! Continue to have a heart of surrender saying, "Here I am, Lord." Trust the Lord to provide and fulfill His promises through you.

---

[7] Constable, 296.

> **And all the nations of the earth will be blessed by your offspring because you have obeyed My command. —Genesis 22:18**
>
> Further Scripture: Psalm 84:11; Hebrews 11:17; James 1:2–4

## Questions

1. In Genesis 22:1–12, how was Isaac a picture of Christ? (John 19:17–18; Hebrews 11:17, 19)

2. Why was it crucial that Abraham did not withhold his son Isaac from what God told him to do? (Genesis 22:16–18; Hebrews 11:19; James 2:21)

3. The Lord provided a substitute sacrifice in Genesis 22:13–14. Why then, in verse 14, did Abraham call that place, "The Lord Will Provide" (future tense)?

4. In Genesis 22:18, God promised a blessing to all nations through what? What does this blessing look like? (Luke 1:72–75)

5. The Lord referred to Isaac in Genesis 22:2, 12, 16 as Abraham's "son, your only son," although he also had a son named Ishmael. Why did the Lord refer to Isaac as his only son? (Genesis 21:10; 1 Corinthians 15:45–47)

6. What did the Holy Spirit highlight to you in Genesis 22 through the reading or the teaching?

# Lesson 11: Genesis 23—24
## *Seed*: Finding a Wife for Isaac

## Teaching Notes

### Intro

In Genesis 22, God tested Abraham by telling him to sacrifice his son Isaac. As we continue this study, we'll see this ongoing thread of the seed. Genesis 23 revealed that Sarah died at the age 127. In verses 4–6, Sarah was given a special burial site. In verses 11–20, Abraham purchased from Ephron the Hittite, for 400 shekels of silver, the field and the cave of Machpelah, where he buried Sarah.

### Teaching

*Genesis 24:1*: God had blessed Abraham "in everything." God's promises from Genesis 12 and Gen 15 were beginning to come to fruition. God was not done with His promises in the Old Testament. Now Isaac had to carry on the seed. And if there was a seed, there had to be a seed bearer, a wife. In Genesis 24, God provided a seed bearer for Isaac. It was not just through the man but also through the woman, that the *Seed* would continue.

*Genesis 24:2*: Abraham instructed his servant to swear that he would go back to Abraham's land and his family to find a wife for Isaac. By looking back at Genesis 15:2–3, while we can't know for sure who this servant was, it could have been Eliezer. The phrase, "place your hand under my thigh" can be translated literally as my loins/genitals. Why? It was not a homosexual act. It indicated a source of life.

*Genesis 24:3–6*: This was the most crucial mission for the seed to continue. Abraham established three conditions for his servant to follow:

- Don't select a wife from the Canaanites. Why? Because Ham's descendants were the Canaanites, who would become servants to Shem and Japheth. They worshipped Baal and Asherah (Deuteronomy 7:1–6). The seed bearer could not believe in false gods.

- Select her from Abraham's family.
- Don't take Isaac back to Abraham's former home.

*Genesis 24:7*: Abraham told his servant that God was going ahead of him to prepare the way. God is always ahead of the curve. Even though Adam and Eve sinned, God already had a plan ready to go. God knew what would happen with Ham, and He knew the *Seed*, Christ, would come through Shem. God is always going to trump and overcome our inadequacies.

*Genesis 24:8*: If this plan to find a wife for Isaac didn't work, the servant was released from it, but he still had to give a report. Romans 14:12 says, "So then, each of us will give an account of himself to God." Whether we are the servants responsible for preparing the way for the wife or preparing the way for Christ, we are going to have to give a report. Are we obedient to the conditions God outlines? We all have assignments to complete. In 1 John 2:28, we are told to remain in Him so we won't be ashamed before Him at His coming. As God's servants, we can't produce the outcome, but we are expected to be obedient to what He is asking us to do.

*Genesis 24:9–11*: Abraham's servant committed to the task assigned to him. He agreed to follow the conditions. Camels were very uncomfortable to ride, but they were a sign of wealth. Ten camels were a lot. Abraham's servant made the camels kneel beside a well outside of town. This was the time of day when women went out to draw water. A camel can drink 25 gallons! With ten camels, they needed 250 gallons of water.

*Genesis 24:12–17*: This was one of the first prayers in Scripture for specific guidance. The servant prayed, "Give me success." Success can be defined as God showing up. The Hebrew word *hesed* is commonly translated as "loving-kindness," "kindness," or "love." The servant prayed that God would continue His loyalty to His existing relationship with Abraham. The servant was praying as the women came out to draw water. This prayer was not about the servant. It had everything to do with everyone else. The servant understood the big picture of what God was doing here. This was exactly what happened to Ruth with Boaz. God is going to intervene when your heart is right with the Lord. Warren Wiersbe describes the life of this servant: He was praying, he asked for help, he kept his eyes open, and while he was praying, God answered his prayer.[1] Isaiah 65:24 says, "Even before they call, I will answer; while they are speaking, I will hear." When we pray

---

[1] Warren W. Wiersbe, *The Bible Exposition Commentary: Genesis–Deuteronomy* (Colorado Springs: David C. Cook, 2001), 108.

expectantly, God answers. "Before he had finished speaking, there was Rebekah." The servant ran to meet her. The servant knew in his heart this was the woman he had prayer for. Sometimes the Lord just deposits within you a heart connection. Sometimes, you just know.

*Genesis 24:18–21*: Rebekah not only offered water for the servant, but also offered to water the camels. Imagine carrying two 5-gallon buckets 25 times. Wiersbe noted, "Make every occasion a great occasion, for you can never tell when someone may be taking your measure for a larger place."[2] In other words, when you are doing something small, you can never tell when someone is watching and ready to elevate you to a higher place. God honored Rebekah to become a *Seed* bearer in the line of Christ. When we walk out the smallest little details in life, we are honoring Christ. And sometimes God will take that small thing and give you more (Luke 16:10). The servant silently watched Rebekah to see if she was going to finish the task, if she was going to honor what she said.

*Genesis 24:22–27*: The servant gave Rebekah an abundance of gifts. Bethuel was Isaac's cousin. And suddenly, another qualifier was fulfilled. Rebekah was from Abraham's family. I think Rebekah blew the servant away. When we walk by faith, we never know what it's going to look like, but I think when we walk by faith, God always goes above and beyond (Ephesians 3:20). The servant bowed down and worshipped the Lord because Rebekah was better than he imagined. What started in a prayer ended in a prayer! God answered his prayers. What is cool about the rest of this story is that it all unfolded, everything came together, and Rebekah was the one.

*Genesis 24:60*: Here's what happened to Rebekah. When her family sent her with the servant to become Isaac's wife, they blessed her: "Our sister, may you become thousands upon ten thousands. May your offspring possess the gates of their enemies." Because Rebekah was ready and willing, the seed continued. Christ is coming back. Will you be a servant who helps people get ready?

## Closing

Let's go back to the power of prayer. I think there's something to this and to the promise of how it fits with us. We must start believing and walk into our answered prayers. In Mark 11:24, Jesus said, "Therefore I tell you, all the things you pray and ask for—believe that you have received them, and you will have them." In John 15:7, Jesus said, "If you remain in Me and My words remain in you, ask whatever you want, and it will be done for you." In 1 John 5:14–15,

---

[2] Wiersbe, 108.

John wrote, "Now this is the confidence we have before Him: Whenever we ask anything according to His will, He hears us. And if we know that He hears whatever we ask, we know that we have what we have asked Him for." Psalm 66:9 says, "He keeps us alive and does not allow our feet to slip."

We must start praying for more from the Lord! In 1 Samuel 1:27, Hannah received the son for whom she prayed. In Psalm 118:21, the psalmist proclaimed, "I will give thanks to You because You have answered me and have become my salvation." In Psalm 5:3, David said, "At daybreak I plead my case to You and watch expectantly." Wasn't that what happened here with Abraham's servant? He prayed and expected, and God answered. This provided an incredible picture of a father getting a bride ready for his son who was waiting. It's a picture of God who is getting His bride—the church—ready for Christ, who is waiting to return.

Warren Wiersbe broke all of Genesis 24 into four sections: "The will of the father" to want this, "the witness of the servant" to do this, "the willingness of the bride," and "the welcome of the bridegroom."[3] This was such a beautiful picture of a marriage, not just of Isaac and Rebekah, but also of the church and Christ. Are you a servant who is willing to prepare the way? Are you a bride who is preparing for Christ's return?

---

## The Daily Word

Abraham's servant sought the Lord after he received orders from Abraham to go and find a wife for Isaac. The servant immediately appealed to the Lord in prayer before beginning this crucial task of finding a seed-bearer.

In the same way, the Lord longs for you to come to Him. He promises He will answer you. He promises when you ask, you will receive. And yet, why do believers so often turn to the Lord as the final step in obedience, walking in their own strength? Today, pause and ask the Lord for help before you go and do the tasks the Lord has for you.

**"Lord, God of my master Abraham," he prayed, "give me success today, and show kindness to my master Abraham." —Genesis 24:12**

Further Scripture: Psalm 91:15; Jeremiah 33:3; Matthew 7:7

---

[3] Wiersbe, 107–10.

## Questions

1. Abraham lived in the land God had promised to his descendants. Yet according to Genesis 23:4, how did he view himself in regard to dwelling there? (Hebrews 11:9)

2. Although Abraham had two sons, his son Isaac carried the *Seed*, Christ, and partook in the covenant and promise (Genesis 17:21; Hebrews 11:18). What else did Isaac receive? How did this parallel with Christ? (Genesis 24:36; Ephesians 1:22)

3. In Genesis 24:2–6, what three qualifications did Abraham give his servant for finding a wife for Isaac? Why did Abraham not want Isaac to marry a Canaanite woman? (Genesis 9:24–27)

4. Abraham told his servant in Genesis 24:7 that the Lord would "send His angel [messenger] before you." Do you think this one who was sent ahead to make the way for the bride of Isaac could have been the pre-incarnate Christ? (Genesis 24:30) Why or why not?

5. How do you see Isaac, Rebekah, and Abraham's servant symbolizing the Bride and the Bridegroom?

6. In Genesis 24:35, how did Abraham's servant describe Abraham to his relatives?

7. What did the Holy Spirit highlight to you in Genesis 23—24 through the reading or the teaching?

# Lesson 12: Genesis 25—26
*Seed*: The Birth of Jacob and Esau

## Teaching Notes

### Intro

Most people look at the sin and the fall, but we know that there's so much more through Christ.

### Teaching

*Genesis 25:7–9*: Verses 7–9 reveal that Abraham died when he was 175 years old, and he was buried in the cave of Machpelah where Sarah was buried. Verses 12–18 provide the record of Ishmael's sons, and verses 19–26 provide the record of the sons of Isaac. Because of the conflict between the seed of the serpent and the *Seed* of the woman, Christ, there was this constant tension, and we'll see that today.

*Genesis 25:21*: "Isaac prayed to the Lord on behalf of his wife because she was childless." Abraham modeled prayer, his servant modeled prayer, and now Isaac prayed because Rebekah was barren. Why did he pray? He was carrying the seed, and if Rebekah was barren, there would be no descendants. The Lord heard his prayer. Praying means intercession; Isaac went to battle on behalf of his wife. Rebekah was barren for at least 20 years after their marriage. Constable said, "God closed her womb for that time, so that the chosen family would recognize her children as the fruit of His grace, rather than simply the fruit of nature."[4] Maybe God waited so He could get the glory, so everyone could see Him intervening. Bruce Waltke said, "Theirs is not a natural but a supernatural seed."[5]

*Genesis 25:22*: Obviously, Rebekah was pregnant with at least two children. She inquired of the Lord. This wrestling of her children was painful, which pointed back to Genesis 3:15–16: "I will intensify your labor pains." Rebekah was feeling the physical pain of Adam and Eve. She was carrying the *Seed*, but it was not easy.

---

[1] Thomas L. Constable, *Expository Notes of Dr. Thomas Constable: Genesis*, 317, https://planobiblechapel.org/tcon/notes/pdf/genesis.pdf.

[5] Bruce Waltke, *Genesis: A Commentary* (Grand Rapids: Zondervan, 2001), 357.

The pain continued throughout her life, as shown when Rebekah said to Isaac, "I'm sick of my life because of these Hittite women. If Jacob marries a Hittite woman, what good is my life?" (Genesis 27:46). Rebekah's whole purpose in life was to be the *Seed* bearer. She felt this tension in the beginning (Genesis 25:22) and the end (Genesis 27:46). But just as Abraham had to walk by faith, so did Rebekah. All of us have to go through our own tensions. In her case, her two boys were always fighting. Rebekah endured the pain because she was called for a purpose—to carry Jacob and Esau.

*Genesis 25:23–26*: God reminded Rebekah of her purpose: two nations would come from her womb. Prophetically, the younger would take the lead. There were indeed twins, as Rebekah already knew, in her womb. Esau meant "hairy one." He was also called Edom, which meant "reddish" (v. 30). Jacob came out grasping Esau's heel. Jacob meant "heel holder." Isaac was 60 years old when they were born.

*Genesis 25:27–28*: Esau became an expert hunter, an outdoorsman. Jacob was a quiet man, or a plain man, who stayed at home. Abraham died when the twins were about 15 years old, so they got to spend time learning from their grandpa and hearing his stories. Surely, Abraham talked about the land and the blessing. Isaac had a heart for Esau because he liked the food Esau hunted. Isaac was already going down the wrong path. Isaac went for the fleshly things . . . the "taste" of wild game. Rebekah loved Jacob. Parental favoritism always divides the family. Bruce Waltke said: "A marriage made in heaven can end in dysfunction when a spouse gives priority to taste in the mouth over a voice in heart."[6] Isaac's whole taste for food trumped the perspective of the seed. God was using imperfect people, and with time, their perspectives got skewed. I think Rebekah saw it coming the whole time. Constable said: "Adam failed in eating, Noah in drinking, and Isaac in tasting."[7] I think if it wasn't for Rebekah, who knows how this could have ended up. God used a woman to sustain the seed. We tend to think of the patriarchs—Abraham, Isaac, and Jacob—but if it wasn't for Rebekah, Isaac would have been in trouble.

In God's plan, you may not ever be the name that everyone knows, but you can play a super important role in keeping it going. We can see a parallel here with the Prodigal Son and the Father's heart—Esau, the older brother, and Jacob, the outcast. Jacob was plain; he was civilized, domesticated, a homebody. In the NET Bible, David Sharpe said Jacob's name implied he was calm and

---

[6] Waltke, 363.

[7] Constable, 320.

even-tempered.[8] That same language could also imply "blameless."[9] In Proverbs 29:10, the same word is translated "upright." This implied the mentality that this upright person Jacob had.

*Genesis 25:29–32*: Jacob cooked the stew because he was a plain person, a homebody. Esau, the hairy outdoorsman, came in from the field. Esau was exhausted and famished, so he needed food. This action was premeditated on Jacob's part. It was extreme. In this culture, the birthright was essential. In *Understanding the Genesis*, Nahum Sarna described the importance of a birthright, which included the privilege of being chief of the tribe or family. The one with the birthright was the bearer of the blessing of Yahweh's promises. He received possession of land. He held the covenant fellowship that God intended for the firstborn. He received a double portion of inheritance. And he was the spiritual leader of the family.[10]

*Genesis 25:33*: Jacob was smart; he made Esau swear. Esau gave up his birthright because he looked to the flesh. The second you look to the flesh, you begin to function in the seed of the serpent, not the *Seed* of the woman. You have to have a spiritual perspective. Be careful about giving up what God is entrusting to you. He'll just give it to someone else. If you don't walk it out, He'll find someone else.

The firstborn of the womb was important. The firstborn of the womb was always consecrated to the Lord. In Exodus 13:12, Moses relayed God's command: "You are to present to the Lord every firstborn male of the womb. All firstborn offspring of the livestock you own that are males will be the Lord's." Deuteronomy 18:4 further specified, "You are to give him the firstfruits of your grain, new wine, oil, and the first sheared wool of your flock." But Esau effectively said, "I don't care." That's functioning in the seed of the serpent, functioning in the flesh. Esau didn't present anything to God; he just wanted to know what he could have for himself. In 1 Corinthians 15:20–23, Christ is identified as "the firstfruits of those who have fallen asleep." Did Jacob and Rebekah force the hand of God to get the blessing? Or were they just aware that something wasn't right, and they were ready to take the opportunity when it presented itself?

*Genesis 25:34*: Esau despised his birthright because he gave it up. And when Esau gave it up, Jacob got it. Was Jacob in the wrong? Remember the Amorites who hadn't sinned enough (Genesis 15:16)? Maybe this was God's way of continuing the promise. We don't have to agree with it or understand it. It was the prophetic

---

[8] NET Bible, https://net.bible.org/bible/Genesis+25, footnote for Gen. 25:43.

[9] NET Bible, footnote for Gen. 25:43.

[10] Nahum M. Sarna, *Understanding Genesis* (Skokie, IL: Varda Books, 1966), 185; quoted in Constable, 321.

word that God spoke to Rebekah playing out. Constable pointed out that Jacob's "scheming to obtain the birthright and the blessing was unnecessary, because God had already promised that *he* would become the dominant nation."[11] Did Jacob need to scheme to make it happen? Dr. Constable would say no. Perhaps God prophesied it simply because He knew it was going to happen, even though Jacob's scheming was wrong. Whatever your view, the incident seems to show that God's plan doesn't always have to be pretty in our eyes. Sometimes you can't see what God's doing right now.

## Closing

It might not look pretty, but God was setting the stage for the *Seed* to continue. And in this case, it was coming through Rebekah and Jacob.

## The Daily Word

The story of Jacob and Esau was not without sin, and yet the Lord used them and their mother Rebekah when He set the stage for the *Seed*, Christ, to continue.

Even when people fall, we can—and we must—*trust* that God is able to work in and through the difficult situation. The key is to stay the course. Keep the faith. As we walk out our faith in Christ, we can hold on to the hope in Christ, knowing His plan prevails. Praise the Lord!

**And the LORD said to her: "Two nations are in your womb; two people will come from you and be separated. One people will be stronger than the other, and the older will serve the younger." —Genesis 25:23**

Further Scripture: Psalm 130:5–8; Proverbs 19:21; Romans 8:28

## Questions

1. Why was Genesis 25:23 significant? Which one of Isaac's sons was the "older" and which one was the "younger"? (Romans 9:12; Genesis 25:25–26)
2. Which of Isaac's sons carried the *Seed*, Christ: Esau or Jacob? (Genesis 25:23, 29–34)
3. In Genesis 25:28, why do you think Rebekah "loved Jacob"? What was Isaac's motivation for loving Esau?
4. In Genesis 25:29–34, what exchange took place between Jacob and Esau? Do you think Jacob was wrong to take the birthright from Esau?

---

[11] Constable, 318.

5.  What did God promise Isaac in Genesis 26:3–4? How did this relate to His promises to those who carried the *Seed*, Christ, before Isaac? Are you included in this blessing? (Genesis 12:3, 7; 18:18; 22:17–18; Galatians 3:29)

6.  What did Isaac do in Genesis 26:17–19? What symbolic significance did this action carry?

7.  What did the Holy Spirit highlight to you in Genesis 25—26 through the reading or the teaching?

# Lesson 13: Genesis 27—28
## *Seed*: How Jacob Stole Esau's Birthright

## Teaching Notes

### Intro

The *Seed*, Christ, came from Adam to Noah to Shem to Abraham and Sarah to Isaac and Rebekah to Jacob. And in Genesis 25, Esau sold his birthright to Jacob for a bowl of stew.

### Teaching

*Genesis 27:1–2*: The battle that started in Rebekah's womb continued. Isaac was 100 years old at this point; Scripture said he lived to be 180. Abraham lived to 175. Nobody knows the day of his death. Isaac did not end well. Abraham finished well because he looked for a wife for Isaac to continue the blessing. King David handed off the building of the temple to Solomon. Paul laid the groundwork for Timothy to be successful. But here we have Isaac who just wanted good food. Who else in Scripture didn't finish well? Judas, Lot, Gideon, Noah, Samson, King Saul, King Solomon, Demas (walked with Paul, then he went back to his old ways). Isaac did not finish strong. How will we finish?

*Genesis 27:3–4*: Remember Esau was the hunter, so Isaac's request wasn't strange. Six times in this chapter, Isaac referenced this tasty food. At this time, most blessings were public, not private. For instance, in Genesis 49:1, Jacob publicly blessed his sons. What did Isaac have to hide? It's almost like he knew this wasn't of the Lord but wanted to do it anyway. Isaac was a man who had prayed and pressed in, but now he had started to go the opposite direction. Isaac wasn't functioning by faith, but instead depended on:

- His sense of taste (Genesis 27:4, 9, 25).
- His sense of touch (Genesis 27:21).
- His hearing (Genesis 27:22).
- His sense of smell (Genesis 27:27).

*Genesis 27:5–8*: Isaac functioned in his flesh, not by faith and in the Spirit, and he missed it. Everything he did was focused on his natural senses, not faith, and Rebekah knew how to take advantage of this. Rebekah spoke into her favorite son, Jacob. In verse 6, she never referred to Isaac as her husband or Esau as her son. There was no connection there anymore. Rebekah knew the prophecy, but she was no longer functioning in faith either. She was scheming and lying to walk into the prophecy.

*Genesis 27:9–10*: Rebekah and Jacob didn't want to wait for the blessing; they had to get it themselves. This was reminiscent of Sarah and Abraham with Hagar. There was this constant impatience to receive the blessing. Not only did Jacob purchase the birthright, but now he was stealing the blessing. Really the blessing is about the same as the birthright. There's not much difference. Later, when Esau wanted to inherit the blessing and birthright, he was rejected. According to Hebrews 12:17b: "he was rejected because he didn't find an opportunity for repentance, though he sought it with tears."

*Genesis 27:11*: Jacob knew he would get caught. He knew doing this in a deceiving way wasn't right. Warren Wiersbe said, "Faith is living without scheming, and faith means obeying God no matter how we feel, what we think, or what might happen."[1] Were Jacob and Rebekah walking by faith in this moment? No! Why? Because they were lying and scheming. They didn't have to lie and scheme for the prophecy to be fulfilled. There is a weird tension when there's a prophecy spoken over you. How much do you let the Lord unfold and how much do you walk out? As humans, we live in this tension. First Thessalonians 5:20 says not to despise prophetic utterances. How do we embrace them in such a way that we walk them out but don't force them?

What we do know, is that Jacob knew it was wrong to deceive. Satan is known as the deceiver (2 Corinthians 11:3). The opposite of the seed of the serpent is the *Seed* of truth. Jesus is the truth (John 14:6). If there's a prophetic word, you don't have to deceive to make it happen. You can walk into it in truth. But God, to continue the seed, used imperfect people.

*Genesis 27:12–15*: Jacob knew he was acting as a deceiver. And he knew the promise of Genesis 12:3: "If you curse me, you'll be cursed, if you bless me, you'll be blessed." When Jacob didn't want to do this, Rebekah insisted. Everything about this feels off. Rebekah was lying and deceiving. She knew Jacob was going to steal the blessing, and she was OK with that.

---

[1] Warren W. Wiersbe, *The Bible Exposition Commentary: Genesis–Deuteronomy* (Colorado Springs: David C. Cook, 2001), 121.

*Genesis 27:16–19*: Rebekah covered everything—Jacob's neck and hands—and had Jacob wear Esau's clothes. Rebekah did all this. Go back to Genesis 24:60. This was the godly, beautiful Rebekah who watered all the camels. I believe Rebekah had this in mind the whole time. I believe she knew what she was doing, and she went after the blessing. Perhaps Rebekah believed Isaac was dying, and she feared that Jacob would miss it, so she intervened. When God gives you a blessing and a prophetic word of that magnitude, it just becomes part of who you are. Jacob was after the blessing.

*Genesis 27:20–26*: How many lies did Jacob tell? (1) His name (v. 19); (2) said he did as Isaac told him (v. 19); (3) "my game" (v. 19); (4) he gave credit to God in his lying (v. 20); (5) he again claimed to be Esau (v. 24); and (6) his kiss was hypocritical (v. 26). Isaac blessed Jacob because of Jacob's "goat" hands. Jacob continued lying. He again claimed to be Esau (v. 24) This was reminiscent of Judas and Jesus. Lie after lie after lie, ending with a kiss (vv. 25–26) Rebekah knew the blessing was coming (Genesis 24:60) and that it had to come to Jacob, not through Esau. It took six lies to get there (v. 27).

*Genesis 27:28–29*: This was an awesome picture of what the Promised Land was going to look like. We already know the descendants of Ham were going to serve the descendants of Shem and Japheth. Isaac's blessing was just like Genesis 12: "Those who curse you will be cursed, and those who bless you will be blessed." Don't miss this—talking about "the nations" even speaks into Matthew 28:19–20 and how the nations will receive the gospel when we go to the ends of the earth.

*Genesis 27:30–33*: Isaac couldn't stop trembling. Verse 33 describes Isaac's trembling as uncontrollable, with great excess of trembling. I believe there are root sins that, if we don't cut them off, get passed down to our kids. Abraham lied to Abimelech about Sarah, Isaac had lied to Abimelech about Rebekah, and now Isaac and his sons participated in the lies.

*Genesis 27:34–35*: Human sin can impact everything. The Israelites demanded a king, and they got Saul. Rahab lied to protect the spies in Joshua 2:4–5. Her family was spared because she lied to protect the Israelites. Matthew 1:1–5 contains the historical record of Christ. Rahab was the prostitute in the lineage of Christ. I believe the same thing happened with Jacob and Rebekah. God still used two people who lied to continue the lineage of Christ. I'm not saying it's right or it's justified. It happened.

*Genesis 27:36–38*: When Esau realized that Isaac had blessed Jacob, he begged for Isaac's blessing. Yet Hebrews 12:16–17 explains that Esau was the immoral and irreverent one. Later, when he wanted to inherit the blessing, he was rejected. It's so strange that we see these six lies Jacob used to steal the blessing, and yet when we get to the faith chapter in Hebrews, it's Esau who was called the immoral and irreverent one. I think this proves the point that Esau was in the wrong, and Jacob and Rebekah needed to do everything they could to preserve the seed. It was the opposite of the blessing (vv. 39–40).

## Closing

When all was said and done, God used lies and deception from Rebekah and Jacob because of something Esau did wrong. God knew what He was doing through those two to preserve the lineage of Christ.

## The Daily Word

As you walk with the Lord, remember His promises to Jacob on his journey. Remember the Lord's promise to you because you are on a journey with Him as well. What promises are you holding on to today?

**Look, I am with you and will watch over you wherever you go. I will bring you back to this land, for I will not leave you until I have done what I have promised you. —Genesis 28:15**

Further Scripture: Exodus 3:12; Psalm 121:5; Romans 8:31

## Questions

1. In Genesis 27:1–29, Rebekah prepared food for Isaac and assisted Jacob in pretending to be his brother before Esau could complete his assigned task. What did Rebekah know that motivated her to do this? (Hebrews 12:16–17)
2. In Genesis 27:4, 21–22, 25, and 27, by what senses did Isaac function rather than functioning by faith? What can you learn from this?
3. What blessings did Isaac give Jacob in Genesis 27:26–29? What blessings did he give Esau in Genesis 27:38–40? What is the difference between the two blessings? (Hebrews 11:20)
4. What did Rebekah say to Isaac in Genesis 27:46? Why did she say this?
5. Although Rebekah and Jacob protected the *Seed*, Christ, through lying and deception, do you think they were justified in doing so?

6. How was Jacob's dream of a ladder in Genesis 28:12 a picture of Jesus? (John 1:51; Ephesians 1:10; Colossians 1:20)

7. Like Abraham and Isaac, what things did the Lord promise to Jacob in Genesis 28:13–15? How were the promises to Abraham fulfilled through Isaac and Jacob? (Hebrews 6:14; Galatians 3:8–9, 16; Matthew 1:2)

8. What did the Holy Spirit highlight to you in Genesis 27—28 through the reading or the teaching?

# Lesson 14: Genesis 29
## *Seed*: The Line of Judah Came Through Leah

## Teaching Notes

### Intro

In the last lesson, we learned that Jacob stole the birthright and the blessing. Esau was so angry he wanted to kill his brother. Rebekah told Jacob to flee to her brother Laban in Haran because she knew what Esau planned to do (Genesis 27:41–43). Isaac blessed Jacob and told him not to take a Canaanite wife (Genesis 28:1). So, the Messianic prophecy would continue through Jacob (vv. 3–4). Esau did the opposite of what Isaac wanted and married a Canaanite. The seed of the serpent and the *Seed* of the woman continued to rage against each other. The Edomites (descendants of Esau) would war against the Israelites (descendants of Jacob). It would be an ongoing battle (vv. 8–9). Jacob had a dream of angels going up and down a ladder. The Lord spoke to Jacob and blessed him, promised him the land, and reaffirmed that he was the chosen one (vv. 10–12). This is the backdrop of Genesis 29.

### Teaching

*Genesis 29:1*: Jacob knew he was carrying the seed, but he didn't have a seed bearer (a wife). The first thing Abraham's servant did was pray. Jacob, however, continued his journey from Beersheba to Haran, a walking distance of 400–450 miles. The Hebrew here implies, "he lifted up his feet."[1] You can't go where God's called you to if you don't move your feet. Jacob needed to find a wife. Scripture says marriage can be an option; it's not commanded. For Jacob, however, it was not an option. He knew he needed a seed bearer.

*Genesis 29:2–4*: Three flocks of sheep surrounded a well that was covered with a stone. Usually it took two to three men to move this stone (v. 2). Jacob asked the shepherds where they were from and they responded, "Haran" (v. 3). The whole point of Jacob going through this process was to look for a wife. As he questioned the shepherds, Jacob found out he had already reached his

---

[1] Bruce Waltke, *Genesis: A Commentary* (Grand Rapids: Zondervan, 2001), 400.

destination (v. 4). Praise God! This was the guy Jacob had been looking for (v. 5). Then Rachel appeared, coming with sheep. Unbelievers would call this a coincidence. But believers would realize God's hand was on Jacob (v. 6).

*Genesis 29:7–10*: At the well, Jacob told the shepherds what they needed to do. He didn't want the shepherds around when he talked to Rachel (v. 7). The shepherds didn't want to go. Maybe they were waiting for more help or were just lazy (v. 8). Jewish tradition says Jacob was a giant. He "manned up" and rolled the stone away by himself. This was a pretty powerful picture of what he could do for Rachel. There was something about Jacob and stones. Jacob laid his head on a stone when he had the dream, and he anointed the stone when it was over. He wanted to remember all God had done (Genesis 28:18–19). Later in Genesis 31:45–53, his covenant with Laban would be marked with stones as a witness to their agreement. Jacob used rocks as markers whenever God showed up.

*Genesis 29:11*: This is the only time in Scripture where a man and woman kissed. Jacob wept loudly because he realized he had found success. Contrast Jacob's response to Genesis 24:26–27. When Abraham's servant saw he had found success, he bowed down and worshipped the Lord. But when Jacob kissed Rachel and wept loudly, he didn't praise God. He didn't praise God because he didn't pray to God. It seems like Jacob did everything in his own strength. He didn't seem to include God, and he didn't praise God.

*Genesis 29:12–15*: When Jacob met Laban, "Jacob told him all that had happened" (v. 13). Did Jacob leave out the part about his deception of Isaac and Esau, which necessitated his journey to Haran? Laban disregarded the family relationship between him and Jacob. All Laban wanted was what he could get out of an economic relationship.[2] Waltke described Laban as "an oppressive lord over an indentured servant paying off a bride price."[3]

*Genesis 29:16–21*: Leah was the older daughter, and Rachel was the younger daughter (v. 16). Leah's eyes were ordinary, which could mean "delicate, weak, soft." Waltke said it could mean she lacked the sparkle that culture prized as beautiful. In contrast, Rachel was shapely and beautiful. Leah meant "cow" and Rachel meant "ewe." Laban treated his daughters as commodities he could bargain.[4] Jacob loved Rachel, so he agreed to work seven years for her (v. 18). This was a strange answer from Laban, but Jacob was not in a spiritual condition to

---

[2] Waltke, 404.

[3] Waltke, 405.

[4] Waltke, 405.

discern that something was off (v. 19). Seven years felt like nothing to Jacob because of his love for Rachel (v. 20). Jacob was not in the right mindset. He was not thinking about continuing the *Seed*, Christ. He was only thinking about his desires. Jacob had worked for seven years for Rachel, and he wanted to make her his wife.

*Genesis 29:22–24*: Laban threw a great feast, and although Jacob had worked seven years for Rachel, not Leah, Laban gave Leah to Jacob that night. How could Jacob not know it was Leah? Several possible explanations have been offered. The tent was dark. The bride entered the tent completely veiled.[5] It was just like when Jacob pretended to be his older brother. And now it was coming back full circle. Rebekah had Jacob pretend to be his older brother. Now Laban had Leah pretend to be the younger sister.[6] It was customary for the father to give a slave girl to his married daughter. So Laban gave Leah the slave girl Zilpah, whose name meant "small nose."

*Genesis 29:25–27*: The next morning, Jacob asked Laban: "Why have you deceived me?" When Jacob said this, I wonder if the Holy Spirit came upon him and convicted Jacob of his own deception. As Jacob took advantage of Isaac's bad eyesight, Laban took advantage of the darkness of Jacob's tent. One of the commentators said Laban took the prize for being despicable.[7] How was Laban's deceit any different from what Jacob did to Isaac? Maybe it was the length of time that it played out. Laban said that in their culture it was the custom to give the firstborn daughter in marriage first. Jacob had now lived among these people for seven years. Why didn't Jacob pick up on something? Sailhamer said, "Jacob had planned to take Rachel as his wife. But God intended him to have Leah."[8] Laban explained it was not their custom to give the younger daughter in marriage before the firstborn. In Leviticus 18:18 (obviously written after these events), the Mosaic Law said a man was not to marry two sisters. Why? Because it causes crazy rivalry!

*Genesis 29:28–30*: It seems Rachel was given to Jacob after seven days, and then he worked seven more years for Laban (v. 28). Here again we see the custom of giving the servant to the married daughter. Bilhah meant "carefree" (v. 29). Strangely enough, Jacob did the same thing his parents, Isaac and Rebekah, had done. He showed favoritism. He favored Rachel. Polygamy and bigamy were

---

[5] Waltke, 405.
[6] Waltke, 405.
[7] NET Bible, https://net.bible.org/bible/Genesis+29, footnote for Gen. 29:26.
[8] John H. Sailhamer, *The Pentateuch as Narrative* (Grand Rapids: Zondervan, 1992), 195.

never God's will. It was just Adam and Eve. Any time you add to what God's plan is, it just gets messy. But God continued to move anyway. I think the work Jacob had to do for 14 years was brought on himself because of his deception of Isaac and Esau (Proverbs 3:12; Galatians 6:7; Hebrews 12:5–6). I believe God still disciplines His people to take care of unresolved sin. I think this adjustment from seven to fourteen years was disciplining for Jacob. God was faithful to keep the *Seed* going, but He disciplined Jacob in the process. God was refining Jacob, and He was beginning to do something special with him. We see this play out at the end of Genesis 29 with the sons of Jacob.

*Genesis 29:31–35*: Jacob preferred Rachel, so God opened Leah's womb because she was unloved (v. 31). Leah quickly had four sons: Reuben, Simeon, Levi, Judah. These sons were part of the 12 tribes of Israel. Leah probably felt unworthy and unloved, yet God chose to use her. Do you understand the magnitude and significance of Leah giving birth to Judah? Matthew 1:2 reveals that Judah is in the lineage of Christ! Hebrews 7:14 says Judah was the one God chose to carry the *Seed* through. The seed from Jacob and the seed-bearer Leah, was traced to Christ. Judah came from Leah, not Rachel.

## Closing

The *Seed* came through the woman no one wanted and pointed to the lineage of the tribe of Judah. God can redeem any situation. The root of David, the Messiah, came through the tribe of Judah (Revelation 5:5).

## The Daily Word

As you walk with the Lord, may you praise His name. Leah waited to praise the Lord until her fourth son was born. How long will you wait to give praise to the Lord in the midst of your day? The Lord is with you.

**And she conceived again, gave birth to a son, and said, "This time I will praise the LORD." Therefore she named him Judah. Then Leah stopped having children." —Genesis 29:35**

Further Scripture: Psalm 34:1; Ephesians 5:20; 1 Thessalonians 5:18

# Questions

1. What was the symbolic significance of the sheep, shepherd, well, and stone in Genesis 29:1–8? (Matthew 28:2; Mark 16:2–4; John 4:14; 10:11)

2. Describe the differences between Leah and Rachel based on Genesis 29:17. Why was it significant that God chose to use Leah? (1 Corinthians 1:28)

3. In Genesis 29:23, why didn't Jacob realize he was making love to Leah and not Rachel?

4. Why do you think Laban gave Leah to Jacob in marriage instead of honoring his promise in Genesis 29:19–20 (seven years work in exchange for Rachel)? What did Laban know that caused him to do this?

5. Leah gave birth to four sons in Genesis 29:31–35. Which one of Leah's sons carried the *Seed*, Christ? (Genesis 29:31–35; Matthew 1:2; Luke 3:33; Hebrews 7:14; Revelation 5:5)

6. Do you think Jacob's extra seven years of work for Laban could have been discipline from the Lord for his actions toward Esau in Genesis 26—28? (Galatians 6:7; Proverbs 3:12; Hebrews 12:5–6)

7. What did the Holy Spirit highlight to you in Genesis 29 through the reading or the teaching?

# Lesson 15: Genesis 30
## *Seed*: The Twelve Tribes of Israel

## Teaching Notes

### Review

Jacob and Laban came to an agreement that after seven years of working Laban's land, Jacob would marry Laban's daughter, Rachel (Genesis 29). After seven years passed, Laban deceived Jacob and tricked him into marrying his other daughter, Leah. Sailhamer wrote, "Jacob had planned to take Rachel as his wife, but God intended him to have Leah."[1] Every time Jacob tried something, God seemed to have another plan. Today, we look at the 12 tribes of Israel and how they came through Jacob. It can be confusing to see how God would use chaos to bring control. Still, God would use imperfect people to bring a perfect plan to fruition.

### Teaching

*Genesis 29:31*: The Lord saw that Leah was unloved, so He opened her womb. Leah's first son was *Reuben* (#1), which means, "See a son!" Leah hoped that after giving Jacob a son, he would love her. In Numbers 34 is the description of the land that was given to the 12 sons of Jacob (the 12 tribes of Israel) promised in Genesis 12:1–3. If you look at a map, you will see that Reuben wasn't blessed with much. Reuben brought disgrace to his family when he slept with his father's concubine, Bilhah (Genesis 35:22). Through his actions, Reuben implied he wanted Jacob's authority and inheritance. Genesis 49 records that Reuben was not blessed because of this sin.

*Genesis 29:33*: Leah conceived and gave birth to a second son. Remember, the whole point of the seed was that there had to be a seed-bearer so the lineage of Christ could continue. The name *Simeon* (#2) means, "the One who hears." Simeon was a troublemaker. When Simeon heard that his sister, Dinah, was raped (Genesis 34:24–31), he sought revenge by going into the rapist's city and killing all the males (Genesis 34:25). Simeon's actions led to harsh words from Jacob: "May I never enter their counsel" (Genesis 49:5).

[1] John H. Sailhamer, *The Pentateuch as Narrative: A Biblical-Theological Commentary* (Grand Rapids: Zondervan, 1992), 195.

*Genesis 29:34*: Leah conceived yet another son named *Levi* (#3), which means "attached." Leah's identity was not in the Lord but in the approval of her husband. Levi was not given land because he became "attached" to the priesthood. The Levites would not be given land because God would be their portion and inheritance among the Israelites, and the firstfruits offered to the Lord would be their provision. Levi participated with Simeon in murdering the Hivites (Genesis 34:25). Simeon got the bad rap, and Levi seemingly got away with his part without punishment.

*Genesis 29:35*: Leah conceived and gave birth to her fourth son, *Judah* (#4), which means, "Praise the Lord." Leah said, "This time I will praise the Lord!" Judah would eventually bring about healing to the family, through Leah, bringing blessing and reconciliation to the world. Judah becomes the *Seed*, Christ. Jesus is called the Lion of the tribe of Judah. Jesus is the full picture of the Old and New Testament (Revelation 5:5).

*Genesis 30:1–5*: Rachel became jealous of Leah and said to Jacob, "Give me sons, or I am about to die!" The phrase "I am about to die," seems to be used to make dramatic pleas (Genesis 25:32; 27:46). Rachel's envy led to issues. Leah and Rachel saw only each other, not God. Jacob became angry and told Rachel, "I can't control this." Rachel gave her slave Bilhah to Jacob because tradition called for giving a slave to the husband if the wife was barren. Three women in Scripture who are referred to as *both* wives and concubines: Hagar, Keturah, and Bilhah. Bilhah conceived and gave Jacob another son.

*Genesis 30:6*: Rachel's servant Bilhah has a son, *Dan* (#5), which means, "God has vindicated me." Rachel believed God had finally vindicated her. The tribe of Dan doesn't get a whole lot of land in the Promised Land and Dan is not listed in the tribes to be sealed (Revelation 7:4–8). The tribe of Dan did not have much faith. Scripture tells us in Judges 18 that the tribe of Dan didn't really take their land because they fell into idolatry.

*Genesis 30:7–8*: Bilhah bore Jacob a second son, Naphtali. Keep in mind that Rachel was not conceiving here; it was Bilhah. In Rachel's mind, she was competing with her sister. This was why this child was named *Naphtali* (#6), which means, "struggle." In Genesis 49:21, Naphtali is described as a doe set free who bears beautiful fawns. There's this mentality of a swift runner, of freedom and bravery and Jesus started His ministry in the land of Naphtali (Matthew 4:13–16), which fulfilled the prophecy in Isaiah 9:1–2.

*Genesis 30:9–11*: When Leah saw she was done having children, she gave her slave Zilpah to Jacob, who conceived and bore a son, *Gad* (#7), which means, "What good fortune!" Zilpah didn't praise the Lord; she saw the birth of her son as luck. Gad is listed multiple times in the Old Testament and was known as a strong man of war (1 Chronicles 12:8). Elijah the Tishbite was from Gad (1 Kings 17:1).

*Genesis 30:12–14*: Leah's slave, Zilpah, had a second son, Asher. The name *Asher* (#8) means, "blessed, happy," or "I'm happy to be envied." Leah's whole point here was the hope that people would say she was better than Rachel. The motivations of Jacob's wives were off, but God continued to use them. Asher was given fertile soil in the Promised Land. God uses imperfect people to point to the perfect Christ. Reuben, the first son of Leah, went to the fields and found some mandrakes and brought them to his mother Leah. When Rachel saw the mandrakes, she asked if she could have some. Mandrakes are a member of the nightshade family that also includes the tomato and potato plants. Eventually the mandrake produces strong, pleasant fragrances that supposedly help people to conceive. This fruit is also referred to as an aphrodisiac (Song of Solomon 7:13). Rachel wanted the mandrakes because she was still barren.

*Genesis 30:15–16*: Leah became indignant: "You've taken my husband, now my son's mandrakes!" Rachel traded Leah a night with her husband for some fruit. After working, Jacob came home and Leah immediately approached him saying, "I've hired you with my son's mandrakes." Waltke wrote, "This is actually the fourth 'commercial' exchange in the Jacob cycle (cf. exchange of birthright, exchange of blessings, exchange of wives, exchange of husband for sex-by-hire). In the first two Jacob is the victimizer; in the last two, the victim."[2] Fokkelman wrote, "The family's life is rotten and broken by the dehumanizing atmosphere of service wages."[3]

*Genesis 30:17–21*: God honored Leah and she conceived a fifth son, *Issachar* (#9), which means, "hired" or "He rewards." Leah now had five sons! Issachar was described as a fighting man (Numbers 2:5–6), and the tribe of Issachar were the ones, "who understood the times and knew what Israel should do; they were watchmen" (1 Chronicles 12:32). Each of the 12 tribes had a different role. Leah conceived and bore a sixth son, *Zebulun* (#10), which means, "God has

---

[2] Bruce K. Waltke and Cathi J. Fredricks. *Genesis: A Commentary* (Grand Rapids: Zondervan, 2001), 413.

[3] J. P. Fokkelman, *Narrative Art in Genesis* (Eugene, OR: Wipf & Stock, 2004), 140; quoted in Paul Vrolijk, *Jacob's Wealth: An Examination Into the Nature and Role of Material* (Leiden, Netherlands: Koininklijke Brill, 2011), 159.

presented/honored/acknowledged me." Zebulun had three sons and more than 57,000 fighting men for war (Numbers 2:7–8). The land of Zebulun was where Jesus started His ministry (Matthew 4:13–16; Isa 9:1–2). After the 14 years Jacob worked for Laban, Leah bore a daughter Dinah. The other sons (listed thus far) were probably born during those 14 years.

*Genesis 30:22*: Then God remembered Rachel and allowed her to conceive a child. Rachel's first son was *Joseph* (#11), which means, "increase; may He add." Rachel's mentality was not thanks, but "give me more!" Joseph is described as, "a man who has the spirit of God in him, intelligent, wise, strong, well built, handsome" (Genesis 41:38–39). Acts 7:9 says, "God was with him." God used Joseph to spare his entire family and the Israelites. Jacob blessed Joseph's two sons, Ephraim and Manasseh, so he received a double blessing! Later, Rachel had another son *Benjamin* (#12), which means, "son of my right hand." Rachel died while giving birth to Benjamin. God shielded and blessed Benjamin. The Benjamin tribe was described as ravenous wolves (Genesis 49:27).

## Closing

These 12 tribes of Israel established everything for the Messiah! God used four women who were a disaster. These four women kept jockeying and struggling for a position with their husband, Jacob, and all they had to do was look to the Lord. And yet, God used them even through their wrong motives. God can redeem any situation to point to Himself.

## The Daily Word

When you read about Jacob's 12 children by four different women, or about how he became prosperous from spotted, striped, and speckled sheep and goats, doesn't it appear messy and complicated? It may seem deceiving, conniving, or even corrupt—but the Lord worked, despite all of this, for the Seed, Christ, to continue.

Even in our mess, even in the fall of man, the Lord is working and has a plan. As you trust Him and hold on to hope, His plan will prevail—even in the middle of the mess.

**Rachel said, "God has vindicated me; yes, He has heard me and given me a son," and she named him Dan. —Genesis 30:6**

Further Scripture: Psalm 33:11; Proverbs 19:21; Isaiah 46:10

# Questions

1. List each of Jacob's children and divide them by his four wives/concubines. What does each name mean? (Genesis 29:31–35; 30:1–24)

2. What was motivating Leah and Rachel to have more children? (Genesis 30:1–24; Proverbs 23:17; Psalm 127:4-5)

3. What do the names of Jacob's children reveal to you about Leah and Rachel's heart at the birth of each child?

4. What is the significance of Jacob's sons? (Genesis 49:1–28; Numbers 24:13–29; 1 Chronicles 12:23–38; Revelation 7:4–8)

5. In Genesis 30:25–34, Laban and Jacob negotiated whether Jacob would stay with Laban or take his family back to his homeland. Do you think Jacob made the right decision? (Genesis 31:3, 10–13)

6. Laban and Jacob agreed that Jacob would take certain types of sheep, lambs, and goats in exchange for staying on Laban's land. How did Jacob take advantage of Laban in Genesis 30:35–43?

7. What did the Holy Spirit highlight to you in Genesis 30 through the reading or the teaching?

# Lesson 16: Genesis 31
## *Seed*: Jacob Considers Returning to his Homeland

## Teaching Notes

### Intro

Our goal is that the Word of God we are studying *goes out* from us. We should not just be sponges, hoarding His words for ourselves. In Genesis 30, Jacob had 11 sons and was ready to move on, but Laban didn't want him to leave. It was decided that Jacob's wages, before he left, were to be speckled and spotted sheep and goats (vv. 25–43). While Laban left on a three-day trip, Jacob started peeling bark and setting the peeled branches in troughs when the animals mated. Somehow Jacob thought this superstitious act would give him what he wanted. There was no trust in the Lord!

### Teaching

*Genesis 31:1–2*: Laban's sons were saying, "Jacob has taken what belongs to us!" There was jealousy that started to come into play. We know Laban is the one who cheated Jacob, but God's hand was on Jacob. Jacob sensed something was off and said Laban's face was "not with him." The Lord was with him, but Laban was not. Envy and jealousy took root, just as it had with Jacob's wives.

*Genesis 31:3*: God told Jacob to leave Paddan-aram and go back to Canaan, the land of his fathers. Wiersbe addressed how God told Jacob it was time to leave this way: "Through inner witness of our hearts, the outward circumstances of life, and the truth of His Word."[1]

How God addressed Jacob (and addresses us!):

- Inner witness of our heart
- Be careful! The heart can be deceitful (Jeremiah 17:9).
- If we delight in the Lord, He will give us our heart's desire (Psalm 37:4).

---

[1] Warren W. Wiersbe, *Be Authentic (Genesis 25-50): Exhibiting Real Faith in the Real World* (Colorado Springs: David C. Cook, 1997), 55.

74

- Jacob knew the promises of Abraham and Isaac, and he wanted to see God do what He promised.
- Outward circumstances of life
- The Word of God
- Jacob was reminded of the promise at Bethel (Genesis 28:12–15).
- Jacob is told to go back to Esau (Genesis 31:2–4).
- God tells Jacob to go back to Bethel (Genesis 35:1).
- Jacob is instructed to move to Egypt (Genesis 46:1–4).

Repeatedly, Jacob was instructed to do different things. God was fulfilling His promise! It all goes back to Genesis 12:1–3. The promise goes from Abraham to Isaac to Jacob. When God told Jacob to go back to the land, Jacob had to be feeling like the promise was getting closer.

*Genesis 31:4–9*: For the first time, it seems like Jacob was in control of his own household, not Rachel and Leah and their jealousy. Jacob called Rachel and Leah to where the flocks were, an isolated environment. He wanted to make sure Rachel and Leah were behind him and not their father. Remember from verse 2 that Laban was different toward Jacob. This was the first time Jacob took ownership of his own faith! Not buying things, selling things, or tricking people. Jacob recognized God was on his side. Jacob explained to his wives that Laban had changed his wages, but *God* changed the flocks. Just like in verse 5, Jacob credited God! Psalm 119:105 shows us that God directs our steps. Everywhere that Jacob was going, God was directing it. There was an anointing and calling on Jacob's life, even in his imperfection. Jacob was finally realizing that it's all about God!

*Genesis 31:10–11*: God spoke to Jacob through a dream. God still speaks through dreams (Joel 2:28–29; Acts 2:17–19). Has the day of the Lord come? No! Then the dreams and visions and prophecies are still going to happen. God will speak to us through dreams and visions, and it will always line up with the truth of His Word. For example, Muslims are coming to know the Lord through dreams and visions. Jacob's response to his dream was "Here I am!"

*Genesis 31:12–13*: In Jacob's dream, an angel appeared and said, "Lift up your eyes, I want to show you!" God was going to provide for Jacob; it had nothing to do with superstition. God is the One who provides. God reminded Jacob of his first dream in Bethel where Jacob made a vow to God.

*Genesis 31:14–16*: Jacob proclaimed all that God had done, and now Rachel and Leah proclaimed what their father Laban had *not* done. The wives looked at Laban's actions in the past, present, and future.[2] They decided, "Jacob you're right! Our dad has done nothing for us, but God has." God had given Jacob these two women who chose to stand behind him.

*Genesis 31:17–18*: Jacob woke up the next day and put his wives and children on camels. Jacob only had 11 children at this time: Reuben, Simeon, Levi, Judah, Isaachar, Zebulun, Gad, Asher, Dan, Naphtali, and Joseph.

Jacob acted in haste. We know we are not supposed to act in haste. Isaiah 28:16, "The one who believes will be unshakable." We shouldn't have to act in haste when we trust the Lord. Jacob fled Laban at a much slower pace than when he fled Esau. This time, Jacob had all his family and possessions. It took Laban seven days to catch up (Genesis 31:23).

*Genesis 31:19:* While Laban was shearing sheep, usually a day of celebration and blessing, Rachel stole her father's idols. Rachel either wanted to punish her dad, or she did not fully trust the Lord, as she held on to some false beliefs. Laban's idols were most likely two- to three-inch figurines, which could have been considered charms, and possibly were figures of departed ancestors or false gods. It was even believed these idols could be used in helping people be fruitful. Maybe Rachel took them because she thought they would give her children. Remember at this point she had not had Benjamin yet.

*Genesis 31:20–21:* Jacob was deceptive again. He left in haste, not trusting the Lord. Why did Moses (author of Genesis) refer to Laban as an Aramean at this point? I believe God is showing there were two distinct people groups here. Jacob fled to his homeland and to safety. Laban came after them, and Rachel got away with stealing the idol. In the end, Jacob and Laban make a covenant.

## Closing

For the first time, Jacob recognized that God was in this. And Leah and Rachel were standing with him. There was this beginning process of them realizing that God was up to something. Genesis 31:42 states, "If the God of my father, the God of Abraham, the Fear of Isaac [the 'awesome one'], had not been with me, certainly now you would have sent me off empty-handed. But God has seen my affliction and my hard work, and He issued His verdict last night." Jacob finally started to see that God's hand was on him. What you can learn from Jacob is that

---

[2] Bruce F. Waltke and Cathi J. Fredricks, *Genesis: A Commentary* (Grand Rapids: Zondervan, 2001), 426.

you need to give yourself patience as God is speaking to you. God will continue to speak to you. God's hand is on you, and it will not leave you.

## The Daily Word

God showed up in dreams to both Laban and Jacob, reminding them that He was with them even in the middle of their sinful ways. God sees, and He knows our hearts. God sees our sin—even when we deny it or think we can cover it up and escape. He still sees us.

Why do we try to hide? The Lord loves you and will never leave you. Come before Him as you are. Let Him transform you.

**If the God of my father, the God of Abraham, the Fear of Isaac, had not been with me, certainly now you would have sent me off empty-handed. But God has seen my affliction and my hard work, and He issued His verdict last night. —Genesis 31:42**

Further Scripture: Proverbs 4:25–26; Isaiah 1:18; Matthew 6:22

## Questions

1. Do you think the Lord speaking to Jacob in Genesis 31:3 could be the pre-incarnate Christ?

2. What do you think Rachel's motivation was to take Laban's gods/idols in Genesis 31:19? (John 2:8; Isaiah 46:5–7; Psalm 96:4–6)

3. Do you think Jacob made the right decision to flee from Laban in secret with his family in Genesis 31:19–21? What would you have done in this situation?

4. Why do you think God told Laban "don't say anything to Jacob" in Genesis 31:24? Did Laban obey God? (Genesis 31:29, 43–44)

5. How do you see Jacob's reverence for God and relationship with God begin to solidify in Genesis 31? (Compare to his actions in Genesis 27—30)

6. What did the Holy Spirit highlight to you in Genesis 31 through the reading or the teaching?

# Lesson 17: Genesis 32—33
*Seed*: Jacob Wrestling with God

## Teaching Notes

### Intro

As Jacob and his family were on their way back to Canaan, God's angels met Jacob. These angels could be similar to the angels in Genesis 28 where God released the promise to Jacob in Bethel, and God reiterated His promise of Genesis 12:1–3.

### Teaching

*Genesis 32:1*: God's angels met Jacob on His way back to Canaan. Hebrews 1:13–14 shows us the role of angels as messengers and ministering spirits sent out to serve. God sends His angels to have our back! I believe God is sending angels wherever we go as we advance the kingdom of God.

*Genesis 32:2*: Jacob saw the angels and recognized he was in God's camp! When Jacob called this place a camp, he implied that there was a great army of angels there. Jacob called this place, *Mahanaim*, which meant, "double camps, two camps." God sent a massive number of angels. What a comfort that should have been, to know that God was with them!

*Genesis 32:3*: Jacob sent out messengers to his brother Esau. There is a debate among theologians as to who these messengers were. Some argue angels were sent. That could have been, but we can't conclusively know for sure. Jacob sending messengers to Esau was a big deal! Jacob hadn't seen Esau since he had stolen Esau's birthright and blessing. The reason Jacob had fled was because Esau had been ready to kill him. It is important to remember that if God has promised something for you, no one can keep it from you (Romans 8:31). Jacob finally recognized that God was with him!

*Genesis: 32:4*: The messengers relayed Jacob's message meant for Esau. The message started with "my lord Esau." Jacob was nervous as he addressed his brother. It is almost as if Jacob's trust was in the outcome of his own planning rather than the Lord's plan. Jacob's message seemed too brief, with almost no detail. Jacob communicated that he had stayed with Laban and had been delayed.

*Genesis 32:5*: Jacob had tried to find favor with Esau. Three times besides this one, Jacob asked for favor. First, in Genesis 33:8, "So Esau said, 'What do you mean by this whole procession I met?' 'To find favor with you, my lord,' he answered." Second, in Genesis 33:10, "But Jacob said, 'No, please! If I have found favor with you, take this gift from my hand. For indeed, I have seen your face, and it is like seeing God's face, since you have accepted me.'" Third, in Genesis 33:15, "Esau said, 'Let me leave some of my people with you.' But he replied, 'Why do that? Please indulge me, my lord.'"

*Genesis 32:6–8*: The messengers returned to Jacob to declare that Esau and 400 men were coming to see Jacob. Four hundred men was a typical number for a militia. Throughout Scripture there is a constant theme of numbers. For example, 1 Samuel 22:2 and 25:13—both passages mention the number 400. Jacob was afraid. Jacob divided the people with him, his family, into two camps, so that if one was attacked, the other could escape. Remember in verse 2, Jacob had named the spot they were in *Mahanaim*, which means "double camps, two camps." God knew this was going to happen, and He went ahead of Jacob. God used Jacob's imperfection and accomplished His perfect plan. Wiersbe wrote, "A guilty conscience often makes us see the darkest possible picture."[1] There had been no inner healing between Jacob and Esau.

*Genesis 32:9–12*: In these verses, Jacob actually turned to the Lord! He addressed God in prayer because God had gotten him to that point in time. Jacob recognized God, confessed, and then petitioned. This petition was huge because Jacob didn't want the blessing, the seed, to stop. It was not just about Jacob anymore; it was about his family and his children. Jacob wanted God to preserve the seed. Jacob reminded God of His promise. Jacob pleaded with God—God, you've promised me descendants! You can't wipe us out (Genesis 28:14–16)! When you realize the promises of God's call in your life—how much are you willing to petition for what He's asked you to do?

*Genesis 32:13–23*: Jacob listed all the animals he was going to give his brother—550-580 animals. He sent the animals with his slaves, divided into two groups. Each group had the same speech to give to Esau. I think Jacob was still sucking up, addressing him as "your servant Jacob, my lord Esau" and giving him

---

[1] Warren W. Wiersbe, *The Bible Exposition Commentary: Genesis–Deuteronomy* (Colorado Springs: David C. Cook, 2001), 132.

the best of the best. Jacob wanted to appease and soften Esau with all the gifts. Jacob sent the gifts ahead to Esau, while he himself stayed behind. During the night, Jacob took his family and female slaves to cross the river, in an attempt to keep them safe. For Jacob's family to cross the river at night was just as dangerous as facing 400 militiamen. I can't help but wonder, what about God's camp? The angels? And God's promise to be with Jacob? It feels as though Jacob kept going back and forth, trusting God and then trying to make it happen on his own.

*Genesis 32:24*: With his family across the river, Jacob was left alone. This is when God showed up! The real battle was about to take place. Wiersbe quotes Walter Savage Lander, who wrote, "Being left alone is the audience chamber of God"[2] Finally, there were no distractions for Jacob—no wives arguing over children, no camels, and no children fighting. Alone, Jacob wrestled "a man" until daybreak. Jacob had been stripped of everything, his whole family, possessions, and was utterly alone (Hosea 12:2–4). As a child, Jacob wrestled with his brother, and now he wrestled with God. Jacob wrestled with God in human form, the pre-incarnate Christ.

*Genesis 32:25–27*: When the man could not defeat Jacob, He dislocated Jacob's hip. If God is all-powerful, how was Jacob winning? My only conclusion is that God let him. Just the fact that God dislocated his hip socket shows it was God. He removed Jacob's strength and revealed a weakness. The limp would always remind Jacob of God wrestling with him. Interestingly, God came as a traveler when Abraham was a pilgrim, as a soldier when Joshua was a general, and as a wrestler because Jacob was always wrestling. I think this was Jacob's love language. Jacob went from a physical battle to a verbal battle: "I will not let You go unless You bless me." Jacob was constantly trying to get something out of every situation! God asked Jacob his name. God wanted a confession! Remember the last time he was asked his name was when Isaac asked who he was, and he lied Genesis 27:18–19). Jacob's name was equated with cheating (Genesis 27:36). God wanted to redeem Jacob's name.

*Genesis 32:28–32*: Because Jacob prevailed, God renamed him Israel. "Renaming marked a change of direction and context for an individual. It does not always mark a change of character or inner person."[3] Notice throughout the Old Testament that whenever Moses made a reference to Jacob, it was in line with the

---

[2] Wiersbe, 133.

[3] Eugene F. Roop, *Believers Church Bible Commentary: Genesis*, vol. 2 (Scottsdale, PA: Herald Press, 1987).

flesh. When Moses referenced "Israel," it usually was in line with the Spirit. Jacob needed inner healing, and God was his *Deliverer*.

Did Jacob wrestle with the pre-incarnate Christ? Hosea 12 said it was God. Exodus 33:20 said that no one can see God and live. Judges 13:21–22 said that the mentality was that whoever sees God face-to-face would die. The only conclusion I have is that Jacob didn't see God the Father, but he saw God the Son. Jesus came in some form and wrestled with Jacob. Israel walked away limping. In our weakness, God is made strong!

## Closing

As Jacob was made weak, God was made strong. In Genesis 33, Jacob and Esau end up meeting, and a truce takes place. God continued to move through Jacob. Through imperfect people, God's perfect plan continues. And that's for the *Seed*, Christ, to continue through all generations (2 Corinthians 12:9–10).

## The Daily Word

Jacob was "greatly afraid and distressed" to meet his brother Esau, whom he hadn't seen in years (Genesis 32:7). He prayed and asked the Lord to rescue him, remembering the Lord's promise and calling on his life. The Lord answered Jacob's prayer.

Turn your fears and apprehensions over to the Lord today. If He is leading you to a place of reconciliation, He will provide, and He will answer you. Cry out to the Lord, and watch Him move in your life.

**Then Jacob said, "God of my father Abraham and God of my father Isaac . . . Please rescue me from the hand of my brother Esau, for I am afraid of him; otherwise, he may come and attack me, the mothers, and their children. You have said, 'I will cause you to prosper, and I will make your offspring like the sand of the sea, which cannot be counted.'" —Genesis 32:9, 11–12**

Further Scripture: Genesis 33:10; Psalm 56:3; Isaiah 41:10

## Questions

1. In Genesis 32:1 we see the angels of the Lord come to meet Jacob. What are reasons God might send angels to us? (Numbers 22:31–32; 2 Kings 6:16–17; Psalms 34:7; 91:1; Hebrews 1:14)

2. Jacob restated a promise that was given to him from God in his prayer in Genesis 32:12. Why is it important to remind God's promises to us in prayer?

How does it benefit us? (Numbers 23:19; Lamentations 3:22–23; Romans 4:21; Hebrews 6:13–18; 1 Thessalonians 5:24)

3. In Genesis 32:24–25, Jacob did not initiate the "wrestling" match, but the Man (Jesus pre-incarnate?) did. Why do you think He started this match, and what do you think He wanted from Jacob?

4. When did Jacob realize he wasn't wrestling with an ordinary man? (Genesis 32:25–26, 30)

5. What was the result of this match? (Genesis 32:28; 35:10; 1 Kings 18:31)

6. What did the Holy Spirit highlight to you in Genesis 32—33 through the reading or the teaching?

# Lesson 18: Genesis 34—35
## *Seed*: Jacob's Delay in Following God's Instructions

## Teaching Notes

### Intro

Even though we're imperfect people, God still uses us to help further the *Seed*, Christ. The path of the *Seed* at this point was: Abraham —> Isaac —> Jacob —> 12 sons, 1 daughter.

### Teaching

*Genesis 34:2–30*: Dinah, Jacob's daughter, was raped by Shechem, which caused some serious anger among the brothers. Their outrage was not just about Dinah, but Israel! Shechem wanted to marry Dinah, so he made an agreement with Simeon and Levi that all the males in his village would be circumcised. The men were circumcised, and on their third day of recovery, Simeon and Levi entered the village and killed every male. Jacob's other sons plundered the city. Jacob told Simeon and Levi, "You have brought trouble on me" (v. 30). Jacob had the seed of the serpent mentality again and was concerned about losing his seed because of what his sons had done.

*Genesis 35:1*: God told Jacob to move again from Canaan and settle in Bethel. The move to Canaan happened ten years earlier (Genesis 28), when Jacob set up a stone and made a promise to make the Lord his God in Bethel. But Jacob didn't go. Now God told Jacob to do what He had said. Even though Jacob had heard from the Lord, he didn't finish the instructions. After he had encountered Esau, Jacob arrived in Shechem and stayed (Genesis 33:18). And this is where Dinah was raped. Did Jacob's delay bring destruction to his family?

God told Jacob to go, but he delayed. Multiple times, men of God were told to go back: Abraham—Genesis 13; Isaac—Genesis 26; David—2 Samuel 12; Jonah—Jonah 3; and Peter—John 21

*Genesis 35:2–5*: Before leaving for Bethel, as God had instructed, Jacob told his family to remove all foreign gods, become purified, and change their clothes. But Rachel had stolen her father's idols. Jacob had implied he wanted his family to have a new beginning. Scripture emphasizes the cleansing of impurities (Psalm 51:2,7; Isaiah 1:16; 2 Corinthians 7:1; 1 John 1:9). New garments are an image of cleansing (Isaiah 64:6; Genesis 3:21). Jacob proclaimed that God had answered his prayers! Jacob made a public confession again that God was with them!

Jacob took up the idols and buried them. Jacob buried the idols at the oak near Shechem, the same place where God appeared to Abram after he entered the land (Genesis 12:6). When Jacob and his family began to move, a terror from God came over the cities around them as soon as they set out! A true revival will never imply that people are just sitting! Wiersbe wrote, "When God's people are doing God's will in God's way, they can depend on God's provision and protection."[1]

*Genesis 35:6–7*: Jacob renamed Bethel and recognized God. Waltke wrote that, at this time, "The covenant family retains their separation from Canaanites, their witness to them, and symbolically claim the land based on God's promises."[2] They declared that they were not part of the Canaanites and that they followed the God of Abraham, Isaac, and Jacob. Jacob and his family believed God was going to fulfill His promise to them. Was this the first revival? Maybe. They gave up their idols, purified themselves, and walked it out to Canaan.

*Genesis 35:8–17*: Deborah, Rebekah's nurse, who had a strong presence in the family, died and was buried. It is a big deal for her to be listed here; most likely, she was an integral part of Jacob's life. God spoke life into Jacob again. The Lord was overemphasizing that the *Seed* was coming through Abraham, Isaac, and Jacob. God gave Jacob the name "Israel." We know God did this when Jacob wrestled with Him. Our memory can be so short that we can have an encounter with God one day and still need another one the next day. These people were no different. God said, "I am God Almighty!" (El Shaddai). God told Jacob to be fruitful and multiply, reminding him that a nation would come from him and that kings would descend from him (2 Samuel 7:12). Like Genesis 12 when God met with Abram, He was physically present when He withdrew from Jacob.

*Genesis 35:14–15*: Jacob marked with a stone the place where he had spoken with God and named it Bethel (v. 15). Pouring out a drink offering was a symbol of dedication, giving everything one had (2 Samuel 23:16; Philippians 2:17).

---

[1] Warren W. Wiersbe, *Be Authentic (Genesis 25-50): Exhibiting Real Faith in the Real World* (Colorado Springs: David C. Cook, 1997), 82.

[2] Bruce K. Waltke and Cathi J. Fredricks, *Genesis: A Commentary* (Grand Rapids: Zondervan, 2001), 473.

*Genesis 35:16–17*: They set out from Bethel. But God never told them to leave. Rachel had given birth to their last son, and the labor was difficult. It was difficult because of Genesis 3 and the fall of Adam and Eve. She had reaped the consequence of sin.

*Genesis 35:18*: Rachel named her son "Ben-oni," meaning, "son of sorrow, son of trouble" but Jacob renamed him "Benjamin," or "son of my right hand." Rachel died in childbirth. Did judgment come on Rachel because they left Bethel or because of her past comments? We're not sure, but when Jacob had been disobedient, there were consequences (for example, Dinah's rape and Rachel's death). God's power always trumps who we are (our imperfectness), but we still have consequences for our sin. Wiersbe said, "Life is a mosaic of lights and shadows, joy and sorrows; and the same baby that brought Rachel and her husband joy also brought tears."[3]

*Genesis 35:19–21*: Rachel was buried on the way to Ephrath (Bethlehem). Jacob was now referred to as Israel. Moses chose when to refer to him as Israel and when to refer to him as Jacob. While they lived in that region, Reuben slept with Bilhah, his father's concubine and his mother's slave. There was no clear reason as to why Reuben did this. The Law said, "A man is not to marry his father's wife; he must not violate his father's bed" (Deuteronomy 22:30). Because of what he did, Jacob cursed him and told him he would no longer excel. Reuben lost his blessing (Genesis 49:3–4).

*Genesis 35:22–26*: The 12 tribes of Israel are listed again: Reuben, Simeon, Levi, Judah, Issachar, Zebulun, Joseph, Benjamin, Dan, Naphtali, Gad, Asher (vv. 22–26).

*Genesis 35:27–29*: Isaac lived 180 years. When he died, Esau and Jacob came together and buried their father.

## Closing

Somewhere amidst all of this, the *Seed* continues.

---

[3] Wiersbe, 84.

## The Daily Word

Jacob watched his only daughter be taken advantage of by men who wrongly pursued her. Then he watched his sons retaliate and kill those men. During this time, Jacob turned to God. He remembered God's promise that God would be with Jacob wherever he went.

Even in the midst of your shortcomings or in the middle of hardship, cry out to the Lord! Look back on God's faithfulness in your life and remember the times when the Lord stood with you. God promises we will not be forsaken. He has even more plans ahead for you!

**So Jacob said to his family and all who were with him, "Get rid of the foreign gods that are among you. Purify yourselves and change your clothes. We must get up and go to Bethel. I will build an altar there to the God who answered me in my day of distress. He has been with me everywhere I have gone." —Genesis 35:2–3**

**Further Scripture:** Psalm 120:1; Matthew 28:20; 2 Peter 3:9

## Questions

1. Why do you think Dinah went out to see the daughters of the land in Genesis 34:1?

2. How did Dinah's brothers react to what happened to her in Genesis 34:2? Were they justified in their plan of revenge? Why or why not? Whose seed is being acted out in their plot?

3. How does Jacob set a good example of following God for his family in Genesis 35:2–3? Have you experienced similar things in your family?

4. What is the significance of God appearing to Jacob again to remind him He had changed Jacob's name to Israel? (Genesis 32:28; 35:9–10)

5. God was gracious toward Jacob when he made mistakes or was too concerned about his own reputation (Genesis 34:30). How does this story of God's blessing and restoration give you hope? (Genesis 35:9–15)

6. What did the Holy Spirit highlight to you in Genesis 34—35 through the reading or the teaching?

# Lesson 19: Genesis 36—37
## *Seed*: Joseph Sold into Slavery

## Teaching Notes

### Intro

We've defined the book of Genesis with one word—*Seed*. Throughout Genesis 1—35, the *Seed* of the woman points to Christ. How was this *Seed* communicated? Through multiple people . . . Abraham and his wife Sarah; Isaac and his wife Rebekah; and Jacob and his wives Leah and Rachel. This is Jacob's lineage. We know that the *Seed*, Christ, the Messiah, comes through Judah (Genesis 29; 2 Samuel 7:12; Revelation 5:5).

### Teaching

*Genesis 36*: In this chapter, 43 verses are dedicated to the lineage of Esau who came from the same line as Jacob. Esau had three wives, five sons (vv. 1–8), and ten grandsons (vv. 9–14). His lineage is packed with chiefs: political and military (vv. 15–19); the chief of the Horites who came from the Edomites who intermarried (vv. 20–30); kings of Edom (vv. 31–39); and a list of related chiefs (vv. 40–43). The lineage of Esau is massive compared to Jacob's. Constable said "that secular greatness develops faster than spiritual greatness. Consequently, the godly must wait patiently for the fulfillment of God's promises."[1] God will still keep His promises through the 12 tribes of Israel (Jacob).

*Genesis 37:1–2*: Verse 1 states that Jacob stayed in the land of Canaan. In verse 2, the 12 sons of Jacob, the 12 we identified in chapter 35, were working together as shepherds. At this point, Joseph was working directly with Dan, Naphtali, Gad, and Asher—just the five of them. Joseph took a bad report about his brothers back to his father, Jacob. A bad report means it had to be about some seriously bad behavior. When Dinah was raped, all of Jacob's sons did the plundering. It was in their DNA. This wasn't the first bad step the brothers of Joseph had made.

---

[1] Thomas L. Constable, *Expository Notes of Dr. Thomas Constable: Genesis*, 395, https://planobiblechapel.org/tcon/notes/pdf/genesis.pdf.

Wiersbe suggests, "The presence of Joseph in the home didn't create problems so much as revealed them."[2]

*Genesis 37:3–4*: Verse 3 states Israel loved Joseph more. Parental favoritism is never good. Jacob gave Joseph a robe of many colors. There's only one other time a robe of this type is mentioned in Scripture (2 Samuel 13:18). When Joseph showed up in his new robe, all the brothers—not just Dan, Naphtali, Gad, and Asher—recognized the favoritism and hated Joseph.

*Genesis 37:5–8*: Joseph *then* had a dream, and when he told it to his brothers, they hated him even more (v. 5). Was Joseph completely clueless? Why would he share these dreams? We've already considered that God still gives dreams and visions (Joel 2:28) and that God speaks through the old and the young (Acts 2:17). In verse 6, Joseph shares his dream: "There we were, binding sheaves of grain in the field. Suddenly, my sheaf stood up, and your sheaves gathered around it and bowed down to my sheaf" (v. 7). And they hated him still more (v. 8).

*Genesis 37:9–14*: Joseph had another dream and told his brothers again: "This time, the sun, moon, and 11 stars were bowing down to me" (v. 9). In this dream, the sun was his father, the moon was his mother, and the stars were his brothers, so now the whole family would be bowing down to him. His father (Jacob-Israel) rebuked him (v. 10), but pondered it (maybe like Mary pondered the events of Jesus' birth?) (v. 11). Look at the growing controversy in these verses: jealousy, conflict, darkness, anger—all aimed at Joseph. Was Joseph walking in faith or foolishness to tell his brothers these things? Biblical commentator Meir Sternberg says, "God's future agent and mouthpiece in Egypt could hardly make a worse impression on first appearance: spoiled brat, talebearer, braggart!"[3] Joseph's brothers were pasturing flocks in Shechem (where Dinah was raped). When Jacob told Joseph to check on his brothers, he responded, "I'm ready!" There's a lot to Joseph's response. Joseph was sent from Hebron to Shechem to see his brothers, a 50- to 60-mile distance and a three-day journey, just to report back to his father. That makes you think that Joseph had proven to be good at reporting.

*Genesis 37:15–17*: In verse 15, it says "a man" found Joseph wandering in a field. Joseph had never been far from home, so he had no idea where he was going. Joseph's brothers had moved to Dothan (v. 17). Note that in Psalm 105:17, God had sent a man ahead of them. Joseph, who became a slave, was sent. Why were

---

[2] Warren W. Wiersbe, *Be Authentic (Genesis 25-50): Exhibiting Real Faith in the Real World* (Colorado Springs: David C. Cook, 1997), 92.

[3] Meir Sternberg, *The Poetics of Biblical Narrative: Ideological Literature and the Drama of Reading* (Bloomington: Indiana University Press, 1985), 98.

Jacob's sons pasturing flocks 50 to 60 miles away? Why would they go to a dangerous place like Shechem? Why would Jacob send Joseph alone with his coat?

*Genesis 37:18–22*: The brothers saw Joseph, probably his robe, from far off, and before he could get to them, the brothers planned to kill him. Who starts that kind of conversation? Murder was already in their hearts. Constable suggested that the brothers "may have actually wanted to alter the will of God as revealed in Joseph's dreams."[4] In verse 20, the brothers say, "Here come's that dreamer!" In this account, Joseph's dreams got him into the pit. Thirteen years later, interpreting dreams will get Joseph out of the pit of jail. Reuben (the firstborn) tried to rescue Joseph (v. 21, possibly to make up for the wrong he had done in sleeping with his father's concubine, Bilhah).

*Genesis 37:23–27*: Joseph received no welcome. Instead, the brothers took off his robe and threw him into the empty pit (vv. 23–24). Then they sat down to eat (v. 25). These brothers were heartless. When you have a hard heart, you'll do anything (Jeremiah 17:9). The next time they have a meal together is with Joseph in Egypt. In Genesis 42:21, as we see the brothers pleading not to bring Benjamin to Egypt when they came back, they were probably thinking back to this moment in time. A caravan came along (v. 25b). Reuben had been the spokesman, but now Judah, whom the seed passes through, spoke up (v. 26). The brothers "not only sold their brother, but in their brother they had cast out a member of the seed promised and given to Abraham, Isaac, and Jacob."[5] They were from the *Seed* of the woman, but they were functioning in the seed of the serpent. Puett wrote, "Kidnapping and selling humans into slavery is a crime that is considered a capital offense,"[6] placing the offense as equal to murder.

*Genesis 37:28–35*: The price of 20 pieces of silver was common for anyone from age five to 20 sold as a slave. When Reuben found out what happened to Joseph, he was in complete distress. The brothers dipped Joseph's robe in the blood of a slaughtered goat. Constable said, "Jacob had deceived his father with the skin of a goat. Now his sons were deceiving him with the blood of a goat."[7] When Jacob examined the robe, he recognized it and said, "some ferocious animal has devoured him" (v. 33). One writer stated the "vicious animal" was actually

---

[4] Constable, 402.

[5] Carl Friedrich Keil, *Bible Commentary on the Old Testament*, vol. 1 (Edinburgh, Scotland: T & T Clark, 1872), 332.

[6] Terry L. Puett, *Institute of Biblical Studies: The Book of Genesis* (Pueblo, CO: T&L Publications, 2013), 509.

[7] Constable, 404.

Joseph's brothers. Jacob still mourned for his son 20 years later (Genesis 42:36). Jacob refused comfort (v. 35). Jacob mourned not only the loss of his son but Joseph's lost role in God's plan (1 Chronicles 5:2).

*Genesis 37:36:* We know Joseph is an illustration of Christ. Wiersbe described Joseph as "beloved by his father and obedient to his will; hated and rejected by his own brethren and sold as a slave; falsely accused and unfairly punished; finally elevated from the place of suffering to a powerful throne, thus saving his people from death."[8] Even though Joseph had to go through all this, so did Christ. Genesis 50:20 states: "You planned evil against me; God planned it for good to bring about the present result—the survival of many people." Joseph was in the lineage to save all his brothers! Even though Judah carried the *Seed*, Christ, Joseph had to save his brother.

## Closing

Daniel 4:35 records that God is in control: "All the inhabitants of the earth are counted as nothing, and He does what He wants with the army of heaven and the inhabitants of the earth. There is no one who can hold back His hand or say to Him, 'What have You done?'" (Romans 8:28). God will not allow the *Seed* to be destroyed.

## The Daily Word

Reuben and Judah went against the popular opinion of Joseph's brothers. They both spoke up, voiced their concerns about killing Joseph, and offered a different option. In the end, their courage to speak up saved Joseph's life and ultimately saved the lives of the brothers and the *Seed*, Christ, as well.

The Lord may put you in a position to speak up. Trust the voice of the Holy Spirit inside you, and take courage. Speaking up in obedience may ultimately save a life . . . even if you never know it!

**When Reuben heard this, he tried to save him from them. He said, "Let's not take his life." . . . Then Judah said to his brothers, "What do we gain if we kill our brother and cover up his blood? Come, let's sell him to the Ishmaelites and not lay a hand on him, for he is our brother, our own flesh," and they agreed. —Genesis 37:21, 26–27**

Further Scripture: Esther 4:14; Psalm 31:24; Luke 21:15

---

[8] Wiersbe, 92.

## Questions

1. When Jacob and Esau's property had become too large for the area to sustain them both, how was this issue settled (Genesis 36:6–7)? How did God use this situation to fulfill His promise to the seed of Abraham? (Genesis 28:4)

2. Even though Joseph's brothers were jealous of him because their father loved him more than them (Genesis 37:3–4), what was Joseph's response when Jacob/Israel wanted to send him to his brothers (Genesis 37:13)? How does Joseph's response parallel Christ? (John 4:34)

3. In Genesis 37:18, what was the brothers' motivation (Genesis 37:4,11)? How does this event compare to what happened to Christ? (Matthew 12:14; 27:18; John 11:53)

4. In chapter 37 of Genesis, we see several more similarities between Joseph and Jesus. Can you find at least two not already mentioned?

5. How do Joseph's brothers react when he told them about his dreams (Genesis 37:5,10–11)? Does it appear that they believed the dreams were from God? How did his father, who also had dreams from God, react to hearing Joseph's dreams? (Genesis 31:11; 37:10–11)

6. What did the Holy Spirit highlight to you in Genesis 36—37 through the reading or the teaching?

# Lesson 20: Genesis 38
*Seed*: The Sons of Jacob

## Teaching Notes

### Intro

We have had all sorts of drama from Abraham to Isaac to Jacob! Lying, deceiving, selling things, sex with other people, wives, and concubines . . . and it doesn't stop here!

Jacob's new name was Israel, and he had 12 sons. One of his sons was Judah, whose mother was Leah. Christ came from the lineage of Judah. At this point in time in Scripture, Joseph has just been sold as a slave and taken into Egypt. Judah was the one who suggested it.

### Teaching

There were 13 years between when Joseph was sold as a slave to when he was placed on the throne. Then, there were the seven years of plenty and the two years of famine before the reconciliation with Joseph's family. So, there were 22 years from the pit to reconciliation. In chapter 38, Joseph was in slavery, and Judah was just living his life. Genesis 38 is a window into the life of Judah.

*Genesis 38:1–5*: Judah left his brothers and moved away (which was a problem). He then took a Canaanite as his wife (that was another problem). They had a son and named him Er. Victor P. Hamilton wrote, "Their relationship to each other is conveyed in six verbs: three for him (he meets her, marries her, and has intercourse with her, v. 2), and three for her (she conceives, bears a son, and names a child, v. 3)."[1] Judah's wife had two more sons Onan and Shelah.

*Genesis 38: 6–10*: Judah found a wife for Er named Tamar. Er was evil, so the Lord put him to death. Judah insisted his other son Onan sleep with Tamar because he had to fulfill his brotherly duty. This was not a strange request! It was a custom. Deuteronomy 25:5–6 reveals the background: "When brothers live on the same property and one of them dies without a son, the wife of the dead man

---

[1] Victor P. Hamilton, *The Book of Genesis: Chapters 18-50* (Grand Rapids: Eerdmans, 1995), 433.

may not marry a stranger outside the family. Her brother-in-law is to take her as his wife, have sexual relations with her, and perform the duty of a brother-in-law for her. The first son she bears will carry on the name of the dead brother, so his name will not be blotted out from Israel."

Onan knew the offspring would not be his, so he took precautions to ensure Tamar would not get pregnant. Onan was evil in the eyes of the Lord, so he was put to death. Dr. Thomas Constable wrote, "Onan was frustrating the fulfillment of God's promises to Abraham, Isaac, and Jacob."[2]

*Genesis 38:11*: After Onan's death, Judah sent Tamar to her father's house "to wait on Shelah to grow up." But Judah had no intentions of giving him to her. He viewed Tamar as the reason his sons had died, not because of their own evil deeds.

*Genesis 38:12–15*: Judah's wife, the daughter of Shua, died (v. 12). Tamar heard that Judah had gone to shear sheep. She knew Judah had no intention of giving Shelah to her as a husband, so Tamar changed her appearance and went to meet Judah. She knew the relations were supposed to stay within the family (vv. 13–14). Since Shelah wasn't going to be given to her, Tamar knew Judah was the only one left. Tamar played the role of a prostitute in order to preserve her family line (v. 15). Judah began to negotiate what he would pay to sleep with Tamar. Tamar was trying to raise up the seed. Judah carried the seed. Tamar was essential to the lineage of Christ.

*Genesis 38:16–19*: Tamar got Judah to give her his signet ring, cord, and staff. She was to hold all of these things until Judah paid her with a goat. All of these things were proof of Judah's identity. Judah slept with Tamar, and she became pregnant. Tamar was a shrewd woman.

*Genesis 38:20–23*: Judah honored his word and tried to send a goat to Tamar. Judah really just needed his stuff back. He could not find her anywhere. Judah was probably really sick to his stomach at this point realizing he couldn't get his items back. Sin always catches up with you!

*Genesis 38:24–25*: Three months later, after hearing about Tamar's behavior, Judah's first response was to burn her to death. Judah might have thought, "Finally we have a way to get rid of her!" As Tamar was being brought out to her death, she sent Judah his items back. The deceiver is actually being deceived.

---

[2] Thomas L. Constable, Expository Notes of Dr. Thomas Constable: Genesis, 409, https://planobiblechapel.org/tcon/notes/pdf/genesis.pdf.

*Genesis 38:26–27*: Judah said, "She is more in the right than I, since I did not give her to my son Shelah. Literally, "she is righteousness, not I." Bruce Waltke wrote, "She [Tamar] risks her life for family fidelity," because of that risk the lineage will continue.[3] Tamar gave birth to twins—maybe to compensate for her lack from Er and Onan.

*Genesis 39:28–29*: The two sons from Tamar and Judah were Perez and Zerah. The lineage of Christ continued through Tamar and Judah and Perez! In Matthew's genealogy of Jesus, he recorded: "Judah fathered Perez and Zerah by Tamar, Perez fathered Hezron, Hezron fathered Aram" (Matthew 1:3).

Ruth 4:18 is the beginning of the genealogy of Perez: "Perez fathered Hezron. Hezron fathered Ram, who fathered Amminadab. Amminadab fathered Nahshon, who fathered Salmon. Salmon fathered Boaz, who fathered Obed. And Obed fathered Jesse, who fathered David."

## Closing

This is messy, but the seed continues. Warren Wiersbe identified four areas to explain why this messy story of Tamar was included in Genesis:

(1) *History*: The lineage of the seed continued through Perez and Tamar.

(2) *Morality*: This story shows just how dangerous it was for God's people in Canaan.

   Joseph said no to Potiphar's wife, but Judah slept with a strange woman. Judah tricked his father, Jacob, with a piece of clothing. Tamar tricked Judah the same way.

(3) *Community*: The Israelites lived in community under God's covenant agreement. When Judah separated himself from his brothers and left the community of God's people, he got in trouble by joining himself to a foreigner's wife. Genesis 24:3–4 said: "And I will have you swear by the Lord, God of heaven and God of earth, that you will not take a wife for my son from the daughters of the Canaanites among whom I live, but will go to my land and my family to take a wife for my son Isaac."

(4) *Grace*: Even though the people in this patriarchal period were deliberately disobedient, God still used them. God showed them the grace described in 1 Corinthians 1:26–31, "Brothers, consider your calling: Not many are wise from a human perspective, not many powerful, not many of noble birth. Instead, God has chosen what is foolish in

---

[3] Bruce K. Waltke and Cathi J. Fredricks, *Genesis: A Commentary* (Grand Rapids: Zondervan, 2001), 515.

the world to shame the wise, and God has chosen what is weak in the world to shame the strong. God has chosen what is insignificant and despised in the world—what is viewed as nothing—to bring to nothing what is viewed as something, so that no one can boast in His presence. But it is from Him that you are in Christ Jesus, who became God-given wisdom for us—our righteousness, sanctification, and redemption, in order that, as it is written: The one who boasts must boast in the Lord."

The bottom line is, God takes nothing and turns it into something!

## The Daily Word

As we read the story of Judah and Tamar, we see the Lord use broken people to continue the *Seed*, Messiah. Despite Judah and Tamar's sin, God still used them. It is interesting how the Lord doesn't use Joseph, Judah's brother, with a seemingly grander life story, to carry the *Seed*, Christ.

If you ever feel as though you don't measure up or you've made too many mistakes, remember God knows what He is doing. He can use anyone's life story for His will and for His glory. He is the perfecter of our faith. God will use you today!

**Judah recognized them and said, "She is more in the right than I, since I did not give her to my son Shelah." And he did not know her intimately again.**
**—Genesis 38:26**

Further Scripture: Isaiah 43:7; 2 Corinthians 12:9; Hebrews 12:2

## Questions

1. In Genesis 38:2, what did Judah do that went against what Abraham established in Genesis 24:3? How do we see these actions bring brokenness and loss to Judah?

2. Why did Judah withhold his son Shelah from marrying his daughter-in-law Tamar? (Genesis 38:11) Did his actions make things better or worse?

3. Why do you think Tamar asked specifically for the three items from Judah in Genesis 38:17–18? How do these items save her life? (Genesis 38:25–26)

4. In the midst of this mess, what seed-bearer (one who bears the seed) does God use to continue the bloodline? (Genesis 38:29; Matthew 1:3)

5. Does Judah look like the best choice for God to use to continue the lineage of Christ (the promised *Seed*)? What does this tell us about God?

6. What did the Holy Spirit highlight to you in Genesis 38 through the reading or the teaching?

# Lesson 21: Genesis 39—40

*Seed*: God Blesses Joseph in Everything He Does

## Teaching Notes

### Intro

As we study Scripture, our goal is to paint the complete picture of the Messiah. Our word for Genesis is *Seed*. Genesis 3:15 says, "I will put hostility between you and the woman, and between your seed and her seed. He will strike your head, and you will strike his heel." The *Seed*, Christ, permeates the book of Genesis. We've studied: Abraham and Sarah; Isaac and Rebekah; Jacob and Leah; Judah and Tamar; and Perez.

There was a 22-year window from when Joseph was thrown into the pit and when he and his brothers reunited in Egypt. Now we go back and look at Joseph, who had been thrown into a pit and taken to Egypt.

### Teaching

*Genesis 39:1*: In Egypt, Potiphar bought Joseph for 20 pieces of silver. Warren Wiersbe wrote, "The Egypt in which Joseph found himself was primarily a land of small villages inhabited by peasants who worked the land and raised grain and vegetables."[1] Egypt was located on the Nile River. The only two main cities around, at this point, were On and Memphis. Egypt practiced a lot of religious superstition and worshiped at least 2,000 gods. The community was made up of great builders. They actually developed the 365-day calendar! Egyptians had created established medicines and successful embalming techniques. During these times, slavery was prominent.[2]

*Genesis 39:2*: Joseph didn't get lost! He was not thrown in the pit and forgotten about. The Lord was with him! Joseph became successful serving. He wasn't out serving in the fields; God placed him serving prominent people. The ongoing theme of chapter 39 is that the Lord was with Joseph, and this is stated four

---

[1] William W. Wiersbe, *The Bible Exposition Commentary: Genesis–Deuteronomy* (Colorado Springs: David C. Cook, 2001), 146.

[2] Wiersbe, 146.

different times (Genesis 39:2–3, 21, 23). When you see Abraham, Isaac, and Jacob, you know the Lord's hand was on them and now it was true with Joseph!

Even though Judah carried the seed, Joseph was essential. The 11 brothers were in big trouble, and God used Joseph to save them. Joseph was the partial fulfillment of Genesis 12:3, which states, "All the peoples of the earth will be blessed through you." Joseph went from pit to prison to a palace—all because of the promise.

*Genesis 39:3–4*: The Lord made everything Joseph did prosper. Joseph and Potiphar did everything together. It is like what Joshua was to Moses or Elisha was to Elijah. They had that much interaction. Joseph lived out the prophet's words in Jeremiah 29:7: "Seek the welfare of the city I have deported you to. Pray to the Lord on its behalf, for when it has prosperity, you will prosper." Joseph sought the welfare of the city where God had placed him. I think we play the victim card too much: "Woe is me!" We must deal with it, pray for it, and God will honor it.

*Genesis 39:5:* The Lord blessed Potiphar and his household because of Joseph (Genesis 12:1–3)! Potiphar trusted Joseph because he had a pure heart. Joseph was well built and handsome (v. 6). Proverbs 22:29 says, "Do you see a man skilled in his work? He will stand in the presence of kings. He will not stand in the presence of unknown men." Joseph used the talents he had been given (Matthew 25:21). I just wonder sometimes if Jesus had been talking about Joseph.

The challenge in our lives is to consider: What are we doing with what God has given to us? Luke 16:10: "Whoever is faithful in very little is also faithful in much, and whoever is unrighteous in very little is also unrighteous in much." The *Seed*, Christ, was preserved because Joseph was faithful in the small things.

*Genesis 39:7–9*: After a while, Potiphar's wife lifted up her eyes to Joseph and looked at him with desire. Waltke wrote, "Sarna also captures the dramatic irony: 'She, the mistress of the house, is a slave to her lust for her husband's slave.'"[3] Joseph refused her, though it was a no-win situation. Joseph showed respect and care for Potiphar. Joseph recognized that this would be a sin against God.

*Genesis 39:10*: Although Potiphar's wife approached him day after day, he refused. Commentary writer John H. Sailhamer wrote, "The Joseph narratives are intended to give balance to the narratives of Abraham, Isaac, and Jacob. Together, the patriarchal narratives and the Joseph narrative show both God's faithfulness

---

[3] Bruce K. Waltke and Cathi J. Fredricks, *Genesis: A Commentary* (Grand Rapids: Zondervan, 2001), 520.

in spite of human failure and the necessity of an obedient and faithful response on the part of human beings."[4]

We cannot give in to the seed of the serpent (James 1:13–17; Luke 22:40; Matthew 6:13; 1 Corinthians 10:13). If Joseph could say no to temptation, so can we. God always provides a way out! Genesis 4:6–7 says, "Then the LORD said to Cain, 'Why are you furious? And why do you look despondent? If you do what is right, won't you be accepted? But if you do not do what is right, sin is crouching at the door. Its desire is for you, but you must rule over it.'"

Satan is coming after us. Sin is crouching at the door. Sin's desire is for us, but we must rule over it. Tamar was persistent to continue the seed. Joseph was persistent to flee from sin (2 Timothy 2:22).

*Genesis 39:11–12*: Potiphar's wife grabbed him, but Joseph fled, leaving behind his garment. Wiersbe wrote, "As the puritan preacher said, 'Joseph lost his coat, but he kept his character.'"[5] Joseph's garment would have been a mid-calf length shirt with a tunic that resembled a really long T-shirt that went down past his rear end. We have to be careful who we hang out with (Proverbs 5:1–8).

*Genesis 39:13–20*: Potiphar's wife accused Joseph of trying to sleep with her, using his garment as proof. Satan will use seductive people to mess up everything. When Potiphar heard, he was furious and "burned with anger" (v. 19). Joseph was thrown into prison. He went from the pit to prison.

*Genesis 39:21*: God gave Joseph favor with the prison guard. Psalm 105:18 describes Joseph's situation: "They hurt his feet with shackles; his neck was put in an iron collar." It's crazy how God can take someone from a pit to a prison and still keep His promise. God didn't remove Joseph from suffering but remained with him in the midst.

*Genesis 39: 22–23*: All the prisoners were put under Joseph's authority. God was with Joseph and gave him favor even in the prison. Joseph didn't force the situation or run ahead of the situation, he embraced it and allowed the prosperity to unfold. Even when it didn't look good, we knew that the promise of the *Seed* would continue to unfold.

---

[4] John H. Sailhamer, *The Pentateuch as Narrative* (Grand Rapids: Zondervan, 1992), 234, 235.

[5] Wiersbe, 147.

*Genesis 40*: The cupbearer and baker were thrown into the prison as well. They had dreams Joseph interpreted. The cupbearer was freed and supposed to remember Joseph when he was released, but he didn't.

## Closing

Even as Joseph was faithful in the small things, God used that to continue the promise, and saved a nation. It's an incredible story of following the seed all the way through the book of Genesis.

## The Daily Word

The Lord was with Joseph, and whatever he did prospered. Joseph found favor with his boss, Potiphar, who put Joseph in charge of all he owned. Joseph also found favor with the prison warden when he was unjustly imprisoned. Whether at a high place in life or low place in life, the Lord was with Joseph. Joseph remained steadfast in the Lord no matter his circumstances.

The Lord promises to be with you wherever you are. Do not base your feelings today on your circumstances. He delights in you, and He has plans for you.

**But the LORD was with Joseph and extended kindness to him. He granted him favor in the eyes of the prison warden. —Genesis 39:21**

Further Scripture: Psalm 139:7–10; Isaiah 26:3–4; Zephaniah 3:17

## Questions

1. In Genesis 39:2, 3, 21, and 23, we see that the Lord was with Joseph. Do you think it would be easy for Joseph to not believe that considering his current circumstances? [Examples: his brothers' betrayal, selling him into slavery, relatives purchasing and reselling him, having an Egyptian master (think Hagar)]

2. How does Genesis 39:1–6 reveal God's favor? Have you ever seen God's favor revealed in a way you didn't expect? (2 Corinthians 5:7)

3. Do you believe God was orchestrating Joseph's difficult circumstances in order to fulfill His purpose? If so, do you see the same thing at work in your own life?

4. We saw Joseph flee from a compromising situation to keep his integrity and yet was accused and punished. Do you feel a sense of injustice at this part of the story? Who is an even better example of total innocence and bearing punishment? (2 Corinthians 5:21; 1 Peter 2:21–23)

5. When two of Pharaoh's officials were dejected, Joseph showed concern for them. How did the chief cupbearer return the favor Joseph requested in Genesis 40:14, 23?

6. What did the Holy Spirit highlight to you in Genesis 39—40 through the reading or the teaching?

# Lesson 22: Genesis 41—42
*Seed*: Joseph's Brothers in Egypt

## Teaching Notes

### Intro

We finish the first book of the Bible this week! Joseph's purpose in Genesis was to preserve the seed. In Genesis 39—40, God was with Joseph and gave him favor and success.

### Teaching

*Genesis 41*: Two years after the cupbearer was released from prison, Pharaoh had a dream that needed interpretation. The cupbearer remembered Joseph, and Pharaoh pulled Joseph out of prison. Joseph interpreted Pharaoh's dream to mean there would be seven years of abundance and then seven years of famine. Joseph gave a strategy in response to the dream. Joseph suggested that Pharaoh place a man over the land in Egypt to store up grain during the years of abundance. Pharaoh exalted Joseph to that role.

Remember, 13 years earlier Joseph was in a pit, and now here he was in a palace. God's promise to preserve the seed was happening through Joseph. Pharaoh gave Joseph a wife and a new name, Saphenath-paneah, meaning, "God speaks, and He lives." Joseph was 30 years old when he began to implement the interpretation of the dream. He was in charge of everything except what Pharaoh ate.

Joseph had two sons: Manasseh, meaning "forget" and Ephraim, meaning "fruitful." These two sons became part of the 12 tribes. Gideon came from the tribe of Manasseh. Joshua came from the tribe of Ephraim. God was expanding Joseph's role and his family. Joseph was storing up the grain in all the storehouses all over Egypt. When the famine spread across the land, Joseph opened up the storehouses and sold grain. All the nations came to Egypt to buy grain. The seed was in jeopardy because of the famine. Genesis 12:3: "All the peoples on the earth will be blessed through you." Joseph was playing a part in that promise!

*Genesis 42:1–2*: Jacob's whole family was in danger. The trip to Egypt was a dangerous trip. Wiersbe wrote, "For one thing, the trip to Egypt was long (250–300 miles) and dangerous, and a round trip could consume six weeks' time. Even after arriving in Egypt, the men couldn't be certain of a friendly reception. As foreigners from Canaan, they would have been vulnerable and could have been arrested and enslaved."[1] Jacob knew there was more going on: "Then the Lord said to Abram, 'Know this for certain: Your offspring will be foreigners in a land that does not belong to them; they will be enslaved and oppressed 400 years.'" (Genesis 15:13)

*Genesis 42:3–8*: Ten of Jacob's sons were sent to Egypt to buy grain. Jacob kept Benjamin home because he was the only link left to Rachel. Israel's sons were a part of every nation coming to Egypt. This was a national identity, a people group. Keep in mind that Israel didn't became a nation until May 14, 1948.

Joseph sold grain to all peoples. It's intriguing that Joseph was right there when the brothers came. God had to have orchestrated that! The brothers bowed down before Joseph. The dream! The sheaves bowing down (Genesis 37:7–9)! Twenty-one years later, the dream came to fruition. Joseph didn't want to blow his cover yet, so he spoke to them harshly. They didn't recognize Joseph—it was 21 years later, and he was dressed as an Egyptian.

*Genesis 42:9*: Joseph accused them of being spies. That was a normal accusation or thought of that time. Bruce Waltke wrote, "Frontier guards at Egypt's Asian border routinely checked travelers to discover spies who might herald an imminent attack."[2] Even in Israel today, they're always watching for someone who might be coming to attack. Joseph accused them of being spies four times in this dialogue.

*Genesis 42:10–15*: Joseph kept digging because he wanted more information. The brothers defended themselves. Why did they say 12 brothers? They still count Benjamin, at home with Jacob, and Joseph, who they think is dead. Joseph judged them to be spies and tested them. He told them they would not leave Egypt until their younger brother came. Joseph wanted to see Benjamin! In American society, you're always innocent until proven guilty. In Egypt, we see the opposite. The brothers were guilty until proven innocent.

*Genesis 42:16–20:* Joseph was going to send the brothers to get Benjamin, but first, he imprisoned them all for three days. Maybe this is a taste of what he experienced in the prison for three years. On the third day, Joseph approached his brothers and spoke to them. This was the first time in this dialogue that

---

[1] Warren W. Wiersbe, *The Bible Exposition Commentary: Genesis–Deuteronomy* (Colorado Springs: David C. Cook, 1997), 151.

[2] Bruce K. Waltke and Cathi J. Fredricks, *Genesis: A Commentary* (Grand Rapids: Zondervan, 2001), 543.

Joseph acknowledged God verbally. "I fear God," Joseph declared. This would be a highly unusual statement for an Egyptian to make. One brother was to stay back, and the rest were to go back to get Benjamin.

*Genesis 42:21–23*: The brother's consciences were kicking in. They remembered their guilt from what they had done to Joseph. They concluded that this was why trouble had come to them. They discussed how Joseph had been in deep distress in the pit (Genesis 37) and regretted their decision. Reuben essentially said, "I told you!" They didn't know Joseph had been listening or understanding because there had been an interpreter between them.

*Genesis 42:24*: Joseph lost it and wept. Joseph showed emotion over his family through weeping six times: (1) when he heard his brothers (Genesis 42); (2) when he saw Benjamin (Genesis 43); (3) when he revealed himself to his brothers (Genesis 45); (4) when he saw his father for the first time (Genesis 45); (5) when his father died (Genesis 50); and (6) when his brothers were fearful (Genesis 50).[3] This showed Joseph's true character. Joseph kept Simeon in prison, likely because he realized that Reuben had defended him. Remember what Simeon and Levi did? At Schechem, they killed all the men for raping Dinah.

*Genesis 42:25–32*: Joseph handed their bags back with money—he played mind games. The brothers were fearful when they realized the money was in their bag. They questioned: "What is this God has done to us? Why is God judging us? Is it all catching up with us?"

*Genesis 42:33–35*: The brothers told Jacob the story of what happened in Egypt. They had to bring back Benjamin. At this point, everything had been laid on the table. The brothers realized the money had been returned to all of their sacks, and they were really nervous.

*Genesis 42:36–37*: Jacob said something we've all been thinking, "You've deprived me of my sons (Joseph and Simeon)! Now you want Benjamin?" Jacob was placing the guilt on his sons. Reuben offered his two sons as security. This is reminiscent of Lot offering his two virgin daughters (Genesis 19:8).

*Genesis 42:38*: Jacob did not want Benjamin to go. He allowed Benjamin to go, saying, "I know I don't have an option, but if it ends badly, I'm done."

---

[3] Wiersbe, 153.

# Closing

Here we see Joseph living out the interpretation of the dreams, the sheaves bowing down, the seven years of abundance and then the seven years of famine. The nations had come to Joseph. His family had come to Joseph. Why? Because Joseph had been called to save the seed. Judah could not have continued on without Joseph.

Even as Joseph was faithful in the small things, God used that to continue the promise and saved a nation. It's an incredible story of following the *Seed* all the way through the book of Genesis.

# The Daily Word

During Joseph's "rise to success," he turned all the attention toward God. The common theme of Joseph's explanations about wisdom or understanding was God. Joseph feared God. He referenced God above himself, and he did not receive the accolades or the credit.

May you remember that God is in all things, and in Him, all things hold together. Do you pat yourself on the back and receive the praise, or do you remember that everything comes from God? Today, give God all the honor and thanksgiving.

**Joseph answered Pharaoh. "It is God who will give Pharaoh a favorable answer." —Genesis 41:16**

Further Scripture: Genesis 42:18; Colossians 1:17; James 1:17

# Questions

1. How would you have interpreted Pharaoh's two dreams in Genesis 41:1–7? What was Joseph's outlook on accomplishing this task? (Genesis 41:16)

2. Joseph was imprisoned in Genesis 39:20. Which of Joseph's actions ultimately led him from prison to the events of Genesis 41:41? What can you learn from this?

3. Why do you think Joseph received expedited favor from the Lord (Genesis 39:1–6; 41:37–40)? Can you think of a time when you have seen God do this in your life?

4. What motivated Joseph's brothers in Genesis 42:21–22? Do you think there was truth to what they said—that distress had come on them because of their previous actions?

5. Why did Joseph accuse his brothers of being spies when he knew they weren't? (Genesis 42:8–14)

6. Why do you think Joseph chose the instruction in Genesis 42:15–20 as the "honesty test"?

7. What did the Holy Spirit highlight to you in Genesis 41—42 through the reading or the teaching?

# Lesson 23: Genesis 43—44

*Seed*: Joseph's Brothers Return to Egypt

## Teaching Notes

### Intro

Joseph was saving the seed that was established in Genesis 3 and carried through Abraham, Isaac, and Jacob. God had put Joseph in place in Egypt to hand out food for all those who had none. Remember there had been seven years of plenty and now they were experiencing seven years of famine. Genesis 43 is set in the midst of the famine.

### Teaching

*Genesis 43:1*: The famine in the land was severe. Remember the brothers had previously come to Joseph for food. Joseph told them he would keep Simeon until they brought their younger brother, Benjamin, to him.

*Genesis 43:2–4*: When Israel (Jacob) and his sons had used up all the grain, Jacob told them to go back to Egypt to buy food. Judah reminded Israel that they were to take Benjamin back with them. That was the only chance they had of seeing "the man" (Joseph) and getting access to more food. The tribe of Judah was finally standing up! Judah told Jacob that if he would send Benjamin with them, they would go back to Egypt.

*Genesis 43:5–7*: Judah reiterated that they would not go without Benjamin. If they didn't take Benjamin, they wouldn't get anything. Israel asked the brothers why they had caused so much trouble. Why did they even tell the man they had another brother? The brothers now answered together, telling Israel that the man prodded them. They said, "the man" (Joseph) asked them lots of questions about their father and if they had another brother. The brothers defended themselves, "We answered him accordingly. How could we know that he would say, 'Bring your brother here'?" (v. 7).

*Genesis 43:8*: Judah asked his father to send Benjamin with them so they would not die. If the brothers didn't go back to Egypt, everyone would die from starvation. Israel had to send Benjamin. The seed would have stopped if they hadn't gone. The seed that had been promised in Genesis 12, 15, 17, and 25 would stop if the family operated in fear.

*Genesis 43:9–10*: Judah promised he would be responsible for Benjamin. Waltke wrote, "I will bear blame before you all my life. The Hebrew literally reads, I have sinned . . . if he violates the agreement. Judah is willing to take whatever penalty Jacob wishes to inflict on him for the rest of his life, and the patriarch can and will treat his sons harshly."[1] Judah valued the seed and realized that if they did nothing, this family was done.

If we're not careful, this is the American Church. We can't stay stagnant inside a building, or it will die. This was a great example of where Jacob needed to release his sons and say "GO" and not be afraid. They wasted time arguing with Israel. Judah said they could have gone and come back twice already. They were afraid to address the issues that really needed to be addressed, and it wasted time.

*Genesis 43:11*: Because Judah spoke up, they finally had a plan. Jacob told them to take the best products of the land as a gift to Joseph. Where were they getting these "best products" from? They were in the middle of a severe famine! It tells me this family was still wealthy. God's hand was still obviously on this family.

The brothers were to take: balsam, honey, aromatic gum, resin, pistachios, and almonds. When I think about Israel, I think about honey. Look at the following Scriptures:

- A land flowing with milk and honey (Exodus 3:8,17).
- Honey is a source of sweetening (Exodus 16:31; Proverbs 24:13).
- Honey is a prized gift (Psalms 19:10; 119:103; Song of Solomon 4:11).
- Honey is medicinal (Proverbs 16: 24).
- Honey never goes bad.
- Honey is a gift (2 Samuel 17:29).

*Genesis 43:12–14*: Jacob told the brothers to take twice the amount of money and their brother and return at once. This statement from Jacob did not sound like a man of God who claimed the promises of God. What I hear is a man who sat down in sorrow and didn't function in faith. Both Esther and Jacob spoke out

---

[1] Bruce K. Waltke and Cathi J. Fredricks, *Genesis: A Commentary* (Grand Rapids: Zondervan, 2001), 554.

of desperation (Esther 4:16). Esther spoke in desperation *with* faith. Shadrach, Meshach, and Abednego, like Esther, also spoke from a place of desperation *and* faith, in contrast to Jacob (Daniel 3:16–18).

*Genesis 43:15–16*: When the brothers stood before Joseph with Benjamin, it reminds me of Abraham and Isaac. They were nervous and afraid that they might lose their brother. Joseph was excited about having another interaction with his brothers. Dr. Tom Constable pointed out that the brothers had three problems to face: (1) The brothers were carrying a lot of money and didn't know if they would be accused of stealing; (2) they wondered if Simeon would be released from prison; and (3) they worried they might lose Benjamin.[2]

*Genesis 43:17–22*: The brothers were taken to Joseph's house, and they were afraid. They knew Egyptian slaves were kept in the dungeon of officers' houses (Genesis 40:3). They explained to Joseph's steward about the money.

*Genesis 43:23–24*: You knew this was Joseph's steward because he talked like Joseph. No Egyptian steward would talk like this unless Joseph was talking to the Lord around him. Simeon was brought out to them. This was a turning point for his brothers!

*Genesis 43:25–31*: They got their gift ready for Joseph and bowed to the ground before him. Joseph kept living out the dream (Genesis 37). Now the 11 brothers were bowing down. Joseph started to ask questions. He was wise in how he stewarded the conversation. Verse 28 says, "And they bowed down to honor him." Who were they honoring? Jacob or Joseph? In verse 29, the phrase "When he looked up," suggests Joseph was bowing down as well. Joseph wept over the sight of Benjamin, but not in front of everyone.

*Genesis 43:32–34*: Joseph was served the meal at his own table. The brothers were served the meal at a different table, and the Egyptians were served at a third table. Culturally, they would not have eaten together. The brothers were seated before Joseph in order by age and were astonished by their treatment. They were served from Joseph's table, but Benjamin received five times as much. The 12 brothers were eating and drinking together. There was a unity that had started to take place, and yet the brothers still had no clue who Joseph was.

---

[2] Thomas L. Constable, *Expository Notes of Dr. Thomas Constable: Genesis*, https://www. planobiblechapel.org/tcon/notes/html/ot/genesis/genesis.htm.

*Genesis 44:1–13*: Joseph commanded his steward to put his silver cup in the top of Benjamin's bag. Joseph set it up so that the brothers would be accused of stealing. The brothers were so sure they were clean that they told the steward to search their stuff. The cup was found in Benjamin's bag. The brothers were so distraught that they tore their clothes. They then returned to the city.

*Genesis 44:14–34*: The brothers fell on the ground before Joseph. Judah pleaded before Joseph. Joseph said Benjamin would be his slave. The rest of the brothers could return to their father. Again, this was a complete set-up. He had to get his father back. Judah begged Joseph to let him switch places with Benjamin.

## Closing

These two chapters set up chapter 45. They are a cliffhanger for what happens next!

## The Daily Word

Judah pleaded with Joseph to allow him to take the place of their brother, Benjamin, as a slave. Judah longed to spare his brother and explained to Joseph how their father Jacob would die of sorrow if they returned without Benjamin. Judah displayed a selfless, sacrificial love, allowing Joseph to see into this brother's heart.

Judah was the seed-bearer for Christ, who is our ultimate example of selfless and sacrificial love. You are called to love others as Christ loved. Is the Lord asking you to show this selfless and sacrificial love toward someone in your life today?

**Now please let your servant remain here as my lord's slave, in place of the boy. Let him go back with his brothers. —Genesis 44:33**

Further Scripture: John 15:13; Philippians 2:3–5; 1 John 3:16

## Questions

1. Joseph's servant greeted them in Genesis 43:23. How can you see Joseph's character influencing his servant? How are those you are surrounded by influenced by you?

2. In Genesis 43:26, we see 11 of Joseph's brothers bowed down before him. Joseph's dream continued to unfold (Genesis 37:9). Have you seen God reveal pieces of a complete picture/dream in your life? How can you wait patiently for a dream to be fulfilled?

3. Why do you think Joseph wanted Benjamin to stay with him and become his slave in Genesis 44:2, 10–17?

4. How would you have responded to Judah's plea in Genesis 44:18–34?

5. How was Joseph protecting the *Seed*, Christ in Genesis 43—44? (Genesis 45:7)

6. What did the Holy Spirit highlight to you in Genesis 43—44 through the reading or the teaching?

# Lesson 24: Genesis 45—46
*Seed*: Joseph Reveals His Identity

## Teaching Notes

### Intro

We are seeing the end of Genesis, and it's just beginning. The last lesson saw the climax of the situation with Joseph and his brothers. Judah tried to take leadership in the situation by begging Joseph to let him trade places with Benjamin, who had been accused of stealing the silver cup. Commentator Bruce Waltke said, in regard to Judah's speech to Joseph at the end of chapter 44, "He proves to Joseph, once hateful and selfish, they are now motivated by love for one another. [The brothers] have integrity within themselves and with one another."[1] Judah's response to Benjamin's predicament and his speech proved he and his brothers had changed.

### Teaching

*Genesis 45:1–2*: Joseph's composure and passion could no longer be contained, so he sent everyone away. Joseph signified that this longtime family feud was coming to an end. Joseph had now cried three times: (1) when he first saw his brothers; (2) when he saw Benjamin; and (3) now, when he revealed his identity. Joseph identified himself as a member of this family, no longer as an Egyptian (Hebrews 11:22). All of Pharaoh's household heard him weep.

*Genesis 45:3–4*: The brothers were terrified. The word "terrified" here has the same feel as when used in Exodus 15:15; Judges 20:41; and Psalm 48:5. "Terrified" gives the sense of being afraid of joining a battle. Wiersbe noted that this man now standing before the brothers was claiming to be someone whom they thought was dead. This claim caused them to wonder, "If this is Joseph, why has he been treating us like this?" Considering the implications of either possibility, they were speechless."[2] Joseph needed them to come closer. There would be no more family secrets.

---

[1] Bruce K. Waltke, *Genesis: A Commentary*. (Grand Rapids: Zondervan, 2001).

[2] Warren W. Wiersbe, *Be Authentic (Genesis 25-50) ): Exhibiting Real Faith in the Real World* (Colorado Springs: David C. Cook, 1997), 142.

*Genesis 45:5*: We've said all along, *Joseph was the man to preserve the seed*, and Joseph himself explained that here in verse 5, "God sent me ahead of you to preserve life." God sent Joseph ahead to Egypt as a forerunner to preserve life and ultimately to preserve the lineage of Christ. We all have the role of forerunner (Luke 1:17; Isaiah 40:3–5; Malachi 3:1; 4:5–6; Hebrews 6:19–20). Waltke noted, "This statement [God sent me] is the theological heart of the account of Jacob's line. God directs the maze of human guilt to achieve His good and set purposes. Such faith establishes the redemptive Kingdom of God."[3] God took all the brothers' sin and guilt and used it to point to Christ.

W. H. Griffith Thomas wrote, "Happy is the man whose eye is open to see the hand of God in every-day events, for to him life always possesses a wonderful true joy and glory."[4] Everyday serves as an opportunity to point others to Christ. Joseph did this over and over (Genesis 50:19–21). Romans 8:28 was Joseph's heart. His purpose was to save the seed and to be a forerunner. He had to go through some really hard things to save his people.

*Genesis 45:6–8*: Joseph was not just a forerunner. He was also sent to establish a remnant. Victor P. Hamilton says, "It may well be, in the deliverance of his brothers and his father, that Joseph perceives that more is at stake than the mere physical survival of twelve human beings. What really survives is the plan of redemption announced first to his great grandfather."[5]

*Genesis 45:9–11*: Joseph sent for his father, Jacob, with a sense of urgency. When Abraham was told to leave his home to follow God, he was told to take nothing. Jacob was told to bring everything. If Jacob's family didn't come, they would likely die because the famine was going to last for five more years.

*Genesis 45:12*: Why did Joseph make a distinction between Benjamin's eyes and his brothers' eyes? Waltke says Benjamin was the only credible source.[6] He was the only one who wasn't a part of what took place before. Joseph spoke to them in Hebrew. This is one of the most profound illustrations of when life looks bad, but God has a much bigger picture. Whether you are the brother or Joseph, don't give up, keep your eye on the *Seed*, Christ.

---

[3] Waltke, 563.

[4] W. H. Griffith Thomas, *Genesis: A Devotional Commentary* (London: Religious Tract Society, 1908), 3:40.

[5] Victor P. Hamilton, *The Book of Genesis: Chapters 18-50*, The New International Commentary on the Old Testament (Grand Rapids: Eerdmans, 1995), 576.

[6] Waltke, 564.

*Genesis 45:13–15*: Here is a picture of Psalm 85:10: "Faithful love and truth will join together; righteousness and peace will embrace." Love, truth, righteousness, and peace are in the presence of the 12 brothers. What were the similarities between Joseph and Jesus? (1) Jesus was rejected the first time when He came to earth (John 1:11; 5:43). (2) Joseph was rejected the first time when his identity was hidden. But when he revealed himself, he was accepted the second time. (3) People will accept Christ the second time (Zechariah 12:10—13:1). When Christ comes back the second time, the Jewish people will realize who He is and will weep and mourn. They will see that He is coming to wash away their sin and impurity.

*Genesis 45:16–27*: Pharaoh blessed Joseph's family; "I will bless those who bless you and curse those who curse you" (Genesis 12:3). Joseph, who had his coat taken away and was thrown into a pit, gave his brothers clothes. Joseph was once sold for silver, and now he gave his brothers silver. Joseph was constantly forgiving and gave abundantly (Luke 6:29–30). The brothers told Jacob that Joseph was alive. Jacob was "stunned." Here, "stunned" meant that his heart fainted, it grew cold, or it might have even gone numb. Jacob might have had a heart attack. The one who Jacob thought was dead was now alive. Jesus, rejected once and thought to be dead, came alive. As soon as God showed up and Jacob saw the wagons, the tangible evidence of his sons' words, Jacob was revived. Joseph and Jacob would have 17 years together in which they could enjoy being a family.

*Genesis 46:1–2*: Jacob left Hebron and went about 20 miles northeast to Beer-sheba where God spoke to him in a vision. There is a difference between a dream and vision. In a dream, the person is sleeping. In a vision, the person is awake and tangibly seeing something (Joel 2:28–29; Acts 2:17–18). Dreams and visions will continue until Christ returns.

*Genesis 46:3*: Jacob knew the prophecy from Genesis 15:13, that his people would be enslaved for 400 years. God massaged Jacob's heart and spoke to him through a vision. Abraham, Isaac, and Jacob all had encounters with the Lord in Beer-sheba (Genesis 21:32–33; 26:23–25). Repeatedly, Abraham and Isaac heard God promise that He would make them into a great nation (Genesis 12:2; 15:13–14; 17:6; 18:18; 21:13–18). Jacob needed to hear God's promise too.

*Genesis 46:4–34:* God promised He wouldn't keep Jacob in Egypt. God would allow him to die in his own land, Canaan, and Joseph would be with him. This is the last revelation where God spoke to someone in Genesis. The next revelation will be in Exodus, almost 430 years later, to Moses at the burning bush. Jacob's fear was gone. The entire family went to Egypt. The firstborn sons of Jacob's lineage are listed. Judah was now the son who was sent ahead by Jacob to meet

Joseph, the forerunner for the family, as the family comes to Egypt. Joseph and Jacob were reunited after more than 20 years. God used Joseph to speak into the life of his father. Pharaoh gave Jacob what he had promised for Jacob's family: the land of Goshen.

## Closing

When things don't look good, God still shows up. One man, Joseph, saved his brothers, his father, the seed, and, in reality, all of us.

## The Daily Word

You only see part of the picture God is writing in your life today. Once again, Joseph gave God credit for redeeming his life so his entire family could be preserved and delivered.

When the Lord provides restoration, it is emotional and powerful because it is all God, just as it was in Joseph's family. Today, hang on to this hope. Do not fear even if those around you are not walking with the Lord. Remember, He is with you. Trust Him.

**God sent me ahead of you to establish you as a remnant within the land and to keep you alive by a great deliverance. —Genesis 45:7**

Further Scripture: 2 Samuel 22:2–3; Psalm 18:50; Psalm 89:4

## Questions

1. Why did Joseph encourage his brothers to not be angry with themselves over selling him into slavery? (Genesis 45:5; 50:20)

2. How did Joseph's experience of being sold by his brothers, God's plan (Genesis 45:8) for the ultimate purpose of saving them, show us a picture of Christ? (John 3:17; Acts 5:30–31; Hebrews 5:8–9)

3. Israel set out with all he had in response to Joseph's call to come with a sense of no turning back. Do you see a parallel to our call to come to Christ? (Matthew 19:21, 27–29; Luke 5:10–11, 27–28; 9:23)

4. Joseph knew, according to Genesis 45:11, that in order for his family to survive the famine and not become impoverished, he needed to provide for them. In what way is that a representation of Christ and His kingdom? (Matthew 6:33; Romans 8:32; 2 Corinthians 9:8; Philippians 4:19)

5.  God instructed Israel in a vision of the night to not be afraid to go down to Egypt. Why might Israel have been fearful? (Genesis 15:13)

6.  What did the Holy Spirit highlight to you in Genesis 45—46 through the reading or the teaching?

# Lesson 25: Genesis 47—48

*Seed*: Jacob Blesses Ephraim and Manasseh

## Teaching Notes

### Review

In the book of Genesis, we've gotten to the point where Joseph was reunited with his father Jacob and his brothers. Genesis 47 continues Joseph's story. In verses 1–10, Pharaoh met Joseph's brothers, and they were given the land that was promised. Pharaoh met Joseph's father, and Jacob blessed Pharaoh, speaking life into him. In verses 11–25, the family settled in Goshen. They were fruitful and become numerous, even during the years of famine. God's hand was clearly on this family. In Genesis 47:28, the final details of Jacob's life are given: Jacob lived in Egypt for 17 years and lived to be 147 years old. As he neared his death, he released a prophetic word, asking Joseph not to bury him in Egypt.

### Teaching

*Genesis 48:1–3*: Joseph still had a job to do—he was still overseeing things in Egypt. Joseph was told his father had become weaker, so he took his two sons, Manasseh and Ephraim, to Jacob.

Jacob walked through what God had done in his life and then blessed Joseph's sons. He reiterated the promises that we've been seeing throughout Genesis.

*Genesis 48:4*: Jacob was sharing what God had given him. The promises he had received included: making him a great nation, being fruitful and numerous, and giving him land as an eternal possession to future descendants. Commentator Victor P. Hamilton wrote, "Jacob may be losing his health, but he is not losing his memory."[1]

*Genesis 48:5*: As he lay dying, Jacob wanted to bless his sons. Jacob blessed his grandsons, Manasseh and Ephraim, as well. They were technically grandsons, but Jacob counted them as sons. In Genesis 46:7–27, there is a list of 52 grandsons, but Jacob chose these two to add to the tribes.

---

[1] Victor P. Hamilton, *The Book of Genesis: Chapters 18-50*, The New International Commentary on the Old Testament (Grand Rapids: Eerdmans, 1995), 628.

Ephraim and Manasseh's mother was the daughter of a priest to the sun god. Jacob pulled them from that line and into his line. They were "grafted" in. The tribe of Manasseh is listed as a part of the 144,000 in Revelation 7:6. Ephraim got a double blessing. Gideon was from Ephraim. Joshua was from Manasseh.

*Genesis 48:6–12*: Ephraim and Manasseh were counted among Jacob's sons to make the 12 tribes. There were 12 because Levi is not allotted land. Jacob reflected on Rachel and losing her. Joseph honors his father by bowing to the ground.

*Genesis 48:13*: Joseph took Ephraim to Israel's left and Manasseh to Israel's right (right indicated the greater). He was attempting to set the stage for the blessing. Mier Sternberg wrote, "Joseph then firmly stage-manages the blessing scene for his doting father."[2]

*Genesis 48:14*: Jacob took his right hand and rested it on Ephraim's head, and the left on Manasseh, even though Manasseh was the firstborn. Jacob may have been losing his sight, but he was in the right frame of mind. He did what he intended to do.

The right hand brings strength, honor, power, and glory.

- *Exodus 15:2:* "The LORD is my strength and my song; He has become my salvation. This is my God, and I will praise Him, my father's God, and I will exalt Him."
- *Psalm 89:13:* You have a mighty arm; Your hand is powerful; Your right hand is lifted high.
- *Proverbs 3:16:* "Long life is in her right hand; in her left, riches and honor."
- *Ecclesiastes 10:2:* "A wise man's heart goes to the right, but a fool's heart to the left."
- *Matthew 25:33:* "He will put the sheep on His right and the goats on the left."
- *Acts 2:33:* "Therefore, since He has been exalted to the right hand of God and has received from the Father the promised Holy Spirit, He has poured out what you both see and hear."

Other examples of the younger receiving what the older traditionally would: Abel not Cain, Isaac not Ishmael, Jacob not Esau, and Judah not Reuben.

---

[2] Meir Sternberg, *The Poetics of Biblical Narrative: Ideological Literature and the Drama of Reading* (Bloomington: Indiana University Press, 1985), 352.

*Genesis 48:15–16:* Jacob blessed Joseph. Jacob referred to God as His shepherd (Psalm 23; Genesis 49:24; John 10:11). Jacob referred to the Angel of the Lord who redeemed him (Genesis 28:12; 31:11–12; 32:1-3; 32:22–32).

*Genesis 48:17–21:* Joseph thought Jacob's hand placement was a mistake. Eventually Ephraim became the most powerful of the northern tribes. The ten tribes would take on the name of Ephraim (Jeremiah 31:9; Hosea 4:16–17; 7:1). Jacob reminded Joseph that God would be with him (Joseph) and would bring him (Joseph) back to the land of his forefathers.

*Genesis 48:22:* Jacob gave Joseph the mountain slope he took from the Amorites. We never saw Jacob fight the Amorites. Possibilities . . .

- *Genesis 34:* Jacob denounced what happened with Shechem when his sons killed, plundered, and took all the land.

*Genesis 33:18–20:* Jacob purchased land.

Maybe he was referring to when he bought the land, and his sons fought and took it. Now he was giving it to Joseph's sons.

Dr. Tom Constable wrote, "Apparently Jacob gave Joseph the town of 'Shechem,' which he regarded as a 'down payment' of all that God would give his descendants as they battled the Canaanites in the future."[3]

In John 4:5, Jesus came to a town in Samaria called Sychar, which is the same area of Shechem. At the end of Genesis 48, Joseph received his dying father's land, and Jesus walked into this same land that was the property of his heritage.

# Closing

God sets everything up for a purpose. God is very intentional! The Lord wants to give us all mountain slopes to set the stage for more people to see who the Messiah really is.

## The Daily Word

God is a God of the unexpected. Israel never expected to see his son again after hearing the news from the brothers that Joseph was dead. And yet the Lord God is able to bring life from death. Not only did Israel see Joseph again, but he was also able to bless Joseph's sons.

---

[3] Thomas L. Constable, *Expository Notes of Dr. Thomas Constable: Genesis*, 466, https://planobiblechapel.org/tcon/notes/pdf/genesis.pdf.

Joseph expected his father to bless the older son with his right hand, but Israel had other plans for the blessing. Remember, the Lord is faithful, and His ways are higher than your ways. He promises that He is able to do above and beyond anything you can imagine.

**Israel said to Joseph, "I never expected to see your face again, but now God has even let me see your offspring." —Genesis 48:11**

Further Scripture: Ephesians 3:20; Hebrews 11:6, 21

## Questions

1. In Genesis 47:29–31, Israel instructed Joseph to take his remains and bury him in Canaan when he died. How does this reveal Israel's faith in the promises God made to him and his forefathers? (Genesis 46:4; 48:3–4)

2. What was the significance of Israel claiming Joseph's two sons, Ephraim and Manasseh, as his own? (Genesis 48:22; Joshua 16:4; 1 Chronicles 5:1) In Hebrews 11:21, how was Jacob's blessing to these two "sons" an act of faith?

3. Joseph's brothers told Pharaoh in Genesis 47:4 that they had come to *sojourn* in the land of Egypt, which is defined as a temporary stay. Why do you think they used that description?

4. Israel describes God as, "The God who has been my shepherd all my life to this day" (Genesis 48:15). Why do you think he, who was himself a shepherd by trade, described God this way? Read Psalm 23. Do David's words reflect what Israel was conveying?

5. In Genesis 48:4, Jacob recounted the promises of God, including land that He will give Jacob's descendants as an everlasting possession. Do you see this as only physical or might it represent something spiritual? If so, what? (Psalm 37:29; Hebrews 9:15)

6. What did the Holy Spirit highlight to you in Genesis 47—48 through the reading or the teaching?

# Lesson 26: Genesis 49—50
## *Seed*: Jacob Blesses His Sons

## Teaching Notes

### Review

We've made it to the final lesson on the book of Genesis! In the previous chapter, Israel blessed Joseph and blessed Joseph's two sons, Ephraim and Manasseh. Jacob even elevated them to the sons' status, adopting them into the lineage.

### Teaching

*Genesis 49:1–2*: Chapter 49 is often referred to as the "Blessing" chapter, but it's more of a prophetic chapter. Israel spoke into the 12 tribes. The gift of prophecy is meant to encourage, edify, and comfort us. Look at 1 Corinthians 14. This is a different context, but I feel like this is what Jacob was about to do. The phrase "in the days to come" is very similar to the language of "in the last days" (Isaiah 2:2).

*Genesis 49:3–32*: Jacob gave a blessing to each of his sons:

(1) *Reuben* was the firstborn, whose mother was Leah. Although Reuben was the first son, he would not excel. Remember in Genesis 35:22, Reuben slept with Jacob's concubine Bilhah after Rachel's death. When discussing the word "turbulent," Bruce Waltke wrote, "The Hebrew root means to be insolent, proud, undisciplined, reckless, uncontrollable or unstable."[1] Isaiah 57:20 really describes Reuben and the instability of his life. Reuben was constantly causing problems (Genesis 49:3–4).

(2) *Simeon* and *Levi*, whose mother was Leah, killed all the Shechemite males in response to Shechem raping their sister (Genesis 34). There would be a loss to their power, and they would be scattered all over. Simeon was eventually absorbed into Judah, and Levi never got any land (Genesis 49:5–7).

---

[1] Bruce K. Waltke and Cathi J. Fredricks, *Genesis: A Commentary* (Grand Rapids: Zondervan, 2001), 606.

(3)  *Judah*, whose mother was Leah, became the leader of all the tribes (Judges 1:1–12; 20:18). Judah had four major enemies: (1) Philistines—West. (2) Edomites—East, (3) Amalekites—South, and (4) Babylonians and Assyrians—North (Genesis 49:8–9). Judah was a young lion (Numbers 24:9; Micah 5:8). Bruce Waltke wrote, "Jacob blessed Judah with the rewards of wisdom: kingship, dominion, eternity, prosperity."[2] The Messiah came from Judah (Hebrews 7:24; Revelation 5:5). Jacob didn't even want to be with Judah's mom, Leah. The theme throughout Genesis is: God choosing someone else. God always has a bigger picture in mind.

"The scepter will not depart from Judah or the staff from between his feet until He whose right it is comes and the obedience of the people belong to Him." Most Jews called this person "He" or "Shiloh." The name "Shiloh" means the promised Messiah. Remember in Genesis 38, Judah slept with Tamar and gave up the scepter, the staff, and the signet ring. But even though Judah was willing to give up the scepter and staff, God gave it back. Through the tribe of Judah, this scepter will never depart (Genesis 49:10). The scepter is a symbol of the royal command—the right to rule. 2 Samuel 7:16 states that the Davidic Kingdom will last forever. Numbers 24:17 states the *Seed*, the star, and the scepter came from the line of Judah.

When we read Genesis 49:11, we have to realize that no one did the things stated in this scripture, unless they were prosperous and wealthy. And riding the donkey is a royal mentality. Zechariah 9:9 states that only the kings ride on donkeys. Matthew 21:5 is an incredible picture of the coming Messiah. The one to come would be handsome, well built, and taken care of. The *Seed* came through Noah, then through Shem, then Abraham, Isaac, Jacob, Judah, David, and then the Messiah was born in Bethlehem (Micah 5:2).

(4)  *Zebulun*, whose mother was Leah, lived by the seashore but never owned a port. Warren Wiersbe wrote, "Zebulun was located on an important route that carried merchandise from the coast to the Sea of Galilee and to Damascus . . . For the most part, the Jews weren't seafaring people, but the tribe of Zebulun did business with the Phoenicians east of them and provided goods to the people west of them"[3] (Genesis 49:13). In Deuteronomy 33:18–19, Moses reiterated this prophetic word that Zebulun drew wealth from the sea. Matthew 4:13 and Isaiah 9:1–2 both point out that Jesus did ministry in the land of Zebulun.

---

[2] Waltke and Fredricks, 607.

[3] Warren W. Wiersbe, *Be Authentic (Genesis 25-50): Exhibiting Real Faith in the Real World* (Colorado Springs: David C. Cook, 1997), 166–167.

(5) *Issachar*, whose mother was Leah, birthed the tribe of Issachar, which was made up of farmers and preferred agriculture. Wiersbe wrote, "The image in Genesis 49:14—15 is that of a strong people who weren't afraid to carry burdens."[4] The sons of Issachar were always watching, sensing God's will (1 Chronicles 12:32). Wiersbe wrote, "This tribe produced no great heroes, but their everyday labor was a help to others. After all, not everyone in Israel was called to be a Judah or a Joseph!"[5] (Genesis 49:14—15).

(6) *Dan*, whose mother was Bilhah. This tribe couldn't drive out the Philistines. They were known as dangerous and aggressive people, who would strike unexpectedly. In Ezekiel 38, Dan is included in the kingdom but not in Revelation 7. Verse 16 is the first time you see the phrase "tribes of Israel" (Genesis 49:16—18).

(7) *Gad*, whose mother was Zilpah. Gad would live a troubled life but was given a good portion of land (Genesis 49:19).

(8) *Asher*, whose mother was Zilpah, would make food fit for a king. The tribe of Asher could not drive out inhabitants. They become an agricultural people. The tribe of Asher was the most blessed, and their land is fertile (Genesis 49:20).

(9) *Naphtali*, whose mother was Bilhah. The tribe of Naphtali was made up of free-spirited people ("fawns"), writers or messengers that could write and speak. Zebulun and Naphtali became home base for where Jesus did ministry around the Sea of Galilee (Matthew 4). Wiersbe refers to the tribe of Naphtali as "ideal messengers"[6] (Genesis 49:21).

(10) *Joseph*, whose mother was Rachel (Genesis 49:22—23). Joseph was fruitful and his fruitful vine went beyond the "wall" (v. 22). In verse 24 we see another reference to the Messiah: "the Mighty One of Jacob . . . the Shepherd." Over and over, Joseph depended on the Mighty One, the Shepherd, to get him through life. Praise the Lord Joseph was going to save all of this! Some have taken this prophecy and said there will be blessings below the ground in the form of oil. The blessings happened at the head of Joseph's family. The head of Joseph was now Manasseh and Ephraim (Genesis 49:25—26). Everywhere else in the Middle East there is oil, except in Israel. I believe because of Genesis 49 that oil will be found in the land (given to the tribes of Manasseh and Ephraim) of Joseph. The Lord's hand was on Joseph.

---

[4] Wiersbe, 167.

[5] Wiersbe, 167.

[6] Wiersbe, 169.

(11) *Benjamin*, whose mother was Rachel (Genesis 49:27). The tribe of Benjamin has a reputation for bravery in war (Judges 3:15–30; 5:14). There is this "loose cannon" mentality. For example, Saul, first king of Israel, came from Benjamin. Saul, who became the Apostle Paul, was from Benjamin. If they trusted in the Lord, they were good. If they didn't, they were crazy.

*Genesis 49:29–33*: Jacob instructed his sons to take him back to Canaan to be buried where Abraham, Sarah, Isaac, Rebekah, and Leah were buried.

*Genesis 50:1–26*: Joseph buried his father. The brothers were nervous Joseph would repay them for what they had done to him, but Joseph reassured them. Joseph died at the age of 110. He made the Israelites take an oath that they would carry his bones out of Egypt and back to the land of Canaan.

## Closing

God is not done yet. There are Messianic believers today who represent each one of these tribes. My prayer is that we become the Josephs: going ahead, preserving the *Seed*, serving as a forerunner, and raising up a remnant.

The beauty of all this is that we got to experience these lives in 50 chapters, and we got to see what would happen to them because of what they experienced in life. The one word for Genesis is *Seed*!

## The Daily Word

In his final days of life, Jacob, the father of the 12 tribes of Israel, blessed each of his sons by name. He honestly pointed out their characters and remembered events in their lives. He also spoke into their future days.

How much more does your heavenly Father love you? The heavenly Father sees you. He knows when you fall down. He knows when you give in to temptation. And yet your heavenly Father loves you and wants to bless you. May you receive His love and walk in it. The Father loves you.

**These are the tribes of Israel, 12 in all, and this was what their father said to them. He blessed them, and he blessed each one with a suitable blessing.**
**—Genesis 49:28**

Further Scripture: Romans 8:38–39; Ephesians 1:3–4; 1 John 3:1

# Questions

1.  What did Jacob realize about himself in Genesis 49:2, before he blessed his children? Would you consider this recognition of who he was in the Lord as spiritual maturity? Are you confident in who you are in Christ? (John 1:12; 15:15; Romans 5:1; Ephesians 1:5)

2.  In Genesis 49:5, Simeon and Levi received the same blessing. Why? (Genesis 34:25–29) Jacob did not punish them at the time of their crime, but he and God remembered their sin. Why do you suppose Jacob chose this particular time to bring their sin to light?

3.  Which of Judah's blessings point to the *Seed*, Christ, in Genesis 49:8–10? (Numbers 24:17; Psalm 2:6–9; Revelation 5:5; 22:16)

4.  Jacob seemed to have come to an understanding of who God was by Genesis 49. What are the five titles he gave God in Genesis 49:24–25?

5.  How did Joseph resemble Christ in Genesis 50:19–21? (Acts 5:30–31; Hebrews 7:25)

6.  Jacob said Benjamin was a ravenous wolf in Genesis 49:27. Who else from the tribe of Benjamin had this reputation? (Judges 3:15–23; 1 Samuel 9:1–2; 14:47–52; Acts 8:1–3, Romans 11:1)

7.  What did the Holy Spirit highlight to you in Genesis 49—50 through the reading or the teaching?

# Lesson 27: Exodus 1
## *Deliverer:* Pharaoh Oppresses Israel

## Teaching Notes

### Intro

Lesson 27 is the first lesson of Exodus! We get to reveal to you our new painting! In Genesis, the one word for Christ, was *Seed.* For the book of Exodus, our word is *Deliverer.*

Eugene Merrell wrote that the purpose of Exodus is "to celebrate God's gracious deliverance of His chosen people Israel from Egyptian slavery to freedom of covenant relationship with Him."[1] The word "exodus" means "exit, a way out, departure."

### Teaching

*Exodus 1:1–4:* This gives us a cool picture of the families of Israel. Reuben, Simeon, Levi, and Judah were Leah's sons. Issachar and Zebulun were also sons of Leah. Benjamin was a son of Rachel. Dan, Naphtali, Gad, and Asher were sons of Bilhah and Zilpah (Genesis 46:8–27).

*Exodus 1:5:* Joseph was missing from the family picture in the previous verse. Why? He was already in Egypt. Remember, God had sent Joseph ahead to prepare the way. This number 70 is significant:

Genesis 10:1–32: 70 nations
Exodus 24:9: 70 elders of Israel
Numbers 11:16: 70 other elders
Judges 1:7: 70 submissive kings
1 Samuel 6:19: 70 men who were struck down
Judges 8:30: Gideon had 70 sons (Gideon is the most famous son from Manasseh.)
2 Kings 10:1: Ahab had 70 sons
Jesus, in different versions, sent out 70 or 72 witnesses.

---

[1] Eugene Merrell, Exodus Sermon Series (Copley, OH: Covenant of Grace Church, 2017), https://cogc.org/sermon_series/exodus-saved-for-gods-glory/.

God started with 12 tribes and with the 12 disciples. He brought 70 into the land of Egypt!

*Exodus 1:6–7*: Joseph and his generation died out, but the Israelites continued to multiply. The 70 people from verse 5 became so numerous they filled the land. The prophetic word we read about in Genesis was beginning to take place here in Exodus 1:7. Did they even know they were walking out prophecy (Genesis 12:1–3)? At the time of the Exodus, scholars predict the numbers to be 600,000 men 20 years old and up, and more than 2 million when women and children are counted. Abraham's descendants were beginning to fulfill the prophecy of being as numerous as the grains of sand.

Our word for Exodus is *Deliverer*. If there was going to be an exit from Egypt, someone was going to have to lead them. The question was, who? Joseph and all of his brothers were gone.

*Exodus 1:8–10*: A new Pharaoh ruled the land and did not care for the Israelites. He became concerned about the great number and strength of Israel. The seed of the serpent and the *Seed* of the woman were at war again.

*Exodus 1:11*: Pharaoh oppressed them with forced labor. This was the fulfillment of Genesis 15 and was the start of 400 years of oppression. When I read this verse, I think of Genesis 15:13, "Your offspring will be foreigners in a land that does not belong to them." That land was Egypt!

Remember when Joseph was about to enter Egypt and God told him not to be afraid? The Israelites were now building supply cities for Pharaoh. When I see this, I get excited about how true God is to His word.

*Exodus 1:12–13*: The more the Israelites were oppressed, the more they multiplied and spread. Oppressed means to be crushed. The Egyptians were forcing them into submission. The Israelites were worked ruthlessly. Ezekiel 34:4 says, "you have ruled the Israelites with violence and cruelty."

*Exodus 1:14*: The Israelites were given difficult work, such as making bricks and mortar. They also had to do all kinds of field work. This was super difficult labor! Slavery is not from the Lord! Remember labor was instituted back in Genesis 3:17–19 after the fall. Now we're seeing an extreme perversion of this labor as slavery.

*Exodus 1:15–16*: The Israelites were fighting back by multiplying. Then Pharaoh decided he needed to control the population growth. He asked the midwives to kill the Israelite sons. But if God said Abraham's descendants were going to continue to grow, they were going to continue to grow.

*Exodus 1:17*: These were not Egyptian midwives; they were Hebrew. Their allegiance was to God, not Pharaoh. Shiphrah and Puah (the Hebrew midwives), were heroes because they submitted to God and not to man. In Romans 13, we see we are to submit to the government, except when asked to do something that goes against God.

This was the first time you see civil disobedience in Scripture. The Israelites were refusing to obey the law because there was a higher good involved.

Having the "Fearing God" mentality:

- Genesis 20:11: Abraham lied about Sarah being his sister because he thought the Egyptians did not fear God.
- Genesis 22:12: Abraham was willing to sacrifice Isaac because he feared God.
- Genesis 42:18: Joseph feared God and sent his brothers to get Benjamin.

The fear of the Lord is the beginning of wisdom (Proverbs 9:10). Colossians 2:2–3 says Jesus is actually the wisdom of God. So, if the fear of the Lord is the beginning of wisdom, when you fear God, you're beginning to understand and embrace the Messiah as well. And these two women were doing this. If a Hebrew midwife could reject the King of Egypt, why can't I walk this out in faith without fear?

*Exodus 1:18–21*: Pharaoh asked them, "Why have you done this"? Did they lie? Rahab did. Rachel did. But it was for the Lord's purpose.

What was modeled from these two Hebrew women began to spread throughout all of the Israelite people (Exodus 18:21; Exodus 20:20). The Lord was good to the midwives because the midwives feared God. He gave them their own families (vv. 20–21). He blessed their work, and then He blessed them. Psalm 127:3: "Sons are indeed a heritage from the Lord, children, a reward." They are not to be killed. Abortion is not of the Lord! Children are a reward from the Lord.

Pharaoh, not liking how the Hebrew women responded, commanded all his people across the country of Egypt to start killing the Hebrew sons.

## Closing

How does this fit into being a *Deliverer*? You have to have the bad news in order to understand the good news. You have to understand sin and death to experience new life.

In Exodus 1, you see bondage, slavery, and oppression. At some point, they had to be delivered. Over the course of 40 chapters, we will walk through that process. How were the Israelites going to be delivered?

## The Daily Word

The Lord used the midwives in a mighty way to expand the Hebrew people. The midwives overcame the fear of man and chose to fear God.

When you fear God, you are not dependent on yourself or on things you can control. Instead you live with awe and respect that God is able to handle it all. The Lord longs for you to fear Him and promises to fulfill your desires.

How would you complete this sentence for yourself today? *Since I feared God, God gave me [fill in the blank].*

**So God was good to the midwives, and the people multiplied and became very numerous. Since the midwives feared God, He gave them families. — Exodus 1:20–21**

Further Scripture: Exodus 1:17; Psalm 145:19; Luke 1:50

## Questions

1. What is the definition of Exodus? How does Exodus highlight the need for a *Deliverer*?
2. God's plan to birth a nation is beginning to take shape (Exodus 1:7). Why was the new king of Egypt upset about this (Exodus 1:8–10)?
3. What did the king of Egypt make the Israelites do in Exodus 1:11–14? How did the Israelites respond to the Egyptian's oppression (Exodus 1:12)? How do you respond when persecuted?
4. Why would the king of Egypt call for the Hebrew midwives to put the sons to death but not the daughters? (Exodus 1:9–10, 15–16; Acts 7:18–19)
5. Did the midwives comply with the king? How was God honored through their actions? Can you think of any examples today where someone obeyed God rather than man? (Acts 4:19; 5:29; Romans 13:1–5)
6. How did God bless the midwives' obedience (Exodus 1:20–21)?
7. What did the Holy Spirit highlight to you in Exodus 1 through the reading or the teaching?

# Lesson 28: Exodus 2—3
## *Deliverer:* Moses and the Burning Bush

## Teaching Notes

### Intro

In Exodus, our word is *Deliverer.* The Lord is going to deliver us through the Lamb, the staff, the hyssop and the oil, and the sky. Moses wrote the first five books of the Bible, the Pentateuch—Genesis, Exodus, Leviticus, Numbers, and Deuteronomy. So now, we get to hear straight from Moses about his own life.

### Teaching

*Exodus 2:1–14*: The Israelites kept multiplying so Pharaoh commanded that all Hebrew sons be thrown into the Nile River. During this time, Amram and Jochebed, a married Hebrew couple, had a son. Jochebed, his mother, hid the baby for three months, but he became too big to continue hiding so she put him in a basket and placed it among the reeds in the Nile River. In some ways, Jochebed had obeyed what the king said; she just added some things to help her child survive, like a basket covered in "asphalt and pitch" (v. 3). Pharaoh's daughter went to bathe in the river. She saw the child and took pity on him. The baby's sister, who was watching from a distance, offered to help find a Hebrew woman to watch the baby and brought his mother. Pharaoh's daughter thought it was a great idea. In fact, she agreed to pay the nurse. The sister's name was Miriam. The baby also had an older brother named Aaron. Pharaoh's daughter named the baby Moses, which means, "drawn out of the water." That is such a prophetic name— Moses' life revolved around water and wilderness. God was just setting the stage. Years later, Moses went to observe his people. Pharaoh had forced the Hebrew people into slavery. Moses saw his people being oppressed. After he witnessed cruelty, Moses killed the Egyptian taskmaster.

*Exodus 2:15–23*: Pharaoh heard about the man whom Moses had murdered and wanted Moses dead. Moses went from being drawn out of the water to fleeing. On his journey, Moses helped some daughters water their flocks at a well and was invited to dinner. Moses stayed with the family and married Zipporah. They gave birth to a son named Gershom, which means, "a foreigner in a foreign land."

While Moses was away on his journey, Pharaoh (most likely Thutmos III) died. He was the one who had imposed the difficult labor onto the Israelites.

*Exodus 2:24–25*: God heard the cries of the people because of their intense labor (Numbers 20:16; Deuteronomy 26:7). Wiersbe wrote, "God's delays aren't evidence of unconcern, for He hears our groans, sees our plights, feels our sorrow, and remembers His covenant. What He promised, He will perform, for He never breaks His covenant with His people. When the right time comes, God immediately goes to work."[1] In the 400-plus years, God remembered His covenant 14 times! He still remembers His covenant with His people, the Israelites (Psalm 105:8). He remembered His holy covenant (Luke 1:72). You and I can play a role in gently reminding the Lord what He has promised us.

*Exodus 3:1–2*: Moses was tending to his flock with Jethro, Moses' father-in-law. Some people think Jethro was his priest name. He was called "Reuel" in verse 18, which was his fatherly house name. Moses went to Horeb, which was also known as Mount Sinai, the Mountain of God. God continually used Bethel, Shechem, and Beersheba. You'll see God do that with Mount Sinai all throughout Exodus.

When God calls us to something, sometimes we go into a period of waiting. Moses wasn't simply sitting around waiting for God to show up. He was working with the flock when "the Angel of the Lord appeared to him in a flame of fire within the bush" (v.2). Moses had been shepherding for 40 years—much like Joseph had to wait 13 years and Paul waited three years. Wiersbe wrote, "It's significant that God calls people who are busy: Gideon was threshing grain (Judges 6), Samuel was serving in the tabernacle (1 Samuel 3), David was caring for sheep (1 Samuel 17:20), Elisha was plowing (1 Kings 19:19–20), four of the apostles were managing their fishing business (Mark 1:16–20), and Matthew was collecting taxes (Matthew 9:9)."[2] The point is that these guys were just doing life, and God showed up. God wants to use willing and obedient people (Proverbs 24:30–33.) The Angel of the Lord appeared to Moses while he was taking care of the sheep. During this time, it was common to see bushes on fire. The uncommon part was that this bush wasn't consumed. The Angel of the Lord showed up to all kinds of people: Abraham (Genesis 22); Jacob (Genesis 31); Moses (Exodus 3); Gideon (Judges 6); Samson's father (Judges 13); Hagar (Genesis 16).

Moses saw this bush not being destroyed and was perplexed. Fire usually brings: (1) Destruction: Think Sodom and Gomorrah (Genesis 18:16—19:29).

---

[1] Warren W. Wiersbe, *Be Delivered (Exodus): Finding Freedom by Following God* (Colorado Springs: David C. Cook, 1998), 23–24.

[2] Wiersbe, 24.

(2) Purification: The burning coal purifies Isaiah's mouth (Isaiah 6:6–7). There is also purification through burning sacrifice. (3) Presence: God is a consuming fire (Hebrews 12:28–29). The lamp was to never go out as a symbol of God's presence (Exodus 27:20–21).

*Exodus 3:3–6*: Moses' name was called twice, to which he replied, "Here I am." God gave very clear direction. He said, "You're going to be in My presence." I want you to know this is not normal! God remembered His covenant with Abraham, Isaac, and Jacob! This hadn't happened since Jacob had an encounter at the end of Genesis. God was reminding them that He was still there and that He had their backs. Moses hid his face, in reverence and awe. Remember, Moses became afraid after killing the Egyptian (Exodus 2:12–14). Moses realized this was the presence of God and it was special. He knew he was experiencing a special moment in his life. In Deuteronomy 33:16, Moses was praying over the Josephites, asking for the favor of Him who was in the burning bush, to be shown to Joseph's descendants.

*Exodus 3:7–10*: God responded, "Deliverance is coming!" Nelson's commentary states, "The listing of the peoples reminds the reader of three things: (1) The land was not just a figure of speech; it was a real place with real people living in its borders. (2) For the inhabitants, their time was nearly up; their cup of iniquity was now full, and God's judgment was about to fall on them (Genesis 15:16). (3) While the land was God's gift, it was not vacant property; the land would have to be seized from the inhabitants. This could be done with the power of God."[3] God told Moses to go so he could lead the Israelites, God's people, out of Egypt.

*Exodus 3:11–15*: Moses came up with five excuses. We'll look at two today. First, "I'm a nobody" (v. 11). Wiersbe wrote, "[Moses] argued with the Lord and tried to escape the divine call to rescue Israel from slavery. In Egypt, 40 years before, Moses had acted like an impetuous horse and rushed ahead of God, but now he is acting like a stubborn mule and resisting God (Psalm 32:9)."[4] God responded with the promise, "I will be with you" (v. 12). Moses' second excuse was, "I don't know your name" (v. 13). God gave him the answers that "I AM WHO I AM" (v. 14), and "I AM has sent me to you." God was with us, is with us, and will always be with us. "The God of Abraham (Genesis 26:24), the God of Isaac, and the God of Jacob has sent me to you." After 400 years of bondage, God is still reminding them of His promise.

---

[3] Earl D. Radmacher, Ronald B. Allen, and H. Wayne House, eds. *Nelson's New Illustrated Bible Commentary* (Nashville: Thomas Nelson, 1999), 92.

[4] Wiersbe, 24–25.

*Exodus 3:16–22*: God was making a connection with the Hebrews. The land of milk and honey is a real place, but they would have to actually engage the people living there. In verse 18, it says the Israelites wanted to worship God on a neutral site so they could worship in purity. As Moses received the plan to free the Israelites, God told them you will not go empty-handed! Just as the Israelites came into Egypt with wagons, they will leave Egypt with plunder (vv. 21–22).

## Closing

God is going to deliver the Israelites from Egypt, using Moses, or in Hebrew, Moshe. God said don't worry; I will always be with you. When I hear this phrase, I AM, I think of how Jesus talked about being I AM as well.

In John 8:52, Jesus was interacting with a group of folks, and the Jews accused Him of having a demon. They said this because Jesus said He would never die. Even Abraham died. Jesus responded, "I do know Him, and I keep His word" (v. 55). Abraham had an encounter with Jesus (v. 56): "Before Abraham was, I am" (v. 58). By using these two words, Jesus just equated Himself as the God of the burning bush.

Eight times in the Gospel of John, Jesus said, "I am" (John 6:35; 8:12, 58; 10:7, 11; 11:25; 14:6; 15:1). Everything is pointing to Jesus being the *Deliverer*. But it started in Exodus with Moses.

## The Daily Word

The Israelites cried out to the Lord while in bondage in Egypt. God heard their groaning and remembered His promises. The story of deliverance began as the Lord heard the cries of their hearts.

When we cry out to the Lord, it means we get honest with God. We turn to Him with everything. Be honest with God about the situation you find yourself in today. He will bring you deliverance and set you free from bondage. In Christ there is freedom. Just be honest with the Lord today.

**After a long time, the king of Egypt died. The Israelites groaned because of their difficult labor, and they cried out; and their cry for help ascended to God because of the difficult labor. So God heard their groaning, and He remembered His covenant with Abraham, Isaac, and Jacob. God saw the Israelites, and He took notice. —Exodus 2:23–25**

Further Scripture: Exodus 3:7–8; Psalm 107:13–14; Galatians 5:1

# Questions

1. How do you see God using a tragic situation for His purpose in Exodus 2:1–10? (Romans 8:28)

2. What blessing from God did Moses' mother receive for her obedience (Exodus 2:9)?

3. Why do you think Moses made the decision to flee the luxury (sin) of Egypt (Hebrews 11:24–27)? Give an example of a time when you walked away from worldly wealth for the cause of Christ.

4. What is an example in Exodus 2 of God listening, caring, and acting on behalf of the Israelites? Have you experienced God doing this in your life? (Exodus 3:7; 6:5; 1 Peter 5:6–7)

5. What evidence is given in Exodus 3:6 that God gives us life after death? (Matthew 22:32; Mark 12:26–27; Luke 20:37–38)

6. What characteristic does God reveal about Himself in Exodus 3:14? How does this point to Jesus? (John 8:24, 28, 58)

7. What did the Holy Spirit highlight to you in Exodus 2—3 through the reading or the teaching?

# Lesson 29: Exodus 4—5
## *Deliverer*: Moses Given Powerful Signs

## Teaching Notes

### Intro

Moses interacted with the Lord in one of the most unique encounters recorded in Scripture. God used Moses to deliver the Israelites from Egypt and to be the deliverer who pointed to Jesus as the *Deliverer*.

### Teaching

*Exodus 4:1–5*: Yesterday we looked at two of the five excuses Moses used when God told him to go to Pharaoh: (1) I'm a nobody; and (2) I don't know Your (God's) name. Today, we'll look at three more excuses Moses gave.[1] The third excuse is Moses claims the elders won't believe him. Moses knew the Jews were always looking for a sign for proof. He also knew that they would need confirmation that God told Moses to throw his staff on the ground. This word "throw" was the same word used when Pharaoh commanded the people to throw the Hebrew babies into the Nile.[2] When Moses obeyed God, the staff became a snake, and Moses ran from it. God told Moses to grab the snake by the tail, and when he did, it instantly became a staff again. Sign #1: The staff became a snake and then it became a staff again. God did this *so that* the Israelites, especially the elders, would believe. Although Moses had offered an excuse, God provided a sign so that the elders would believe in the God of Abraham, Isaac, and Jacob.

*Exodus 4:6–8*: As commanded, Moses put his hand inside his cloak, and it became leprous. Then God told Moses to put his hand back into his cloak and his hand was healed. Sign #2: Moses' hand became leprous, and then the leprosy was healed. Since they didn't believe the first sign, God gave "the evidence of the second sign."

---

[1] Warren W. Wiersbe, *Be Delivered (Exodus): Finding Freedom by Following God* (Colorado Springs: David C. Cook, 1998), 183.

[2] Victor P. Hamilton, *Exodus: An Exegetical Commentary* (Grand Rapids: Baker Academic, 2011), 71.

*Exodus 4:9*: Sign #3: If they didn't believe the first or the second signs, Moses was instructed to take water from the Nile and pour it on dry ground where it would turn to blood. The Nile was the source of water for everything!

*Exodus 4:10*: Fourth, Moses said he was not a fluent speaker. Moses was focused on himself, not on the Lord. Wiersbe said, "True humility isn't thinking poorly of ourselves; it's simply not thinking of ourselves at all but making God everything."[3] Hamilton listed four reasons why Moses' arguments could have been legitimate: maybe Moses wanted to avoid God's will; maybe Moses really did have a speech defect; maybe Moses truly had difficulty speaking Hebrew (he was raised Egyptian); and maybe Moses was just nervous with public speaking.[4] Wiersbe said, "Moses was clothing his pride and unbelief in a hollow confession of weakness."[5]

*Exodus 4:11–12*: God responded, effectively saying, "I made your mouth! I will teach you what to say." The Spirit of the Father speaks through us! When we claim we won't know what to say to people on the streets, we're saying that the Holy Spirit is not adequate to speak through us.

*Exodus 4:13–14*: Fifth, Moses asked God to send someone who could do the job. This was the first time the Lord really showed His anger. When God spoke of His plans to destroy the earth and all He had made, He didn't say He was angry; He said He was "grieved in His heart" (Genesis 6:6). Moses wrote, "Who understands the power of Your anger? Your wrath matches the fear that is due You" (Psalm 90:11). In Exodus 34:6, God said: "Yahweh—Yahweh is a compassionate and gracious God, slow to anger and rich in faithful love and truth." Though God was angered by Moses' excuses, He said that He could use Aaron to speak for Him. Wiersbe said, "One of the most painful judgments that God can send is to let His own people have their way."[6]

*Exodus 4:15–17*: "You will speak with him and tell him what to say. I will help both you and him to speak and will teach you both what to do." Moses doubted his ability to speak for God, but God assured Moses He would tell him everything he should say and do. "He will speak to the people for you. He will be your spokesman, and you will serve as God to him. And take this staff in your hand that you will perform the signs with." Moses was instructed to take his staff and his brother and go where God directed him.

---

[3] Wiersbe, 184.
[4] Hamilton, 73.
[5] Wiersbe, 184.
[6] Wiersbe, 184.

*Exodus 4:18–21*: Moses had now lived for 40 years in Midian. He went to explain to Jethro, his father-in-law, that he wanted to return to Egypt to see if any of his relatives were still living. His father-in-law blessed him to go in peace. (In contrast to Laban and Jacob, when Jacob snuck away, and Laban chased after him.) Moses didn't tell the whole story though. All the men who wanted to kill Moses were now dead. This was the same imagery of Christ with King Herod. When Herod died, Jesus (and His family) could leave Egypt and go back to Israel. The threat was gone. God wanted Moses to pursue what God called him to do, and that was to deliver God's people. Walking out your calling is pretty special. Moses spent 40 years learning all of these things, and now God told him to go. God told Moses: "When you go back to Egypt, make sure you do all the wonders before Pharaoh that I have put within your power. But I will harden his heart so that he won't let the people go." Even as Moses started his journey to Egypt, God told Moses it wasn't going to work.

*Exodus 4:22–26*: God told Moses to say to Pharaoh, "Israel is My firstborn son." Now we're talking about a people group, not just Jacob. Israel was God's chosen people. In Jeremiah 31:9, God said, "I am Israel's Father, and Ephraim is My firstborn." In Hosea 11:1, God called Israel, "My son." God said He would kill Pharaoh's firstborn son because Pharaoh would refuse to let God's firstborn, Israel, leave Egypt! The promise to kill the firstborn was a big deal. As Moses and his family began the journey from Midian to Egypt, the Lord confronted Moses and "sought to put him to death." Moses had neglected to circumcise one of his sons, probably his second son Eliezer. Genesis 17:1–11 specified that circumcision was the sign of God's covenant with them. Zipporah was the one who saved the day. Biblical scholar, Cassuto, said Zipporah removed God's judgment from Moses and her family by righting Moses' disobedience. His wife Zipporah knew the covenant. She saved the *Deliverer*.[7] First Timothy 3:4–5 indicates that when God uses someone publicly, they have to be obedient at home as well! If Moses didn't clean up his family, he would not be adequate to lead God's people. If you don't manage your household, I believe God withholds the calling on your life.

*Exodus 4:27–31*: Greeting each other with a kiss was a normal custom of the time. Romans 16:16 included the instruction to "greet one another with a holy kiss." Moses met up with Aaron and told him everything God had sent him to say and showed Him the signs God had commanded him to do. The brothers went together to speak with the elders of the Israelites. Aaron repeated everything

---

[7] U. Cassuto, *A Commentary on the Book of Exodus*, trans. Israel Abrahams (Jerusalem: Magnes Press, 1983), 59–61; quoted in Thomas L. Constable, *Expository Notes of Dr. Thomas Constable: Exodus*, 56, https://planobiblechapel.org/tcon/notes/pdf/exodus.pdf.

Moses was told *and* performed the signs for the people as well. When you don't feel as though you're adequate to do the Lord's work, He'll find someone else. If the Lord is calling us to do something, let's be the ones to walk it out. The Israelites believed, and they bowed down and worshipped God. Belief will always lead to bowing down and worshipping the Lord.

## Closing

In Exodus 5, the elders believed, and they approached Pharaoh and began to walk this out. Wiersbe listed three questions that summarize Exodus 5: (1) Pharaoh: Why should I obey the Lord?—Exodus 5:2; (2) Pharaoh: Why should your people stop working?—Exodus 5:4,14; and (3) Moses: God, why did You send me?—Exodus 5:22–23.[8]

Tomorrow we get the opportunity to dig into Exodus 6. I'm excited about unfolding how Moses, as deliverer, points to the *Deliverer*, Yeshua.

## The Daily Word

The Lord called upon Moses to help deliver the Israelites. Moses responded with doubts, feelings of inadequacy, and excuses about why he should not be the one. Despite Moses' excuses, the Lord still used him. God explained to Moses in detail how He would help him.

You may have similar excuses as to why you should not be the one the Lord uses in the area He is calling you. Moses didn't think he could speak to people, but the Lord still used him in a mighty way! If the Lord has called you to something, trust that He will equip you with everything you need.

**You will speak with him and tell him what to say. I will help both you and him to speak and will teach you both what to do. He will speak to the people for you. He will be your spokesman, and you will serve as God to him. — Exodus 4:15–16**

Further Scripture: 2 Corinthians 3:5; Philippians 2:13; Hebrews 13:20–21

## Questions

1. Why do you think God chose the three signs in Exodus 4:1–9 as the signs for Moses?

---

[8] Wiersbe, 186–87.

2. Have you experienced someone not believing or accepting the Word of God without a sign? What was your response? (Mark 16:15–18; John 4:48; 6:30; 20:30–31)

3. What were the five excuses Moses gave to God in Exodus 3:11–14 and 4:1–17? Can you think of a time when you have given a similar excuse to the Lord?

4. Why do you think God hardened Pharaoh's heart in Exodus 4:21? Was Pharaoh responsible for his decisions? If not, who was? Do you struggle with this?

5. Why was God going to kill Moses in Genesis 4:24–26? Who and what saved Moses from being killed?

6. How do you see the need for a *Deliverer* in Exodus 4—5?

7. What did the Holy Spirit highlight to you in Exodus 4—5 through the reading or the teaching?

# Lesson 30: Exodus 6
*Deliverer:* God Promises Deliverance

## Teaching Notes

### Intro

God used Moses as the deliverer to point His people to Yahweh, the true *Deliverer*. Remember God had given the signs—the staff turning to a snake, the leprous hand, and turning water to blood—and the Israelites had believed Aaron and Moses. But when they went to Pharaoh, he refused to let them go. Moses ended chapter 5 saying, "God, why did you ever send me?"

You should, in your calling, always expect opposition and misunderstanding from other people. As servant leaders, you have to spend time with the Lord. Moses did this in chapter 5, expressing his frustration with God.

### Teaching

*Exodus 6:1–2*: God answered Moses: "Now you are going to see what I will do to Pharaoh: he will let them go because of My strong hand; he will drive them out of his land because of My strong hand." In His answer to Moses, twice God said, "because of My strong hand." Seven times in His answer to Moses, God said, "I will" (vv. 1, 6, 7, 8). Then God spoke to Moses. Most likely, Moses heard God's voice audibly. In His response to Moses, multiple times God said, "I am Yahweh" (vv. 2, 6, 7, 8). (Exodus 33:11; Deuteronomy 34:10.)

*Exodus 6:3–8*: God continued to talk with Moses and explained that while He had appeared to Abraham, Isaac, and Jacob, He had never revealed His name Yahweh to them (as He had to Moses). God stated that He remembered His covenant with them and that He had heard Israel's groanings from Egypt. God promised to free Israel from slavery in Egypt and deliver them to the land He swore to Abraham, Isaac, and Jacob—the Promised Land. Within this passage, we're basically transitioning from Abraham to Moses.

Sailhamer said Exodus 6 provided an outline of the Pentateuch (the first five books of the Bible).[1]

---

[1] John H. Sailhamer, *The Pentateuch as Narrative* (Grand Rapids: Zondervan, 1992; ePub Edition 2017), 251.

(1) God established His covenant with Abraham, Isaac, and Jacob (Exodus 6:4).

(2) In Genesis 12:1–3, God made a covenant with Abram that was confirmed in Genesis 15; Genesis 17; and Genesis 22.

(3) In Genesis 15, God told Abram his descendants would live as foreigners in another land (Paul said this too).

(4) God remembered His covenant (Exodus 6:5).

(5) God promised to deliver His people (Exodus 6:6).

(6) God promised to adopt Israel as His nation (Exodus 6:7).

(7) This pattern would be repeated in the New Covenant.

(8) In Luke 4:18–19, Jesus quoted Isaiah 61:1 when He said, "The Spirit of the Lord is on Me . . . to proclaim freedom to the captives." Jesus, the *Deliverer*, came to set people free.

(9) We have been adopted into Christ (Ephesians 1:5).

(10) God promised to bring Israel into the Promised Land (Exodus 6:8).

The land in Israel is really important because, when you give up land, it goes against the covenant God established in the Pentateuch. This is why, as believers, we want to support that Israel gets and keeps the land.

*Exodus 6:9–12*: When Moses told the Israelites what God had said to him, they didn't listen. Remember the context: the Israelites had not been set free yet. When God commanded Moses to go to Pharaoh and tell him to let the Israelites leave his land, Moses wanted to know why Pharaoh would listen to him if his own people didn't. Moses pulled the classic victim card: Pharaoh wouldn't listen "since I am such a poor speaker."

*Exodus 6:13*: Rather than continue to debate Moses' claims of inadequacy, God reaffirmed His commands. Scripture pauses here to give the genealogy of Moses and Aaron. Francis Schaeffer said, "There are no little people in the Bible."[2] They're all important.

*Exodus 6:14–16*: These verses provided the lineage of three of Jacob's sons by Leah: Reuben, Simeon, and Levi. Verse 16 named Gershon, Kohath, and Merari as Levi's three sons. (By continuing to follow the lineage, we will see that Moses and Aaron are Levites.)

---

[2] Francis Schaeffer, *No Little People* (Wheaton, IL: Crossway Books, 2003), 10.

*Exodus 6:17*: This verse named Gershon's sons, who were Levi's grandsons.

*Exodus 6:18*: This verse named Kohath's sons, who were also Levi's grandsons. Amram was named as Aaron and Moses' father in verse 20.

*Exodus 6:19*: This verse named Merari's sons, who were also Levi's grandsons.

*Exodus 6:20*: Amram married his father's sister, Jochebed (which meant he married his aunt). She bore him two sons: Aaron (older) and Moses (younger). They also had Miriam (Moses' sister), who was also a major part of the deliverance (Micah 6:4).

*Exodus 6:21–22*: These verses named the sons of Izhar and the sons of Uzziel, who were Moses' cousins.

*Exodus 6:23*: Aaron married Elisheba (the daughter of Amminadab, a well-known family in the tribe of Judah). Aaron was in the lineage of the Levites, who became the priests of Israel. Elisheba was from the tribe of Judah (Numbers 1:7, 2:3). Judah eventually led to David and eventually to the Messiah. In Aaron's family, the lineage of the Levites and Judahites came together.

*Exodus 6:24*: Korah (the son of Izhar, see verse 21) was a cousin to Moses. Korah led a rebellion against Moses (Numbers 16). Numbers 26:11 revealed that when Korah and all the men who rebelled against Moses died, the sons of Korah survived. These sons of Korah wrote Psalms 84, 85, and 87. The sons of Korah give us hope that we don't have to continue in our father's bad decisions. Some of you don't have a positive lineage, and that's OK.

*Exodus 6:25*: Aaron's son Eleazar was the father of Phinehas, who was a hero in Numbers 25. These are the heroes and the heads of the Levite family.

*Exodus 6:26–27*: God instructed "this Aaron and Moses" to bring the Israelites out of Egypt, so Moses and Aaron were the ones who spoke to Pharaoh. Wiersbe said, "God's calling always means God's enabling."[3]

Hamilton connected the fulfillment of the prophecy in Genesis 15:13–16 to this listing of genealogy in Exodus 6:14–25.[4] Exodus 6:16 described the first

[3] Warren W. Wiersbe, *Be Delivered (Exodus): Finding Freedom by Following God* (Colorado Springs: David C. Cook, 1998), 187.

[4] Victor P. Hamilton, *Exodus: An Exegetical Commentary* (Grand Rapids: Baker Academic, 2011), 110.

generation. Gershon, Kohath, and Merari were Levi's sons who lived in bondage. Exodus 6:18 named the second generation. Amram was the son of Kohath and the father of Aaron and Moses. Exodus 6:20 named the third generation. Aaron and Moses were the sons of Amram and Jochebed. Exodus 6:23 named the fourth generation. Aaron's sons Nadab, Abihu, Eleazar, and Ithamar would be among those delivered to the Promised Land.

## Closing

Everything pointed to the *Deliverer*. Can you believe it? The lineage of the Levites pointed to the Messiah! One little name, Elisheba (Aaron's wife), was the daughter of Amminadab and the sister of Nahshon, who were both in the lineage of Christ (Luke 3:32–33).

## The Daily Word

God did not deliver the Israelites the first time around, and Moses voiced his frustration. God responded forthrightly to Moses, explaining who He was and about all His promises. God told Moses He revealed Himself to Abraham, Isaac, and Jacob as "God Almighty," but to Moses, God said, "I Am Yahweh," meaning "I Am Who I Am." This name described His fullness—His eternal existence, sovereignty, unlimited power, and omnipresence. This should have ended Moses' excuses and given him the confidence he needed to press on with the mission God had given him.

What about you? Is it enough to know God Almighty, Yahweh, I Am Lord, is with you and will bless you along the way? Or will you continue to give the Lord excuses as to why you can't follow Him? Remember, He is the great I Am.

**Then God spoke to Moses, telling him, "I am Yahweh. I appeared to Abraham, Isaac, and Jacob as God Almighty, but I did not reveal My name Yahweh to them." —Exodus 6:2–3**

Further Scripture: Isaiah 46:9–10; John 8:58; Revelation 1:8

## Questions

1. What did God reveal to Moses in Exodus 6:3 that He had not revealed to Abraham, Isaac, and Jacob? Why was this name significant?

2. What things did the Lord promise to the Israelites through Moses in Exodus 6:6–8? What was Moses sent to deliver the Israelites from? How was this a picture of Christ? (Luke 4:18; Romans 11:26; Colossians 1:13–14)

3. What was the Israelites' response to the Lord's promises? (Exodus 6:9)? Can you think of a time when you have responded to the Lord in this manner?

4. Why was it significant that Moses and Aaron came from a Levite clan/family line?

5. In both Exodus 6:12 and 30, Moses brought up the same concern—that Pharaoh wouldn't listen to him because of his speech. Did God still use him despite his weaknesses? How can you use this to encourage others?

6. What did the Holy Spirit highlight to you in Exodus 6 through the reading or the teaching?

# Lesson 31: Exodus 7—8
## *Deliverer:* Plagues 1–4

## Teaching Notes

### Intro

These are the classic chapters in Exodus. We're talking about the plagues. The point of these plagues was that God used this man who didn't feel adequate to deliver His people. Exodus 6:30 says: "But Moses replied in the LORD's presence, 'Since I am such a poor speaker, how will Pharaoh listen to me?'"

### Teaching

*Exodus 7:1–3*: "The LORD answered Moses, 'See, I have made you like God to Pharaoh, and Aaron your brother will be your prophet'" (v. 1). This was a ridiculous statement! God believed in Moses despite his doubt and complaining. "You must say whatever I command you" (v. 2). "But I will harden Pharaoh's heart and multiply My signs and wonders in the land of Egypt" (v. 3). God offered no further details about hardening Pharaoh's heart or how He would multiply His signs and wonders. These signs were going to be a reminder of God's powerful presence that would be in front of Pharaoh day in and day out. Nelson's commentary described these signs and wonders as "irrefutable works" that God would do to "demonstrate His power and authenticate His agents, Moses and Aaron."[1]

*Exodus 7:4*: God told Moses that Pharaoh wouldn't listen, so God would then "put My hand" on the Egyptians and bring "the divisions of My people the Israelites out of the land of Egypt." Divisions could be equated with armies or tribes—meaning the 12 tribes of Israel. One commentator said the Egyptians needed to be brought to their knees and the Israelites needed to see that He alone is God.[2] Imagery of the hand was not pleasant; this was an image of God's wrath. Similar language was used in the New Testament to describe the Pharisees' desire to get their hands on Jesus because they wanted to kill Him (Luke 20:19; Mark 14:46).

---

[1] Earl Radmacher, Ronald B. Allen, and H. Wayne House, eds. *Nelson's New Illustrated Bible Commentary* (Nashville: Thomas Nelson, 1999), 98.

[2] Victor P. Hamilton, *Exodus: An Exegetical Commentary* (Grand Rapids: Baker Academic, 2011), 95–96.

*Exodus 7:5–8*: "The Egyptians will know that I am Yahweh" (v. 5). Why did this judgment need to take place (Exodus 12:12)? Why did God need to bring the Israelites out? They were beginning to worship the Egyptian gods (Ezekiel 20:7–9). "So, Moses and Aaron did this" (v. 6). They didn't add to God's directions; they did what God said. They walked it out together. In verse 8, the Lord spoke to Moses and Aaron together for the first time.

*Exodus 7:9–11*: "When Pharaoh tells you, 'Perform a miracle,' tell Aaron, 'Take your staff and throw it down before Pharaoh. It will become a serpent.'" This staff was used as a form of deliverance for the people. Moses was a shepherd. Jesus is the Good Shepherd. This was an image of the everyday people God used to do extraordinary things. "So Moses and Aaron went in to Pharaoh and did just as the Lord had commanded." Did the staff really become a snake? Some commentators think it could have been a reptile, crocodile, or a monster. Constable pointed out that this began the period of the miracles. We see four periods of miracles throughout Scripture: Moses through Joshua, Elijah and Elisha, Christ and the apostles, and finally the two witnesses in Revelation[3] (Mark 16:17). Signs and wonders will happen, but we can't make them happen. "But then Pharaoh called the wise men and sorcerers—the magicians of Egypt, and they also did the same thing by their occult practices." This was the dark side of the miracles. They had their little bag of tricks.[4] They possessed occult knowledge. Scripture says Satan can masquerade himself as light (2 Corinthians 11:14). We can always expect Satan to try to mimic what God is able to do. Wiersbe said, "Satan can empower his people to perform 'lying wonders'"[5] (2 Thessalonians 2:9–10). Wiersbe said: "Pharaoh's attitude was, 'Anything Jehovah can do, we can do better!'"[6] (Matthew 24:24; Revelation 13:11–16). We are going to see deception from the enemy all the way from Moses' time to the end times. We should expect it and test things (1 John 4:1).

*Exodus 7:12*: "Each one threw down his staff, and it became a serpent. But Aaron's staff swallowed their staffs." Staffs is plural; Aaron's staff ate them all. God's staff overpowered their staffs, Satan's staffs, instantly. Why? The seed needed to be delivered, and nothing would get in the way of setting the people free. You're

---

[3] Thomas L. Constable, *Expository Notes of Dr. Thomas Constable: Exodus*, 74–75, https://planobiblechapel.org/tcon/notes/pdf/exodus.pdf.

[4] Radmacher et al., 99.

[5] Warren W. Wiersbe, *The Bible Exposition Commentary: Genesis–Deuteronomy* (Colorado Springs: David C. Cook, 2001), 188.

[6] Wiersbe, 188.

always going to see these counterfeit situations—even in the New Testament: false brethren and counterfeit Christians everywhere we go (Romans 10:1–3); false brothers (2 Corinthians 11:26); a false gospel (Galatians 1:6–9). As we get closer to the end times, we have to be careful of false gospels today. Our God will always overcome their false truth.

*Exodus 7:13–16*: "However, Pharaoh's heart hardened, and he did not listen to them, as the Lord had said." Over and over again, we will see that Pharaoh's heart is hardened. Three times over the course of the plagues, Moses and Aaron were told to go to Pharaoh in the morning. "Tell him: Yahweh, the God of the Hebrews, has sent me to tell you . . ." Of the ten plagues, Pharaoh was warned about seven. Three plagues struck his nation without warning.

*Exodus 7:17*: "I will strike the water in the Nile with the staff in my hand, and it will turn to blood." The Nile was their source of water for everything. One commentator has explained this could have happened naturally between the red soil and red algae.[7] But the Scriptures say blood, so I believe it was blood. The word, "strike" was used three more times. This imagery of striking the Egyptians happens in Exodus 2:12, when Moses strikes the Egyptian dead; in Exodus 17:6, when Moses strikes the rock, and in Exodus 12, when God strikes the firstborn.

*Exodus 7:18–19*: The fish would die, the water would stink, and the Egyptians would be unable to drink water from the Nile. Through this plague, God was showing His authority over the earth (v. 18). Then God turned the waters throughout Egypt into blood—"the rivers, canals, ponds, and all their water reservoirs . . . even in wooden and stone containers." Not just one little area was affected; everything became blood, even water in the containers that weren't connected to the water source (v. 19). Wiersbe said: "This was a judgment on the Nile River itself, which was treated like a god, and on Hapi, the god of the Nile, and Isis, the goddess of the Nile."[8]

*Exodus 7:20–22*: "Moses and Aaron did just as the Lord had commanded." Even the psalmists wrote about what God had done in Psalms 78:43–44 and 105:29. The fish in the Nile died, and there was blood throughout the land of Egypt. "But the magicians of Egypt did the same thing by their occult practices. Pharaoh's heart hardened, and he would not listen to them, as the Lord had said." How was it possible that the Egyptians did the same thing if the water was already blood? Maybe God was talking about surface water and not the water underground,

---

[7] Radmacher et al., 100.

[8] Wiersbe, 189.

so they dug up some water (v. 24). But we know it was false because they used occult practices. What Pharaoh's magicians should have done, if they were that powerful, was to reverse what Moses and Aaron had done.

*Exodus 7:23–25*: "Pharaoh turned around, went into his palace, and didn't even take this to heart." Pharaoh didn't care that his people were dying with no water. "All the Egyptians dug around the Nile for water to drink" (v. 24). This was where we got the idea that maybe God only changed the surface water. "Seven days passed after the Lord struck the Nile." This was either seven days of bloody water or seven days until the next plague. This is the only time frame described in the ten plagues other than the three days of darkness in the ninth plague (Exodus 10:21–23).

## Closing

Hebrews 10:31 says, "It is a terrifying thing to fall into the hands of the living God!" Pharaoh walked a very fine line because he rejected God and hardened his own heart. He also brought destruction on his own people and his own family. Moses was a part of this. Moses and Aaron helped deliver the people so that they could be free. Why? They needed to be free so the Messiah could come into the picture.

## The Daily Word

Why did the Lord allow the awful plagues to afflict Egypt? So the Egyptians would know that the Lord was God and the Israelites would know Him as their deliverer.

The Lord is your deliverer too. Because of sin, everyone deserves death, but the Lord delivered the world through His Son Jesus. He will also deliver you from difficult situations in your life so you will know He is the Lord. Is there anything in your life today the Lord might be allowing in order to prove He is your deliverer? Turn to Him and let Him deliver you.

**The Egyptians will know that I am Yahweh when I stretch out My hand against Egypt, and bring out the Israelites from among them. —Exodus 7:5**

Further Scripture: 2 Samuel 22:1–4; Psalm 34:7–8; Galatians 5:1

## Questions

1. What were the first four plagues in Exodus 7—8? Why do you believe God started with these particular plagues? Do you think there was significance to the order of the plagues?

2. What do you think God meant in Exodus 7:1 when He talked with Moses?

3. What were the "judgments" mentioned in Exodus 7:4 intended to accomplish for Pharaoh and the Egyptians (Exodus 7:1–5)?

4. Which plague was the first to convince the magicians that God had to be the One sending the plagues? Did this change their attitude toward Him? Why do some people acknowledge the power of God but refuse to worship Him (Romans 1:18–25)?

5. What was the significance of God releasing the fourth plague in Exodus 8:20–30 on the Egyptians but not on the Israelites? What was God revealing to both groups about themselves—Pharaoh and the Egyptians, and the children of Israel? (Exodus 11:7; John 15:19; Romans 1:1; 2 Corinthians 5:17; 1 Peter 2:9)

6. What did the Holy Spirit highlight to you in Exodus 7—8 through the reading or the teaching?

# Lesson 32: Exodus 9—10
## Deliverer: Plagues 5–9

## Teaching Notes

### Intro

In the previous lesson, we began talking about the ten plagues—the water turned into blood, frogs covering the land, a plague of gnats (which the Egyptian magicians could not replicate), and a plague of flies which affected the Egyptians but not the Israelites. Wiersbe said: "Another reason for the display of His wonders during the plagues is that the Jews might be able to tell the greatness to come about the awesome power of their great God."[1]

### Teaching

*Exodus 9:1–3*: God sent Moses to tell Pharaoh, "This is what Yahweh, the God of the Hebrews, says: Let My people go, so that they may worship Me." Notice that God again referred to Himself as "Yahweh, the God of the Hebrews." God warned Pharaoh what would happen if he refused to let the Israelites go. "The Lord's hand will bring a severe plague against your livestock in the field—the horses, donkeys, camels, herds, and flocks."

*Exodus 9:4*: As in the previous plague, God made a distinction between the livestock of the Egyptians and the livestock of the Israelites. MacArthur said this was a direct attack on the false gods of the Egyptians.[2] The Egyptians prized the bull Apis as a sacred animal, identified as the son of the goddess Hathor, and was assigned a significant role in her worship. Apis was also considered to serve as the intermediary between humans and other powerful gods such as Pitah (god of craftsmen and architects), Osiris (god of the afterlife), and Atum (finisher of the world). Evidence suggests Apis was the first god of Egypt. God told the Israelites to settle in Goshen where He would take care of them (Genesis 45:9–11). God had brought not just the people but their animals into Goshen,

---

[1] Warren Wiersbe, *The Bible Exposition Commentary: Genesis–Deuteronomy* (Colorado Springs: David C. Cook, 2001), 188.

[2] John MacArthur, *The MacArthur Bible Commentary* (Nashville: Thomas Nelson, 2005), 94.

and He protected them. God also took the animals out of Egypt in the Exodus (Exodus 12:37–38).

*Exodus 9:5–11*: "And the Lᴏʀᴅ set a time, saying, 'Tomorrow the Lᴏʀᴅ will do this thing in the land'" (v. 5). God gave Pharaoh a 24-hour warning: "The Lᴏʀᴅ did this the next day. All the Egyptian livestock died, but none among the Israelite livestock died" (v. 6). Imagine being an Egyptian farmer, not being aware of this conversation between Pharaoh, and Moses and Aaron, and walking out to the field to see all of your livestock dead (v. 3). Pharaoh sent out messengers to see if what Moses and Aaron said was true. Although Pharaoh saw the truth, he still hardened his heart. Nothing fazed him. He feared no one! God told Moses and Aaron: "Take handfuls of furnace soot, and Moses is to throw it toward heaven in the sight of Pharaoh" (v. 9). Black soot symbolized the blackness of the skin in the disease.[3] The Israelites were probably still making bricks, and they put the soot in a kiln to make the bricks. Moses took something that had been part of their bondage and threw it toward heaven to bring judgment on the Egyptians. Remember, there was a pattern of warning before some plagues and no warnings before others: (1) water to blood—warning; (2) frogs—warning; (3) gnats—*no warning*; (4) flies—warning; (5) livestock—warning; (6) boils—*no warning*. "So they took furnace soot and stood before Pharaoh. Moses threw it toward heaven, and it became festering boils on man and beast." These boils were a "rash, which occurs in summer, chiefly toward the close of the time of the overflowing of the Nile, and produces a burning and pricking sensation upon the skin which give strong twitches and slight stinging sensations, resembling those of scarlet fever."[4] The magicians had the boils as well, which were so painful that they could not stand before Moses (2 Timothy 3:8).

Exodus 9:12–13: "But the Lord hardened Pharaoh's heart and he did not listen to them." This was the first time the hardening of Pharaoh's heart was attributed to God. Constable said, "If a person continues to harden his own heart, God will then harden it further in judgment"[5] (Proverbs 29:1). Notice the repetition as the seventh plague is introduced (see underlined phrases in the verse): "Then the Lord said to Moses, 'Get up early in the morning and present yourself to Pharaoh. Tell him: This is what Yahweh, the God of the Hebrews says: Let My people go, so that they may worship Me.'"

---

[3] Thomas L. Constable, *Expository Notes of Dr. Thomas Constable: Exodus*, 89 https://planobiblechapel.org/tcon/notes/pdf/exodus.pdf.

[4] Carl Friedrich Keil and Franz Delitzsch, *The Pentateuch*, trans. James Martin, 3 vols., Biblical Commentary on the Old Testament, reprint ed. (Grand Rapids: Eerdmans, n.d.), 1:487; quoted in Constable, 90.

[5] Constable, 90.

*Exodus 9:14–19*: God promised to send *all* His plagues against Egypt—with one purpose—so they would know there was no one like God. God planned to bring His full force against Pharaoh. The word "all" is used 12 times in this statement. "By now I could have stretched out My hand and struck you and your people with a plague, and you would have been obliterated from the earth" (v. 15). Remember the use of the word "strike" in previous lessons. Although God had the power to strike them, Wiersbe noted, "In His mercy God decides to still spare them."[6] God identified His whole purpose in allowing Pharaoh and the Egyptians to live: "to show you My power and to make My name known in all the earth" (v. 16; Romans 9:17). God said Pharaoh was still acting arrogantly against the Israelites by refusing to let them go. Hamilton said that God had a plan for Pharaoh[7] (Jeremiah 29:11). "Tomorrow at this time I will rain down the worst hail that has ever occurred in Egypt from the day it was founded until now" (v. 18). God warned them and even told them to bring their animals into shelter. Pharaoh had to respond to God. Hamilton said, "Those are always the two options when a word from God goes forth to any people: obey/disobey, listen/do not listen, respond/ ignore, fall at his feet and worship him/unless I see I will not believe, soften your heart/harden your heart."[8]

*Exodus 9:20–26*: Even Pharaoh's officials realized God was real and began turning against Pharaoh. Those who didn't take God seriously left their servants and livestock in the field. "Moses stretched out his staff toward heaven, and the Lord sent thunder and hail. Lightning struck the earth, and the Lord rained hail on the land of Egypt" (v. 23). John McArthur said it was a "violent electrical thunder storm that brought unusual lightning and these fireballs that zigzagged down on earth, bringing destruction on anything they touched."[9] This plague was a picture of what will happen in the future; it was just a taste of what's coming in the end (Revelation 8:7). "The hail, with lightning flashing through it, was so severe that nothing like it had occurred in the land of Egypt since it had become a nation." Everything that happened was a foreshadowing—it is coming again (Revelation 16:21). Hail struck through Egypt, bringing death and destruction of man, beast, plant of the field and every tree. Only in Goshen were the Israelites safe (v. 26). All of these plagues did not happen to God's people. In Exodus 10:23 (the plague of darkness), the Israelites had light when everyone else had darkness. God was clearly making His name known as the God of the Hebrews.

---

[6] Wiersbe, 95.

[7] Victor P. Hamilton, *Exodus: An Exegetical Commentary* (Grand Rapids: Baker Academic, 2011), 150.

[8] Hamilton, 151.

[9] MacArthur, 96.

*Exodus 9:27–35*: Pharaoh sent for Moses and Aaron, admitted his sin, and proclaimed Yahweh as the Righteous One. While Pharaoh sounded sincere, it didn't lead to repentance. Greenberg said, "He acknowledged guilt but went right on being guilty."[10] Moses called Pharaoh out, pointing out that neither he nor his officials feared Yahweh. Constable said, "Fearing Him means bowing in submission to Him as sovereign over all the earth."[11] Pharaoh only gave lip service to God. The ripe crops of flax and barley were destroyed, but the wheat and the spelt (raw wheat) were not destroyed because they are later crops. Moses left Pharaoh and the city, and then extended his hands to God and everything stopped. But Pharaoh *and* his officials hardened their hearts. Pharaoh would not let the Israelites go.

*Exodus 10:* This chapter gives details of the eighth and ninth plagues: the plague of locusts and the plague of darkness.

## Closing

God is giving us the Light. He's giving us the Spirit. He wants us to experience the fullness of God. Let's not be like the Egyptians and Pharaoh and say, "No, I don't want that." He has given us a *Deliverer*. We can't act like we're in bondage when we've been given life.

## The Daily Word

Pharaoh's heart was hardened, and he resisted letting the Israelites go. As a result, the Lord continued to multiply signs and wonders in the land of Egypt, specifically through the ten different plagues.

Just as the Lord saw Pharaoh's hardened heart, the Lord sees your heart. He longs for your heart to be surrendered to His ways. Even still, He will show His power and make His name known in all the earth. He is the great I Am.

**However, I have let you live for this purpose: to show you My power and to make My name known in all the earth. —Exodus 9:16**

Further Scripture: Exodus 7:3; Psalm 67:1–2; Matthew 6:10

---

[10] Moshe Greenberg, *Understanding Exodus*, 2nd ed. (Eugene, OR: Cascade Books, 2013), 129; quoted in Hamilton, 151.

[11] Constable, 92.

# Questions

1. According to Exodus 9:4, how many of the Israelite's livestock died in the plague? What characteristics of God were revealed as He continually protected the Israelites and their possessions?

2. What was Pharaoh's motivation when he asked Moses to pray (Exodus 8:8, 28; 9:27–28)? Has someone who isn't a Christian ever asked you for prayer? What does this reveal to you about that person?

3. In Exodus 9:15–16, what did God reveal to Pharaoh through Moses? What can you learn from this (Romans 9:17)?

4. What was the outcome for the Israelites due to God hardening Pharaoh's heart?

5. In Exodus 9:27–28, what was wrong with Pharaoh's repentance? What is the difference between worldly and biblical repentance (2 Corinthians 7:10)?

6. What did the Holy Spirit highlight to you in Exodus 9—10 through the reading or the teaching?

# Lesson 33: Exodus 11
*Deliverer:* The Final Plague Threatened

## Teaching Notes

### Intro

We're covering the tenth and final plague today. Let's review the nine plagues described in Exodus 7—10: (1) water turned to blood, (2) frogs, (3) gnats, (4) flies, (5) death of livestock, (6) boils, (7) hail, (8) locusts, and (9) darkness. Childs, a biblical commentator, said the events in chapter 11 were the culmination of the plagues and the beginning of Passover tradition.[1]

### Teaching

*Exodus 11:1*: God had never told Moses how many plagues it would take. Now, God did reveal this plague would be the last and then Pharaoh would let them go. Moses saw the end was coming. Notice God said Pharaoh would "drive you out." This phrase is translated from "nega," which is a generic term for plagues, diseases, injuries. It is a noun referring to when something touches. Remember when God "touched" Jacob's thigh (Genesis 32:25)? Now God was going to "touch" the Egyptians in a way that would be drastic. The Egyptians had already experienced this touch from God to some degree. In Genesis 12:17, "The LORD struck Pharaoh and his household with severe plagues because of Abram's wife Sarai." God brought this judgment because of what the Egyptians had done to His people. Hamilton said this was the same concept described in Proverbs 6:32–33, which allowed a husband to inflict a "touch" on an adulterer.[2]

*Exodus 11:2*: God told Moses to tell all the men and women of Israel to ask their Egyptian neighbors for silver and gold jewelry. This was not a small request. In 991 BC, they found a buried necklace that weighed more than 42 pounds. This was a lot of plunder! God had promised this to Moses earlier (Exodus 3:22). And in Exodus 12:36, it actually happened.

---

[1] Brevard S. Childs, *The Book of Exodus* (Louisville: Presbyterian Publishing, 1974, 2004), 161.

[2] Victor P. Hamilton, *Exodus: An Exegetical Commentary* (Grand Rapids: Baker Academic, 2011), 165–66.

*Exodus 11:3*: "The LORD gave the people favor in the sight of the Egyptians. And the man Moses was highly regarded in the land of Egypt by Pharaoh's officials and the people." The Israelites had been through a lot of grief, and now the Lord poured out His favor on them. Remember when Pharaoh's officials realized the hail was coming and they brought in their livestock because they feared God and believed what Moses said? Here again, the people feared God because of what they saw happening. Pharaoh was the only one who didn't see it.

Moses was "highly regarded" in Egypt. This was the same language used in Esther 9:4 that described Mordecai as "highly regarded" by the people of Persia.[3] You can see when God's favor is on a business or ministry or household. This happened to Moses because he was obedient, and he stayed the course.

*Exodus 11:4*: Moses said, "This is what Yahweh says: 'About midnight I will go throughout Egypt.'" We typically think of bad things happening at midnight. However, a couple of positive events occurred at midnight in Scripture: Psalm 119:62 encourages us to "rise at midnight to thank You for your righteous judgments." Acts 16:25 described Paul and Silas praying and singing hymns to God at midnight while all the prisoners listened to them. Notice the statement "I will go," meaning the Lord would go through Egypt. This was preparation for or foreshadowing the Incarnation.[4] God would go throughout Egypt and bring deliverance to the Israelites.

*Exodus 11:5*: No ifs, ands, or buts—when God executed His judgment, every firstborn male in the land of Egypt would die. Pharaoh would not escape this judgment. No more hierarchy. It would affect everyone, including the livestock. Throughout Genesis, we talked about the value and importance of the firstborn. Think of Cain and Abel, Jacob and Esau, and the 12 tribes of Israel. Constable said the firstborn sons were the sign of a nation's strength and vigor. The family lines came through the firstborn son.[5] Remember that the Levites were considered the firstborn sons. Dozeman summarized these events:[6] (1) Time: about midnight, (2) Content: firstborn males in Egypt, (3) Scope: across the board, and (4) Outcome: great cry of anguish; innocent children will die (v. 6).

---

[3] Hamilton, 167.

[4] Earl Radmacher, Ronald B. Allen, and H. Wayne House, eds., *Nelson's New Illustrated Bible Commentary* (Nashville: Thomas Nelson, 1999), 105–106.

[5] Thomas L. Constable, *Expository Notes of Dr. Thomas Constable: Exodus*, 99, https://planobiblechapel.org/tcon/notes/pdf/exodus.pdf.

[6] Thomas B. Dozeman, *The Eerdmans Critical Commentary: Exodus* (Grand Rapids: Eerdmans, 2009), 249.

*Exodus 11:6*: "Then there will be a great cry of anguish through all the land of Egypt such as never was before, or ever will be again." This makes me think of Noah and the rainbow. Many have questioned how a just God could randomly kill firstborn children. Constable provided five possible arguments:[7] (1) Whatever God does is right because He's God; (2) God is the sustainer and giver of life, so He's righteous in withdrawing life from any creature; (3) God can take life as well as give it; (4) Humans are sinners and sin results in death, so God is just in punishing people; and (5) God didn't kill all of the kids.

*Exodus 11:7*: "But against all the Israelites, whether man or beast, not even a dog will snarl, so that you may know that Yahweh makes a distinction between Egypt and Israel." Israel was going to be saved. But for Egypt, every firstborn would be gone. God was going to deliver the *Seed* in this process. God was going to pass over the Israelite firstborn males.

*Exodus 11:8*: Moses left Pharaoh's presence in fierce anger. When I think of anger, I think of Jesus' anger at the temple. Scripture says it was a righteous anger. I feel this anger was righteous as well. Moses was sick of the evil that was taking place. In addition to this instance, Moses showed anger several other times but always with a clear head.[8] In Exodus 16:20, he became angry when the Israelites gathered more than a day's worth of manna. In Leviticus 10:16, he became angry with Aaron's sons when sacrifices weren't done properly. In Numbers 16:15, he became angry when the sons of Korah rebelled against his leadership. Only once did Moses show hot-headed anger. In Numbers 20:10–12, he struck the rock in Meribah in anger to draw forth water for the Israelites who were complaining. In this case, Moses' anger prevented God from showing His holiness, so Moses was not allowed to lead Israel into the Promised Land.

When sin is present, sometimes it's OK to be angry. At what point is there going to be a righteous anger that builds up in you? When is the church going to get it? When are we going to admit that what we're doing is not radically impacting our culture? We're not giving up our lives for the Lord! I just want to say sometimes, "Church, soften your hearts"! I'm angry at the Pharaohs in America. I'm ready for a move of God. When you're honest, can you say you've given it all up for Him?

*Exodus 11:9–10*: Though Pharaoh witnessed God's power in the wonders Moses and Aaron performed, he refused to let the Israelites go. You know what gives me hope when people don't listen? God gets to show His power, and He gets the glory. I want to see God demonstrate His power. Moses and Aaron were obedient.

---

[7] Constable, 100–101.

[8] Hamilton, 168.

# Closing

Sailhamer said, "By means of the last plague, then, the writer is able to bring the Exodus narratives into the larger framework of the whole Pentateuch and particularly that of the early chapters of Genesis. In the midst of the judgment of death, God provided a way of salvation for the promised *Seed* (Genesis 3:15). Like Enoch (Genesis 5:22–24), Noah (Genesis 6:9), and Lot (Genesis 19:16–19), those who walk in God's way will be saved from death and destruction."[9]

God honored His promise to deliver the *Seed*, and it was going to come in a unique way—Passover. God was going to pass over the Israelites, save His people, and strike down the Egyptians.

## The Daily Word

Even after nine plagues afflicted Egypt, Pharaoh's heart remained hardened. He would not let the Israelites go. The Lord gave Moses instructions about the tenth and final plague that would kill all the firstborns in the land of Egypt. The Lord continued to reveal His power and control in the midst of the situation.

In a similar way, the Lord says you will have trials in this life and will suffer. However, He uses these times in your life to restore, confirm, strengthen, and establish you in Christ. May you take heart in the midst of hardship, trusting the Lord has overcome the world. He is working in you so you will have the strength to endure even more.

**The LORD said to Moses, "Pharaoh will not listen to you, so that My wonders may be multiplied in the land of Egypt." —Exodus 11:9**

Further Scripture: John 16:33; James 1:2–3; 1 Peter 5:10

## Questions

1. In Exodus 11:7, the Lord wanted them to know He made a distinction between Egypt and Israel. What were several "distinctions" described in the first 11 chapters of Exodus?

2. The Lord told Moses in Exodus 11:1 that after "one more plague" Pharaoh would let them go. Why do you think God sent all the other plagues on Egypt if this last one would cause Pharaoh to send them away? Or do you think it was the culmination of them all (Romans 9:17)?

---

[9] John H. Sailhamer, *The Pentateuch as Narrative* (Grand Rapids: Zondervan, 1992), 258.

3. Why do you think the Israelites were instructed by God to ask their Egyptian neighbors for articles of silver and gold (Exodus 11:2)?

4. The whole process of deliverance, which unfolded in Exodus 11, was not an instant event. In the midst of your trials, how have you seen God bring deliverance?

5. In reference to Exodus 11:7, do you think the Lord still makes a distinction between Israel and their persecutors? Can you name any specific event?

6. What did the Holy Spirit highlight to you in Exodus 11 through the reading or the teaching?

# Lesson 34: Exodus 12—13
## *Deliverer:* The Passover

## Teaching Notes

### Intro

The Passover was really the death of the firstborn of the Egyptians, but the Lord *passed over* the Israelites. Moses and Aaron helped deliver God's people; that ultimately pointed to the *Deliverer*, the Messiah. God brought about ten plagues: (1) water turned to blood; (2) frogs; (3) gnats; (4) flies; (5) death of livestock; (6) boils; (7) hail; (8) locusts; (9) darkness; and (10) death of the firstborn. Exodus 12 records God's instructions for the Passover and the death of the firstborn. Because Pharaoh's heart was hardened, God used the plagues to make His name known (Romans 9:17).

### Teaching

*Exodus 12:1–2*: God instructed Moses and Aaron to establish a new religious calendar for the Israelites that began in the month of the Passover, the March/April time frame. This month was called Abib, which means "ear month," when grain was in the ear, meaning it was almost harvest time.[1] At the end of the Babylonian captivity, this month was renamed Nisan (Nehemiah 2:1; Esther 3:7). Today, the Israelites use a civil calendar that begins at Rosh Hashanah in September/October. God was starting something new for Israel, which was marked by a change in the calendar. This makes me think that when you embrace Messiah as your Savior, you get a whole new calendar, a whole new beginning.

*Exodus 12:3–5*: God instructed each household to select an unblemished one-year-old male animal (sheep or goat) on the tenth day of the month. Smaller families were instructed to join together and choose an animal "according to what each person will eat." To be considered unblemished, the animal could have no faults, no defects, and no injuries.

---

[1] Thomas L. Constable, *Expository Notes of Dr. Thomas Constable: Exodus*, 105, https://planobiblechapel.org/tcon/notes/pdf/exodus.pdf.

*Exodus 12:6*: This animal was kept until the fourteenth day of the month, and then the whole community slaughtered the animals at twilight. Keeping the animals for four days allowed them to be sure they were perfect. Then the sacrifice of these animals would protect the Israelites in the Passover. The lamb reminds us of the time when God asked Abraham to sacrifice Isaac and Isaac's question to Abraham as they made preparations: "Where is the lamb for the burnt offering?" (Genesis 22:7).

This sacrificial lamb also foreshadows Christ as the sacrificial lamb. When John the Baptist saw Jesus approach him for baptism, he said, "Here is the Lamb of God, who takes away the sin of the world" (John 1:29). When the Ethiopian eunuch read from Isaiah 53, he wanted to know who was "led like a sheep to the slaughter" (Acts 8:32), so Philip told him the good news about Jesus. Just as Isaiah 53:7 described, Jesus "was oppressed and afflicted, yet He did not open His mouth. Like a lamb led to the slaughter and like a sheep silent before her shearers, He did not open His mouth." Peter described Jesus as a lamb without defect or blemish (1 Peter 1:18–20). In Revelation 5:5–6, John "saw One like a slaughtered lamb" standing before the throne of God. Scripture tells us that Jesus met the qualifications of an unblemished lamb. Jesus did not know sin (2 Corinthians 5:21). "He did not commit sin, and no deceit was found in His mouth" (1 Peter 2:22). There was no sin in Him (1 John 3:5). Jesus is the Lamb of God. He's perfect. He's God in human form.

*Exodus 12:7*: They were told to take some of the blood of the innocent lamb and put it on the top (lintel) and sides (posts) of the door. Wiersbe said, "It wasn't the *life* of the lamb that saved the people from judgment, but the *death* of the lamb."[2] Likewise, Jesus' death is what gives us life. Jesus came "to give His life—a ransom for many" (Matthew 20:28). When Jesus established the New Covenant, He said, "This is My blood that establishes the covenant; it is shed for many for the forgiveness of sins" (Matthew 26:28). Jesus is the good shepherd who "lays down his life for the sheep" (John 10:11). We have been redeemed and forgiven through His blood (Ephesians 1:7), for Jesus gave Himself as a ransom for all (1 Timothy 2:5–6). "Without the shedding of blood there is no forgiveness" (Hebrews 9:22–23), so Jesus redeemed people for God by His blood (Revelation 5:9). Exodus 12 is a complete foreshadow of Christ's sacrifice for our sins.

*Exodus 12:8–11*: God gave specific instructions for consuming the Passover meal. The lamb had to be roasted and eaten that evening, along with unleavened bread and bitter herbs. Every part of the lamb, including the head, legs, and inner

---

[2] Warren W. Wiersbe, *The Bible Exposition Commentary: Genesis–Deuteronomy* (Colorado Springs: David C. Cook, 2001), 198.

organs had to be consumed. Any leftovers had to be burned up. The Lord's Passover had to be eaten in a hurry, and the Israelites had to be dressed for travel with sandals on their feet and staff in hand.

*Exodus 12:12–13*: God passed through the land of Egypt that night to execute His judgment against all the gods of Egypt by striking the firstborn male of both man and beast. The Israelites would be protected from this plague by the distinguishing mark of the lamb's blood on their doorposts and lintels.

*Exodus 12:14–20*: God instructed Israel to celebrate the Passover every year as a memorial to this night. They were instructed to remove all yeast from their homes and eat only unleavened bread for seven days. For this entire week they would "observe the Festival of Unleavened Bread" to remember how God brought them out of Egypt. They could do no work other than preparing food, and on the first and seventh days, they were commanded to hold "a sacred assembly." Those who disobeyed these instructions were to be cut off from Israel.

*Exodus 12:21–23*: Moses instructed the Israelites to select and slaughter the Passover animal, then dip a cluster of hyssop into the blood and spread the blood over the doorposts and lintels of their homes. When the Lord passed through Egypt, He would "not let the destroyer enter your houses to strike you" when He saw the blood. Wiersbe said, "Our faith may be as weak as the hyssop, but it's not faith in our faith that saves us, but faith in the blood of the Savior."[3]

Could "the destroyer" in verse 23 be the pre-incarnate Christ?[4] In Numbers 22:31, "the Lord opened Balaam's eyes, he saw the Angel of the LORD (Jesus) standing in the path with a drawn sword in His hand. Balaam knelt and bowed with his face to the ground." In Isaiah 37:36, "the angel of the LORD went out and struck down 185,000 in the camp of the Assyrians." Exodus 23:20–23 said God would send an angel before the Israelites to protect them and bring them into the Promised Land, and to wipe out the Amorites, Hittites, Perizzites, Canaanites, Hivites, and Jebusites. To protect may mean to defend Israel and kill the enemy. Jesus could be the Destroyer preparing the way to point to Himself. Jesus had all kinds of roles in the Old Testament. He wasn't always speaking; maybe He was wrestling, revealing Himself in a burning bush, wiping out people in order to prepare a way for His people. Revelation 19:11–14 reveals Jesus as a powerful warrior who "judges and makes war in righteousness" as He leads the armies of

---

[3] Wiersbe, 199.

[4] Earl Radmacher, Ronald B. Allen, and H. Wayne House, eds., *Nelson's New Illustrated Bible Commentary* (Nashville: Thomas Nelson, 1999), 108.

heaven in battle. Jesus is not always this peaceful person; He'll do what it takes to deliver His people.

*Exodus 12:24–28*: Moses conveyed God's command to observe this Passover ritual every year so they could teach their children how God struck the Egyptians and delivered them from captivity. So, the Israelites did as God commanded.

*Exodus 12:29–36*: Passover happened. The Israelites were set free through a perfect little lamb. God struck the firstborn in Egypt, and Pharaoh drove the Israelites out of Egypt. Just as God had promised, the Egyptians gave the Israelites silver and gold jewelry and clothing as they sent them out of Egypt. And that lamb would eventually become Jesus.

*Exodus 12:37–42*: The Israelites began the journey to the Promised Land. Josephus said there could have been up to 2 million people (600,000 men plus their families) who traveled with their flocks and herds. The "ethnically diverse crowd" could have included Egyptians who married Jews or Egyptians who feared God. These are the people who, over time, had become part of the Israelite community though they were from other lands. "Then He brought Israel out with silver and gold, and no one among His tribes stumbled. Egypt was glad when they left, for the dread of Israel had fallen on them" (Psalm 105:37–38). After 430 years in Egypt, the Israelites were delivered! They were going to the Promised Land.

Jude 1:5 explained, "Now I want to remind you, although you once fully knew it, that Jesus, who saved a people out of the land of Egypt, afterward destroyed those who did not believe." So, who delivered the people out of Egypt? The Lord! Jesus! God will go to any extremes, through Jesus Christ, to save His people.

*Exodus 13*: This chapter restated God's command to consecrate the firstborn to Him (v. 2), described their route out of Egypt (vv. 17–18), revealed that Moses brought Joseph's bones with them (v. 19), and emphasized that the Lord went ahead of them in a pillar of cloud/fire to lead them (vv. 21–22). But there's no pillar without the blood of the lamb.

## Closing

God is in the business of deliverance, and my prayer is that each one of you have been delivered from the bondage of sin and death through the blood of Christ.

## The Daily Word

After the tenth plague, Pharaoh finally let the Israelites go. As the Israelites began their journey out of Egypt, the Lord was very intentional. First God led them on a specific route, not the shortest, but the best one for His people. Then God said He would take care of His people. Finally, God went before the people to lead them.

Remember, God is the same yesterday, today, and forever. Therefore, the same is true for your own journey. The Lord's path is the best one for you, even if it's not the shortest or the easiest. The Lord will care for you. The Lord is going before you and is with you day and night. So keep on walking one step at a time!

**When Pharaoh let the people go, God did not lead them along the road to the land of the Philistines, even though it was nearby; for God said, "The people will change their minds and return to Egypt if they face war." So He led the people around toward the Red Sea along the road of the wilderness.
—Exodus 13:17–18**

Further Scripture: Exodus 13:21; Proverbs 3:5–6; Hebrews 13:8

## Questions

1. Exodus 12:12 states, "and against all the gods of Egypt I will execute judgments—I am the LORD." We know they were false gods with no power, so what do you think this verse means?

2. According to Exodus 12:2, the Lord instructed Moses to reset the calendar to begin with the month of their deliverance out of Egypt. Why do you think God established this?

3. In Exodus 12, the Passover lamb was a type pointing to Christ, the Lamb of God (John 1:29). What details about the Passover lamb can you find that point to a detail about Christ? (Psalm 34:20; John 19:36; 2 Corinthians 5:21; 1 Peter 1:18–20; Revelation 5)

4. What do you think was the significance of the ordinance not allowing any foreigners to partake in the Passover Feast? (Exodus 12:43; Numbers 9:14; 1 Corinthians 11:26–27)

5. Moses instructed the people that on the first day of the Feast of Passover, all leaven was to be removed from their houses (Exodus 12:14–15), for whoever ate anything leavened would be cut off from Israel. What was the importance of removing the leaven? (Exodus 12:15, 20; 13:3; John 6:48, 51; 1 Corinthians 5:7–8)

6. Explain what it meant when the Lord told Moses, "the first offspring of every womb among the sons of Israel, both of man and beast; it belongs to Me" (Exodus 13:2).

7. In addition to the Passover lamb, what other deliverer do you see in chapter 12? (Exodus 12:51; Acts 7:36; 13:17)

8. What did the Holy Spirit highlight to you in Exodus 12—13 through the reading or the teaching?

# Lesson 35: Exodus 14—15
## *Deliverer:* Crossing the Red Sea

## Teaching Notes

### Intro

In the Passover, we see an incredible picture of the unblemished lamb that pointed to Christ, the Ultimate Passover. Because "Christ our Passover had been sacrificed" (1 Corinthians 5:7), we too have been delivered. As we continue our study, the Israelites had been set free, and now the Lord was leading them out of Egypt. He didn't lead them along the road but led them toward the Red Sea through the wilderness (Exodus 13:17–18).

### Teaching

*Exodus 14:1–4:* Can you imagine the logistical challenge of leading 2 million people through the wilderness? Psalm 103:7a says God "revealed His ways to Moses." After leading Israel on the wilderness route instead of along the road, God told them to camp facing the sea. Wiersbe pointed out, "The Jewish people were told what God wanted to do, but God revealed to Moses why He was doing it."[1] The Israelites will soon be trapped between the Red Sea and the approaching Egyptian army. God arranged a trap so He would get the glory in the wilderness and the Egyptians would know that He was Yahweh (v. 4). How many times have you heard, "This is a Red Sea moment!"? In those times, we find ourselves in situations where we need God to show up and reveal His glory through the situation.

*Exodus 14:5–10:* Once the Israelites left Egypt, Pharaoh and his officials soon realized they had released their free labor force! So Pharaoh gathered his troops and chariots and pursued the Israelites, who were celebrating and praising God as they left Egypt. Josephus said there were probably 50,000 horsemen, 200,000 footmen, and all of them were probably armed. While archeologists have searched for this area, they have not found the exact location. When Israel realized Pharaoh was chasing them, they were terrified and cried out to God for help.

---

[1] Warren W. Wiersbe, *The Bible Exposition Commentary: Genesis–Deuteronomy* (Colorado Springs: David C. Cook, 2001), 204.

*Exodus 14:11–12*: How quickly the Israelites forgot the plagues and everything God had done to bring them out of Egypt! Instead of continuing to trust in God, they turned on Moses and asked if he had led them out of Egypt to die in the wilderness. They claimed it would be better to serve Egypt than die by the sea. Scripture recorded the Israelites' continual complaints against Moses. In Exodus 5, they complained when Pharaoh punished them after Moses and Aaron first requested their release. In Exodus 16, they complained about the lack of food, and in Exodus 17, they complained about the lack of water for themselves and their flocks. Josephus wrote that it got so bad that the Israelites wanted to stone Moses. It doesn't matter who you are, Moses or Jesus, if you're a deliverer, they'll come after you. Sometimes the church sounds like we've forgotten that we've been delivered and have passed from death to life by the blood of the Lamb. Let's walk by faith and stop complaining and grumbling! When we function in a position of faith, we win. But when we function in a position of fear and grumbling and whining, we lose.

*Exodus 14:13–14*: With the strongest backbone ever, Moses stood up to the people and told them, "Don't be afraid. Stand firm and see the Lord's salvation . . . The Lord will fight for you; you must be quiet." As Wiersbe said, fear can either energize or paralyze.[2] In this context, the word "salvation" (*yeshû'â*) means "space" or "room." Nelson's commentary says, "The people were under great pressure, squeezed between the waters before them and the armies of Pharaoh behind them. Salvation would relieve the pressure in a most dramatic way."[3] All Israel had to do was stand still and watch God work on their behalf. Scripture recorded other times when God worked miraculously in Israel (1 Samuel 17:47; 2 Chronicles 20:15–17; Zechariah 14:3). Like the Israelites, sometimes we have to stand firm in our faith to see God work. I think the church in America has tried to create our own salvation. We've tried to fight our own battles and then incorporate the Lord at the end. How about we just stand and wait for the Lord to do the fighting?

*Exodus 14:15–18*: God told Moses to stop crying out to Him and to break camp and keep moving! Instead of remaining paralyzed by fear, they needed to move forward expecting God to show up and miracles to happen. Then God told Moses what to do and what the results would be. "Lift up your staff, stretch out your hand over the sea, and divide it so that the Israelites can go through the sea on dry ground" (v. 16). God planned to take Israel through the sea! Then, through the

---

[2] Wiersbe, 204.

[3] Earl Radmacher, Ronald B. Allen, and H. Wayne House, eds., *Nelson's New Illustrated Bible Commentary* (Nashville: Thomas Nelson, 1999), 112.

destruction of Pharaoh's army, God would be glorified, and the Egyptians would know He was Yahweh. To get to the land flowing with milk and honey, we've got to pass through the sea, which means we've got to walk by faith.

*Exodus 14:19–20*: Remember, the Destroyer in the Passover could have been Jesus. Now we see Jesus in this role again. The Angel of God, who had been in the pillar of cloud leading Israel, moved to stand between Israel and Pharaoh's army. Compare this to Isaiah 63:8–9: "He said, 'They are indeed My people, children who will not be disloyal,' and He became their Savior. In all their suffering, He suffered, and the Angel of His Presence saved them. He redeemed them because of His love and compassion; He lifted them up and carried them all the days of the past." Exodus 13:21; 14:19; 23:20–23; 32:34; and 33:2 all describe the Angel of the Lord who went before Israel to deliver them, protect them, guide them, and drive out their enemies. Deuteronomy 8:2 says God did this the entire 40 years Israel wandered in the wilderness. The Presence of God, the Angel of God, was in the pillar of cloud and fire. And the Angel of the Lord is Jesus.

*Exodus 14:21–25*: Moses stretched his hand over the sea and God parted the waters; so the Israelites crossed over on dry ground "with the waters like a wall to them on their right and their left" (v. 22). Can you imagine watching the sea form into walls and then walking through them on dry ground? When the Egyptians followed them, God created great confusion in their army, and they tried to get away from Israel "because Yahweh is fighting for them" (v. 25). The Egyptians recognized God was at work. That's when you know it's God. You don't have to tell people; they just know it.

*Exodus 14:26–28*: God told Moses: "Stretch out your hand over the sea so the waters may come back on the Egyptians, on their chariots and horsemen." So, Moses stretched out his hand and God caused the waters to completely cover and destroy Pharaoh and his army. Hamilton compared this event to the story in Mark 5:1–20, where Jesus transfers "demons from a possessed man into 2,000 pigs, who promptly rush down a steep bank into a lake and drown."[4] In both cases, God's power was revealed.

*Exodus 14:29–31*: Israel walked through the sea on dry land and then saw God's great power displayed against the Egyptians. The people then feared God and believed in Him and His servant Moses. This Red Sea moment radically transformed the culture of the Israelites. Why? Because they depended on the Lord

---

[4] Victor P. Hamilton, *Exodus: An Exegetical Commentary* (Grand Rapids: Baker Academic, 2011), 220.

in faith, and God used Moses to deliver them out of bondage. God would once again bring forth a *Deliverer* out of Egypt. Matthew 2:13 says an angel of the Lord told Joseph to take Mary and Jesus to Egypt to avoid Herod's killing spree of male babies in Israel. Matthew 2:15 says, "He stayed there until Herod's death, so that what was spoken by the Lord through the prophet might be fulfilled: Out of Egypt I called my Son."

I believe God used Moses and his faith to deliver the Israelites, which then led to the lineage of Christ. I think the mentality here was *"Out of Egypt I called my Son."* Hosea 11:1 says, "When Israel was a child, I loved him, and out of Egypt I called my son," which foreshadowed Jesus' sojourn in Israel to escape Herod's massacre and return to Israel after Herod died.

## Closing

I love watching the Lord tie in all of Scripture. Moses' faith led to the ultimate *Deliverer*, Jesus Christ, who was called out of Egypt to set all of us free. I promise all of us will have "Red Sea moments" at some point. When you do, just stand still and watch the Lord fight for you. Exodus 15 recorded the Israelites singing praises to God about how He saved them in Exodus 14.

## The Daily Word

Shortly after the Israelites left Egypt, Pharaoh's heart hardened once again. He pursued the Israelites until they came to a dead end, facing the Red Sea. The Israelites were frightened and cried out to the Lord. In their minds, they had nowhere to turn. And yet, this created another opportunity for God to reveal He is the Lord, the great I Am. In His power, the Lord parted the Red Sea. He saved the Israelites and crushed the Egyptians.

Are you at a place in life that feels like a Red Sea moment? Do you feel as though you have nowhere to turn? Remember, the Lord is with you. The Lord will fight for you. He has a plan. Like the Lord said to the Israelites, "Be quiet," and trust He will bring victory to your situation in a way you never expected!

But Moses said to the people, "Don't be afraid. Stand firm and see the LORD's salvation He will provide for you today; for the Egyptians you see today, you will never see again. The LORD will fight for you; you must be quiet." —Exodus 14:13–14

Further Scripture: Exodus 14:31; Deuteronomy 20:4; Romans 8:31

# Questions

1. Read Exodus 14:13. How do you see the Egyptians symbolizing the bondage of sin and our ultimate deliverance from this bondage (Romans 6:6b–7)?

2. We saw God fighting for the Israelites (Exodus 14:15, 25) and the Egyptians trying to flee. When have you called on the Lord to fight for you in a situation that looked hopeless and He delivered?

3. The children of Israel complained to Moses in Exodus 14:11 because they saw the enemy closing in (Exodus 14:10) and they reacted out of fear, in spite of all they had seen the Lord accomplish. Have you ever taken your eyes off God and reacted out of fear when you've been under the enemy's attack?

4. In Exodus 15:13, Moses' song declared that in His lovingkindness the Lord led the people whom He had redeemed. What does the word lovingkindness mean? Who ultimately redeemed us, and how does He lead us? (Psalm 23:1–3; John 10:3–4; 14:6)

5. What did the Holy Spirit highlight to you in Exodus 14—15 through the reading or the teaching?

# Lesson 36: Exodus 16—18

## Deliverer: Water from the Rock and Amalekite Defeat

## Teaching Notes

### Intro

Exodus is the story of the Israelites "exiting" slavery. So far, we've seen God part the Red Sea, the Israelites praise God for this miracle, and God's provision for the people.

### Teaching

*Exodus 17:1*: The Israelites numbered 2 million people and had 40 stops on their wilderness journey (Numbers 33). Constable said, "They wanted [God] to act as they dictated, rather than waiting for Him to provide as He had promised." The Israelites were testing the Lord instead of having the Lord test them[1] (1 Corinthians 10:9–10).

*Exodus 17:3*: The Israelites' hearts were still in Egypt. They forgot who God is and what He'd done. Wiersbe says every experience can "become either a test that can make us better or a temptation that can make us worse."[2] *Any* situation can be used for His glory (Romans 8:28)!

*Exodus 17:4*: This became a pattern: tough situation, people complained, and Moses took his difficulties to the Lord. As a leader, Moses was consistent: in the midst of their complaints, he went to the Lord on their behalf (Exodus 32:30); he went to the tent to meet with the Lord (Exodus 33:8); and he prayed for the people when things got tough (Numbers 11:2). Moses was the deliverer. God used him to bring the Israelites out of Egypt, and he pointed people to God's presence. When we face hard times, we should point people to God's presence (Psalm 46:1).

---

[1] Thomas L. Constable, *Expository Notes of Dr. Thomas Constable: Exodus*, 152, https://planobiblechapel.org/tcon/notes/pdf/exodus.pdf.

[2] Warren Wiersbe, *Be Delivered (Exodus): Finding Freedom by Following God.* (Colorado Springs: David C. Cook, 1998), 104.

*Exodus 17:5–7*: Moses' staff turned into a snake and turned the Nile to blood in Egypt. Moses stood before the people with the elders and God stood on the rock at Horeb. Massah meant testing or proof; Meribah meant murmuring or dissatisfaction. Many passages recorded the grumbling and complaining of the Israelites. (Exodus 15; 16; 17; Numbers 14; 16; 17.) Yet God met their needs every time (Psalms 78:15–16; 105:41). It took one night for the Israelites to get out of Egypt but 40 years to get Egypt out of the Israelites.

*Exodus 17:8–9*: Amalek came and fought against Israel. God promised to give them the land, but He didn't promise to just hand it over to them. They were going to have to fight to take it. The Amalekites were pirate-like people (v. 8). This is the first reference to Joshua. He will be mentioned 200 times. Moses was already beginning to entrust the deliverer mentality to Joshua (v. 9). A true leader will always empower others.

*Exodus 17:10*: Joshua didn't complain. He did what Moses told him to do. Moses, Aaron and Hur went to the top of the hill. Moses and Aaron were the sons of Amram and Jochebed. Hur was the son of Caleb and Ephrath (1 Chronicles 2:19). He could have been the grandfather of Bezalel (Exodus 31:2), the architect of the tabernacle. Aaron and Moses were Levites. Hur was in the lineage of Judah. The Levites and Judah were working together. Josephus claimed that Hur could have been the husband of Miriam.[3]

*Exodus 17:11–12*: Moses' hands dictated the outcome. When Moses sat down, Aaron and Hur held his hands up. Josephus called the Amalekites the most warlike of the nearby nations.[4] The Israelites' first fight was with the toughest opponent possible.

We can do nothing apart from Him (John 15:5). Victory is not dependent on us but on God. I love the image that Moses is praying. We need to be interceding for the Lord to be victorious. This must have been a tiring process for Moses' strength to have left him, because even when he was old, he was known to be strong (Deuteronomy 34:7). Zwemer called prayer "the gymnasium to the soul."[5] We too are told to lift up our hands to the Lord (Psalms 28:2; 44:20; 63:4).

---

[3] Josephus, *Antiquities of the Jews*, book 3, chapter 2, https://www.biblestudytools.com/history/flavius-josephus/antiquities-jews/book-3/chapter-2.html.

[4] Josephus.

[5] Samuel M. Zwemer, quoted in Warren W. Wiersbe, *The Wiersbe Bible Commentary: Old Testament*. (Colorado Springs: David C. Cook, 2007), 176.

*Exodus 17:13*: Because of Moses, Aaron, and Hur's intercession, Joshua defeated the Amalekites. It was a team effort. Josephus wrote that no Hebrews died, but an innumerable number of Amalekites perished.[6] The Israelites were not seasoned fighters. This was a miracle! Intercession was essential! Moses is a type of Christ, as a picture of *Jesus'* intercession for us (Hebrews 7:25). The Holy Spirit also intercedes on our behalf (Romans 8:26–27).

*Exodus 17:14*: God wanted Joshua to remember this moment. Moses was instructed to write things down three times in Exodus and two times in Numbers. The Israelites had a tendency to forget. What God told Moses to write down had not fully come to fruition yet. It was a prophecy. God was going to blot out their memory later.

*Exodus 17:15–16*: Moses built an altar and named it, "The Lord Is My Banner." The Lord would be at war with Amalek from generation to generation. Scripture records five other times Israel fought the Amalekites (Numbers 14; Judges 6; 1 Samuel 15; 30; 2 Samuel 8). The prophecy seems to be fulfilled in 1 Chronicles 4:42–43. Exodus 17 is a picture of Moses being the deliverer.

*Exodus 18*: Jethro and the rest of Moses' family came to Moses. They got caught up on all God had done for the people. Aaron and the elders ate a meal with Moses' family. Jethro noticed that Moses was tired, so he told Moses to surround himself with other leaders. Moses did what his father-in-law said, as any humble leader should do.

## Closing

God is in the business of setting people free, and He loves to use you and me to do it.

## The Daily Word

Moses' arms were heavy: literally and figuratively. He could no longer lead the people alone. Aaron helped him to speak. Hur and Aaron supported his hands during the battle with Amalek. Then the Lord sent his father-in-law Jethro to advise him in the area of delegation and leadership. Jethro came from the outside and assessed the situation from his perspective.

Moses received assistance with humility. Are you facing a task too heavy for you? Are you overwhelmed? You are not alone. Seek the Lord. He will send the

---

[6] Josephus.

help and insight you need when the task seems too big. Receive it, and God will be with you.

**You will certainly wear out both yourself and these people who are with you, because the task is too heavy for you. You can't do it alone. Now listen to me; I will give you some advice, and God be with you. —Exodus 18:18–19**

Further Scripture: Exodus 18:24; Psalm 34:17; Matthew 11:28

## Questions

1. What did the Lord provide for the Israelites in Exodus 16? What was their response? (Exodus 16:20, 27; Numbers 11:4–6) Can you think of a time when you responded to the Lord's provision like the Israelites?

2. How does manna in Exodus 16 foreshadow Christ? According to John 6:48–51, how does Jesus surpass manna from heaven?

3. Was the Rock of Horeb (Exodus 17:6) a foreshadowing of Christ? (Psalm 105:41; 1 Corinthians 10:1–4)

4. Do you see Moses lifting up his hands on behalf of the Israelites in Exodus 17:10–16 as a picture of prayer? What does lifting hands to the Lord represent? (Psalms 28:2; 63:4; 141:2) Do you ever lift your hands in prayer? Why or why not?

5. How do you see Moses as a deliverer for the Israelites in Exodus 16—18? Can you think of any parallels to Christ as *Deliverer*?

6. What did the Holy Spirit highlight to you in Exodus 16—18 through the reading or the teaching?

# Lesson 37: Exodus 19—20

*Deliverer*: Israel at Mt. Sinai: God's Treasure, Kingdom of Priests, and Holy Nation

## Teaching Notes

### Intro

Many will say Exodus 19 is the heart of the Pentateuch. We've gone through the Abrahamic Covenant and seen how, through Abraham, Isaac, and Jacob, God had a special plan for His people (Genesis 12:1–3). The Abrahamic Covenant does not stop until the Messiah comes back. But as the Abrahamic Covenant continues on, God decided to interject another covenant, the Mosaic Covenant. This is where Moses was used as a deliverer for God's people and for His *Seed*. The Israelites had been through the plagues and the parting of the Red Sea. They had daily manna and quail, and now God said, "I want to show you now that I am *with* you." Here Moses began to hear the voice of God even more clearly.

### Teaching

*Exodus 19:1–3*: The Israelites were in the wilderness of Sinai, where Moses was looking for the mountain God promised! Can you imagine what it would have been like for two million people to camp at the base of this mountain? The southeast part of Sinai Peninsula is called Jebel Musa, the "mountain of Moses." Josephus recorded that it was the highest mountain in the Peninsula. Verses 3–6 are the heart of the Pentateuch. God gave Moses the message to give to the Israelites. This was the same guy who said he couldn't talk, and now God was telling him to go communicate to everyone.

*Exodus 19:4–5*: Moses had his own speechwriter—God! Why use the imagery of the eagle? Wiersbe wrote, "The adult birds [eagles] stay near the fledglings and, if they fall, carry them on their strong wings until the young birds learn how to use their wings, ride the air current, and enjoy the abilities God gave them."[1] Wiersbe also says, "Eaglets illustrate three forms of freedom: (1) Freedom *from* (they are

---

[1] Warren W. Wiersbe, *Be Delivered (Exodus): Finding Freedom by Following God* (Colorado Springs: David C. Cook, 1998), 120.

175

out of the nest, which to us is redemption). (2) Freedom *in* (they are home in the air, which to us is maturity). (3) Freedom *to* (they can fulfill their purpose in life, which to us is ministry)."[2] God viewed the Israelites three ways. *First, they were God's special treasure*[3] (Deuteronomy 7:6; 14:2; Psalm 135:4). They didn't do anything to deserve it; God has chosen them. This was the Mosaic Covenant: Israel as God's treasured possession. God has not stopped viewing them as His treasured possession. God's hand was so clearly on Israel right here.

The Abrahamic Covenant is *unconditional*; it's by faith. God will pour out His blessing, making the descendants endless. The Mosaic Covenant is a *conditional* covenant, a covenant for a limited period of time. It began with Moses and ends with Christ. When Jesus came, the law was replaced with the New Covenant. The Mosaic Covenant that was being established was a means for sanctification, rules for living, and redemption for the people (Galatians 3:19.) The Mosaic Law was instituted until the Messiah would come. We needed something to serve as a guideline for our sins. The Mosaic Covenant was a track. The Israelites now had a responsibility to fulfill in order to receive God's blessings. The difference in this conditional covenant is that they were still God's people; they just missed out on what He had in store for them.

*Exodus 19:6: Second, they were God's kingdom of priests.*[4] This is the first time you'll see "kingdom" referring to God's rule through man on earth.[5] This happened as priests depended on their faith in God. The priests' role is to stand between God and the people. They were going to become a nation of mediators between God and other nations.[6] They were to be a nation that is different—a serving nation, not a ruling nation. Isaiah 61:6: "But you will be called the LORD's priests; they will speak of you as ministers of our God; you will eat the wealth of the nations, and they will boast in their riches." They had to change their mindset to "we're not going to have kings, but priests." Aaron and his sons became priests (Exodus 28—29). Aaron would carry the 12 tribes in stones on his breast piece every time he went before the Lord.

*Third, they were God's holy nation.*[7] The word "holy" means set apart or different. They were holy because they were devoting themselves to God and

---

[2] Wiersbe, 120.

[3] Thomas L. Constable, *Expository Notes of Dr. Thomas Constable: Exodus*, 173, https://planobiblechapel.org/tcon/notes/pdf/exodus.pdf.

[4] Constable, 173.

[5] Constable, 173–74.

[6] John I. Durham, *Exodus*, Word Biblical Commentary series (Waco: Word Books, 1987), 263; quoted in Constable, 174.

[7] Constable, 174.

separating themselves from sin. Six times in Leviticus it says, "Be holy for I am holy!" God reiterated in Exodus 22:31, "Be My holy people." The Israelites were going to reflect God's holiness. It is important to remember these three phrases are the heart of the Pentateuch: God's special treasure, His kingdom of priests, and His holy nation. God has not stopped viewing Israel as a holy nation, as a kingdom of priests, or as a special treasure. Constable wrote, "Israel could have become a testimony to the whole world, of how to live under the government of God."[8] But the problem was, over the course of time, they only experienced a partial blessing because they only showed a partial time of obedience.

*Exodus 19:7–12:* Moses delivered this speech with his three talking points: special treasure, kingdom of priests, holy nation. "However, they overestimated their own ability to keep the covenant, and they underestimated God's standards for them."[9] Because the Israelites agreed to these things, they needed to start this process. In verse 10, the Lord told Moses to "Consecrate the people today and tomorrow" by the Israelites bathing themselves and changing their clothes, which reflected a new beginning. On the third day, God would come down. Wiersbe points out that Moses put up barriers to keep the people away from the mountain and posted guards with authority to kill anyone who crossed the barriers. [10]

*Exodus 19:13–15:* God continued to put things in order to keep the Israelites from touching the mountain. At this point, all the Israelites knew that God could not be touched. But when the Messiah comes, it's the complete opposite! John 1:14 says, "The Word became flesh." In the Mosaic Covenant, there was a distance required to stay away from Yahweh the Almighty God. Matthew 1:23 emphasizes, "God *with* us." I understand why Jewish people sometimes have a hard time turning to the Messiah. Their mindset has always been that God is holy and can't be approached. But through the New Covenant, Jesus provides a way for us to approach God with boldness (Hebrews 10:19–25). No longer do we have this mountain or distance in front of us. Remember it took three days for this process to be completed. God issued a temporary prohibition against sexual relations as the Israelites went through the process of cleansing. God was not saying sex is bad but to keep their eyes on Him.

*Exodus 19:16–25:* The Israelites had to be consecrated. They'd washed their clothes, abstained from sexual relations, and had not touched the mountain. The cloud covered the mountain, and Moses shuddered (Hebrews 12:21). Moses

---

[8] Constable, 174

[9] Constable, 175.

[10] Wiersbe, 124.

spoke and the Lord addressed him. Again, Moses was back and forth from the people and back up to God on the mountain. Who were the priests at this point? Aaron and his sons hadn't been instituted yet. They were probably young men who offered sacrifices before God, probably the firstborns (Exodus 24:5). Exodus 19 shows us a covenant that was beginning to take place. There were two types of covenants in Moses' day[11]: Parity (a formal contract between two equals), and Suzerainty (a covenant between a sovereign and his subjects). The Suzerainty covenant had a preamble (v. 3), historical prologue (v. 4), statement of general principles (v. 5), consequences of obedience (vv. 5–6), and consequences of disobedience. The covenant here was totally familiar to the Israelites.

## Closing

*Exodus 20* outlines the Ten Commandments. There were a whole lot more than just ten. Wiersbe wrote, "They had documented 613 commands in the law, 248 positive and 365 are negative."[12] Over time, the Israelites begin to see that they couldn't keep this pace up. A *Deliverer* was needed to come in and pull them from this covenant to ultimately set them free.

### The Daily Word

Three months after their deliverance from Egypt, the children of Israel set up camp at Mount Sinai. God reminded them of their deliverance with a picture of His tender love for them, saying, "How I carried you on eagles' wings and brought you to Me." Then on the third day, as the consecrated people stood at the foot of the mountain, God revealed Himself in a powerful display. The mountain was in smoke. The Lord descended upon it in fire. The whole mountain quaked violently. The sound of a trumpet grew louder and louder.

Pause for a minute and imagine this: the tender love of a heavenly Father and the majestic power of an Almighty God. He alone is exalted over all. As you seek the Lord today, watch for Him to reveal Himself to you in tender love and powerful splendors.

**Mount Sinai was completely enveloped in smoke because the LORD came down on it in fire. Its smoke went up like the smoke of a furnace, and the whole mountain shook violently. As the sound of the trumpet grew louder and louder, Moses spoke and God answered him in the thunder. —Exodus 19:18–19**

---

[11] Constable, 176.

[12] Warren W. Wiersbe, *The Wiersbe Bible Commentary: Old Testament* (Colorado Springs: David C. Cook, 2007), 66.

Further Scripture: Exodus 19:4; 1 Chronicles 29:11; Isaiah 40:31

## Questions

1. What is the Mosaic covenant (begins in Exodus 19)? Has the Mosaic covenant ended? If so, when?

2. How did God see the Israelites according to Exodus 19:5–6? Do you see parallels to Christians today? (1 Peter 2:4–5, 9–10)

3. Do you think the Israelites responded to Moses' message of what the Lord commanded with honesty in Exodus 19:7–8?

4. Name the Ten Commandments. Why do you think God chose to put these in place?

5. Why did Jesus quote the Ten Commandments listed in Exodus 20:1–17 during His ministry? (Matthew 5:27; 15:4; 19:18–19)

6. How could you use the Ten Commandments to share Christ with someone?

7. What did the Holy Spirit highlight to you in Exodus 19—20 through the reading or the teaching?

# Lesson 38: Exodus 21

*Deliverer*: Ordinances Regarding Slaves and Personal Injury

## Teaching Notes

### Intro

Our whole theme for Exodus is "The *Deliverer*." Jesus was the one who delivered the people out of Egypt. Yes, He used Moses. But the big picture is that it was Jesus who sets the captives free (Luke 4). The Mosaic Covenant was a conditional covenant the Lord made with the Israelites. Exodus 20 states the Ten Commandments. God gave these key guidelines to the Israelites. Then He continued to go on and give a total of 613 ordinances.

### Teaching

*Exodus 21:1*: The Ten Commandments were good, but God had a whole lot more as well. What we're going to read now are specific cases that were given in more detail than the Ten Commandments. How does studying the ordinances reveal to us Jesus, the *Deliverer*? God was trying to govern their heart issues. He was trying to change their mindsets and thinking, which would lead to changing their heart condition. We have to remember, they've been wandering around the wilderness, and God wanted to create a culture for them.

*Exodus 21:2*: Verses 2–6 are about slavery. Why this mindset of the Hebrews having slaves? They just came out of slavery. It's actually more about the servant mindset than a slave. They were to be released after six years. Likely, the Hebrew slaves became slaves because they were indebted to someone. For example, Jacob worked for Laban in order to marry Rachel and Leah. Paul urged Philemon to treat Onesimus as a friend and brother as he worked for him (Philemon 15). Constable wrote, "Slavery as a social institution becomes evil when others disregard the human rights of slaves."[1] God was creating guardrails that value human rights.

---

[1] Thomas L. Constable, *Expository Notes of Dr. Thomas Constable: Exodus*, 204, https://planobiblechapel.org/tcon/notes/pdf/exodus.pdf.

*Exodus 21:3–6*: If a slave wanted to stay with his family, there was a procedure. The slave would have an ear pierced with an awl, which signified the slave belonged to his master for life. An awl is a long sharp tool used in leather working. Nelson writes, "The slave would be taken before judges, where he would be given the opportunity to declare his intentions." [2] The slave would be *intentionally* giving up his life to serve his master in order to stay with his wife and children.

MacArthur points out that at this point the slave would remain as a servant.[3] After coming out of the culture of slavery in Egypt (where the Israelites were treated harshly and put in bondage), God was teaching the Israelites that slaves and servants had lives of value. Servants and slaves were to be treated in this way, not like in Egypt.

*Exodus 21:7–10*: Now we are going to look at the female side of slavery. When a father sold his daughter, she had no authority. This was in the context of marriage. The father-in-law could not sell her to foreigners. If the daughter is sold, the father-in-law must treat her as a daughter, according to the customs. After being married to the son, the son can decide to get a second wife. He cannot treat his first wife differently from his second wife. He still has to provide food, clothing, and marital rights.

*Exodus 21:11*: If the woman was not provided for, she could leave. After six years, a male slave could leave, but this was the only time the female slave could leave. In Genesis, Leah gave Zilpah to Jacob as a wife (Genesis 30:9). Jacob then must treat Zilpah according to this law—the same way he treated Leah. God had to put ordinances in place to guide their behaviors.

*Exodus 21:12–14*: Now we are going to look at what was essentially capital punishment. Genesis 9:6 says, "Whoever sheds man's blood, his blood will be shed by man, for God made man in His image." Constable wrote, "God regarded the sanctity of human life greater than the sanctity of place."[4] In the ancient east, they could kill someone, leave, and hide. God's law required that the one who intentionally killed someone would die.

Unintentional homicide resulted in the banishment to cities of refuge. See Numbers 35 and Deuteronomy 19 for cities of refuge. Premeditated murder resulted in the killer being put to death. John Davis wrote, "Life, in essence, is

---

[2] Earl D. Radmacher, Ronald B. Allen, and H. Wayne House, eds., *Nelson's New Illustrated Bible Commentary* (Nashville: Thomas Nelson, 1999), 125.

[3] John F. MacArthur, *The MacArthur Bible Commentary* (Nashville: Thomas Nelson, 2005), 116.

[4] Constable, 206.

the property of God; the possession of it is leased to human beings for a number of years . . . [A killer has] violated one of the essential laws of God and forfeits the right to the possession of life."[5]

*Exodus 21:15–19*: One who struck his mother or father would be punished by death. Why was this so drastic? It was an act of breaking one of the Ten Commandments! God was establishing a culture of respect. The Code of Hammurabi, which was around during Babylonian times, stated that a person who struck his father would have his hand cut off. Kidnappers were also put to death. Where does kidnapping fit in the Ten Commandments? Kidnapping is stealing. Now we're getting into bodily punishment issues. If you got in a fight, you had to pay workman's compensation. Nobody can keep up with all of these laws! And if you were guilty, you'd be put to death. Praise the Lord for the Messiah, our *Deliverer*!

*Exodus 21:20–21*: If an owner kills his slave, his punishment is simply to lose his slave. Verse 21, "He is his owner's property." This is difficult. I thought we were discussing that slaves were not to be considered property, but servants? Moses wrote this. Didn't he kill someone?

*Exodus 21:22–23*: Life for life mentality here. People use this as a pro-abortion verse, because if the baby died, only a fine was required; but if the woman was harmed, it was eye for an eye, life for a life. The Lord knew from the very beginning that life was existent both in and outside the womb. A fetus is a person:

- Psalm 51:5: "I was sinful when my mother conceived me."
- Psalm 58:3: "The wicked go astray from the womb."
- Psalm 139:13–15: "You knit me together in my mother's womb."

*Exodus 21: 24–28*: How did this eye for eye, tooth for tooth work? Most commentators would say this was figurative, meaning you would pay for what you took. The more and more you study this culture, you see a lot about paying out for what was lost. For the rest of this, it's about taking ownership of what was done wrong.

*Exodus 21:33–36*: It is all about payment and giving compensation for what was done wrong. Everything was being made equal. You have to compensate fully. It was a justice deal.

---

[5] John Davis, *Moses and the Gods of Egypt* (Grand Rapids: Baker Book House, 1971), 221.

# Closing

There were so many ordinances that people just couldn't keep up with them—613 ordinances. The pressure that the Jewish people must carry today is a radical weight. That's a heavy weight that they may not even know the fullness of. Even if you can name all 613 ordinances, you can't keep them.

The deal is that we have been delivered from that weight! All of this is going to point to the coming Messiah, and our need for Him! Because he's already come, it's time to let these things go so we can walk in full freedom!

## The Daily Word

After God gave Moses the Ten Commandments on Mount Sinai, He detailed specific ordinances for Moses to share with the people. These ordinances were the framework for judging and resolving civil disputes. The Israelites were fresh out of slavery, and the Lord knew they needed this framework for living in their newfound freedom.

Where do you turn for the framework regarding right and wrong in your life? Do you seek after the world, or do you seek the Word of God for insight? The Word of God is living and effective and sharper than any double-edged sword (Hebrews 4:12). Seek God's Word for answers, and He will show you the way.

**These are the ordinances that you must set before them. —Exodus 21:1**

Further Scripture: Psalm 103:7; Psalm 119:105; Hebrews 4:12

## Questions

1. Exodus 21:17 was repeated in Leviticus 20:9 and was quoted by Jesus in Matthew 15:4 and Mark 7:10. What does it mean to curse your father or your mother?

2. What do you think, "Eye for eye, tooth for tooth, hand for hand, foot for foot," mean in Exodus 21:24? In Jesus' teaching in Matthew 5:38–42, how did He change this law?

3. In what way is Galatians 6:7 similar to or different from Exodus 21:23–25? (Romans 12:17–20)

4. God's first words from Sinai in Exodus 20:1 declared that He was, "The LORD your God," who brought them out of slavery. After the Ten Commandments were given, who was the first person/people whose rights were dealt with? Is this significant (Exodus 21:2–11)?

5. Moses' father-in-law Jethro, advised him to teach the statutes and laws to the people, and we see these written in Exodus 21—23 (Exodus 18:14–24). Who in your life do you seek counsel from? Do they point you to the Word of God?

6. What did the Holy Spirit highlight to you in Exodus 21 through the reading or the teaching?

# Lesson 39: Exodus 22

*Deliverer:* Ordinances Regarding Theft, Crops, and Personal Property

## Teaching Notes

### Intro

God was revealing himself through Abraham, Isaac, and Jacob and through the *Seed* of the woman. Yesterday we talked about the ordinances. God was intervening and implementing these conditions so the Israelites would know how to handle the situations they deal with.

### Teaching

*Exodus 22:1*: Verse 1 discusses stealing animals. Why so drastic? What happened to "cattle for cattle" or "a sheep for a sheep"? Animals were their livelihood—their means of living. Five times the cost for cattle, and four times for sheep.

Second Samuel 12:6 says, "Because he has done this thing and shown no pity, he must pay four lambs for that lamb." This was David unknowingly pronouncing judgment on himself for sleeping with Bathsheba. Wiersbe wrote, "The prophet Nathan saw King David as a sheep stealer and Bathsheba as a stolen lamb, for adultery is thievery" (1 Thessalonians 4:1–7).[1] David, because of this sin, experienced fourfold punishment:

- 2 Samuel 12:18—David's child died
- 2 Samuel 13:28–29—Amnon was murdered (David's son)
- 2 Samuel 18:14—Absalom was murdered (David's son)
- 2 Samuel 13:14—Tamar was raped (David's daughter)

Yes, this was practically talking about the sheep, but it was also revealing God's just nature and a spiritual principle.

---

[1] Warren W. Wiersbe, *The Wiersbe Bible Commentary: Old Testament* (Colorado Springs: David C. Cook, 2007), 186.

*Exodus 22:2–3*: If someone was breaking in at night and an Israelite killed him, there was no guilt. There was guilt, however, if there was bloodshed in daylight. Wiersbe wrote, "To kill the thief in daylight would be an unnecessary expression of revenge."[2] A thief had to make full restitution or be sold as a slave.

*Exodus 22:4–5*: Repayment was double. The ordinances in verses 1–4 were about stealing animals. One was to repay with the *best* of his own field. There were no fences back then, just boundary markers (Deuteronomy 19:14). Because there were no fences, naturally the animals will just come across the boundary. Proverbs 22:28 says, "Don't move an ancient boundary marker that your father set up."

*Exodus 22:6–8*: The one who started a fire had to repay the damage. The word meaning "full restitution" is seen six times in Exodus 22. The Hebrew word *shalan* means, "to make whole or complete." It's tied closely to the word "shalom" for peace. When you bring full restitution, that peace begins to come into play. It all comes down to a heart condition.

*Exodus 22:9*: We've gone from stealing animals to stealing crops, and now we're talking about personal belongings. Right away I think of Solomon and his wisdom with the baby (1 Kings 3:16–28). Who is really right, and where's the heart condition?

It also makes me think of Joseph and his brothers who sold Joseph into slavery and then lied to their father (Genesis 37:25–36). I want to keep going back to the heart condition. It's weird to me how jealousy and bitterness led the brothers in doing this to Joseph and their father. When we see wrong behavior (for example, stealing from your neighbor), there's a heart condition underneath it.

*Exodus 22:10–15*: No restitution was needed if there was truly no wrong done. If someone was entrusted with something, and they didn't take care of it, they had to pay it back. The loss was covered by the rental price. Remember, the Israelites were wandering around in the wilderness, so they needed structure and regulations.

*Exodus 22:16–17*: A girl was the property of her father. When a young couple had premarital sex, a man then had to marry the girl and give a dowry to the father-in-law. If the father refused to give the daughter to him, the man still had to pay the bridal price. The bridal price could be 100 silver shekels (Deuteronomy 22:19).

---

[2] Wiersbe, 186.

In our generation, for some reason, people think it's ok to have premarital sex and live together before marriage. It's sin, and it will lead to all sorts of problems. Genesis 2:24 states that when two people have sex, they become one flesh. God designed it for one man and one woman. Look at Sodom and Gomorrah; God did not design it for man and man or woman and woman (Genesis 19). The body of Christ needs to begin declaring the truth.

*Exodus 22:18–24*: Black magic was an attempt to override God's will and was punishable by death. Sexual intercourse with animals was punishable by death. In all of this, the greatest temptation Israel had was idolatry.

God said, "I want to protect the vulnerable—the foreigners, the widows and orphans." God would hear their cries and His anger would burn. If they didn't care for widows and orphans, they would be killed; and then their wives and children would become widows and orphans.

*Exodus 22:25–27*: Proverbs 28:8, "Whoever increases his wealth through excessive interest, collects it for one who is kind to the poor." If the Israelites would focus on the Lord and not themselves, they would naturally bless others. Quit thinking about yourself but think of others! That's really Jesus' message: love God and love others.

*Exodus 22:28–30*: In Acts 23:4–5, Paul apologized for speaking against the high priest (referencing Exodus 22). God's commands: be generous, don't delay the obedience, let the animals get stronger for seven days, and don't try to hold back what I'm asking of you.

*Exodus 22:31*: Finally, God said, "Be My holy people." Remember the things from the heart of the Pentateuch (Exodus 19:5–6).

- You're My special treasure.
- You're a kingdom of priests.
- You're a holy nation.

God commanded, don't eat the meat of a mauled animal—you are a holy person. The righteous doesn't have to beg for food (Psalm 37). God was going to provide food for them.

# Closing

These ordinances continually point the Israelites back to the Lord. God was saying: "Do you remember how I've delivered you through the innocent lamb? Through the hyssop and the blood on the post? Through the staff that has set all of you free from the plagues? Through the pillar of cloud by day and fire by night? I want you to act like I've delivered you! I want you to act like I've got your back in the wilderness. I will take care of you." God is in all of it. All of this points to the Messiah.

## The Daily Word

The Lord continued to give Moses ordinances for the people of Israel. The Lord knew the nature of His people; He cared for them and explained what consequences would follow their actions. And then, in the middle of explaining the ordinances to Moses, the Lord revealed His character and His heart.

Better than any earthly father, God is your heavenly Father, and He loves you. If you cry out to the Lord, He will listen to you. He is compassionate. He cares for you, and He understands your needs. He longs for you to call out to Him, and He promises He is there to rescue you.

**If you ever take your neighbor's cloak as collateral, return it to him before sunset. For it is his only covering; it is the clothing for his body. What will he sleep in? And if he cries out to Me, I will listen because I am compassionate. —Exodus 22:26–27**

Further Scripture: Psalm 91:15; Psalm 103:8; 2 Corinthians 1:3

## Questions

1. Ordinances are given in Exodus 22:7–8 in regard to a man being a steward of his neighbor's money or goods. How do you take care of what's put in your charge?

2. Several of the ordinances in Exodus 22 deal with theft, and one of the Ten Commandments is, "You shall not steal." In light of Luke 6:29b, how should we respond to someone who has stolen from us? Would this be difficult for you to do?

3. Does God's degree of protection of foreigners, orphans, and widows in Exodus 22:21–24 surprise you? Explain why you think He is so protective of them (Deuteronomy 10:18; 24:19; Psalm 68:5; Isaiah 1:17; James 1:27). How does this challenge you?

4. The Israelites were warned in Exodus 22:28 not to curse God or the ruler of their people. Do you think this applies even if a ruler is corrupt? (1 Kings 21:10; Acts 23:5; Romans 13:1–5)

5. In Exodus 22:31, God called men to be set apart/different: to not eat the meat that was torn by beasts in the field. What else comes to your mind when you read the words, "You shall be holy to Me"? (Leviticus 11:44–45; Psalm 96:9; Hebrews 12:14; 1 Peter 1:16)

6. What did the Holy Spirit highlight to you in Exodus 22 through the reading or the teaching?

# Lesson 40: Exodus 23—24

*Deliverer:* Festivals of Unleavened Bread, Harvest, and Ingathering

## Teaching Notes

### Intro

At Mount Sinai, God gave Moses not just the Ten Commandments but also specific ordinances for how to deal with specific situations. Yesterday, we talked about ordinances dealing with theft of animals, crops, and personal belongings. In all of this, God wants us to be holy.

### Teaching

*Exodus 23:1–9:* These laws are about honesty and justice. These ordinances are harder to live by than to read. They help us to overcome sin. An example of this would be Jezebel, who did what this ordinance warns about; she integrated herself into the situation and killed the innocent and just (1 Kings 21:7–10). The point here is don't kill the innocent and just. Then the Lord said to not take a bribe. There are worlds out there living by injustice and bribes, and God doesn't want that to happen.

*Exodus 23:10–11:* Verses 10–17 talk about the feasts. The Lord commanded the Israelites to leave their land to rest in the seventh year. Why? So the poor among them could eat from their fields. They're actually still in the wilderness, not yet in the land where this will take place. The principle is, while you rest, God will use that to bless others.

*Exodus 23:12–14:* God gave everybody a time to breath, even animals, slaves, and foreigners. God reminded His people throughout these ordinances—No idols! God wanted the Israelites to celebrate a festival for Himself three times a year.

*Exodus 23:15:* *The Festival of Unleavened Bread* celebrates no sin. Leaven (yeast) is a symbol of sin. The Lord commanded the Israelites to find an unblemished lamb on the tenth day and sacrifice it on the fourteenth day. The festival began on the Passover (day 14) and lasted 15–21 days. The month of Abib was roughly in March or April. The exodus had begun! That's what all 12 tribes were to celebrate three times a year. God had set them free! (Exodus 12:15–16; Leviticus 23:6; Numbers 28:17)

Over and over, Moses wrote about this festival. In order to connect with the Jewish people, we need to understand the festivals! Because of the Passover and the Exodus, we have a Messiah! We need to understand our own heritage!

*Exodus 23:16a*: *The Festival of Harvest* has a time frame of 50 days after Passover (May/June-ish). It was also known as the Feast of Weeks and Pentecost. All 12 tribes were to celebrate! This happens when the firstfruits of the harvest are ready (Exodus 34:22; Leviticus 23:15–21). The Israelites were to bring two loaves of bread (with yeast), seven unblemished lambs, one young bull, and two rams (these are the firstfruits to present to the Lord). God said, "Don't forget what I've done." The Day of Pentecost was the day the Holy Spirit came to the Church (Acts 2:1). They celebrate this festival for 50 days, seven weeks from Passover to Pentecost, by bringing the best of the best to the Lord in the festival. Don't hold back what you're presenting to the Lord!

*Exodus 23:16b*: *The Festival of Ingathering* is also known as the Festival of Booths or Tabernacles. The time frame for this festival is September/October (Deuteronomy 16:13; Leviticus 23:34). The Israelites were celebrating how God brought them out of the 40 years in the wilderness where they lived in booths/tabernacles/tents. In Israel today, they celebrate by building little booths on their balconies and sidewalks. They're celebrating that God delivered them from 40 years in the wilderness.

*Exodus 23:17–19*: The women and children were not excluded from these festivals. The fat was the best part of the offering. Young goats were a favorite food of the people. To cook it in milk made it taste better, but to cook the goat in the milk of its mother would reveal an attitude of sin in the heart. And it was reflective of a Canaanite ceremony. Wiersbe wrote, "[this] milk was then sprinkled on the trees and fields to help promote fertility."[1] God had to explain these things. One commentator writes, "This was disrespect for the God-given relationship between parent and offspring."[2]

---

[1] Warren W. Wiersbe, *Be Delivered (Exodus): Finding Freedom by Following God* (Colorado Springs: David C. Cook, 1998), 145.

[2] F. B. Meyer, *A Devotional Commentary on Exodus* (Grand Rapids: Kregel, 1978), 270.

*Exodus 23:20*: The Angel was going before the Israelites and then would move behind them at the Red Sea. Eleven times in the Old Testament the Angel shows up (the pre-incarnate Christ) (Genesis 32:1–2, 24–32; 48:16; Exodus 3; 14:19; 23:20; Joshua 5:13–15; Judges 6:11, 22; 13:3–4; 1 Kings 19:7; Isaiah 37:6; Daniel 3:25). God was present with Abraham, Isaac, and Jacob, and He was going to do the same with Moses and His people.

*Exodus 23:21–29*: Jesus was showing up for the Israelites (Jude 5)! The Lord was the one who was delivering His people from Egypt (Isaiah 7:18; Deuteronomy 7:20). God was the one who went ahead. God's timing is so good! We have to trust Him!

*Exodus 23:30–33*: Let things happen in God's timing, even if it's slow. In life, who wants little by little? Everybody wants the land now. Meyers wrote, "'Little by little' does the work of God proceed through the individual soul. 'Little by little' do the conquests of the cross win over the world. 'Little by little' is the unfolding purpose of Redemption made manifest to men and angels."[3] Little by little let the purpose of redemption manifest itself throughout the earth. Little by little God has a plan. We want it all now, but God has it differently.

God set the borders for the land. He kept reminding them: Keep your eyes on Me, not on other gods, or it will be a trap. Over and over again, God said, "I'm with you, just trust Me in the timing and keep your eyes on Me; celebrate Me through the festivals, and I'll go with you one day at a time."

*Exodus 24*: Moses told the elders all of the ordinances. They said, "We'll do it!" and set up an altar and performed offerings. They read the covenant and sprinkled the blood on the people. Moses and Joshua went up. Moses in verse 18 goes up into the cloud where the Lord was and stayed there for 40 days and 40 nights.

## Closing

As you go through the readings of Exodus, the Lord will speak to you about what you need to hear. Keep pressing in. Even in the ordinances, God wants to speak to you. I'm greatly encouraged by how God says, "Celebrate all that I've done in your life. And as you do, remember, I'm with you, little by little."

## The Daily Word

After Moses shared the entirety of the law with the Israelites, they agreed to do all the Lord had spoken and be obedient. Then Moses went up the mountain where

---

[3] Meyer, 281–82.

the glory of the Lord rested on Mount Sinai, and a cloud covered it. To the eyes of the people, the appearance of the glory of the Lord was like a consuming fire.

Do you ever picture God as a consuming fire, able to consume and utterly destroy? It's an image of God deserving of our reverence and awe. He will conquer our enemies and wipe out evil. Even so, grace is available to all who receive it freely through His Son Jesus. Allow the Consuming Fire to fight for you while you stand in awe of His power.

**The appearance of the LORD's glory to the Israelites was like a consuming fire on the mountaintop. —Exodus 24:17**

Further Scripture: Deuteronomy 9:3; Psalm 50:3; Hebrews 12:28–29

## Questions

1. What are some laws God gave in Exodus 23:1–9? Knowing Jesus is the same yesterday, today, and forever (Hebrews 13:8), how do these laws translate today?

2. How did the law of the sabbatical year set the Israelites apart (Exodus 23:10–11)? Were the Israelites successful in keeping this law? What was their punishment? (Leviticus 26:32–35; 2 Chronicles 36:21)

3. What were the three festivals the Israelites were commanded to keep? What is the significance of each one (Exodus 23:14–16)?

4. In Exodus 23:16, God said to bring the firstfruits of their labor they had sown in the field. What do you think this looked like?

5. What are your thoughts on the angel in Exodus 23:20 being the pre-incarnate Christ? What were the blessings and promises given by God through the angel (Exodus 23:22–30)?

6. In John 1:18, it states no one has seen God at any time. That being true, what do you think they saw in Exodus 24:10–11?

7. What did the Holy Spirit highlight to you in Exodus 23—24 through the reading or the teaching?

# Lesson 41: Exodus 25

*Deliverer*: Directions for the Tabernacle:
Ark, Mercy Seat, Table, and Lampstand

## Teaching Notes

### Intro

In Exodus, we looked at the *Deliverer*, Christ, who will deliver His people out of bondage. The Israelites were wandering around the wilderness, and God began to give them direction. He gave them the Ten Commandments and ordinances about how to live. He also revealed His heart to them; they were His treasure, kingdom of priests, and holy nation.

In Exodus 24:18, Moses had received all commandments and ordinances, and entered the cloud as he went up the mountain. He remained there 40 days and 40 nights.

### Teaching

*Exodus 25:1*: The Lord revealed something to Moses that was absolutely incredible. He revealed how He was going to dwell among His people. At this point, the Israelites weren't even allowed to touch the mountain, remember?

*Exodus 25:2*: Moses was to take an offering from everyone willing to give. This was a form of worship. Sometimes it's easier to give than to obey. God even calls it out, "I desire obedience more than sacrifice." God wanted to take an offering for a place where the Israelites could experience God's presence.

*Exodus 25:3–7*: Moses collected specific items for the offering. The Israelites had to make their colors: blue (shellfish), purple (snails), and scarlet (powdered eggs and worms). Moses also collected fine linen; the Egyptians had a good reputation for fine linen. Where do you think all of these offerings came from? Egypt (Exodus 12:35–36)!

It was never the Israelites' money anyway. Our money is not ours. You become a funnel as finances come in and out for how the Lord wants to work in and through your life. The abundance of items the Israelites brought for the making of the sanctuary is an incredible picture that people must be willing to give. There was more than enough (Exodus 36:3–7). To me, that is people giving from their heart (2 Corinthians 9:7). People were bringing specific things for a specific purpose.

*Exodus 25:8–9*: There are four terms Scripture uses for what the people were going to be building:

(1) *Sanctuary* is symbolic and means a center for His presence where the Shekinah glory will dwell. This is the same mentality as the holy ground at the burning bush. Glory means "weight." You feel the weight of His presence.

(2) *Tabernacle* is the same thing as sanctuary, just different terminology. This has the same mentality as a dwelling place for God. It looked no different from other nomad tents.

(3) *Tent of Meeting:* This is another term for the sanctuary or the tabernacle (Exodus 26:36; 29:42; 35:21).

(4) *Tabernacle of Testimony:* All four of these are different words for the same place (Exodus 38:21; Numbers 9:15). Every term implies God's presence is dwelling amongst the people. God was going to get more specific about what was going inside the tabernacle.

*Exodus 25:10–15*: The first thing made was the Ark of the Covenant, an "ark of acacia wood." Acacia wood is straight, not porous, and not susceptible to mold or insects. Acacia is hard-grained and orange-brown in color. It was covered with gold. Joshua 2:1 mentions an acacia grove (called Shittam in some Bible versions). The Israelites were commanded not to touch the Ark. Remember, Uzzah was immediately struck down when he touched the Ark (2 Samuel 6:6–7).

*Exodus 25:16–22*: Inside the Ark of the Covenant were the Ten Commandments (tablets of testimony), the golden pot of manna (Exodus 16:32–34), and Aaron's budded staff (Numbers 17). Then the Israelites made a mercy seat of pure gold. MacArthur explained that the "lid or cover of the ark was the 'mercy seat' or the place at which atonement took place. Blood from the sacrifices [on the mercy seat] stood between God and the broken law of God."[1] "Mercy" means, propitiation or sacrifice. Jesus became our propitiation. The mercy seat served as the propitiation for the Israelites, but it no longer exists (1 John 2:2). *Jesus* Himself is the propitiation for our sins! This is the beginning stage of pointing people to the

---

[1] John MacArthur, *The MacArthur Bible Commentary* (Nashville: Thomas Nelson, 2005), 121.

Messiah! A lamb would be sacrificed once a year, on the Day of Atonement (Yom Kippur), and its blood would be put on the mercy seat.

*Exodus 25:23–30*: The Israelites built the Table of Showbread (the table of acacia wood). The plates, cups, pitchers, and bowls were made out of pure gold, and held the bread of the Presence on the table before God at all time. Only the priests ate the bread of the Presence (Leviticus 24:5–9). Twelve loaves of bread were placed there to represent the 12 tribes. This is expressive of Christ ultimately becoming our Bread of Life. When Jesus said this to the Jews, He was pointing to the bread of the Presence, which they were familiar with (John 6:32–36). All these aspects of the earthly tabernacle pointed to the Messiah.

*Exodus 25:31–40*: Moses was receiving these instructions spelled out to him by God. The Israelites made a golden lampstand that had six branches, three on each side, in addition to the center lamp. It is also called the Menorah. They would see this light as they walked into the tabernacle. It was made of 75 pounds of gold and was the light for the priests who were serving in the Holy Place. The oil was essential to keep it burning. Part of the priest's role was to keep the lamp burning continually (Exodus 27:20–21). Jesus said, "I am the light of the world" (John 8:12). The golden lampstand never went out, and Jesus says the same thing: "You will never walk in darkness again."

God warned the Israelites to be careful to make everything according to the patterns shown. God showed Moses the pattern on the mountain. Moses was trusted to deliver God's people and part of that process was to assist the Israelites into His Presence.

## Closing

Hebrews 8:5–6 says: "These serve as a copy and shadow of the heavenly things, as Moses was warned when he was about to complete the tabernacle. For God said, 'Be careful that you make everything according to the pattern that was shown to you on the mountain'. But Jesus has now obtained a superior ministry, and to that degree He is the mediator of a better covenant, which has been legally enacted on better promises."

Moses' pattern that he received from the Lord was a copy and shadow of the better pattern, *Jesus*!

# The Daily Word

While on Mount Sinai, the Lord gave Moses specific instructions for construction of the Ark of the Covenant. The Ark served as the place for the presence of God to be with the Israelites at all times. It seems somewhat bazaar for God to place Himself in a tent and inside a box so He could be near His complaining and grumbling people. But our God is humble and merciful. He draws near to sinners.

Thankfully for the new covenant believers, God continues to promise He will always be with us and dwell within us as the power of the Holy Spirit. Today, give thanks for God's presence, which is always with you.

**They are to make a sanctuary for Me so that I may dwell among them. You must make it according to all that I show you—the pattern of the tabernacle as well as the pattern of all its furnishings. —Exodus 25:8–9**

Further Scripture: Exodus 25:22; Psalm 139:7–10; Matthew 11:29

## Questions

1. God is a very detailed God, and Moses took good notes. Practically speaking, how do you suppose Moses kept up with all the details God gave him (Hebrews 8:5)? Do you write down what the Lord tells you?

2. Are you able to describe a few ways the Ark of the Covenant points to Christ? If so, what are they (Hebrews 8:5)?

3. In Exodus 25:1–2, who was instructed to give an offering? When you feel prompted to give an offering to the Lord, how do you respond (2 Corinthians 9:6–7)?

4. What was the ultimate purpose for the tabernacle?

5. God told Moses to put the Testimony (Law) inside the Ark before the law was even given. Why do you think God did this? Do we have enough faith to walk in obedience before we completely understand God's purpose? Why or why not (2 Corinthians 5:7)?

6. What did the Holy Spirit highlight to you in Exodus 25 through the reading or the teaching?

# Lesson 42: Exodus 26

*Deliverer:* Directions for the Tabernacle:
Curtains, Planks, Bars, Veil, and Screen

## Teaching Notes

### Intro

The Lord encountered Moses on the mountain for 40 days and 40 nights, while He revealed to Moses the pattern for building the tabernacle (also called the sanctuary, the tent of meeting). The Ark consisted of the Ten Commandments, a golden pot of manna, and Aaron's budding staff. On top of the Ark was the mercy seat.

In the tabernacle, there was the Table of Showbread and the Golden Lampstand. Exodus 26 is the continuation of what Moses was told to build.

### Teaching

*Exodus 26:1–6:* The first 14 verses give details about the curtains. The colors blue, purple, and scarlet are used 20 times in Exodus in this specific order. The design of cherubim was to be worked into the curtains (Genesis 3:24; Isaiah 37:16). Cherubim are the representation of God's presence wherever they go. God was describing it from His view. There were to be ten curtains of the blue, purple, and scarlet for the tabernacle itself.

*Exodus 26:7–14:* There were to be 11 "curtains of goat hair for a tent over the tabernacle" (v. 7). Whenever the prophets put on goat hair, it always symbolized separation from sin (Leviticus 16). These curtains were made of rich black fabric and were costly. The covering of ram skins and a covering of manatee (or badger) skins were even waterproofed.

*Exodus 26:15–25:* These verses describe the planks of acacia wood for the tabernacle. Were these planks solid boards or frames? Tenon and mortise were the parts that fit the planks together. If this mattered to God's chosen people in the Old Testament, it should matter to us. I think we've blown off the Tanakh and the Torah for too long. This is important to God!

*Exodus 26:26–30*: God loves detail. He loves when you do something, and you do it well. God said to Moses, "I want you to remember and set this up exactly how I've told you to do it!" Sometimes God tells us to do something, and we feel like we can cut corners. But Psalm 119:25 says, "Revive me according to Your word" (NASB). When you work through the details, He has something way bigger in mind.

*Exodus 26:31–35*: These verses gave instructions for the veil. It was to be blue, purple, and scarlet "with a design of cherubim worked into it" (v. 31). The Israelites were to put the Ark of the Testimony behind the veil. The veil was to create a separation between the Holy Place and the Most Holy Place. The Most Holy Place (or Holy of Holies) contained the Ark of the Covenant and the mercy seat. The Holy Place was where the lampstand and the table were located. According to Arthur Pink:

"This order 'blue, purple and scarlet' is repeated over 20 times in Exodus and is never varied . . . The 'blue' is the color of heaven and speaks of Christ as the Son of God. The 'scarlet' is both the color of sacrifice and human glory. The 'purple' is a color produced by mixing together blue and scarlet. Without the purple, the blue and the scarlet would have presented too vivid a contrast to the eye; the purple coming in between them shaded off the one extreme from the other. Now the antitype of these colors is found in the incarnate Christ. He was both God and man, and yet these two vastly dissimilar natures unite in one perfect Person. The 'purple,' then, coming in between the 'blue' and the 'scarlet' tells on the perfect blending or union of His two natures."[1]

When Jesus died, the veil was torn! And we now have access to the New Covenant. We now have access to the Presence of God (Matthew 27:50–51). God told Moses to construct the veil with blue, purple, and scarlet, but He had His Son in mind the whole time (Mark 15:37–38). For the Jew, the access to the Father is now split and torn and their religion is now done (Luke 23:45–46).

The veil is all about Jesus! It represents His flesh (Psalms 27:4). This is what the Israelites wanted—to be in His presence in the tabernacle (Psalm 26:8). But now *Jesus* is the way, the truth, and the life. The Orthodox Jews long to be in the courts of the Lord, but it's no longer there! Jesus has torn the veil. We come into the Presence of God through Christ.

All of this points to the Messiah, and it started through a mountaintop experience on which God revealed the pattern to Moses. Ultimately, God knew His Son would cry out, the veil would be torn, and the Jews would no longer have to seek His presence in that house. They would have it in Christ.

---

[1] Arthur W. Pink, *Exposition of the Gospel of John* (Grand Rapids: Zondervan, 1975), 600.

All of the Psalms cry out for more of the tabernacle, more of the Presence. And Jesus said, "I am more." It's a pretty awesome picture that the tabernacle points to Christ:

- All of His fullness now dwells in Christ (Colossians 1:19)!
- Everything we think is of God is now in Christ (Colossians 2:9).
- We have access to everything in Christ (Colossians 2:3).
- If you're seeking Him, you'll find every single spiritual blessing (Colossians 3:1).
- We don't need to go to a sanctuary, a tabernacle, or a tent. All of the blessings now come through Christ (Ephesians 1:3). [2]

## Closing

Sometimes it's hard to imagine that through the tabernacle, the Lord would point all this out. Slow down. If we look deep enough, we'll see the Messiah there because He is the Word of God.

## The Daily Word

The Lord gave Moses detailed instructions for building the Tabernacle and creating the veil, which would hold the Ark of the Covenant. The Tabernacle served as a church in the wilderness for the Israelites, a place where the Lord's presence stayed among the people. In the construction details, the number fifty was used several times and was often seen when two things are united or joined together.

The number fifty is a definition of the word *Pentecost* and can signify fullness. Fifty is related to the coming of God's Holy Spirit and symbolizes deliverance or freedom from a burden. As you study the Tabernacle and the Lord's presence among His people, pray for the Holy Spirit to bring freedom to your life, releasing you from any burdens you carry. May you find joy in the presence of the Lord.

Make 50 loops on the one curtain and make 50 loops on the edge of the curtain in the second set, so that the loops line up together. Also make 50 gold clasps and join the curtains together with the clasps, so that the tabernacle may be a single unit. —Exodus 26:5–6

Further Scripture: Exodus 26:10–11; Psalm 16:11; Colossians 1:19–20

---

[2] Warren W. Wiersbe, *The Bible Expository Commentary: Genesis–Deuteronomy* (Colorado Springs: David C. Cook, 2001), 239.

## Questions

1. In Exodus 26:1, God instructed Moses about the ten curtains. What were the three colors God told Moses to use? What do you think was the significance of these three colors?

2. In addition to the ten curtains already discussed, Moses was instructed to make 11 more. What were the reasons for these additional curtains (Exodus 26:7)?

3. Silver is mentioned often in Scripture, as it is in Exodus 26:19. How do you see silver being used in the following Scriptures? (Exodus 21:32; Leviticus 5:15, 27:3; Numbers 18:16; Matthew 26:15)

4. What went on the Ark of the Testimony in the Most Holy Place (Exodus 26:34)? How does this point to Christ (Romans 3:23–26)?

5. Only the high priest could enter the Holy of Holies once a year (Hebrews 9:7). Knowing this, how does the truth in Hebrews 9:12 encourage you? How could you use this to encourage someone else (Hebrews 10:11–14)?

6. What did the Holy Spirit highlight to you in Exodus 26 through the reading or the teaching?

# Lesson 43: Exodus 27—28
*Deliverer:* The Priestly Garments

## Teaching Notes

### Intro

We're continuing to look at the instructions the Lord gave Moses for building the tabernacle. Exodus 26 described how the ten inner curtains and 11 outer curtains were designed and installed over the upright planks and cross bars. God gives details of the veil and the embroidered screen for the entrance. Exodus 27 described the altar of burnt offering and its utensils, the courtyard, and the lampstand filled with oil. God instructed Moses to appoint Aaron and his sons to serve as the holy priests to operate and maintain the holy things inside the tabernacle.

As a quick review, in Exodus 19:3–6, God referred to the Israelites in three different ways: (1) as God's special treasure, (2) as a kingdom of priests (all of the Israelites were priests in so many regards, but God also established specific priesthood in the Levites), and (3) a holy nation.

### Teaching

*Exodus 28:1:* Following God's instructions, Moses appointed his brother Aaron and his four sons (Moses' nephews) to serve as priests before God. Constable gave four specific roles of the priests: (1) maintaining the holy place of the tabernacle by burning incense, trimming the lamps, and replacing the showbread; (2) maintaining the tabernacle courtyard, including offering sacrifices, keeping the fire burning, and removing the ashes; (3) inspecting and appraising the people and their sacrifices; and (4) teaching the Mosaic Law, counseling the people, and deciding difficult cases.[1]

Nadab and Abihu offered unauthorized fire in the tabernacle and were burned to death before the Lord (Leviticus 10:1–2). Following that incident, Eleazar and Ithamar served as priests according to the instructions God set forth. The role of the priests was to serve God, which was emphasized no less than five times in Exodus and Leviticus. The rest of this chapter described their priestly garments, which would become their uniform for serving.

---

[1] Thomas L. Constable, *Expository Notes of Dr. Thomas Constable: Exodus*, 251, https://planobiblechapel.org/tcon/notes/pdf/exodus.pdf.

*Exodus 28:2*: God then gave Moses specific instructions for making holy garments for the priests. Wiersbe said these holy garments "gave the priests dignity and honor . . . revealed spiritual truths relating to their ministry . . . and if the priests didn't wear the special garments, they might die."[2]

If you're not focused on your role to serve God, it can go by the wayside. Ezekiel said the priests permitted people to worship idols, and the Israelites were sent into exile in Babylon as a result. As leaders inside the church, this is a serious responsibility. We don't want to lead God's people by the wayside. That's why we need revival.

*Exodus 28:3–5*: Moses conveyed the instructions to skilled craftsmen who then created the priests' clothing: "a breastpiece, an ephod, a robe, a specially woven tunic, a turban, and a sash . . . [using] gold; blue, purple, and scarlet yarn; and fine linen" (vv. 4–5). Remember, the blue-purple-scarlet represents Christ in His humanity and divinity.

*Exodus 28:6–14*: These garments were so important that the priests could be killed if they didn't wear them (Exodus 28:43). The Ephod was made with fine linen and "embroidered with gold, and with blue, purple, and scarlet yarn" (v. 6). It was joined together by two shoulder pieces and held in place by an "artistically woven waistband" (v. 8). An onyx stone was engraved and attached to each shoulder with gold filigree settings. The onyx stone on the right shoulder was engraved with the names of these six tribes: Reuben, Simeon, Levi, Judah, Dan, and Naphtali (who were Jacob's first six sons). The onyx stone on the left should was engraved with the names Gad, Asher, Issachar, Zebulun, Joseph, and Benjamin (Jacob's younger sons). As the high priest, Aaron would carry these stones on his shoulders as a memorial to the Israelites. Filigree is delicate jewelry metalwork made with tiny beads or twisted thread, or a combination of both, arranged in artistic motifs and soldered together or to the surface of an object. In addition to the settings, gold filigree was used to create two braided cords that were also attached to the settings. Aaron's garments would remind him of his role to present the people to the Lord.

*Exodus 28:15–21*: The embroidered breastpiece was "square and folded double, nine inches long and nine inches wide" (v. 16) and was made with the same materials and workmanship as the ephod. The breastpiece was used for making decisions. It contained four rows of three stones set in gold filigree, with each

---

[2] Warren W. Wiersbe, *The Bible Exposition Commentary: Genesis–Deuteronomy* (Colorado Springs: David C. Cook, 2001), 240.

different stone engraved with the name of one of the tribes of Israel. Therefore, when the priest entered the holy place, he carried the names of the tribes on his shoulders and on his heart. Malachi 3:17 says, "'They will be Mine,' says the LORD of Hosts, 'a special possession on the day I am preparing. I will have compassion on them as a man has compassion on his son who serves him.'" The term "special possession" can mean special jewels.

*Exodus 28:22–28*: The breastpiece was attached to the ephod at the shoulders and the waistband with gold braided chains threaded through gold rings on its corners. Look at the detailed instructions God gave to Moses. Everything had to be carefully made according to God's design.

*Exodus 28:29–30*: Whenever Aaron entered the sanctuary, he carried the names of the tribes over his heart. What did it look like when Jesus and Paul carried people in their hearts? When we carry people in our hearts before God?

Within the breastpiece, the priest carried the Urim and Thummim to be used for making decisions. The Urim began with the first letter of the Hebrew alphabet and the Thummim began with the last letter of the Hebrew alphabet. Some think these items represented casting lots: Urim for "no," and Thummim for "yes." All we know for certain is that somehow God spoke through these instruments to provide divine guidance for the Israelites (Leviticus 8:8; 1 Samuel 28:6).

*Exodus 28:31–35*: The robe was made from blue yarn. It was worn under the ephod, the breastpiece, and the shoulder pieces. The hem of the robe was decorated with gold bells alternated with pomegranates made from blue, purple, and scarlet yarn. The priests wore the robe whenever they ministered, and the bells would sound as they entered and exited the sanctuary of the Lord. Why? If the bells made no sound, the people would know the priest died in the Most Holy Place. They tied a long rope to the priests' ankle in case he died while in the Most Holy Place then they could pull him out without having to go inside.

*Exodus 28:36–38*: A pure gold medallion engraved with HOLY TO THE LORD was fastened to a blue cord and attached to the turban. The priest wore this to be acceptable to the Lord and so they could "bear the guilt connected with the holy offerings that the Israelites consecrate" (v. 38).

*Exodus 28:39–43*: God included instructions for the priests' tunic, turban, sash, and headband, also made from fine linen and beautifully embroidered, to give the priests "glory and beauty" (v. 40). To cover their nakedness, the priests wore linen undergarments from the waist to the thighs. Moses was commanded to "anoint, ordain, and consecrate" Aaron and his sons to serve God as priests. Whenever the priests entered the tent of meeting or approached the altar, they had to wear these garments so they would not die.

## Closing

The priests had to come to the table with a pure heart, represent the people without guile, and worship without deviating from the commands. Jesus is our High Priest. We no longer need the high priests who had to enter the tabernacle for the people because we have Jesus, our forever High Priest. Hebrews 4:14 confirms that Jesus is our High Priest.

Hebrews 2:17: "Therefore, He had to be like His brothers in every way, so that He could become a merciful and faithful high priest in service to God, to make propitiation for the sins of the people."

## The Daily Word

God gave Moses detailed instructions for building the courtyard of the tabernacle. The tabernacle was a place for the people to present themselves before the Lord. Only the priests could approach the altar, and they had to wear very specific priestly clothing.

As a believer in Christ, you are a priest with Christ in you, set aside from others. You are clothed in garments of salvation and robes of righteousness. It's nothing you have to earn or even put on yourself. It's a gift from Him. Live freely, clothed in the righteousness of Christ and in His presence all day long! He loves you. He has called you as a priest to reflect His love and give Him glory!

**These are the garments that they must make: a breastpiece, an ephod, a robe, a specially woven tunic, a turban, and a sash. They are to make holy garments for your brother Aaron and his sons so that they may serve Me as priests. . . . These must be worn by Aaron and his sons whenever they enter the tent of meeting or approach the altar to minister in the sanctuary area, so that they do not incur guilt and die. This is to be a permanent statute for Aaron and for his future descendants. —Exodus 28:4, 43**

Further Scripture: Psalm 100:4; Isaiah 61:10; Galatians 3:27

## Questions

1. How was Aaron a type of Christ (Hebrews 5:4–6; 9:7–14)?
2. What was the purpose of priestly garments (Exodus 28:3)?

3. List the garments they needed to make in Exodus 28:4. Do you think there is value in wearing special clothing/garments to worship the Lord today?

4. When Aaron entered the Holy Place, he bore the names of the sons of Israel over his heart (Exodus 28:29–30). He was not only called to work on behalf of the Israelites but also to love them. Who are the people that you "carry over your heart" when you talk with the Lord?

5. What were a few of the ordinances for Aaron and his sons to approach the Holy Place as priests? Why was the Lord so specific about how He wanted things to be done?

6. What did the Holy Spirit highlight to you in Exodus 27—28 through the reading or the teaching?

# Lesson 44: Exodus 29
*Deliverer*: The Instructions of the Holy Priests

## Teaching Notes

### Intro

God gave Moses instructions for building and equipping the tabernacle. He commanded Moses to set aside Aaron and his sons as priests and to make the priestly garments they were to wear as they served at the tabernacle. Now God explained how to consecrate the priests to serve Him.

### Teaching

*Exodus 29:1–4*: Before Aaron and his sons could serve as priests before God, they had to be consecrated. To be consecrated means to be set apart, to be made sacred for the specific purpose of serving God. First, Moses had to gather a young bull, two unblemished rams, unleavened bread, cakes, and wafers made from fine wheat flour. He then brought Aaron and his sons to the entrance of the tent of meeting where they were washed with water. Nelson's commentary pointed out that bathing the priests "symbolized the necessity of cleanness before the Lord. Bathing was a rare luxury in the desert of Sinai."[1]

Sin was represented in the Bible in many ways. Isaiah 1:4–6 said disease and sickness represented sin. In the New Testament, darkness and death represented sin. Isaiah 1:16 equated dirt with sin and urged people to wash and cleanse themselves from their evil deeds. In future lessons, the laver will be revealed as a basin where the priests washed their hands and feet before ministering to God. Much later, Jesus said that those who had once bathed completely would then need to clean just certain parts (John 13:10).

*Exodus 29:5–7*: The priests were washed and clothed. Baptism symbolizes being washed and then putting on the robe of righteousness. When our sins are forgiven, we put on new clothes! Jesus is the One who delivers us from our sin so we can come before the Lord. Next the priests were anointed by pouring anointing oil over their heads (Psalm 133:2–3). In the Old Testament, the anointing came

[1] Earl D. Radmacher, Ronald B. Allen, and H. Wayne House, eds., *Nelson's New Illustrated Bible Commentary* (Nashville: Thomas Nelson, 1999), 136.

to the priests, the prophets, and the kings. The anointing was "a symbol that God granted them the Holy Spirit for power and service."[2]

In Luke 4:17–18, Jesus quoted prophecy from Isaiah to reveal that He was anointed as the high priest to serve and do God's work. You don't have to be a priest from the Old Testament to be anointed! You have already been anointed! *We are* the holy priesthood today! Scripture says when you believe in the death, burial, and resurrection of Jesus, the oil has been poured out on your head. In 1 John 2:20, 27, believers are told they have been anointed by the Holy One. The anointing doesn't leave us and can be trusted to teach us all truth.

This priesthood pointed to the Messiah as the High Priest and also to us as the new holy priesthood. The oil was a symbol of the Holy Spirit in the Old Testament. In the Old Testament, the Holy Spirit would come and go. Numbers 11:29 revealed the people in the Old Testament longed for the Holy Spirit. But the Spirit only comes to people through the Messiah and allows them to walk in the empowerment of the priesthood.

*Exodus 29:8–9*: After anointing Aaron, Moses clothed Aaron and his sons with the tunics, sashes, and headbands. They were then permanently appointed to the priesthood. The word "ordain" meant "to fill one's hands, to empower." Nelson's commentary pointed out that kings were empowered when they filled his hands with the rod "as the symbol of his political power."[3]

*Exodus 29:10–12*: After the priests were washed, clothed, and anointed, they were forgiven.[4] Aaron and his sons made a sin offering by laying their hands on the head of the bull, which was then slaughtered at the entrance of the tent of meeting. Moses applied some of the bull's blood to the horns of the altar and poured out the remaining blood at the base of the altar. Nelson's commentary emphasized that Moses wasn't just throwing out the extra blood—everything Moses did was intentional and important.[5]

*Exodus 29:13–14*: The fat portions and the kidneys of the bull were burned on the altar, but its flesh, hide, and dung were burned outside the camp. As you read about the burning of these things, keep in mind that Jesus became our sin offering, our sacrifice. In Isaiah 53, a chapter many Jews won't even read, we learn that Jesus bore our sickness (v. 4) and was pierced for our transgressions (v. 5). Jesus

---

[2] Warren Wiersbe, *The Bible Exposition Commentary: Genesis–Deuteronomy* (Colorado Springs: David C. Cook, 2001) 243.

[3] Radmacher et al., 136.

[4] Wiersbe, 243.

[5] Radmacher et al., 136.

was punished because of our sin (v. 6–7); He was our sin offering. When we turn to Him, we are healed by His wounds (v. 5).

In Matthew 26:28, Jesus said, "This is my blood that . . . is shed for many for the forgiveness of sins." His life was the portrayal of the sin offering the priests had to offer every day. God "made the One who did not know sin to be sin for us" (2 Corinthians 5:21a). This sin offering the priests offered every single day pointed to Jesus, who is our sin offering once and for all (1 Peter 2:24). Jesus Christ set us free from our sins by His blood (Revelation 1:5–6).

*Exodus 29:15–18*: Next Aaron and his sons made a fire offering to the Lord. They laid their hands on the first ram, slaughtered it, sprinkled its blood on all sides of the altar, and then cut the ram into pieces, washed them, and burned the whole ram on the altar, which produced a pleasing aroma to the Lord. Wiersbe said the priests had been washed, clothed, anointed, forgiven, and now they were being dedicated.[6]

*Exodus 29:19–21*: After Aaron and his sons laid their hands on the second ram, it was slaughtered, and its blood was placed on their right earlobes, right thumbs, and right big toes. Wiersbe said now the priests were marked with blood.[7] Nelson's commentary offered this insight: Anointing of the ear represented hearing of the Word of God; anointing the thumb represented doing the work of God; and anointing the feet represented walking out the will of God.[8] The remaining blood was sprinkled on the altar. Some of that blood was mixed with oil and then sprinkled on Aaron and his sons' bodies and garments to make them holy (v. 21).

Jesus was marked by the blood. And when we embrace Him, then we, too, are marked by the blood. We are allowed to enter His presence because we are marked by His blood. Romans 12:1 tells us to present ourselves as living sacrifices, holy and pleasing to God, as our spiritual act of worship.

*Exodus 29:22–25*: Wiersbe said the priests were then fed. Aaron and his sons held portions of the ram along with one loaf of bread, one cake of bread, and one wafer of unleavened bread, and waved them as a presentation offering for the Lord, which signified, "God is My provider!" In John 4:34, Jesus said, "My food is to do the will of Him who sent Me." As priests today, we must never stop feeding from the Lord, tasting, and seeing that He is good!

---

[6] Wiersbe, 243.

[7] Wiersbe, 243–44.

[8] Radmacher et al., 137.

*Exodus 29:26–46*: To complete their consecration, every day for seven days, the priests sacrificed a bull as a sin offering to atone for their sins and to purify the altar (vv. 35–37). Then as priests, they offered a lamb every morning and at twilight (vv. 39–41). Each day they ministered before God by beginning and ending the day with sacrifice.

## Closing

Wouldn't that be cool if we focused on the sacrifice Christ made for us in the morning when we woke up and at night when we went to sleep? Thank You, Jesus, for delivering me. Then we might realize that as the holy priesthood, we've been washed, clothed, anointed, forgiven, dedicated, marked by the blood, and fed.

## The Daily Word

The Lord described to Moses exactly how Aaron and his sons should prepare to become priests; they would go through a time of consecration and offer sacrifices for the people. After these specific instructions, God made it clear that He would dwell among the people so they would know He was the Lord their God.

In the New Testament, consecration is for every believer as he or she presents and surrenders his or her life as a living sacrifice to the Lord. It's saying, "Lord, I am living for You. I am no longer living for myself, the world, or anything else. Use me for Your glory." In your sacrifice to Him, as His chosen priest, remember the Lord dwells within you, He is the Lord your God!

**I will consecrate the tent of meeting and the altar; I will also consecrate Aaron and his sons to serve Me as priests. I will dwell among the Israelites and be their God. And they will know that I am Yahweh their God, who brought them out of the land of Egypt, so that I might dwell among them. I am Yahweh their God. —Exodus 29:44–46**

Further Scripture: Romans 12:1; 2 Timothy 2:21; 1 Peter 2:9

## Questions

1. How did the daily sacrifices in Exodus 29:38–41 foreshadow Christ (John 1:29, 36)?
2. What do you think it would have been like to be a priest, like Aaron, offering daily sacrifices to the Lord (Exodus 29:38)? How does the truth in Hebrews 10:11–14 encourage you?

3. In Exodus 29:19–21, Aaron and his sons needed to mark themselves with the blood of the ram. Why did they need to do this? What do you think was significant about the specific body parts marked with the blood? Do you consider yourself marked by the blood of Christ? (Ephesians 1:7; Hebrews 12:24; Revelation 7:14)

4. What was the "wave offering" in Exodus 29:24, 26? Why do you think God wanted the priests to do this?

5. The consecrated bread was only to be eaten by priests (Exodus 29:32). Read Matthew 12:3–8 and Mark 2:23–27. Why do you think it was acceptable for David to eat the consecrated bread (1 Samuel 21:1–9)?

6. What did the Holy Spirit highlight to you in Exodus 29 through the reading or the teaching?

# Lesson 45: Exodus 30—31

*Deliverer*: Skilled Workers and the Sabbath

## Teaching Notes

### Review

While Moses met with the Lord for 40 days, he received all of the Lord's instructions for the tabernacle. According to Exodus 29:45, this tabernacle was so important because God said, He "will dwell among the Israelites and be their God. And they will know that I am Yahweh their God, who brought them out of the land of Egypt, so that I might dwell among them. I am Yahweh their God." In this tabernacle, they would see God dwelling with them, and they could be in His presence. In Exodus 30, God continued to instruct Moses to build additional furnishing for the tabernacle: the altar of incense (vv. 1–10); the atonement money, which the poor and rich had to pay (vv. 11–16); the laver or bronze basin (vv. 17–21); the anointing oil (vv. 22–33); and the sacred incense (vv. 34–38). So, who was going to build this?

### Teaching

*Exodus 31:1–2*: God told Moses He had chosen Bezalel to lead the work. Bezalel means "in the shadow of God."[1] Bezalel was the grandson of Hur, whom many believe was Miriam's husband. If so, Bezalel was the grandson of Miriam.[2] He was from the tribe of Judah! The man who built the tabernacle was from the lineage of the Messiah. Our word for Jesus in Exodus is *Deliverer*. In a weird way, Bezalel served as a deliverer for the Messiah.

The tent of meeting allowed the people to experience the presence of God, and it pointed to the Messiah. God effectively said to Bezalel, "Put on a hard hat and some work boots because I have work for you." Bezalel was called to serve God as a construction foreman. Never minimize any calling on your life.

*Exodus 31:3*: God filled Bezalel with the Spirit to give him "wisdom, understanding, and ability in every craft." This was an incredible picture of how a

---

[1] Thomas L. Constable, *Expository Notes of Dr. Thomas Constable: Exodus*, 264, https://planobiblechapel.org/tcon/notes/pdf/exodus.pdf.

[2] Constable, 264.

construction worker pointed to the coming King. At this point in the Old Testament, the Holy Spirit was specifically mentioned only two times before. Genesis 1:2 described the Spirit of God hovering over the waters. In Genesis 41:38, Pharaoh recognized that Joseph had God's Spirit in him. Isaiah 11:2, a messianic prophecy, says, "The Spirit of the LORD will rest on Him—a Spirit of wisdom and understanding, a Spirit of counsel and strength, a Spirit of knowledge and of the fear of the LORD." Acts 2:1–13 described the events of Pentecost when believers were filled with the Holy Spirit. When you're filled with the Holy Spirit, the gifts of the Spirit will become active in your life, as they did in Bezalel's life.

In the Old Testament, God gave the Holy Spirit for specific times and purposes. In the New Testament, believers receive the Holy Spirit when they believe in the death, burial, and resurrection of Christ (Acts 4:8; Ephesians 5:18). When we trust in Christ, we have the indwelling of the Spirit, and He never leaves us. But we are encouraged to ask Him to continually fill us up. The more we have of Him, the more glory is given to God.

*Exodus 31:4–5*: God gave Bezalel the gifts he needed to do the job God had for him. All of us have natural abilities, and when the Spirit of God comes into our lives, He fans those natural abilities to be used for Him. One example was described in 1 Samuel 16:13–23. After Samuel anointed David, "the spirit of the Lord took control of David from that day forward" (1 Samuel 16:13). David knew how to play the harp, and God used the harp to relieve Saul of the evil spirit. When the Spirit of God takes over in our lives, our natural abilities can be exercised for the glory of God! We need to learn how to hear from the Holy Spirit. When we open ourselves up to Him, we begin to see the Lord work in new ways in our lives.

*Exodus 31:6*: God also chose Oholiab, from the tribe of Dan, to work with Bezalel. Oholiab meant "tent of the father, one who lives closely with God." Dan was the firstborn son from Jacob's concubines. Samson would later be born from the tribe of Dan. The Danites were known as craftsmen who could build things. Many years in the future, Huram-abi, a skillful man from the tribe of Dan, would help build Solomon's temple (2 Chronicles 2:13). God "placed wisdom within every skilled craftsman" (v. 6), not just within Bezalel and Oholiab. These guys were in tune with the Lord, and they were instructed to build a whole lot of incredible things so the Israelites could experience the presence of God. These were everyday guys, which makes me think of the 12 sons of Israel, the 12 tribes, who were just normal guys. And the disciples were average, everyday men as well, like tax collectors and fishermen. But when the Spirit of God came upon them, He empowered them! Revelation 21:12–15 says these men will be remembered in the New Jerusalem. "The names of the 12 tribes of Israel's sons will be inscribed on the gates" (Revelation 21:12), "and the 12 names of the Lamb's 12 apostles" will be on the 12 foundations of the city walls (Revelation 21:14).

*Exodus 31:7–11*: God gave specific instructions for setting up the tent of meeting and the placement of all its furnishings, as well as the garments for the priests, and the anointing oil and incense. The skilled workmen completed all this work exactly as God commanded.

*Exodus 31:12–13*: While emphasizing the importance of following His instructions for the tabernacle, God commanded Moses to "Tell the Israelites: You must observe My Sabbaths, for it is a sign between Me and you throughout your generations." Even in the midst of building a place for God to dwell with them, God wanted them to rest in His presence. There were no other cultures that practiced this.[3]

*Exodus 31:14–15*: God considered observing the Sabbath so important, that whoever profaned it or did any work on that day would be cut off from the people and put to death. God commanded that the Sabbath be observed as a day of complete rest dedicated to the Lord.

*Exodus 31:16*: This command was so new that the Israelites weren't sure what was work and what wasn't. Numbers 15:32–35 recorded that a man went to pick up wood on the Sabbath and was brought before Moses and Aaron for violating the Sabbath. God then instructed Moses to put the man to death by stoning him outside the camp. Remember that the manna fell daily except on the Sabbath. On the sixth day, the Israelites had to gather double portions so that they didn't have to work on the Sabbath. The Sabbath was a day to celebrate!

*Exodus 31:17*: The Sabbath was a sign between God and His people, not the people and the church.[4] On the Sabbath, they were commanded to stop working and come before the presence of the Lord to rest.

Do we see anything about holding a worship service on the Sabbath? Sometimes we take things out of context and we don't really understand what they mean. In Isaiah 1:13, God told the Israelites, "Stop bringing useless offerings. Your incense is detestable to Me. New Moons and Sabbaths, and the calling of solemn assemblies—I cannot stand iniquity with a festival." Apparently, some of their assemblies weren't pleasing to God. In Hosea 2:11, God said He would

---

[3] Constable, 265.

[4] Constable, 266.

put an end to Israel's celebrations. In this context, God didn't say put together a worship service—He said rest.

*Exodus 31:18*: God "finished speaking with Moses on Mount Sinai" and gave him the tablets with the Ten Commandments that He wanted the Israelites to live by. The phrase "inscribed by the finger of God" was an example of anthropomorphism, when a quality of God was expressed in human characteristics. The emphasis is that the word of God was delivered to the man of God, and now that man of God was supposed to deliver it to all of the Israelites. These Ten Commandments would be stored in the tabernacle that Bezalel and Oholiab were going to build.

## Closing

Everybody played their unique part! Moses received the Word, the skilled craftsmen built the tabernacle, and the priests served in the tabernacle.

## The Daily Word

In order for the building instructions God gave Moses to be completed, the Lord specifically chose the craftsmen for service. God filled them with His Spirit and with wisdom, understanding, and ability for their calling as craftsmen.

May you find comfort trusting that when God has a plan for His people and calls you to something, He will provide everything you need and will empower you through His Spirit. When you work as unto the Lord, His power will fill you and equip you. Remember, He goes before everything He has commanded you to do!

**Look, I have appointed by name Bezalel son of Uri, son of Hur, of the tribe of Judah. I have filled him with God's Spirit, with wisdom, understanding, and ability in every craft to design artistic works in gold, silver, and bronze, to cut gemstones for mounting, and to carve wood for work in every craft. I have also selected Oholiab son of Ahisamach, of the tribe of Dan, to be with him. I have placed wisdom within every skilled craftsman in order to make all that I have commanded you. —Exodus 31:2–6**

Further Scripture: Joshua 1:9; 1 Corinthians 12:4–8; Colossians 3:23

# Questions

1. Where was the Altar of Incense to be placed? What was God's function for this altar (Leviticus 16:12–13)?

2. Why was Aaron the one chosen to burn the incense to the Lord? (Exodus 28:1; 1 Samuel 2:28)

3. What was the altar of incense in Exodus 30:7 a picture of (Revelation 5:8; 8:3–4)? What does this reveal to you about God's desire for us?

4. In Exodus 30:9, God said not to put a "strange" incense (or burnt offering or grain offering or pour a drink offering) on the altar. What did this mean (Leviticus 10:1–3)? How can you tie this into how we serve or worship the Lord today?

5. Read Exodus 31:1–5. Why did God fill Bezalel with the Holy Spirit? What role(s) has God wired you to do in the kingdom of God?

6. What did the Holy Spirit highlight to you in Exodus 30—31 through the reading or the teaching?

# Lesson 46: Exodus 32—33

*Deliverer*: Moses Intercedes for the People

## Teaching Notes

### Intro

The word we have used to describe the Messiah in all of Exodus is *Deliverer*. Why? Because we believe Jesus is the One who delivered the people out of bondage in Egypt. Jude 5 says, "Now I want to remind you, though you know all these things: The Lord first saved a people out of Egypt and later destroyed those who did not believe." Moses came down from the mountain with all the instructions from the Lord that were written on the tablets by the finger of God. But during this time, the Israelites had become impatient, so they built a golden calf.

### Teaching

To quickly summarize Exodus 32: Aaron led the Israelites in fashioning a golden calf from the jewelry they had taken from the Egyptians. When God saw the Israelites worshipping the golden calf, He was so angry He wanted to destroy the Israelites and start over with Moses (v. 10). Moses played a role like Christ, and he interceded with God for the people (v. 11). When Moses came down from the mountain and saw the calf and the Israelites dancing before it, he smashed the tablets written by the finger of God (v. 19). Moses called "whoever is for the Lord" to stand with him, and the Levites gathered around him (v. 26). Moses commanded the Levites to kill their brother, friend, and neighbor: 3,000 men were struck dead (vv. 27–28). Then God "inflicted a plague on the people for what they did with the calf Aaron had made" (v. 35). This was the first judgment the Lord brought on His people: the killing of 3,000 men (v. 28) and the plague (v. 35). Sin always leads to death (Romans 3:23; 1 John 5:16–17)! The second judgment is in Exodus 33: God didn't want to go with the Israelites on their journey to the Promised Land.

*Exodus 33:1–2*: Notice that God referred to the Israelites as "the people you [Moses] brought up from Egypt." God reminded Moses of His promise to Abraham, Isaac, and Jacob even in the midst of the Israelites' rebellion. God promised to send "an angel" ahead of them to drive out the people in the land. However, this angel was *not* the angel of the Lord.

*Exodus 33:3–6*: Because God was angry, He would not go with Israel because He "might destroy you on the way" (v. 3). Sin had created a barrier between Israel and God. When the Israelites heard this, they mourned and didn't put on their jewelry. Possibly this was the remaining jewelry from Egypt that hadn't been used to create the calf. After all God had done for the people, they had the audacity to worship a golden calf! God remained separated from them until He decided what to do with them.

Isaiah 59:2 says, "But your iniquities have built barriers between you and God, and your sins have made Him hide His face from you so that He does not listen" (2 Thessalonians 1:9). In this Old Testament mentality, there was a penalty of eternal separation from the Lord's presence and His glorious strength because of sin. But in the New Testament era, nothing can separate us from the love of God through *Jesus* (Romans 8:38–39)!

*Exodus 33:7–11*: God's third judgment against Israel was telling Moses to set up a tent of meeting outside the Israelite camp. (This wasn't the tabernacle, as it had not been built.) God moved Himself outside, away from the Israelites. Moses was allowed to meet God in the tent, but the Israelites could only watch while Moses entered the tent, and the pillar of cloud came down and covered the opening of the tent. Hamilton said, "When Moses 'goes out', God (in the pillar) comes down."[1] Perhaps when they saw the pillar of cloud, they remembered everything God had done for them. Whenever they saw the pillar of cloud, they bowed in worship at the doors of their own tents while God "spoke with Moses face to face, just as a man speaks with his friend" (v. 11). Other passages describe this friendship between Moses and God. Deuteronomy 34:10 says, "No prophet has arisen again in Israel like Moses, whom the Lord knew face to face." While Moses met with God, Joshua remained inside the tent of meeting. He was learning; he was soaking in the presence of the Lord.

*Exodus 33:12–13*: Moses continued to intercede for Israel, which reminds me of the widow in Luke 18:1–8, who persisted in making her requests before the judge. The Father wants to bless us; the question is, "Are we asking?" Moses pleaded for God to remember "this nation is Your people." Moses was an incredible example of how to negotiate with the Lord in prayer. He asked God, "Please teach me

---

[1] Victor P. Hamilton, *Exodus: An Exegetical Commentary* (Grand Rapids: Baker Academic, 2011), 563.

Your ways." Psalm 103:7 says God answered Moses' prayer: "He revealed His ways to Moses, His deeds to the people of Israel."

*Exodus 33:14–17*: God said, "My presence will go with you, and I will give you rest." The word "presence" is interchangeable with the word "face," and "rest" meant the Promised Land. Moses continued this dialogue with God by saying the other nations would not know Israel was God's people unless God went with them because His presence "distinguished" Israel from "all the other people on the face of the earth" (v. 16). God promised to go with Israel because Moses found favor in God's sight and God knew him by name. God knows each of us by name. He knows everything about us.

*Exodus 33:18*: Moses asked to see God's glory. "Glory" means "holiness." Moses wanted to experience God like he had never experienced God before. When Moses first met God at the burning bush, he took off his shoes and experienced God's glory, but he hid his face "because he was afraid to look at God" (Exodus 3:1–6). Now he wanted more!

*Exodus 33:19–23*: God said He would pass in front of Moses and proclaim the name Yahweh before him, but He also told Moses: "You cannot see My face, for no one can see Me and live." Judges 13:22 recorded that Samson's father was afraid he and his wife would die because they had seen God. God told Moses to stand on a rock. God said He would put Moses into the crevice of a rock and cover him until He had passed by, then remove His hand so Moses could see His back. God would not allow His face to be seen. God allowed Moses to experience His glory but not all of it.

Moses showed us that when we seek His face, God will respond. Where are we seeking God's face? How are we seeking His presence? Scripture invites us to seek God's face:

- 1 Chronicles 16:11: "Search for the LORD and His strength; seek His face always."
- 2 Chronicles 7:14: "And My people who are called by My name humble themselves, pray and seek My face, and turn from their evil ways, then I will hear from heaven, forgive their sin, and heal their land."
- Psalm 27:8: "LORD, I will seek Your face."
- Psalm 105:4: "Search for the LORD and His strength; seek His face always."

# Closing

The Lord showed Himself in a mighty powerful way to Moses while he was protected in the cleft of a rock. Moses was pretty exhausted. He was tired of the people and was exhausted by the people complaining and doing the wrong things. And yet he still interceded on their behalf. Wiersbe said, "When God's servants are discouraged and disappointed because of the sins of their people, the best remedy for a broken heart is a new vision for the glory of God."[2] To overcome disappointment, we need a dose of the glory of God.

Things were a mess until Moses interceded and stood on a rock to experience the glory of God. Fast forward to today and the New Covenant. If you need the medicine of encouragement, you need to go before the Lord and seek His face until you experience His glory. But it doesn't always have to look like it did for Moses. In 1 Kings 19:11–12, while Elijah waited in the cleft of the rock, God was not in the wind or the earthquake or the fire; He was in the whisper.

## The Daily Word

After God's anger rose up against the Israelites because they chose to make and worship a calf-god, Moses and God had an honest, face-to-face talk, like friends. Despite His great frustration, God showed an even greater and more intimate love for Moses and His people by continuing to lead and deliver them.

The Lord loves you deeply, no matter your shortcomings. Even when it seems He would want to walk away from you, He will draw near to you as you draw near to Him. The Lord longs for you to know Him in a personal, honest, face-to-face way. Do you talk to the Lord as though He were a friend? As you follow the Lord and spend time speaking with Him, the closer you will be to Him, like friends.

**The Lord spoke with Moses face to face, just as a man speaks with his friend. —Exodus 33:11**

Further Scripture: John 15:12–15; James 2:23; James 4:8

---

[2] Warren W. Wiersbe, *The Bible Exposition Commentary: Genesis–Deuteronomy* (Colorado Springs: David C. Cook, 2001), 247.

# Questions

1. Why did Aaron lead the way in making the golden calf? What was God's response (Exodus 32:7–10)?

2. Moses interceded for the people twice because of their sin (Exodus 32:11–13, 31–32). What was God's response? Do you have a habit of interceding for others? If not, how does this challenge you?

3. In Exodus 32:32, Moses told the Lord that if He would not forgive the people's sin, to blot his very name out of His book. How does this speak to the spiritual character of Moses? Paul had the same heart in Romans 9:3. How could Moses and Paul's actions compel you to have a deep compassion for the lost? Do you have the faith of Moses or Paul to make a similar plea with God for those in your circle of influence?

4. In Exodus 33:3, God told Moses that he and the people could go to the land promised to them but that God would not be with them. What was your first reaction when you read this? Read Moses' response in Exodus 33:15. If you could have everything you ever wanted or desired here on earth but God was not present, would you be satisfied? Why or why not?

5. What were the people instructed to do if they wanted to seek the Lord in Exodus 33:7? Why do you think Moses had the tent of meeting far from the camp?

6. How can we see Christ as the rock mentioned in Exodus 33:21–22? (Psalm 118:22; 1 Peter 2:4)

7. What did the Holy Spirit highlight to you in Exodus 32—33 through the reading or the teaching?

# Lesson 47: Exodus 34—35
## *Deliverer*: New Stone Tablets

## Teaching Notes

### Review

The Israelites had messed up by worshipping the golden calf. Moses came down from the mountain where he had been meeting with God and smashed the Ten Commandments in his anger. Then God brought a plague and had the Levites kill 3,000 men. Then God said, "I'm not going with you anymore," and moved Moses and the tent outside the camp. Within that context, the Lord began to speak to Moses about the next steps.

### Teaching

*Exodus 34:1–4*: God told Moses to cut two stone tablets to replace the ones he had broken, and on these tablets God would write His words. The next morning, Moses went back up Mount Sinai to meet with God again. Verse 28 of this same chapter, said Moses spent another 40 days and 40 nights with the Lord, during which time he did not eat or drink water. Tomorrow would be a new day, a reminder that God's mercies are new every morning (Lamentations 3:22–23). Many notable events in Scripture occurred in the morning. In Genesis 19:27–28, Abraham woke early in the morning to look over Sodom and Gomorrah. In Judges 6:28, the men of the city rose early in the morning to find Baal's altar torn down. In Job 1:5, Job rose early in the morning to offer sacrifices for his children. In Luke 24:1, the women rose early to return to Jesus' tomb. And that's what's happening in verse 2, God tells Moses, "Be prepared by morning. Come up Mount Sinai in the morning and stand before Me on the mountaintop." Then in verse 3, God says that no one, not Joshua or even the animals, was allowed to go with Moses or be seen anywhere on the mountain. So, Moses took the stone tablets and climbed Mount Sinai to meet with the Lord.

*Exodus 34:5–7*: God came down in a cloud to meet with Moses. Constantly God showed up in a cloud. The *Deliverer* pointed to the Messiah who delivers His people. John 1:14 says, "The Word became flesh and dwelt with us" (ESV). God met with Moses and proclaimed His name Yahweh. This was an epiphany—an appearance of the Lord in a grand descent to encounter humans.

When God passed in front of Moses, He revealed His attributes: compassionate; gracious; slow to anger; rich in faithful love and truth; maintaining faithful love; forgiving wrongdoing, rebellion, and sin; will not leave the guilty unpunished. Moses later shared this description of God with the Israelites at Kadesh-barnea (Numbers 14:17–19). The Jews used this same language to describe God in Nehemiah 9:17–18. When God chose to forgive the Ninevites, Jonah said, "I knew that You are a merciful and compassionate God, slow to become angry, rich in faithful love, and One who relents from sending disaster" (Jonah 4:2). "God has a 'long fuse."[1] God is willing to show His mercy, but He reveals that His wrath comes as well.

*Exodus 34:8–9*: Immediately, Moses bowed down in submission and worshipped. Moses continued to pray for God's presence to go with them and for God's forgiveness of their sin. He interceded on behalf of God's people that God would relent and change His mind. Moses didn't separate himself from the people; he made himself a part of the people. Ezra (ch. 9), Daniel (ch. 9), and Nehemiah (ch. 1) all cried out to God on behalf of the people. Be cautious of any leader who disassociates from the people. Moses didn't do that. Jesus didn't do that.

*Exodus 34:10–14*: God made a covenant to perform wonders for Israel that had never been done "in all the earth or in any nation . . . for what I am doing with you is awe-inspiring" (v. 10). God promised Israel would experience "an awesome thing, namely the conquest of Canaan."[2] But God also gave Israel guidelines for living in covenant with Him. They were forbidden from making treaties with those who lived in the land because they would become a snare to Israel (v. 12). Instead, Israel was required to tear down the altars to the idols, refuse to worship those idols, and to worship only Yahweh because God is a jealous God (v. 14). Wiersbe pointed out that "like cancerous tumors in human bodies, the pagan temples and altars had to be removed and destroyed before the land could be healthy."[3]

*Exodus 34:15–16*: First Guideline: The Israelites were forbidden from making treaties with the inhabitants of the land as that would ultimately lead to worshipping their gods. This was exactly what happened with the golden calf. While

---

[1] Michael P. Knowles, *The Unfolding Mystery of the Divine Name: The God of Sinai in Our Midst* (Downers Grove, IL: InterVarsity, 2012), 98.

[2] Earl D. Radmacher, Ronald B. Allen, and H. Wayne House, eds., *Nelson's New Illustrated Bible Commentary* (Nashville: Thomas Nelson, 1999), 144.

[3] Warren W. Wiersbe, *The Bible Exposition Commentary: Genesis–Deuteronomy* (Colorado Springs: David C. Cook, 2001), 248.

they were in the wilderness, the Israelites went back to their old lifestyle. Nelson's commentary said, "Intermarriage would be the quickest route to compromise with false religion and immoral behavior."[4]

*Exodus 34:17–20*: Second Guideline: The Israelites were commanded to worship God alone. They were forbidden to make "cast images of gods" and were instructed to observe the Festival of Unleavened Bread to remember how God had delivered them out of Egypt. By celebrating what God had done, they would focus on Him.

*Exodus 34:21–26*: They were commanded to rest from their labor on the seventh day even "during plowing and harvesting times." Even when there was lots of work to be done, the Sabbath was a form of celebration! The Festival of Weeks celebrated the firstfruits of the wheat harvest and the Festival of Ingathering celebrated the agricultural year. The Passover commemorated their deliverance from Egypt. When they gathered for these festivals, God promised to protect their land. The Israelites needed markers in their lives to remind them to look to the Lord.

*Exodus 34:27–28*: God instructed Moses to write down "these words" of His covenant with Israel. The Mosaic Covenant was being established. Moses spent 40 days and 40 nights on the mountain with God, neither eating nor drinking water, during which time God wrote the Ten Commandments on the tablets.

*Exodus 34:29–30*: Moses didn't realize that when he was with the Lord, the presence of God shone on his face, in his life. But the Israelites were afraid to come near him because "the skin of his face shone" (v. 30). This makes me think of Jesus on the Mount of Transfiguration (Matthew 17:1–2). Jesus' face shone like the sun!

*Exodus 34:31–33*: But Moses called out to them, and he told them everything he had written down. How long was that conversation? How did Moses gather 2 million people and how could they even hear him? Then Moses put a veil over his face.

*Exodus 34:34–35*: Moses removed his veil when he met with the Lord. When he returned to the people with his face shining, he would tell the Israelites what God had commanded. Then he'd put the veil back on until he went to speak with the Lord again so the people wouldn't see the fading glory.

In 2 Corinthians 3:7–18, Paul addressed this exact interaction. The "ministry of death" (v. 7) was the Ten Commandments (the Mosaic Law). The glory faded from Moses' face because he had to come and go from the presence of God (v. 7). "For if the ministry of condemnation had glory, the ministry of righteousness

---

[4] Radmacher et al., 145.

overflows with even more glory" (v. 9). Those who come to faith under the New Covenant will experience God's glory. "Whenever a person turns to the Lord, the veil is removed . . . we all, with unveiled faces, are looking as in a mirror at the glory of the Lord and are being transformed into the same image from glory to glory" (vv. 16, 18). The veil is set aside in *Christ* (v. 16)!

## Closing

The veil is removed when we turn to our Lord Jesus Christ! We don't have to go back and forth and back and forth. The glory never leaves when we are in the presence of Jesus Christ.

## The Daily Word

Moses spent another 40 days and 40 nights with God on Mount Sinai. This time, he fasted and did not eat or drink. Moses spent time talking with and listening to God. As he came down from the mountain, Moses' face radiated brightly because he had spent time in God's presence.

When you spend time in the presence of God, in His Word, praying, and listening to Him, you will be transformed. The key is taking time away from the distractions of the world to spend time with God. God is a God of transformation! It may be a process, but the more time you abide with Christ, the more you are being made into His image and will reflect His love and His glory!

**As Moses descended from Mount Sinai—with the two tablets of the testimony in his hands as he descended the mountain—he did not realize that the skin of his face shone as a result of his speaking with the Lord.**
**—Exodus 34:29**

Further Scripture: Acts 4:13; Romans 12:2; 2 Corinthians 3:18

## Questions

1. At the beginning of Exodus 34, the Lord instructed Moses to cut out two stone tablets like the ones Moses shattered in Exodus 32:19. Why do you think God didn't make them Himself as He made the first set (Exodus 32:16)? How important were the words written on those stone tablets (Exodus 25:21; 31:18; 34:28)?

2. The Lord described Himself as He passed before Moses in Exodus 34:6–7. Is there anything in this description that you have trouble believing about God in your life right now?

225

3. At the end of Exodus 34:10, the Lord told Moses that it was a *fearful* thing He was going to perform (NASB). Other translations use the words "wonder," "terrible," "awesome," and "awe-inspiring." Would this message frighten you if it was spoken by God to you? Why or why not?

4. In Exodus 34:29–35, the text described that Moses' face glowed because He had been in God's presence (speaking with God). Why do you think Moses put the veil over his face (Exodus 34:30, 33; 2 Corinthians 3:13–16)?

5. Read Exodus 35:30–33. Bezalel was given excellent crafting skills by the Spirit of God. What skills do you recognize in your own life? Have you understood these skills as coming from God (Exodus 31:6; 36:1)?

6. What did the Holy Spirit highlight to you in Exodus 34—35 through the reading or the teaching?

# Lesson 48: Exodus 36

*Deliverer:* Building the Tabernacle

## Teaching Notes

### Review

The priests were supposed to minister every day. According to Acts 19:8–10, Paul had daily discussions with the 12 students at the school of Tyrannus. That's what we're doing through reviveSCHOOL.

In Exodus 34, Moses was given the Ten Commandments. God reestablished His covenant with Israel: Israel was forbidden to make treaties with the Canaanites and commanded to worship only God through the festivals. Moses addressed the people and told them what God had said. His face shone from being in God's presence, so he put on a veil to hide the fact that it was fading.

In Exodus 35, Moses told the Israelites to build a tabernacle. Bezalel and Oholiab led the charge. God told them to collect an offering for the tabernacle.

### Teaching

*Exodus 36:1*: Bezalel, Oholiab, and the skilled people went to work on building the tabernacle as God commanded. Nelson's commentary described the characteristics of these skilled people. Both men and women were among the workers (Exodus 35:20–22, 25). "Their hearts were 'willing' or 'stirred'" (Exodus 35:5, 21–22, 26). They had the skills and giftedness to complete their tasks (Exodus 35:10, 25, 34–35; 36:1–2). "They were generous with their skills . . . [and] possessions" (Exodus 35:5, 22, 29; 36:3–7). Their finished products showed the excellence of their work.[1]

*Exodus 36:2–3*: The skilled people responded immediately to Moses' call to start the work. The workers collected the freewill offerings the Israelites contributed for the construction of the tabernacle. They brought their gifts "morning after morning" (v. 3). There was no campaign . . . the people just contributed.

When people are called, you don't have to convince them. When their hearts are moved, they're going to do the work.

---

[1] Earl D. Radmacher, Ronald B. Allen, and H. Wayne House, eds., *Nelson's New Illustrated Bible Commentary* (Nashville: Thomas Nelson, 1999), 146.

*Exodus 36:4*: The craftsmen came one by one from the work they were doing. They had to leave other jobs to do the work God called them to. At this point in the biblical story, they were constructing the only God-designed building. I believe there is beauty in the work of these skilled craftsmen. Samuel Mather said, "All the arts are nothing else but the beams and rays of the Wisdom of the first Being in the creatures, shining and reflecting thence upon the glass of man's understanding; and as from Him they come, so to Him they tend."[2]

What we do exemplifies how God has wired us, and He gets the glory. In the tabernacle, God used mankind to reveal His beauty. In Psalm 27:4, David said, "I have asked one thing from the LORD; it is what I desire: to dwell in the house of the LORD all the days of my life, gazing on the beauty of the LORD and seeking Him in His temple." Psalm 96:6 says, "Splendor and majesty are before Him; strength and beauty are in His sanctuary." One by one, the skilled workers came to work on something greater. These skilled craftsmen created a place where His beauty could dwell and be displayed. What if people in the church willingly left their posts and came together to display God's beauty?

*Exodus 36:5*: As the craftsmen came together to work, they realized the people had given more than what was needed to construct the tabernacle. The people believed in this calling, and they willingly gave up everything they had. Their actions remind us of what Jesus said in Matthew 6:21, "For where your treasure is, there your heart will be also." When the Spirit of God is working, you don't have to convince anybody. They knew, and they kept giving. The people would show similar generosity in the future. When King Joash issued a call to collect money to "renovate the Lord's temple" (2 Chronicles 24:4), the people responded by giving generously, filling the chest with money each day (2 Chronicles 24:8–11). When people see and sense that God is in something, the money is never short. When King Hezekiah asked the people to give generously so the priests and Levites "could devote their energy to the law of the Lord" (2 Chronicles 31:4), they brought their offerings to the Lord's temple and there was an abundance left over (2 Chronicles 31:10). People will give when they sense the urgency of God moving.

In Matthew 26:6–13, a woman gave everything she had to honor Jesus. "A woman approached Him with an alabaster jar of very expensive fragrant oil. She poured it on His head as He was reclining at the table." In Acts 4:34–35, Luke recorded, "For there was not a needy person among them, because all those who owned lands or houses sold them, brought the proceeds of the things that were sold, and laid them at the apostles' feet. This was then distributed

---

[2] Philip Graham Ryken, *Exodus: Saved for God's Glory* (Wheaton, IL: Crossway, 2015), 1038.

for each person's basic needs." The first century believers didn't have any needs because they took care of each other. In Luke 21:1–4, a widow gave "two tiny coins," and Jesus pointed out that where others gave out of their surplus, she had given everything she had to live on. It's not about what people see! It's about the heart.

In Exodus 36, people gave radically to God of their skills, gifts, and resources. We cannot come to the table stingy! In Matthew 10:39, Jesus said, "Anyone finding his life will lose it, and anyone losing his life because of Me will find it." When God asks you to do something, you have to leave what you're doing and give everything to do what He asks. There has to be sacrifice to walk out your calling. These Israelites gave up everything in order for people to experience the presence of God. It's worth it, but it doesn't mean it's easy.

*Exodus 36:6–7*: Moses had to give an order for the offerings to stop. There were more than enough materials for the people to do all of the work!!

*Exodus 36:8–38*: The people began the work! The ten inner curtains were made as God described (vv. 8–13). The 11 outer curtains made from goat hair were made and assembled as God directed, from "ram skins dyed red and a covering of manatee skins on top of it" (vv. 14–19). The frame was made with planks of acacia wood and set into bases of silver (vv. 20–30). The crossbars were made of acacia wood, overlaid with gold (vv. 31–34). Then the inner veil and outer veil were made according to God's design (vv. 35–36). An embroidered screen was then set at the entrance of the tent (vv. 37–38).

## Closing

A. W. Pink described three meanings of the tabernacle identified by Adolf Saphir.[3] First, the tabernacle provided a visible illustration of the heavenly place where God dwells. Second, the tabernacle was a type of Christ, or a picture of how we can meet God through Jesus Christ. Third, the tabernacle is a type of Christ inside the church because believers are the temple of the Holy Spirit, the presence of God.

When skilled people function out of obedience to what the Lord is asking them to do, it points people to God. The obedience of the Israelites pointed us to our deliverance through the Messiah.

---

[3] Arthur. W. Pink, *Gleanings in Exodus* (Chicago: Moody, 1981), 180.

## The Daily Word

Moses summoned every skilled person the Lord had given wisdom and understanding for building the sanctuary. Their hearts stirred to work and do the tasks at hand. Morning after morning, the sons of Israel brought contributions and offerings to use for construction. Not only did they bring what was sufficient, the people brought more than enough. They listened to their hearts and responded in obedience as the Lord led them.

When the Lord gives a plan for something and calls His people to it, He will make a way. He will equip you with all wisdom and knowledge so you may bear fruit in every good work. Listen to the stirrings of your heart. Respond to the Lord. And remember, in Christ, you will have more than enough.

**So Moses summoned Bezalel, Oholiab, and every skilled person in whose heart the LORD had placed wisdom, everyone whose heart moved him, to come to the work and do it. They took from Moses' presence all the contributions that the Israelites had brought for the task of making the sanctuary. Meanwhile, the people continued to bring freewill offerings morning after morning. . . . The materials were sufficient for them to do all the work. There was more than enough. —Exodus 36:2–3, 7**

Further Scripture: 2 Corinthians 9:8; Colossians 1:9–10; Hebrews 13:20–21

## Questions

1. Why do you think Exodus 36—39 repeated the details God gave the Israelites for making the sanctuary in Exodus 25:8—28:43? (Exodus 39:42–43)

2. Where did much of what the people contributed for the construction of the sanctuary come from? (Exodus 3:22; 11:2; 12:35–36)

3. Contributions for the sanctuary were requested as a freewill offering (Exodus 36:3). What does this mean? (Exodus 35:5–9, 21–22, 29)

4. Why did Moses issue a command for contributions to cease (Exodus 36:6–7)? Do you see this kind of generosity in your community?

5. Did Moses have trouble finding people who were willing to give their time and services for the work needed? What does this say about their hearts?

6. What did the Holy Spirit highlight to you in Exodus 36 through the reading or the teaching?

# Lesson 49: Exodus 37—38
## *Deliverer*: Constructing the Tabernacle

## Teaching Notes

### Review

In Exodus, Moses followed God's instructions for building the tabernacle. Bezalel and Oholiab and the skilled craftsmen began construction of the tabernacle, and that continued in Exodus 37.

Exodus 37 described the furnishings made for inside the tabernacle. The ark was made of acacia wood (vv. 1–5). The mercy seat was made of pure gold (vv. 6–9). The table of showbread was made from acacia wood, and the utensils placed on it were made of pure gold (vv. 10–16). The lampstand was made in one piece from pure hammered gold (vv. 17–24). The altar of incense was made from acacia wood overlaid with horns of pure gold (vv. 25–28). Bezalel also made the holy anointing oil and expertly blended incense (v. 29). They made all these components so the Israelites could experience the presence of the Lord.

### Teaching

*Exodus 38:1*: Bezalel, whose name meant "in the shadow of God," constructed the altar of burnt offering from acacia wood to the exact dimensions God described. Compare these verses to God's instructions given to Moses in Exodus 27:1–8 to see that Bezalel's work was precisely obedient to God's plan. Bezalel was tangibly walking out his calling. It's rewarding to see your work come to fruition in God's design. Moses' obedience led to Bezalel's obedience, which led to the people experiencing the presence of God. Moses never shortchanged God's directions.

*Exodus 38:2*: Bezalel then made horns for the four corners of the altar and overlaid it with bronze. Bezalel built this altar so the Israelites could bring their offerings to the Lord. All their sacrifices pointed to the Messiah. Multiple things took place here on the altar of burnt offering.[1]

---

[1] Philip Graham Ryken, *Exodus: Saved for God's Glory* (Wheaton, IL: Crossway, 2015), 1067–68.

- Whole burnt offerings: every morning and evening the people made a sacrifice of atonement (Leviticus 1).
- Fellowship offerings: the fat parts were offered to God and the rest of the animal was eaten (Leviticus 3).
- Sin offerings: sacrifices for purification and to atone for certain sins (Leviticus 4).
- Guilt offerings: sacrifices for inadvertent offenses (Leviticus 5).
- Day of Atonement: the high priest offered sacrifices for his sin and then the people's sins (Leviticus 16).

*Exodus 38:3–7*: Bezalel followed God's instructions for making the utensils that would be used at the altar of burnt offering. The utensils were made from bronze. The poles used to carry the altar were made from acacia wood overlaid with bronze. Remember, acacia wood is very straight, doesn't warp, and is moisture resistant.

*Exodus 38:8*: Bezalel made the bronze basin (also called brazen laver) from the bronze mirrors gathered from the women who served at the tent of meeting. As slaves in Egypt, the likelihood of the Israelites owning their own mirrors was not good. But when they plundered the Egyptians, they were probably given these bronze mirrors. And now, the Israelite women gave those mirrors as an offering to be used for the tabernacle. Exodus 30:17–20 gave instructions for building and using the basin. It was positioned between the tent of meeting and the altar.

The priests washed their hands and feet in the water in this basin so they wouldn't die when they entered God's presence. This was essential in order to experience the presence of God! This brings to mind the widow's mite (Luke 21:1–4). God saw the heart of the women who gave up their mirrors so the priests wouldn't die when they did their jobs. The women gave up their mirrors; the skilled craftsmen built the basin; all so the priests could make atonement for the people. They all did their part.

The priests needed to be cleansed before approaching the Lord. Philip Graham Ryken drew this parallel. When they received atonement from the offerings on the altar, it was like Passover. When they washed in the basin, that was like the Red Sea moment.[2] The New Testament also points out the importance of washing before God. In Ephesians 5:25b–26, Paul pointed out that Jesus cleanses the church "with the washing of water by the word." In Titus 3:5, Paul said God saves us "through the washing of regeneration and renewal by the Holy Spirit." In

---

[2] Ryken, 1070.

John 13:8, Jesus told Peter, "If I don't wash you, you have no part with Me." God chose to deliver His people through the tabernacle, and it all pointed to Jesus.

*Exodus 38:9–17*: Bezalel continued to follow God's specific instructions as he led the work to create the furnishings for the courtyard according to every detail.

*Exodus 38:18–20*: These verses describe the screen that covered the gate of the courtyard. There was only one entrance to experience the presence of God. Every time I go out to share the gospel, someone always says, "There are multiple ways to God!" But there is only *one way* to God! I believe the tabernacle and the one entrance through the screen is a type of Christ, foreshadowing that He is the only way to God. There was no back door. Jesus emphasized this truth during His ministry.

In John 14:6, Jesus told Thomas, "I am the way, the truth, and the life. No one comes to the Father except through Me." In the Sermon on the Mount recorded in Matthew 7:13–14, Jesus said, "Enter through the narrow gate. For the gate is wide and the road is broad that leads to destruction, and there are many who go through it. How narrow is the gate and difficult the road that leads to life, and few find it." And in John 10:9, Jesus said, "I am the door. If anyone enters by Me, he will be saved and will come in and go out and find pasture."

None of the tabernacle is in existence today. The tabernacle led to the temple, and that's no longer in existence either. If people have no way to offer their sacrifices, there has to be another way—and Jesus said, "I'm the door now. I am the narrow gate."

*Exodus 38:21–23*: Under the direction of Ithamar, son of Aaron, the Levites maintained an inventory of the materials used to build the tabernacle and all of its furnishings. Bezalel and Oholiab had led the skilled craftsmen in the construction. It was done! The tabernacle had been built! Multiple people, out of their obedience to God, opened the doors for us to experience the presence of God.

*Exodus 38:24–28*: Moses recorded that a little more than one ton of gold and well over three tons of silver were used for the project. Each of the 603,550 men gave two-fifths of an ounce of silver. (When a census of Israel was taken in Numbers 1, the number of men who contributed silver for the tabernacle matched the number of men registered in the census.) The bronze used in construction totaled 5,310 pounds (over 2 tons).

# Closing

An incredible amount of money and resources came from everyday people because they believed that God was in this. The skilled workers came together, and they built the tabernacle, a dwelling place where people began to meet with God. And it all started with Moses hanging out on a mountain hearing from the Lord.

## The Daily Word

Once again, Moses, the author of Exodus, inspired by God, recounted the exact details of the Tabernacle construction process. Have you ever wondered why Moses wrote the features out in such full detail—not once but twice? As you compare the two, see how similar and exact the two accounts were. In a similar way, the writers of the New Testament often repeated truths they wanted the early church to understand. Paul said he repeated truths for believers' protection.

Pay attention to the things that repeat or even happen three or four times in your life. God may be trying to get your attention, keep you safe, or make sure you understand something. God is an intentional God. Don't overlook some of the obvious ways He is trying to speak to you.

**Now Bezalel made the ark of acacia wood; its length was two and a half cubits, and its width one and a half cubits, and its height one and a half cubits. —Exodus 37:1 NASB**

Further Scripture: Philippians 3:1; 2 Peter 1:12; Jude 1:5

## Questions

1. God instructed the lampstand to be made "all of one piece" (Exodus 37:17, 22). We know God had a purpose in it. What might that purpose have been (John 14:20; 17:20–21; Revelation 1:20)? What do you think was the source of light in the Holy of Holies?

2. The lampstand was to be made of pure gold (Exodus 37:17). It was the only source of light and was never to go out (Exodus 27:20). Can you see how these details point to Christ? (John 1:9; 8:1; 1 Peter 2:9; Revelation 21:23)

3. Each detail of the courtyard and its gate had significance and symbolic meaning. The colors of the screen (curtain hanging at the entrance) of blue, purple, and red symbolized deity, royalty, and blood sacrifice, respectively. The white curtains around the courtyard represented holiness. How do you see all these details pointing us to the Messiah?

4. No one could enter the courtyard by any way except through the one gate. How does this fact point to Christ? (John 10:9; 14:6)

5. Do you think it was easy for them to make all the articles and furniture for the sanctuary and courtyard according to the exact detail God commanded Moses? Why do you think God spent so much time giving such specific detail about these things? (Exodus 25:8–9; Hebrews 9:11, 24)

6. What part of the tabernacle, if any, did not point to the Messiah in some way? (Exodus 25:8–9)

7. What did the Holy Spirit highlight to you in Exodus 37—38 through the reading or the teaching?

# Lesson 50: Exodus 39
## *Deliverer:* Making the Priestly Garments

## Teaching Notes

### Intro

Exodus is constantly pointing to how we can experience the presence of God. Moses and the Israelites had been instructed to build a tabernacle. In Exodus 37 and 38, the people built all of the individual parts of the tabernacle. Exodus 39 gives the instructions for making the garments for the priests.

### Teaching

*Exodus 39:1*: Ryken wrote, "Vern Poythress describes [the priests] as 'vertical replicas of the tabernacle.'"[1] The yarn on the outside of the tabernacle looked like the yarn of the priests' garments. Even though Aaron made a lot of mistakes and was the guy who made the golden idol, he was now going to lead the charge into God's presence. God can use anyone! He's a redeeming God! Every one of us has made mistakes. Aaron was washed with water to be cleansed to do the work of the Lord (Exodus 40:12). Aaron was a mini tabernacle because of his garments.[2] If you think about it, aren't we all?

*Exodus 39:2–5*: Bezalel was going to make the different aspects of the priestly garments. The first thing he made was the ephod, and then he made the shoulder pads. Basically, the priest served as an ambassador. God was literally appealing through Aaron and his sons (2 Corinthians 5:20), and now, through *us!* We plead on Christ's behalf to be reconciled to God. Then the waistband was made, "Just as the Lord commanded." They were not cutting corners. They honored what the Lord had asked them to do. Do what the Holy Spirit is telling you to do, even if it's weird or doesn't make sense.

---

[1] Phillip Graham Ryken, *Exodus: Saved for God's Glory* (Wheaton, IL: Crossway, 2015), 1076.

[2] David M. Levy, *The Tabernacle: Shadows of the Messiah* (Bellmawr, NJ: Friends of Israel Gospel Ministry, 1993), 160; quoted in Ryken, 1076.

*Exodus 39:6–21*: The onyx stones were engraved with the 12 sons (12 tribes). The Lord said, "I want you to remember who the Israelites are and take them before Me." Next the breast piece was made with 12 stones, which sat over the priest's heart. The priest was to take the people of God before the throne of God.

*Exodus 39:22–29*: Next the robe was made entirely of blue. Then they made the tunic, the turban, and the sash.

*Exodus 39:30–31*: The medallion was made to go on the turban. Everything was, "Holy to the Lord." Everything was for a purpose. David Levy pointed out there are three major reasons we need these garments: (1) the holiness—set apart; (2) the glory—it exalts the priestly office; and (3) the beauty—reflects the Tabernacle.[3] All of it reflects God.

These priests were not perfect. Look at Exodus 32 when Aaron fashioned the golden calf (Psalms 132:9). Aaron and the Levitical priests did everything they could to be clothed in righteousness and, despite all their attempts to come before the presence of the Lord in holiness, they still fell short. In Leviticus, the priests still sinned. They had to make offerings, on their *own* behalf, on a regular basis. We need a high priest who is different. Aaron was the high priest, but Jesus is the great High Priest (Hebrews 4:14; 10:21).

I want to walk you through why Jesus is superior to Aaron the high priest (Philip Ryken)[4]:

- **Jesus serves in a superior *place*** (Hebrews 8:1–2). Jesus is at the right hand of God, not inside the tabernacle veil. He's serving in the true tabernacle, in the heavens.

- **Jesus serves with superior *righteousness*** (Hebrews 7:26–28). He is Holy, innocent, and undefiled. He doesn't need to offer sacrifices daily; He did it once for all, perfected forever.

- **Jesus serves with superior *sympathy*** (Hebrews 4:15–16). Because He can connect with us, we can connect with Him. Approach Him with boldness.

- **Jesus serves with superior *longevity*** (Hebrews 7:23–25). He remains forever and holds His priesthood permanently. Therefore, He is *always* able to save.

- **Jesus is the superior *sacrifice*** (Hebrews 9:12, 25–26). He offers eternal redemption, once for all!

---

[3] Ryken, 1079.

[4] Ryken, 1080–81.

In spite of their holy garments and how they pointed to Jesus, the Levitical priesthood always fell short. But it still points us to Christ (1 Peter 2:4–5, 9; Revelation 1:5b–6). All of this points to us experiencing the presence of God. They needed a priest to represent them before God in the holy tabernacle.

*Exodus 39:32–33*: All the work was finished! The clothes were made and done, "Just as the Lord had commanded." Notice the work wasn't accomplished only by Bezalel, Oholiab, or Moses. It was a team effort that made it possible for others to experience the presence of God. The whole nation was represented here. They brought the tabernacle to Moses.

*Exodus 39:34–41*: The Israelites began to list all the items God had instructed them to build. John MacArthur wrote, "It was fully His architecture and His design at every level of the undertaking."[5] They were bringing these things together that point to the coming Messiah.

*Exodus 39:42–43*: The Israelites had done all the work. They didn't take any shortcuts. Moses inspected it all. Moses blessed the people; and this is the first time we see this in Scripture.

## Closing

Spend some time digging into and comparing the work of Moses to the work of Jesus in Hebrews 3:1–6. Moses as the deliverer points ultimately to Jesus as the *Deliverer*.

## The Daily Word

As you read the detailed instructions for making the ephod, breastplate, and priestly garments, ten different times you see the phrase, "as the Lord commanded Moses." When you read a phrase repeated this many times in one chapter, take notice. The skillful Israelites obeyed everything the Lord commanded. Not one detail was left undone.

In the New Testament, Jesus said the greatest command is to love the Lord with all your heart, soul, and mind and to love others as yourself. Are you obedient to this commandment? Obedience to the Lord is love. As you receive grace from Jesus, you are able to walk out His commands in faith.

---

[5] John F. McArthur, *Exodus and Numbers: The Exodus from Egypt* (Nashville: Nelson Books, 2008), 77.

The Israelites had done all the work according to everything the Lord had commanded Moses. Moses inspected all the work they had accomplished. They had done just as the Lord commanded. Then Moses blessed them. — Exodus 39:42–43

Further Scripture: Matthew 22:35–39; Romans 1:5; 2 John 1:6

## Questions

1. The description of Aaron's priestly garments in Exodus 39 sounds a lot like the description of the tabernacle with regard to materials and colors used. Do you think God had this in mind when He gave Moses the instructions? Why or why not?

2. In Exodus 39, it's written nine times (vv. 1, 5, 7, 21, 26, 29, 32, 42, 43) that everything was made just as the Lord commanded Moses. Have you considered why this was such an important point to make? (Hebrews 8:5)

3. The priestly garments were also called holy garments (Exodus 28:2; 39:4). In Psalm 132:9, the priests were to be clothed in righteousness. Whose righteousness did the garments reflect (Psalm 132:9; Isaiah 61:10; Romans 13:14)? Since we are called priests (1 Peter 2:9; Revelation 1:6; 5:10) in the New Testament, what are our holy garments? (Isaiah 61:10a; Romans 13:14; Colossians 3:12–14)

4. There was a reason for the specific details and directions God gave Moses for the tabernacle and all its furnishings. Can you think of a Biblical example of someone who did not do exactly as God asked? Has God ever called you to do specific things? If so, did you struggle with doing exactly as He asked?

5. What did the Holy Spirit highlight to you in Exodus 39 through the reading or the teaching?

# Lesson 51: Exodus 40
## *Deliverer*: Setting Up the Tabernacle

## Teaching Notes

### Intro

We've studied the book of Genesis, and now we're finishing up the book of Exodus. Yesterday we covered Exodus 39, where the Israelites were told to make the priestly garments. Now it's time to finally put all of this together so God's presence can dwell in the tabernacle.

### Teaching

*Exodus 40:1–4*: This was almost one year after the exodus. God told Moses to set up the tabernacle, bring in the ark, and bring in the table with the lamps. What you're going to hear in Exodus 40 is God's instructions for how to build the tabernacle itself.

*Exodus 40:5–8*: Moses had an impeccable memory. They put everything in place. He said, "Don't do it yet, but get ready." Moses was so in tune with the Lord that he knew how this thing fit together. Did it have to be special water for the basin? It's not like they had a hose to fill it. They were in the wilderness, so they had to haul the water in. There was a whole lot of detail that required Moses to walk by faith as he was told to build the tabernacle.

This was hard work. They didn't have all of the tools we have. They were building what the Lord told them to build, and they were doing it by faith. Now Moses was assembling everything together. He got it all completed and assembled, and then in verse 9, God told him what to do.

*Exodus 40:9–13*: Moses was to anoint everything and consecrate it so *it will be holy*. Aaron and his sons were to wash themselves with water. They were preparing to serve as the Levitical priesthood. Moses was to clothe, anoint, and consecrate Aaron. Moses functioned as prophet, and his brother functioned as priest.

*Exodus 40:14–15*: Moses was to clothe and anoint Aaron's sons as well. Their anointing inaugurates a permanent priesthood. When you believe in Jesus Christ, you are given the indwelling Holy Spirit. Because of the Holy Spirit inside you, you automatically have that anointing (1 John 2:20, 27). The anointing *remains in you*. Remain in Him. Walk in confidence and authority, grace, and humility.

In the Old Testament, Aaron and the priests anointed everything so it would be set apart. But now, we are the anointed; we have been set apart from the world. When you realize the Spirit of God has anointed you, you don't have to convince people.

*Exodus 40:15–18*: Moses was anointing them to do the work God had asked them to do. Moses did everything just as the Lord commanded. Seven times you'll hear this language, "Just as the Lord had commanded him." The tabernacle was now being built! It was assembled and anointed, and everything was coming together. Moses set up the tabernacle.

*Exodus 40:19–30*: Moses spread the tent over the tabernacle and brought in the ark (which contained the testimony), the mercy seat, the table, the bread, and the lampstand. Everything God told him to do at Mount Sinai was happening. Everything was so detailed, what to make and where to put it. God knew exactly where He wanted everything to be—this was His house. They brought in the gold altar, the fragrant incense, the screen, the altar, and the basin with the water. Moses had incredible help!

*Exodus 40:31–34*: Moses, Aaron, and his sons washed their hands and feet. Moses finished the work (v. 33). Moses served as a deliverer in the book of Exodus, and so does Jesus in the book of John (John 19:28–30).

In Genesis, God finished the work of creation (Genesis 2:2). In Exodus, Moses finished the work of the tabernacle so the Israelites could experience God's presence. In John, Jesus finished the work so you and I can come into the Father's presence. The veil has been torn, and it's done. The cloud covered the tent, and the glory filled the tabernacle. Nelson wrote, "The glory of the Lord filling the tabernacle demonstrated His presence with the Israelites, His significance to them, and His awe-inspiring wonder."[1]

*Exodus 40:35–38*: His presence was so thick Moses couldn't go inside. The glory of the Lord filled the tabernacle—all because of one man's faith and obedience to listen on the Mount of Sinai and to listen in the wilderness. We have to be careful because our sins will drive away the glory of God. Whenever the cloud lifted, the Israelites set out. Their journey was just beginning. The cloud lifted and the

---

[1] Earl D. Radmacher, Ronald B. Allen, and H. Wayne House, eds., *Nelson's New Illustrated Bible Commentary* (Nashville: Thomas Nelson, 1999), 149.

Israelites followed (Exodus 13:21–22; Numbers 9:15–23). The cloud was visible to all the house of Israel. They all saw the presence of the Lord.

## Closing

This is the end of Exodus. Your body is a sanctuary of the Holy Spirit. When you walk, you are carrying the presence of God wherever you go.

Philip Ryken presents ten things that describe the role of Jesus in Exodus[2]:

(1) Jesus is the Moses of our salvation—He is the mediator who goes before us.

(2) Jesus is the lamb of our Passover—He is the sacrifice for our sins.

(3) Jesus is our way out of Egypt—He delivers us and baptizes us in the sea of grace.

(4) Jesus is our bread in the wilderness—He gives us what we need daily.

(5) Jesus is our voice f rom the mountain—He declares the law for our lives.

(6) Jesus is the altar of our burning—We offer praise up to Him.

(7) Jesus is the light on our lampstand—He is the Source of our life and light.

(8) Jesus is the basin of our cleansing—He is the Sanctifier of our souls.

(9) Jesus is our Great High Priest—He prays for us at the altar of incense.

(10) Jesus is the blood on the mercy seat—He is the atonement that reconciles us to God.

Jesus is the one who saved the people out of Egypt and He's the One who saves us.

## The Daily Word

When Moses finished work on the tabernacle, God filled it with His glory in the form of a cloud. God placed a cloud over it by day and a fire inside the cloud by night as a sign to the people that He was with them along their journey. These physical signs served as a visible reminder of God's presence. He was with them, and His glory was all around.

Remember, God is with you on your journey. Open your eyes to see God in your midst. And if you don't sense Him, ask Him to reveal Himself to you! The Lord is your Deliverer.

---

[2] Philip Graham Ryken, *Exodus: Saved for God's Glory* (Wheaton, IL: Crossway, 2015), 1103.

> For the cloud of the LORD was over the tabernacle by day, and there was a fire inside the cloud by night, visible to the entire house of Israel throughout all the stages of their journey. —Exodus 40:38
>
> Further Scripture: Judges 18:6; Psalm 25:4–5; Psalm 121:8

## Questions

1. The high priest had to be washed and anointed in order to serve as a priest to God (Exodus 40:12, 13). Where do we see Jesus "washed" and "anointed"? (Matthew 3:13–17; Luke 4:18; Acts 10:38)

2. In Exodus 40:15, the sons of Aaron, and consequently all future priests, were also to be washed and anointed to serve before God. We are also called to be priests (1 Peter 2:5, 9; Revelation 1:6). How are we washed and anointed to serve God? (1 Corinthians 6:11; 2 Corinthians 1:21; Ephesians 5:26; Hebrews 10:22; 1 John 2:27; Revelation 1:5b)

3. Everything that would be used in the tabernacle was to be anointed and consecrated, and it became holy. Consecrate means, "dedicated to a sacred purpose; to set apart; make holy." If we are now the temple (1 Corinthians 3:16) and the Spirit of God dwells in us, how are we consecrated? (2 Corinthians 6:16—7:1; Ephesians 4:20–24; Colossians 3:12–17)

4. In Exodus 40:34, Moses wrote that the glory of the Lord filled the tabernacle. In 2 Chronicles 7:1, after Solomon dedicated the newly built temple, again it says the glory of the Lord filled the temple. Since we are the temple of God, what does our being filled look like (Acts 2:1–4a; 1 Corinthians 6:19–20; Ephesians 5:18–20)? How then should we live?

5. When reading Exodus 40:33, the phrase "so Moses finished the work" points us back to Genesis 2:2 where God "finished the work that He had done." Where else is something of monumental importance being declared finished (John 19:30)? According to this reference, what is finished? (Remember our theme for Exodus: Isaiah 53:4–12; Romans 8:1–4; 1 Corinthians 15:55–57; 2 Corinthians 5:17; Colossians 2:13–15)

6. What did the Holy Spirit highlight to you in Exodus 40 through the reading or the teaching?

# Lesson 52: Leviticus 1—3
## *Atonement*: The Burnt Offering

## Teaching Notes

### Intro

Our goal through the entire Bible is to identify one word in each book that points to the Messiah. Our word for Genesis is *Seed* (Genesis 3:15). Our word for Exodus is *Deliverer* (Jude 5). Now we're in Leviticus. Leviticus means, "He called" or "He names."

Our word for Jesus, in the book of Leviticus, is *Atonement*. The entire old covenant points to Yeshua, the Messiah. Leviticus relates to the Levites, the priests, and contains the requirements of the Mosaic covenant. Gordon Wenham wrote, "It would be wrong, however, to describe Leviticus as a manual for priests. It is equally concerned with the part the laity should play in worship."[1] It's for everyday people.

The Israelites had the tabernacle in the wilderness, and God said He was going to give them more regulations like: When to go to the sanctuary? What to bring? What did the priests need to do? How were they supposed to dress? Only a few chapters in the book were given directly to the Levites. The rest was directed to everyday people for instructions on how to approach the presence of God. Mark F. Rooker wrote, "This is one of the books they teach Jewish children."[2]

Sailhamer says one of the central themes of Leviticus is holiness.[3] God identified the Israelites as: (1) a special possession, (2) a kingdom of priests, and (3) a holy nation (Exodus 19:5–6). In Leviticus, God gave them a manual for how this would happen. The Israelites were in the wilderness, and they didn't know how to interact with the tabernacle. They needed instruction.

---

[1] Gordon J. Wenham, *The Book of Leviticus* (Grand Rapids: Eerdmans, 1979), 3.

[2] See the discussion and critique of the Documentary Hypothesis in Mark F. Rooker, *The New American Commentary: Leviticus* (Nashville: Broadman & Holman, 2000), 23–38.

[3] John H. Sailhamer, *The Pentateuch as Narrative* (Grand Rapids: Zondervan), 323.

# Teaching

*Leviticus 1:1–2:* Moses' audience was the Israelites. Nelson wrote that "offering" means "to bring near that which one brings near to God."[4] Remember, the Israelites didn't know how to approach God. God was teaching them how to approach the throne. All the Israelites had, at that point, were their flocks and herds.

*Leviticus 1:3:* Noah offered burnt offerings on the altar (Genesis 8:20). Abraham was to offer his own son Isaac as a burnt offering (Genesis 22:1). Jethro, Moses' father-in-law, brought a burnt offering to God (Exodus 18:11–12). Even though they didn't have the tabernacle in place, the idea of a burnt offering was not foreign to them. The requirements were an unblemished male from the herd or flock. They had to bring an acceptable offering. Over the course of time, this was going to become a weight. They will eventually be given 613 rules and regulations.

*Leviticus 1:3–9:* The process for burnt offerings:

(1) Present the offering (v. 3).

(2) Lay hands on the animal's head (v. 4).

(3) Slaughter the sacrifice (v. 5). The offerer did the killing here, not the priest, though the priest supervised.

(4) Collect the blood and sprinkle it on the altar (v. 5b). The priests did this. It's all about the blood, because without the blood there was no atonement.

(5) The skinned the burnt offering and cut it in pieces (v. 6). To experience the presence of God, the one with the offering had to do the work.

(6) The priests prepared a fire (v. 7).

(7) Then they arranged the pieces of the sacrifice on the fire (v. 8).

(8) The washed its entrails with water (v. 9a). The people needed direction, a focus.

(9) The priests then burned it all (v. 9b). Purification was by fire. This was what the Israelites were to do in order to approach God in his presence.

*Leviticus 1:10:* The exact same process used for offering a bull (see above) was used for offering a sheep or goat. Loving the Lord and loving your neighbor is

---

[4] Earl D. Radmacher, Ronald B. Allen, and H. Wayne House, eds., *Nelson's New Illustrated Bible Commentary* (Nashville: Thomas Nelson), 153.

more important than all the burnt offerings and sacrifices (Mark 12:33). But these components all pointed to the perfect atonement of Christ.

The one word for all of Leviticus is *Atonement*. I want to give you a quick backdrop on the word atonement:

- When the Israelite put his hand on the head (of the animal) it was so he could be accepted, "to make atonement for him" (Leviticus 1:4).
- Atonement means "to cover."
- Constable describes three meanings of "atonement"[5]:
- Substitution—The animal served in place of the offerer. The perfect animal's blood atoned for the sin of the offerer.
- Imputation—God transferred the guilt of the Israelites and put it onto the animal (when the offerer put his hands on the head of the animal).
- Death—It was required in order for atonement to work. Bloodshed brought atonement.
- They had to go through this whole process in order to be acceptable to God.

*Leviticus 2*: The meal/grain offering.

*Leviticus 3*: The fellowship/peace offering.

## Closing
Leviticus constantly points to Christ, our *Atonement*.

## The Daily Word

While Exodus is like a design manual for the tabernacle, Leviticus is a user manual. It's a codebook for the Law. It begins by describing the burnt offerings, grain offerings, and peace or fellowship offerings. The people sacrificed their most costly possessions or livelihood at the altar as an offering to the Lord. The sacrifices were a soothing aroma to God and allowed the people to be found acceptable by Him. This alone was reason enough to make the sacrifice at the altar.

Disciples who give up everything to follow Christ also make this sacrifice. It, too, is pleasing to God. As you worship God, you are called to present yourself as

---

[5] Thomas L. Constable, *Expository Notes of Dr. Thomas Constable: Leviticus*, 13, https://planobiblechapel.org/tcon/notes/pdf/leviticus.pdf.

a living sacrifice. You are to hold nothing back. Is there anything you are holding back today that needs to be presented to God as a sacrifice in worship to Him? As you lay it down before Him, remember, it will please the Lord.

**Then the LORD summoned Moses and spoke to him from the tent of meeting: "Speak to the Israelites and tell them: When any of you brings an offering to the LORD from the livestock, you may bring your offering from the herd or the flock. . . . He must bring it to the entrance to the tent of meeting so that he may be accepted by the LORD." —Leviticus 1:1–2, 3**

Further Scripture: Mark 8:34; John 12:3; Romans 12:1

## Questions

1. Men were to bring a burnt offering and lay hands on the head of the animal, thus transferring their guilt onto the animal. According to Leviticus 1:4, what was the purpose of this? Can you see this reality in Isaiah 53:12b?

2. "An offering by fire of a soothing aroma to the Lord," is repeated in Leviticus 1—3 (Leviticus 1:9,13,17, etc.). A similar phrase is found in Ephesians 5:2. Do you see a connection? If so, what is it?

3. The Lord instructed the people through Moses in Leviticus 2:13 that the grain offerings be seasoned with salt, and in fact, all offerings were to be offered with salt. How does Mark 9:49–50 relate to this system of offering?

4. How would you define atonement? In Kyle's teaching, he talks about three things that take place during an atoning sacrifice. Name and describe them.

5. What did the Holy Spirit highlight to you in Leviticus 1—3 through the reading or the teaching?

# Lesson 53: Leviticus 4—5
## Atonement: Sin Offering

## Teaching Notes

### Intro

In Leviticus 4, we see God giving Moses more instructions. Moses had just built the tabernacle, and now he and the Israelites needed to know how to use it. God was giving Moses the manual on how to interact with Him and have a relationship with Him. "These are the things that will allow you to be acceptable to Me," God says. So far, we've seen:

- Leviticus 1—burnt offerings
- Leviticus 2—grain offerings
- Leviticus 3—fellowship/peace offerings

In Leviticus 4, God starts to get very specific. He had to get specific because of sin. Rooker wrote, "The root ht' for 'sin' occurs 595 times in the Old Testament, and Leviticus, with 116 attestations, has far more occurrences than any other Old Testament book."[1] Leviticus is going to address the issue of sin. Today in Leviticus 4 and 5, we'll see the root word of sin 53 times. We have to remember that God can actually forgive His people from sin. That's what the sacrifice is all about—receiving atonement through death. Today we're going to identify people groups that were sinning in the Israelites' time.

### Teaching

*Leviticus 4:1–2*: What is unintentional sin? Constable wrote, "This category [unintentional sin] includes sin done: by mistake, in error, through oversight or ignorance, through lack of consideration, negligence, or by carelessness."[2]

---

[1] Mark F. Rooker, *The New American Commentary: Leviticus* (Nashville: Broadman & Holman, 2000), 106.

[2] Thomas L. Constable, *Expository Notes of Dr. Thomas Constable: Leviticus*, 47, https://planobiblechapel.org/tcon/notes/pdf/leviticus.pdf.

Wiersbe wrote, "They [the Israelites] had become defiled or disobedient and didn't realize it. However, ignorance doesn't cancel guilt."[3] Even though sin is unintentional, you're still guilty. Psalm 19:12: "Who perceives his unintentional sins? Cleanse me from my hidden faults." Nelson's commentary says, "Sin that occurred without the sinner realizing it still offended the holiness of God and polluted His earthly dwelling place, just as clothing may be soiled without the wearer knowing it. To be used again, both the clothing and the tabernacle required cleansing."[4]

*Leviticus 4:3–4*: The anointed priests were in charge of the Israelites, so if one of them sinned, he brought guilt on everyone. He was then required to present a sin offering. The priest was to put his hand on the head and slaughter the bull.

*Leviticus 4:5–7*: The priest was to bring the blood into the tent of meeting. Blood is everywhere in Leviticus (Leviticus 3:2; 4:5). Receiving atonement requires death, which always requires bloodshed (Exodus 12:13; Isaiah 1:11; Genesis 25:30; Leviticus 17:11; Hebrews 9:22; Romans 5:9; and 1 Corinthians 11:25).
The priest was to dip his finger in the blood and sprinkle it seven times. This blood was from the bull (v. 3). The priest would do this in front of the veil. Then the priest was to put some of the blood on the altar of fragrant incense. Finally, the priest would pour out the rest of the blood at the base of the altar of burnt offering. The altar of fragrant incense did not typically have blood, but it was needed because this was the sin of the priests. The only other time blood was sprinkled on the altar of fragrant incense was the Day of Atonement (Hebrews 9:4).

*Leviticus 4:8–10*: The offerer was to remove the fat. This is a comparison to the fellowship sacrifice or peace offering.

*Leviticus 4:11–12*: The rest of the bull needed to be brought outside the camp. Hebrews 13:11–15: "For the bodies of those animals whose blood is brought into the most holy place by the high priest as a sin offering are burned outside the camp. Therefore, Jesus also suffered outside the gate, so that He might sanctify the people by His own blood. Let us then go to Him outside the camp, bearing His disgrace. For we do not have an enduring city here; instead, we seek the one to come. Therefore, through Him let us continually offer up to God a sacrifice

---

[3] Warren W. Wiersbe, *The Exposition Bible Commentary: Genesis–Deuteronomy* (Colorado Springs: David C. Cook, 2007), 203.
[4] Earl D. Radmacher, Ronald B. Allen, and H. Wayne House, eds., *Nelson's New Illustrated Bible Commentary* (Nashville: Thomas Nelson, 1999), 156.

of praise, that is, the fruit of our lips that confess His name. Don't neglect to do what is good and to share, for God is pleased with such sacrifices."

Jesus suffered outside the camp so that He could sanctify us with His blood. Jesus is everywhere in Scripture. It all points to Him. The writers of Scripture tie this together through the Holy Spirit.

*Leviticus 4:13–21*: If the *whole community* made a mistake and no one noticed it, then the assembly was to present a young bull as an offering. They were to present a young bull and go through the same process that the priests did (vv.1–12).

The elders would put their hands on the bull, representing the whole congregation. They would sprinkle the blood, put some on the horns, and pour out the rest at the altar. Then they would remove the fat and burn the rest outside the camp. They followed the same process as the sin offering for the priests. The Jewish tradition in this story says that the congregation was the Sanhedrin. The community involved the religious leaders. There was some form of authority in this community for it to require the same level of sacrifice as the priests.

*Leviticus 4:22*: Here we look at how the Israelites were to deal with the sins of a *leader*. Remember, all of this is in regard to *unintentional* sins. Now and forward, you will not see the blood poured around the altar of incense anymore. Now, it was just poured around the altar of burnt offering.

*Leviticus 4:27*: A *common person* was anyone who was not a leader or a priest. Female or male goats were accepted. Why was a female goat acceptable this time? Maybe the common people didn't have as many resources to choose from?

*Leviticus 4:31b*: All of this continued to happen so that the priest could make atonement and the people could be forgiven. How does forgiveness happen? It's always through the blood. Whether you were a priest, part of the community, a leader, or a common person, all could be forgiven through the sin offering.

*Leviticus 5:* Guilt Offerings. All of it points to Christ, our *Atonement*, who sets us free!

# Closing

Hebrews 10:19–22: "Therefore, brothers, since we have boldness to enter the sanctuary through the blood of Jesus, by a new and living way He has opened for us through the curtain (that is, His flesh), and since we have a great high priest over the house of God, let us draw near with a true heart in full assurance of faith, our hearts sprinkled clean from an evil conscience and our bodies washed in pure water."

Through Christ we have a new way to approach God! Because of the blood of Christ, we have been forgiven. Our hearts have been sprinkled, and our bodies have been washed in pure water because of what Christ has done for us.

## The Daily Word

In today's reading, this phrase is repeated: "If a person sins, so the priest shall make atonement on his behalf for his sin which he has committed, and it will be forgiven to him." It is important to understand what this means. Atonement means reconciliation. God provides a way for humankind to come back into a loving, peaceful relationship with Him, despite sin. Because God loves you, He seeks to reconcile Himself to you.

In the Old Testament, the high priests' sacrifices accomplished atonement for themselves and for the people because of sin. In the New Testament, Jesus Christ gave His life as a ransom for you. If you believe in Jesus Christ as your Savior, your sins are forgiven. Today, rest in that promise. Your sins are forgiven as a child of God. Thank the Lord for this free gift of reconciliation to God.

**He must prepare the second bird as a burnt offering according to the regulation. In this way the priest will make atonement on his behalf for the sin he has committed, and he will be forgiven. —Leviticus 5:10**

Further Scripture: Mark 10:45; Romans 5:11; Hebrews 7:27

## Questions

1.  The blood of the sin offering in Leviticus 4:5–6 was taken into the tabernacle and sprinkled in front of the veil. What are your thoughts about why this was done? Read the following verses: 1 Peter 1:2 and Hebrews 10:22. How would you describe these verses in connection with Leviticus?

2.  The body of the sin offering was to be taken outside the camp to be burned by fire (Leviticus 4:11–12). Read Hebrews 13:11–13. How do these verses reference something greater? What do you think verse 13 means?

3.  Some organs of the sin offering were to be removed and offered on the altar to the Lord, specifically the kidneys and the liver with the fat (Leviticus 4:8–10). What are the functions of these organs and fat in the body? Do you see a purpose for these parts to be offered on the altar?

4. The Lord made atonement available not only to those who could afford the animals for sacrifice but to the poor as well (Leviticus 5:7, 11). Does it appear the Lord wanted atonement available to all people once they were aware of their sin? Do you believe this is true for mankind today (Joel 2:32; Acts 2:21; Romans 10:9–13; 2 Peter 3:9)?

5. The New Testament references about sacrifices cannot be fully understood without learning about the sacrificial system. What new insights have you learned by studying the first few chapters of Leviticus (Hebrews 10:1–22)?

6. What did the Holy Spirit highlight to you in Leviticus 4—5 through the reading or the teaching?

# Lesson 54: Leviticus 6

*Atonement:* The Guilt Offering and Continual Fire

## Teaching Notes

### Intro

In Leviticus, we're plowing through a whole lot of offerings. So far, we've covered:

- Leviticus 1—burnt offerings
- Leviticus 2—grain offerings
- Leviticus 3—fellowship offerings
- Leviticus 4—sin offering (priests, community, leaders, common people)
- Leviticus 5—trespass or guilt offering

Remember God gave this manual to tell the Israelites how to engage in worship with Him. Recognize that you need forgiveness, which is only received through the sacrifice of Christ, our *Atonement.*

Israel, in this context, had been in Egypt for a long time and was now traveling through the desert. Nelson's commentary says, "Israel was a refugee nation traveling through the desert."[1] They didn't really have homes as they traveled throughout the desert and they had no rules. So God gave them these regulations and required offerings to guide them. At the end of Leviticus 5, there was the trespass/guilt offering when a person was aware of his guilt or the guilt was suspected.

### Teaching

*Leviticus 6:1–4*: The Lord gave Moses instructions for *guilt offerings.* Remember, this was the manual for these Israelite refugees and was an ongoing conversation between Moses and God. Can you imagine the wilderness conversations? When the Israelites deceived a neighbor, they offended the *Lord!* The offender had to acknowledge he was wrong and return whatever he had stolen from the neighbor. God was giving the Israelites an outlet.

---

[1] Earl D. Radmacher, Ronald B. Allen, and H. Wayne House, eds., *Nelson's New Illustrated Bible Commentary* (Nashville: Thomas Nelson, 1999), 158.

*Leviticus 6:5*: If an Israelite deceived or stole from his neighbor, he had to make full restitution! He also had to add a fifth to its value—20 percent on top of what was taken. This was to be done "*on the day*" he acknowledged his guilt! This happened to Zacchaeus (Luke 19:8). He was willing to pay back four times as much to those he had deceived or stolen from! When they recognized they were guilty, they had to give back whatever they had stolen plus 20 percent. We all have opportunities to go the wrong way. As an encouragement, let's look at how Joseph responded when he had the opportunity to take what did not belong to him (Genesis 39:9; 1 John 4:20).

*Leviticus 6:6–7*: After restitution was made, there was more to be done. Rooker wrote, "Only after restitution had been made with one's fellow man could it be sought with God (6.6)."[2] The American church can learn from this example! We need to go to our brother first when we have wronged him and make it right. Isn't that what we're instructed to do when partaking of communion (1 Corinthians 11:17–34)?

The priest served as an appraiser of sacrifices, "according to your assessment of its value." The unblemished ram they were to bring as a guilt offering to the Lord was to be appropriate for the level of wrong they had done. They had to (1) return the item,

(2) add one-fifth of its value, and (3) make an appropriate guilt offering to the Lord. Sin always costs us more! The sacrifice makes atonement. The Israelite would be forgiven through the blood of the sacrifice. Praise the Lord! He gave them some structure.

*Leviticus 6:8–13*: We talked about the *burnt offering* in Leviticus 1. The fire had to be constantly burning and must not go out! This is going to be a theme as we continue in Leviticus. The priests had been anointed to do this work and they were to change their clothes before bringing out the ashes. When I picture revival, I think of fire and the Holy Spirit.

I want to walk through this image of fire in Scripture:

- Leviticus 9:24: An original fire on the altar from God. It was a perpetual fire that symbolizes perpetual worship. It represents a continual need for Christ, our *Atonement*, and reconciliation. Luke 3:16: John the Baptist said Jesus would baptize with the Holy Spirit and with fire. The fire is burning away the chaff, the guilt, and the sin. A lot of times the

---

[2] Mark F. Rooker, *The New American Commentary Series: Leviticus* (Nashville: Broadman & Holman, 2000), 126.

American Church doesn't want to let the fire burn away the chaff in our lives. There's freedom when the fire of God burns in our lives.

- Romans 12:1–2: Present your bodies as a living sacrifice. If you never allow the baptism of fire, you'll be drowned by sin. The baptism of fire enables you to function in the baptism of the Holy Spirit.
- Jeremiah 20:9: If you don't mention the message of God, it becomes like a fire in your heart, shut up in your bones.
- Psalm 39:3: My heart grew hot within me.

Five times in verses 8–13, the statement "the fire must keep burning; it must not go out" was recorded. Nelson's commentary explained, "Perpetual fire symbolized the continual need for atonement and reconciliation with God, which was the purpose of the offering."[3]

*Leviticus 6:14–23*: The Grain Offering (cereal, food offering) was explained.

*Leviticus 6:24–30*: The Sin Offering was explained.

## Closing

When we acknowledge the guilt we feel when we've done something wrong, we sometimes allow the enemy to creep in and cause us to keep the guilt. But the blood sets us free! Steven Cole wrote, "Satan loves to come in and charge us of being guilty, and then we stay in that position of victim who's fallen short."

In Revelation 12:10, Satan is the accuser of the brethren. In Zechariah 3:1, Satan accused Joshua the high priest. We can't live in this position of guilt! Jesus has set us free! If we hold onto the guilt, we're saying Jesus' blood is not enough.

2 Corinthians 3:17, "Now the Lord is the Spirit, and where the Spirit of the Lord is, there is freedom." When we talk about being baptized in the Spirit and in fire, we're talking about walking in freedom. These guilt offerings in Leviticus 6 brought freedom. But the Israelites had to make the guilt offerings every single time. We only have to do it once.

---

[3] Radmacher et al., 160.

## The Daily Word

You know the feeling of guilt you experience after sinning? You try to ignore it or wish it away, but the guilt lingers and even gets heavier. The Lord spoke to Moses, giving him instructions for "when a person sins." Notice, God didn't say *if* someone sins but *when*. The Lord knew His people would sin. Therefore, He instructed Moses on the guilt offering so the people's sins would be forgiven, and they would no longer incur guilt.

In a similar way, Jesus came to make atonement for your sin. Instead of carrying the burden of guilt and shame, He longs for you to know you are forgiven and can walk in freedom! Turn to Him, confess your sins, and you will be forgiven. He loves you and wants you to let go of the guilt you have been carrying. Be honest with Him today. Let His love wash over you.

**In this way the priest will make atonement on his behalf before the LORD, and he will be forgiven for anything he may have done to incur guilt. — Leviticus 6:7**

Further Scripture: 2 Corinthians 3:17; 2 Corinthians 7:9–10; 1 John 1:9

## Questions

1. Leviticus 6:2 says that a person who sins, sins against the Lord. Why is all sin against the Lord (Psalm 51:4; Luke 5:21)?

2. What was the penalty for lying about or stealing from someone's neighbor (Leviticus 6:4–6; Luke 19:8)? What would happen if believers today humbled themselves to this degree?

3. How did the priest make atonement for the guilty party (Leviticus 6:7)? What are we to do as believers when we sin (1 John 1:9)?

4. Why was the fire on the altar to be kept burning continually (Leviticus 6:12–13)?

5. When could a portion of the sin offering be eaten? When could it not be eaten?

6. What did the Holy Spirit highlight to you in Leviticus 6 through the reading or the teaching?

# Lesson 55: Leviticus 7

*Atonement:* The Fellowship Offering

## Teaching Notes

### Intro

We've been studying the different types of offerings: guilt offering, burnt offering, sin offering, grain offering, and fellowship peace offering. I'd like to slow down and take a look at what we've learned so far.

When God spoke to Moses on Mount Sinai, He said, "This is how I want my people, my treasured possession, my holy priesthood, my holy nation, to engage with Me. I want them to bring forth offerings so they can be cleansed from their sins and experience more of Me."

God taught Moses how the Israelites, whether priests, leaders, or common people, could experience forgiveness. It was all about the blood that provides atonement. Through death, there is life.

Here is a how *Christ* is represented in each of these offerings:

| | | | |
|---|---|---|---|
| Leviticus 1 | Burnt Offering | Atonement | Christ's sinless nature |
| Leviticus 2 | Grain Offering | Dedication / Consecration | Christ wholly devoted to the Father's purpose |
| Leviticus 3 | Fellowship/Peace Offering | Fellowship | Christ was at peace with God |
| Leviticus 4 | Sin Offering | Propitiation | Christ's substitutionary death |
| Leviticus 5—6 | Guilt Offering | Repentance | Christ paid it all for repentance |

Today we're going to discuss the fellowship offering, and it's refreshing. Yes, there's a sacrifice, but there's also a party. And when we slow down, we see that Christ is in all of this.

# Teaching

*Leviticus 7:1–2*: Restitution Offering (or Guilt Offering) is the restoration of something lost or stolen, thus restoring it back to its proper owner. It is offered at the altar of burnt offering.

*Leviticus 7:3–10*: The offerer (the Israelite who sinned) presented the fat. The priest burned it. The priest could eat the meat of the restitution offering, like the sin offering. The priests were actually getting payment through the restitution offering. Grain offerings were also payments for the priests.

*Leviticus 7:11*: The Fellowship Offering (or Peace Offering) was when believers were celebrating peace with God. This was a positive offering. Sometimes it's so easy to focus on our sin, but we need to remember to celebrate the things God is doing in our lives.

*Leviticus 7:12*: The fellowship offering was presented for thanksgiving! Nelson wrote, "Thanksgiving [is] a confession of human dependence on God's grace and mercy, and a praise of the living God."[1] So many of us wallow in our woes and sorrows. Think of what it would mean if we had this perspective of, "Praise God, I'm alive! Praise God, I've been atoned for!"

They celebrated the fellowship offerings by presenting unleavened cakes mixed with olive oil, unleavened wafers coated with oil, or well-kneaded cakes of fine flour mixed with oil. Nelson wrote, "The sacrifice of thanksgiving was a public proclamation of who God is and what He does."[2] I want to be known as the guy who offers the fellowship offering more than any other offering. Moses was saying, "I want you to thank the Lord for what He's doing."

*Leviticus 7:13*: The bread and meat were to be served as a sacrifice. The Israelites were celebrating peace with God and expressing public gratitude to God. Not just saying thanks but expressing thanks to God with material things. Jacob offered a sacrifice and invited his relatives to eat a meal (Genesis 31:54). The fellowship offering included a sacrifice and eating a meal together. Solomon offered a fellowship offering—22,000 cattle and 122,000 sheep—to dedicate the temple (1 Kings 8:62–63). First Moses built the tabernacle, later Solomon built the temple.

---

[1] Earl D. Radmacher, Ronald B. Allen, and H. Wayne House, eds., *Nelson's New Illustrated Bible Commentary* (Nashville: Thomas Nelson, 1999), 161.

[2] Radmacher et al., 161.

*Leviticus 7:14–15*: Heave offerings (not a wave offering) were waved before the Lord to acknowledge that He is the giver of gifts. There were certain types of food that would be lifted up in thanksgiving. There could be no leftovers.

*Leviticus 7:16*: Constable wrote, "There are three types [of fellowship offerings]: 1) Thanks offerings expressed gratitude for an unexpected blessing. 2) Votive offerings expressed gratitude for a blessing granted when a vow had been made while asking for the blessing. 3) Freewill offerings expressed gratitude to God without regard to any specific blessing."[3] The leftovers may only be left one day if he offered a vow or a freewill offering. The Israelites are given an opportunity to have peace with the Lord and celebrate it. Are you at peace with the Lord? The only way you can have it is through Christ!

In Colossians 3:15, we read, "And let the peace of the Messiah, to which you were also called in one body, control your hearts. Be thankful." When we're at peace, it results in thankfulness. If you don't have the peace of Christ, it's time to give control back to Him. Scripture tells us the following:

- Romans 3:23—we all sin
- Romans 6:23—the wages of sin is death; there is no peace

I want us to experience the peace available in Christ! When there's anxiety, give it to Him! So how do we overcome these things that lead to anxiety?

- Romans 5:8—His love takes away the sin and death.

Stop trying to do it on your own! He'll take it! That's what I love about Leviticus. It points to the *Atonement* of Christ, which gives us peace. That's when you can experience the peace offering.

- Ephesians 2:8–9—you are saved by grace through faith; it's a gift.
- Romans 10:9–10—if you confess and believe in Jesus as Lord, you *will be saved* = life

## Closing

When you experience Romans 10:9–10, that's when you experience the fellowship offering; that's when you experience life and peace.

---

[3] Thomas L. Constable, *Expository Notes of Dr. Thomas Constable: Leviticus*, 225–26, https://planobiblechapel.org/tcon/notes/pdf/leviticus.pdf.

# The Daily Word

The people of Israel received instructions on peace offerings, sometimes referred to as fellowship offerings. The peace offering focused on wholeness or completeness. The Israelites would sense completeness with God as they brought sacrifices. Completeness with God can feel like joy and peace of mind, which comes from knowing God is at peace with you. Likewise, Paul instructed believers to present their requests to God with thanksgiving and supplication, and then, the peace of God will cover them completely.

Jesus is your peace and brings completeness to your life. His peace will come upon you when you stop trying to control every situation and instead give every moment over to the Lord. What are you still trying to control that you may need to surrender as a sacrifice to the Lord? Make today a day of surrender, a peace offering to God!

**The LORD spoke to Moses: "Tell the Israelites: The one who presents a fellowship sacrifice to the LORD must bring an offering to the LORD from his sacrifice." —Leviticus 7:28–29**

Further Scripture: Psalm 29:11; Ephesians 2:17–18; Philippians 4:6–7

## Questions

1. What is the difference between a guilt offering and a sin offering (Leviticus 4; 5:14–19)? Which one is considered the most holy (Leviticus 7:1)?
2. Some sacrifices were required at specific places and times. What was unique about the peace and thanksgiving offerings (Leviticus 7:11–14)?
3. Why was the blood to never be consumed (Leviticus 7:26; 17:11)? What was the penalty for doing so (Genesis 9:4–6)?
4. How has Christ fulfilled the burnt, grain, peace, sin, and guilt offerings (Romans 4:25; 5:1; 1 Corinthians 15:20; 2 Corinthians 5:21; Ephesians 5:2)?
5. What did the Holy Spirit highlight to you in Leviticus 7 through the reading or the teaching?

# Lesson 56: Leviticus 8—9
## *Atonement*: The Priestly Ministry Inaugurated

## Teaching Notes

### Intro

Leviticus is a tangible, practical manual that showed the Israelites how to function with God on a regular basis. Remember Bezalel and Oholiab who helped build the tabernacle? God was telling the Israelites how to use the tabernacle to commune with Him. Leviticus 8 and 9 cover the ordination of Aaron and his sons.

### Teaching

*Leviticus 8:1–5*: The whole assembly gathered for the ordination. Since the priests were going to faithfully serve day in and day out, the Lord was going to ordain them. Their role was not only to serve the Lord but also to serve the Israelites.

*Leviticus 8:6–9*: Aaron and his sons were washed with water. Aaron was clothed in the holy garments: sash, robe, ephod, breastpiece, Urim and Thummim, and turban with a gold medallion. These items composed Aaron's uniform. Remember our word for Genesis is *Seed*, Exodus is *Deliverer*, and Leviticus is *Atonement*. The Messiah is the One who will come in and atone for our sins. But for now, the priests were taking care of the atonement process.

*Leviticus 8:10–36*: Aaron and the tabernacle were anointed. Aaron's sons were clothed, and various sacrifices were offered. They were getting ready! The anointing took place. The priests were consecrated. The ram of ordination was being eaten. Once the priests had been ordained, they were told to not go anywhere for seven days.

*Leviticus 9:1–3*: On the eighth day, after seven days of ordination, Moses walked through four major offerings. The first two offerings were a young bull (sin offering) and ram (burnt offering). This was the first time Aaron became a voice for all the Israelites. A male goat (sin offering), calf, and lamb (burnt offering) were also to be sacrificed.

*Leviticus 9:4*: The second type of offering included two separate offerings: the ox and the ram (fellowship offering) and grains mixed with oil (grain offering). Remember, the tabernacle had never been opened for business before! They were getting the whole place ready. He was going to perform the first four offerings to get started. There was a balance between atoning for sin and celebrating peace with God.

This was Aaron who messed up in Exodus 32:1–4 by creating the golden calf. All the way back in Genesis, we saw the chosen ones making mistakes. God uses unlikely people. Now the high priest was going to usher in the presence of God by offering four offerings. Two offerings were to atone for sin and two offerings were to fellowship with God. Remember God's punishment for Aaron's sin of making the golden calf? God told Moses that He wasn't going to go with the Israelites any longer. And look who it was who got to usher in the Lord's presence in the tabernacle—Aaron! God is a redeeming God!

We can't live in the place of guilt! The atonement takes care of that! We have to walk in peace and fellowship with God. Are we willing to let the "golden calves" of our past go? Jesus is! Are we?

*Leviticus 9:5–7*: The community came and stood before the Lord. Moses began to implement all four of the offerings. Remember when we talked about each of the different people groups within the Israelites: the priests, the community, the leaders, and the common people? Aaron was going to present the offering for himself first and then offer the sacrifice for the people. Thus we have to be in a right relationship with the Lord in order for us to do ministry with someone else.

*Leviticus 9:8–11*: The sin offering for Aaron took place. There had to have been some crazy satisfaction to see all that they had built, finally being used for its intended purpose. This was happening as the Lord commanded. Aaron burned the flesh and hide outside the camp. Jesus was sacrificed outside the camp (Hebrews 13:11–13). Aaron was given a second chance, and Jesus gives us one too!

*Leviticus 9:12–16*: The burnt offering took place. Why? The burnt offering was the everyday offering and didn't go outside the camp. Only the sin offering had to go outside the camp. Leviticus 16:5 describes the Day of Atonement where the goat was offered as a sin offering. What was taking place here in Leviticus 9 was foreshadowing the Day of Atonement.

*Leviticus 9:17–21*: The grain offering was made. You can't always stay in a state of celebration, but you also can't always stay in a state of repentance. There has to be a balance. This was Aaron's first day on the job, and he presented the sin offering, the burnt offering, the grain offering, and the fellowship offering.

*Leviticus 9:22*: This was the first time Aaron blessed the people. Who taught this to Aaron? It was because he had been anointed. The Spirit of God was directing his steps and his hands. Aaron raised his hands to bless the people. Numbers 6:24–26 is referred to as the Aaronic Blessing.

*Leviticus 9:23*: Aaron went through the whole process, and now Aaron and Moses went into the tent of meeting. Then they both came out and blessed the people again. The glory of the Lord appeared to all the people! And Moses, too, had experienced God's glory:

- Exodus 3—the burning bush
- Exodus 24—the cloud
- Exodus 33—the rock at Mount Sinai
- Exodus 40—the tabernacle was filled
- Exodus 40—the people were led by the pillar of cloud and fire

In 1 Kings 8, the temple was filled with God's glory. God wants people experiencing His glory. In John 1:14, the Word became flesh and we experienced His glory! We get to experience His glory through our relationship with Christ. Matthew 24:29–30 says He's coming back in glory! "All the peoples . . . will see the Son of Man coming . . . with power and great glory" just like here in Leviticus 9 when "the glory of the LORD appeared to all the people." It's a picture of the coming Messiah!

*Leviticus 9:24*: Fire came from the Lord. All the people saw it! The altar (7.5' x 4.5') was filled with fire! This is what I want. I want to experience His glory and His fire! When you have a relationship with Jesus, you can experience this! He baptizes us with the Holy Spirit and with fire.

Multiple times in the Old Testament, we see God in the fire: in Deuteronomy we see God as a consuming fire; in Psalm 18 we see images of fire; in Ezekiel 1:4 God is like a great cloud with fire flashing back and forth; and in Malachi 3:2, He is like a refiner's fire. I think about the fire coming in Matthew 24:29–30. Christ is coming back. The glory and fire are going to fall. Are you ready? The way I believe you can get ready is through the lesson of Aaron's offerings: the sin offering, the burnt offering, the grain offering, and the fellowship offering. Through Christ's atonement and fellowship with Him, we can be ready.

## Closing

To experience the glory and the fire, you have to be willing to offer yourself to Him. And when you do, you'll experience Him like never before. Because of what Aaron and Moses walked through, all the Israelites got to experience the glory of the Lord.

## The Daily Word

Moses, Aaron, and Aaron's sons did just as the Lord commanded them to do so that the glory of the Lord would appear. The seven-day process of ordination was detailed and involved, but even so, they obeyed every detail. On the eighth day, the Lord honored His word, and the glory of the Lord came as a fire, causing all the people to fall facedown and shout. They worshipped the Lord with humility and joy.

God demonstrated His glory for you through the death, burial, and resurrection of Jesus Christ. May you never cease bowing down in worship to the Lord with humility and joy! As you worship the Lord, you will experience His transforming glory!

**When they came out, they blessed the people, and the glory of the LORD appeared to all the people. Fire came from the LORD and consumed the burnt offering and the fat portions on the altar. And when all the people saw it, they shouted and fell facedown on the ground. —Leviticus 9:23–24**

Further Scripture: Leviticus 9:6; Matthew 17:5–6; Romans 6:4

## Questions

1. Who was Moses anointing for the ordination ceremony? What was the significance of this ordination? Why was everything commanded in this way (Leviticus 8:34)?
2. What was the job of the priests in Israel?
3. Where did Moses and Aaron go after sacrificing the offerings? What happened when they came out (Leviticus 9:22–23)?
4. Where did Moses tell Aaron to go for his sin and burnt offering (Leviticus 9:7)?
5. Aaron raised his hands and blessed the people in Leviticus 9:22. He may have blessed them with the words written in Numbers 6:24–26. How do we know that we have those same promises today (Ephesians 1:3; Hebrews 8:6–7)?
6. What did the Holy Spirit highlight to you in Leviticus 8—9 through the reading or the teaching?

# Lesson 57: Leviticus 10
## Atonement: Unauthorized Offering

## Teaching Notes

### Intro

Leviticus points to the Messiah. Everywhere you look, our one word, *Atonement*, is seen. Remember, Leviticus 9 described Aaron's first day on the job when he made all the offerings: the sin offering and the burnt offering for himself and then the fellowship offering and the grain offering that covered the Israelites. Afterward, Aaron blessed the people, and then he and Moses blessed the people again. Then the fire and glory of the Lord fell. Both pointed to the coming of the Messiah.

In Exodus 28:4, special garments were made for the priests. In Leviticus 8, Aaron and his sons were consecrated and ordained to do the work of the Lord. Yet in Leviticus 10, despite this special anointing, despite seeing the fire fall, Aaron's sons still chose to do their own thing.

### Teaching

*Leviticus 10:1*: Nadab and Abihu presented unauthorized/strange fire to the Lord, which He had not commanded them to do. The entire tabernacle was one *big* commandment. Were these priests already tired of following all the commandments?

*Leviticus 10:2*: "Then fire came from the LORD and burned them to death before the LORD." Immediately, a precedent was set: if you aren't going to follow the Lord's commands, then you're done. Wiersbe described how these two guys were wrong in this situation.[1] First, they were the wrong people to make this offering. The high priest, their father Aaron, was the only one who could make this offering (Exodus 30:7–10). Second, they used the wrong instruments, namely their own fire pans (Exodus 40:9). Third, it was the wrong time. This was only to be offered on the Day of Atonement (Leviticus 16:11). Fourth, they came with the wrong authority. They didn't come with God's authority but on their own. Fifth,

---

[1] Warren W. Wiersbe, *The Bible Exposition Commentary: Genesis–Deuteronomy* (Colorado Springs: David C. Cook, 2001), 264.

they brought the wrong fire. The fire should have come from the altar itself, which had been lit when fire fell down from heaven (Leviticus 16:12). Sixth, they had the wrong motive; they were trying to get their own glory (Leviticus 10:3). Seventh, they came to the table with the wrong energy. There's a good chance they were completely drunk (Leviticus 10:9).

*Leviticus 10:3*: When Moses said, "This is what the LORD meant when He said: 'I will show My holiness to those who are near Me, and I will reveal My glory before all the people,'" Aaron kept quiet. Maybe his silence was caused by shock? Aaron (and all the priests) had a responsibility to maintain. James 3:1 warns: "Not many should become teachers, my brothers, knowing that we will receive a stricter judgment." There's grace today, but teachers are held more accountable. We must take seriously the warning of 1 Corinthians 10:12: "Whoever thinks he stands must be careful not to fall." Sin can creep in when we walk in pride, and it leads to a fall. Hebrews 12:28–29 advises, "Let us hold on to grace . . . [then] we may serve God acceptably."

*Leviticus 10:4–5*: Moses called Mishael and Elzaphan to carry the brothers away from the tabernacle to a place outside the camp! The dead men could not be carried by immediate family because they would become unclean (Leviticus 21:1–2).

As a reminder, neither Moses nor Aaron were perfect; both had messed up. Aaron built the golden calf (Exodus 32), but now he was the high priest. Moses messed up in Numbers 20 and won't be allowed to enter the Promised Land. In 1 Samuel 6:19, God struck down 70 men out of 50,000 because they looked into the Ark of the Covenant. It's hard to understand how God chooses when He strikes people down and when He doesn't. Why those 70? Why strike down Nadab and Abihu? Why couldn't Moses go into the Promised Land but Aaron could still be high priest?

*Leviticus 10:6–7*: Moses told Aaron and his sons, Eleazar and Ithamar, not to mourn their sons/brothers. However, the community would mourn over the tragedy of their deaths. Instead, Aaron and his surviving sons would serve the house of Israel. They weren't allowed to leave the tent of meeting because the anointing oil of the Lord was on them. They had work to do.

God's calling on your life is bigger than your family. In Luke 9:59–60, we see Jesus delivering a hard message to a potential follower about family and the kingdom of God. Jesus told His disciples to leave everything behind to follow Him. Sometimes in America, we elevate our family to the point that we skew what the Lord is calling us to do. It's important to remember that God always has a bigger picture in mind.

*Leviticus 10:8–11*: God told Aaron that he and his sons could not drink wine or beer when they entered the tent of meeting or they would die. This was a permanent statute for Aaron's family. Aaron (and all the priests) had to distinguish between the holy and the common, the clean and unclean. Aaron had to have a clear mind because he was going to teach the Lord's statutes to the people. The priests had to have the gift of discernment, the ability "to distinguish between good and evil" (Hebrews 5:13–14). The priests were distinct from anyone else in the world. They functioned in holiness.

*Leviticus 10:12–15*: Aaron and his remaining sons, Eleazar and Ithamar, proceeded with the offerings to the Lord. They performed the grain offerings and the wave offerings.

*Leviticus 10:16–18*: When Moses realized Aaron and his sons didn't eat the sin offering but had allowed it to burn up instead, he was angry with them. He wanted to know why they didn't follow the instructions to eat the sin offerings in the sanctuary.

*Leviticus 10:19–20*: Aaron responded to Moses' accusation (v. 19) about not following instructions by asking, "Since these things have happened to me, if I had eaten the sin offering today, would it have been acceptable in the LORD's sight?" Constable said Aaron couldn't eat the offering in good conscience, and he wasn't going to try and fool God but instead chose to fast.[2] Aaron banked on God looking at his heart.

## Closing

God wants our obedience, not just our sacrifice. As you walk out God's calling on your life, He understands the seriousness of the calling. As you walk out the call, just breathe. If your heart and your intent is to serve the Lord, He's going to extend grace.

## The Daily Word

Even in the midst of the marvelous presentation of God's glory, Aaron's two sons, who were priests, went against the commands of the Lord and presented unauthorized fire before Him. The Lord gave them immediate judgment and burned them to death.

---

[2] Thomas L. Constable, *Expository Notes of Dr. Thomas Constable: Leviticus*, 84, https://planobiblechapel.org/tcon/notes/pdf/leviticus.pdf.

As a royal priesthood of Christ, even in the middle of doing the work of the Lord, you may be tempted to put "unauthorized fire" before God. You may be tempted to live selfishly in the area of addiction, pride, or the worship of other gods. Remember, as Christ's chosen priests, you are called out of darkness, out of sin, and into His marvelous light, filled with grace and power from the Lord. Resist the temptation to do your own thing. Today, may you draw strength from the Lord to stand strong.

**Aaron's sons Nadab and Abihu each took his own firepan, put fire in it, placed incense on it, and presented unauthorized fire before the LORD, which He had not commanded them to do. Then fire came from the LORD and burned them to death before the LORD. —Leviticus 10:1–2**

Further Scripture: Romans 6:22–23; James 1:13–15; 1 Peter 2:9–10

## Questions

1. What was the unauthorized offering made by Aaron's two sons in Leviticus 10:1–3? Do you think they meant to offer an unauthorized sacrifice? Do you think there was fear in Aaron's family (the priests) of following suit?

2. Why do you think God chose to kill Nadab and Abihu (Leviticus 10:2)? Why does God choose to strike people down at times and at other times extend grace and give a second chance?

3. As priests, Aaron and his sons were held to a high standard. Read James 3:1 and 1 Corinthians 10:12. Are you held to this higher standard (Matthew 18:6; Hebrews 5:11–14)?

4. Why were Aaron and his sons Eleazar and Ithamar not allowed to mourn in Leviticus 10:6–7?

5. What motivated Aaron and his sons not to eat the sin offering that they were told to eat (Leviticus 10:16–20)? Was this the right decision?

6. What did the Holy Spirit highlight to you in Leviticus 10 through the reading or the teaching?

# Lesson 58: Leviticus 11—12

*Atonement:* Clean and Unclean Animals

## Teaching Notes

### Intro

In Leviticus 8, Aaron and his sons were ordained and received their calling. In Leviticus 9, their first day on the job, they made the four offerings. Aaron blessed the people, and then both Moses and Aaron stood at the tent of meeting and blessed the people. Everything seemed to be going well, until Leviticus 10, when Nadab and Abihu decided to do something on their own. They brought an unauthorized offering, and the Lord brought fire on them and killed them. Israel mourned the loss of these two priests. Aaron mourned by fasting, but he still had a job to do. Aaron's role as priest was set apart, as described in Leviticus 10:8–9. The priests could not drink wine or beer when they entered the tent of meeting. They were to distinguish between the holy and the common, the clean and the unclean. They were to teach God's statutes to the people. In Leviticus 11, God gave dietary statutes to Moses and Aaron to share with the Israelites.

### Teaching

*Leviticus 11:1–8*: God revealed dietary guidelines for land animals. "Any animal with divided hooves and that chews the cud" could be eaten (v. 3). But among the animals that have divided hooves or chew their cud, they cannot eat the camel, the hyrax, the hare (different from a rabbit), or the pig. Deuteronomy 14:4–5 provided the positive list of animals they could eat: "the ox, the sheep, the goat, the deer, the gazelle, the roe deer, the wild goat, the ibex, the antelope, and the mountain sheep."

They could not eat the meat or touch the carcass of any unclean animal. Clean meant acceptable to God; unclean meant unacceptable to God. The word "unclean" is mentioned 32 times in Leviticus. The priests were given the task of determining what was clean and unclean, so they had to come to the tent of meeting without drinking. They had to have a clear mind, a clear conscience, and allow the Spirit of God to work.

Why was it even important what Israel ate? John McArthur said, "Israel was to obey God's absolute standard, regardless of the reason for it, or the lack of understanding of it."[1] It was not up to them to understand or discern why God told them to eat or not to eat something. Likewise, we are simply just to obey. The beauty of walking by faith is not trying to figure it all out but to be obedient. Israel's diet was unique so that Israel would not be compromised by the other nations and how they served their false idols.[2] Most other religions integrated animals into their religious services. The Lord was setting Israel apart from their old ways. He removed anything that could possibly lead His chosen people astray and toward the false idols of other nations.

Nelson's commentary explains why Jews and Muslims weren't allowed to eat pig/pork.[3] First, pork was often undercooked; inadequately cooked pork could transmit disease to humans. Second, pigs were often sacrificed to other deities or pagan gods. Being tempted was not sin, but Satan would try to deceive the Israelites. Wiersbe said if they were disobedient in partaking of this unclean animal, they might end up partaking in the false idols.[4] Eating a pig could have led to death, and the Lord didn't want his people anywhere near that. When God said don't taste it, He was asking them to be faithful in obedience to what He had commanded. God was very clearly trying to make His people separate and distinct.

*Leviticus 11:9–12*: God next identified the clean and unclean aquatic animals. The Israelites could eat everything in the water that had fins and scales, for those were considered clean. But anything in the seas or streams that did not have fins and scales were considered unclean and could not be eaten (such as clams, oysters, shrimp, lobster, and eel).

*Leviticus 11:13–19*: God then identified the unclean birds: "You are to detest these birds. They must not be eaten because they are detestable." Detestable might indicate nauseating or gross, something worse than unclean. The eagle, bearded vulture, black vulture, kite, falcon, raven, ostrich, short-eared owl, gull, hawk, little owl, cormorant, long-eared owl, white owl, desert owl, osprey, stork, heron, hoopoe, and bat were unclean and therefore forbidden.

---

[1] John MacArthur, *The MacArthur Bible Commentary* (Nashville: Thomas Nelson, 2005), 148.

[2] MacArthur, 148.

[3] Earl D. Radmacher, Ronald B. Allen, and H. Wayne House, eds. *Nelson's New Illustrated Bible Commentary* (Nashville: Thomas Nelson, 1999), 168.

[4] Warren W. Wiersbe, *The Bible Exposition Commentary: Genesis–Deuteronomy* (Colorado Springs: David C. Cook, 2001), 266.

*Leviticus 11:20–23*: God also identified the clean and unclean flying insects. Winged insects that walk on all fours were unclean and detestable. However, winged insects with jointed legs above their feet that allowed them to hop on the ground were clean and could be eaten. The Israelites were allowed to eat the locust, katydid, cricket, and grasshopper.

*Leviticus 11:24–40*: Whoever touched the carcass of a dead animal was unclean until evening and was required to wash his clothes (vv. 24–25). In verse 26, anyone who touched an animal that did not have a divided hoof and did not chew its cud was unclean until evening. Samson was an example of this in Scripture. He was a Nazarite, which meant he was set apart for God—he knew these lists. Judges 14:5–9 says Samson killed a lion; nothing wrong at this point. But, after some time, he returned and took some honey from the lion's carcass. He ate it and gave it to his parents. He knew it was unclean. Could this be what led to his demise?

Animals that swarm on the ground were unclean, so the weasel, mouse, lizard, gecko, skink, and chameleon were unclean and forbidden. God was serious about uncleanliness. They were commanded to break their pots if touched by one of these unclean animals (v. 33). If their carcasses fell on an oven or stove, they were to be smashed (v. 35).

*Leviticus 11:41–46*: God said the swarming creatures (v. 41) as well as those that moved on their belly or walked on all fours or on many feet (v. 42) were detestable and could not be eaten.

The bottom line for all of these restrictions was that Israel was supposed to be holy and function as a clean nation, not as an unclean nation; they were to function not as a common nation, but as a holy nation. This dietary code was God making the distinction that Israel was a chosen nation. They were to be holy because God is holy. Oftentimes, we come to the Lord saying we want things to look like this, but God says, "No, it's going to look like this."

# Closing

God called the Israelites to be holy, and by following the dietary guidelines listed in Leviticus 11, Israel was set apart. This list shouldn't have been a burden, it was meant to be a privilege. In 1 Peter 1:13–16, we are called to be holy because God is holy.

For this teaching, it is important to understand the culture in Israel, the Jewish people, and the coming Messiah. Our one word for Leviticus is Atonement, how the blood serves as a substitution for us. Imputation takes the guilt that was supposed to be ours and puts it on someone else. All of this pointed to the Messiah.

# The Daily Word

God wanted the Israelites to be holy because He is holy. For the Israelites, it meant eating specific food. God wanted His people to be set apart, and eating this specific way was an outward act of obedience and holiness.

As followers of Christ, you are chosen, and you are holy. You are called not only to be set apart from sin and the world but also to be set apart for God's purposes. Rather than focusing on what you eat or don't eat, choose to put on compassion, kindness, humility, gentleness, and patience. Today, whatever you do, do everything for God's glory.

**For I am Yahweh your God, so you must consecrate yourselves and be holy because I am holy. You must not defile yourselves by any swarming creature that crawls on the ground. For I am Yahweh, who brought you up from the land of Egypt to be your God, so you must be holy because I am holy. — Leviticus 11:44–45**

Further Scripture: Deuteronomy 7:6; 1 Corinthians 10:31; Colossians 3:12

## Questions

1. Define "clean" and "unclean." How does Leviticus 11—12 help you understand God's desire for Israel to be clean and holy (Leviticus 11:44–45)?

2. Have you ever eaten an animal that would be considered "unclean" in Leviticus 11? Jesus came to fulfill the law but not abolish it (Matthew 5:17–20). Do you think the food regulations regarding clean/unclean animals apply today (Romans 14:17)?

3. Why was God so specific about what animals He wanted the Israelites to eat? Why do you think God did not want them to eat the animals He defined as unclean?

4. Why was a woman considered unclean when she gave birth (Leviticus 12:1–2, 6–7)?

5. Read Luke 2:21–24. What did Joseph and Mary do after childbirth in keeping with the law in Leviticus 12?

6. What did the Holy Spirit highlight to you in Leviticus 11—12 through the reading or the teaching?

# Lesson 59: Leviticus 13

*Atonement*: Skin Diseases

## Teaching Notes

### Intro

Yesterday, we made it through the list of clean versus unclean land animals, aquatic animals, swarming animals, insects, and birds. God used clean and unclean animals to set His people apart; this was God's holy nation. Today, we are going through another list: diseases. Remember, in Leviticus 10, the Lord spoke to Aaron and told him the priests could not drink alcohol because they had to distinguish between the holy and the common, the clean and unclean.

### Teaching

*Leviticus 13:1*: God spoke to Moses and Aaron about different skin diseases, and the priests were given specific instructions about how to examine each circumstance. The priests were responsible for examining and determining what was clean and unclean on people and in their fabrics.

*Leviticus 13:2–8*: Constable pointed out that God gave them five sets of tests for examining a variety of diseases of the skin.[1] The first set of tests was for rashes. Anyone with a swelling, scab, or spot on his body had to be examined by the priest who would ultimately decide if the person was clean or unclean.

*Leviticus 13:9–17*: These verses cover a second set of tests for skin disease. If the person had white swelling on the skin, white hairs, or patches of raw flesh in the swelling, the priest pronounced him unclean (vv. 10–11). When the raw flesh changed and turned white, then the priest could pronounce him clean (v. 17).

*Leviticus 13:18–23*: These verses cover a third set of tests for boils on the skin and describe circumstances under which the priest pronounced the person either unclean or clean.

---

[1] Thomas L. Constable, *Expository Notes of Dr. Thomas Constable: Leviticus*, 107, https://planobiblechapel.org/tcon/notes/pdf/leviticus.pdf.

*Leviticus 13:24–28*: These verses cover a fourth set of tests for examining burns on a person's body. Based upon his examination of the burn, the priest pronounced the person unclean. When the burn healed, the priest would pronounce the person clean again.

*Leviticus 13:29–37*: These verses cover a fifth set of tests for examining scaly infections. After examining the affected area, the priest would decide whether the person was clean or unclean.

*Leviticus 13:38–44*: The priests examined people with rashes or baldness to determine whether they were clean or unclean.

*Leviticus 13:45–46*: When someone was determined to be unclean, their clothes must be torn, their hair would hang loose, they must cover their mouth (their upper lip, or mustache), and must call out, "Unclean, unclean!" This was a sign of mourning for they were walking death. No one wanted to be around a person who had a skin disease or leprosy. Wiersbe said at this point the person was taken outside the camp, and people who were outside the camp were away from the presence of God.[2] The ultimate picture was that the person was separated because of sin. Most theologians would say in this context that the disease was the result of some form of sin.

*Leviticus 13:47–59*: These verses guided the priests in examining a variety of fabrics as clean or unclean and stated that unclean fabrics had to be burned.

This list shows us how serious leprosy was for Israel and its importance in Scripture. In Exodus 4:7, Moses put his hand inside his cloak, and it was covered with leprosy. Then he put his hand inside his coat again and the leprosy was healed. In Numbers 12:10, Miriam was stricken with leprosy when she spoke against Moses. In 2 Kings 5, Naaman was an incredible warrior who had been stricken with a skin disease (more on this in a later lesson). So, what do we do with all this information about skin diseases? Wiersbe described how to take all this and apply it to the Israelites and to our lives as well. According to Wiersbe, disease was an illustration of sin.[3]

- Symptoms of sin are deeper than the skin. In Leviticus 13:3–4, the priests examined infection to see if it was deeper than the skin. Jeremiah 17:9 warns us that "the heart is more deceitful than anything else, and

---

[2] Warren W. Wiersbe, *The Bible Exposition Commentary: Genesis–Deuteronomy* (Colorado Springs: David C. Cook, 2001), 271

[3] Wiersbe, 271

incurable—who can understand it?" In Romans 7:18, Paul said that nothing good lived in his flesh, and that even though he desired to do good, there was no ability to do so.

- Expect sin to spread. Leviticus 13:5–7, 34–36, states that a spreading disease was unclean; but when the disease did not spread, the person was OK. James 1:14–15 describes how temptation and evil desire conceive and give birth to sin, which ultimately leads to death.

- Sin very clearly defiles. Leviticus 13:44–45 says that a person whom the priest declared unclean had to cry out "unclean." In Isaiah 6:5, Isaiah declared himself "a man of unclean lips" who lived "among a people of unclean lips." Later he said, "All of us have become like something unclean" (Isaiah 64:6). Sin always leads to defilement. In Psalm 51, David confessed that sin affected his eyes (v. 3), mind (v. 6), ears and bones (v. 8), heart (v. 10), and mouth (vv. 13–14).

- Sin goes to your inner core and everything about you is defiled. That's why David cried out for cleansing (v. 2) and purifying (v. 7). When you are defiled by sin you have to be cleansed.

- Sin isolates. In Leviticus 13:46, the unclean person lived alone outside the camp. In 2 Kings 15:5, King Azariah was afflicted with a serious skin disease and he lived in a separate house by himself. You will know sin has a hold on you when you start isolating yourself.

- Sin is fit only for the fire. Contaminated fabrics had to be burned in the fire (Leviticus 13:52, 55, 57). Mark 9:44 reveals that if you don't have a relationship with Christ and sin is taking over your life, it will lead to the fire. Matthew 25:41 says those who are cursed will be cast "into the eternal fire."

All these symptoms pointed to a greater issue—sin. The Israelites were constantly examined and faced the consequences of their sin.

## Closing

Let's consider the story recorded in Luke 5:12–16. A man had a serious skin disease all over him—it had spread, so he was unclean (v. 12). The man begged Jesus to heal him (v. 12). Even though he was unclean, the man came to Jesus. And although lepers were supposed to go outside the community, Jesus touched him (v. 13). The touching hand of Jesus radically healed this man. He was immediately healed and made clean (v. 13). Jesus told the man to tell no one but to present himself to the priest for examination and to make the offering prescribed by Moses (v. 14). News about Jesus spread quickly, and large crowds came to be healed (v. 15).

A man who was unclean became clean through the touch of Christ. Turn to the Lord. Despite what you are going through, whether sin or sickness, turn to the Lord. Jesus wants to heal you physically, emotionally, and spiritually. He wants to heal every single thing about you. He wants you to be whole. He wants you to be clean. That happens through the blood of Christ.

## The Daily Word

Skin infections and rashes are no fun! If you've ever had even a pimple on your face, you know how awkward and self-aware it makes you. It's hard to imagine the lives of the Israelites, who had to go to a priest for every rash, boil, or skin infection and the humiliation they would have felt from being forced to live outside the community until they were completely healed.

Because of Jesus' love and grace, you belong and are accepted into the body of Christ. Open your eyes to see people on the outside who feel as though they don't belong because of their physical differences. Or maybe you are the one who feels as though you don't belong. Remember, you are forever a part of God's family, and nothing will separate you from His love. May His love shine upon you today.

**He will remain unclean as long as he has the infection; he is unclean. He must live alone in a place outside the camp. —Leviticus 13:46**

Further Scripture: Psalm 139:14; Matthew 5:44–45; Romans 8:38–39

## Questions

1. We have read about some regulations for the priests. These included not drinking wine or beer, distinguishing between holy and unholy, clean and unclean, as well as teaching the Israelites all God's statutes (Leviticus 10:9–11). What was another regulation/role of the priests in Leviticus 13 (Leviticus 13:3, 5–6, 10)?

2. What were the four tests for skin disease (Leviticus 13:2–28)?

3. In Leviticus 13:6, after the priest examined a person on the seventh day, and if the sore had faded, that person would be considered clean. He washed his clothes and was considered clean. What are some incredible promises we have today of being completely washed or cleansed (John 13:8; 1 Corinthians 6:11; Hebrews 10:22; 1 John 1:7)?

4. In Kyle's message, he mentioned that skin diseases could have been symptoms of a bigger problem called sin. How do we know that sin runs deeper than the skin (Ecclesiastes 9:3; Isaiah 64:6; Jeremiah 17:9; Romans 7:18)?

5. Reading about leprous people who were cast out of the camp to live by themselves is depressing, especially when they seemed to have no hope. Share about the hope you have in Christ and His physical or spiritual healing in your life. How is the story in Luke 5:12–16 encouraging to you?

6. What did the Holy Spirit highlight to you in Leviticus 13 through the reading or the teaching?

# Lesson 60: Leviticus 14
## *Atonement:* Cleansing of Skin Diseases

## Teaching Notes

### Intro

Yesterday, we talked about unclean diseases, which in the Bible often revealed sin. By correlating sin to skin disease, it prompts certain images—sin is below the skin, it spreads, it defiles us, and it can ultimately destroy us. That was a lot of bad news. But when there's bad news, there's got to be good news. Leviticus 14 is the good news. God always has a plan; He has an outlet. Jesus is our outlet; Jesus is our *Atonement*, our substitution, our imputation. He took the death we deserve, and now we can have life through His blood. Leviticus 13 described all the things you don't want. Leviticus 14 is about restoration.

### Teaching

*Leviticus 14:1*: Constantly throughout Leviticus, the Lord spoke with Moses, and Moses wrote everything down. Wiersbe said that in this chapter, a procedure for cleansing and restoring the one afflicted by leprosy was revealed.[1] Constable pointed out these procedures were rituals, not cures.[2] This cleansing of disease was not medicine or methods for healing, rather these rituals allowed people to be cleansed.

*Leviticus 14:2–3*: This was the law explaining how people who had been afflicted with skin diseases could be cleansed. Wiersbe described this as a five-step procedure.[3] Because the person with leprosy lived outside the camp, the priest went to the leper to examine him. Scripture reveals that Jesus performed a similar service for us. In Luke 19:10, Jesus said, "For the Son of Man has come to seek and to save the lost." When will we lose the mentality that the lost will come to us? Luke 7:34 says, "The Son of Man has come eating and drinking, and you say, 'Look,

---

[1] Warren W. Wiersbe, *The Bible Exposition Commentary: Genesis–Deuteronomy* (Colorado Springs: David C. Cook, 2001), 271.

[2] Thomas L. Constable, *Expository Notes of Dr. Thomas Constable: Leviticus*, 116, https://planobiblechapel.org/tcon/notes/pdf/leviticus.pdf.

[3] Wiersbe, 271–72.

a glutton and a drunkard, a friend of tax collectors and sinners!'" Jesus showed Himself to be a friend of the leper. He had no problem going outside the camp to those who needed Him. We need to have the mentality to go after the people.

*Leviticus 14:4–7*: When the priest verified the skin disease was gone, he ordered that two live and clean birds, along with cedar wood, scarlet yarn, and hyssop be brought for cleansing the person. The victim then offered the two birds, which was an image of atonement. The first bird was slaughtered, and its blood was sprinkled seven times on the one to be cleansed. This bird represented death. After being dipped into the blood from the first bird, the second bird was released in the open countryside. This second bird represented the freedom that comes through death. This was a picture of substitutionary atonement.

Our freedom comes only through the blood of Christ. John 3:13 and 31 reveal that Jesus came down from heaven. John 6:38 and 42 say Jesus came to earth to do the will of the Father. Atonement is available to us because the Son of Man came to earth, died for our sins, was buried, and was raised on the third day (1 Corinthians 15:1–4). In this process you see purification. Hebrews 9:22 says, "According to the law almost everything is purified with blood, and without the shedding of blood there is no forgiveness." In 2 Kings 5:10–14, Naaman was a leper who washed seven times in the Jordan River, as instructed by the prophet Elisha, and he was made clean. Sometimes we want answers from God in a certain way, but God can do things however He wants.

*Leviticus 14:8–9*: Next the person had to cleanse himself by washing his clothes, shaving off all his hair, and bathing with water. He could then reenter the camp but had to remain outside his tent for seven days. On the seventh day, he cleansed himself again by shaving off all his hair again, washing his clothes, and bathing with water.

*Leviticus 14:10–11*: On the eighth day, he offered the required sacrifices of two unblemished male lambs, an unblemished year-old ewe lamb, and a grain offering before the priest at the entrance to the tent of meeting. Again, the process on its own didn't save or cleanse anyone. This was the process to experience cleansing. The process seems similar to the four sacrifices Aaron offered on the very first day.

*Leviticus 14:12–18*: These verses describe in specific detail how the offerings would be made. The required sacrifices included the restitution offering (also called a trespass or guilt offering). The priest took one male lamb and the olive oil and waved them before the Lord (v. 12). He also made a sin offering and burnt offering (v. 13). The priest then put some of the blood on the right ear lobe, right thumb, and right big toe of the person being cleansed. Next, the priest took some of the olive oil and sprinkled it seven times before the Lord, applied some to the right ear, thumb, and big toe of the person, and put whatever was left on the person's head.

*Leviticus 14:19–20*: The priest then sacrificed the sin offering to make atonement for the person, along with the burnt offering and the grain offering. When the priest made atonement for the person, he was made clean. The imagery of priests anointing people with olive oil became familiar to them. In Mark 6:13, Jesus commissioned His disciples to anoint many people with olive oil and heal them. Jesus took aspects of the law God had given to the priests and carried them over into His ministry. All of this makes us think of a big checklist. There was so much they had to go through. And when this process was done, the priest made atonement, and the person was made clean.

*Leviticus 14:21–57*: Although these verses were not covered in detail, they describe several other ritual cleansings. Verses 21–32 made provision for cleansing for someone who couldn't afford the sacrifices already described. Verses 33–57 describe how contaminated objects could be cleansed as well as the sacrifices to be offered afterwards.

## Closing

Luke 17:11–19 tells the story of ten lepers who were healed by Jesus. Only one realized he was healed and came back to give glory to Jesus. Jesus told him, "Your faith has made you well." This leper experienced the good news. When you have faith, you have the good news. When you have faith, that faith has made you well. You can go from sin and death to experiencing life because you have faith in the Messiah.

## The Daily Word

God made a way for people to come to Him despite their inadequacies and differences. Israelites used the hyssop plant to treat skin diseases or homes with mold to become clean again, no longer a target of judgment. Hyssop was a sign of purity and spiritual cleansing.

God's love is the atonement for our sins. He is the way, the truth, and the life. He makes a way for us when we cannot see it. No matter what you have done or the scars you may bear, you are covered by the grace and love of Jesus Christ. He considers you pure and white as snow. Receive His love for you today.

What is left of the oil in the priest's palm he is to put on the head of the one to be cleansed. In this way the priest will make atonement for him before the LORD. The priest must sacrifice the sin offering and make atonement for the one to be cleansed from his uncleanness. —Leviticus 14:18–19

Further Scripture: Psalm 51:7; John 14:6; John 19:28–30

## Questions

1. People with leprosy lived outside the camp, so the priests went outside the camp to examine them (Leviticus 14:3). How did this give hope to the person with leprosy? How did Jesus respond to those whom others considered unclean? How does He respond today (Luke 5:32; 7:34; 19:10; Romans 5:8)?

2. Why was the shedding of one bird's blood necessary in the ritual for cleansing (Leviticus 14:5–7; Hebrews 9:22)?

3. What was the threefold ritual a person went through to remove the uncleanness and be reintroduced into the community (Leviticus 14:2–8, 9, 10–32)? On what days did they take place?

4. Lepers were considered unclean. If the condition cleared up, they were considered "cleansed." How are our hearts cleansed or purified today (Acts 15:9; 2 Corinthians 7:1; Ephesians 5:26; James 4:8; 1 John 1:7, 9)? Note: If healed of their condition, the blind or crippled were considered "healed" and the lepers were considered "cleansed."

5. What did the Holy Spirit highlight to you in Leviticus 14 through the reading or the teaching?

# Lesson 61: Leviticus 15
## *Atonement*: Bodily Discharges

## Teaching Notes

### Intro

Leviticus 11 described clean and unclean animals. Leviticus 12 dealt with women's menstrual cycles and purification after childbirth. Leviticus 13 talked about skin diseases. Then it got better in Leviticus 14, where the cleansing rituals for people whose skin diseases had healed were described. Remember, the priest went out to the lepers, just like Jesus came to seek and save the lost. We discussed the ritual of cleansing, the process for going from unclean to clean.

### Teaching

*Leviticus 15:1*: The Lord always spoke to Moses and Aaron, the prophet and the priest.

*Leviticus 15:2–15*: These verses address unnatural discharges for males. Remember, the role of the priest included distinguishing between the holy and the common, the clean and unclean (Leviticus 10:10). Whenever a man had a discharge from his body, he was unclean. Commentators say this was probably diarrhea or constipation. Anyone who touched the unclean person or their belongings (bedding, furniture, saddle) had to wash and was also unclean until evening. Commentator John McArthur said any kind of uncleanness—ceremonial, natural, physical, and spiritual—prevented people from worshipping in the tabernacle.[1] In Matthew 23:25–28, Jesus pronounced woes on the Pharisees who focused on outward cleanliness while neglecting internal purity. There's something about this image of physical discharge that is like spiritual discharge. Spiritual discharge is like a religious toxin. A discharge is unnatural whether it is spiritual or physical. When the man was cured of the discharge, he had to wait seven days, wash himself and his clothes, and sacrifice two turtledoves/pigeons to the priest at the tent of meeting.

---

[1] John MacArthur, *The MacArthur Bible Commentary* (Nashville: Thomas Nelson, 2005), 152–53.

*Leviticus 15:16–18*: These verses addressed natural discharges for males. After reading these requirements, you could take the view that a man and woman having sex was a bad thing because they were considered unclean. *But,* notice that nobody has to offer any sacrifices. Within marriage, it was OK to have intercourse; it's not unnatural. They only had to wash and remained unclean until evening. Wiersbe said, "God established marriage for the blessing and benefit of mankind."[2] These verses were a blessing. This was how God designed it. Sex is not sinful. This discharge was messy, but all you had to do was clean it up.

*Leviticus 15:19–24*: These verses addressed natural discharges for females. During menstruation, the woman and all her belongings (bedding, furniture) were considered unclean, as well as anyone who touched her. In 2 Samuel 11:4, David saw Bathsheba when she was bathing to purify herself from her uncleanliness. In Genesis 31:26–35, Rachel took Laban's household idols when Jacob took his family back to his father's land. She put them under her seat on the camel. When she told Laban that she was unclean because of her period, he didn't ask her to get up. Laban knew he would be unclean if he touched her or her belongings.

If a man slept with her during her menstruation and got blood on him, he remained unclean for seven days, and every bed he touched would be unclean. Wiersbe said, "God created sex for pleasure as well as for procreation, but pleasure that isn't disciplined soon becomes bondage and then torture."[3] There were times not to have sexual relations. Hebrews 13:4 instructs us to keep the marriage bed undefiled, keep it clean.

*Leviticus 15:25–30*: These verses addressed unnatural discharges for females. When a woman had a discharge of blood that was longer than her menstruation or at the wrong time for her menstruation, she was unclean and anything she touched was unclean. Wiersbe pointed out, "A prolonged hemorrhage would be both physically painful and religiously disastrous, for the woman would be perpetually unclean."[4] When she was cured of the discharge, after seven days she would bring two turtledoves or pigeons to the priest for him to sacrifice at the tent of meeting to make atonement for her.

An example of this was given in Mark 5:25–34. A woman who suffered from bleeding for 12 years, despite consulting many doctors and spending everything she had for treatment, had become even worse. She heard about Jesus, so she entered the crowd. Everyone she touched became unclean! When she touched

---

[2] Warren W. Wiersbe, *The Bible Exposition Commentary: Genesis–Deuteronomy* (Colorado Springs: David C. Cook, 2001), 1273–1274.

[3] Wiersbe, 274.

[4] Wiersbe, 275.

Jesus' robe, He technically became unclean. But when she touched His robe, instantly the flow of blood ceased. She sensed she had been cured of her affliction. When we pray for healing in others, it's OK to ask them if they sensed or felt anything! Jesus asked who touched Him because He knew that power had gone out from Him. Because of her faith in Jesus, He told her to go in peace for she had been healed.

## Closing

The reality is that we all have to go through the human things. Why do we have all these lists? What good does it do for us to understand the difference between holy and common, clean and unclean? John MacArthur said, "When one considers that God was training a people to live in His presence, it becomes apparent that these rules for maintenance of personal purity, pointing to the necessity of purity in the heart, were neither too stringent nor too minute."[5] We should honor what the Lord is asking because He wants us to be holy. These lists of discharges, natural and unnatural, point to us being holy in real human life.

## The Daily Word

The Lord clearly sees all things, and nothing is hidden from His eyes. Even in the middle of bodily discharge, the Lord knows, He sees, and He makes a way for His people to come back into His holy presence.

In the same way the priests made atonement for the Israelites, Jesus has made atonement for you. He sees the sin you think is hidden from Him. He says, "I am here to forgive you and reconcile you to Myself." He longs for you to have a pure heart and clean hands. Turn to Him, and He will receive you as you are, purifying you with His grace-filled love.

**The priest is to sacrifice one as a sin offering and the other as a burnt offering. In this way the priest will make atonement for her before the LORD because of her unclean discharge. You must keep the Israelites from their uncleanness, so that they do not die by defiling My tabernacle that is among them. —Leviticus 15:30–31**

Further Scripture: Psalm 24:3–4; Hebrews 4:13; 1 Peter 1:22–23

---

[5] MacArthur, 153.

# Questions

1.  Throughout Leviticus 15, if anyone touched an unclean person with a discharge or touched something they sat on or laid on, they also became unclean. Contrast that with Exodus 29:37. What happened if a person touched the altar that had been consecrated?

2.  In Leviticus 15:25 and 27, a woman with an ongoing discharge of blood was unclean, and whomever she touched became unclean and had to change their clothes and bathe. In Mark 5:25–34, a woman in this condition touched Jesus' garment. Do you think He became unclean? Why or why not?

3.  Why do you think Leviticus 15:12 instructed them to break an earthen vessel if someone with a discharge touched it? In 2 Corinthians 4:7–10, believers are referred to as earthen vessels. In our uncleanness (sin), why are we not destroyed (1 John 1:9)?

4.  According to Leviticus 15:31, what was the purpose of the laws in chapter 15? How does Christ separate us from our "uncleanness" so that we will not die (Romans 6:21–22; 1 John 1:7)?

5.  What did the Holy Spirit highlight to you in Leviticus 15 through the reading or the teaching?

# Lesson 62: Leviticus 16

## *Atonement*: Day of Atonement

## Teaching Notes

### Intro

Chapter 16 is the center of Leviticus, and it's in the center, the heart, of the Pentateuch. So far, we've talked about animals, skin diseases, and bodily discharges, and it's been exhausting. We did see hope in chapter 14 with the option for the lepers to be cleansed. Leviticus 16 points to our one word for the book of Leviticus: *Atonement*. This word, atonement, means substitution. It means that Jesus is our substitution. He took what we deserved. Imputation means transfer of guilt. We are sinners, but Jesus took our guilt. Jesus took death so we may have life. *Atonement* is the word that pointed to the Messiah. In this chapter, we see *Atonement* come to life.

### Teaching

*Leviticus 16:1–2*: The Lord spoke to Moses after the death of Aaron's two sons, Nadab and Abihu, and said that Aaron could not go into the Holy Place whenever he wanted (as his sons had done). If you play games with God, you'll die. The Lord wanted them to know how to approach the Holy of Holies correctly. God set the stage. In the Old Testament, this was the Day of Atonement (Yom Kippur), and it was also seen in the New Testament as the Fast (Acts 27:9).

John MacArthur simplified the 15 steps for the Day of Atonement.[1] To make this easier to follow, each step is listed below with the appropriate verse numbers from chapter 16.

(1) The high priest washed and dressed in a specific way (v. 4).

(2) The high priest offered the bull as a sin offering for himself and for his family (vv. 3, 6, 11). This blood took on the guilt and death meant for

---

[1] John MacArthur, *The MacArthur Bible Commentary* (Nashville: Thomas Nelson, 2005), 153–54.

Aaron and his family as a sin offering. In this, Aaron admitted his sins also. In humility, he was being obedient to the Lord.

(3) The high priest entered the Holy of Holies with the bull's blood, the incense, and the fiery coals from the altar of the burnt offering (vv. 12–13). The fire that entered the Holy of Holies had to come from the Lord Himself.

(4) The high priest sprinkled the bull's blood seven times on the mercy seat that was on top of the Ark of the Covenant (v. 14). Mercy seat means "place of atonement." The substitutionary blood was placed on top of the mercy seat and brought about atonement for himself and eventually all of the people of Israel.

(5) The high priest left the Holy of Holies and went back to the courtyard. He cast lots for the two goats: one lot for the Lord and the other for Azazel (vv. 7–8). This was the most important sin offering for the entire year because it covered all their sins, even the ones they had failed to specifically acknowledge!

(6) The high priest sacrificed one goat as a sin offering for the people. It was proper protocol for Aaron to take care of his own sin before offering a sacrifice for the people (vv. 5, 9, 15; Numbers 6).

(7) The high priest reentered the Holy of Holies and sprinkled the blood on the mercy seat and on the Holy Place (vv. 15–17; Exodus 30:10).

(8) The high priest then returned to the altar of burnt offering and cleansed it with the blood of the bull and the goat (vv. 11, 15, 18–19).

(9) The goat that wasn't killed (the scapegoat) was "dispatched" into the wilderness (vv. 20–22). Aaron placed his hands on the goat's head and confessed Israel's sins over it. The scapegoat carried all the sins into the wilderness.

(10) The goat keeper led the scapegoat into the wilderness and was required to cleanse himself (v. 26).

(11) The high priest removed his special clothes. He then washed himself again and put on his regular high priest clothes (vv. 23–24a).

(12) The high priest offered two rams as a burnt offering, one for himself and one for the people (v. 24b).

(13) The fat of the sin offering was burned (v. 25).

(14) The bull, goat, and sin offerings, were carried outside of the camp to be burned (v. 27).

(15) The one who burned the sin offering had to cleanse himself (v. 28).

There's no more tabernacle today. There's actually no more temple today. If there's no tabernacle or temple, there are no more goats to sacrifice. Jewish people are no longer sacrificing animals for their sins. That's because all this pointed to something more. This Day of Atonement pointed to the ultimate substitutionary *Atonement*, Jesus Christ. We no longer have to go through all this because we have the Messiah. This was good for then, but it no longer applies today. How do I know? Because there's no longer a temple, so the Jewish people can no longer find atonement (through these sacrifices). Jesus has taken care of it once and for all. Jesus brings life through His blood (Leviticus 17:11).

Now, let's see what the scapegoat looks like through the lens of Christ:

- Matthew 20:28: Jesus came to give His life as a ransom for many. Jesus was the scapegoat. He took on our sins for us, and He was killed for us.
- John 1:29: John the Baptist recognized Jesus as "The lamb of God who takes away the sins of the world."
- 2 Corinthians 5:21 gives us an ongoing picture of substitutionary atonement. Jesus, who knew no sin, took on our sin. When we don't give Him our sins, things stay inside of us and discharges start happening. We bring things on ourselves when we try to carry the sin ourselves.
- Galatians 1:4: Since there's no longer a temple or a tabernacle, we need someone to take our sin for us. Jesus said, "I will take it for you, I will be your *Atonement*."
- Galatians 3:13: Christ has redeemed us. He took our curse.
- Hebrews 9:28: Jesus was offered once, and His sacrifice paid for the sins of all. The Israelites had to do this process over and over, but not Jesus. When Jesus comes again, He will come bearing salvation.
- Hebrews 10:1–10: The sacrifices on the Day of Atonement had to be made every year because they pardoned sin temporarily. "We have been sanctified through the offering of the body of Jesus Christ once and for all" (v. 10).
- 1 Peter 2:24: Jesus bore our sins when He was crucified so that "we might live for righteousness; you have been healed by His wounds."

The Day of Atonement made sense because it pointed to Jesus, who did all these things so that we can be forgiven.

## Closing

Leviticus 16:12 says, "Then he must take a firepan full of fiery coals from the altar before the LORD and two handfuls of finely ground fragrant incense and bring them inside the veil." The high priest had to take the bull's blood inside the veil (verse 12). In Matthew 27:51, when Jesus' blood was shed, that veil was split in two because the temple was no longer needed. Hebrews 9:15 says, "Jesus is the mediator of a new covenant, so that those who are called might receive the promise of the eternal inheritance, because a death has taken place for redemption from the transgressions committed under the first covenant." Jesus is the answer now. Because of His death, His shed blood, we can receive redemption.

## The Daily Word

The Day of Atonement was a significant annual event for the Israelites. Just in case their sins hadn't been covered by any of the various offerings, this day purified them and allowed them to be clean before the Lord. The Israelites went through many ceremonial steps. They placed their wrongdoings on a goat and sent it into the wilderness in an effort to get rid of their sin.

In the New Covenant, Jesus is the Lamb of God who takes away your sin. As believers in Christ our Messiah, you no longer have to go through the ceremonies and rituals to find freedom and forgiveness. You are freed from your sin and can live in righteousness because of Christ's own sacrifice. Now that's something to celebrate and give thanks for!

**Atonement will be made for you on this day to cleanse you, and you will be clean from all your sins before the LORD. —Leviticus 16:30**

**Further Scripture:** Leviticus 16:22; John 1:29; 2 Corinthians 5:21

## Questions

1. Once a year, the Israelites participated in the Day of Atonement. What was the purpose of it (Leviticus 16:29–30)? For how long were they truly cleansed from their sin? (Hebrews 10:1–4)

2. The high priest had to wash before putting on his "holy garments," which were linen garments like the other priests wore, and not the embroidered ephod or the breast piece with the precious stones. How did this point to Philippians 2:5–7 and Hebrews 2:17?

3. A bull was offered by the high priest as a sin offering for himself and his household before he could atone for the sins of the people. As our High Priest, why didn't Jesus offer a bull, either literally or figuratively? (Hebrews 4:1; 7:26–28)

4. What was the purpose of the scapegoat? (Luke 23:13–25)

5. The high priest put the incense on the fire before the Lord (Leviticus 16:12–13), and the cloud of incense covered the mercy seat. What did the incense represent? (Psalm 141:2; Luke 1:10; Revelation 5:8; 8:3–4)

6. According to Leviticus 16:15, who offered the sin offering? How did Christ fulfill this according to Hebrews 7:27; 9:14, 25–26?

7. Only the high priest could enter the Holy of Holies behind the veil (Leviticus 16:17; Hebrews 9:7). How, when, and why did this change? (Matthew 27:51; Hebrews 4:16; 10:19–20)

8. What did the Holy Spirit highlight to you in Leviticus 16 through the reading or the teaching?

# Lesson 63: Leviticus 17
## *Atonement:* Two Warnings

## Teaching Notes

### Intro

Our one word for Genesis is *Seed.* How did the seed throughout Genesis point to Christ, the *Seed?* Our one word for Exodus was *Deliverer.* Jesus is our *Deliverer* and will deliver His people out of the wilderness. Our one word for Jesus in the book of Leviticus is *Atonement.* In chapter 16, when all the sin was put onto a goat, it brought forgiveness to the people. Leviticus 17 is all about the *blood.*

Hebrews 9:11–14 says that Jesus' blood cleansed us and redeemed us once and for all. Wiersbe cited the work of Leon Morris, which states the word "blood" is found 460 times in all the Scriptures, 362 times in the Old Testament, and 13 times in Leviticus 17.[1] Hebrews 10:10 says, "We have been sanctified through the offering of the body of Jesus Christ once and for all." First Peter 3:18 also emphasized Christ "suffered for sins once for all." First John 2:2 says Jesus was the propitiation for the sins of the whole world. The key verse is Leviticus 17:11: "For the life of a creature is in the blood, and I have appointed it to you to make atonement on the altar for your lives, since it is the lifeblood that makes atonement."

The Time to Revive wristband includes these key Scripture verses from the Old Testament: Ecclesiastes 7:20—SIN. Deuteronomy 24:16—DEATH. Leviticus 17:11—BLOOD. Dr. Martin DeHaan said, "No man ever dies until his blood ceases to circulate."[2] Isaiah 53:5—FAITH. Jeremiah 31:33—LIFE.

### Teaching

*Leviticus 17:1–2*: God told Moses to speak to Aaron, his sons, and all the Israelites. In these verses, God gave two major warnings.

*Leviticus 17:3–9*: Warning #1—Forbidden Sacrifices. Offering sacrifices anywhere other than the entrance to the tent of meeting was strictly forbidden.

---

[1] Warren W. Wiersbe, *The Bible Exposition Commentary: Genesis–Deuteronomy* (Colorado Springs: David C. Cook, 2001), 278.

[2] Martin R. DeHaan, "The Chemistry of the Blood," available from https://www.jesus-is-savior.com/BTP/Dr_MR_DeHaan/Chemistry/01.htm.

Nelson's commentary states this warning did two things.[3] First, God didn't want people killing animals just to kill them on their own. There needed to be purpose and accountability. Second, God was trying to prevent them from offering sacrifices to idols. Even if it really was a sacrifice to the Lord, they still needed to come to the tabernacle to do this, because God is a jealous God (Exodus 20:4–5; 34:14; Isaiah 42:8).

*Leviticus 17:5–6*: Sacrifices could no longer be offered in the open country. They were now offered before the priest at the entrance of the tent of meeting. Fellowship sacrifices meant you had a relationship with the Lord. It was a celebration. Why would they want to do that out in the open if it was a fellowship offering? They would want to do it with other people. They missed the point if they did it themselves. The priest sprinkled the blood on the Lord's altar as a pleasing aroma to the Lord.

*Leviticus 17:7*: "They must no longer offer their sacrifices to the goat demons that they have prostituted themselves with." This means they had offered some sacrifices that were not appropriate. The goat demon was a god the Egyptians and other ancient cultures worshipped.[4] The god may have been represented in the form of goats and satyrs. In Genesis 47:1–6, when Israel settled in Goshen, there was a good chance they entered into this worship of satyrs.[5]

*Leviticus 17:8–9*: Any person, Israelite or foreigner, who offered sacrifices anywhere other than the tent of meeting "must be cut off from his people." There are multiple interpretations for "cut off from his people." The phrase might have meant killed, excommunicated, or taken to a different place. The warning was for them to stop their false worship and bring their offerings to the Lord instead.

*Leviticus 17:10–16*: Warning #2—Eating Blood and Carcasses Prohibited. God promised to turn against anyone who ate blood and to cut him off from his people. This went back to the issue of clean and unclean. Blood was the substitution; it made atonement for the people. None of the people of Israel were allowed to eat blood (v. 12).

[3] Earl D. Radmacher, Ronald B. Allen, and H. Wayne House, eds., *Nelson's New Illustrated Bible Commentary* (Nashville: Thomas Nelson, 1999), 177.
[4] Thomas L. Constable, *Expository Notes of Dr. Thomas Constable: Leviticus*, 144, https://planobiblechapel.org/tcon/notes/pdf/leviticus.pdf.
[5] Radmacher et al., 177.

In John 6:54, Jesus said, "Anyone who eats My flesh and drinks My blood has eternal life." Partaking in Jesus' blood gives us life. Hebrews 9:22 reminds us that shedding of blood has to take place before we can receive forgiveness. Life doesn't come from false worship and sacrificing to idols, so we must not misuse blood because we understand where it comes from.

*Leviticus 17:13–16*: Anyone who hunted down a wild animal or bird was commanded to bury its blood in the dirt. MacArthur said it was customary for hunters to pour out the blood of their kill as an offering to the god of the hunt.[6] This practice was strictly forbidden for God's people.

Leviticus 17 gave two warnings: don't participate in false worship and don't misuse the blood. In the Old Testament, the high priest took care of the blood on their behalf. It's the same with Jesus. If we misuse the blood and try to do it ourselves, it doesn't work.

# Closing

It's appropriate to close this lesson with a discussion of the power of Jesus' blood:

- 1 Peter 1:19: Jesus' blood is precious.
- Romans 5:9: By Jesus' blood, we are justified.
- Ephesians 1:7: In Jesus' blood, we have redemption.
- Revelation 1:5: By Jesus' blood, we are set free.
- Hebrews 13:12: By Jesus' blood, we are sanctified.
- 1 John 1:7: By Jesus' blood, we are cleansed.
- Acts 20:28: Jesus purchased us with His blood.

Leviticus 17 emphasized that we don't have to do anything. Jesus purchased our freedom. He gave us sanctification, justification, and redemption. Jesus cleansed us, washed us, and set us free because He purchased us with His own blood. That is true *Atonement*.

## The Daily Word

The Lord instructed His people once again. This time, He specifically outlined how they were to make sacrifices before Him. The word *blood* is mentioned 13 times in this chapter. The power of blood brings forgiveness in both the Old and New Testaments.

[6] John MacArthur, *The MacArthur Bible Commentary* (Nashville: Thomas Nelson, 2005), 155.

Blood serves as the atonement in your life. God sent His Son Jesus and purchased your forgiveness with His blood. In Christ alone, and in no other, we have abundant life. Seek Him, and you will find life abundantly because of the blood of Christ.

**For the life of a creature is in the blood, and I have appointed it to you to make atonement on the altar for your lives, since it is the lifeblood that makes atonement. —Leviticus 17:11**

Further Scripture: John 10:10; Ephesians 1:7; 1 John 2:2

## Questions

1. The Lord no longer allowed men to offer sacrifices anywhere but before the tabernacle. Why was this? (Leviticus 17:7; Exodus 20:3–6)

2. What was the consequence if they did not follow the Lord's command to bring their sacrifices to the doorway of the tent of meeting? (Leviticus 17:4, 8–9) Why was this so strongly enforced?

3. How were those hunting supposed to deal with their catch according to Leviticus 17:13?

4. Notice that the command to not eat blood included the strangers among them. In Leviticus 17:11, what was the purpose of blood? What was the consequence for those who ate it? (Leviticus 17:10)

5. What did the Holy Spirit highlight to you in Leviticus 17 through the reading or the teaching?

# Lesson 64: Leviticus 18
## *Atonement*: Unlawful Sexual Relations

## Teaching Notes

### Intro

We're continuing in Leviticus with more writing from Moses. And let's be honest, it hasn't been light. As we jump into Leviticus 18, it's building off Leviticus 17. Remember our word for Leviticus is *Atonement*. The blood serves as a substitution for us. It is the blood that allows us to be forgiven so that we can live holy. Leviticus 18 is making sure we are walking in holiness based on the blood in Leviticus 17.

Seven times God told His people, "Please don't act like the other nations. You are My treasured possession, a royal priesthood and holy nation. Act like it." Leviticus 18 really begins to give the Israelites the guardrails to live holy.

### Teaching

*Leviticus 18:1–4*: Yahweh spoke to the Israelites through Moses. These new guidelines would not look like what the Israelites were used to or where they came from. God essentially said, "I want you to look like My people, not where you came from or where you're going. You need to look differently." God knew what they had been exposed to, and so He was instructing them.

God told them what not to do. Now He was going to tell them what to do. God said, "Practice My ordinances." Because God used the word "practice," you can infer that they were probably not always going to get it right. God said, "This is the standard! Because of who I am, this is your standard!"

*Leviticus 18:5*: If they obeyed God's commands, they would live. Is He implying that if you do these things, you'll have salvation? No. MacArthur wrote, "Obedience doesn't save from sin and hell, but it does mark those who are saved."[1] This is an indicator you're walking out your faith.

- Deuteronomy 4:40—You keep the statutes and commands and your children will live.

---

[1] John MacArthur, *The MacArthur Bible Commentary* (Nashville: Thomas Nelson, 2005), 156.

- Deuteronomy 30:11–20—You know this! It's not far off! You can do this! But if you don't, you will perish.
- Genesis—The *Seed*, Christ, is going to carry all the way through to the book of Revelation.
- Psalm 90—The average life is 70 to 80 years.
- Romans 7:10–12—Sin will lead to death and destruction if we're not careful.
- Galatians 3:23–26—The Law was our guardian until Christ; the law points to Jesus!
- Leviticus 18:5—Jesus is the fulfillment for us because only He is able to keep all the statutes and commands!

We can't keep all of His statutes (Romans 3:23), but Jesus has freed us from the curse of the Law and we are now sons of God through faith in Christ Jesus (Galatians 3:10–14, 23–26). So many of us keep doing things in order to receive, but it's about receiving the gift He's already given us.

*Leviticus 18:6*: What does the sanctity or holiness of a marriage relationship look like? Let's look at what it doesn't look like. An example would be no sex with a family member. Sex is an intimate act in which a man and a woman become one flesh (Genesis 2:21–25). First Corinthians 6:16 states that to have sex with someone is to become one flesh with him or her.

*Leviticus 18:7*: God was establishing the guardrails for sex. God designed a male and female to literally fit together and to become one flesh. That's why it's not His design for sex to be between male and male or female and female—it just doesn't fit. The ESV translation says, "You shall not uncover the nakedness of your father, which is the nakedness of your mother" (Genesis 9:20–25). Because of what happened in Genesis 9, Ham was cursed. Many commentators believe some homosexual behavior took place between Ham and his father. Regardless, man is not designed to see man naked.

*Leviticus 18:8–18*: Don't have sex with your mom (v. 7), stepmom (v. 8), sister (v. 9), or granddaughter (v. 10).

This is still an issue today! Unfortunately, molestation by grandparents and parents is too common! We see on the news doctors who take advantage of their patients. This is not how God designed it!

The Israelites were coming out of the Egyptian pagan culture where these things could have been normal. These guidelines were likely new to them (though it's common sense to us today). The reason God was being so specific is because this was a new way of living for the Israelites. Don't have sex with your stepsister, adopted sister (v. 11), or aunt—father's sister (v. 12).

Sometimes in the American church, we just want to skip over the parts of Scripture that make us uncomfortable. Moses was writing these commands, and yet his own father and mother were actually nephew and aunt. Amram (Moses' father) married Jochebed, his aunt (his father's sister). They didn't have these laws yet. This was new! Don't have sex with your aunt, mother's sister (v. 13), aunt-in-law (v. 14), daughter-in-law (v. 15), sister-in-law (v. 16), a woman and her daughter (v. 17), or a woman and her sister (v. 18) (for example, Rachel and Leah).

*Leviticus 18:19–20*: More guidelines: no sex during a woman's menstrual bleeding (v. 19) and also no sex with your neighbor's wife (v. 20).

*Leviticus 18:21*: Molech was a Canaanite god represented by a brawn image with a bull's head and outstretched arms. The image was hollow. They would kindle it with fire and literally place the children on the outstretched arms and sacrifice them. This is also probably somehow related to some sexual perversion with the Canaanites.

*Leviticus 18:22–23*: More guidelines: No man-man sexual intercourse (v. 22). Homosexuality is described as being detestable. It is not of the Lord. Studies have found the average lifespan of a homosexual man is 20 years less than the average of a heterosexual man.[2] Why? Because they're trying to create one flesh outside of God's intended design, and it doesn't work.

That may be how other countries and other people do this, but not the Israelites. The Israelites are God's people. This truth is throughout Scripture, not just in the Old Testament, but also in the New Testament. Also, no sex with an animal (v. 23).

Bestiality is a perversion!

*Leviticus 18:24–30*: The Israelites were not to defile themselves like the other nations! God said, "Keep My statutes. Keep My ordinances. The people of Egypt did these things, but do not defile yourselves by them because I AM Yahweh your God! I am the standard! Be holy as I am holy! Be one flesh . . . man with woman . . . the way I designed." And guess what? It all points to Christ (Ephesians 5:25–33). Christ and the church! When we play games with who we can have sex with within our culture, we're saying Christ is no longer the head.

---

[2] R. S. Hogg, et al., "Modelling the Impact of HIV Disease on Mortality in Gay and Bisexual Men," *International Journal of Epidemiology* 26, issue 3 (1 June 1997): 657–61, https://doi.org/10.1093/ije/26.3.657.

# Closing

The guardrails in Leviticus 18 ultimately point to Ephesians 5 and Christ being the head of our lives and our marriages, as followers of Yeshua. It all goes back to Leviticus 17, the blood and the forgiveness of Christ through His shed blood on the cross, allows us to walk in holiness.

## The Daily Word

Through Moses, the Lord told the Israelites to follow Yahweh's commands. Essentially, the Lord said, "Don't follow the practices of your old ways, and don't follow the practices of the land you are going to inhabit in the future. Instead, follow the commands of your current living situation."

We are often tempted to go back to our old ways, or we want to look ahead to what is on the horizon. In Christ, we are a new creation—the old is gone, and the new has come. We have the power of the Holy Spirit inside us, and we are to live in that power, not in the flesh. Today, don't live the way you used to live. You have a heavenly calling. The Holy Spirit living inside you will give strength for today to walk the ways of the Lord.

**Do not follow the practices of the land of Egypt, where you used to live, or follow the practices of the land of Canaan, where I am bringing you. You must not follow their customs. . . . Keep My statutes and ordinances; a person will live if he does them. I am Yahweh." —Leviticus 18:3, 5**

Further Scripture: 2 Corinthians 5:17; Philippians 3:18–20; Philippians 4:12–13

## Questions

1. In Leviticus 18:1–5, God prefaced what He was about to say in the rest of the chapter. What can you glean from this? (2 Corinthians 6:17–18)

2. Read Romans 10:5–10. How do these verses contrast righteousness by the law, as referenced in Leviticus 18:5, and righteousness by faith? (Galatians 3:12)

3. Do you think there were consequences if someone didn't obey God's instruction in Leviticus 18:5 (Leviticus 18:27–29)? What would an Israelite gain by living according to His "decrees and laws"?

4.  Leviticus 18 gives regulations on unlawful sexual behavior. Are these things still unlawful today (1 Corinthians 6:12; 10:23)? According to Ephesians 5:25–33, what is God conveying through marriage between a man and a woman? How does this help you see why it is so important to God to keep marriage holy?

5.  How could you use Leviticus 18 to share Christ with someone who is in the midst of dealing with an unlawful sexual behavior? How and when would you approach this topic with someone within your circle of influence?

6.  What did the Holy Spirit highlight to you in Leviticus 18 through the reading or the teaching?

# Lesson 65: Leviticus 19
## *Atonement:* Laws of Holiness

## Teaching Notes

### Intro

You made it through another day of Moses' writings about how the Israelites should live. Yesterday we studied Leviticus 18 and a list of who you can and cannot have sexual relations with. God set the Israelites apart as a special treasure, a holy nation, and a royal priesthood.

Here we have the heart of Leviticus: Leviticus 20:26, "You are to be holy to Me because I, Yahweh, am holy, and I have set you apart from the nations to be Mine."

The way this took place was through *Atonement.* They were to offer sacrifices to receive forgiveness. In Leviticus 19, we are going to look at how this nation was to walk in holiness. I'm going to give you a list today of what the Israelites were to do to experience holiness.

### Teaching

*Leviticus 19:1–2*: I want to make sure everyone understands! This message was not just for the priests, it was for all of the Israelites: "Be holy as I am holy!"

*Leviticus 19:3–34*:

(1)  Respect your parents (v. 3): Exodus 20:12.

(2)  Keep Sabbaths (v. 3): No work on the Sabbath (Exodus 20:8). "I am Yahweh your God!" Why did the Israelites have to keep these laws? Because He is Yahweh, their God. He is holy, and He is to be the standard.

(3)  Forsake idols (v. 4): Why? This was part of the culture they had lived in (Exodus 20:4).

(4)  Fellowship/peace offerings (vv. 5–8): This was to be eaten on the first or second day. Remember the thanksgiving offerings, vow offerings, and freewill offerings? God was supposed to get the fatty portions. The priest got the breast and waved it, and then got the right thigh

and heaved it. The offerer participated and ate as well. If it was eaten on the third day, it was repulsive. That would be going against the guardrails God had set.

(5) Have concern for the poor (vv. 9–10): Moses wrote to not reap all the way to the very edge of the fields. This had to be a strange concept because the Israelites were wandering around the wilderness and didn't have any fields yet. But it was coming, and God was preparing them. In Ruth 2:8–23, Ruth got to experience this very thing.

(6) Show honesty and integrity even in regard to business (vv. 11–13). More guidelines: don't steal, don't cheat people, and don't lie or swear falsely (James 5:4; Matthew 20:1). We always want to be the ones who are going above and beyond, not short-changing people.

(7) Protect the physically challenged (vv. 14–15): Judge fairly! Our culture labels people based upon what we wear or how much money we have. God says not to judge based on those things. We have to be different from the world.

(8) Justice and truth in speech (vv. 16–17): Don't spread slander. This can be one of the hardest things for us. We want to talk to our friends about it when someone wrongs us.

(9) Love your neighbor as yourself (v. 18): This is the most quoted Old Testament text in the New Testament. Vengeance does not belong to us; it belongs to the Lord (Deuteronomy 32:35). Love your neighbor as yourself (Matthew 22:37–40). God's standard is that we love Him so that we can love our neighbors. Don't blend worlds. God says He doesn't want things to mix. Why? Deuteronomy 7:3–6 says when we blend these worlds, it turns us away from God. This included a law regarding intercourse with a slave (vv. 20–22).

(10) Five-year fruit tree (vv. 23–25): Some commentators say it takes three years to overcome the uncleanliness. The fourth year, the firstfruits are to be offered to the Lord as a praise offering. In the fifth year the fruit could be eaten. This is a picture of the Lord's patience with us as He transforms us. Relax if you don't see instant fruit right away. Have the five-year fruit tree perspective. As you praise Him, the fruit is going to come.

(11) Dignified mourning (v. 28): There were unethical ways to mourn, like gashing or cutting their skin and marking their bodies (Jeremiah 16:6; Jeremiah 47:5). Ethical mourning is seen in Isaiah 22:12.

(12) Forsake magic and witchcraft (v. 31).

(13) Respect for elderly (v. 32).

(14) Loving treatment of aliens (vv. 33–34): We all were, at one point, for-eigners (v. 34b).

## Closing

We're going through these standards because this is how God wants us to live. But even more so, Jesus wants us to live like this. Jesus said, "Don't assume that I came to destroy the Law or the Prophets. I did not come to destroy but to fulfill" (Matthew 5:17).

Jesus came to fulfill Leviticus 19. At least seven different times, Jesus referenced Leviticus 19 in His teaching throughout the New Testament, such as:

- Leviticus 19:2: "Be holy because I am Holy."
- Matthew 5:48: "Be perfect therefore as your heavenly Father is perfect."
- Leviticus 19:3: "Respect your mother and father."
- Matthew 19:19: "Honor your father and your mother!"

There's this constant correlation between the Old Testament Law and Jesus' teaching. Jesus didn't come to wipe it out; He came to fulfill everything that was spoken in Leviticus 19.

## The Daily Word

God instructed Moses to speak directly to the entire Israelite community. He restated the Ten Commandments. After each commandment, the phrase, "I am Yahweh," is repeated. When you read something over and over in a chapter, pay attention. "I am Yahweh," can be translated, "I Am Who I Am," and highlights God as the author of these holiness laws. The Lord also commanded the Israelites to be holy because He is holy.

You are called to be an imitator of Christ. Because God is holy, and God is who He says He is, you are to love others and live your life as a sweet aroma of Christ.

The LORD spoke to Moses: "Speak to the entire Israelite community and tell them: Be holy because I, Yahweh your God, am holy." —Leviticus 19:1–2

Further Scripture: Leviticus 19:18; Matthew 5:48; Ephesians 5:1–2

# Questions

1. In Leviticus 19, laws are repeated and specified, and new laws are given. Why is it so important for God to remind and specify things He has already said? What is an example of this in your life?

2. The command to "love your neighbor as yourself" (Leviticus 19:18) is the most quoted Old Testament law in the New Testament (Matthew 5:43–44; 22:39; Mark 12:31). How does this challenge you? What are practical ways you can "love your neighbor as yourself"?

3. Read Leviticus 19:23–25 about the fruit tree. What was the timeline for this tree? How does this challenge you in your life?

4. In Leviticus 19:33–34, how could you apply this to situations going on in the world today regarding immigration? How can you apply this personally?

5. Considering that Jesus didn't come to abolish the law but to fulfill it (Matthew 5:17–20), do you think these commands are still applicable to you today? How about not cutting the sides of your hair (v. 27) or not having tattoos (v. 28)? What does your righteousness "surpassing that of the Pharisees and teachers of the law" in Matthew 5:20 mean to you?

6. What did the Holy Spirit highlight to you in Leviticus 19 through the reading or the teaching?

# Lesson 66: Leviticus 20

*Atonement:* Punishment for Molech Worship and Sexual Offenses

## Teaching Notes

### Intro

In Leviticus 18, we studied whom the Israelites could and could not have sexual relations with. Then, in Leviticus 19, we looked at laws for holiness. Now in Leviticus 20, they almost run parallel. We're going to get into the punishments—what happens if they didn't live according to the standards.

### Teaching

*Leviticus 20:1–2*: This message was not just for the Levitical priests but was for all the Israelites. Who was Molech? Molech was a metal image, heated red hot as fire, that the Canaanites would worship and place their children, as a sacrifice, in the arms of this image (2 Kings 23:10; 2 Chronicles 33:6; Jeremiah 32:35).

*Leviticus 20:3–5*: The Lord was essentially saying to the Israelites, "If you do go back and don't listen to Me, you will be punished. You will die." If the Israelites saw a child sacrifice and didn't put that person to death, then God would turn against that family.

The reason the Israelites wouldn't turn in the person sacrificing his own children was that their priorities were skewed, and they cared more about their family and friends than about God. Jesus updated this in Luke 14:26: "If anyone comes to Me and does not hate his own father and mother, wife and children, brothers and sisters—yes, and even his own life—he cannot be My disciple." We tend to filter everything based on how people will perceive us and what causes us fear. We can't do that and be Jesus' disciples! The phrase "cut you off" means there would be constant punishment for not living according to God's standard. When you don't live according to God's standard, it leads to sin. Sin often begins with a desire. It then leads to deception, which leads to disobedience, and ultimately death (James 1:15).

Gordon Wenham shares examples from Exodus, Leviticus, and Numbers of the punishment of stoning[1]:

- If an Israelite gorged an ox = stoned to death
- Practice of divination or sorcery = stoned to death
- Blasphemy = stoned to death
- Plowing on Sabbath = stoned to death
- Idolater = stoned to death
- Adultery = stoned to death

*Leviticus 20:6*: If a person turned "to mediums or spiritists" (v. 6), God would "turn against that person and cut him off" as punishment. Going against God's standard of holiness meant punishment was inevitable, and it separated the Israelites from God's standard. I think the more we interact in this world, the more we realize that people don't even think about a standard anymore. As soon as you say that 100 percent of the Bible isn't true, you've strayed away from the standard, and you separate yourself from the holiness of God.

*Leviticus 20:7–8*: Moses told the people to consecrate themselves and to be holy! They became consecrated when they chose to move toward God's standard. Yahweh has set His people apart!

*Leviticus 20:9–10*: Moses said that screaming curses against parents was punishable by death (2 Samuel 16:5; Job 3:1), and that person's blood was on their own hands (Proverbs 20:20; Mark 7:9–10). The Israelites were not to curse their parents but to honor them. And for the man and woman caught in adultery, both were to be put to death. You'd think that knowing they would be put to death would keep them from doing it!

*Leviticus 20:11–12*: If a man slept with his father's wife (Leviticus 18), he must be put to death. They knew the law; their blood was on their own hands. If a man slept with his daughter-in-law, both must be put to death. They knew the law (Leviticus 18); the guilt for their death is their own.

*Leviticus 20:13–14*: If a man slept with a man, he had to be put to death. In this context, as an Israelite, if they committed the sin, they would die as punishment. As an Israelite, if they messed up, they would die. There was not a whole lot of hope in that—unless they kept the standard, and that was a whole lot of weight.

---

[1] Gordon J. Wenham, *The Book of Leviticus* (Grand Rapids: Eerdmans, 1979), 277ff.

If a man married a woman and her mother, they were to be burned with fire. Commentators say they were probably stoned first and then burned with fire, possibly because they didn't want to do a burial in this situation. Judah accused Tamar of prostitution and declared she should be burned, but he was the one who had slept with her, which meant he should be burned too (Genesis 38:24).

*Leviticus 20:15–18*: If a man had sexual intercourse with an animal, both the man and the animal were to be killed. If a woman had sexual intercourse with an animal, both were to be killed. If a man married his sister, they were disgraced and cut off publicly. There were to be no sexual relations with an aunt either. There will always be a punishment, whether death or being cut off from the tribe.

*Leviticus 20:19–25*: We can go through this laundry list of "If you do this sin, it will catch up with you." I promise you, if an Israelite committed a sin, it would catch up with them, so they were to keep the statutes and ordinances. Why? To keep the Israelites pure and holy. They needed to be ready to go into the land, so it wouldn't "vomit them out." They had to distinguish the clean from the unclean. Basically, God said, "Don't become contaminated" (Leviticus 10:10). Remember the clean and the unclean.

*Leviticus 20:26*: Why did the Israelites go through all these lists and talk about these punishments? Because they were to be holy as God is holy! God had set them apart to be HIS! We've been talking about the *Seed*, the *Deliverer*, and Jesus being our *Atonement*. God does all this so we can be set apart and be His! This hasn't stopped. God hasn't said, "Oh, okay, I'm done with the Israelites." God still has a plan for the Israelites! And His plan is, "I want you to be holy as I am holy." God has a standard and He wants us to follow it.

The problem was the Israelites had a hard time keeping the standard. For example, Saul, who was supposed to live according to God's standards, didn't (1 Samuel 28:3–9). When things didn't look good, look at what Saul did. When Saul was feeling the pressure and didn't hear answers from the Lord, he caved in. He sent for a medium. Saul's response was not to wait for the Lord.

*Leviticus 20:27*: "A medium must be put to death." Saul left the standard, and he knew the standard. I think that's the issue with all of us. We know the standard, but we keep letting sin get in the way.

## Closing

Praise the Lord, we have an answer! We don't have to live in sin any longer. We don't have to deal with this punishment. The apostle Paul reveals hope and freedom in Romans 8:1: "No condemnation now exists for those in Christ Jesus." Because of Jesus becoming a sin offering for us, this punishment, this death that we were destined for is gone. We no longer have to play these games, "should I or should I not?" God has already taken care of it all. The blood that was shed on the cross has set you and me free. Every once in a while, you and I are going to sin. But we don't have to stay in the sin. We can come back to the standard because of the cross of Christ that allows us the freedom and for-giveness that we need every day. I don't have to stay in the position of being an adulterous person, a drunkard, or a liar. I don't have to stay in the position of being a labeled sinner.

While we were yet sinners, Christ died for us. And He came to give us a relationship with Him.

## The Daily Word

The Lord gave black-and-white statutes to the people so they would be set apart. He longed for His people to be holy as He is holy. For example, if a man com-mitted adultery with a married woman, both the woman and the man were to be put to death. Oh, how far from these commands our culture has come today. It should be emphasized that this was the Old Testament law.

Yes, in Christ, you are forgiven and covered by the blood of Jesus. Yes, His grace washes over you. But even as New Testament believers, you are to resist temp-tation, flee from evil, and do what is right in the eyes of the Lord. Please don't give the enemy a foothold. If you are married, please love, respect, and honor your spouse. Fill yourself up with the Spirit daily so you will not give into the flesh.

**If a man commits adultery with a married woman—if he commits adultery with his neighbor's wife—both the adulterer and the adulteress must be put to death. —Leviticus 20:10**

Further Scripture: Ephesians 5:18, 25; James 4:7

## Questions

1. Leviticus 20:5–6 describes people "prostituting themselves." What are the two situations described? What does the phrase "giving their offspring to Molech" mean?

2. Adultery carried a severe penalty (Leviticus 20:10). James referred to those he'd written to as "adulterers" (James 4:4). Who were they committing adul-tery with? What might this look like in our current culture (1 John 2:15)?

3. After listing the customs of the nations that the Lord detested (Leviticus 20:1–23), Moses reminded the Israelites that He had set them apart from the nations (Leviticus 20:24, 26). Why did He then use the word "therefore" to talk about clean and unclean animals, birds, and creeping things (Leviticus 20:25)? How are believers today to be separated from the world (John 17:14–18; 2 Corinthians 6:14—7:1)?

4. According to Leviticus 20:21, it is abhorrent for a man to marry his brother's wife. When is this not only permitted but commanded (Genesis 38:8; Deuteronomy 25:5; Mark 12:19; Luke 20:28)? What happened to John the Baptist when he told Herod it was not lawful to have his brother's wife (Mark 6:16–18)?

5. Both Leviticus 20:22 and Genesis 4:11–12 describe land using personification (giving it human characteristics). What do you think these verses mean?

6. What did the Holy Spirit highlight to you in Leviticus 20 through the reading or the teaching?

# Lesson 67: Leviticus 21
## *Atonement*: Holy Conduct of Priests

## Teaching Notes

### Intro

Most commentators describe Leviticus 21 as an instruction manual for the priests. Yes, they had been given clothes, they had been given some specific assignments from Leviticus 10, and they had been anointed and ordained, but there was still a lot more. They needed a manual for everyday life. Could priests get married or not? What was all this supposed to look like?

McArthur says, "Laws for the priests are given, which demanded a higher standard of holy conduct than for the general Israelite."[1] So we are going to elevate, in this context, high priests and priests and what was expected of them, in order to see forgiveness happen in their lives and the lives of all Israelites. Priests were not perfect. They still messed up. We know what was asked of them.

### Teaching

*Leviticus 21:1–2*: The Lord instructed Moses to speak to Aaron's sons, the priests. They were not to make themselves ceremonially unclean by being with a dead person among their relatives, except in the case of their mother, father, son, daughter, brother, or immediate family member. (Later, we will see Aaron's priestly sons, Nadab and Abihu die because of disobedience, while Eleazar and Ithamar remained obedient.)

*Leviticus 21:3–4*: Another exception would have been a young unmarried sister who wouldn't have had anyone to take care of her. What if an in-law dies? The priests wouldn't have to do anything. They were not to defile themselves by taking care of them.

*Leviticus 21:5*: The priests were not to improperly mourn. They were to have no superstitious marks of grief like the pagans did. The priests were not to do anything to indicate that they weren't holy. An example of what this could look like is 1 Kings 18:28.

[1] John MacArthur, *The MacArthur Bible Commentary* (Nashville: Thomas Nelson, 2005), 158.

*Leviticus 21:6*: Priests were to follow the standard that God had set—to be holy to God. By making bald spots, shaving the edges of their beards, making gashes and marks, they were profaning the name of God. The priests were not to come to the Lord in this way. In order to present the fire offerings (food to God), they were to be holy. It's like they were learning as they went. This happened in Leviticus 10 and now Moses was writing about it.

*Leviticus 21:7–8*: Priests could not marry a woman who had been defiled by prostitution or who had been divorced by her husband. Why? It would bring another flesh to them; it was unclean (Genesis 2:24; Mark 10:8). They had to make sure that if they got married, whomever they married had to enter the union holy, like themselves.

There is tension between ministry and marriage. We have family, and yet we've been called to this ministry. There is going to be tension, and you should expect it.

When you are thinking about getting married, consider 2 Corinthians 6:14–18. Do not marry an unbeliever and do not marry people to change them; it's dangerous ground. Israel was told over and over not to blend and mix these worlds. Today this means not to mix belief systems (for example, Islam and Christianity), not races. God said to the priest, "don't defile yourself, just stay single and understand you are holy! You have been set apart."

*Leviticus 21:9*: If the priest's daughter messed up one time, she was done and was burned up. There was no room for grace. This goes back to the standard God wanted for His priests, the leaders of the tabernacle . . . holiness.

*Leviticus 21:10–12*: Aaron, the high priest, could not defile himself and leave his post when his sons died. His calling was very high because the consecration of the anointing oil was on him. He could not leave his post to bury his sons. Aaron loved his kids, so the ministry/marriage tension was high right at that moment.

*Leviticus 21:13–15*: If a priest were to marry, he was to marry a woman who was a virgin. A holy union needed to take place. There was a love connection between God and Israel (Ezekiel 16:8–14). God said, "I have chosen to marry you Israel. We are a perfect fit." The Lord married His chosen people (Jeremiah 31:32; Isaiah 54:5).

This image of God and Israel can't be broken. It's a one-flesh deal. God isn't going to part with them. He isn't done. He won't divorce the Israelites. Israel turned away from God then kept going back, over and over again (Hosea 2:7). God constantly woos them back and says, "I am still here." The priest's relationship with his wife or soon-to-be wife needed to be pure.

*Leviticus 21:16–23*: It was not an option for a priest to represent the Lord if he had defects. A priest was not qualified to come into God's presence if he had a defect.

## Closing

Jesus hung out with the people who had defects! Jesus hung out with people who looked funny (Luke 14:21). He intentionally went after these people. Jesus was the perfect priest (Hebrews 7:26). He was also the perfect victim (Hebrews 9:14). This is how we can connect with Him. The perfect High Priest offered Himself without blemish (1 Peter 1:19). Jesus was perfect. Jesus could have stayed right there, inside the tabernacle. Safe. Clean. He could have let the defective people stay out (1 Peter 2:22). Yet Jesus did the opposite! As a victim, Jesus gave up His life and came out to those who desperately needed Him.

This is an awesome picture of the change from the Old Testament to the New Testament. We don't need a tabernacle. Romans 5:8 says, "While we were yet sinners." While we have a defect of pride. While we have a defect of lust. While we have a defect of impatience. You name the defect—it doesn't matter! God proves His own love for us in that while we are still dealing with these defects, still dealing with these sins (not physical defects), Christ died for us. The High Priest has now come to us! No more stuff getting in the way of us having access to the Father.

## The Daily Word

If any of Aaron's descendants throughout the generations had a physical defect, they could not come near to present food offerings to God. They couldn't go near the curtain or approach the altar. Give thanks today for the blood of Jesus the Messiah, the ultimate High Priest, who without defect or blemish cleansed you from your sin so you could spend forever with the eternal God.

Jesus came to serve and to heal those with physical defects. May you love others the way Jesus loves others, even those who look differently from the way you look. Jesus paid the price for everyone!

The LORD spoke to Moses: "Tell Aaron: None of your descendants throughout your generations who has a physical defect is to come near to present the food of his God. No man who has any defect is to come near: no man who is blind, lame, facially disfigured, or deformed." —Leviticus 21:16–18

Further Scripture: Matthew 4:24; Hebrews 9:14; 1 Peter 1:18–19

# Questions

1. Why do you think there were specific regulations for the priests (Leviticus 21:1–24)? Does this seem harsh or unfair? Do you think of your pastor or spiritual leader with a similar expectation? Should you (1 Timothy 3:2–10; Titus 1:6–9)?

2. The high priest had even more required of him than a priest. Why was he not allowed to be in the presence of a dying or dead relative, including his parents (Leviticus 21:10–12)?

3. The high priest had to marry a virgin; he could not marry a widow, a divorced woman, or a woman defiled by prostitution. If the high priest was a type of Christ, then who would his bride point to (2 Corinthians 11:2; Ephesians 5:27, 31–32)? What does this regulation reveal to us about what God requires of us?

4. No priest among the descendants of Aaron with a defect could serve in the offering of sacrifices to God (Leviticus 21:16–23). How is this a picture of us as believers (Isaiah 53:5; Ephesians 4:15–25; Hebrews 10:14)?

5. What does it mean to profane the sanctuary of God (Leviticus 21:12)? Since we are the temple of the Holy Spirit, what would profaning this temple look like (1 Corinthians 3:16–17)?

6. What did the Holy Spirit highlight to you in Leviticus 21 through the reading or the teaching?

# Lesson 68: Leviticus 22
*Atonement:* Separation of the Priests

## Teaching Notes

### Intro

Remember when we brought in a Jewish person who knew everything about Leviticus? I want you to feel qualified to teach and share with others. I want you to feel like you can teach on Leviticus 22 today. Hopefully, you wouldn't run in fear. Hebrews 5—6 says we should no longer be teaching on the elementary things, but we should be teaching on things that are deep and mature in the Lord.

Here is a list of the commentaries I use in these studies:

- *The John MacArthur Bible Commentary*
- *Nelson's New Illustrated Bible Commentary*
- *New American Bible Commentary* by Mark F. Rooker (who wrote only on Leviticus)
- *The World Biblical Commentary* by John E. Hartley
- *JPS Torah Commentary*

Before you read any of the commentaries listed above, the first place you need to go to is the Holy Spirit. Scripture says you don't need anyone to teach you; let the Holy Spirit teach you (John 14:26).

### Teaching

*Leviticus 22:1*: Remember, Leviticus 22 is an instruction manual of how the priests were supposed to be living their lives as holy men. Sometimes when you go through the routines of ministry over and over, it can become lifeless. Moses warned the priests not to become lifeless. Wiersbe recorded, "Novelist George McDonald said 'Nothing is so deadening to the divine as a habitual dealing with outsiders of holy things.'"[1] We're going to walk through the three things Wiersbe

---

[1] Warren W. Wiersbe, *The Wiersbe Bible Commentary: Genesis–Deuteronomy* (Colorado Springs: David C. Cook, 2007), 225.

says were to keep the priests from becoming lifeless: First, let's make sure we are not becoming unclean priests.[2]

*Leviticus 22:2–4*: Moses was to tell Aaron and his sons to deal respectfully with the holy offerings. If anyone approached the holy offerings unclean, he would be cut off. Sometimes that meant he would be killed, and sometimes it meant removing him and putting him someplace else. None of Aaron's descendants who had a skin disease (leprosy) or discharge could eat of the holy offerings until they were clean.

*Leviticus 22:5–7*: If a priest was made unclean, he would remain unclean until evening and would not eat of the holy offerings unless he had bathed his body with water. Not only was water a part of the cleansing process, but so was time. When sunset came, only then would he become clean. Then he would be able eat of the holy offering, for that was his food.

*Leviticus 22:8*: A priest was not to eat an animal that died naturally or was mauled by wild beasts. Ordinary people could, but priests were to be set apart. Remember the whole goal was that the Lord was setting them apart.

*Leviticus 22:9*: The Lord wanted the priest to keep His instructions. A priest could actually go along with this routine and his life be a mess. That's called hypocrisy. Hypocrisy goes on in the church. That's why I believe we need a move of God. In order to be a priest, a man could not be a part of these things that are unclean. In Matthew 23:25–27, Jesus described religious hypocrisy.

*Leviticus 22:10–16*: Second, there could be unqualified guests.[3] While the priest might want to bless others, the commandment said not to feed people. The priests couldn't feed guests. Only their immediate family could eat of the sacrificed food. Sometimes, being set apart means saying no to the things you really want to do.

If priests purchased someone (a slave), that person could not partake. If a priest's daughter was married to someone outside the family (son-in-law), she could not eat either. If the daughter became widowed or divorced, had no children to take care for her, and returned to the house to live, then the father could share the food with her. The priests were not to profane the holy offerings.

*Leviticus 22:17–30*: Third, make sure you are not allowing unacceptable sacrifices.[4] Fellowship sacrifices were to be unblemished sheep or cattle. Someone bringing an

---

[2] Wiersbe, 226.

[3] Wiersbe, 226.

[4] Wiersbe, 226.

unacceptable sacrifice may be thinking, "Oh, it's okay if that sheep is missing an ear." If we are not careful, we can go from the standard, which is constant, to sin (Malachi 1:13). Second Samuel 24:24 says God is worthy of our best. Stop trying to cut corners in your walk with the Lord. Only what's perfect is acceptable.

*Leviticus 22:31–33*: The Lord said, "Keep My commands and do them. I am the LORD. Do not profane My holy name." According to Nelson's commentary, "God's person, His name, His present action in sanctifying His people, and His past action in rescuing them from slavery in Egypt, all were given as the basis of Israel's worship."[5] The Lord continued to say, "I am your God! Trust Me on these standards that I am asking you to do! I am the One who brought you out of Egypt."

## Closing

Where are you giving God your best? Where are you with reviveSCHOOL and your reading? Are you bringing your obedience to the table?

Leviticus 22 reminds us to bring our best and to stick to the manual. What does the Word of God say? We need a holy priest. There is one Priest who has it all figured out:

- Hebrews 7:26: "For this is the kind of high priest we need: holy, innocent, undefiled, separated from sinners, and exalted above the heavens."
- Hebrews 9:14: "How much more will the blood of the Messiah, who through the eternal Spirit offered Himself without blemish to God, cleanse our consciences from dead works to serve the living God?" We are now allowed to serve the living God!
- Ephesians 5:27: "He did this to present the church to Himself in splendor, without spot or wrinkle or anything like that, but holy and blameless."

We depend upon the High Priest to live holy and blameless, and His name is Jesus.

## The Daily Word

Following the regulations from the Lord was a serious matter. The phrase, "That person will be cut off from My presence; I am Yahweh," may be hard for some to fathom, as it is spoken from a kind, loving, gracious, Father God. And yet that's how seriously the Israelites were to take the regulations.

---

[5] Earl D. Radmacher, Ronald B. Allen, and H. Wayne House, eds., *Nelson's New Illustrated Bible Commentary* (Nashville: Thomas Nelson, 1999), 185.

Can you imagine being cut off from the Lord's presence? A life of complete darkness: no hope, no glimpse of the light. Today, give thanks for the Lord's presence. Give thanks for the Holy Spirit's presence in your life every day, all day, wherever you go! In His presence you will find rest, peace, and hope from an all-knowing, all-powerful Lord and Savior. And thanks to Jesus' atonement, nothing will ever separate us from His presence.

**Say to them: If any man from any of your descendants throughout your generations is in a state of uncleanness yet approaches the holy offerings that the Israelites consecrate to the LORD, that person will be cut off from My presence; I am Yahweh. —Leviticus 22:3**

Further Scripture: Psalm 16:11; Psalm 139:7–10; Romans 8:38–39

## Questions

1. Why was it important for a priest not to minister in a ceremonially defiled (unclean) state (Leviticus 22:2–3)? What was Israel to know about drawing close to God (Leviticus 22:9)?

2. How can we know that the old covenant was a shadow of the better new covenant? (Colossians 2:16–17; Hebrews 8:4–13; 10:1)

3. In Leviticus 22:7, God stated that a person can be clean again when the sun goes down, signifying the start of the Jewish day. What promise reminds us that we can begin each day with new mercies from the Lord (Lamentations 3:22–23)?

4. Who could and could not eat of the sacred offerings mentioned in Leviticus 22:10–13? There is a different attitude toward slavery in Israel than in American history. How do you see God's compassion toward slaves in Leviticus 22:11?

5. According to Leviticus 22:31–33, we are to honor His Name and be obedient to His Word. How are you living that out in your life today?

6. What did the Holy Spirit highlight to you in Leviticus 22 through the reading or the teaching?

# Lesson 69: Leviticus 23—24
*Atonement:* The Sabbath and the Feasts

## Teaching Notes

### Intro

Leviticus 23 and 24 are about a calendar. Wiersbe wrote, "God gave Israel a calendar that was tied to the rhythm of the seasons and the history of the nation. It was an unusual calendar because it not only summarized what God had done for them in the past, but it anticipated what God would do for Israel in the future."[1] There were seven feasts and festivals. Some of these feasts and festivals were more celebratory than others. I want to unfold these seven feasts and festivals, and how every one of them points to the Messiah.

### Teaching

*Leviticus 23:1–2*: We hear people mention Yom Kippur. It is one of God's appointed festivals. They all point to the Messiah. God wanted them to have appointed times on their calendar to celebrate and remember. It could last for one day, several days, or several weeks.

*Leviticus 23:3–4*: Every seventh day, the Israelites were to do no work. This was not to be mistaken for the festivals. Anything that involved work could not be done. Today in old city Jerusalem, you can't even carry a camera on the Sabbath. We observe Sunday because that was the day Jesus came back to life. Don't get hung up on what day it is, but take a day of rest. Find your own Sabbath. These sacred assemblies were to be proclaimed at their appointed times.

*Leviticus 23:5*: Passover is on the first month at twilight on the fourteenth day of the month (March/April) and is celebrated for only one day. The Israelites were to kill the perfect lamb, take hyssop and dip it in the blood, and put it on the doorposts and lintels of their homes. This was first done in Egypt so that the Spirit of Death would pass over their firstborn children inside the home.

---

[1] Warren W. Wiersbe, *The Bible Exposition Commentary: Genesis–Deuteronomy* (Colorado Springs: David C. Cook, 2007), 227.

In Matthew 26:17, Jesus celebrated the Passover. How does the Passover point to Christ? First Corinthians 5:7 says to clean out the old yeast before making a new batch. We are indeed unleavened, for Christ our Passover Lamb has been sacrificed. Jesus came to fulfill the Old Testament.

*Leviticus 23:6*: The Festival of Unleavened Bread was on the fifteenth day of the same month and lasted for seven days (March/April). During these days, one was to eat unleavened bread. Yeast was symbolic for sin. No yeast meant no sin.

*Leviticus 23:7–8*: The first day held a sacred assembly, and they were not to work. The Israelites were to present a fire offering for seven days. Then, on the seventh day, they held a sacred assembly and were not to work. The first and seventh days were the same. They were to eat unleavened bread every single day. There are three festivals that the males are required to participate in, and this is one of them. Second Corinthians 5:21, "He made the One who did not know sin to be sin for us, so that we might become the righteousness of God in Him." Unleavened bread speaks to the sinlessness of Christ.

*Leviticus 23:9–14*: Firstfruits was celebrated in March or April. The Israelites were to bring the best of the barley harvest. The priest waved the sheaf to the Lord, thanking Him for the harvest. For just one day, the Firstfruits was celebrated on the sixteenth day of the first month of Nisan, right in line with Passover and the Festival of Unleavened Bread. MacArthur says, "Firstfruits symbolized the consecration of the whole harvest to God and was a pledge of the whole harvest to come."[2] First Corinthians 15:20 says, "But now Christ has been raised from the dead, the firstfruits of those who have fallen asleep." The firstfruits point to the resurrection of Christ. Christ is the firstfruits of those who have fallen asleep.

*Leviticus 23:15–22*: Pentecost was celebrated seven complete weeks from the day they brought the sheaf offering, counting 50 days until the day after the seventh Sabbath. They were to present a new grain offering to the Lord in May/June. "Fifty" in Greek means Pentecost. The Israelites were to bring two loaves of bread baked with yeast, four quarts of flour, seven male lambs, a year old and without defect, one young bull, and two rams. Then they would sacrifice one male goat as a sin offering and two lambs that were a year old as a fellowship offering.

The priest would wave two lambs before the Lord as a wave offering together with the bread as firstfruits. They made a proclamation and were not to do any work. This was the wheat harvest. They were not to reap to the very edges of the

---

[2] John MacArthur, *The MacArthur Bible Commentary* (Nashville: Thomas Nelson, 2005), 160.

land but were to leave them for the poor people. Acts 1:5 says, "For John baptized with water, but you will be baptized with the Holy Spirit not many days from now." Acts 2:4 says, "Then they were all filled with the Holy Spirit and began to speak in different languages, as the Spirit gave them ability for speech." This was another festival that was mandatory for the males to participate in. In the Christian mindset, this starts with Easter and extends for 50 days.

*Leviticus 23:23–25*: Festival of the Trumpets was celebrated on the seventh month on the first day of the month for one day (Sept/Oct). This was one complete day of rest, commemoration, and jubilation. There was a sacred assembly and an offering made to the Lord by fire. In Israel, this is known as Rosh Hashanah and you will see people blowing trumpets. Matthew 24:31 says, "He will send out His angels with a loud trumpet, and they will gather His elect from the four winds, from one end of the sky to the other." Israel's regathering by Christ has not taken place yet. This is the *second coming* of the Messiah.

*Leviticus 23:26–32*: On the Day of Atonement, everybody would put their sins on one goat and then send that goat into the desert. They would then kill a second goat. This was celebrated on the tenth day of the seventh month (Sept/Oct) for just one day. This was the day of repentance. Jews know it as Yom Kippur. They had a sacred assembly and did no work. The Israelites were to practice self-denial and present a fire offering. They were making atonement for themselves before the Lord. First Corinthians 15:3 says, "For I passed on to you as most important what I also received: that Christ died for our sins." Ephesians 5:2 says, "And walk in love, as the Messiah also loved us and gave Himself for us, a sacrificial and fragrant offering to God."

*Leviticus 23:33–44*: Festival of Tabernacles was also known as Festival of Booths and was celebrated on the fifteenth day of the seventh month (Sept/Oct) and lasted for seven days. On the first day, they were not to do any work as they celebrated that God brought the people out of Egypt and put them in booths. They made little booths out of trees and lived in them for the seven days. This was another festival that all males must attend (Deuteronomy 16:16). They still do this today. You can walk down their sidewalks and see the booths. Zechariah 14:16 says, "Then all the survivors from the nations that came against Jerusalem will go up year after year to worship the King, the Lord of Hosts, and to celebrate the Festival of Booths." This has not happened yet. Zechariah was prophesying.

# Closing

These are the seven festivals, and they all point to Jesus! Pretty cool picture. There's a lot more here that we will cover tomorrow.

## The Daily Word

The phrase "sacred assembly" occurs eleven times in just one chapter. These assemblies served as a time for people to set aside their routine work and activities and focus on worshipping the Lord. The Lord described each of the eight different days designated as sacred assemblies, such as Passover, the Festival of Unleavened Bread, and the Day of Atonement. You too were created to worship the Lord. It may be through fasting, sacrifices and offerings, rejoicing in His goodness, or resting in His promises.

As a New Testament believer, you are no longer instructed to celebrate these specific sacred assemblies; however, Paul instructs believers to rejoice always and in everything give thanks. Today, give thanks, and remember the Lord's faithfulness in your life. Give thanks for the trials that have strengthened your faith and the joys in life that display God's goodness and kindness. The Lord is worthy of your praise and thanksgiving!

**The LORD spoke to Moses: "Speak to the Israelites and tell them: These are My appointed times, the times of the LORD that you will proclaim as sacred assemblies." —Leviticus 23:1**

Further Scripture: Lamentation 3:22–23; 1 Corinthians 10:31; 1 Thessalonians 5:16–18

## Questions

1. Name the seven annual feasts Israel celebrated as listed in Leviticus 23.

2. What was the significance of the one-week celebration of the Festival of Unleavened Bread (Exodus 12:14–20)? How has Christ fulfilled this celebration (1 Corinthians 5:7–8)?

3. How long did the Feast of Harvest occur after Passover (Leviticus 23:15–16)? How were the Israelites commanded to celebrate Feast of Harvest (also known as Pentecost)? How was the celebration of Pentecost described in the New Testament (Acts 2:1–4)? The Feast of Harvest was a joyous celebration. How can you continually celebrate your joy in the Holy Spirit (Romans 14:17)?

4. The details for the priests regarding the Day of Atonement are found in Leviticus 16. What was the responsibility of the people during this day (Leviticus 23:26–32)?

5. Look for the connection in the following questions regarding the festivals and Christ: During what festival was Jesus crucified (Leviticus 23:5; John 19:14)? During what festival was He buried and then resurrected?

6. What did the Holy Spirit highlight to you in Leviticus 23—24 through the reading or the teaching?

# Lesson 70: Leviticus 25
## *Atonement*: Sabbath Years and Jubilee

## Teaching Notes

### Intro

Yesterday, we learned about the Sabbath's importance and the seven feasts the Israelites were commanded to celebrate. The purpose of the Sabbath and the feasts was to remember what God had done and would do for the Israelites. Every festival also points to the Messiah. As a recap, the seven festivals are:

(1) Passover
(2) Feast of Unleavened Bread
(3) Firstfruits
(4) Pentecost
(5) Feast of Trumpets
(6) Day of Atonement
(7) Feast of Booths

God gave the Israelites a new calendar. Today, we're going to dive into what this looked like over the course of 50 years.

### Teaching

*Leviticus 25:1–2*: We know God is the one who owns the land (v. 2). We will also see that God owns the people (v. 55). Wiersbe noted that God truly is the "landlord."[1] As the landlord, God wants to be sure His people know what to do. Verses 1–7 and 18–22 outline God's rules for rest for the land.

*Leviticus 25:3*: The Israelites were to "sow your field for six years," that is, to plant six years of crops.

---

[1] Warren W. Wiersbe, *Be Holy (Leviticus): Becoming "Set Apart" for God* (Wheaton, IL: Victor Books, 1996), 149.

*Leviticus 25:4*: The seventh year was to be a Sabbath of complete rest. The Israelites were to work the land for six years. But in the seventh year, they were to do no work—they were not to sow the field or prune the vineyard in the seventh year. They were not to touch the land.

*Leviticus 25:5*: They were instructed not even to reap what grew on its own.

*Leviticus 25:6–7*: They could feed themselves, their slaves, their hired hands, the foreigners who stayed with them, and the livestock from what the land produced in the Sabbath year. Why is it healthy to give land rest? If you continually work it, you're breaking it down so that it doesn't have any natural nutrients left. Constable said that God didn't want the Israelites to "work the land to death."[2] Why was it important to stop working for the seventh year? It was a time to regather themselves and be refreshed.

*Leviticus 25:8–17*: Not only did the land rest, but both land and financial debts were released (Deuteronomy 15:1–11). Each year, during the Feast of Booths, all Israel assembled and read from the book of law (Deuteronomy 31:9–13). God wanted the Israelites to go back to the law so they could do it for another six years. Over the course of time, the Israelites forgot the law and festivals and didn't follow them anymore (Jeremiah 25:8–11). They stopped doing all this. The whole land would become conquered by their enemies. Why? Because they didn't obey God's law. When there's a standard that God has given (Leviticus 18), and we don't follow it, there's always a consequence (Leviticus 20). God told them to let the land rest. Instead, they played god and were so thickheaded about working the land that they worked it to death. So God sent them away for 70 years.

*Leviticus 25:18*: "You are to keep My statutes and ordinances." Apparently, that didn't happen. Because they didn't keep God's ordinances, they missed out on the blessings of verse 19.

*Leviticus 25:19*: "The land will yield its fruit so that you can eat, be satisfied, and live securely in the land." They lost their land because they didn't keep the Sabbath. They lost their land because they kept doing the work.

*Leviticus 25:20–21*: God promised to take care of the Israelites by giving them so many crops in the sixth year that it would be enough for three years!

---

[2] Thomas L. Constable, *Expository Notes of Dr. Thomas Constable: Leviticus*, 200, https://planobiblechapel.org/tcon/notes/pdf/leviticus.pdf.

*Leviticus 25:22*: Why did the Israelites need provision for three years? Since they wouldn't sow in the seventh year, they would sow in the eighth year, but the crop wouldn't come until the ninth year. They needed provision for years six, seven, and eight. God was not only going to provide for seven years but for the next 50 (Leviticus 25:8)! But the Israelites didn't trust the Word of the Lord. All of this was just for the seven-year time period, but let's look at the Year of Jubilee by going back to verse 8.

*Leviticus 25:8–12*: Moses outlined seven sets of seven years in which the seventh year was a Sabbatical year. In the 50th year, the trumpet blew on the Day of Atonement. This was the day the high priest went before the Lord to sacrifice the animals for atonement. Holiness was even present in the Israelite calendar. The Year of Jubilee was holy.

*Leviticus 25:13–17*: Wiersbe identified four words that God called for during the Year of Jubilee:

(1) Repentance (v. 9): God called for repentance on the Day of Atonement.
(2) Release (v. 10): They were to make sure everyone had been released!
(3) Rest (v. 11): They were not to sow, reap, or harvest but to eat what had been given to them.
(4) Restoration (vv. 13–17): Of both property and land.[3]

*Leviticus 25:18–23*: Fruit came from observing the Sabbath years and Year of Jubilee. God owned the land, so it was never permanently sold. The poor and the rich were equal. No one could ever have more than another for the long term because everything evened out in the Year of Jubilee. When a person walks through this process of repentance, release, rest, and restoration, they have been revived!

## Closing

Do you want to know how you ultimately get this revival? Isaiah prophesied that a coming Messiah was going to do these things. The Spirit of the Lord has anointed the Messiah to bring good news to the poor, heal the brokenhearted, and proclaim liberty for the captives and freedom for the prisoners (Isaiah 61:1). Isaiah described what happened in the Year of Jubilee! He went on to say, "and to proclaim the year of the LORD's favor." The year of the Lord's favor was the Year of Jubilee!

---

[3] Wiersbe, 153.

The Israelites went through a time of repentance, release, rest, and restoration so they could start all over again, and I believe the way that we start all over again (according to Luke 4) is by turning to Christ. We turn to Him for freedom! The way we experience the Year of Jubilee in our own lives is through Jesus Christ.

## The Daily Word

The Lord gave Moses clear instructions for the Israelites to observe a Sabbath rest for the land every seventh year. The Lord explained in detail how this would work. The Israelites would have a sufficient crop every sixth year to provide enough to carry them through the Sabbath year and even the year following the Sabbath. God promised the Israelites would live securely in the land if they kept His statutes and ordinances and carefully observed them. Can you imagine physically not working for an entire year, trusting the Lord to provide everything you need? And yet, what was their alternative? They could have taken matters into their own hands, doing what they wanted and what they thought best.

In the same way, the Lord instructs you to rest in Him, trusting He will provide as you follow His ways. So why is it so hard to let go of control, rest with unwavering faith in God's promises, and do things His way? Today, seek the Lord for rest, and trust in His ways and His plans for your day. Let go of control and walk by faith.

**But there will be a Sabbath of complete rest for the land in the seventh year, a Sabbath to the LORD: you are not to sow your field or prune your vineyard. You are not to reap what grows by itself from your crop, or harvest the grapes of your untended vines. It must be a year of complete rest for the land. . . . You are not to cheat one another, but fear your God, for I am Yahweh your God. You are to keep My statutes and ordinances and carefully observe them, so that you may live securely in the land. —Leviticus 25:4–5, 17–18**

Further Scripture: Psalm 147:7–9; Matthew 6:24; Matthew 11:28–29

## Questions

1. When does the Sabbatical year occur? When does the Jubilee year occur? (Leviticus 25:2, 8–9)
2. Why did God command the Israelites to give the land a Sabbath of complete rest on the seventh year (Leviticus 25:4)? What was God's blessing for obeying this command? (Leviticus 25:20–22)

3. In Leviticus 25:23, God reminded the Israelites that the land actually belonged to Him and that they were just foreigners. How did that bring them hope? How does knowing this world isn't our home give us hope? (Exodus 19:5; 1 Chronicles 29:15; Hebrews 11:13–16)

4. Were the Israelites faithful to keep the Sabbath years for the land? What was their punishment (Leviticus 25:4; 26:34, 43; 2 Chronicles 36:21; Jeremiah 25:11)? How have you been a good steward of God's land?

5. What was the incredible promise that God gave for obeying His command about the land (Leviticus 25:18–22)? What promises has the Lord made to you and fulfilled because of your obedience and His faithfulness?

6. What did the Holy Spirit highlight to you in Leviticus 25 through the reading or the teaching?

# Lesson 71: Leviticus 26
## *Atonement*: Covenant Blessings and Discipline

## Teaching Notes

### Intro

Today, we are studying Leviticus 26. As a reminder, Moses wrote Leviticus. Our one word in Genesis was *Seed*, and we saw how the seed pointed to the Messiah. Our one word in Exodus was *Deliverer*, and we saw Jesus as the Deliverer of His people bringing them out of Egypt. Our one word in Leviticus is *Atonement*. This word, atonement, means substitution, imputation, or death. Jesus took on our guilt and sin and died on our behalf.

### Teaching

*Leviticus 26:1*: God forbade Israel from making and worshipping idols or carved images—"for I am Yahweh your God." The Mosaic covenant was conditional. This meant the people had to do something for God to keep His covenant. Nelson's commentary pointed out that good leaders make sure their people know what they should and should not do, as well as clearly state the consequences for keeping or not keeping those expectations.[1] In Leviticus 26, Moses established what the Israelites were supposed to do, and what they were supposed to refrain from doing, to fulfill the covenant of the Lord. He also clarified the consequences if they didn't fulfill the commands of the Lord. Wiersbe offered four reasons why the Israelites should have obeyed God's commands: (1) "Because of who God is"; (2) "Because of what God did"; (3) "Because of where God dwells"; and (4) "Because of what God promised."[2]

*Leviticus 26:2*: "You must keep My Sabbaths and revere my sanctuary; I am Yahweh." God rested after six days of creation (Genesis 2:2) and declared the seventh day as holy (Genesis 2:3). God also established the Sabbath as a day of rest for the Israelites (Exodus 20:8–10). Thus, to revere something means to honor it.

---

[1] Earl D. Radmacher, Ronald B. Allen, and H. Wayne House, eds., *Nelson's New Illustrated Bible Commentary* (Nashville: Thomas Nelson, 1999), 190.

[2] Warren W. Wiersbe, *The Bible Exposition Commentary: Genesis–Deuteronomy* (Colorado Springs: David C. Cook, 2001), 301–302.

Because God dwelt in His sanctuary (the tabernacle), the Israelites could be in His presence.

*Leviticus 26:3–5*: Moses set forth God's conditions: "If you follow My statutes and faithfully observe My commands." When the Israelites were faithful, God promised to give them rain at the right time so the land would yield an abundant food supply. In fact, the land would produce so much that threshing would continue until the grape harvest, which would continue until it was time to sow again. God promised them plenty of food to eat as they lived securely in the land. However, they constantly tried to make it rain by worshipping Baal.

*Leviticus 26:6–8*: God made additional promises to Israel: I will make peace in the land. You will lie down with nothing to frighten you. I will remove dangerous animals. No sword will pass through your land. When we talk about Israel today, we don't see this. Since there's no peace in Israel right now, maybe it's because they are not doing these things. God's presence among them would enable them to pursue and overpower enemies who far outnumber them: "Five of you will pursue 100, and 100 of you will pursue 10,000."

*Leviticus 26:9*: God's promise to make them fruitful so they multiplied in number brought His previous promises to mind. In Genesis 1:28, God blessed Adam and Eve: "Be fruitful, multiply, fill the earth, and subdue it." In Genesis 12:1–3, God promised Abram, "I will make you into a great nation, I will bless you, I will make your name great, and you will be a blessing. I will bless those who bless you, I will curse those who treat you with contempt, and all the peoples on earth will be blessed through you." In Genesis 15:5, God promised Abram that his offspring would be as numerous as the stars in the sky.

*Leviticus 26:10–13*: God promised not to reject them, but to dwell with them and walk among them. God promises that He will not reject us. If you feel the spirit of rejection, it is not from Jesus, but the enemy. In Exodus 32, Aaron and all the Israelites messed up when they made the golden calf. But even though they messed up, God said, "I . . . will be your God, and you will be My people." Paul repeated God's restriction against idol worship and His promise to dwell among His people in 2 Corinthians 6:16. God broke their bonds of slavery in Egypt so they could live in freedom. He did the same for us. God wants a relationship with us every single day so we can experience His presence. Why wouldn't you sign up for this?

*Leviticus 26:14–17*: Beginning in verse 14, God described the consequences the Israelites would face if they failed to obey God and broke their covenant with

Him. MacArthur said the "wasting disease" could have been tuberculosis or leprosy.[3] Their eyes would fail, and life would ebb away. They would sow seed that their enemies would eat. When God turned against them, they would be defeated by their enemies. They would flee even though no one chased them.

*Leviticus 26:18–22*: If these conditions didn't cause Israel to obey God, He promised to discipline them "seven times" for their sins. The phrase "seven times" was repeated in verses 21, 24, and 28. God would make the sky like iron (no rain) and the land like bronze (hard ground) so it could not produce a crop. If Israel acted with hostility toward God, He would multiply the plagues "seven times" for their sins. God would send wild animals to attack them and their livestock, which indicated an extreme economic downturn.

*Leviticus 26:23–26*: If Israel refused to accept God's discipline, He would strike them seven times for their sins. He would bring the swords of foreign nations "to execute the vengeance of the covenant." God would send pestilence among them and deliver them into enemy hands. God would cut off their supply of bread so that ten women would have to use the same oven. They would not have enough food to eat.

*Leviticus 26:27–33*: If Israel didn't obey, then God would act with "furious hostility" and discipline them "seven times" for their sins. The famine would be so great that they would eat the flesh of their sons and daughters. Such cannibalism was described in 2 Kings, Lamentations, and Jeremiah. God spelled out the consequences of their failure to keep the covenant. He would destroy their high places, cut down their altars, and pile their dead bodies on their idols. God would reject them! He would reduce their cities to ruin, refuse to smell the pleasing aroma of their sacrifices, devastate the land, allow their cities to become ruins, scatter them among the nations, and allow other nations to chase after them.

*Leviticus 26:34–39*: God scattered the Israelites into exile (Assyrian and Babylonian) so He could restore the land because they didn't honor the Sabbath. Those left behind were so fearful of their enemies that even the sound of a leaf brought them fear. They stumbled over each other as they fled before their enemies. They perished among the nations because of their sin.

*Leviticus 26:40–46*: God knew the Israelites would sin against Him, so He offered an option that allowed them to restore their relationship with Him: "But

---

[3] John MacArthur, *The MacArthur Bible Commentary* (Nashville: Thomas Nelson, 2005), 163.

if they will confess their sin and the sin of their fathers—their unfaithfulness that they practiced against Me." When they confessed their sins, God promised to remember His covenant with Jacob, Isaac, and Abraham. God promised not to reject, destroy, or break covenant with the Israelites because He would remember His covenant with their fathers, whom He brought out of Egypt. What was God saying? God promised to give them a second chance.

## Closing

The cross is our second chance. To the Israelites, it didn't make sense that God would continually pour out His love for them. They were always messing up, but so do we. In the Old Testament they had the blood because they sacrificed animals on the Day of Atonement to receive forgiveness. But we don't have to do that anymore because Jesus said that He is our second chance. God is always giving us another option. Today my prayer is that you will take that option and turn to Him.

## The Daily Word

If the Israelites followed God's statutes and faithfully observed His commands, the Lord promised to bless them abundantly. Not only would He bless the work of their hands, but His presence would also be with them, bringing them ultimate peace and freedom. They had a choice to follow God or go their own way. God even gave them a second chance through confessing their sins, offering blood sacrifices, and turning back to Him. God desires strongly for His people to follow Him and trust Him.

The same is true today. The Lord, through the blood of Jesus, longs for you to follow Him and His ways each day. In Him, there is freedom, love, and peace. As a believer, the Holy Spirit takes residence in you, and He is with you always. Rest in that promise today, and make a choice to seek the Lord your God with all your heart, soul, mind, and strength.

**I will place My residence among you, and I will not reject you. I will walk among you and be your God, and you will be My people. I am Yahweh your God, who brought you out of the land of Egypt, so that you would no longer be their slaves. I broke the bars of your yoke and enabled you to live in freedom. —Leviticus 26:11–13**

Further Scripture: Isaiah 57:15; 1 Corinthians 3:16; 1 John 4:12

# Questions

1. What was the Mosaic covenant (Leviticus 26; Deuteronomy 28)? How did this differ from the covenants God made with Abraham (Genesis 17:1–14) and other biblical covenants? (Genesis 9:8–17)

2. If the Israelites obeyed what God commanded in Leviticus 26:1–3, they would be rewarded for their obedience with the promises outlined in verses 4–13. Do you find conditional rewards based on obedience hard to comprehend? What is your reward for obedience to the Lord now (Matthew 25:21; Galatians 6:9; Colossians 3:23–24)? How does this encourage you to be obedient to what God asks of you?

3. In verses 14–39, God explained what He would do as a result of disobedience to His commands in verses 1–3. However, in verses 40–42, He gave them an opportunity to receive pardon from their punishment. What is our final pardon of eternal punishment and condemnation today? (John 3:16; 14:6; Acts 4:11–12; 1 John 1:9)

4. Paul quoted Leviticus 26:12 in 2 Corinthians 6:16. How do these verses challenge and encourage you? Why do you think Paul chose to quote this verse to the Corinthians?

5. What did the Holy Spirit highlight to you in Leviticus 26 through the reading or the teaching?

# Lesson 72: Leviticus 27
## *Atonement:* Dedicating Persons and Things

## Teaching Notes

### Intro

Welcome to the final lesson in Leviticus! After 72 lessons this might be one of the hardest. This lesson is about vows. When we think of vows, we think of wedding vows. We just studied Leviticus 26 where God said, "If you keep My commands, then I'll give you an abundance of food, My presence, and peace in the land, but if you don't do these things, then I will bring terror, disease, war, and hostility." Now, Moses addressed making vows. Vows had nothing to do with the Law. R. K. Harrison said, "A vow to God placed a person or property in a special consecrated relationship which stood outside the formal demands of the law."[1] Vows represent a special deal that someone makes with God.

Constable gave these descriptions of vows:

(1) We are not commanded to make vows at all.

(2) Vows are natural desires of people who make them because they love God or want something from Him.

(3) God expected His people to make vows.

(4) God expected them to actually keep their vows.[2]

Moses recorded some extreme guidelines for the Israelites who made vows to the Lord. The importance of keeping a vow is confirmed throughout Scripture. Proverbs 20:25 says, "It is a trap for anyone to dedicate something rashly and later to reconsider his vows." Before you flippantly make a vow to God, give it some thought. Ecclesiastes 5:4–5 says, "When you make a vow to God, don't delay fulfilling it, because He does not delight in fools. Fulfill what you vow.

---

[1] R. K. Harrison, *Tyndale Old Testament Commentary: Leviticus* (Downers Grove, IL: InterVarsity, 1980), 235; quoted in Thomas L. Constable, *Expository Notes of Dr. Thomas Constable: Leviticus*, 219, https://planobiblechapel.org/tcon/notes/pdf/leviticus.pdf.

[2] Constable, 218.

Better that you do not vow than that you vow and not fulfill it." When you make a vow to the Lord, you had better make sure you are going to do it.

Jesus also addressed the importance of carefully considering the vow we make to follow Him. In Luke 14:26–31, Jesus said: "If anyone comes to Me and does not hate his own father and mother, wife and children, brothers and sisters—yes, and even his own life—he cannot be My disciple. Whoever does not bear his own cross and come after Me cannot be My disciple. For which of you, wanting to build a tower, doesn't first sit down and calculate the cost to see if he has enough to complete it? Otherwise, after he has laid the foundation and cannot finish it, all the onlookers will begin to make fun of him, saying, 'This man started to build and wasn't able to finish.' Or what king, going to war against another king, will not first sit down and decide if he is able with 10,000 to oppose the one who comes against him with 20,000?"

If you make a vow, then your lifestyle, words, and actions better back it up. When you commit yourself to following after the Lord, you have to count the cost. That's what Moses was after. That's what Jesus is after.

## Teaching

*Leviticus 27:1–4*: God gave Moses specific instructions for the Israelites who made a special vow to the Lord. Making a special vow to dedicate persons to the Lord required payments to the priests of different amounts based on the age and sex of the person dedicated. For the 20- to 60-year-old age range, the cost was 50 shekels of silver for males and 30 shekels for females.

*Leviticus 27:5–6*: For those aged five to 20 years old, the cost was 20 shekels for a male and ten shekels for a female. If the person was one month to five years old, the cost was five shekels for a male and three shekels for a female. The parents made this vow before the Lord for the child. Later in Scripture, we see this demonstrated in the life of Hannah. In 1 Samuel 1:8–11, Elkanah saw Hannah crying and refusing to eat because she was distressed over her barrenness. Hannah went to the tabernacle where she prayed and wept before the Lord and pleaded, "LORD of Hosts, if You will take notice of Your servant's affliction, remember and not forget me, and give Your servant a son, I will give him to the LORD all the days of his life, and his hair will never be cut" (v. 11). Hannah made a vow to God, which she fulfilled after Samuel was born.

*Leviticus 27:7–8*: If the person was 60 years and older, the cost was 15 shekels for a male and ten shekels for a female. Those who were too poor to pay the assessment presented the person to the priest, who then set the value according to what the one who made the vow could afford.

*Leviticus 27:9–13*: Next, God talked about offering animals in their vows. When offered as part of a vow, the animal became holy, so the person could not exchange or make a substitution, either good or bad, for the offered animal. If the vow involved an unclean animal, one that was not acceptable as an offering, the priest would determine its value. If the owner wanted to redeem the unclean animal, he had to add one-fifth to its value.

*Leviticus 27:14–25*: These verses addressed vows made with property. When a man consecrated his house to the Lord, the priest assessed its value. To redeem the house, the man had to pay the entire value plus one-fifth. When a man consecrated any part of his field to the Lord, its value was assessed at 50 shekels to every five bushels of barley seed required to plant it. If the field was consecrated in the Year of Jubilee, its value remained as set. If consecrated after the Year of Jubilee, the priest determined the value according to the number of years that remained until the next Year of Jubilee. If the person who consecrated the field wanted it back, he had to pay the value plus one-fifth, and ownership transferred back to the man who consecrated it.

*Leviticus 27:26–29*: Some things were not redeemable. No one could consecrate the firstborn of their livestock because it already belonged to the Lord. If it was an unclean animal, it could be bought back by adding one-fifth to its value. Nothing that a man devoted to the Lord, whether man, animal, or land, could be sold or redeemed. A person could not take back his vow to the Lord. If he did, he would be put to death.

*Leviticus 27:30–34*: A tithe of everything from the land, grain from the soil or fruit of the trees, belonged to the Lord. If a man wanted to redeem any of his tithe, he had to add one-fifth to its value. Every tenth animal of a shepherd's flock was holy to the Lord. God gave Moses these commands for the Israelites on Mount Sinai.

Wiersbe said there were three types of tithes that the Jews offered:

- A tithe to the Levites/priests (Numbers 18:21–32)
- A tithe that was "brought to the sanctuary and eaten before the Lord" (Deuteronomy 14:22–27)
- "A tithe every three years to the poor"[3] (Deuteronomy 14:28–29)

---

[3] Warren W. Wiersbe, *The Bible Exposition Commentary: Genesis–Deuteronomy* (Colorado Springs: David C. Cook, 2001), 305.

A tithe was money committed to the Lord, but a vow didn't always mean that.

## Closing

God expects us to keep our commitments to Him. We need to be honest with our dealings with Him. We are no different from the Israelites. We all need redemption, but it only comes through the great High Priest Himself. As Peter said, "For you know that you were redeemed from your empty way of life inherited from the fathers, not with perishable things like silver or gold, but with the precious blood of Christ, like that of a lamb without defect or blemish" (1 Peter 1:18–19).

What we have been talking about throughout the whole book of Leviticus is redemption through the blood of Christ. I don't think we realize how much Christ has done for us. Jesus said, "I am your *Atonement*. I am your lamb without blemish." Leviticus is a book with a lot of dos and a lot of don'ts, but what I love about it is that there is hope. And this hope comes through the blood of Christ, and we all need to be redeemed.

## The Daily Word

As Leviticus comes to an end, God gave Moses final commands for the Israelites. Specifically, they discussed making vows to the Lord and how the vows could be redeemed (essentially breaking the vows through a determined sum of money).

As believers, there is a cost to following Christ. Jesus said if you want to be His disciple, you must bear your own cross and follow Him. Jesus said believers who do not count the cost and hold loosely to all earthy things cannot be His disciples. However, in all this, the beautiful truth is that Christ gave His life for you. Through His precious blood, Jesus came as the atonement for sinners. And life with Christ is free and full when you surrender all and follow Him. He is our forever hope.

If the vow involves one of the animals that may be brought as an offering to the LORD, any of these he gives to the LORD will be holy. —Leviticus 27:9

Further Scripture: Luke 14:27, 33; 1 Peter 1:18–19

## Questions

1. What is a vow? What are examples of vows that you have made in your life?
2. What payment was to be made to the priest when making a vow (Leviticus 27:2–8)? Why do you think God instituted a payment system for making vows?

3. Read Ecclesiastes 5:3–7. How does this help you understand how God sees vows? What is the difference between making a vow to God and one made to men?

4. What does it mean to "redeem" something in Leviticus 27 (vv. 13, 15, 19, 27–28, 31)? What price was paid in order to redeem something? How does this compare to Christ in 1 Peter 1:18–19?

5. Do you see your decision to follow Jesus as a vow? What does God expect of us when we vow to follow Jesus? (Luke 14:25–33)

6. What did the Holy Spirit highlight to you in Leviticus 27 through the reading or the teaching?

# Lesson 73: Numbers 1—2
*Rock*: The Census of Israel

## Teaching Notes

### Intro

Welcome to our study on the book of Numbers—36 chapters where we talk about lots and lots of numbers. The writers weren't super creative with the title because they were going to talk about numbers. It all pointed to one thing, the Messiah.

- In Genesis, the *Seed* pointed to the Messiah.
- In Exodus, the *Deliverer* was actually the Messiah who pulled the Israelites out of Egypt into freedom.
- In Leviticus, the *Atonement* was the blood of Christ that allows us to be free.

Now here we are in Numbers, and our one word is *Rock*. Let's look at 1 Corinthians 10:1–4 where Paul wrote, "Now I want you to know, brothers, that our fathers were all under the cloud, all passed through the sea, and all were baptized into Moses in the cloud and in the sea. They all ate the same spiritual food, and all drank the same spiritual drink. For they drank from a spiritual rock that followed them, and that rock was Christ."

In Numbers, they were going from one generation to the next generation. They were in the wilderness, and the *Rock* they were partaking from was Christ. Jesus was their foundation. Jesus was their base.

### Teaching

*Numbers 1:1*: Moses was the writer. From Numbers 20 through the end of the Pentateuch (the end of Deuteronomy), covers one year, which included the rest of Moses' life. The Israelites had been here in the Wilderness of Sinai at least 11 months (Exodus 19:1) after their departure from Egypt.

*Numbers 1:2*: Wiersbe said Moses was given an order to "take a census of the men available to serve in the army."[1] Every male in the community would be counted by tribe by clan and by family. In Exodus 30:11–12, God told Moses, "When you take a census of the Israelites to register them, each of the men must pay a ransom for himself to the LORD as they are registered. Then no plague will come on them as they are registered." Exodus 38:25–26 tallied the silver collected and counted 603,550 men. Keep this number in mind as we read Numbers 1.

*Numbers 1:3–4*: Only men who were 20 years and older and able to serve in the army were counted. The purpose was to get the men ready for war. Moses didn't complete this census alone.

*Numbers 1:5–15*: One man from each tribe was named to assist Moses:

- Elizur from the tribe of Reuben (Jacob's firstborn and son of Leah).
- Shelumiel from the tribe of Simeon.
- Nahshon from the tribe of Judah (from the family tree of David according to Ruth 4:20).
- Nethanel from the tribe of Issachar.
- Eliab from the tribe of Zebulun.
- Elishama from the tribe of Ephraim (son of Joseph).
- Gamaliel from the tribe of Manasseh (son of Joseph).
- Abidan from the tribe of Benjamin.
- Ahiezer from the tribe of Dan.
- Pagiel from the tribe of Asher.
- Eliasaph from the tribe of Gad.
- Ahira from the tribe of Naphtali.

*Numbers 1:16–19*: These men were the leaders of their tribes—the heads of Israel's clans. They were like Jesus' 12 disciples. Moses and Aaron, along with these men who had been designated by name, called the whole community together on the first day of the second month. One by one, the men who were 20 years and older were listed by name according to their clan and family. They did just as the Lord commanded.

*Numbers 1:20–43*: Moses registered the Israelite males 20 and older who could serve in the army:

[1] Warren W. Wiersbe, *The Bible Exposition Commentary: Genesis–Deuteronomy* (Colorado Springs: David C. Cook, 2001), 313.

- Reuben's tribe = 46,500 men
- Simeon's tribe = 59,300 men
- Gad's tribe = 45,650 men
- Judah's tribe = 74,600 men
- Issachar's tribe = 54,400 men
- Zebulun's tribe = 57,400 men
- Ephraim's tribe = 40,500 men
- Manasseh's tribe = 32,200 men
- Benjamin's tribe = 35,400 men
- Dan's tribe = 62,700 men
- Asher's tribe = 41,500 men
- Naphtali's tribe = 53,400 men

The tribe with the fewest members was Manasseh (32,200) and the largest tribe was Judah (74,600). Don't overlook the simple facts that they had to count these people and retain this information.

*Numbers 1:44–46*: These were the men counted by Moses and Aaron and the 12 leaders of Israel; each one represented his family. All were men 20 years and older who were able to serve in Israel's army. The total number equaled 603,550. Compare that back to Exodus 38:25–26.

*Numbers 1:47–51*: God instructed Moses not to register or count the Levites, but to appoint them over the tabernacle, its furnishings, and everything in it. They were charged with transporting and caring for the tabernacle and everything associated with it. Whenever the Israelites made camp, the Levites camped around the tabernacle. Whenever the Israelites moved, the Levites were responsible for moving the tabernacle and its furnishings. If anyone else touched any of these items, they had to be put to death. There were priests, and then there were Levites, each group with different roles. The Levites took care of everything around the tabernacle while the priests did the offerings. The Levites were the ones who stayed back and served the Lord in this way. They were not part of the army who fought on the battlefields. The Levites were the logistical crew.

*Numbers 1:52–54*: The Israelites camped out under the banners of their family tribes. The Levities camped around the tabernacle of the testimony so no wrath would fall on the Israelites. The Israelites did everything just as the Lord commanded Moses.

# Closing

How does this apply to us? We all have our own lanes. We all have our own roles to fill so God gets the glory. God is glorified when everybody comes together. These are the tribes in the church today according to Ephesians 4:11–13: "And He personally gave some to be apostles, some prophets, some evangelists, some pastors and teachers, for the training of the saints in the work of ministry, to build up the body of Christ, until we all reach unity in the faith and in the knowledge of God's Son, growing into a mature man with a stature measured by Christ's fullness."

When we walk in the sweet spot where God has put us, then God gets the glory. We will continue this dialogue of how important every person is in order for God to get the glory.

## The Daily Word

The Lord commanded Moses and Aaron to take a census of the entire Israelite community, counting their names one by one. The Lord was bringing order to the Israelites and beginning to build Israel's army. Pay attention as you read the names and numbers in each ancestral house. Can you imagine counting all those people one at a time? No computers, no paper or pens; still, the Lord commanded that each name be counted one by one. The task was worth the time and effort to the Lord.

In the same way, the Lord knows your name. He has an ultimate plan for you. No matter what community you belong to, you have a role and are important to the entire body of Christ. He's counting on you to bring Him glory!

**Take a census of the entire Israelite community by their clans and their ancestral houses, counting the names of every male one by one. —Numbers 1:2**

Further Scripture: Isaiah 43:1; John 10:14; Ephesians 4:11–12

## Questions

1. The theme for Numbers is *Rock*. How do you see Jesus in 1 Corinthians 10:1–4?

2. In Numbers 1:1, the Lord spoke to Moses in the tent of meeting in the Wilderness of Sinai. Does this encourage you that no matter what situation or circumstance you are in (even wilderness-like situations), God still wants to speak to you?

3. What did God ask Moses to do in the first few verses of Numbers? These were all sons of Jacob (Israel). Why was Levi left off the list? (Numbers 1:47–51)

4. Numbers 2 organized the tribes around the tabernacle. As a review, what did the Most Holy Place represent? What was kept there? (Exodus 25:21–22; Hebrews 6:19–20)

5. God assigned each tribe's leaders the land where they would camp around the tabernacle. In what order did the tribes set out when they traveled to a new destination? What was God's purpose for doing this? Are you able to see God's purpose for you right now? (Proverbs 19:21; Philippians 2:12–13) Why or why not?

6. What did the Holy Spirit highlight to you in Numbers 1—2 through the reading or the teaching?

# Lesson 74: Numbers 3
*Rock*: The Levitical Census

## Teaching Notes

### Intro

Yesterday we read through 12 names that represented one man from every tribe. Every name matters to God. In Numbers 1, God used these 12 men, with the help of Moses and Aaron, to count 603,550 soldiers 20 years and older who were able to serve in the army. The Israelites were getting ready for something—to protect the people of Israel. In Numbers 2, they were told how to move forward. They were told which tribe would move first, and then who would go next, etc. It just shows you how detailed God is. Today, we are going to look at how Numbers 3 instructed the Levites to serve.

### Teaching

*Numbers 3:1–4*: Notice that Moses flipped the names and put Aaron first, because the book of Numbers is about the priests. It was not about Moses, but Aaron and his family, the Levites. Aaron had four sons. Aaron's sons were ordained to serve as priests. The firstborn Nadab and his brother, Abihu, died when they offered unauthorized fire before the Lord (Leviticus 10:1–3). Nadab and Abihu had no sons, so their family line ended. Eleazar and Ithamar served as priests under the direction of their father Aaron, which implied Nadab and Abihu didn't follow Aaron's instructions. Numbers 20:22–29 says Eleazar became high priest when Aaron died.

*Numbers 1:5–10*: God gave Moses instructions for the Levites. Moses presented the Levites to Aaron to assist him by performing duties for Aaron and the entire community. The Levites were charged with caring for all the furnishings of the tent of meeting and attending to the service of the tabernacle. Their role was to serve. At God's direction, Moses assigned the Levites to Aaron and his sons to serve and assist them exclusively. Aaron and his sons served as priests, but any unauthorized persons who came near the sanctuary were to be put to death.

*Numbers 3:11–13*: The Lord said He had taken the Levities, out of all the Israelites, as His firstborn. Out of the 2 million people, the Levites belonged to God. When God struck down all the firstborn in Egypt, He consecrated, or set apart, every firstborn in Israel to Himself. Review God's statement to Moses in Exodus 13:1–2: "The LORD spoke to Moses: 'Consecrate every firstborn male to Me, the firstborn from every womb among the Israelites, both man and domestic animal; it is Mine.'"

*Numbers 3:14–16*: God commanded Moses to register every Levite one month old or older by family and clan. So Moses counted them as he was commanded. Note that Moses had no help this time.

*Numbers 3:17–20*: Levi had three sons: Gershon, Kohath, and Merari. Gershon had two sons, Libni and Shimei. Kohath had four sons, Amran, Izhar, Hebron, and Uzziel. Merari had two sons, Mahli and Mushi.

*Numbers 3:21–26*: Moses counted the sons of Gershon one month old or more. The whole tribe of Gershon numbered 7,500. These clans camped behind the tabernacle on the west side. Eliasaph, son of Lael, was appointed as the leader of the Gershonites. The Gershonites' duties were to care for the tabernacle, the tent, its coverings, the screen for the entrance to the tent of meeting, the courtyard hangings, and the ropes.

*Numbers 3:27–32*: The Amramites, Izharites, Hebronites, and Uzzielites were the Kohathite clans. The whole tribe of Kohathite numbered 8,600. They were responsible for the care of the sanctuary. They had the most important job because they were taking care of the holy objects. The Kohathites camped on the south side of the tabernacle.

*Numbers 3:33–37*: The Merari clans were Mahlites and Mushites. The whole tribe of Merari numbered 6,200. They camped on the north side of the tabernacle (Numbers 2:25). The Merarites were assigned to take care of the wooden framed things, the supports, the crossbars, the posts, the bases, and all related equipment. Zuriel, son of Abihail, was the leader of the Merarites.

*Numbers 3:38*: Moses, Aaron, and his sons camped on the east side of the tabernacle, in front of the tent of meeting, toward the sunrise. They were responsible for the care of the sanctuary. Any unauthorized person who approached the sanctuary would die.

*Numbers 3:39*: The total number of Levite men one month old or older was 22,000. By reading ahead in Numbers 4, we learn that Moses later counted "men from 30 years old to 50 years old, everyone who was qualified for work at the tent of meeting" (Numbers 4:3, 23, 30, 35, 39, 43, 47). After the men were picked at age 20, it took five years until they were ready for service. It was basically an apprentice program. Who was doing all this work? Who was evaluating all these animals? According to Numbers 8:24: "In regard to the Levites: From 25 years old or more, a man enters the service in the work at the tent of meeting." The men were qualified at the age of 30, but they started at the age of 25. They were in training for five years to learn all the duties of the priesthood so they could screen and help the priest. Numbers 4:36 said 2,750 men were qualified to serve from the Kohathite tribe. Numbers 4:40 said 2,630 men were qualified to serve from the Gershonite tribe. Numbers 4:44 said 3,200 men were qualified to serve from the Merarite tribe.

Nelson's commentary provided these observations about the Levites:

(1) They were numbered separately from other tribes.

(2) They were obviously appointed to ministry in the worship of God rather than soldiers.

(3) They were given certain restrictions for the way they were to conduct their life.

(4) They represented the firstborn gift of God.

(5) They live in their own cities.

(6) Their end goal was to serve Aaron and his sons and the Lord.[1]

*Numbers 3:40–43*: God then commanded Moses to count every firstborn male Israelite one month old or more and make a list of their names. God then claimed the Levites for Himself in place of every firstborn among the Israelites. The total number of firstborn males one month old or more totaled 22,273.

*Numbers 3:44–48*: Now Moses was told to take the Levites in place of all the firstborn Israelites. The total firstborn Israelites (22,273) minus the total Levites (22,000) meant the firstborn Israelites outnumbered the Levites by 273. To redeem these 273 Israelites, five shekels were collected for each (273 people x 5 shekels) and given to Aaron and his sons as a redemption price.

---

[1] Earl D. Radmacher, Ronald B. Allen, and H. Wayne House, eds., *Nelson's New Illustrated Bible Commentary* (Nashville: Thomas Nelson, 1999), 199.

*Numbers 3:49–51*: Moses collected the redemption money for those in excess of the ones redeemed by the Levites. Moses collected 1,365 shekels and gave the money to Aaron and his sons just as God commanded.

## Closing

The 22,000 Levites represented the firstborn. They were to surround the tabernacle for God. That makes me think of the ultimate firstborn, the *Rock*. The *Rock* is Jesus. Jesus is also the firstborn. Colossians 1:15 says, "He is the image of the invisible God, the firstborn over all creation." When Jesus was little, He was brought up to Jerusalem to be presented to the Lord as a firstborn. Luke 2:22–23 recorded the event: "And when the days of their purification according to the law of Moses were finished, they brought Him up to Jerusalem to present Him to the Lord (just as it is written in the law of the Lord: Every firstborn male will be dedicated to the Lord)."

## The Daily Word

After the Lord gave commands and job assignments to all the Israelites, He focused on the 22,000 Levites. The Levites' job was to assist Aaron and his sons by attending to the service of the tabernacle. They were specifically instructed to take care of all the furnishings. What a role!

Many times, jobs that deal with the "caring of things" go unnoticed in life until something is dirty, out of place, or falling apart. Then you realize how important it is to have a group serving and caring behind the scenes. The world may not view these roles as important or highly esteemed, but as followers of Christ, you are called to serve just as Jesus came to serve. If you are following the Lord and His plans for your life, there's no better place to be, even if it involves scrubbing toilets!

**The LORD spoke to Moses: "Bring the tribe of Levi near and present them to Aaron the priest to assist him. They are to perform duties for him and the entire community before the tent of meeting by attending to the service of the tabernacle." —Numbers 3:5–7**

Further Scripture: John 12:26; Romans 12:4–7; Galatians 5:13

# Questions

1. What were the names of Aaron's two sons who died? Why did they die (Leviticus 10:1–2; Numbers 3:4)? How was this the wrong kind of offering/worship? How does God command us to worship Him today? (John 4:23–24)

2. God referred to the whole nation of Israel as a "kingdom of priests" (Exodus 19:5–6). Who did He set apart to care for the tabernacle? What were some of their roles?

3. The church you attend may not have thousands of people in it like the tribe of Levi. Can God still use a small body of Christ to do His work? How so? (Judges 7:7; 1 Corinthians 1:25; 2 Corinthians 12:9)

4. Why were all the firstborn sons of Israel one month old or older counted? Who were the Levites a substitute for (Numbers 3:41)? How does this point to Christ as the firstborn of all creation? (Colossians 1:15)

5. What did the Holy Spirit highlight to you in Numbers 3 through the reading or the teaching?

# Lesson 75: Numbers 4

*Rock*: Duties of the Kohathites, Gershonites, and Merarites

---

## Teaching Notes

### Intro

Let's look back at Numbers 1. Why did the Israelites have to count the 12 tribes? They had to identify the males over the age of 20 who were eligible to serve in the army. Today, both male and female serve in the Israeli army, but at this time of the Israelites, just the men served. The census totaled 603,550. The Levites were exempt from the military. Their position was to work around the tabernacle and alongside Aaron and his sons. Numbers 2 told each tribe where to camp around the tabernacle. Numbers 3 described how Aaron and the priest were different from the Levites. The Levites did everyday work because they were God's first-born people. They got everything ready for Aaron, Eleazar, and Ithamar. They did so for 40 years!

I love Mindi's painting: the rock, the cloud, the feet, the native flower of Israel. This represents the *Rock*, Christ. First Corinthians 10:4 describes Jesus' role in the wilderness: "And all drank the same spiritual drink. For they drank from a spiritual rock that followed them, and that rock was Christ." I want you to have this picture of the *Rock*. Every time the Israelites put their feet down, that *Rock*, Christ, supported them in the wilderness. Today, we are going to talk more about the role of the Levites in Numbers 4.

### Teaching

*Numbers 4:1–3*: This time, Moses was named first even though Aaron was older by three years. God told Moses to count the Kohathite men aged 30 to 50 years old who could work at the tent of meeting. This differed from the census in Numbers 3:15, which counted every male one month old and older. Numbers 8:24 said, "In regard to the Levites: From 25 years old or more, a man enters the service in the work at the tent." The writer of 1 Chronicles 6:2–3 also documented the Levite generations: "Kohath's sons: Amram, Izhar, Hebron, and Uzziel. Amram's children: Aaron, Moses, and Miriam." Aaron and Moses were from the Levite tribe.

*Numbers 4:4–6*: Whenever the Israelite camp moved, the Kohathites were responsible for the most holy objects. Eleazar was the overseer for the Kohathites. First, Aaron and his sons covered the ark of the testimony with the screening veil, then covered it with a covering made from manatee skin, and then spread a cloth of solid blue over it and put the poles in place.

*Numbers 4:7–10*: Over the table of the Presence, they spread a blue cloth and put the plates, cups, bowls, and pitchers for the drink offering and the bread offering. Over these, they spread a scarlet cloth, covered that with coverings made from manatee skin, and put its poles in place. This reminds us of the instructions in Exodus when they built the tabernacle with the blue and scarlet. Later we will get into the purple. The priests wore the same colors as the tabernacle. They covered the lampstand with its lamps, snuffers, firepans, and jars of oil with a blue cloth, and then placed everything in a covering made from manatee skin and put the poles in place.

*Numbers 4:11–14*: After covering the altar and its furnishings with a blue cloth, wrapped with manatee skin, they put them on a carrying frame. They removed the ashes from the bronze altar, spread a purple cloth over it, placed all equipment on it, and then covered it with manatee skin and set the poles in place. All of these instructions were super important. Everyone had an important role to play in transporting the tent of meeting.

*Numbers 4:15–20*: After Aaron and his sons covered all the holy objects, the Kohathites carried them. But if the Kohathites touched any holy thing they would die! This actually happened in 2 Samuel 6:6–7: "When they came to Nacon's threshing floor, Uzzah reached out to the ark of God and took hold of it because the oxen had stumbled. Then the LORD's anger burned against Uzzah, and God struck him dead on the spot for his irreverence, and he died there next to the ark of God." Eleazar, the son of Aaron the priest, had oversight over the oil of the light, the fragrant incense, the daily grain offering, and the anointing oil. Because Eleazar was the overseer of the entire tabernacle and everything in it, he was the overseer of the Kohathites. The Lord said to Moses and Aaron, "Do not allow the Kohathite tribal clans to be wiped out from the Levites." Aaron and his sons had to make these preparations and then assign each man his work and transportation duty. The Kohathites could not look at the holy things or they would die.

*Numbers 4:21–28*: God then told Moses to take a census of the Gershonites by family and clan, registering each man 30 to 50 years of age who could work in the tent of meeting. This Gershonite clan was assigned the service of transporting the tabernacle curtains, the tent of meeting with its covering and the outer coverings made from manatee skins, the screen for the entrance to the tent of meeting, the hangings of the courtyard, the screen for the entrance at the gate of the courtyard that surrounded the tabernacle and alter, along with the ropes and all the equipment used in its service. They were responsible for these things and did everything at the command of Aaron and his sons. They were under the direction of Ithamar, son of Aaron, the priest. The Gershonites were assigned the coverings. They had responsibility for everything on the outside.

*Numbers 4:29–33*: God then told Moses to count the Merarites by family and clan, registering each male 30 to 50 years of age who could work in the tent of meeting. The Merarites were assigned the work of carrying the frame for the tent of meeting, the supports of the Tabernacle, its crossbars, posts, and bases as well as the posts of the surrounding courtyard with their bases, tent pegs, ropes, all their equipment and everything related to their use. They were responsible for the framework. The Merarites were also under the direction of Ithamar, son of Aaron, the priest.

These were the home bases of the three clans: The Kohathites were on the south side of the tabernacle. The Gershonites were on the west side of the tabernacle. The Merarites were on the north side of the tabernacle.

*Numbers 4:34–37*: Moses and Aaron registered 2,750 Kohathite men 30 to 50 years old to serve in the work of the tent of meeting by taking care of the holy objects. From ages 25 to 30, they were taught how to interact with the holy objects. Numbers 3:28 registered every Kohathite man: "Counting every male one month old or more, there were 8,600 responsible for the duties of the sanctuary."

*Numbers 4:38–41*: Moses and Aaron registered 2,630 Gershonite men 30 to 50 years of age to serve at the tent of meeting. Numbers 3:22 registered every Gershonite man: "Those registered, counting every male one month old or more, numbered 7,500."

*Numbers 4:42–49*: Moses and Aaron registered 3,200 Merarite men 30 to 50 years of age to serve at the tent of meeting. Numbers 3:34 registered every Merarite man: "Those registered, counting every male one month old or more, numbered 6,200." Altogether, 8,580 men from 30 to 50 years of age were assigned transportation duty.

# Closing

In 2 Timothy 2:2, Paul told Timothy: "And what you have heard from me in the presence of many witnesses, commit to faithful men who will be able to teach others also." We are to teach others about our faith.

When I see the Merarites, I see 3,200 men who could train 3,200 more. I see a discipleship process. I see multiple people in order to get the work done. If we're not careful in the American church, we may think we're the only ones qualified and we're not training up more people. Our job is to be fruitful and multiply, and I actually think that means in the area of ministry. This is an incredible example of training someone for five years. Jesus did this for three years with 12 guys, and one of those guys didn't even get it.

Look at the Apostle Paul in Acts 19. He poured into 12 men daily for two years. All of Asia heard the Word of the Lord. You should never run out of Gershonites, Kohathites, or Merarites because a disciple is always making a disciple. A practical question wherever you serve: "Are you always looking to replace yourself?" Jesus did it with 12. Paul did it with 12. As more are trained, more can experience the presence of God. Very simply, go find a disciple that you can teach so they can begin to teach somebody else.

## The Daily Word

The Lord assigned the Kohathites, the Gershonites, and the Merarites to transportation duties. They were given specific tasks to complete in the process of transporting the tent of meeting. As the Lord outlined specific transportation assignments, it was a reminder that He was in the details of life. Previously God said He would go ahead of Moses and the Israelites in a pillar of cloud and a pillar of fire, so the Israelites knew they would be moving. Then He gave them detailed instructions on how to build the tent of meeting. If God commanded the Israelites to build it and said they would be moving, then it only made sense that God had transportation details taken care of!

Remember, if the Lord has called you to something, He is going to have a plan for all the delicate details. The Lord promises He will counsel you and show you the way to go. Doesn't that give you great relief? God has a plan!

**Their registered men numbered 8,580. At the LORD's command they were registered under the direction of Moses, each one according to his work and transportation duty, and his assignment was as the LORD commanded Moses. —Numbers 4:48–49**

Further Scripture: Exodus 13:21; Exodus 35:10–11; Psalm 32:8

# Questions

1. Name the three Levite clans. How many were in each clan? (Numbers 4:34–45)

2. When Aaron and his sons took down the items of the tabernacle, why did they cover everything with manatee skin?

3. In verses 18–20, what did the Lord command them to do so that the Kohathites would live and not die when they entered and approached the most sacred items?

4. Numbers 4:20 said the Kohathites must never look at or touch the sacred objects or they would die. Why do you think that was? (Numbers 4:15; 2 Samuel 6:6–7)

5. What did the Holy Spirit highlight to you in Numbers 4 through the reading or the teaching?

# Lesson 76: Numbers 5—6
## *Rock*: The Nazirite Vow

## Teaching Notes

### Intro

Our goal is to be able to take these lessons and tell the story to somebody else. To take Genesis and tell somebody, "Did you know the *Seed*, Christ, is found in Genesis?" or, "Did you know, in Numbers, Christ is the *Rock*?" How is *Rock* the word for Numbers? In 1 Corinthians 10:3–4, Paul said, "They all ate the same spiritual food, and all drank the same spiritual drink. For they drank from a spiritual rock that followed them, and that rock was Christ."

### Teaching

Numbers 5 specifically explains how the Israelites would deal with unclean people. Verses 2–3 said anyone in the camp who had a skin disease, a discharge, or was defiled by a corpse must be sent outside the camp. Then at the end of Numbers 5, the Israelites were told how to deal with an adulterous situation. Numbers speaks right to our lives. It can be applied to today. Numbers 6 is about vows. Harrison said, "A vow to God placed a person or property in a special consecrated relationship which stood outside the formal demands of the law."[1] A vow was not part of the Ten Commandments or the 613 Jewish laws. Wenham said making vows was not commanded but was a natural desire within the hearts of people who loved God and wanted something from God.[2]

*Numbers 6:1–6*: God gave Moses instructions for men and women who made a special vow, a Nazirite vow, to the Lord. Nazirite means "to separate." When someone made a special vow, they were to separate themselves from the daily routine. Someone making a Nazirite vow had to abstain from wine, beer, grape juice, grapes, and raisins. As long as he was a Nazirite, he could not eat anything that

---

[1] R. K. Harrison, *Tyndale Old Testament Commentary: Leviticus* (Downers Grove, IL: InterVarsity, 1980), 235; quoted in Thomas L. Constable, *Expository Notes of Dr. Thomas Constable: Leviticus*, 219, https://planobiblechapel.org/tcon/notes/pdf/numbers.pdf.

[2] Gordon J. Wenham, *New International Commentary on the Old Testament: The Book of Leviticus* (Grand Rapids: Eerdmans, 1979), 337.

came from the grapevine, not even the seeds or skins. He could not cut his hair during his time of consecration and was forbidden from going near a dead body. The requirements for the Nazirite vow were similar to those of the high priest. Both, the Nazirite and the high priest, were called to set themselves apart from the norm. Leviticus 10:9 addresses the high priest: "You and your sons are not to drink wine or beer when you enter the tent of meeting, or else you will die; this is a permanent statute." I don't see where it was ever said to the high priest to not cut their hair. Leviticus 21:11–12 forbade priests from going near dead persons or making themselves unclean. Today, going through a 40-day fast would compare to a Nazirite vow. There's something about going to the extreme to experience a deeper relationship with God.

*Numbers 6:7–12*: During his period of consecration, he could not defile himself even if a family member died (vv. 7–8). In the midst of tough times, God raised up a man of God to take a vow. Judges 13:1–5 explained that the angel of the Lord appeared to Manoah and his wife to tell them of the son they would bear. "It is true that you are unable to conceive and have no children, but you will conceive and give birth to a son. Now please be careful not to drink wine or beer, or to eat anything unclean; for indeed, you will conceive and give birth to a son. You must never cut his hair, because the boy will be a Nazirite to God from birth, and he will begin to save Israel from the power of the Philistines" (Judges 13:3b–5). Sampson was a person whom God called to a Nazirite vow.

The Nazirite set himself apart from everyone else, but not in an arrogant way, and he dedicated himself to God. If someone suddenly died near him, and the Nazirite was accidentally defiled, then he had to shave his head on the seventh day. On the eighth day, he had to bring two turtledoves or young pigeons to the priest at the tent of meeting. The priest offered one as a sin offering and the other as a burnt offering. This made atonement for the Nazirite (notice the Nazirite was not labeled an unclean person) for being in the presence of a dead body. On that same day, the Nazirite consecrated his head again and rededicated his time of consecration to the Lord. He then brought a year-old male lamb as a restitution offering. The previous period of consecration didn't count; he must start all over (Numbers 6:12).

*Numbers 6:13–21*: The Nazirite then came to the entrance to the tent of meeting to present an offering to the Lord: an unblemished year-old male lamb as a burnt offering, an unblemished year-old female lamb as a sin offering, an unblemished ram as a fellowship offering, together with a grain offering, drink offering, basket of unleavened cakes, and unleavened wafers coated with oil (vv. 14–15). The priest presented these to the Lord and sacrificed the Nazirite sin offering and burnt offering (v. 16). The priest offered the ram as a fellowship sacrifice, together with the basket of bread, the grain offering, and drink offering (v. 17). The Nazirite shaved his head at the entrance to the tent of meeting and put the hair in the fire as a fellowship sacrifice (v. 18). The priest took the boiled shoulder of the ram, one unleavened cake, and one unleavened wafer and put it into the hands of the Nazirite after he had shaved his head (v. 19). The priest waved them as a presentation offering before the Lord. It was a holy portion for the priest, in addition to the breast of the offering and the thigh of the contribution (v. 20). With his vow fulfilled, the Nazirite could now drink wine (v. 20). I think every person in the church should go through a Nazirite vow. What would a Nazirite vow look like for me?

Other people of the Bible who went through Nazirite vows:

John the Baptist: Luke 1:13–17 revealed God's plan for John the Baptist to be a Nazirite for his entire life. "But the angel said to him: Do not be afraid, Zechariah, because your prayer has been heard. Your wife Elizabeth will bear you a son, and you will name him John. There will be joy and delight for you, and many will rejoice at his birth. For he will be great in the sight of the Lord and will never drink wine or beer. He will be filled with the Holy Spirit while still in his mother's womb. He will turn many of the sons of Israel to the Lord their God. And he will go before Him in the spirit and power of Elijah, to turn the hearts of fathers to their children, and the disobedient to the understanding of the righteous, to make ready for the Lord a prepared people."

Paul: Acts 18:18 revealed that Paul also took a Nazirite vow. "So Paul, having stayed on for many days, said goodbye to the brothers and sailed away to Syria. Priscilla and Aquila were with him. He shaved his head at Cenchreae because he had taken a vow."

Other verses that reveal the importance of making and keeping vows to God:

- Proverbs 20:25: "It is a trap for anyone to dedicate something rashly and later to reconsider his vows."
- Luke 14:28 says we must count the cost before we make a vow: "For which of you, wanting to build a tower, doesn't first sit down and calculate the cost to see if he has enough to complete it?"
- Ecclesiastes 5:4–5 says we must fulfill the vows we make: "When you make a vow to God, don't delay fulfilling it, because He does not delight in fools. Fulfill what you vow. Better that you do not vow than that you vow and not fulfill it."
- Jonah 2:9: "but as for me, I will sacrifice to You with a voice of thanksgiving. I will fulfill what I have vowed. Salvation is from the Lord!"

- Psalm 22:25 said when we make a vow, we should honor it because we fear the Lord: "I will give praise in the great congregation because of You; I will fulfill my vows before those who fear You."
- 1 Corinthians 9:19–23 revealed that Paul did whatever it took to have a relationship with God so that others might also have a relationship with God.

## Closing

The heart behind a vow is the desire to experience more of the Lord and, at times, so others can experience the gospel as well. When people make a vow, there are benefits for the one taking the vow and for the kingdom of God. The Nazirite vow is a homerun for anyone who understands the importance and value of a vow (it is not necessarily about the wine or the cutting of hair). Just talk to the Lord and see if there is anything you need to do differently to have a deeper, closer relationship with Him so you can hear clearly from Him, and so that others can greatly benefit from the gospel.

## The Daily Word

After giving instructions regarding purity laws and vows, it was almost as though the Lord paused and took a deep breath. Again, God spoke to Moses with instructions for Aaron and his sons on how to bless the Israelite people. This Aaronic blessing brings protection, favor, deliverance, hope, and more.

God continues to be the example to follow of how to deal with people. Even in the midst of details and structure, remember to pause and see the people around you as human beings with emotions and feelings. Sometimes life's details keep you so busy that you may forget to bless people. No matter where you are today, pause for just a minute, and bless someone with the love of Jesus.

**The LORD spoke to Moses: "Tell Aaron and his sons how you are to bless the Israelites. Say to them: May Yahweh bless you and protect you; may Yahweh make His face shine on you and be gracious to you; may Yahweh look with favor on you and give you peace. In this way they will pronounce My name over the Israelites, and I will bless them." —Numbers 6:22–27**

Further Scripture: John 1:16; 2 Corinthians 9:11; Philippians 2:4

355

# Questions

1. In Numbers 5:2–3, God commanded Moses to put every leper, anyone with a bodily discharge, or anyone who had been defiled by the dead out of the camp. Why do you think He commanded this?

2. What did the jealousy offering consist of (Numbers 5:15)? Why would this be presented to the priest? What was the outcome of this offering? (Numbers 5:27–28)

3. What was the purpose of having no wine, vinegar, strong drink, grapes, or grape juice when one made a Nazirite vow? (Judges 13:5–7)

4. Who do you think is a form of a Nazirite in modern times? Men/women? Do you think Jesus could be a Nazirite? Why or why not?

5. Becoming a Nazirite is a vow of vows. Have you ever made a vow to God or someone else? Were you able to fulfill that vow? Why or why not?

6. What does the priestly blessing in Numbers 6:24–26 mean to you? Do you think verse 27 sounds like Genesis 12:3?

7. What did the Holy Spirit highlight to you in Numbers 5—6 through the reading or the teaching?

# Lesson 77: Numbers 7
*Rock*: Offerings from the Leaders

## Teaching Notes

### Intro

You've made it through a whole week of finishing with Leviticus and beginning Numbers. God has a plan with names and numbers. In Numbers 6, we talked about the Nazirite vow. In Numbers 1, God raised up 12 men to count the number of males 20 years and up in each tribe as they prepared to fight in the first Israeli army. God took this Levite tribe, the Kohathites, Gershonites, and Merarites, and the priests, Moses and Aaron, to allow Israel to experience the presence of God in the tabernacle.

### Teaching

*Numbers 7:1–3*: When Moses finished setting up the tabernacle, he anointed and consecrated it and all its furnishings, along with the altar and utensils. Referring back to Exodus 40:17 gives us more details: "The tabernacle was set up in the first month of the second year, on the first day of the month." At this time, the leaders of Israel, the heads of their ancestral houses, presented an offering. They were the tribal leaders who supervised the registration (vv. 1–2). They brought six covered carts and 12 oxen, a cart from every two leaders and an ox from each and presented them in front of the tabernacle, on the east side.

*Numbers 7:4–6*: At God's command, Moses accepted these offerings to be used in the work of the tent of meeting. He distributed them to the Levites according to their needs for serving the tent of meeting.

*Numbers 7:7–9*: Moses gave the Gershonites two carts and four oxen. The Gershonites transported the fabrics and the coverings. They needed the covered wagons and oxen to carry this stuff. Moses gave the Merarites four carts and eight oxen. They transported all the framework. They probably moved a lot more stuff, so they needed more carts and oxen. Moses didn't give any to the Kohathites. They took care of the holy objects, and those were to be carried on their shoulders. God provided what the Levites needed to take care of the tabernacle.

*Numbers 7:10–11*: The leaders also presented the dedication gift for the altar when it was anointed. Each day one leader from each tribe presented his offering for the dedication of the altar. Since there were 12 tribal leaders, there were 12 days of presenting offerings.

*Numbers 7:12–17:* On the first day, Nahshon, son of Amminadab from the tribe of Judah, presented his offering. In Numbers 2:3, Judah was the first tribe to be assigned a place around the tabernacle. Nahshon brought one silver dish weighing three and one-quarter pounds and one silver basin weighing one and three-quarters pounds, both full of fine flour mixed with oil for a grain offering (v. 13). He brought one gold bowl weighing four ounces, full of incense (v. 14); one young bull, one ram, and one male lamb a year old for a burnt offering (v. 15); one male goat for a sin offering (v. 16); and two bulls, five rams, five male breeding goats, and five male lambs a year old for a fellowship sacrifice (v. 17). In total, Nahshon brought 21 animals. This was only the first day of the offerings from the tribal leaders.

*Numbers 7:18–83*: The remaining 11 tribal leaders presented the same offerings on these days. This was the same progression Moses described in Numbers 2 as the 12 tribes were placed around the tabernacle.

- Day 2: Nethanel, the leader of Issachar, presented his offering.
- Day 3: Eliab, the leader of the Zebulunites, presented his offering.
- Day 4: Elizur, the leader of the Reubenites, presented his offering.
- Day 5: Shelumiel, the leader of the Simeonites, presented his offering.
- Day 6: Eliasaph, the leader of the Gadites, presented his offering.
- Day 7: Elishama, the leader of the Ephraimites, presented his offering.
- Day 8: Gamaliel, the leader of the Manassites, presented his offering.
- Day 9: Abidan, the leader of the Benjaminites, presented his offering.
- Day 10: Ahiezer, the leader of the Danites, presented his offering.
- Day 11: Pagiel, the leader of the Asherites, presented his offering.
- Day 12: Ahira, the leader of the Naphtalites, presented his offering.

The names were incredibly important because they indicated that God knew every Israelite's name. In the same way, God knows the name of every believer today. Consider the support of these Scripture verses:

- John 10:3: "The doorkeeper opens it for him, and the sheep hear his voice. He calls his own sheep by name and leads them out." I believe God knows your name.

- Luke 10:20: "However, don't rejoice that the spirits submit to you, but rejoice that your names are written in heaven." Our names are listed in the heavenly register.

- Philippians 4:3: "Yes, I also ask you, true partner, to help these women who have contended for the gospel at my side, along with Clement and the rest of my coworkers whose names are in the book of life." Our names are written in the book of life.

- 1 Corinthians 10:4: "and all drank the same spiritual drink. For they drank from a spiritual rock that followed them, and that rock was Christ." That *Rock* is what gets us into the book of life.

- In 2 Samuel 23, David listed the names of his mighty men because each was important to him.

- In Romans 16, the Apostle Paul listed 26 names of people who helped him in his ministry.

Each person is important to God and to His work. If you don't remember someone's name, ask them. Names are important, and calling someone by their name makes them feel valued.

*Numbers 7:84–88*: When you take all 12 days, the dedication gifts from the Israeli leaders equaled:

- 12 silver dishes—each weighing three and one-quarter pounds
- 12 silver basins—each weighing one and three-quarter pounds
- 12 gold bowls—each weighing four ounces
- The total weight of the silver articles was 60 pounds, measured by the standard sanctuary shekel.
- The total weight of the gold bowls was three pounds.
- All the livestock for burnt offerings totaled 12 bulls, 12 rams, 12 male lambs a year old with their grain offering
- 12 male goats for sin offerings
- All livestock for the fellowship sacrifices totaled 24 bulls, 60 rams, 60 male breeding goats, and 60 male lambs a year old. This was the dedication gift for the altar after it was anointed.

*Numbers 7:89*: When Moses entered the tent of meeting to speak with the Lord, he heard the voice speaking to him from above the mercy seat that was on the ark of the testimony, from between the two cherubim. This was how God approved of what Moses had done.

## Closing

Mark 12:42–44 says, "And a poor widow came and dropped in two tiny coins worth very little. Summoning His disciples, He said to them, 'I assure you: This poor widow has put in more than all those giving to the temple treasury. For they all gave out of their surplus, but she out of her poverty has put in everything she possessed—all she had to live on.'"

You can never out give God. Second Corinthians 9:7 said, "Each person should do as he has decided in his heart—not reluctantly or out of necessity, for God loves a cheerful giver." I see a generous people who saw that God had gotten them to this point, and they were so grateful. In Numbers 7, I see a generous nation that said, "Yes Lord, it's Yours."

## The Daily Word

When Moses finished setting up the tabernacle, he anointed and consecrated it, along with all the furnishings, the altar, and its utensils. Afterwards, the leaders of Israel presented an offering in front of the tabernacle. The Lord commanded Moses to accept this offering. Then the Lord told Moses to use the offering for specific purposes. Finally, Moses gave the offering to specific people.

The Lord presented a model for receiving offerings. It is a great example to keep in mind as you receive gifts from God. If the Lord allows something to be given to you, then accept it. Open your eyes to why the Lord gave it to you so you know how to use it. And, if there is anyone you need to pass the gift along to, do so. Remember, all good and perfect gifts are from the Lord. Give thanks for God's goodness today!

The LORD said to Moses, "Accept these from them to be used in the work of the tent of meeting, and give this offering to the Levites, to each division according to their service." —Numbers 7:4–5

Further Scripture: Psalm 84:11; James 1:17; 2 Corinthians 9:8

# Questions

1. In Numbers 7:2–3, the 12 tribes brought the first gifts: oxen and carts. These were distributed to the Levite divisions. Why did some Levites receive more than others? Why did the Kohathites not receive anything (Numbers 7:9)? How is this a picture of God's provision?

2. What were the 12 days of gifts? Why do you think each tribe gave exactly the same gift? What was the purpose of these offerings?

3. What parallels can we draw between the generous giving of the Israelites in Number 7 and the giving in Acts 4:32–35 and Mark 12:42–44? Considering that God loves a cheerful giver (2 Corinthians 9:7), do you always give willingly and generously when prompted by God?

4. Why was it important that God knew the name of each person who gave and exactly what they were offering? John 10:3 states that the Good Shepherd calls His sheep by name. How does it make you feel to know that God knows your name? How can you share this truth with others?

5. Moses met with God and heard His voice from above the mercy seat (Numbers 7:89). How important is it for us to hear from God? What are some ways you can hear His voice more clearly?

6. What did the Holy Spirit highlight to you in Numbers 7 through the reading or the teaching?

# Lesson 78: Numbers 8—9

*Rock*: The Second Passover and Guidance by Cloud

## Teaching Notes

### Intro

God continues to speak to us in multiple ways.

### Teaching

*Numbers 8:1–26*: These were instructions on how Aaron was to set up of the lamps, build the lampstands, and keep the light in the holy place. Instructions were given for dedication and consecration of the Levite firstborn. Also, age parameters for Levites to serve as priests were set.

*Numbers 9:1–3*: The second Passover: This was the beginning of the second year after departure from Egypt. It was the Israelites' second time to commemorate the time in Egypt when the spirit of death passed over them (Exodus 12:1–32). They were to celebrate through the generations. It was a joyous occasion. The appointed time was in the first month, on the fourteenth day (Day of Unleavened Bread), at twilight. John MacArthur identified twilight as "the time between the day and the beginning of the next."[1] Twilight was a peaceful time when the day's duties were over.

*Numbers 9:4–5*: Israel did all that the Lord commanded Moses. They had a party in the wilderness of Sinai, in a dusty, lifeless place. The generations continued to observe the Passover. Note that Passover always points to the coming Messiah. In fact, Matthew 26:17 says, "On the first day of Unleavened Bread the disciples came to Jesus and asked, 'Where do You want us to prepare the Passover so You may eat it?'"

Jesus celebrated the Passover. John the Baptist was paving the way (John 1:29). Jesus was celebrating the Jewish Passover at the beginning of His ministry (John 2:13). Jesus still celebrated the Passover at the end of His life (Luke 22:15). 1 Corinthians 5:7 seems to bring it altogether.

---

[1] John MacArthur, *The MacArthur Bible Commentary* (Nashville: Thomas Nelson, 2005), 174.

Jesus Christ is the Passover Lamb. He shed His blood as the atonement (substitution, imputation, death) for our sins. Christ died, and the Passover took place so that we could have life. Israel was commanded to keep observing the Passover every single year because Christ was going to come and "pass over" for us. God wanted there to be a natural transition.

*Numbers 9:6–8*: Some men, because of a human corpse, could not celebrate the Passover. Those in that situation, with a proper heart attitude, went to Moses and asked if it was possible to be included in the festivities. In humility, Moses went to the Lord with their request. Moses didn't try to make the decision himself. In leadership and in our own lives, how much better would it be if we always went to the Lord first before a decision is made?

*Numbers 9:9–12*: The Lord answered Moses that one may go ahead and observe the Passover if unclean because of a corpse or on a distant journey but not with the people. They were to keep all the statutes commanded. But they were to celebrate the Passover in the second month (not the first), on the fourteenth day, at twilight. They were also to eat the lamb with unleavened bread and bitter herbs, and nothing was to be left until morning. Finally, they were not to break any of the lamb's bones.

The command to not break any of the lamb's bones foreshadows the coming of the Messiah:

- 1 Corinthians 5:7: Paul talked of Jesus being our Passover.
- John 1:29: We also know Jesus is *the Lamb*.
- Exodus 12:46: Israel was not to break any of the bones of the sacrificial lamb.
- Psalm 34:20: "He protects all his bones; not one of them is broken."
- John 19:31–36: The care of the body of Jesus:
  - Verse 31: The Jews were in a hurry for the bodies to be taken down before the Sabbath and requested Pilate have the three men's legs broken before being taken away.
  - Verse 32: The two men on either side of Jesus were still alive; their legs were broken.
  - Verse 33: Jesus was dead, so they saw no point in breaking His legs. Jesus, the Passover Lamb, would have no broken bones.
  - Verses 34–35: The soldiers pierced Jesus' side, and declared Him dead. All that saw knew He was dead.
  - Verse 36: And "Scripture would be fulfilled: Not one of His bones will be broken."

Moses wrote of this. The Psalmist wrote of this. John wrote this. All point to the fact the original Passover lamb foreshadowed Jesus' role as the *Passover Lamb*. That is why Israel was instructed to celebrate every year, so they would not forget.

*Numbers 9:13–14*: A man was to observe the Passover if he was eligible. If he chose not to, he would be cut off and would bear the consequence of his sin. Foreigners residing with Israelites could participate, and the same statutes and ordinances would apply.

*Numbers 9:15–23*: The tabernacle was set up, and starting that day, a cloud covered the tent of testimony. The cloud would appear like fire shown at night. It remained this way continuously. Whenever the cloud lifted, the Israelites were to pull up camp and follow the cloud until it stopped. As long as the cloud remained over the tabernacle they stayed, but when it moved, they moved as the Lord commanded. Whether it was one night, two days, a month or longer, they camped at the Lord's requirement in His command to Moses, moving when the cloud moved, and stopping when and where the cloud stopped.

# Closing

Over and over, God was establishing trust. Here are a couple of examples:

- Exodus 13:21–22: The Lord had established trust with the Israelites with the presence of the pillar of cloud by day and the pillar of fire by night.
- Exodus 16:1: Trust was established in going from one place to the next. The Israelites, over and over again, were sensing, seeing, and living out God's presence.
- Exodus 33:9: Moses, not just the Israelites, had to depend on the Lord speaking to him and over and over, God showed up. He will always be with us wherever we go.
- Psalm 18:9: God showing up in the clouds is an incredible sign that God's presence is wherever we go.
- Matthew 17:5: Even in the New Testament, the people experienced God speaking on behalf of the Messiah in a cloud, preparing people for His message.
- Matthew 24:30: A sign in the clouds will happen for us as well! In Numbers 9, the Israelites were told to live day and night by following the cloud of God's presence. Now, we are watching for the Son of Man to come "on the clouds!"

All of this points back to Christ. As Jesus went in the clouds, He is coming back in the clouds (Acts 1:9–11)! We need to be ready and waiting for the Messiah (Revelation 1:7). Every eye of both those who are alive and those who have died is going to see him. Every eye . . . not just a couple or a chosen group but every eye! Church, all over the world, be ready! We have to watch and wait for His return. We have to hold the things we have (cars, houses, families, etc.) loosely. We have to be ready to move. We have to be ready to listen to the Spirit of God and have the mentality to always be watching (Matthew 24:42).

Like those in Numbers 9, as followers of Yeshua (Jesus), we are filled with the Spirit and need to be ready, moving when the cloud moves. We need to be watchmen because we do not know when our Lord is coming back! Get ready to follow His presence!

## The Daily Word

The Israelites prepared to celebrate the second Passover a year after they first observed Passover in Egypt. Some men came to Moses with questions after hearing the commands on how to observe this sacred assembly. When they asked Moses for clarification, Moses responded with, "Wait until I find out what the Lord commands concerning you." Moses could have just answered on his own or told the men how he thought the Lord would answer. Instead, Moses paused and told the men to wait. Then Moses confidently asked the Lord, believing the Lord would have an answer for the men.

How often do you rush into making decisions or giving answers to people in your life without seeking the Lord's counsel? In this situation, Moses provided a great example of not rushing into an answer or giving advice without seeking the Lord first and foremost. As believers, you have the Holy Spirit dwelling inside you ready to counsel you moment by moment. Walk this out in your own life today, and watch the Lord guide you in all ways.

**These men came before Moses and Aaron the same day and said to him, "We are unclean because of a human corpse. Why should we be excluded from presenting the Lord's offering at its appointed time with the other Israelites?" Moses replied to them, "Wait here until I hear what the Lord commands for you." Then the Lord spoke to Moses: "Tell the Israelites . . ."
—Numbers 9:6–10**

Further Scripture: Psalm 32:8; John 14:26; James 1:5

# Questions

1. How is the instruction to not break any of the lamb's bones in Numbers 9:12 a foreshadowing of Christ (Exodus 12:46; Psalm 34:20; John 19:36)?

2. What does it mean to be "under the cloud" in 1 Corinthians 10:1? (Numbers 9:15–23)

3. The Israelites were waiting for the Lord's direction in the form of the cloud to direct their every step (Numbers 9:15–23). In what way(s) do you sense God directing your steps (Psalm 37:23; Proverbs 16:9)?

4. What did the Holy Spirit highlight to you in Numbers 8—9 through the reading or the teaching?

# Lesson 79: Numbers 10—11
*Rock*: Trumpets and Complaints

## Teaching Notes

### Intro

In Numbers 9, we saw how the cloud always led the people. Chapter 10 is about silver trumpets and how they were essential in declaring how to move. Today, we have many ways we hear from God: through the Word of God, through the Holy Spirit, and through pastors, teachers, and other Christians.

### Teaching

*Numbers 10*: Trumpets declared to the people when to come together. In this chapter, the silver trumpets declared to Israel how God wanted them to move. The sound of the trumpet will also be heard when Jesus comes back (1 Thessalonians 4:16–17). It is going to be the sound of heaven, and He is coming back!

*Numbers 11:1*: The people of Israel still had not learned to trust God's provision. In Exodus 15:22–24, three days after they had been delivered from slavery, they started complaining. We are the same. Over and over, we see God move, and still we complain. The people complained *openly* about hardship. God's anger burned and He sent fire, burning intensely.

*Numbers 11:2–5*: The fire got their attention, so they went to Moses to complain. Moses prayed to the Lord and the fire died down. This place was named Taberah, meaning "fire had blazed among them." It was a warning, and Nelson's commentary says it was purifying.[1] Then they complained about food. "Contemptible people" were the foreigners who joined the Israelites who had a strong craving for other food.

*Numbers 11:6*: "But now there is nothing for us to look at but manna," they complained. "Our appetite is gone." Such extremeness! Ten chapters later (Numbers 21:5), the Israelites hadn't changed. They were still complaining. Wiersbe wrote,

---

[1] Earl D. Radmacher, Ronald B. Allen, and H. Wayne House, eds., *Nelson's New Illustrated Bible Commentary* (Nashville: Thomas Nelson, 1999), 207.

"Jesus taught that wherever the Lord 'plants' His true children, the devil comes along and plants counterfeits."[2]

As soon as we forget God has cared for us, and we start complaining, we stop trusting.

> 2 Peter 2:1–2: Contemptible people's heresy is that we want different food or more food. This seems small, but this is how it gets started. The second you start looking to your own strength, you will continue to seek your own desires and agenda.
>
> Galatians 2:4: This isn't the lost outside the walls, it comes from within the church.
>
> 2 Corinthians 11:13–14: Be alert! Christ is coming back. Be aware of those appearing as an angel of light, like Satan. Be careful, church!
>
> Jude 4: Men are stealthily coming into our churches, complaining and campaigning to change the truth, implementing false teaching.

Be careful, the complaining card can turn into denying Jesus Christ. Love the people, but do not compromise just to appease them; tell them truth.

*Numbers 11:7–10*: Moses described the manna and said that it was good. The Israelites just had to gather and prepare; there would be just enough. Exodus 16:33 gave instructions for the golden pot of manna so the Israelites would not forget how God provided. Complaining spread from family to family and many cried at their tents. The Lord was angry, and Moses was provoked.

*Numbers 11:11–14*: Moses pointed out that God appointed him to this leadership position and that he (Moses) hadn't actually birthed the Israelites. This is one of the times in the Old Testament when God is portrayed as a female giving birth to the people. Moses told God, "This is your baby, not mine. You nurse them." Moses just wanted to give them meat so they would shut up. Moses was done with them.

---

[2] Warren W. Wiersbe, *The Bible Exposition Commentary: Genesis–Deuteronomy* (Colorado Springs: David C. Cook, 2001), 328.

*Numbers 11:15*: Moses basically said, "If I have to put up with this just kill me, I'm done or, if I've done my job, don't let me see misery, take it away." In 1 Kings 19:4, Elijah hit a wall, sat down under a broom tree and asked to die. When leaders hit a wall, they have to decide whether to go on or not.

*Numbers 11:16–17*: Moses received help. Seventy men were brought in to help Moses. The anointing on Moses, in part, was taken from him and put on these men. God was going to help Moses by imparting the gift on these 70 also.

*Numbers 11:18–20*: Moses told the Israelites: "Get ready! Tomorrow you will have meat! Purify yourselves. You are going to eat." They would have meat not one day but for a whole month. There would be so much meat, it would come out of their nostrils and be nauseating. God was saying, "Do not question Me again."

*Numbers 11:21–24*: Moses tried to comprehend feeding meat to 600,000 soldiers, not to mention women and children. Moses knew he didn't have enough animals for meat, even if the fish of the sea were counted. It was a promise. Do not limit God's power but wait and see. Game on! Moses told the people. And God brought in the 70 men.

*Numbers 11:25*: The Lord descended in the cloud. The elders received some of the spirit that was in Moses. They released the word and began to prophesy, that one time only. Eugene Merrill wrote, "Prophesying here does not refer to prediction or even proclamation but to giving (in song or speech) praise and similar expressions without training."[3] The same thing happens in 1 Samuel 10:9–10. This is what happened to the 70.

*Numbers 11:26–29*: Eldad and Medad were listed among the men but were not present. Yet, the same spirit came upon them also. A young man reported about them prophesying. Joshua wanted them stopped. Moses told Joshua not to be jealous on his account—all people need to be prophets and speak what the Lord tells them to speak (1 Corinthians 14:1–5). We should desire these gifts and bless those who do so and receive them.

*Numbers 11:30–32*: Moses and the elders returned to camp. Wind from the sea brought quail that flew about three feet off the ground for about 20 miles beyond camp, in all directions. Israelites had to catch and kill this meat. For two days

---

[3] Eugene Merrill, *The Zondervan Pictorial Encyclopedia of the Bible* (Grand Rapids: Zondervan, 1957), 227.

and a night, they gathered quail. The minimum amount a family gathered was 50 bushels.

*Numbers 11:33–35*: God sent the meat but also a severe plague (Psalms 78:31; 106:15). The reality is that the plagues were from the Lord. God killed some of the best men. The Israelites buried the men who craved the meat then they moved on to Hazeroth and remained there.

## Closing

Wiersbe wrote, "To ignore the Word, treat it carelessly, or willfully disobey it is to ask for the discipline of God (Hebrews 12: 5–11)."[4] We must depend, not on the world, but on the Word of God (Jeremiah 15:16). This is what a prophet does. This is what a person of God does, and that should be enough!

## The Daily Word

The Israelites complained about hardship, and the Lord's anger literally burned among them, consuming parts of the camp. Then some became dissatisfied with the manna the Lord had provided. They wanted something different—they wanted meat. In response, the Lord gave them quail, and the people who complained for a different type of food died while eating it. Have you noticed a pattern yet? The people become dissatisfied, God answers, and the people are still dissatisfied. How exhausting!

The Lord longs for you to find your satisfaction in Him alone. You are to crave God's presence in your life more than anything else. The lies of the enemy will tell you otherwise. Today, examine your heart, and ask the Lord if you are craving things of this world for satisfaction rather than Him. Remember, in the Lord's presence there is fullness of joy.

The Lord answered Moses, "Is the Lord's power limited? You will see whether or not what I have promised will happen to you." —Numbers 11:23

Further Scripture: Psalm 16:11; Jeremiah 15:16; Philippians 2:13–15

---

[4] Wiersbe, 329.

# Questions

1. What were the silver trumpets used for? (Numbers 10:1–10)

2. Moses persuaded Hobab to continue the journey when he wanted to go back to his old land and people (Numbers 10:31). In what ways have others encouraged you to stay on the journey God has for you? What has been your response?

3. In Numbers 11:14, Moses told God that his current role was too much of a burden to carry on his own. When have you felt like a role you held was too much of a burden for you?

4. God told Moses to summon 70 elders and explained that He would put some of the Spirit that Moses carried on them (Numbers 11:17). Have you ever been in a situation where you felt like delegation was the only option? In what practical ways does God lighten your burdens when you ask Him to?

5. When the elders received some of the Spirit that Moses carried, they prophesied, but only one time. (Numbers 11:25) Why were they able to prophesy only once? How did Moses' words in Numbers 11:29 ultimately become fulfilled in Acts 2? Why was it important for the Spirit to assist the 70 elders in their new role?

6. What did the Holy Spirit highlight to you in Numbers 10—11 through the reading or the teaching?

# Lesson 80: Numbers 12—13
## *Rock*: Scouting Out Canaan

## Teaching Notes

### Intro
We've made it through 80 days!

### Teaching
*Numbers 12:1–3*: Miriam and Aaron criticized Moses regarding who he married. This is the only time mentioned in the Bible that Miriam fell. They asked why God only spoke through Moses. They questioned Moses' leadership and God heard! Moses was the humblest man on earth.

*Numbers 12:4–14*: God called Moses, Aaron, and Miriam out to the tent of the meeting. Miriam suddenly had leprosy. Moses pleaded to God on behalf of Miriam. Miriam was confined outside of camp for seven days.

*Numbers 13:1–15*: God instructed Moses to send one man from each tribe to scout Canaan. Twelve scouts were sent. Deuteronomy 1:21 records the scouts were not to be afraid or discouraged. Moses chose the scouts—the able bodied, athletic men, the Navy Seals:

(1)  Shammua, Tribe of Reuben
(2)  Shaphat, Tribe of Simeon
(3)  Caleb, Tribe of Judah
(4)  Igal, Tribe of Issachar
(5)  Hoshea, Tribe of Ephraim
(6)  Palti, Tribe of Benjamin
(7)  Gaddiel, Tribe of Zebulun
(8)  Gaddi, Tribe of Manasseh
(9)  Ammiel, Tribe of Dan
(10) Sethur, Tribe of Asher
(11) Nahbi, Tribe of Naphtali
(12) Geuel, Tribe of Gad

*Numbers 13:16–20*: Moses renamed Hoshea, "Joshua." Hoshea means "desire for salvation." Joshua means "the Lord saves, He is salvation." Joshua and Jesus become two forms of the same name. Nelson's commentary says Moses changed Hoshea's name to Joshua to symbolize the act of ritual adoption.[1]

Moses told the scouts where to go. They were to check out the land and the people, describing what they were like. Few or many? Strong or weak? Is the land good or bad? Cities? Encampments or fortifications? Trees, no trees? Fruit, no fruit? They were to be courageous and bring back some fruit.

*Numbers 13:21–22*: They scouted the Wilderness of Zin to Rehob, to the entry of Hamath, 87 miles total. Through Negev to Hebron (the place to be!), which was built seven years before Zoan in Egypt. Abraham built an altar there (Genesis 13:18). Abraham and Isaac were buried there (Genesis 49:31). David's capital was there (2 Samuel 2:11). Caleb's inheritance was there (Joshua 14:13).

*Numbers 13:23–25*: At the Valley of Eshcol, the spies cut down a single cluster of grapes and put it on a pole. This picture is actually the Israeli Ministry of Tourism's logo. Two men carried the grapes on a pole. They also collected pomegranates and figs. Eshcol was named because of the grapes cut there. The scouts returned after 40 days.

*Numbers 13:26–27*: Reporting Back: A Fruit Report: They showed them the fruit to prove that indeed, it was a land flowing with milk and honey. Many times, this had been talked about:

- Exodus 3:8: Fruit and enemies
- Exodus 3:17: Out of affliction to land of milk and honey
- Exodus 13:5: I am going to give it to you
- Exodus 33:3: Go to the land of milk and honey

Enemies were mentioned each time. God always prepares us for what is ahead.

*Numbers 13:28–29*: A Fear Report: The cities were large and fortified and the people were strong. The descendants of Anak were there! They were big, tall warriors. Also, the Amalekites, Hittites, Jebusites, Amorites, and, oh yeah, the Canaanites were there.

---

[1] Earl D. Radmacher, Ronald B. Allen, and H. Wayne House, eds., *Nelson's New Illustrated Bible Commentary* (Nashville: Thomas Nelson, 1997), 252.

*Numbers 13:30–33*: Caleb stood and quieted the people. He said, "We must go up and take possession of the land because we can certainly conquer it." Caleb was saying he believed this could happen and the land could be theirs. The ten spies did not believe this because the men of Canaan appeared stronger. They had no faith.

They gave a negative report—a fear report. They repeated that the men were huge. The Anak were descendants of Nephilim. The Nephilim were there! Again, their report was, "We seemed like grasshoppers."

## Closing

If God promises us something, He's going to allow it to come to fruition! When you look at your scouting, which way do you report? 2 Timothy 1:7 says, "For God has not given us a spirit of fearfulness, but one of power, love, and sound judgment." We have a promise and power, love, and a sound mind from God. Does it matter who is against us? This is how we combat fear.

Kadesh-barnea was the place known for the scouting report. It was base camp for the spies before getting ready to go into the land. Kadesh was also the place of Korah's rebellion against Moses (Numbers 16). Miriam is buried here (Numbers 20:1). Moses dishonored God by striking the rock (Numbers 20:8–12). It seems like a place of rebellion and resistance, and yet God promised fruit over and over again.

Wiersbe says, "A faith that cannot be tested, cannot be trusted."[2] God tests our faith to help us make sure its genuine, and that it helps us grow (1 Peter 1:1–9). A tested faith makes us become more like Him. God tells us to cross the sea, to take the land, because it's ours, but it requires radical faith!

- Romans 4:21: "Because he was fully convinced that what He had promised He was also able to perform."
- Hebrews 11:6: "Now without faith it is impossible to please God."

At this point, we know that at least ten of the men said, "No way, it can't be done." But Caleb stood up and declared the Israelites could take the land. The scouting report had nothing to do with the scouting, but it had everything to do with whether or not the Israelites had faith that God would keep His promise.

---

[2] Warren W. Wiersbe, *The Bible Exposition Commentary: Genesis–Deuteronomy* (Colorado Springs: David C. Cook, 2001), 333.

# The Daily Word

God commanded Moses to send 12 men to scout out the land of Canaan. After 40 days, they returned to the Israelites with two different reports. The majority of the scouts came back fearful, intimidated, and with negative attitudes about going into the land. But Caleb spoke up, full of faith, believing they could certainly conquer the land.

Whenever the Lord leads you into new situations, you can choose to respond with a negative or positive attitude. You can choose to fear or have faith. You can choose to believe you are defeated before it even begins, or you can choose to believe you are a conqueror in all situations. With God by your side, and the power of the Holy Spirit within you, you have all you need for seemingly impossible situations. Remember, with God, all things are possible. God has not given you a spirit of fear but of love, power, and sound judgment. Walk in these promises today as the Lord leads you to new adventures!

**Then Caleb quieted the people in the presence of Moses and said, "We must go up and take possession of the land because we can certainly conquer it!" But the men who had gone up with him responded, "We can't go up against the people because they are stronger than we are!" —Numbers 13:30–31**

Further Scripture: Luke 1:37; Romans 8:37; 2 Timothy 1:7

## Questions

1. In Numbers 12:1–2, Aaron and Miriam spoke against their brother Moses (1 Chronicles 16:22; Psalm 105:15). What comparison did the Lord make between Moses and other prophets in Numbers 12:6–8?

2. The Lord said in Numbers 12:7 that Moses was faithful in all God's household. This was later quoted in Hebrews 3:2. In Hebrews 3:1–6, what two people were being compared? What were their relationships to God (Hebrews 3:5–6)?

3. Moses was a type of Christ, pointing to one greater than him (Numbers 12:7; Deuteronomy 18:15; Acts 7:37). The people did not listen to Moses very well, often complaining and speaking against him. According to Deuteronomy 18:15, were they instructed to listen to the promised prophet? Read Acts 3:22–23. What will happen to those who will not listen or heed the word of the coming prophet, which is Christ?

4. In Numbers 13:2, a leader of each tribe was sent as a spy into the Promised Land to bring back a report. The majority gave a bad report (Numbers 13:32), and its effect on the people was fear (Numbers 14:1–3). Why do you think they chose to believe they were like grasshoppers rather than what God had promised (Genesis 17:8; 35:12; Exodus 6:8; Numbers 13:2). What does this tell you about the responsibility on leaders to filter what they see and hear through God's promises and His Word (2 Corinthians 1:20; 5:7)? Can you think of a time when you have listened to a "bad report"? How did that work out for you?

5. Caleb, son of Jephunneh, stood up against the bad reports given by the other spies, speaking faith and victory. Have you ever stood against the majority for what you believe, relying on God's promises rather than reacting to fear of man?

6. What did the Holy Spirit highlight to you in Numbers 12—13 through the reading or the teaching?

# Lesson 81: Numbers 14
*Rock*: The People Rebel

## Teaching Notes

### Intro

When we started Numbers, we talked about the formation of the Israelite army. Everything was counted and everyone was counted. Yesterday, we started talking about the 12 scouts going into the land.

### Teaching

Wiersbe talks about five blatant sins in Numbers 13—14.[1] We can learn much from Israel's sins:

(1) Doubting God's Word (Numbers 13:1–25)
- Israel doubted God's promise
- In the American church, how many times do we doubt promises can happen today?

(2) Discouraging other people (Numbers 13:28–29, 31–33)
- False reporting
- People of the land were too big

(3) Defying God's will (Numbers 14:1–10)
- Israel's refusal to enter Canaan

(4) Deserving of God's judgment (Numbers 14:11–38)
- Judgment on Israel's rebellion

(5) Disobeying God's Command (Numbers 14:39–45)
- Tried to compensate for their sin

*Numbers 14:1–2*: The spies reported that the Israelites couldn't take possession of the land. The people wept, and there was more complaining. They wished they had died in the wilderness.

---

[1] Warren Wiersbe, *The Bible Expository Commentary: Genesis–Deuteronomy* (Colorado Springs: David C. Cook, 2001), 331–35.

*Numbers 14:3*: The Israelites started thinking they had it better in Egypt. What they had in Egypt seemed better than the unknown that was waiting for them in the Promised Land.

*Numbers 14:4*: There was talk of appointing a leader to head back (1 Corinthians 10:10; Philippians 2:14). Every day, we have a choice: Is this life-giving or life-taking? The Israelites had an opportunity to trust God and be blessed beyond imagination, but instead, they listened to a negative report.

*Numbers 14:5*: Moses and Aaron fell on their faces before the whole assembly. Moses and Aaron responded in humility. This seems to become a pattern when men of God, sensing something from the Lord, hit the ground (Numbers 16:4, 22, 45; 20:6).

*Numbers 14:6–8*: Joshua and Caleb tore their clothes and responded in humility. They were dismayed at what was unfolding. These two men began to oppose the grumbling people. Joshua and Caleb believed God would do what He promised.

*Numbers 14:9*: Joshua and Caleb were saying, "Don't be afraid, we can devour them." The time of Genesis 15:16 was coming. Joshua and Caleb radically stepped up. They are good examples of being in the world but not of the world. At what point will we start acting confident in the Lord?

*Numbers 14: 10–16*: The whole community (possibly 2 million) threatened to stone Joshua and Caleb, but the glory of the Lord showed up. When the people of God act like the people of God, the Lord shows up. God asked, "When are these people going to get it? I will destroy them and start over with you, Moses." Moses had a heart for his people. He reminded God that Egypt would hear of the annihilation.

*Numbers 14:17–19*: "The Lord is slow to anger and rich in faithful love, forgiving wrongdoing and rebellion" (v. 18), but Israel would not go unpunished. This was consistent with God's faithful love from Egypt until now. Moses interceded for Israel, praying, "I love the people of God, so God, in keeping with the love that delivered Israel from Egypt, please pardon the wrongdoing of these people!" Moses prayed like Nehemiah, who prayed for God to spare Jerusalem.

*Numbers 14:20–21*: God heard and pardoned them (Psalm 130:4). Forgiveness always leads to the fear of God. God said, "I forgive them, but there will be judgment."

*Numbers 14:22*: No man who had experienced the deliverance journey or seen the Lord's glory would enter into the Promised Land. They tested God ten times, rejecting His provision:

(1) Exodus 14: Red Sea crossing
(2) Exodus 15: Marah, the bitter water
(3) Exodus 16: Hungered for more
(4) Exodus 16: Ignored Moses coming
(5) Exodus 16: Manna again
(6) Exodus 16: Didn't want to collect manna for the Sabbath
(7) Exodus 17: Complained about water again
(8) Exodus 32: Mount Sinai, the golden calf
(9) Numbers 11: Raged against the Lord for meat
(10) Numbers 13: Refused to believe the good report

*Numbers 14:23*: God said, "If you despised Me, you will not enter." The Israelites would suffer the consequences of their sin.

*Numbers 14:26–38*: The corpses of all those who were 20 years and older would fall in the wilderness. It was a death march. Only the children would experience Canaan. Joshua and Caleb would be the only adults to enter the Promised Land.

*Numbers 14:39–45*: There was grief, but no repentance. The Israelites decided they would go ahead and go in themselves. Moses warned them that they would be defeated, but the Israelites did it anyway. Moses stayed in camp; God did not go with them.

## Closing

Moses warned the people that the Lord would not be with them if they went. We need to learn from the Israelites. When we get out of line with the will of God, it is better to fall on our face before God than to try to fix it in our own will and strength. It is time for humility in the body of Christ. It is time for humility in the church. It's time to admit there might be things out of alignment in the American church. Let's consider pulling back; God might not be with us. It takes radical humility. Joshua and Caleb had it. Moses and Aaron had it.

Wiersbe wrote, "The British Anglican minister F. W. Robertson (1816–1853) was right when he said that obedience was the organ of spiritual knowledge."[2] When we are obedient, we can actually walk it out and know the will of God. Wiersbe wrote, "If we aren't willing to obey, God isn't obligated to reveal His will to us."[3] When you walk in the Spirit; the Spirit will set you free (John 8:32).

## The Daily Word

Out of the 12 men who scouted the land for 40 days, only Caleb and Joshua remained alive. The Lord saw that Caleb had a different spirit and had followed the Him completely. Caleb walked in faith and humility. He mourned alongside Moses, Aaron, and Joshua for the sins of the Israelites. He had faith that God would be with him and the Israelites in this new land.

Can you imagine if the Lord said those words about you? "[Fill in your name] has followed Me completely." When God leads you to something, do you fully trust Him and His faithfulness, or do you waiver and doubt? Today, make the choice to trust that God will be with you always, and with humility, follow Him completely. The Lord is rich in faithful love, a love that will never fail you.

**But since My servant Caleb has a different spirit and has followed me completely, I will bring him into the land where he has gone, and his descendants will inherit it. —Numbers 14:24**

Further Scripture: Numbers 14:18; Psalm 119:133; James 4:6

## Questions

1. The Israelites grumbled against Moses and Aaron upon hearing the bad reports from the spies. As believers, how can we keep ourselves from reacting in fear when life feels frightening?

2. Moses and Aaron's response in Numbers 14:5 was to fall on their faces. In verses 13–19, Moses interceded on behalf of the congregation. Have you seen this pattern throughout the journey out of Egypt? Which are you most like: the complainers, quick to give up, or Moses, who interceded for those who had sinned?

3. What happened to the ten spies who brought back a bad report based on fear rather than faith (Numbers 14:36–37)? Why were Joshua and Caleb not included?

---

[2] Wiersbe, 334.

[3] Wiersbe, 334.

4. According to Hebrews 3:19, what was the reason the Israelites were not able to enter the Promised Land?

5. The day after hearing the consequence for their sin, what was the Israelites' plan (Numbers 14:40)? What was Moses' response?

6. What did the Holy Spirit highlight to you in Numbers 14 through the reading or the teaching?

# Lesson 82: Numbers 15—16
## *Rock*: Korah's Rebellion

## Teaching Notes

### Intro

Yesterday's lesson taught about the 12 scouts. While ten men of God said, "Wait!" Joshua and Caleb said, "Go!" Because ten spies said "No," God decided to punish all of Israel. The Israelites would wander around until their deaths. Only the ones under the age of 20 would live to see the Promise Land. Joshua and Caleb depended on the Lord's promises but the rest of the Israelites didn't depend on those promises. Look what happened; the rest of the Israelites didn't make it into the Promise Land.

### Teaching

*Numbers 15:1–29*: The Israelites wouldn't enter the Promise Land, but their children would (vv. 1–5). There were laws about offerings when they enter the land (vv. 6–16.) They were to do the wave offering (vv. 17–21) and were also instructed on what to do about unintentional sin (vv. 22–29).

*Numbers 15:37–41*: The Lord commanded Moses to have the Israelites make tassels for their garments to remind them to obey and remember the Lord's commands. Today, this would be similar to wearing a cross necklace, a special coin, or having a sign in your home. Sailhamer wrote, "As the laws increase and constraints grow, the people seem less willing or capable of following them."[1] As the laws increased, the Israelites were going to rebel, and this is what you are going to see in Numbers 16.

*Numbers 16:1–2*: Korah, Dathan, and Aniram, along with 250 Israelite men, who were well-known leaders, became insolent and rose up against Moses. According to Wiersbe, the Kohathites carried the tabernacle furniture.[2] They camped out on the south side, so they were hanging out with the Gadites, Reubenites, and

---

[1] John H. Sailhamer, *The Pentateuch as Narrative* (Grand Rapids: Zondervan, 1992), 391.

[2] Warren W. Wiersbe, *The Wiersbe Bible Commentary: Genesis–Deuteronomy* (Colorado Springs: David C. Cook, 2007), 249.

Simeonites. I think of Numbers 12 when Miriam and Aaron both questioned Moses' authority (Numbers 12:8; Proverbs 13:20; 1 Corinthians 15:33).

*Numbers 16:3*: This group of 250 came together and questioned Moses and Aaron: "Why do you think you are the only holy ones? The whole community is holy. You have gone too far" (Exodus 19:5–6). The reality was that there had to be someone in authority (Romans 13:1).

*Numbers 16:4–7*: When Moses heard their complaints, he fell facedown. Moses told them that tomorrow the Lord would choose who was holy and who could come close to Him. Korah and his followers were to take firepans. The next day they were to put fire and incense in the firepans before the Lord. The man the Lord would choose would be the one who was holy. "It is you Levites who have gone too far!" (v. 7). The Lord judges righteously. First Peter 2:23 and Luke 22:42 show how Jesus responds when people question Him. He's the *Rock* we can rely on with our lives.

*Numbers 16:8–11*: Moses said to the Levities, "Isn't it enough that God has separated you from the rest of the Israelite community? He has brought you near to Himself to do the work of the tabernacle. But now you are trying to get the priesthood also? It is against the Lord that you are doing this. Why are you complaining against Aaron?" When you do the Lord's work, you should fully expect to be hated (Genesis 37:4; John 15:18–19; 1 John 3:12–13). When you come to serve, that's when He elevates you (Mark 10:45).

*Numbers 16:12–15*: Moses sent for Dathan and Abiram, but they wouldn't come out. They said, "Isn't it enough that you took us out of a land of milk and honey to bring us to a desert to lord over us? Will you gouge out the eyes of our men? We won't come out!" Moses became very angry, and he asked the Lord to not accept their offering.

*Numbers 16:16–19*: Moses told Korah to appear before the Lord on the next day with all his men and Aaron. Each one was to bring a firepan with incense in it (that would be 250 firepans) and present them before the Lord. So Korah and all his men, plus Moses and Aaron, took their firepans with incense and stood at the entrance to the tent of meeting. The glory of the Lord appeared to the whole community.

*Numbers 16:20–23*: The Lord spoke to Moses and Aaron. He told them to separate themselves from the whole community because He was going to consume them instantly. But Moses and Aaron fell facedown and asked the Lord not to consume the whole community because of the 250 men. The Lord told Moses to tell the community to get away from the dwellings of Korah, Dathan, and Abiram. They were to get away from those wicked people.

*Numbers 16:25–27*: Moses went to Dathan and Abiram and the elders of Israel who followed him. He warned the whole community to get away from the tents of these wicked men—to get away from anything that belonged to them or they would be swept away because of their sin. Then Dathan and Abiram, with their wives, children, and infants, came out of the tents and stood at the entrance.

*Numbers 16:28–30*: Moses told them the Lord had sent him; it was not of his own will. If these people died naturally, then the Lord hadn't sent him. If the Lord brought something unprecedented and the ground swallowed them with all that belonged to them and they go down alive to Sheol, the Israelites would know Korah and his followers had despised the Lord.

*Numbers 16:31–34*: Just as Moses finished speaking, the ground split open (1 Samuel 14:15; 1 Kings 19:11). God can use whatever physical means: clouds, fire, lightening, or thunder to do what He wants to do. The earth swallowed them and their households, as well as all of Korah's people and their possessions (Jude 1:11). This was known as one of the ultimate rebellious groups in all of the Old Testament. The earth then closed over them and they vanished from the assembly. At their cries, all the people around fled for fear of being swallowed up also.

*Numbers 16:35–38*: Then fire came from the Lord and consumed the 250 men and their incense (Hebrews 10:31). The Lord spoke to Moses, "Tell Eleazar to gather the firepans, for they are holy, and scatter the fire far away. Make them into hammered sheets for the altar." The firepans were holy because they had been presented to the Lord. They would serve as signs to the Israelites.

*Numbers 16:39–41*: Eleazar took the bronze firepans and had them hammered into plating for the altar. It was a reminder that no unauthorized person outside the lineage of Aaron should approach to offer incense before the Lord. The next day the entire Israelite community complained that Moses and Aaron had killed the Lord's people. There was no fear of God.

*Numbers 16:42–46*: Moses and Aaron went to the front of the tent of meeting to dialogue with God. Again, God wanted to consume the Israelite community instantly. Moses and Aaron once again fell facedown on behalf of the people. Moses told Aaron to take the firepan and put fire and incense in it. He was instructed to go the community and make atonement for them because God was going to bring a plague.

*Numbers 16:47–50*: Aaron did as Moses said. Aaron saw that the plague had begun, and people were beginning to die. Aaron stood between the dead and the living and the plague halted. Aaron was the intercessor. Already 14,700 people had died, plus the number from the Korah incident. More would have died if Aaron hadn't acted as an intercessor with the incense. Aaron returned to Moses at the entrance to the tent of meeting.

## Closing

This just makes me think of Jesus. Jesus just runs right into the middle of our camp (Romans 5:8; Ezekiel 22:30; Hebrews 7:25). God wanted to wipe them out many times. I love how Aaron runs into the middle of everything to stop the craziness. That is exactly what Jesus does for us.

## The Daily Word

The Israelite community continued to act in rebellion toward God. Korah, a Levite, along with 250 prominent Israelite men and leaders of the community, questioned Moses and Aaron's ordained positions as leader and priest. Three different times Moses' and Aaron's reactions to the rebellion were to fall facedown before the Lord. They sought the Lord in complete humility and surrender on behalf of the Israelite people. Even when the people criticized Moses and Aaron, they continued to seek the Lord's mercy to save the people and not penalize the entire nation of Israel.

What do you do when you are desperate for the Lord to move? Do you fall on your face before Him in complete surrender? Moses and Aaron knew the power of the Lord, and they came before Him with all they had. Whatever you are facing today, fall on your face before the Lord in worship and complete surrender, expecting Him to move powerfully in your situation!

**But Moses and Aaron fell facedown and said, "God, God of the spirits of all flesh, when one man sins, will You vent Your wrath on the whole community?" —Numbers 16:22**

Further Scripture: Galatians 2:20; Hebrews 11:6; James 4:10

# Questions

1.  What were the "special gifts/offerings" the people could present as a pleasing aroma to the Lord?

2.  What was the punishment the Lord told Moses had to be carried out against the man gathering wood on the Sabbath? By whom? (Numbers 15:35–36)

3.  In Numbers 16, who conspired and rebelled against Moses (and therefore, God)? Why do you think they did it?

4.  What did Moses tell them to do in Numbers 16:6–7? What happened to these men in verses 31–33?

5.  In Numbers 16:36–38, what did the Lord tell Moses to do with the incense burners? Why?

6.  The very next morning, the people were complaining again. What did the Lord do? What did Moses tell Aaron to do to counteract it?

7.  What did the Holy Spirit highlight to you in Numbers 15—16 through the reading or the teaching?

# Lesson 83: Numbers 17—18
*Rock*: Aaron's Staff That Budded

## Teaching Notes

### Intro

Today, we are studying Numbers 17 and 18. What stands out from the previous chapters is how Moses and Aaron still wanted to bless the people, even after they rebelled. Korah's rebellion was one of the worst rebellions in Scripture. They didn't trust Moses and Aaron, so God opened up the earth to swallow them and then brought fire to burn up the 250 followers. In chapter 17, God said that if the Israelites need more proof that He was with them, then He would give them more proof.

### Teaching

*Numbers 17:1–3*: The Lord instructed Moses. Here we see this dialogue again, that there was a test coming. Moses was to speak to the Israelites and to take one staff from each leader of the 12 tribes. Then he was to write the name of each man on his staff and write Aaron's name on the Levite's staff. There was one staff for all of the houses of Israel.

*Numbers 17:4–5*: Next, Moses was to place the 12 staffs in the tent of meeting in front of the testimony (the Holy of Holies). Aaron was the only one who saw into the Holy of Holies. The Lord instructed, "The staff of the man I choose will sprout and I will rid Myself of the Israelites' complaints that they have been making about you."

*Numbers 17:6–7*: Moses asked the Israelites to give him a staff from each leader of the 12 tribes. Aaron had done a couple of dumb things, for example the golden calf (Exodus 32:4). He had a wife and had four sons, two of whom had died. God was going to show all the Israelites that this man, Aaron, was His chosen vessel. Keil and Delitzsch wrote that "A man's rod was a sign of position as a ruler in the house and congregation."[1] In the story of Esther, if the king didn't lower

---

[1] C. F. Keil and Franz Delitzsch, *The Pentateuch*, trans. James Martin, 3 vols., Biblical Commentary on the Old Testament, reprint ed. (Grand Rapids: Eerdmans, n.d.), 3:114.

his scepter to her, she wasn't allowed to come forward. The staff was a symbol of power and authority. Moses placed the staffs before the Lord in the tent of the testimony.

*Numbers 17:8*: The next day, Moses entered the tent of testimony and saw that Aaron's staff, which represented the house of Levi, had not only sprouted but had budded, blossomed, and produced almonds. The staff went from dead to sprouted. Wenham wrote, "Almonds blooms early with white blossoms and its fruits were highly prized."[2]

> Genesis 43:11: "Then their father Israel said to them, 'If it must be so, then do this: Put some of the best products of the land in your packs and take them down to the man as a gift—some balsam and some honey, aromatic gum and resin, pistachios and almonds.'" They were taking this to Joseph. The color white also symbolizes purity, holiness, and God himself.
>
> Isaiah 1:18: "'Come, let us discuss this,' says the LORD. 'Though your sins are like scarlet, they will be as white as snow.'" God was showing purification and fruit at the same time. They go hand in hand.
>
> Daniel 7:9: "As I kept watching, thrones were set in place and the Ancient of Days took His seat. His clothing was white like snow, and the hair of His head like whitest wool." White always represents the presence of God.
>
> Revelation 20:11: "Then I saw a great white throne and One seated on it. Earth and heaven fled from His presence, and no place was found for them." Wenham wrote that, "Jeremiah the prophet associates almonds with watching."[3]
>
> Jeremiah 1:11–12: "Then the word of the LORD came to me, asking, 'What do you see, Jeremiah?' I replied, 'I see a branch of an almond tree.' The LORD said to me, 'You have seen correctly, for I watch over My word to accomplish it.'"

---

[2] Gordon J. Wenham, "Aaron's Rod (Numbers 17:16–28)" (*Zeitschrift für die Alttestamentliche Wissenschaft*, 1981), 140.

[3] Wenham, 280–81.

*Numbers 17:9–12*: Moses brought the staffs out for each man to look at. The Lord told Moses to put Aaron's staff back in front of the tent of testimony as a sign to the rebellious. He was to keep it as a sign to end their complaining or they would die. We all need reminders that point us to the Lord. Moses did as the Lord commanded him. Maarsingh wrote, "Just as God could make an apparently dead rod miraculously bear fruit, so he could elect a line of descendants like any other and enable it to render priestly service fruitfully."[4] Wiersbe wrote, "As usual, the Israelites overreacted when they heard the news."[5] The Israelites lamented, "We will die. We are lost."

*Numbers 17:13*: The Israelites questioned, "Anyone who comes near the tabernacle will die. Are we all going to die?" Aaron had had this staff all his life:

> Exodus 7:8–10: "The LORD said to Moses and Aaron, 'When Pharaoh tells you, "Perform a miracle," tell Aaron, "Take your staff and throw it down before Pharaoh. It will become a serpent."' So Moses and Aaron went in to Pharaoh and did just as the LORD had commanded. Aaron threw down his staff before Pharaoh and his officials, and it became a serpent."

> Exodus 7:19: "So the LORD said to Moses, 'Tell Aaron: Take your staff and stretch out your hand over the waters of Egypt—over their rivers, canals, ponds, and all their water reservoirs—and they will become blood. There will be blood throughout the land of Egypt, even in wooden and stone containers.'"

> Exodus 8:15–16: "But when Pharaoh saw there was relief, he hardened his heart and would not listen to them, as the LORD had said: Then the LORD said to Moses, 'Tell Aaron: Stretch out your staff and strike the dust of the earth, and it will become gnats throughout the land of Egypt.'"

Could it be that the Israelites finally saw the wretchedness and sinfulness of their lives? Wiersbe wrote that "the Lord gave Israel three reminders to encourage

---

[4] B. Maarsingh, *Numbers: A Practical Commentary*, trans. John Vriend, Text and Interpretation Series (Grand Rapids: Eerdmans, 1987), 63.

[5] Warren W. Wiersbe, *The Bible Exposition Commentary: Genesis–Deuteronomy* (Colorado Springs: David C. Cook, 2007), 340.

them to obey His law and submit to His will: the tassels on their garments, the brass plates on the altar, and Aaron's rod in the Holy of Holies."[6]

## Closing

What does the Lord give us as a parallel, so we are obedient with Him? Wiersbe wrote:[7]

- The Word of God (John 17:17): "Sanctify them by the truth; Your word is truth."
- The Holy Spirit (1 Corinthians 6:19–20): "Don't you know that your body is a sanctuary of the Holy Spirit whom you have from God? You are not your own, for you were bought at a price. Therefore, glorify God in your body."
- The Lord's Supper (1 Corinthians 11:23): "For I received from the Lord what I also passed on to you: On the night when He was betrayed, the Lord Jesus took bread, gave thanks, broke it, and said, 'Take, eat. This is My body, broken for you. Do this in remembrance of Me.'"
- Interceding Savior (Hebrews 4:14–16): "Therefore, since we have a great high priest who has passed through the heavens—Jesus the Son of God—let us hold fast to the confession. For we do not have a high priest who is unable to sympathize with our weaknesses, but One who has been tested in every way as we are, yet without sin. Therefore, let us approach the throne of grace with boldness, so that we may receive mercy and find grace to help us at the proper time."

So, we can go from dead to becoming alive (Romans 8:11). All of this comes from a simple picture of a dead stick that now has fruit. Numbers 18 just talks about the provision for the priesthood, then gets into support for the priests.

---

## The Daily Word

From among 12 staffs, one belonging to the head of each ancestral house, the Lord chose Aaron's. Overnight, it was Aaron's staff that miraculously went from being a lifeless piece of wood to sprouting, forming buds, blossoming, and producing almonds! Then the Lord commanded that Aaron's staff be placed in front of the testimony as a sign to the rebels in the community, putting an end to their complaining about whom the Lord had appointed for priestly service.

---

[6] Wiersbe, 340–41.

[7] Wiersbe, 341.

As believers, the Lord has called you by name. Through Christ, you go from death to life. Just as the white blossoms on the staff symbolized purity and holiness to the Aaronic priests, you too, as a chosen member of the royal priesthood of Christ, are to be holy and live pure in Christ. As you remain in Christ, you will produce much fruit. Today, when you walk out your calling, remember that the Lord's presence, the Holy Spirit, resides in you at all times. You are not alone. His rod and staff will comfort you.

**The next day Moses entered the tent of the testimony and saw that Aaron's staff, representing the house of Levi, had sprouted, formed buds, blossomed, and produced almonds! —Numbers 17:8**

Further Scripture: Psalm 23:4; Romans 8:11; 1 Peter 2:9

## Questions

1. Why did the Lord tell Moses to gather the 12 wooden staffs, one from each tribe?

2. In Numbers 18:7, what did the Lord give Aaron and his sons? What happened to any unauthorized person who got too close to the sanctuary?

3. God allotted a portion of the most holy offerings that were not burned in the fire. Which offerings did that include?

4. Why did the Lord tell Aaron that his priests would not receive an allotment of land?

5. In Numbers 18:29, it said to be sure to give the Lord the best portions of the gifts. Why do we give the best to the Lord?

6. What did the Holy Spirit highlight to you in Numbers 17—18 through the reading or the teaching?

# Lesson 84: Numbers 19—20
## Rock: Years of Wandering: Purification Rituals

## Teaching Notes

### Intro

We have talked about the scouts giving bad reports as well as the Israelites complaining, and complaining some more. Had we not been doing reviveSCHOOL, I don't think I would have seen the value of Aaron's rod in the tent of meeting. The whole goal of reviveSCHOOL is to experience God in a new and refreshing way that will impact the entire community. You have to walk this thing out, live this thing out. In Numbers 19, we are going to talk about the purification rituals of the red heifer.

### Teaching

*Numbers 19:* If the Israelites killed a red heifer, they could use the ashes and purify the water. There was clean and unclean. If they touched a corpse, they could use these ashes in the water to bring about cleanliness. The Israelites needed instruction on how to walk. The whole book of Numbers is teaching people constantly how to exercise what God was telling them to do and how to walk this thing out. The tassels, the manna, the rod—all were reminders that God was with them.

*Numbers 20:1*: This chapter takes place at the end of the Israelites' wilderness journey. This was year 40. The whole Israelite community arrived at the Desert of Zin in the first month and settled in Kadesh. Miriam died and was buried there. Miriam was the famous sister. She interacted with Pharaoh's daughter, got Moses to be fed, and saved his life. In Exodus 15:21, she led the praises of women at the Red Sea. In Exodus 12, we see the only issue Moses had with Miriam was a brother-sister fight. The Lord's hand was clearly on Miriam.

*Numbers 20:2–5*: There was no water in the Desert of Zin. The Israelites assembled against Moses and Aaron. They quarreled with Moses saying, "If only we had perished when our brothers died." Again, this was a lack of trust. Then they called the place evil. The Israelites started to bring up all the things they had had in Egypt: grain, figs, grapevines, and pomegranates. They lamented, "And there is no water to drink!" Their hearts were still in Egypt. Their hearts were in the world (1 John 2:15–16).

*Numbers 20:6–10*: Moses and Aaron went to the entrance to the tent of meeting and fell facedown. The glory of the Lord appeared to them. Wiersbe explained that basically God said He was going to reveal the game plan.[1] The Lord instructed Moses to take the staff, and he and Aaron were to gather the assembly. Moses was to speak to the rock, and before their eyes, it would pour out water. The water would be for the community and livestock. Moses took the staff just as the Lord commanded. Moses and Aaron gathered the assembly together in front of the rock. Moses got angry at the Israelites and said, "Must we bring water from this rock?"

*Numbers 20:11*: Moses raised his hand and struck the rock twice with his staff. Water gushed out and the community and livestock drank. The Lord told him to speak to the rock, not strike it. It wasn't for Moses to do the work but the Lord. This was an impulsive sin that kept him from getting into the Promised Land (Exodus 17:6). Maybe through instinct, Moses fell back to the Exodus 17 model. I think the *rock* is essential to this story in Numbers 20 (Deuteronomy 32:4, 15, 18; Psalms 18:2; 31:3; 42:9; 106:32–33; 1 Corinthians 10:4; Hebrews 9:26–28).

*Numbers 20:12–13*: Now as Wiersbe wrote, there was a painful discipline coming.[2] The Lord said that because they did not trust Him to show His holiness then, this community would not enter into the land. These were the waters of Meribah where the Israelites quarreled with the Lord, and God showed His holiness to them.

*Numbers 20:14–17*: Now the Israelites were moving toward Kadesh. Moses sent a message to the king of Edom referring to them as family and addressing him as brother. Moses told the king all they had been through with the Egyptians and requested permission to travel through their land. Moses promised the Israelites would not go through any field or vineyard or drink water from their wells.

*Numbers 20:18–20*: Edom replied that they must not travel through their land or they would confront them with a sword. The Israelites replied that they would stay on the main road, with their livestock, and if they drank any of

---

[1] Warren W. Wiersbe, *The Bible Exposition Commentary: Genesis–Deuteronomy* (Colorado Springs: David C. Cook, 2007), 344.

[2] Wiersbe, 344.

their water, they would pay for it. They only wanted to travel through on foot. Edom insisted they must not travel through, so they came out to meet them with a large military force.

*Numbers 20:21–24*: Edom refused to allow the Israelites through, so the Israelites turned away from them. The Israelites came to Mount Hor. The Lord spoke to Moses and Aaron at Mount Hor, on the border of Edom. Aaron was to be gathered to his people. He would not be allowed to enter the land because both he and Moses rebelled against the commands of the Lord at the waters of Meribah.

*Numbers 20:25–26*: Aaron was to go up to Mount Hor with his son, Eleazar. Aaron was to remove his garments and put them on Eleazar. Aaron would be gathered to his people and he would die there. Moses climbed Mount Hor in the sight of the whole community. This reminds you of Abraham and Isaac. The Israelites were moving from the old generation to the new generation.

*Numbers 20:28–29*: As soon as they put Aaron's garments on Eleazar, Aaron died. Then Moses and Eleazar came down the mountain. Scripture doesn't say they brought Aaron's body down. Moses and Eleazar couldn't touch Aaron's dead body because they were high priests. The whole community mourned for 30 days over Aaron's passing. John Wesley wrote, "God buried His workers, but His work always goes right on."[3]

## Closing

Do you know how many times Moses told the people to trust in the Lord? This one time he messed up, and look what happened. Moses was a man of faith.

- Hebrews 11:23: "By faith, after Moses was born, he was hidden by his parents."
- Hebrews 11:24: "By faith Moses, when he had grown up . . ."
- Hebrews 11:27: "By faith he left Egypt behind."
- Hebrews 11:29: "By faith they crossed the Red Sea."

Moses couldn't give the Israelites their inheritance; they had to proceed with faith (Galatians 3:18). I know this is a stretch. What if it comes from Joshua? Moses couldn't cross over to the land, but Joshua could. Joshua served as the transition piece. Jesus is the only one who can get us into the Promised Land. He

---

[3] John Wesley; quoted in Wiersbe, 345.

is our *Rock*. In Numbers 20, Miriam died, Aaron died, and Moses died spiritually because he lost his promise. We will get into how Joshua points to the Messiah over the course of time.

## The Daily Word

Once again, the Israelites complained and grumbled to Moses and Aaron about a lack of water. Once again, Moses and Aaron fell on their faces and sought help from the Lord. And once again, the Lord responded with a plan to display His miraculous provision. The Lord instructed Moses to speak to a *rock* while the Israelites watched, and the *rock* would yield water. However, Moses raised his hand and struck the *rock* twice with his staff. Moses clearly did not follow the exact commands of the Lord. Yet God displayed mercy, and the *rock* still produced water for the people. Moses acted in anger and impatience. This act of disobedience caused God to prevent Moses from entering the Promised Land.

Although God is a forgiving God, there are consequences for behavior. Your actions demonstrate your trust in God's faithfulness. As you walk in the Spirit, you are filled with the fruit of the Spirit: love, joy, peace, patience, kindness, goodness, faith, gentleness, and self-control. If your life lacks one or more of these, take a minute today to come before the Lord. Spend time in His presence, read through His Word, worship Him with thanksgiving, confess anything that comes to mind, and allow Him to fill you up. When you are refreshed with the Spirit, you will be strengthened for the journey ahead.

**Then Moses raised his hand and struck the *rock* twice with his staff, so that a great amount of water gushed out, and the community and their livestock drank. But the LORD said to Moses and Aaron, "Because you did not trust Me to show My holiness in the sight of the Israelites, you will not bring this assembly into the land I have given them." —Numbers 20:11–12**

Further Scripture: 2 Corinthians 12:9–10; Galatians 5:22–23a; Ephesians 5:18

## Questions

1. When Eleazar took the red heifer outside of town to slaughter it, what needed to be thrown into the fire with the remains? (Numbers 19:6)
2. Do you think the red heifer is a type of Christ? Why or why not? How does the blood atone for sins? (Hebrews 9:13–14)

3. What did the Lord command Moses and Aaron to do in Numbers 20:8? Did they do it? What punishment did they receive? Can you think of a time when you didn't listen to the exact words God said, but rather did it your own way?

4. Who did Moses and Aaron take with them when they went up Mount Hor? Why?

5. What did the Holy Spirit highlight to you in Numbers 19—20 through the reading or the teaching?

# Lesson 85: Numbers 21—22
*Rock*: March of Israel: The Bronze Snake

## Teaching Notes

### Intro

Yesterday, we talked about Numbers 20 and the two people who died, Miriam and Aaron. Moses got mad, and instead of trusting in the Lord and speaking to the rock, he struck it. The consequence of hitting the rock was Moses was not allowed to enter the Promised Land.

### Teaching

*Numbers 21:1*: Arad is an actual town in the Negev (the wilderness) in Israel. Today 60 percent of Israel's land is in the Negev, but only 7 percent of the people live in that area today. When the Canaanite king of Arad, who lived in Negev, heard the Israelites were coming on the Atharim road, he attacked and captured some of them. The Atharim road was probably the road the two spies later took when Joshua sent them to spy out the land.

*Numbers 21:2*: "Then Israel made a vow to the LORD." The Israelites were committing to give themselves to God by making this vow. If the Lord delivered the Canaanites into their hands, they would completely destroy their cities. The word "destroy," according to Wiersbe, meant, "to devote something completely to the Lord, wiping out the people and their cities and giving all the spoils to God."[1]

*Numbers 21:3*: The Lord heard the prayer of the Israelites and gave the Canaanites over to them. The Israelites completely destroyed the Canaanites and named the place Hormah.

*Numbers 21:4:* When God sent the Israelites out from Mount Hor, along the route of the Red Sea, to go around Edom, the people grew impatient on the way. Their impatience contrasted sharply with the patience shown by others. Abraham waited 25 years for his son. Joseph waited 13 years to go from the

---

[1] Warren W. Wiersbe, *The Bible Exposition Commentary: Genesis–Deuteronomy* (Colorado Springs: David C. Cook, 2007), 347.

pit to the palace. Moses waited 40 years, and walked around with people in the wilderness. David waited 15 years to become king. Jesus waited 30 years to implement His ministry. This was the first time this generation of Israelites encountered the Canaanites, and they didn't handle it well. God is always taking us through a process. He has much to teach us through the afflictions we face. Instead of asking why or quitting, we should ask God what He is teaching us. Romans 5:3–4 encourages us to rejoice in our afflictions because they produce endurance, proven character, and hope. Hebrews 6:11–12 explains the importance of persevering: "Now we want each of you to demonstrate the same diligence for the final realization of your hope, so that you won't become lazy but will be imitators of those who inherit the promises through faith and perseverance."

*Numbers 21:5*: The people spoke against God and Moses, complaining about the lack of bread and water and "this wretched food." Because they tested God, He sent poisonous snakes that bit them, and many people died. First Corinthians 10:9 says, "Let us not test Christ as some of them did and were destroyed by snakes." God had continually promised to give the land to the Israelites (Numbers 15:1–2), but they constantly forgot His promises. In Exodus 16, God sent manna and quail every day. God continued to feed them every day despite their whining and complaining. Psalm 78:25 revealed, "People ate the bread of angels. He sent them an abundant supply of food." God gave them the best of the best, yet they complained: "Contemptible people among them had a strong craving for other food. The Israelites cried again and said, 'Who will feed us meat?'" (Numbers 11:4). Commentators Keil and Delitzsch said these snakes, with red spots on their bodies, are still around today, affecting the Bedouins.[2]

*Numbers 21:7–8*: The people came to Moses and said they had sinned against him and God. They asked Moses to intercede with God for them, so Moses prayed for the people. God told Moses to make a snake image and mount it on a pole so that anyone who was bitten could look at it and recover.

*Numbers 21:9*: Moses made a bronze snake and put it on a pole so that whenever someone was bitten, they could look at the bronze snake and recover.

Scripture says this was a picture of Jesus:

---

[2] Carl Friedrich Keil and Franz Delitzsch, "Commentary on Numbers 21," https://www.studylight.org/commentaries/kdo/numbers-21.html.

- John 3:14: "Just as Moses lifted up the snake in the wilderness, so the Son of Man must be lifted up." The only way people can be saved from the bite of death is because Jesus was lifted up. Jesus had to be infected by sin, and He actually had to die.
- Hebrews 9:27–28: "And just as it is appointed for people to die once—and after this, judgment—so also the Messiah, having been offered once to bear the sins of many, will appear a second time, not to bear sin, but to bring salvation to those who are waiting for Him." Jesus is now the image of death, but when we look through His death, we will get life.
- Romans 10:13: "For everyone who calls on the name of the Lord will be saved." The pole with the snake had to be out in the camp, just like Jesus had to be a part of the world.
- Acts 4:12: "There is salvation in no one else, for there is no other name under heaven given to people, and we must be saved by it."
- John 14:6: "Jesus told him, 'I am the way, the truth, and the life. No one comes to the Father except through Me.'" No one could force someone to look at the snake on the stick. Each person had to do that himself.
- Isaiah 45:22: "Turn to Me and be saved, all the ends of the earth. For I am God, and there is no other."
- Ephesians 2:8–9: "For you are saved by grace through faith, and this is not from yourselves; it is God's gift—not from works, so that no one can boast."

## Closing

My friends from Wausau, Wisconsin, made me a soapbox. I love this soapbox. So, I'm going to get on my soapbox for a minute here. I'm so tired of people saying you have to do this, this, and this to be saved. There is no Jesus plus. It's just Jesus! We've made it harder than it has to be. Just look at the snake on the stick. Just look at Jesus on the cross.

First Corinthians 1:18–25 tells us: "For the message of the cross is foolishness to those who are perishing, but it is God's power to us who are being saved. For it is written: I will destroy the wisdom of the wise, and I will set aside the understanding of the experts. Where is the philosopher? Or wise? Where is the scholar? Where is the debater of this age? Hasn't God made the world's wisdom foolish? For since, in God's wisdom, the world did not know God through wisdom, God was pleased to save those who believe through the foolishness of the message preached. For the Jews ask for signs and the Greeks seek wisdom, but we preach Christ crucified, a stumbling block to the Jews and foolishness to the Gentiles. Yet to those who are called, both Jews and Greeks, Christ is God's power and God's wisdom, because God's foolishness is wiser than human wisdom, and God's weakness is stronger than human strength."

The Israelites were on a journey. They started complaining. They tested God. Finally, God brought His wrath and sent the snakes. Once they finally recognized their sin and repented, God said He would save them. All they had to do was look to Him. He tells us, "Look to Me, and I will save you." This pointed to the coming Messiah.

We all sin, and our sin leads to death. The snakebite will lead to death. Ephesians 2 says all we have to do is believe in Jesus. Once we say "Jesus, I'm in," we will have life. That is the message Moses gave. That is the message Jesus gave. That is the message of Numbers 21.

## The Daily Word

The Israelite people grew impatient because of the journey, and they spoke against God. So the Lord sent poisonous snakes among the people, and their bites caused many Israelites to die. Once again, the people pleaded for help, and Moses interceded with the Lord on their behalf. And once again, the Lord showed mercy and grace to the Israelites by creating a way to rescue them from the snakes. The Lord instructed Moses to make a bronze serpent and set it up on a pole. When those bitten by snakes looked at the pole, they recovered, and their bites were healed.

Think about how this parallels with the saving grace of Jesus. When life gets to be too much and the journey feels beyond what you can bear, you may complain to God and forget His faithful promises. But God has an ultimate plan. He sent Jesus to be lifted up on the cross. Everyone on the journey who looks up to Him is saved from death, healed of sins, and freed from bondage. In looking up to Christ and believing in Him, you will have eternal life. Turn to Christ and look up to Him, giving thanks for His many promises in your life.

**Then the LORD said to Moses, "Make a snake image and mount it on a pole. When anyone who is bitten looks at it, he will recover." —Numbers 21:8**

Further Scripture: Isaiah 45:22; John 3:14–15; Acts 4:12

## Questions

1. Do you find it hard to believe that God ("destroyer/destroying angel," 1 Corinthians 10:9–10) could have killed the Israelites for complaining (Numbers 21:6)? Why do you think God sent the venomous snakes?

2. How was it possible that looking at a bronze serpent on a pole saved an Israelite from death (Numbers 21:8–9)? How did this bronze serpent ultimately point to Christ (John 3:14–15)? Do you find it interesting that a serpent, typically a symbol for death, was the image that ultimately saved the Israelites from death?

3. What was the "Book of the LORD's Wars" starting in Numbers 21:14?

4. Read 2 Peter 2:15–16 and Jude 11. How do you reconcile what God instructed Balaam to do in Numbers 22:20 with these two passages? Why was Balaam's decision to go with Balak the wrong choice?

5. When Balaam's donkey saw the Angel of the Lord (Numbers 22:23), it would not move forward on the path toward Balak, but Balaam was unable to see the angel until Numbers 22:31. Are there times when God tried to interfere in your path with a "donkey" but ultimately needed to reach you in a more direct way? Why do you think God stopped Balaam but eventually let him move forward? (Numbers 22:35)

6. What did the Holy Spirit highlight to you in Numbers 21—22 through the reading or the teaching?

# Lesson 86: Numbers 23—24
## *Rock*: Balaam Blesses Israel

## Teaching Notes

### Intro

In Genesis, we saw the *Seed*, Christ. In Exodus, Moses the deliverer pointed to the ultimate *Deliverer*, who is Christ. In Leviticus, the *Atonement* was the sacrifices and offerings made at the tabernacle. In Numbers, we're talking about the *Rock*. In 1 Corinthians 10:4, Paul said, "All drank the same spiritual drink. For they drank from a spiritual rock that followed them, and that rock was Christ." In Numbers 21, we alluded to Christ being that snake on the stick so when people were bitten, they could look at it and be healed. Before we get to Numbers 23, let's look at how Wiersbe summarized Numbers 22:[1]

- Numbers 22:1–20: The King's Request: Balak, son of Zippor the king of Moab, asked Balaam to put a curse on the Israelites because word had spread concerning how powerful the Israelites had become.

- Numbers 22:21–30: The Donkey's Resistance: The donkey didn't want to go because the Angel of the Lord was standing in the way. There's a really good chance that this angel was the Lord. Balaam beat the donkey three times to make it go. The donkey then talked to Balaam.

- Numbers 22:31–35: The Angel's Revelation: The Lord opened Balaam's eyes to see the Angel of the Lord. The angel said, "What you are doing is evil in My sight. The donkey saw Me and turned away from Me these three times. If she had not turned away from Me, I would have killed you by now" (vv. 32–33). Balaam recognized he had sinned because he did not know the angel was there (v. 34). The Angel of the Lord told him to go with the donkey but only say what he was told to say (v. 35).

- Numbers 22:36–41: Balak and Balaam: Balak came out to meet Balaam at the edge of town (v. 36). Balaam said that he could only speak what came from God (v. 38). Balaam went with Balak when Balak sacrificed

---

[1] Warren W. Wiersbe, *The Bible Exposition Commentary: Genesis–Deuteronomy* (Colorado Springs: David C. Cook, 2007), 350.

cattle and sheep (vv. 39–40). This was a part of the occult process. The next morning Balak took Balaam to Bamoth-baal to look at the Israelite camp.

## Teaching

*Numbers 23:1–12*: The First Oracle: An oracle was a message communicated by a medium. Here Balak picked a sorcerer to tell them what he wanted to hear concerning the Israelites. Balaam told Balak to build seven altars and prepare seven rams, one for each altar. Balaam told Balak to wait by the offerings while he went to see if God would speak to him. God met with Balaam and gave him a message for Balak. Balaam returned to Balak and proclaimed this first poem, or oracle, from God:

- Balak asked me to put a curse on Israel, but I can't curse the Israelites because the Lord has not cursed them (vv. 7–8).
- The Israelites have been set apart (v. 9).
- I can't even comprehend the vastness of the Israelites. I actually want to be like them (v. 10).

When Balak complained that Balaam had blessed Israel instead of cursing them, Balaam answered that he could only say what the Lord put in his mouth. This is just a small example of what is going on in the country of Israel today. Iran wants to annihilate, blowup, and remove Israel from the face of the earth. That was basically Balak's goal. God intervenes because His hand is on the people of God. Nothing touches His people.

*Numbers 23:13–26*: The Second Oracle: Balak took Balaam to another place to view the Israelites in hopes that Balaam would curse the Israelites for him. So Balak took him to Lookout Field. Again, they built seven altars and sacrificed seven rams, one for each altar. Balaam told Balak to stay with the offering while he met with the Lord. Notice this time he didn't say "maybe" but "while" I meet with him. The Lord met with Balaam and put a message in his mouth. Balaam returned and proclaimed the second oracle:

- Pay attention to what I say! (v. 18).
- God will not change His mind (v. 19).
- I have received a command to bless and cannot change it (v. 20).
- There will be no disaster for Jacob or trouble for Israel, for the Lord rejoices over them (v. 21).

- There would be no magic curse against Jacob (v. 23).

*Numbers 23:27—24:9*: The Third Oracle: Balak took Balaam to the top of Peor, which overlooked the wasteland, hoping that Balaam could put a curse on them from there. Balak built another seven altars and offered a bull and ram on each (vv. 27–30). Since Balaam saw that the Lord wanted to bless Israel, he did not seek omens as in the past. As Balaam looked down at the Israelite camps tribe by tribe, the Spirit of God came upon him (vv. 1–2). The Spirit of God came upon an evil man, one who was coming after the Israelites. This shows that everybody can be touched and blessed by the Lord. Balaam then proclaimed the third oracle:

- The Lord began the oracle by calling Balaam "the man whose eyes are opened." As John MacArthur said, God's Spirit had given him understanding.[2]
- Balaam heard the words of God, saw a vison from the Almighty, and fell into a trance with his eyes uncovered (v. 4). A vision occurs when you are awake. A dream occurs when you are asleep.
- "How beautiful are your tents, Jacob . . . They stretch out like river valleys, like gardens by a stream, like aloes the LORD has planted, like cedars beside the water" (vv. 5–6).
- Water will flow from their buckets; their seed will have abundant water (v. 7). Tom Constable said water was a source of "physical refreshment" and blessing.[3] Proverbs 5:15–17 confirmed this. Balaam was saying if Balak and the Moabites thought there were a lot of Israelites now, more were coming.
- The Israelites' king would be greater than anybody else. Nothing could touch these people (vv. 7–8).
- "Those who bless you will be blessed and those who curse you will be cursed" (v. 9). In Genesis 12:3, God told Abram: "I will bless those who bless you, I will curse those who treat you with contempt, and all the peoples will be blessed through you." Genesis 49:9 recorded Israel's blessing on Judah: "Judah is a young lion—my son, you return from the kill. He crouches; he lies down like a lion or a lioness—who dares to rouse him?" Do not mess with God's people.

Once again, Balak was furious with Balaam because three times he blessed Israel instead of cursing them. When Balak sent him home without payment,

---

[2] John MacArthur, *The MacArthur Bible Commentary* (Nashville: Thomas Nelson, 2005), 186.

[3] Thomas L. Constable, *Expository Notes of Dr. Thomas Constable: Numbers*, 145, https://planobiblechapel.org/tcon/notes/pdf/numbers.pdf.

Balak said the messages were sent to him, and even if Balak gave him a house full of silver and gold he could not go against the Lord. Balaam then released a fourth oracle.

*Numbers 24:15–19*: The Fourth Oracle: Balaam predicted the Messiah:

- In the future, he saw a star that would come from Jacob. Matthew 2:1–2 said the wise men came from the east because they "saw His star in the east and have come to worship Him."
- An evil man, Balaam, prophesied the coming Messiah in the picture of a star.
- The scepter was going to rise from Israel. The scepter was also the symbol of a king. Psalm 89:27 says, "I will also make him My firstborn, greatest of the kings of the earth."

# Closing

God planned for the Messiah to come from Israel and, ultimately, to save the world. As we get into the fifth, sixth, and seventh oracles, Balak's whole purpose, according to Ron Allen, a professor at Dallas Seminary, was: "One nation will rise and supplant another, only to face its own doom. In contrast there is this implied ongoing blessing on the people of Israel and their sure promise of a future Deliverer who will have the final victory."[4]

Balaam pointed ultimately to the truth that victory would come through this *Deliverer*. When a donkey told him to stop, Jesus (the Angel of the Lord) intervened and told Balaam to tell them everything He told him. Balaam was the unknown servant God used, just as God used other unknowns. David was the little shepherd boy. Nehemiah was the cupbearer. Mary was the teenage girl in Nazareth. Peter was a fisherman. Gideon was the least of the least. Moses was a murderer. Despite all these folks not having a superhero cape, God used them. And God can use you to point people to the Star!

## The Daily Word

The Lord got Balaam's attention when He opened the mouth of a donkey and allowed the donkey to speak to Balaam. From the time Balaam met with the Angel of the Lord in the middle of a road, he spoke only the messages God put in his mouth, even when it was not the message King Balak expected to hear. The Lord used Balaam to point Balak and Israel to the coming Star, the King, Christ the Messiah.

[4] Ronald B. Allen, *The Expositor's Bible Commentary: Numbers*, rev. ed. (Grand Rapids: Zondervan, 2012), 336.

If the Lord can speak the message of truth through a donkey and a hired servant, then remember, He can speak through anyone. If the Lord lays a message on your heart as you meet with Him, be obedient and bold, and share it with others. God can use anyone to be His mouthpiece. Your adequacy comes from God, not yourself.

**Balaam said to Balak, "Stay here by your burnt offering while I seek the LORD over there." The LORD met with Balaam and put a message in his mouth. Then He said, "Return to Balak and say what I tell you." So he returned to Balak, who was standing there by his burnt offering with the officials of Moab. Balak asked him, "What did the LORD say?" —Numbers 23:15–17**

Further Scripture: Numbers 24:17; 2 Corinthians 3:5; 2 Corinthians 11:5–6

## Questions

1. What did Balak want Balaam to ask God to do to the Israelites (Numbers 23:7, 11)? Why was Balak so intent on having that done?

2. Balak tried to pay Balaam to gain the favor of God (Numbers 22:17). What did Balak notice about where the success of the Israelites came from?

3. In Balaam's first oracle from God, he stated that the Israelites were set apart from other nations (Numbers 23:9). Are you set apart as a Christian today? What does it mean to be set apart (Psalm 4:3; Romans 1:1; 2 Corinthians 6:17; 1 Peter 2:9; 1 John 4:4)?

4. Human relationships often fail us, and circumstances are constantly changing. How can you take comfort in Numbers 23:19 (Isaiah 40:8; 55:11; James 1:17)?

5. When Balaam first asked the Lord about meeting with Balak, God's answer was no (Numbers 22:12). But God said yes when Balaam asked again (Numbers 22:20). Then the Angel of the Lord blocked Balaam's way and almost killed him (Numbers 22:32–33). Why did God do this? Do you believe Balaam was being obedient? Why or why not? (Numbers 31:16; Revelation 2:14)

6. What did the Holy Spirit highlight to you in Numbers 23—24 through the reading or the teaching?

# Lesson 87: Numbers 25—26
*Rock*: The Doctrine of Balaam

## Teaching Notes

### Intro

Yesterday, we talked about a donkey; Balaam, a prophet no one thought God would use; and Balak, a king who tried to bring curses on God's people. We will see how God's hand was on the Israelites. Then we get to Numbers 25 and the Israelites get in trouble all over again!

### Teaching

*Numbers 25:1*: While the Israelites were in the Acacia Grove, the men started having sexual relations with the Moabite women. Have you noticed that when people get bored, they get in trouble? John MacArthur said the Acacia Grove was a region across the Jordan River from Jericho where Israel eventually invaded Canaan.[1] Joshua 2:1a confirmed, "Joshua son of Nun secretly sent two men as spies from the Acacia Grove, saying, 'Go and scout the land, especially Jericho.'"

*Numbers 25:2–3*: "The women invited them to the sacrifices for their gods, and the Israelites ate and bowed in worship to their gods." Now the Israelites joined in Moab's religion. Scripture says two become one flesh (Genesis 2:24). When you have relations with a woman, you are effectively saying I'm OK with what she believes and how she lives her life. Israel aligned itself with Baal of Peor (v. 3a). This became a continual stumbling block for Israel. Judges 2:13 revealed, "They abandoned Him and worshiped Baal and the Ashtoreths." In 2 Kings 17:16, "They abandoned all the commands of the LORD their God. They made cast images for themselves, two calves, and an Asherah pole. They worshiped the whole heavenly host and served Baal." Jeremiah 2:8 revealed, "The priests quit asking, 'Where is the LORD?' The experts in the law no longer knew Me, and the rulers rebelled against Me. The prophets prophesied by Baal and followed useless idols." Therefore, the Lord's anger burned against Israel (v. 3b).

---

[1] John MacArthur, *The MacArthur Bible Commentary* (Nashville: Thomas Nelson, 2005), 187.

*Numbers 25:4–5:* The Lord told Moses to take all the leaders and execute them in broad daylight (v. 4). Nelson's commentary says, "Israel had been seduced into joining the worship of Baal."[2] The men gave in to lust, and it opened the door to false worship. When we pursue the lust of our eyes, it's an open door for Satan to come into our lives. When we give in to one little thing, then sin is off and running. This time, Moses told the judges to kill each man who aligned himself with Baal (v. 5). Moses didn't fall on his face and pray for God to spare these men.

*Numbers 25:6–9:* When an Israelite man brought a Midianite woman to his relatives in the sight of Moses and the Israelites while they were weeping at the entrance to the tent of meeting, Phinehas, son of Eleazar, got up and took a spear in his hand (vv. 6–7). This man flaunted his sin before his nation and God. Phinehas followed them into the tent of meeting and drove the spear through the man and the woman, through the woman's belly (v. 8a). They flaunted their sin in God's house, so Phinehas killed them while they were having sex. Then the plague on the Israelites stopped, but 24,000 died in this plague (vv. 8b–9).

*Numbers 25:10–11:* The Lord told Moses that Phinehas had stopped His wrath toward the Israelites. The Lord then granted Phinehas a covenant of peace. Psalm 106:30–31 explained, "But Phinehas stood up and intervened, and the plague was stopped. It was credited to him as righteousness throughout all generations to come." When you hear of the 24,000 dying in this plague, it draws your attention back to the 23,000 who were killed for worshipping the golden calf.

*Numbers 25:13:* Because of Phinehas's zeal for God, Phinehas made atonement for Israel, and the covenant of peace would be a perpetual priesthood for him. Phinehas's killing atoned for the Israelites' sin.

*Numbers 25:14–15:* The name of the slain Israelite man was Zimri, the leader of a Simeonite house. The Midianite woman was Cozbi, the daughter of Zur, head of one of their tribes. These two thought they were untouchable and could get away with whatever they wanted to do.

*Numbers 25:16–18:* The Lord told Moses to attack the Midianites and strike them dead. Nelson's commentary said, "God commanded Moses to institute a holy war against Midian in retaliation."[3] Remember that Moses' wife was a

---

[2] Earl D. Radmacher, Ronald B. Allen, and H. Wayne House, eds., *Nelson's New Illustrated Bible Commentary* (Nashville: Thomas Nelson, 1999), 224.

[3] Radmacher et al., 224.

Midianite. Her father, Jethro, was a priest of Midian. Yet God told Moses to attack Midian.

## Closing

When you let the lust of your eyes take over, you slowly open the door for more. Every time you open that door, you stray away from Christ to false worship. Scripture says this over and over:

- Proverbs 5:3–8: "Though the lips of the forbidden woman drip honey and her words are smoother than oil, in the end she's as bitter as wormwood and as sharp as a double-edged sword. Her feet go down to death; her steps head straight for Sheol. She doesn't consider the path of life; she doesn't know that her ways are unstable. So now, my sons, listen to me, and don't turn away from the words of my mouth. Keep your way far from her. Don't go near the door of her house." When you open the door to cheat on God in one area, it opens the door for more. As people of God, we have to resist temptation and call others to resist temptation.
- Hebrews 13:4: "Marriage must be respected by all, and the marriage bed kept undefiled, because God will judge immoral people and adulterers."
- 1 Corinthians 6:18: "Run from sexual immorality! 'Every sin a person can commit is outside the body.' On the contrary, the person who is sexually immoral sins against his own body." Billy Graham always had someone go into his hotel room and check it out when he traveled. You have to always be on the lookout. That's why it's always safest to travel in pairs.
- 1 Corinthians 10:13: "No temptation has overtaken you except what is common to humanity. God is faithful, and He will not allow you to be tempted beyond what you are able, but with the temptation He will also provide a way of escape so that you are able to bear it."
- 1 Corinthians 6:19–20: "Don't you know that your body is a sanctuary of the Holy Spirit who is in you, whom you have from God? You are not your own, for you were bought at a price. Therefore, glorify God in your body." When someone has an affair, they are cheating on the Lord.
- 1 John 1:9: "If we confess our sins, He is faithful and righteous to forgive us our sins and to cleanse us from all unrighteousness." If you are at this point you can start over. God can forgive you. Nobody is exempt from thinking he is invincible.

The Women Living Well website offers ten suggestions to help keep you from giving into temptation.[4]

(1) Beware of your old boyfriends and girlfriends.

(2) Draw boundaries on who you will talk to and what is appropriate.

(3) Avoid dressing to get attention from the other gender.

(4) Never be alone with a person of another gender.

(5) Confess your temptations to the Lord out loud.

(6) Tell somebody about your temptations.

(7) Don't become close emotionally to someone of the opposite sex other than your spouse.

(8) If you are emotionally connected to somebody right now, then end the relationship.

(9) Don't assume your secret feelings won't be found out. Secrets always get revealed.

(10) Your sin always impacts somebody else.

Beware of falling into temptation! The Israelites did it. What makes us think we are any different? Let's not be the Zimris or the Cozbis. Through studying Numbers 25 and 26, my prayer is that the Holy Spirit would speak to and touch everyone listening to this message. Ask God to reveal things to you, and then come clean.

## The Daily Word

The Israelites were in the mountains of Moab near the Jordan River Valley. In the middle of the camp, the Israelites gave in to temptation, and in this case, their sexual desires. In response, God's anger burned against the Israelites. He wanted to kill all the men who had aligned themselves with the god Baal of Peor. However, one man, Phinehas, noticed what was happening and stood up for what was right. In his zealousness, he killed a man and woman having sexual relations near the entrance of the tabernacle, a place reserved for the sacred presentation of offerings to God. Because of Phinehas's bold and courageous act against this sin, the Lord ended the plague, and no one else was killed. A line was drawn in the sand, and there was a shift in the rebellion of Israel.

---

[4] Courtney Joseph, "When You Are Tempted to Have an Affair," Women Living Well Ministries, June 18, 2015, https://womenlivingwell.org/2015/06/when-you-are-tempted-to-have-an-affair/.

Who are you in this harsh reality? Are you the one giving in to temptation and living in sin? Or are you the one zealous enough to follow the Lord and stand up for what is right? The world and Satan want to lure you into sinful ways: an emotional or sexual affair, sex before marriage, or the temptation of pornography. You know it is not from the Lord, but you have grown numb to sin and enjoy the temporary pleasures it brings. As followers of Christ, draw a line in the sand today. Turn away from the darkness of sin and walk into the light of Christ. The Lord will welcome you with open arms of forgiveness. If you see a brother or sister stumbling in this area, be zealous and say something. Don't stand by and watch them live in sin. Be a light for Jesus today!

**The LORD spoke to Moses, "Phinehas son of Eleazar, son of Aaron the priest, has turned back My wrath from the Israelites because he was zealous among them with My zeal, so that I did not destroy the Israelites in My zeal." — Numbers 25:10–11**

Further Scripture: Psalm 106:30–31; 1 Corinthians 10:13; Galatians 6:1

## Questions

1. Balaam could not speak a curse on the Israelites as Balak desired. Why was the anger of the Lord now aroused against them in Numbers 25? Did they know God would not approve of their actions? (Exodus 34:15–16)

2. It was obvious in Numbers 25:4 and 9 that the Lord takes sin very seriously. Why does God not tolerate sin (Isaiah 59:2; Habakkuk 1:13; Matthew 6:2; 1 Corinthians 15:34)? Do you take sin as seriously as God does?

3. Phinehas was described as "zealous for his God." (Numbers 25:11, 13) The word "zealous" was also used to describe Elijah (1 Kings 19:10, 14) and Saul before he became Paul (Acts 22:3; Galatians 1:14). How are these descriptions of being zealous the same? How are they different?

4. Who were the only two people to be included in both the first and second census? Why were they the only two who survived? (Numbers 14:29–32)

5. How did asking Moses to take a second census show God's faithfulness to the promises He made to Abraham? (Genesis 12:1–3)

6. What did the Holy Spirit highlight to you in Numbers 25—26 through the reading or the teaching?

# Lesson 88: Numbers 27—28

## *Rock*: Laws of Inheritance

## Teaching Notes

### Intro

We are almost done with the book of Numbers. Although we didn't discuss Numbers 26, this chapter really is about numbers, specifically, the second census. The Israelites needed to count everyone older than 20 years old.

The end of chapter 26 designated inheritance of land by tribe: "The LORD spoke to Moses, 'The land is to be divided among them as an inheritance based on the number of names. Increase the inheritance for a large tribe and decrease it for a small one. Each is to be given its inheritance according to those who were registered in it. The land must be divided by lot; they will receive an inheritance according to the names of their ancestral tribes. Each inheritance will be divided by lot among the larger and smaller tribes'" (Numbers 26:52–56).

The Levites' inheritance was different from the rest of the clans. They would be scattered and would not get land: "'These were the Levites registered by their clans: the Gershonite clan from Gershon; the Kohathite clan from Kohath; the Merarite clan from Merari. These were the Levite family groups: the Libnite clan, the Hebronite clan, the Mahlite clan, the Mushite clan, and the Korahite clan" (Numbers 26:57–58).

### Teaching

*Numbers 27:1–2*: The daughters of Zelophehad approached Moses. Their names were Mahlah, Noah, Hoglah, Milcah and Tirzah. They stood before Moses, Eleazar the priest, the leaders, and the entire community at the entrance to the tent of meeting.

*Numbers 27:3*: They told Moses their father, Zelophehad, died in the wilderness but wasn't among Korah's followers. He wasn't a part of the rebellion but died due to his own sin.

Zelophehad could have died several ways:

- Numbers 11:33: "While the meat was still between their teeth, before it was chewed, the LORD's anger burned against the people, and the LORD struck them with a very severe plague."
- Numbers 21:6: "Then the LORD sent poisonous snakes among the people, and they bit them so that many Israelites died."
- Numbers 25:1: "The people began to have sexual relations with the women of Moab."
- Numbers 25:9: "But those who died in the plague numbered 24,000."

It is important to note that Zelophehad had no sons.

*Numbers 27:4*: Zelophehad's daughters asked why they shouldn't get land because their father had no sons. They wanted property among their father's brothers. These five women believed in the promises of God. They were bold. The Old Testament describes several other bold women:

- Zipporah: "On the trip, at an overnight campsite, it happened that the LORD confronted him [Moses] and sought to put him to death. So Zipporah took a flint, cut off her son's foreskin, and threw it at Moses' feet. Then she said, 'You are a bridegroom of blood to me!'" (Exodus 4:24–25)
- Deborah: "She summoned Barak son of Abinoam from Kedesh in Naphtali and said to him, 'Hasn't the LORD, the God of Israel, commanded you: "Go, deploy the troops on Mount Tabor, and take with you 10,000 men from the Naphtalites and Zebulunites? Then I will lure Sisera commander of Jabin's forces, his chariots, and his army at the Wadi Kishon to fight against you, and I will hand him over to you."'" (Judges 4:6–7)
- More bold women: Ruth, Hannah, Abigail, and Esther.

*Numbers 27:5–6*: Moses brought the case before the Lord like he had done previously in Leviticus 24:1–11. Moses had to bring situations before the Lord nearly every single day.

*Numbers 27:7–8*: The Lord told Moses to give the daughters of Zelophehad hereditary property among their father's brothers. The Lord also said that when a man died without sons, they transferred his inheritance to his daughter. Daughters were not included in inheritances until this moment.

*Numbers 27:9–10*: If a man had no daughter, his inheritance went to his brothers. If a man had no brothers, his inheritance went to his father's brothers.

*Numbers 27:11*: If a man's father had no brothers, his inheritance went to the nearest relative of his clan. The Bible speaks about inheritance a lot:

- "We have also received an inheritance in Him, predestined according to the purpose of the One who works out everything in agreement with the decision of His will." (Ephesians 1:11)
- "Knowing that you will receive the reward of an inheritance from the Lord. You serve the Lord Christ." (Colossians 3:24)
- "Therefore, He is the mediator of a new covenant, so that those who are called might receive the promise of the eternal inheritance." (Hebrews 9:15)
- "And into an inheritance that is imperishable, uncorrupted, and unfading, kept in heaven for you." (1 Peter 1:4)
- "And the Israelites would see that Moses' face was radiant. Then Moses would put the veil over his face again until he went to speak with the LORD." (Exodus 34:35)

Eternal inheritance in Christ won't fade. This eternal inheritance that we are given is imperishable, uncorrupted, and unfading.

*Numbers 27:12–17*: Moses was told to go up to the mountain and look at the land the Israelites would be given. The Lord told Moses that after he saw the land, he would die. The Lord reminded Moses that when the community quarreled in the Wilderness of Zin, both he and Aaron rebelled against the Lord's command. Moses would never receive the land he was promised.

*Numbers 27:18–23*: The Lord told Moses that Joshua had been picked to replace him. Moses put his hands on Joshua and commissioned him.

## Closing

We will get to the inheritance that we have been promised. Even though Moses didn't make it to his inheritance here on earth, I promise he will be in heaven with us. All of this points to the eternal picture.

# The Daily Word

The daughters of Zelophehad stood before Moses and boldly asked for their father's property. The women came from a father whom the Lord had killed in the wilderness because of his sin. Despite their family's sin, the Lord answered the women's bold request by giving them their inherited property.

The Lord knows everything about your past and your present, and He still loves and cares for you. In Christ, you are no longer called an orphan; you are called God's child. When you put your hope in Christ, you receive an inheritance in Him that is imperishable, uncorrupted, and unfading. It will be yours forever as you walk with Jesus. So walk boldly, like these women, in the promise of your inheritance as a son or daughter of the King of kings and Lord of lords.

**"Why should the name of our father be taken away from his clan? Since he had no son, give us property among our father's brothers." Moses brought their case before the LORD, and the LORD answered him, "What Zelophehad's daughters say is correct. You are to give them hereditary property among their father's brothers and transfer their father's inheritance to them." — Numbers 27:4–7**

Further Scripture: John 14:18; Ephesians 1:11–12; 1 Peter 1:4

## Questions

1. Does the case Moses took before the Lord regarding the daughters of Zelophehad (Numbers 27:1–7) and the Lord's decision seem consistent with how you see women treated in the Old Testament? Do you think females were generally treated with value in this culture? Why or why not?

2. Why did the Lord tell Moses to go up to the mountain of Abarim in Numbers 27:12?

3. Do you think it was difficult for Moses when the Lord reminded him of his rebellion at the waters of Meribah of Kadesh (Numbers 27:14)? Is it difficult for you to reflect on your own past sin when reminded by others or by the Holy Spirit?

4. What was Moses' concern when told he would soon "be gathered to his people" (he would die) (Numbers 27:15–17)? Whose words does Moses' response in this passage reflect (John 10:3–4, 9–11)?

5. What will be different with Joshua when he seeks the Lord's will or judgment versus when Moses sought it (Numbers 27:5–6, 21a)?

6. What did the Holy Spirit highlight to you in Numbers 27—28 through the reading or the teaching?

# Lesson 89: Numbers 29—30
## Rock: Calendar of Public Sacrifices

## Teaching Notes

### Intro

Yesterday, we saw Moses at 120 years old pass the baton of leadership of Israel to Joshua. Going into Numbers 28, we expected a full-on battle. Instead, Moses jumped into offerings and sacrifices again. God was ingraining the value of the calendar in the minds of the people. He instructed them to observe these feasts to not lose their focus. God wanted them to know that the heart behind their entire calendar was worship.

The calendar started in Numbers 28 (see the chart at the end of the lesson). Priests, who were of the Levitical tribe, had a set number of years they were to serve. Priests started serving at the age of 25 and retired at 50. After turning 50 years old, they were permitted to assist but not actually do the work.

### Teaching

*Numbers 29:1–6:* During the Feast of the Trumpets, the Israelites were to do no work, hold a sacred assembly, and offer burnt offerings. An acceptable offering was an unblemished animal—a young bull, a ram, and seven male yearling lambs—and one goat that would be offered as a sin offering for oneself. The trumpet sounded at the beginning of the new civil year (Rosh Hashanah) of the Jewish calendar.

The priests also blew a trumpet to gather people together, to sound an alarm, or announce a battle. Short and long blasts were used to get the people's attention. Israel was going to be scattered but eventually regathered together in the end times at the sound of a trumpet.

- "On that day the LORD will thresh grain from the Euphrates River as far as the Wadi of Egypt, and you Israelites will be gathered one by one. On that day a great trumpet will be blown, and those lost in the land of Assyria will come, as well as those dispersed in the land of Egypt; and they will worship the LORD at Jerusalem on the holy mountain" (Isaiah 27:12–13).

- "Immediately after the tribulation of those days . . . Then the sign of the Son of Man will appear in the sky . . . He will send out His angels with a loud trumpet, and they will gather His elect from the four winds, from one end of the sky to the other" (Matthew 24:29–31).
- The elect are called together (1 Thessalonians 4).

*Numbers 29:7*: The Day of Atonement (Yom Kippur) was the highest and holiest of holy days. It was also a celebration that used the scapegoat, which was released into the wilderness, taking with it the sins of the people (Leviticus 16:10). The Israelites offered burnt offerings of unblemished animals, either one young bull, one ram, seven male yearling lambs, and one male goat.

In Numbers 28—29, the Lord put together a structure so the leadership could implement the sacrifices as the people entered the land. This did not include all the personal sacrifices that were to be offered regularly. Unlike Leviticus 23, in these chapters we learn more about the sacrifices than the event itself. The Passover was the only feast in full implementation at this time.

*Numbers 29:12–39*: The Feast of Tabernacles (Feast of Booths) is still celebrated today. It is a seven-day festival. Notice the consistency of the unblemished animals offered with exception of the bulls.

| Numbers | Occasion | Also known as | Bulls | Rams | Lambs | Goats |
|---------|----------|---------------|-------|------|-------|-------|
| 28:3–8 | Daily | | | | 2 | |
| 28:9–10 | Every Sabbath | Shabbat | | | 2 | |
| 28:11–15 | 1st Day of the month | | 2 | 1 | 7 | 1 |
| 28:17 25 | Passover | Feast of Unleavened Bread | 2 | 1 | 7 | 1 |
| 28:26–31 | Pentecost | Feast of Weeks | 2 | 1 | 7 | 1 |
| 29:1–6 | Feast of Trumpets | Rash Hashanah | 1 | 1 | 7 | 1 |
| 29:7–11 | Day of Atonement | Yom Kippur | 1 | 1 | 7 | 1 |
| 29:12–39 | Feast of Tabernacles | Feast of Booths | | | | |
| | | Day 1 | 13 | 2 | 14 | 1 |
| | | Day 2 | 12 | 2 | 14 | 1 |

| | | Day 3 | 11 | 2 | 14 | 1 |
|---|---|---|---|---|---|---|
| | | Day 4 | 10 | 2 | 14 | 1 |
| | | Day 5 | 9 | 2 | 14 | 1 |
| | | Day 6 | 8 | 2 | 14 | 1 |
| | | Day 7 | 7 | 2 | 14 | 1 |
| | | Day 8 | 1 | 1 | 7 | 1 |

*Numbers 29:40*: "So Moses told the Israelites everything the LORD had commanded him."

## Closing

Gordon Wenham observed, "Over the course of one year, 113 bulls, 1,086 lambs, tons of flour and thousands of bottles of oil are used. And that is just what is prescribed, the public sacrifices! It does not include the individual offerings."[1]

Warren Wiersbe laid out three points for all these sacrifices to help answer the questions: What do you do with all this? How is this practical?

(1) All of these sacrifices are fulfilled in Christ (Hebrews 10:1–18).

(2) The nation of Israel could not have functioned without the priests at that time (Hebrews 4:14–16).

(3) Sacrifices are extremely expensive.[2]

Praise the Lord we do not have to remember any of this! We literally can come before Jesus because we know He gave up Himself so we can go back to Him.

## The Daily Word

Once again Moses instructed the Israelites on everything the Lord commanded regarding sacrifices and offerings. Every year during the many festivals, the Israelites gave up their resources in the form of sacrifices and offerings to make atonement for their sins. This was all the Israelites knew in the way of atonement.

---

[1] Gordon Wenham, *Numbers: An Introduction and Commentary*, vol. 4 of Tyndale Old Testament Commentary (Downer's Grove, IL: Inter-Varsity, 1981), 197.

[2] Warren W. Wiersbe, *Be Counted (Numbers): Living a Life that Counts for God* (Colorado Springs: David C. Cook, 1999), 162.

However, in the New Testament, Christ came and offered a sacrifice for sin forever. With His life, He paid the price of sin once and for all. Through this one offering, Jesus has perfected forever those who are sanctified in Him. You are forgiven forever; therefore, sacrifices and offerings are no longer necessary. Praise the Lord for this sacrificial act of love.

**"You must offer these to the LORD at your appointed times in addition to your vow and freewill offerings, whether burnt, grain, drink, or fellowship offerings." So Moses told the Israelites everything the LORD had commanded him. —Numbers 29:39–40**

Further Scripture: Ephesians 5:2; Hebrews 10:10–12, 17–18

## Questions

1.  Why did the Lord have Moses repeat the commands about the offerings during special days and weeks in the seventh month (Leviticus 16:29; 23:24, 34; Numbers 29)? What details did the Lord give in these chapters which had not been given earlier (Leviticus 23:34–43)?

2.  When a woman made a vow to the Lord, at what point could her father (or husband if she was married) forbid her to keep those vows (Numbers 30:5, 8)? Were there any circumstances listed by which a man could get out of fulfilling a vow he had made to the Lord (Numbers 30; Deuteronomy 23:21)? What does this say about God's protection of women from guilt over being unable to honor a vow or rash statement by which she had bound herself?

3.  Read Matthew 5:33–37. Describe what you think Jesus meant by these instructions.

4.  What did the Holy Spirit highlight to you in Numbers 29—30 through the reading or the teaching?

# Lesson 90: Numbers 31
*Rock*: War with Midian

## Teaching Notes

### Intro

Yesterday we talked about the calendar of sacrifices in Numbers 29. While chapter 30 was not referenced, it provided instructions about regulations on vows, making vows, keeping them and communication to each other. We are in a transition period in chapter 31. Warren Wiersbe wrote, "This battle would be a 'dress rehearsal' for the battles Israel would fight in the land of Canaan."[3] This was also the last battle for Moses before he died. Joshua had received the baton from Moses and now the children of Israel began walking it out.

### Teaching

*Numbers 31:1–2*: The Lord spoke to Moses and told him to execute vengeance! Deuteronomy 32:35 states that vengeance belongs to God, but now God was telling Israel to go execute His vengeance on Midian. Why the Midianites? They were the people group that enticed Israel, luring them away by both physical and spiritual seduction. God told Israel to take vengeance on the Midianites. Then Moses would die and be with his people.

*Numbers 31:3–4*: Moses told the people they were going to go fight and to equip some of the men. The Lord was with the Israelites and they were to execute the Lord's vengeance. Moses stood with the authority of a general. All 12 tribes were to send 1,000 men. Twelve thousand men were equipped for war.

*Numbers 31:5–7*: Phinehas, the son of the priest Eleazar, was the warrior leading the charge. Phinehas, had taken action by killing the Israelite Zimri and the Midianite woman Cozbi, thus stopping the plague of death on Israel (Numbers 25:6–15). The Israelites waged war and killed every male. Think of the bloodbath when thousands and thousands are killed!

---

[3] Warren W. Wiersbe, *The Wiersbe Bible Commentary: Old Testament* (Colorado Springs: David C. Cook, 2007), 297.

*Numbers 31:8–9*: The Israelites killed the Midianite kings: Evi, Rekem, Zur, Hur, and Reba. They also killed Balaam, whose donkey spoke to him as an angel blocked his path (Numbers 22:22–27). Balaam was either a causality of war or still hanging out with the Midianites. The Israelites took all the women and children captive. They plundered all their cattle, flocks, and property. Imagine trying to gather and organize all this stuff.

*Numbers 31:10–11*: All cities and camps were burnt, and nothing remained. Captives and spoils of war were gathered. This was a full-on battle.

Few of us are in combat battles against physical enemies. Our enemy is not flesh and blood or seen with the naked eye. We are fighting the world, the flesh, or the things Satan throws at us. When we wake every morning, we are in a battle (Ephesians 6:10–11). We have to put on the full armor of God and be on high alert so that we do not end up like Balaam who released a blessing only to fall back into his old way. We tend to forget we are in a battle. It's spiritual warfare. If you believe in angels, you have to believe in demons and that demonic activity is trying to come at you from any direction to knock you down (Ephesians 6:12–13). Like the Israelites, we must be prepared and equipped for war.

*Numbers 31:12–14*: The warriors brought all the spoils of battle to Moses and Eleazar and to all the Israelite community. They wanted to share their success. Moses, Eleazar, and the leaders met them outside the camp. Moses became furious with the officers and commanders of the army.

*Numbers 31:15–16*: Every Midianite female was left alive. But the army had brought the problem back to camp! The females were the ones who seduced the Israelite men. This was the cause of the Peor incident (Numbers 25). This is why a plague had been on Israel.

*Numbers 31:17–20*: Now the army had to kill all male children. The Midianite seed would be cut off. The army was also to kill every woman who had had sexual relations. These women were the issue. This had to take time figuring who had been in sexual relations and who hadn't. Moses was not messing around; this was serious. They could keep the virgin females for themselves.

The men of battle needed to remain outside camp until they purified themselves from touching the dead. They had to purify everything: garments, leather goods, things made out of goat hair, and wood products.

*Numbers 31:21–23*: A legal statute from God was presented. It was a command, not an option. Anything that could withstand fire was to be purified with it. For example: gold, silver, bronze, iron, tin, and lead. This was the only time fire was required for the purification process. All the rest was to be passed through the water.

The refiner's fire is a purification process. Being purified is powerful. The junk is cleaned up:

- Malachi 2:17; 3:1–2: Think of the gold, silver, iron, etc. from Numbers 31:23.
- Malachi 3:3–4: He knows they can withstand the fire. The Lord will again be pleased as in the past times.
- Malachi 3:5: These will not withstand the fire of judgment: sorcerers and adulterers, those that swear falsely and cheat the wage earner, oppressors of the widows and fatherless, and denier of justice to foreigners.
- Malachi 3:6: God has not changed; we need to clean up the junk. Let's see who can withstand a refiner's fire.

Read Matthew 3:11–12. You get to experience the Holy Spirit, the presence of God in your life, and the fire of God. It is an awesome picture. When you experience the Holy Spirit in your life, you will be able to express the manifestation of the gifts of the Spirit working through you—the gifts of service, the gift of prophecy, of teaching, the gift of administration, of hospitality, all of these things. But it doesn't happen if the fire of God is not burning within you, burning off the chaff, burning the sin, burning these things that are not of the Lord. If the baptism of fire is not constantly burning within, you will not manifest the Holy Spirit in a way that brings glory and honor to Him.

Those of Israel who went out into battle and brought back the plunder had to send it through the fire so God could use it. It is the same with our mentality; it is the same with us as we go out into the battle. We must understand we have the Spirit of God and the fire of God. That fire of God is going to burn away anything that is not of God and should not be there: pride, greed, lust, false worship, envy, or anything else that is not of the Lord.

*Numbers 31:24–25*: When the Israelites purified themselves with water and with fire, they would be clean. Only then could they enter the camp. The plunder was divided.

# Closing

We are all in the battle, a spiritual battle, for which we need to be equipped. We need to be equipped in full, head-on battle gear. We have to put on the armor of God. The Spirit of God and the fire of God burning in us fuel the armor of God. This is the only way we can withstand the battle and remain strong!

## The Daily Word

The Lord instructed Moses about how the Israelites were to execute vengeance upon the Midianites, who had allowed sexual sin to creep into the Israelite camp. This battle destroyed all the impure people. After the Israelites succeeded in this battle, they went through a purification process for themselves and the goods they obtained before they were allowed back into the community.

God desires purity from His people. You are called into a battle every day. When you go through the daily battle, a purification process naturally occurs in your life. Anything in you that is not of the Lord will not last during the battle. These difficult times help to get rid of pride, lust, selfishness, control, and other fleshly desires that may have crept into your life. What will the Lord purify in your life? The Lord allows you to go through the fire so that you may reflect more of Him. Today let your heart take courage, for the battle belongs to the Lord.

**The LORD spoke to Moses, "Execute vengeance for the Israelites against the Midianites. After that, you will be gathered to your people." . . . "Also purify everything: garments, leather goods, things made of goat hair, and every article of wood." . . . "After that, you may enter the camp." —Numbers 31:1, 20, 24**

Further Scripture: 1 Samuel 17:47; Malachi 3:2–3; Ephesians 6:10–13

## Questions

1. In Numbers 31:8, the warriors killed the kings of Midian. Who were the five slain? Who was the sixth person killed?

2. After the battle, what did the army take as their spoils (Numbers 31:9–11)? Why was Moses angry with them in verses 14–18?

3. Why were the men made to stay outside the camp for seven days (Numbers 31:19)? What were the two separate ways they had to purify the items they took (v. 22–24)?

4. At the end of Numbers 31, the spoils were to be divided. How did the Lord tell them to divide what they took?

5. What did the Holy Spirit highlight to you in Numbers 31 through the reading or the teaching?

# Lesson 91: Numbers 32
*Rock*: Transjordan Tribe Request

## Teaching Notes

### Intro

Israel had just fought the battle with the Midianites. God had given them His vengeance. They were to clean house and kill everyone, but the soldiers brought back the women and children. Moses had to tell them to kill all the male children and any woman who had sexual relations with a man (the Midianite women lured Israelite men: Numbers 25; 31:16–17). This is the backdrop of all the dynamics that were going on. Joshua was now in charge, Moses had just completed his last battle and was about to die, and the children of Israel were preparing to enter the Promised Land.

### Teaching

*Numbers 32:1–5*: Reubenites and Gadites were livestock people. They saw the land where they were presently camped as great land to raise livestock. They were settling for good land when, in reality, God had better land across the Jordan River. The Gadites and Reubenites went to Moses, Eleazar (Aaron's son, the new high priest), and leaders of the community. They asked to stay and settle in this land. They didn't want to cross the Jordan.

Jeff Hart (a guest at this Bible study session) commented: It has the feel of the American church. We are comfortable where we are, at a place where everything is nice, "I'm just going to stay here." These tribes seemed to be saying, "I'll fund you to do it, but don't make us go" (Proverbs 3:1–6).

*Numbers 32:6–13*: It was possible that Moses was very quick to answer, "What are you thinking?" Moses started to question the intention of the Gadites and Reubenites, so he compared this conversation to the spy report. They were no different from their fathers who discouraged the people from the Promised Land. Then, Moses recounted the story of the spies and wandering in the wilderness for 40 years.

*Numbers 32:14–17*: Moses called them a brood of sinners. They were adding to the Lord's anger against their fathers. If they decided to turn away, all would be destroyed. The Gadites and Reubenites began to clarify the situation by dialoguing. They liked the land, but first they wanted to build some sheepfolds and dwellings. Then they would send their fighting men to go with the Israelites to fight. The women and children would stay in the cities.

*Numbers 32:18–19*: They would fight with Israel until all tribes possessed their inheritance. Then they would return back to their homes east of the Jordan. Ray Sturdivant (a guest at this Bible study session) said, "The problem with compromise is that it sounds really rational and good, but compromising is devastating to your relationship with God."

*Numbers 32:20–24:* Moses said, "I hear your negotiation." Then he instructed the Reubenites and Gadites to send their armed men until the enemy is driven out. Only then could they return to this land with no other obligations. Moses said, "Go ahead and do what you have proposed, but keep your promise." If the promise was broken, it would be a sin against the Lord. Moses was done dialoguing; he just gave them a free pass.

*Numbers 32:25–27*: The Gadites and Reubenites agreed. The men would go to war while their dependents stayed in Gilead. It feels like a political response: "Okay, then, we're in, we'll do as you say." We'll find further in Scripture that east of the Jordan River was a highly invaded land. Even today the west side (Iron Dome) has the protection of the Lord's hand.

*Numbers 32:28–29*: Since Moses couldn't go into the Promised Land, he brought in leadership to finish the land deal. The Reubenites and Gadites gave up land. That was not a good land deal; you do not give up land in Israel. In Genesis 12:3, God promised to make Israel a great nation, to bless those who bless them, and to curse those who don't.

*Numbers 32:30–32*: Moses said to the leaders, "Make sure you fight with Israel." If not, they would have to settle in Canaan. The Gadites and Reubenites agreed so they could keep their "hereditary" possession in the east. This sounds like a compromise.

*Numbers 32:33–41*: Half of the tribe of Manasseh decided to jump in! It seemed they had scored a serious deal. However, this was not how God designed it, and greed led them out of God's will. They were given the kingdoms of Sihon (Amorites) and Og (Bashanites) and the surrounding area. Moses gave them the land.

The leadership (Joshua, Eleazar) said they would implement this. The tribes of Gad, Reuben, and half of Manasseh (that was a rift in itself, a split tribe) began building and fortifying cities and sheepfolds. They were separating themselves from the rest of the tribes. Constable wrote, "Distance from the other tribes later produced misunderstanding and disunity (Joshua 22)."[1]

## Closing

Warren Wiersbe tells us of four types of people:[2]

- Some of us are like the older Jews who perished. We never made it to the Promised Land.
- We heard the promises, but we never made it.
- Some of us are like the ten spies. We came into the land, saw its wealth, but failed to enter.
- We like it, this sounds good, but we're not going in.
- Then there are the Transjordan tribes—the Gadites, Reubenites and half of Manasseh.
- Hey, we are going to enter, but we just don't want to stay.
- Then, there is the new generation who gets to enter the land and experience the promises.

This is the challenge to anyone enrolled in reviveSCHOOL—online or over the radio. We want to be the new generation. We want to be the people who embrace the promises given to Abraham, Isaac, and Jacob. We want to say we'll walk into the land regardless of what it looks like. We believe the Word of God is true. We believe He is setting a path for us. All we have to do is simply walk it out.

Here is the challenge: Are you the Jew who never made it in? Are you the spy who said no way? Are you of the Transjordan tribes who like it right where you are? Or are you of the new generation who gets to experience the promise He has for all of us?

---

[1] Thomas L. Constable, *Expository Notes of Dr. Thomas Constable: Numbers*, 179, https://planobiblechapel.org/tcon/notes/pdf/numbers.pdf.

[2] Warren W. Wiersbe, *The Bible Exposition Commentary: Genesis–Deuteronomy* (Colorado Springs: David C. Cook, 2001), 367.

## The Daily Word

The Reubenites and the Gadites came up with their own plan for their families and livestock, and it didn't include crossing the Jordan River with the rest of the Israelites. They liked the land they were on and decided it was best for them. As a result, they didn't think they needed to go into battle or into the Promise Land with the other tribes. Moses was upset with their lack of trust and loyalty to God's original plan.

As followers of Christ, Jesus calls you to keep your hands to the plow and follow Him by faith. However, temporary things may tempt you to stop walking by faith. You are called to walk by faith and to trust in the Lord with all your heart, not depending on your strength. Today, you may be in a place where you are tempted to rely on your own strength. Be encouraged to press on in faith, trusting that the Lord's plan will be the best for your life! He loves you, and His plan is incredible!

**They said, "If we have found favor in your sight, let this land be given to your servants as a possession. Don't make us cross the Jordan." But Moses asked the Gadites and Reubenites, "Should your brothers go to war while you stay here?" —Numbers 32:5–6**

Further Scripture: Proverbs 3:5–6; Luke 9:62; 2 Corinthians 5:7

## Questions

1. In Numbers 32, what two tribes wanted to stay on the east side of the Jordan, rather than cross to the Promised Land?
2. What compromise did those two tribe's leaders come up with in verses 16–18? Are there times when you have compromised something the Lord asked you to do? Did you recognize it right away?
3. What land was given to the now two and a half tribes? What were the names of the cities they were given (Numbers 32:33–42)?
4. What did the Holy Spirit highlight to you in Numbers 32 through the reading or the teaching?

# Lesson 92: Numbers 33
*Rock*: From Egypt to Jordan

## Teaching Notes

### Intro

Our job is to stand on the *Rock* that is Christ. First Corinthians 10:4 says, "And all drank the same spiritual drink. For they drank from a spiritual rock that followed them, and that rock was Christ." In the wilderness, the *Rock*, Christ, was present. In Numbers 32, we saw how the Gadites, Reubenites, and half the tribe of Manasseh didn't want to depend upon the Lord. They decided to just stay where they were instead of following the presence of God. That leads us into Numbers 33.

### Teaching

*Numbers 33:1–10*: Chapter 33 covers the stages of the Israelites' journey as they came out of Egypt by their military divisions (v. 1). God commanded Moses to record their journey (v. 2) by identifying the starting points when God showed up and moved them to the next stage. We'll cover six cycles today. God instructed Moses to write these down because the Israelite people kept forgetting what God had done for them (Deuteronomy 4:9; 6:12; 8:2; Psalm 143:5).

Think about the different ways God has asked the Israelites to remember things:

- The Passover and feasts
- The jar of manna in the tabernacle
- Aaron's rod that bloomed, budded, and provided fruit
- The Ten Commandments
- The tassels on their robes

(Luke 22:19 and 1 Corinthians 11:25 show that Jesus takes this same mentality for remembrance of Himself.)

Back to Numbers 33:3–4, Moses wrote down the starting points for the stages of their journey: They departed from Rameses on the fifteenth day of the first month, the day after Passover, while the Egyptians were burying their first-born, which God had struck down. The Israelites then left Rameses and camped out at Succoth (v. 5). They left Succoth and camped at Etham, on the edge of the wilderness (v. 6). They left Etham, turned back to Pi Hahiroth, to the east of Baal Zephon, and camped near Migdol (v. 7). They left Pi Hahiroth, passed through the sea and into the desert, and after three days camped at Marah (v. 8). The Israelites departed Marah and came to Elim where there were 12 springs and 70 palm trees, and they camped there (v. 9). They departed Elim and camped by the Red Sea (v. 10). Notice that when they arrived at the Red Sea, they had nowhere else to go. This first part of their journey took them from Rameses to the Red Sea, and they were led by the cloud.

*Numbers 33:11–17*: The Israelites departed from the Red Sea and camped in the Desert of Sin and in the process moved from chaos to having some organizational structure (v. 11). They departed the Wilderness of Sin and camped at Dophkah (v. 12). They departed Dophkah and camped at Alush (v. 13). After Alush they went to Rephidim, where there was no water to drink (v. 14). They departed Rephidim and camped in the Desert of Sinai (v. 15). Then, the Israelites departed the Desert of Sinai and camped at Kibroth-Hattaavah (v. 16). The Kohathites had to pack up the tabernacle each time they moved and then set it back up before the holy objects arrived (Numbers 4:4; 10:21). This ended the second period of their journey.

How did the Israelites know when to leave and move on to the next camp? Numbers 9:17 explains that, "Whenever the cloud was lifted up above the tent, the Israelites would set out; at the place where the cloud stopped, there the Israel-ites camped" (Numbers 9:20). This is a great image of depending on the presence of God.

*Numbers 33:18–31*: Beginning in verse 18 is the third part of the journey, and it records the history from the spies being sent to the Desert of Paran. Then, during the fourth period, the Israelites moved from Kadesh to Bene-jaakan (vv. 26–31).

*Numbers 33:32–49*: The fifth period of the journey covers the desert journey the Israelites took to Edom and documents the death of Aaron. The sixth period of the journey follows the Israelites from Punon to the plains of Moab. Other theo-logians would divide the journey into 42 stages. Interestingly, Moses wrote 42 times that they had departed from one place and camped at another.

*Numbers 33:50–53*: On the plains of Moab, the Lord spoke to Moses (v. 50) and emphasized that when the Israelites entered Canaan, they must drive out all the inhabitants and destroy all their idols and high places (vv. 51–52). God emphasized that they should take possession and settle the land because it was the land He had given to them (v. 53). God reminded them that this land was their inheritance (v. 54). But the instructions also came with warning: If the Israelites didn't drive out the inhabitants of the Promised Land, they would harass the Israelites (v. 55) and become "thorns in your eyes and in your sides." Plus, God would punish the Israelites for their failure to do as He directed them (v. 56).

## Closing

All of this leads to Romans 8:14: "All those led by God's Spirit are God's sons." This means we must be led by the Spirit of God. If you don't depend on the Holy Spirit, what are you doing with your walk with Christ? Are you sitting there like a Reubenite or Gadite saying, "I don't really want to go to the Promised Land"? If you want to be led by the Lord, you have to have more of the Holy Spirit. God wants us to experience more of His presence. He wants us to trust Him and His leading, not ours.

## The Daily Word

The Israelites needed to start fresh in the land the Lord was giving them. The Lord knew if they left any of the previous inhabitants in the land, those inhabitants would become stressful to His people, like thorns in their eyes and sides.

Sometimes in life, when you start a new job, move to a new home, or begin at a new school, you may try to merge the previous people, places, or things with the new ones. You want to make both sides happy and avoid causing pain or heartache to anyone. However, in reality, it may lead to unhappiness on both sides, creating a stressful situation. The Lord was commanding the Israelites to eliminate all of the old ways and just start fresh. Maybe you need to hear this today. Make the hard decision and start fresh. Be strong and courageous as you take steps forward. The Lord will work it out for good!

**But if you don't drive out the inhabitants of the land before you, those you allow to remain will become thorns in your eyes and in your sides; they will harass you in the land where you will live. And what I had planned to do to them, I will do to you. —Numbers 33:55–56**

Further Scripture: Numbers 33:52–53; Proverbs 16:1–4; Romans 8:28

# Questions

1. How did the Israelites know the timing of when to camp and when to depart each location (Numbers 9:17)?

2. Looking back at the stages in the Israelites' journey out of Egypt (Numbers 33), which do you feel were the most pivotal for them?

3. The journey from Egypt to the Promised Land was a long journey. Describe the emotions you think the Israelites may have felt throughout the process: beginning, middle, and end?

4. A recount of significant moments is recorded in Numbers 33. Read the instruction God gives the Israelites in Deuteronomy 4:9 and 6:12. What are significant things/moments along your journey that God is calling you to remember? What things have you experienced or learned that you are now teaching or passing down to the next generation or to your children?

5. What did the Holy Spirit highlight to you in Numbers 33 through the reading or the teaching?

# Lesson 93: Numbers 34
## Rock: Boundaries of the Promised Land

## Teaching Notes

### Intro

In the book of Numbers, the Israelites were taught to trust God, to remember God, and to accept that He would always be with them. Why? Because they were going to be entering a new place and would need to remember all that God had done for them. Numbers 33 was a time of memories. Numbers 33:53 says, "He says you are about to take this land and settle in it, for I have given you the land to possess." Genesis 15:18–21 promised, "On that day the LORD made a covenant with Abram, saying, 'I give this land to your offspring, from the brook of Egypt to the Euphrates River: the land of the Kenites, Kenizzites, Kadmonites, Hittites, Perizzites, Rephaim, Amorites, Canaanites, Girgashites, and Jebusites." Everything in Israel, even today, is about land and territories. Anytime Israel negotiates for land today, they are messing with prophesy.

### Teaching

*Numbers 34:1–12*: The Lord told Moses that when the Israelites entered the land of Canaan, it would be allotted to them as an inheritance with these borders (1 Kings 8:56). The southern border would begin at the Wilderness of Zin along the boundary of Edom, and the eastern border would be the Dead Sea (v. 3). The boundary would turn south on the Ascent of Akrabbim, proceed to Zin, and end south of Kadesh-barnea. The boundary would then go to Hazar-addar and proceed to Azmon, where it would turn to the brook of Wadi of Egypt and end at the Sea (vv. 4–5).

Israel today doesn't go all the way down. The western side would be along the coastline of the Mediterranean Sea (v. 6). Joshua 14—19 describes it a little differently, breaking the land up into the tribal lands.

The northern border would be from the Mediterranean Sea to Mount Hor, then from Mount Hor to Hamath, and the border will reach Zedad. The border will go to Ziphron and end at Hazar-enan (vv. 7–9). No matter where other countries are today, Israel will eventually have this land again. It's a matter of Scripture (Numbers 13:21; Ezekiel 47:15–17).

The eastern border will start from Hazar-enan to Shepham, from Shepham to Riblah east of Ain, down the eastern slope of the Sea of Chinnereth, and then the border will go down the Jordan and end in the Dead Sea (vv. 10–12). This is the land defined by all it borders (Genesis 15:18–21; Joshua 1).

*Numbers 34:13–19*: Moses explained to the Israelites that this was the land that nine and a half tribes would receive. The tribes of Reubenites and Gadites and half of Manasseh were not with them, because they stopped before reaching the Promised Land across the Jordan (vv. 13–15). Then Moses gave the names of the men he was appointing to distribute the land: Eleazar the priest and Joshua son of Nun (vv. 16–19).

*Numbers 34:20–29*: Each of the tribes were to send one leader to help distribute the land, and they are named in verses 20–28:

(1) Caleb, from the tribe of Judah

(2) Shemuel, from the tribe of Simeon

(3) Elidad, from the tribe of Benjamin

(4) Bukki, from the tribe of Dan

(5) Hanniel, from the tribe of Manasseh

(6) Kemuel, from the tribe of Ephraim

(7) Eli-zaphan, from the tribe of Zebulun

(8) Paltiel, from the tribe of Issachar

(9) Ahihud, from the tribe of Asher

(10) Pedahel, from the tribe of Naphtali

## Closing

We can use these ten leaders as an encouragement to us to go out and tell people there is an inheritance waiting for them . . . eternal life through Christ.

> Hebrews 9:15: "Therefore, He is the mediator of a new covenant, so that those who are called might receive the promise of the eternal inheritance, because a death has taken place for redemption from the transgressions committed under the first covenant."

They are given a land; we are given an eternal promise.

> 1 Peter 1:4: "And into an inheritance that is imperishable, uncorrupted, and unfading, kept in heaven for you."

This inheritance is never going away.

> Ephesians 1:11: "We have also received an inheritance in Him, predestined according to the purpose of the One who works out everything in agreement with the decision of His will."

> Ephesians 1:18: "I pray that the perception of your mind may be enlightened so you may know what is the hope of His calling, what are the glorious riches of His inheritance among the saints."

How can we even think about not sharing this with somebody else? I pray that you begin to understand the hope of His calling, and that you would begin to experience the glorious riches of His inheritance, so that you can say there's an inheritance waiting for you as well. The best way to get ready for the inheritance is to make sure everyone else knows about the inheritance as well.

## The Daily Word

The Lord gave Moses specific instructions on how to communicate the inheritance of the land to the Israelites. Even though they were walking into the Promised Land and knew they had an inheritance coming, Moses still needed to communicate the inheritance to the people, detailing the borders and assigning a leader from each tribe to distribute the land.

As a believer, you have an inheritance from the Lord—eternal life. Like Moses, you need to communicate to others about this inheritance. Don't keep this knowledge to yourself or assume others already know the details of your inheritance in Christ. This is one inheritance that is available for everyone to receive! Some people may never know about the inheritance of Jesus Christ unless you share it!

**The LORD spoke to Moses, "Command the Israelites and say to them: When you enter the land of Canaan, it will be allotted to you as an inheritance with these borders." —Numbers 34:1–2**

Further Scripture: Numbers 34:13; Ephesians 1:18–19; Hebrews 9:15

## Questions

1. Why was it important for the Lord to detail the borders of the Promised Land for the Israelites?

2. When a man from each tribe was needed to help divide up the land (Numbers 34:18), why do you think God appointed them rather than having Moses choose them? (Numbers 34:29; 1 Samuel 16:7b)

3. What did the Holy Spirit highlight to you in Numbers 34 through the reading or the teaching?

# Lesson 94: Numbers 35—36
*Rock*: Towns for the Levites

## Teaching Notes

### Intro

This is the end of the study on the book of Numbers. For every book of the Bible we have studied so far, we have identified one word to represent the Messiah. In Genesis, we have the *Seed* through Adam and Eve. In Exodus, Moses' writings are about the *Deliverer*, about how Moses delivered his people, and how Jesus delivered us in the New Testament. In Leviticus, we have *Atonement*, and how Christ serves as our atonement. In Numbers, we have the *Rock*, and the Messiah is our *Rock*. First Corinthians 10:4 says, "And all drank the same spiritual drink. For they drank from a spiritual rock that followed them, and that rock was Christ."

In Numbers 34, Moses was instructed to write down the 42 different stages God has taken

the Israelites through. Every step of the way, God was with them. At the end of Numbers 34, they were about to walk into the Promised Land.

### Teaching

*Numbers 35:1–5*: The Lord spoke to Moses in the plains of Moab (v. 1) and told Moses to command the Israelites to give cities and pastures from their inheritance to the Levites (v. 2). The cities would be for the Levites to live in and for their herds and flocks of animals (v. 3). The pasturelands of the cities were to extend from 500 yards on every side (v. 4). To determine these boundaries, they were to measure 1,000 yards outside the city to the east, south, west, and north with the city in the center (v. 5).

*Numbers 35:6–8*: The cities given were to include six cities of refuge, plus the 42 other cities (v. 6). The Levites were given 48 cities in all, plus pastureland (v. 7). Joshua 20:7–8 lists these six cities of refuge. Within these six refuge cities, those who had murdered someone would be safe. In Israel today, no one owns any land; it is all rented from the state. The Levites were scattered throughout the Promised Land, and each tribe was given up to four cities. Exodus 19:5–6 explained, "'Now if you will listen to Me and carefully keep My covenant, you will be My own possession out of all the peoples, although all the earth is Mine, and you will be My kingdom of priests and My holy nation.' These are the words that you are to say to the Israelites." (John 4:21–23: Jesus is saying that you are holy wherever you are.) Some commentators suggest that some of these Levitical cities were actually hamlets, or a few small houses clustered together. Each tribe was to give a certain number of cities based on their size (v. 8).

*Numbers 35:9–15*: The Lord told Moses to explain to the Israelites that when they crossed the Jordan into the land of Canaan, they were to designate cities to serve as cities of refuge. If a person killed someone unintentionally, then he had a place to flee to for safety (vv. 9–11). These designated cities would provide refuge from an avenger, so the one who killed would not be executed until he stood trial (v. 12). The Israelites were to select six cities of refuge, three cities across the Jordan river and three in Canaan (vv. 13–14), where an Israelite, alien, and sojourner, who unintentionally killed someone, could go (v. 15).

*Numbers 35:16–21*: In verses 16–21, additional instructions were given about how to treat someone who murdered someone else. If someone struck another person holding an iron object causing death, he was a murderer and must be put to death (Genesis 4:15; 9:5). If someone used a stone and caused someone to die, he, too, was judged to be a murderer and must be put to death (v. 17). If someone used a wooden object that caused someone to die, he was also judged to be a murderer and must be put to death (v. 18). In each case, a blood relative was to be the avenger of the murdered person and was to kill the murderer (v. 19). If anyone, in hatred, pushed a person or threw an object at him with malicious intent, which caused death, the one who struck him must be put to death because he was judged a murderer (v. 20–21).

*Numbers 35:22–25*: If someone accidentally pushed a person or threw an object without malicious intent and was not an enemy and the person died, the assembly was to determine guilt or innocence according to these ordinances (vv. 22–24). The assembly was to protect those found innocent from the hand of the avengers. The assembly would return him to the city of refuge he fled to, and he must live there until the high priest died. People from the city of refuge were set free with the high priest's death. Constable explained, "The death of the high priest atoned for the sins of the manslayers . . . like an animal sacrifice did."[1]

---

[1] Thomas L. Constable, *Expository Notes of Dr. Thomas Constable: Numbers*, 190, https://planobiblechapel.org/tcon/notes/pdf/numbers.pdf.

# Closing

At the end of chapter 35, God explained that the Israelites could not buy their atonement sacrifices to get released earlier. Wiersbe says, "Guilty sinners today can flee by faith to Jesus Christ and find refuge from the judgment of God. Because Jesus is the ever-living High Priest, salvation is secure forever; for He ever lives to make intersession for them."[2]

> Hebrews 6:18: "So that through two unchangeable things, in which it is impossible for God to lie, we who have fled for refuge might have strong encouragement to seize the hope set before us."
>
> Hebrews 7:25: "Therefore, He is always able to save those who come to God through Him, since He always lives to intercede for them."
>
> Romans 8:1: "Therefore, no condemnation now exists for those in Christ Jesus."

We are not stuck in cities of refuge. We have been set free through Christ.

## The Daily Word

At the end of the book of Numbers, leaders from the clan of Manasseh returned to Moses and questioned the decision made regarding the inheritance of Zelophehad's daughters. Moses answered the command of the Lord and affirmed that the leaders were right. Then Moses relayed a new command from the Lord concerning Zelophehad's daughters, their inheritance, and whom they should marry. Moses responded in humility, and he sought the Lord for wisdom before answering.

Have you ever been questioned by someone who wanted a different answer from the one you originally gave? It takes great humility to say someone else is right because that implies you were wrong. No one likes to be wrong. However, when the Lord is your *rock* and your strong foundation, being right or wrong will not faze you. As you make Christ your solid foundation, acknowledging Him and all His ways whether you are right or wrong, you will not be shaken. Today, allow the Lord to be your *rock*, and your ways will not be shaken.

---

[2] Warren W. Wiersbe, *The Bible Exposition Commentary: Genesis–Deuteronomy* (Colorado Springs: David C. Cook Publishers, 2001), 369.

So Moses commanded the Israelites at the word of the LORD, "What the tribe of Joseph's descendants says is right. This is what the LORD has commanded concerning Zelophehad's daughters." —Numbers 36:5–6

Further Scripture: Psalm 16:8; Psalm 62:6–8; 1 Corinthians 10:3–4

## Questions

1. Once again, God made sure the Levites would be provided for when the Israelites took possession of the land (Numbers 35:2–3). Why did He do this (Numbers 18:21, 23–24; Joshua 13:14, 33)?

2. What were the cities of refuge (Numbers 35:9–12)? How long could a person who had killed someone be safe in these cities of refuge (Numbers 35:12; Deuteronomy 19:11–12)? What if he were found guilty of murder (Numbers 35:16–18)?

3. Who was responsible for putting to death the person found guilty of murder (Numbers 35:19–21)?

4. If the man who accidentally killed someone left the city of refuge, what risk did he take (Numbers 35:26–28)?

5. The "manslayer" living in a city of refuge could return to the land of his inheritance upon whose death (Numbers 35:28)? How does this point to Christ (John 6:37; Hebrews 6:18; 7:23–25)?

6. Because inheritance of the land needed to stay within the tribe to whom it was allotted, daughters who inherited their father's land were instructed to do what (Numbers 36:6–8)? Does this apply to us today, and if so, how (1 Corinthians 7:39b; 2 Corinthians 6:14)?

7. What did the Holy Spirit highlight to you in Numbers 35—36 through the reading or the teaching?

# Lesson 95: Deuteronomy 1—3
## *Prophet:* Journey to the Promised Land

## Teaching Notes

### Intro

We have gone through four books of the Pentateuch, and Deuteronomy is the fifth and final book that was written by Moses. Deuteronomy means "Second Law." Deuteronomy 17:18 says, "When he is seated on his royal throne, he is to write a copy of this instruction for himself on a scroll in the presence of the Levitical priests." Moses was supposed to make a second copy of the book of laws as his will or obituary. He was not going with them because of striking the rock in anger. Moses painted a picture over and over that God was with the Israelites, He was still with them, and He will be with them.

In our paintings, we have one word for each book of the Bible: Genesis—*Seed*, Exodus—*Deliverer*, Leviticus—*Atonement*, and Numbers—*Rock*. For Deuteronomy, the word is *Prophet*. Deuteronomy 18:15 says, "The Lord your God will raise up for you a prophet like me from among your own brothers. You must listen to him."

Jesus is that *Prophet* that Moses was talking about. "For Jesus is considered worthy of more glory than Moses, just as the builder has more honor than the house. Now every house is built by someone, but the One who built everything is God. Moses was faithful as a servant in all God's household, as a testimony to what would be said in the future. But Christ was faithful as a Son over His household. And we are that household if we hold on to the courage and the confidence of our hope" (Hebrews 3:3–6). Jesus quoted from every book in the Pentateuch, from eight of the prophets, and from the book of Deuteronomy 16 times.

### Teaching

*Deuteronomy 1:6–46:* The beginning of this chapter explained how God was going to honor His promises and bring forth leadership to make these things unfold (vv. 6–18). The Israelites' disobedience at Kadesh-barnea was covered in verses 19–46.

*Deuteronomy 2*: The Israelites journeyed through the Transjordan area, along the east side of the Jordan River.

*Deuteronomy 3:1–7*: Moses released his first sermon, reliving what had already happened on the journey. As they went up the road to Bashan, Og, king of Bashan, came out against the whole army (v. 1). The Lord had already said not to fear King Og because He had already given him over to the Israelites. The Lord also told the Israelites to do to King Og the same as they had done to King Sihon (v. 2). The Lord handed over Og, king of Bashan, and the whole army to the Israelites, and there were no survivors (v. 6). The cities were all captured at one time—60 in all (v. 4). Despite being fortified with high walls, gates, and bars, and a large number of rural villages (v. 5), all the cities were completely destroyed, along with the men, women, and children, as it had been done in Sihon (v. 6). Bashan was famous for their oaks (Isaiah 2:13) and livestock (Isaiah 32:14). All was subject to plunder (v. 7). Warren Wiersbe described the victories over Og and Sihon as "preparation for the battles they would fight when they arrived in Canaan."[1]

*Deuteronomy 3:8–11*: The Israelites then took the land from across the Jordan from Amon Valley to Mount Hermon (vv. 8–10). All the cities of the plateau were Gilead, Bashan, Salecah and Edrei (v. 10). "Only Og king of Bashan was left of the remnant of the Rephaim. His bed was made of iron. Isn't it in Rabbah of the Ammonites? It is 13 feet six inches long and six feet wide by a standard measure" (v. 11).

*Deuteronomy 3:12–20*: The Israelites took possession of the land, settled it, and gave it to the Reubenites, the Gadites, and half the tribe of Manassah (vv. 12–13), who wanted the land for their livestock (v. 19). Jair, a descendant of Manasseh, renamed Bashan to Jair's Villages, after himself (v. 14). Moses told them they must cross over and help fight with the Israelites for their land, and lead the way (v. 18):

> Deuteronomy 12:10: "When you cross the Jordan and live in the land the Lord your God is giving you to inherit, and He gives you rest from all the enemies around you and you live in security . . ." They would find rest when there was victory.

---

[1] Warren W. Wiersbe, *The Bible Exposition Commentary: Genesis–Deuteronomy* (Colorado Springs: David C. Cook, 2001), 379.

> Deuteronomy 25:19: "When the Lord your God gives you rest from all the enemies around you in the land the Lord your God is giving you to possess as an inheritance . . ."

*Deuteronomy 3:21–29*: Wiersbe explained that the Israelites first had to prepare for more battles, begin to settle into the land, and then begin the transfer of leadership from Moses to Joshua (vv. 21–22).[2] Joshua had already seen everything the Lord had done and knew that the Lord would do the same to all the kingdoms they entered.

> Numbers 27:18: "The Lord replied to Moses, 'Take Joshua son of Nun, a man who has the Spirit in him, and lay your hands on him.'"

In Exodus 33, we saw how Joshua was a servant to Moses. He had been trained in every way possible, ownership had been transferred, and now Joshua was ready to run. Moses begged the Lord to let him cross over to the Promised Land, but the Lord answered that He was angry with Moses because he would not listen. According to verse 26, the Lord told Moses, "Do not speak to Me about this matter." The Lord did allow Moses to look over into the Promised Land from the top of Mount Pisgah (v. 27). After Moses viewed the Promised Land, he was instructed to commission Joshua (v. 28).

## Closing

Moses prepared the people by telling them that a *Prophet* was coming, and he also prepared Joshua to lead the charge. In the New Testament, I think of John the Baptist preparing the way for someone greater, who was coming. John baptized Jesus, and it was like a transfer of "here we go."

Deuteronomy 1 starts with a review about how the Lord was going to honor His promises. Then, there was the peoples' rebellion at Kadesh-barnea because they didn't trust God. In Deuteronomy 2, we saw the journey through the Transjordan and how the Lord gave the Israelites victory over Sihon and Og. Finally, in Deuteronomy 3 we saw the battles with the inhabitants of the land before going into the Promised Land. Then, Moses turned his leadership over to Joshua, but God allowed him to see the Promised Land.

---

[2] Wiersbe, 379.

## The Daily Word

In the opening chapters of the book of Deuteronomy, Moses readied the people for what was ahead. As he prepared the new generation of Israelites for the Promised Land, Moses reminded them of all that had taken place up to this point. In doing so, Moses recalled how he pleaded with the Lord to "please" reconsider the decision to not allow him into the Promised Land. But the Lord said no once again. Even so, God softened His answer and allowed Moses to see the land with his own eyes by going to the top of Pisgah, overlooking the land.

Have you ever asked the Lord to reconsider His decision for your life? "Can I please move back to my old home?" "Will you please make my child well again?" "Can I please have my job back?" It's hard to not have what you want or what you think is best for your life, but God promises He has a plan and will work all things together for good. It may not always make sense at the time, but choose to rest in the Lord, trusting that He has plans not to harm you but to give you a hope and a future.

**At that time I begged the LORD . . . Please let me cross over and see the beautiful land on the other side of the Jordan, that good hill country and Lebanon. —Deuteronomy 3:23, 25**

Further Scripture: Isaiah 55:8; Jeremiah 29:11; Romans 8:28

## Questions

1. In the first chapter of Deuteronomy, who was Moses telling this history to?

2. In Deuteronomy 3:6–7, who did the Israelites destroy? What did they keep?

3. In Deuteronomy 3:25–26, Moses asked the Lord to be allowed to cross the Jordan and see the Promised Land. The Lord said, "*No,*" and not to ask again. Why was Moses told no (Numbers 20:8–12)?

4. When Moses was denied crossing into the Promised Land, what did the Lord tell him to do in verses 27–28? Was this a final blessing for Moses? Why or why not?

5. What did the Holy Spirit highlight to you in Deuteronomy 1—3 through the reading or the teaching?

# Lesson 96: Deuteronomy 4—6

*Prophet*: Instructions Before Entering
the Promised Land

## Teaching Notes

### Intro

Moses began his sermon in Deuteronomy 1—3. He talked directly to the young
Israelites, reminding them of the battles they had gone through and telling them
that Joshua would be taking over.

### Teaching

*Deuteronomy 4*: This chapter provides instructions on how to live as wise people
(vv. 1–40), what the cities of refuge were and what they were for (vv. 41–43), and
because they were a people who forgot things, Moses went over the instructions
again (vv. 44–49).

*Deuteronomy 5*: This chapter provides information of the Lord's covenant with
His people (vv. 1–5), the Ten Commandments (vv. 6–22), and that Moses was
the mediator between the Israelites and God (vv. 23–33).

Deuteronomy 6 is an important chapter for the Israelites and for the Jewish
culture today. Wiersbe explained that "God gave His law not only to guide people individually but also for a nation collectively."[1] There were 613 laws given,
and the religious leaders were taking those laws and adding traditions to the point
that it became unbearable. Israel today is depressing because the people can't live
up to all the laws and regulations. Acts 15:10 talks about the yoke of the law on
the Jews. Galatians 5:1 says that Christ has set us free from that weight; Psalm
119:14, 45, 103, 105 also talk of the riches and sweetness in the law. Even within
the law there is freedom.

*Deuteronomy 6:1–3:* Moses said that the teachings from God were to follow the
Israelites into the Promised Land (v. 1). They were to fear the Lord their God so

---

[1] Warren Wiersbe, *The Bible Exposition Commentary: Genesis–Deuteronomy* (Colorado Springs:
David C. Cook, 2001), 388.

their sons and grandsons would have a long life (v. 2). Moses told them to listen and follow God's commands carefully so they would prosper and multiply in the land of milk and honey.

> Deuteronomy 4:40: "Keep His statutes and commands, which I am giving you today, so that you and your children after you may prosper and so that you may live long in the land the LORD your God is giving you for all time."

> Deuteronomy 18:5: "For Yahweh your God has chosen him and his sons from all your tribes to stand and minister in His name from now on."

If the Israelites chose to do something outside the will of God, it could shorten their lives.

*Deuteronomy 6:4—6:* These verses are called the Shema and are directed to "the Lord Your God." The Israelites were instructed to love the Lord their God with all their heart, soul, and strength. Jesus quoted this in Matthew 22:37 (also found in Mark 12 and Luke 10). Deuteronomy 11:1: "Therefore, love the Lord your God and always keep His mandate and His statutes, ordinances, and commands." These were words to be kept in their hearts (Deuteronomy 11:18; Psalms 37:31; 40:8; Jeremiah 31:33).

> Colossians 3:16: "Let the message about the Messiah dwell richly among you, teaching and admonishing one another in all wisdom, and singing psalms, hymns, and spiritual songs, with gratitude in your hearts to God."

Most people don't share the Word of God because they fear what they will say. If the Word of God is inside of us, the Holy Spirit will speak through you. We don't have to worry about what we will say.

*Deuteronomy 6:7—9:* Moses instructed the Israelites to repeat these commands to their children and to talk about them when they sat in their houses, walked along the road, woke in the morning, and retired at night. Further, he told them to bind them on their hands and foreheads as a visual symbol of their obedience. These symbols are phylacteries, which are boxes that contain small scrolls of Scripture. They are worn while in prayer. Jews still wear these today.

Moses also told them to write the commands on the doorposts of their houses and gates in what is called a Mezuzah, a small vessel that was (and is) attached to the doorposts. Inside the Mezuzah is a small scroll with Deuteronomy 6:4–9, 11, 13, 21, and God's name, Shaddai. Sadly, when the object becomes more important than what's in the heart, the point of the Shema has been totally missed.

*Deuteronomy 6:10–19*: Moses reminded the people that when they walked the land God promised, they must not forget their God. They were to fear God and worship Him and not follow other gods for their God is a jealous God. They were not to test their God as they had at Massah and were to observe all the commands, decrees, and statutes He had given them. Therefore, the people were to do what is right and good in God's sight so they could enter the land promised to their fathers and drive out their enemies.

*Deuteronomy 6:20–25*: Moses told the people that when their sons asked the meaning of the decrees, statutes, and ordinances, they were to tell them that they had been slaves in Egypt that had been brought out by God, after He had inflicted great signs and wonders on Pharaoh and his household. Also, they were to tell their sons that God had brought them to the land He had given their fathers and that He had commanded them to follow those statutes and to fear Him. Finally, Moses reminded them that righteousness would be theirs if they followed these commands. Nelson's commentary put it this way: "Moses didn't offer people a works-righteousness by keeping the law. Righteousness, the right relationship with God. God initiates this relationship, and His children respond to it as an expression of love"[2] (Romans 7:10; James 2:10; Romans 10:1–10; Galatians 3:11–13).

# Closing

If you get anything out of this message, let it be that righteousness does not come before faith, but rather, faith leads to righteousness. Moses went over the instructions that God had given the Israelites to follow before going into the Promised Land. He told them to remember the Ten Commandments that God had given them and the covenants the Lord had made with them. In Deuteronomy 6, Moses instructed the Israelites to keep the Lord's commands by writing them on their hearts. They were to remember that their God is a jealous God. They were to remind their children of what the Lord did for them in Egypt. Righteousness would be theirs if they followed the Lord's commands.

---

[2] Wiersbe, 388.

## The Daily Word

Moses gave the Israelites the most important commandment to remember before they entered into the Promised Land. They were to love the Lord with all their heart, soul, and strength. These verses are known as the *Shema* and are the greatest commandments. The words from the Lord were to be in their hearts. Yes, teach them to your children. Yes, talk about them when you come and go. Yes, bind them to your hand and forehead. Yes, write them on the doorposts of your house and gate. But first, put them in your heart.

As brothers and sisters in Christ, the Lord is interested in your heart relationship with Him, not about the law or the outward appearance. First examine your heart and your love for the Lord. Living Christ's love on the outside will happen naturally when your heart is filled up with a love for Christ.

**Listen, Israel. The LORD our God, the LORD is One. Love the LORD your God with all your heart, with all your soul, and with all your strength. These words that I am giving you today are to be in your heart. Repeat them to your children. Talk about them when you sit in your house and when you walk along the road, when you lie down and when you get up. Bind them as a sign on your hand and let them be a symbol on your forehead. Write them on the doorposts of your house and on your gate. —Deuteronomy 6:4–9**

Further Scripture: Proverbs 4:23; Proverbs 21:2; Luke 6:45

## Questions

1. In Deuteronomy 4:24, Moses told the people that the Lord their God is a consuming fire, a jealous God. What and who is God jealous for/of?

2. When you read Deuteronomy 4:29, how does it make you feel? Do you see yourself seeking God this way? Why or why not?

3. Where else in the Pentateuch do you see these same commandments listed in Deuteronomy 5?

4. In Deuteronomy 6:16, the Israelites were told to not tempt the Lord their God, and this is quoted in Matthew 4:7 and Luke 4:12. What do you think tempting the Lord looks like?

5. What did the Holy Spirit highlight to you in Deuteronomy 4—6 through the reading or the teaching?

# Lesson 97: Deuteronomy 7—9
*Prophet*: Remember What You Have Been Taught

## Teaching Notes

### Intro

Deuteronomy means the "Second Law." Deuteronomy 17:18: "When he is seated on his royal throne, he is to write a copy of this instruction for himself on a scroll in the presence of the Levitical priests." This was not a new law; it was just reinstating what they had already been told by their forefathers. Moses was preaching this sermon at the Plains of Moab to the young Israelites. Deuteronomy 6 explains that this law had to be on the Israelites' hearts first.

### Teaching

*Deuteronomy 7*: This chapter provides tangible instructions about the conquest of the Promised Land.

*Deuteronomy 8:1–10*: Moses reminded the Israelites the importance of following God's commands so they would live and multiply and take possession of the Promised Land (v. 1). He then reminded the Israelites of the 40-year journey God had taken them through in the wilderness (v. 2). Moses used the word "remember" four times over the next few chapters, emphasizing the Israelites' response to what God had done for them in the past. Wiersbe points out that "the devil tempts us to bring out the worst in us, but God tests us to bring out the best in us":[1]

> 1 Peter 1:6–7: You rejoice in this, though now for a short time you have had to struggle in various trials so that the genuineness of your faith—more valuable than gold, which perishes though refined by fire—may result in praise, glory, and honor at the revelation of Jesus Christ.
>
> James 1:3: "Knowing that the testing of your faith produces endurance."

---

[1] Warren W. Wiersbe, *The Bible Exposition Commentary: Genesis–Deuteronomy* (Colorado Springs: David C. Cook, 2001), 395.

> Psalm 17:3: "You have tested my heart; You have examined me at night. You have tried me and found nothing evil; I have determined that my mouth will not sin."
>
> Psalm 66:10: "For You, God, tested us; You refined us as silver is refined."
>
> Revelation 2:23: "I will kill her children with the plague. Then all the churches will know that I am the One who examines minds and hearts, and I will give to each of you according to your works."

Moses pointed out that God had humbled His people by letting them go hungry (v. 3), and then giving them manna, something their fathers had not even known of. All this, so that His people might learn that they did not live on bread alone (Matthew 4:4; John 4:34). Wiersbe said that "each morning during their wilderness journey, God sent the Jewish people "angels' food" to teach them to depend on Him for what they needed."[2] God has given us a teachable spirit to receive His teachings.

In verse 4, Moses reminded the Israelites that while on that journey their clothes did not wear out and their feet did not swell. Wiersbe points out that this was a sign of God's care for them.[3] Jesus expressed God's care in Matthew 6:31–33: "So don't worry, saying, 'What will we eat?' or 'What will we drink?' or 'What will we wear?' For the idolaters eagerly seek all these things, and your heavenly Father knows that you need them. But seek first the kingdom of God and His righteousness, and all these things will be provided for you" (Nehemiah 9:21; Psalm 37; 1 Peter 5:7).

In verse 5, Moses reminded the Israelites that God had been disciplining them as a father would his son. Wiersbe states that "discipline is an evidence of God's love and of our membership in God's family."[4] Discipline implies we don't have an option; testing gives us an option. When God disciplines us, we will see fruit.

> Hebrew 12:5–11: "And you have forgotten the exhortation that addresses you as sons: My son, do not take the Lord's discipline lightly or faint when you are reproved by Him, for the Lord disciplines the one He loves and punishes every son He receives. Endure suffering as discipline: God is dealing with you as sons. For what son is there that a father does not discipline? But if you are without discipline—which all

---

[2] Wiersbe, 395.

[3] Wiersbe, 396.

[4] Wiersbe, 396.

receive—then you are illegitimate children and not sons. Furthermore, we had natural fathers discipline us, and we respected them. Shouldn't we submit even more to the Father of spirits and live? For they disciplined us for a short time based on what seemed good to them, but He does it for our benefit, so that we can share His holiness. No discipline seems enjoyable at the time, but painful. Later on, however, it yields the fruit of peace and righteousness to those who have been trained by it."

Moses then repeated the instructions that were most important to the Israelites. They were to keep God's commands by walking in His ways and by fearing Him. Then, God would give them abundance in the Promised Land (vv. 6–7). Moses told the Israelites that God was going to pour out His blessings on them, and that they should remember His commands (vv. 10–14).

## Closing

Deuteronomy 9 is about Israel's history and future—Israel's self-righteousness and rebellion, and Moses' intercession. Moses continued to remind the Israelites of the Lord's commands. He wanted them to remember all that they had gone through, and all that the Lord had taught them. Over and over again, Moses instructed the Israelites to look at all God had done and to keep His commands so they would be blessed. The Lord had tested, taught, and disciplined the Israelites during the 40 years in the wilderness.

## The Daily Word

As the Israelites approached the Promised Land, Moses reminded them of God's faithfulness to them over the years: deliverance out of bondage in Egypt and His provision and power through their wandering in the wilderness.

Whenever you prepare to enter a new season, take time to reflect and remember God's faithfulness in your life. Take note of the specific wonders of His power and tender care along the way. And as you look ahead to the future with its unknowns, do not be afraid. Remember, God is the same yesterday, today, and tomorrow. He will be with you all the days ahead in faithful, powerful ways!

**Do not be afraid of them. Be sure to remember what the LORD your God did to Pharaoh and all Egypt: the great trials that you saw, the signs and wonders, the strong hand and outstretched arm, by which the LORD your God brought you out. The LORD your God will do the same to all the peoples you fear. —Deuteronomy 7:18–19**

Further Scripture: Psalm 77:11–12; Psalm 98:3; Hebrews 13:8

# Questions

1. Why did God tell the Israelites not to intermarry with other nations? What were the consequences of disobeying? (Deuteronomy 7:3–4; 2 Corinthians 6:14)

2. In Deuteronomy 7:1–2, Moses told the Israelites that the nations they were to drive out were greater and mightier than them. Whose strength were they to rely on? How do you react when facing something greater or mightier than you? Recall a time when God's strength carried you through a situation mightier than you. (2 Corinthians 12:9)

3. Why was Israel chosen as God's holy people (Deuteronomy 7:6–8)? Why does God choose us (Romans 5:8; 1 Corinthians 1:9; 1 Peter 2:9)? How do you feel knowing God loves you this much?

4. Why did God humble and test the Israelites (Deuteronomy 8:2–5; Romans 5:3–5)? How do you react when He tests your faith or disciplines you?

5. Jesus spoke the words written in Deuteronomy 8:3b when He was being tempted by Satan (Matthew 4:4). How are we to live this out in our life?

6. What did the Holy Spirit highlight to you in Deuteronomy 7—9 through the reading or the teaching?

# Lesson 98: Deuteronomy 10—12
## Prophet: Covenant—Remember and Obey

## Teaching Notes

### Intro

My prayer is that the Lord would continue to speak to you and that this study is not a legalistic thing but about the heart condition. Remember, God is going to test your heart. After He tests you, He teaches you. Some of us are going through a discipline phase right now, but after that comes the fruit.

### Teaching

*Deuteronomy 10*: The covenant was renewed (vv. 1–11), and the Israelites were told what it would take to walk this out (vv. 12–22).

*Deuteronomy 11*: The Israelites were to remember the things God had done for them and to obey His instructions. They were told they would be a blessing if they obeyed and a curse if they did not.

*Deuteronomy 12:1–7*: MacArthur observes that "Moses then explained specific laws that would help the people subordinate every area of their lives to the Lord."[1] Moses instructed them to follow these statutes and ordinances. They had not gotten into the Promised Land yet, but they been told it was already theirs (v. 1). When they arrived, they were to destroy completely all the nations that were worshipping their gods, everywhere—the mountains where they worshipped their false gods and the trees that symbolized fertility (v. 3), and their altars, their pillars, and their carved images (v. 4). This would allow the Israelites to worship the Lord. We don't have Asherah poles today, but we do have to be careful that things don't pull us away from the Lord (Ephesians 4:27). Instead, they were to go to the place of God's choosing for the tabernacle (v. 5).

---

[1] John MacArthur, *The MacArthur Bible Commentary* (Nashville: Thomas Nelson, 2005), 214.

The tabernacle moved from place to place:

- Joshua 18:1: "The entire Israelite community assembled at Shiloh where it set up the tent of meeting there; the land had been subdued by them."
- Joshua 18:10: "Joshua cast lots for them at Shiloh in the presence of the LORD where he distributed the land to the Israelites according to their divisions."
- Joshua 8:30: "At that time Joshua built an altar on Mount Ebal to the LORD, the God of Israel."
- Joshua 24:1: "Joshua assembled all the tribes of Israel at Shechem and summoned Israel's elders, leaders, judges, and officers, and they presented themselves before God."
- 1 Samuel 7:6: "When they gathered at Mizpah, they drew water and poured it out in the LORD's presence."
- 1 Samuel 21:1–6: "David went to Ahimelech the priest at Nob. Ahimelech was afraid to meet David, so he said to him, 'Why are you alone and no one is with you?' David answered Ahimelech the priest, 'The king gave me a mission, but he told me, "Don't let anyone know anything about the mission I'm sending you on or what I have ordered you to do." I have stationed my young men at a certain place. Now what do you have on hand? Give me five loaves of bread or whatever can be found.' The priest told him, 'There is no ordinary bread on hand. However, there is consecrated bread, but the young men may eat it only if they have kept themselves from women.' David answered him, 'I swear that women are being kept from us, as always when I go out to battle. The young men's bodies are consecrated even on an ordinary mission, so of course their bodies are consecrated today.' So the priest gave him the consecrated bread, for there was no bread there except the bread of the Presence that had been removed from the presence of the LORD. When the bread was removed, it had been replaced with warm bread."
- 2 Samuel 6:12: "It was reported to King David: 'The LORD has blessed Obed-edom's family and all that belongs to him because of the ark of God.' So David went and had the ark of God brought up from Obed-edom's house to the city of David with rejoicing."
- Psalm 132:13–14: "For the LORD has chosen Zion; He has desired it for His home: 'This is My resting place forever; I will make My home here because I have desired it.'"

The tabernacle moved from place to place, even after the Israelites settled into the Promised Land. The takeaway from this was to tear down the altars, smash the pillars, cut down the carved images of gods and wipe out their names. I know we don't have altars and carved images, but there may be places in your life where you might be tempted by the devil. Remove them! Ephesians 4:27 explains: "and don't give the Devil an opportunity."

Let's take a right turn here. Look at John 2:18–22: "So the Jews replied to Him, 'What sign of authority will You show us for doing these things?' Jesus answered, 'Destroy this sanctuary, and I will raise it up in three days.' Therefore, the Jews said, 'This sanctuary took 46 years to build, and will You raise it up in three days?' But He was speaking about the sanctuary of His body. When He was raised from the dead, His disciples remembered that He had said this. And they believed the Scripture and the statement Jesus had made."

The tabernacle later became the temple, but the sanctuary Jesus was talking about is Himself. John 1:14 says, "The Word became flesh and took up residence among us." We went from a portable tabernacle to a stationary temple to Christ in us. In Deuteronomy 12:5, Moses was giving a prophetic word about Jesus becoming the sanctuary and then dwelling within us. 1 Corinthians 6:19 says, "Don't you know that your body is a sanctuary of the Holy Spirit who is in you, whom you have from God? You are not your own." Now, your body is a sanctuary of the Holy Spirit. Hebrews 5 and 6 say we should be teaching this message in order to equip others—we are a walking sanctuary of the Holy Spirit wherever we go!

*Deuteronomy 12:8*: Do what is right in His eyes, not yours. We don't have the authority to do what is right in our own eyes and not do what is right in His eyes. That's what happened to the Israelites:

> Judges 17:6: "In those days there was no king in Israel; everyone did whatever he wanted." Judges 21:25: In those days there was no king in Israel; everyone did whatever he wanted." Proverbs 12:15: "A fool's way is right in his own eyes, but whoever listens to counsel is wise." Proverbs 14:12: "There is a way that seems right to a man, but its end is the way to death." Proverbs 16:2: "All a man's ways seem right to him, but the Lord evaluates the motives." Proverbs 21:2: "All a man's ways seem right to him, but the Lord evaluates the motives."

*Deuteronomy 12:9–11*: The Israelites hadn't received the land yet. When they come into the land, they must turn to Him in the place of His choosing. When we realize that we are functioning as a sanctuary of the Holy Spirit, we have nothing to worry about.

# Closing

God wanted the Israelites to seek Him. Ultimately, that's what Jesus is saying: "I am the way, the truth and the life" (John 14:6). When you come to Jesus, you become the sanctuary of the Holy Spirit. You now have Him inside of you.

## The Daily Word

Out of all the peoples of the Earth, the Israelites were blessed and chosen by God to be His. From the highest heavens above to everything on the earth below, it all belongs to the Lord.

As a follower of Christ, the Lord chose you—yes, you—to love and bless and call His own. You are chosen. You are set apart. You are known. You are loved beyond what you can imagine. The Lord called you out of darkness and into His marvelous light. Breathe in these grace-filled truths, and let all the lies of the enemy fall to the side. Today, proclaim the praises of the Lord God Almighty!

**The heavens, indeed the highest heavens, belong to the LORD your God, as does the earth and everything in it. Yet the LORD was devoted to your fathers and loved them. He chose their descendants after them—He chose you out of all the peoples, as it is today. —Deuteronomy 10:14–15**

Further Scripture: Deuteronomy 14:2; Jeremiah 1:5; 1 Peter 2:9

## Questions

1. Moses created a great visual, whether he meant to or not, of Israel breaking God's commandments when he broke the two tablets of the Ten Commandments (Exodus 32:19; Deuteronomy 10:2). How do you see God's grace in replacing the tablets and His desire for us to have His written word (Deuteronomy 10:3–5; 2 Timothy 3:16)?

2. After everything the Lord had done for the Israelites, what were the only things He was asking of them (Deuteronomy 10:12–13; Micah 6:8)? What does this look like in your own life?

3. God commanded the Israelites to do something that only He could do in them. What has always been God's concern for us even from the beginning (Genesis 1:26; Deuteronomy 10:16; Jeremiah 4:4; Luke 10:27; Romans 2:29)?

4. Meditate on God's character described in Deuteronomy 10:17–21. How can you be more like Him in these areas described (Psalms 68:5; 146:9; Acts 10:34)?

5. Read Deuteronomy 11:18–20. What does God desire for us to do in the home? How important is passing on God's truth to the next generation? What are the consequences for not passing it down? Are we seeing those consequences in our own generation? Why or why not?

6. What did the Holy Spirit highlight to you in Deuteronomy 10—12 through the reading or the teaching?

# Lesson 99: Deuteronomy 13—14
*Prophet*: False Prophets

## Teaching Notes

### Intro

Deuteronomy 12:32 says, "You must be careful to do everything I command you; do not add anything to it or take anything away from it." The law can't be added to or taken away from. It is what it is. This is the transition into Deuteronomy 13, where Scripture says to beware of false prophets and teachers who lure you into false thinking and to follow them instead of following Christ.

### Teaching

What is a prophet? Eugene Merrill defines a prophet as "a spokesperson for God who represent Him before others."[1] Prophets were proclaimers (Exodus 4:15–16) and forthtellers (Exodus 7:1). Aaron will fulfill the role of high priest; he will also communicate as a prophet.

*Deuteronomy 13:1–5*: Warren Wiersbe talks about three types of temptations to consider in Deuteronomy 13. The first is the temptation from false prophets (vv.1–5).[2] Moses described the false prophet as someone who comes with a dream or proclaims a sign or wonder that required the worship of other gods (vv. 1–2). In verse 4, Moses said to not only follow God but to fear Him. They were to "keep His commands and listen to His voice; you must worship Him and remain faithful to Him" (v. 4). For information on testing, see 1 Peter 1:6–7; James 1:2–4; Matthew 7:15; 2 Corinthians 11:3–4; and 1 Timothy 1:6–7. There are times when we're going to be refined and tested and we have to rely on the Word of God, not on these false things. The false teachers will perish and go away. Our job is to test everything we hear and align it with God's Word.

---

[1] Eugene Merrill, *Deuteronomy: An Exegetical and Theological Exposition of Holy Scripture*, New American Commentary (Nashville: Holman, 1994), 230; quoted in Thomas L. Constable, *Expository Notes of Dr. Thomas Constable: Deuteronomy*, 93–94, https://planobiblechapel.org/tcon/notes/pdf/deuteronomy.pdf.

[2] Warren W. Wiersbe, *The Bible Exposition Commentary: Genesis–Deuteronomy* (Colorado Springs: David C. Cook, 2001), 407.

Moses said false prophets must be put to death because they were taking people away from God (v. 5). In Deuteronomy, the phrase "purge the evil from you" is used eight times. Why? Because people that turn others away from God are detestable to Him (1 Corinthians 5:6–8, 13). Wiersbe says that "just as a surgeon removes cancerous tissue from a patient's body to keep it from spreading, so the local body of believers must experience surgery, no matter how painful, to maintain the spiritual health of the church."[3] No matter how painful, the person who is turning others away from God has to be removed or it will get worse. Constable says, "God permitted prophets to utter false prophecies in order to test His people's love, specifically to see if they would remain loyal to Him."[4] God allows false prophets to come into the environment to test the love of His people for their Lord.

To keep God's commands and hear His voice (v. 4) means to understand that the Holy Spirit is constantly speaking to us, directing us based on the Word of God. He will never contradict, add to, or remove any portion of Scripture. A false mentality, received from the evil spirit world, will lead people away from God and the truth. There is no way around it. The people receive it because of their flesh, because of the world they operate in, or from the evil spirit world. Think of Pharaoh's magicians that Moses interacted with (Exodus 7; 11; 22). They were receiving things that actually mimicked the truth. Be alert, know the truth, and be careful you don't fall because of information from false prophets.

*Deuteronomy 13:6–11*: The second temptation Wiersbe gives that the Israelites had to face was the temptation from family and friends (vv. 6–11).[5] Verses 7–8 say to keep the friends and family members as far away as possible, and it emphasizes not to spare or shield someone who would lead you down a false path. This includes not "going along with it" just because you feel sorry for them; not even listening to what they have to say; not touching horoscopes or experiencing something enticing you know nothing about; not giving in just because you want to "be there for them" or "help" them.

Solomon's wives created problems for him. King Solomon had 700 wives (including Pharaoh's daughter) and 300 concubines (from many nations) whom he was attached to and loved (1 Kings 11:1–3). They were all from nations that they were not supposed to intermarry with. These women lured and turned Solomon's heart away from God (Matthew 10:21). Jesus said this would happen—this constant tension as you continue to walk with the Lord. Our ministry hears questions like this all the time: "Why do you want to follow Jesus and give

---

[3] Wiersbe, 408.

[4] Thomas L. Constable, *Expository Notes of Dr. Thomas Constable: Deuteronomy*, 95, https://planobiblechapel.org/tcon/notes/pdf/deuteronomy.pdf.

[5] Wiersbe, 408.

everything up?" "Come back, you'll be fine. You do not have to do this all the time." "You don't have to raise your support, that's silly." We need to love God more than our family. It's our family that, sometimes, tries to lure us back from our actual calling (Matthew 10:34–36).

As brothers, Moses and Aaron felt immediate tension when Aaron was caught worshipping the golden calf (Exodus 32). Division between brothers happened instantly. Be careful of advice from family and friends that goes against what we know to be truth. At times, we are called to actually hate our family and it sounds drastic (Luke 14:26). We must be in tune with God's word so that we are always growing in discernment.

Verse 9 commands that the idolater—the one who created the temptation—be killed and all the people were to join in. The command continues in verse 10—to stone the idolater to death. Although others were not enticed, the idolater was still guilty. Why be so extreme? So that all Israel will hear and know not to do anything this evil again (v. 11). They were to kill anyone who tried to turn them from the Lord. God wanted the Israelites to know He's serious about people following Him and being aligned with the Word.

*Deuteronomy 13:12–18*: Wiersbe's list of temptations has one more to add: the third temptation is the temptation of many.[6] In verse 14, three key actions are given to identify these idolaters: Inquire, Investigate, and Interrogate. Together, these words mean to do it thoroughly. If it is found that the people tried to lure them away from God, they were to die by the sword (vv. 15–16). In fact, everything in the city was to be completely destroyed, including the inhabitants and livestock. They were even to create a mound of the spoils of the city and burn it. Nothing of the ruin was to remain or be carried out of the city for personal gain. In verse 18, Moses explained that mercy and multiplication would be given to those who obeyed God and kept His commandments. The passage ended with: "doing what is right in the sight of the Lord your God."

# Closing

Temptation comes from false prophets. Temptation comes from family and friends. Temptation comes from many. This means, Church, be aware. Satan is doing everything he can to kill, steal, and destroy your belief in Him; your belief that this thing is true. God wants us to do right in the sight of the Lord. How do you do this? Simple: Inquire, investigate, and interrogate everything that comes through your lens with the Word of God.

---

[6] Wiersbe, 408.

## The Daily Word

Moses continued to give instructions to the Israelites regarding the days ahead in the Promised Land. Over and over, Moses reminded them to love the Lord their God with all their hearts and warned them not to follow false prophets or have other gods. Moses commanded the Israelites to follow God and fear Him. As the Israelites kept His commands and listened to His voice, they displayed their love for their Lord.

The same is true for believers today. As you draw closer to Jesus, you will become more attune to hearing His voice and keeping His commands because you love Him and desire to obey Him. Just as a sheep hears the voice of its shepherd and walks toward that voice, we are to follow our Shepherd's voice. What is He saying to you today?

**You must follow the LORD your God and fear Him. You must keep His commands and listen to His voice; you must worship Him and remain faithful to Him. —Deuteronomy 13:4**

Further Scripture: John 10:27; John 14:15; Revelation 3:20

## Questions

1. Deuteronomy 13:1–3 addresses false prophets and dreamers. Have you experienced a false prophet or someone who skews the message about Jesus? What did they say, and how did you respond?

2. Is it possible for a false prophet to announce a future sign or wonder that ends up taking place? How do you distinguish between a false prophet and a true prophet (Matthew 7:15–20; 24:24; 2 Timothy 4:3–4; Jeremiah 23:16)?

3. Read Matthew 10:35–37 and Luke 14:26–27. How do these verses tie in with Deuteronomy 13:6–11? In what ways can those closest to you (that is, friends and family) lead you astray from what God is calling you to? How can/do you respond to this today?

4. What were the Israelites instructed to do with the tithe of their produce in Deuteronomy 14:22–29?

5. What did the Holy Spirit highlight to you in Deuteronomy 13—14 through the reading or the teaching?

# Lesson 100: Deuteronomy 15—16
## *Prophet*: Celebrating Freedom from Bondage

## Teaching Notes

### Intro

We've made it to Lesson 100! Genesis, Exodus, Leviticus, Numbers, and now, the book of Deuteronomy. One hundred lessons of plowing through the Pentateuch. Moses was the writer for the last 100 days. We've been through some tough stuff, like Leviticus. In Deuteronomy 16, we're going to talk about festivals and feasts again. The first section of Deuteronomy 15 feels like Leviticus again as it covers debts being cancelled, the requirements for lending to the poor, and about releasing the slaves every seventh year (vv. 1–18). Then in verses 19–23, there is a discussion of giving up firstborns.

### Teaching

*Deuteronomy 16: The Importance of the Calendar*

Why the emphasis on the calendar? Warren Wiersbe explains, "God gave Israel a unique calendar to help His people remember who they were and to encourage them to review all He had done for them."[1] We are a people of forgetfulness, but God doesn't want the Israelites to forget what He did years ago, decades ago, or even centuries ago.

On the calendar, some dates were already established. On the seventh day of the calendar week, no one was to work. Every seventh year was the Sabbath year, and no one was to work. Every fiftieth year, there was no work, only celebration! There are three specific feasts the Lord said were especially important. There are seven festivals total, but we will talk about three of the feasts here.

*Deuteronomy 16:1*: The first instruction to the Israelites is to observe the month of Abib, which is the first month of the religious calendar (their Independence Day). They would observe the celebration of their release into freedom from Egypt (v. 1). The first festival is The Passover Feast, which celebrates their freedom from slavery and from Egypt (Exodus 12:8).

---

[1] Warren W. Wiersbe, *The Bible Exposition Commentary: Genesis–Deuteronomy* (Colorado Springs: David C. Cook, 2001), 415.

*Deuteronomy 16:2*: The Israelites were to sacrifice a Passover animal. How does this point to the Messiah? The hyssop flower was to be dipped in the blood of the sacrificed lamb and spread on the doorposts and lintel of each home. That blood allowed the spirit of death to pass over a household so that the death of the firstborn of that family did not occur (Exodus 12). God had set His people free and wanted them to celebrate life! Tom (on staff with TTR) gave me this sheet of paper that says: "The angel of death made his way through the land killing the firstborn of every home. But, he 'passed over' all the homes covered by the blood of the lamb."

Passover was really about Christ, but the Jews don't know it yet (1 Corinthians 5:7). For us, the Passover Feast is about remembering the death of Christ on the cross at Calvary. Jesus was the fulfillment of the Old Testament Passover because that death has already taken place. Remember that some of the feasts have not yet been fulfilled. Now the Passover Feast occurs during our calendar months (the Roman/Gregorian calendar) of March and/or April. Abib is also the first month of the religious new year.

*Deuteronomy 16:3–8*: The Israelites were not to eat leavened bread with the Passover, but should eat unleavened bread for seven days (v. 3). The Festival of Unleavened Bread reminds the Jews of how they had to leave Egypt in a hurry and couldn't wait for the leaven to make the bread rise. Unleavened bread meant "bread of hardship."

The unleavened bread of Passover points us to Jesus. Leaven represents sin. Not having "sin" present in the bread represents the sinlessness of Christ (2 Corinthians 5:21). Christ had no sin, but He became the representation of sin for us. Israelite homes were to be free of all yeast during this time. Back to the sheet of paper Tom gave me: "Sin and a Holy God cannot abide together, nor can a Holy God allow sin to go unpunished. The feast lasted seven days. The first and last were special Sabbath days." All males were expected to participate in the Passover festival and the Feast of Unleavened Bread.

Verse 4 says no yeast could even be in the territory for the seven days of Passover and no meat that was sacrificed in the evening could be kept until morning. Further, the Israelites were told not sacrifice in any town God was giving them (v. 5). They were to sacrifice only in the tabernacle, the place "where Yahweh your God chooses to have His name dwell" (v. 6). And they were to do this at twilight, the same time of day they exited Egypt. In verse 7, they were told to cook and eat the meal at the place of God's choosing and then return to their tents in the morning. In verse 8, they were told to eat no leavened bread for six days. The Passover Lamb represents Jesus Christ. Christ is the lamb who died for us. John 1:29 identifies Jesus as "the Lamb of God, who takes away the sin of the world!"

John the Baptist was preparing the way and said to look—Look! There He is, the Lamb of God who takes away our sin!

Note how "the Lamb" and "sin of the world" are represented together and how the festival of the Passover, the lamb, and the unleavened bread overlapped! First Peter 1:19 says, "but with the precious blood of Christ, like that of a lamb without defect or blemish." Over and over in Scripture, this is the picture of Christ taking upon Himself the punishment we deserved.

*Deuteronomy 16:9–13*: The Festival of Weeks was scheduled seven weeks from the start of harvest and was a celebration. They were instructed to give in proportion to how God had blessed them. Everybody was to celebrate the harvest "—you, your son and daughter, your male and female slave, the Levite within your gates, as well as the foreigner, the fatherless, and the widow among you" (v. 11).

We, too, are to celebrate! We are to celebrate going from the old life to the new life. We are to celebrate going from this point of being slaves to having been set free. Wiersbe says it's celebrating what we were and what we now are.[2]

## Closing

Why do we celebrate (Matthew 16:6; Mark 8:15; 1 Corinthians 5:7–8; 2 Corinthians 7:1; Galatians 5:9; 2 Timothy 2:19)? We are no longer celebrating with old yeast. Malice and evil aren't an option for us anymore. Wiersbe says to beware of the yeast of compromising with the things we used to do. We are no longer celebrating how we lived in hypocrisy. Even though our past was lived out in malice, evil, hypocrisy, and unbelief, we now celebrate our freedom. We can now celebrate walking free of all these things. The Israelites were physically set free from Egyptian bondage, and we are physically and spiritually set free from sins of the past. Christ is always the one that does the cleaning up.

Going back to 1 Corinthians 5:8, I leave you with this: "Therefore, let us observe the feast, not with old yeast or with the yeast of malice and evil but with the unleavened bread of sincerity and truth."

---

[2] Wiersbe, 416.

## The Daily Word

Moses continued to instruct the Israelites on how to live in the Promised Land. He commanded the Israelites to be generous to others and not have stingy hearts. The Lord is generous, giving good gifts to His children. How much more can His children be generous in return by not holding on to things?

Ask the Lord today for a generous heart. Ask Him to reveal areas in your life that need greater generosity. You can give your time, your resources, your possessions, even your entire life as an offering to the Lord. The more you walk in a spirit of generosity, the more the Lord will bless you through it all. The Lord loves a cheerful giver!

**Give to him, and don't have a stingy heart when you give, and because of this the LORD your God will bless you in all your work and in everything you do. —Deuteronomy 15:10**

Further Scripture: Luke 11:13; 2 Corinthians 9:7; 1 Timothy 6:18–19

## Questions

1. In Deuteronomy 15:12–18, at what point could a slave be set free? What were they to be given? What happened if the slave chose to stay with the family?

2. At the end of every seven years, a release was made. In Deuteronomy 15:1–3, who was released of what? Who was the exception to this release?

3. In Deuteronomy 15:7–11, the Lord spoke to the Israelites about caring for the poor and canceling debts. If you were to compare that time period with the present, are we as a society upholding these commands of the Lord? Why or why not?

4. In Deuteronomy 16:5–6, the Israelites were told to not sacrifice within their city gates but in the place of the Lord's choosing. Where is the place the Lord chose for these sacrifices?

5. What did the Holy Spirit highlight to you in Deuteronomy 15—16 through the reading or the teaching?

# Lesson 101: Deuteronomy 17—18
## *Prophet*: Priests and Prophets

## Teaching Notes

### Intro

The word for Deuteronomy is *Prophet*, and we'll talk about the role of the prophet today. Deuteronomy 17:18–19 talks about the scroll the prophet was to write upon and copy the Word of God. The prophet's release of those words is the backdrop of Deuteronomy 18.

### Teaching

*Deuteronomy 18:1–2*: As Moses wrote instructions for the prophets, he outlined the importance of the role of the priests. The whole tribe of Levi will receive no land when they enter the Promised Land and they will be dependent upon people's provision as they gave offerings (v. 1). Constable describes the Levite priests as "sojourners among the other Israelites . . . had their own cities," but received none of the land inheritance of the other tribes of Israel.[1] The Lord was the Levites' inheritance (v. 2; Matthew 6:33).

As the Levites walked out their priestly role, they couldn't be worried about provision, about where their food and money would come from. This was of the Lord; it was not their choosing (Deuteronomy 10:8–9). Moses was reiterating God's promise to the tribe of Levi. At the beginning of the Time to Revive Ministry, it felt weird to be asking for money and donations to continue to go and share the gospel and make disciples. It felt weird to go into Walmart and buy food with money people gave. It felt like everyone was watching. But if you have the mentality of a Levite, then God has specifically called you to this role. When people within the body of Christ help support this calling, you as a Levite, will understand more fully that God is your portion. It takes a while to navigate those waters, and it probably felt weird to some of the Levites at first.

*Deuteronomy 18:3–8*: When oxen, sheep, or goats were sacrificed, priests were given the shoulder, jaws, and stomach. Further, priests were given the firstfruits of

---

[1] Thomas L. Constable, *Expository Notes of Dr. Thomas Constable: Deuteronomy*, 114, https://planobiblechapel.org/tcon/notes/pdf/deuteronomy.pdf.

grain, wine, oil, and wool of sheared sheep (v. 4). As representatives of the Messiah and called into service by God, they were given the firstfruits (v. 5). There was no turning back for the Levites because this was their calling (v. 6).

I'm not going into much detail on this section because I want to save enough time to cover what I think is the most important verse in all of Deuteronomy. Just understand that, up to this point, we've been talking about the Levitical priests.

*Deuteronomy 18:9–13*: The first set of instructions for prophets were things they were not to do: do not imitate detestable customs or occult practices; do not participate in child sacrifice, divination, fortune telling, omens, sorcery; do not cast spells, consult medium/familiar spirits, or call up the dead (vv. 9–11). All of this was so abominable in God's sight that He was "driving out the nations before you because of these detestable things" (v. 12). Therefore, when coming into communities where God had already driven out these practices, don't bring them back in. He was telling them to beware of people luring them away or wanting to bring back past detestable practices. Instead, they were to come before God with a pure heart (v. 13).

Amidst all these detestable things, consider the Shema (Deuteronomy 6:4–9). Deuteronomy 6:5–6: "Love the Lord your God with all your heart, with all your soul, and with all your strength. These words that I am giving you today are to be in your heart." If this verse is on your wall or in a box, it can become legalistic if it's not in your heart. Amid all the negativity, have a heart condition for all things of God, and be different from the world.

*Deuteronomy 18:14*: The prophets were told to not give in to false prophets or they would become an abomination (v. 14). They were not to meddle in the ways of the land they went into (Exodus 22:18; Leviticus 17:7). These are two pictures of what God was saying again and again: "Don't go back to the old, I want you to experience something new." This is why we have celebrations; we were there and now we are here.

*Deuteronomy 18:15*: "The Lord your God will raise up for you a prophet like me from among your own brothers. You must listen to him." God was going to raise up a *Prophet* like Moses from one of the tribes.

Qualities of this *Prophet* include: Being an Israelite, called by God, empowered by the Holy Spirit, God's spokesman, authorized to speak in the Lord's name, a good shepherd over God's people, and authenticated by signs. The likeness of Moses points to Jesus. Moses was an Israelite, was called by the Lord, had the Spirit came upon him, was a spokesperson, was authorized, was a good shepherd, and was authenticated by signs. Moses was a prophet, and the one coming would have similar qualities and characteristics[2]:

| Likeness | Moses | Jesus |
|---|---|---|
| Spared in infancy | Exodus 2:1–10 | Matthew 2:13–15 |
| Renounced a royal place | Hebrews 11:24–27 | Philippians 2:5–8 |
| Compassion for people | Numbers 27:15–17 | Matthew 9:36 |
| Made intercession on behalf of others | Deuteronomy 9:18 | Hebrews 7:25 |
| Mediator of a covenant (middle man) | Deuteronomy 29:1 | Hebrews 8:6–7 |

John the Baptist, Peter, and Stephen all talked about Jesus being the *Prophet* of Deuteronomy 18:15 (John 1:19–27, 43–45; 5:45–47; 6:14–15; 7:40). Not only did John the Baptist prepare the way, but John recorded Philip saying, "We found Him, the one that Moses wrote about" (John 1:43–45). Over and over the signs pointed to Jesus' coming (Acts 3:17–20; 7:37; Hebrews 3:1–6).

## Closing

Everything pointed to Jesus being greater than the prophet Moses, and Moses agreed. Moses told the people: "There is going to be a *Prophet* coming and I need you to listen to Him. I, Moses, do not save people, only He can." Deuteronomy 18 was speaking of the signs of the coming Messiah's arrival.

## The Daily Word

Moses made a bold statement in the middle of talking about pagan prophets with the Israelites. Confidently, Moses said God would raise up a prophet like himself, and all must listen to the prophet that is to come. Fast forward to the New Testament where John, Peter and Stephen all refer to Moses as a prophet. They go on to confirm Jesus, not only as a *Prophet* but the promised Messiah. Moses came as a faithful servant in God's household to write about the law. And while Jesus' life parallels Moses' life in many ways, Jesus came so we may have eternal life.

As believers, you receive freedom, grace, and eternal life in Jesus Christ, the Promised Prophet. God raised up this Prophet, the Messiah, for you to listen to! What is Jesus saying to you today?

[2] Samuel J. Schultz, *Deuteronomy*, Everyman's Bible Commentary (Chicago: Moody, 1971), 7; quoted in Constable, 118.

The LORD your God will raise up for you a prophet like me from among your own brothers. You must listen to him. —Deuteronomy 18:15

Further Scripture: John 1:45; Acts 7:37; Hebrews 3:5–6

## Questions

1. If someone was caught worshipping other gods, the sun, moon or stars, what was their punishment according to Deuteronomy 17:2–7? Why do you think that more than one witness was required (Deuteronomy 19:15; Hebrews 10:28)?

2. In the event of a legal matter where a decision could not be made, it had to be presented to the Levitical priests. What would happen if someone chose to reject the verdict that was handed down (Deuteronomy 17:11–13)?

3. In Deuteronomy 18:9–12, what characteristics of people groups were listed as examples of detestable people to the Lord?

4. In Deuteronomy 18:15–19, God revealed He was giving the Israelites a *Prophet*. What reason did God give for raising up a new *Prophet*? Are Moses' words in Deuteronomy 18:15 pointing to Jesus or Moses' successor (John 1:21; 6:14; 7:40)?

5. In Deuteronomy 18:22, what did the Lord say about how they would know if a prophecy was from Him or not?

6. What did the Holy Spirit highlight to you in Deuteronomy 17—18 through the reading or the teaching?

# Lesson 102: Deuteronomy 19—20
*Prophet*: Preparing for Battle

## Teaching Notes

### Intro

Deuteronomy 19 deals with the cities of refuge in Canaan. It also explains how to deal with intentional and unintentional manslaughter, the role of neighbors, and how evil can be purged with two to three witnesses. Eugene Merrill identified Deuteronomy 20 as "a manual of warfare."[1] The Israelites hadn't gone into the land or even put together an army. First they had the manual, and then the army.

### Teaching

*Deuteronomy 20:1*: The manual begins with, if the opposing army was larger than the Israelites, they should not be afraid. God had continually shown up for the Israelites, and He was with them as they entered the Promised Land. Instead, they needed to walk by faith because the battle was God's (Exodus 15:3; Deuteronomy 20:4; Psalm 20:7).

*Deuteronomy 20:2–4*: Before the battle even began, the priest was to come forward and address the army (v. 2) and then the priests would blow the trumpets (Numbers 10:8–9). In verse 3, the message the priest was to deliver was "Do not be cowardly. Do not be afraid, alarmed, or terrified." This message was given to the patriarchs as well (Genesis 15:1; 46:3; Exodus 14:13; Isaiah 41:10; Luke 1:13, 30). Each of these were walking into new territory, into the unknown, in faith. Sometimes in the anxiety and worry of the moment, we think we have to do something ourselves. "For the LORD your God is the One who goes with you to fight for you against your enemies to give you victory" (v. 4). So the priest served as the mediator between the army and God. First Chronicles 27:5 shows the importance of priests in the battle.

---

[1] Eugene Merrill, *Deuteronomy: An Exegetical and Theological Exposition of Holy Scripture*, New American Commentary (Nashville: Broadman & Holman, 1994), 282; quoted in Thomas L. Constable, *Expository Notes of Dr. Thomas Constable: Deuteronomy*, 122, https://planobiblechapel.org/tcon/notes/pdf/deuteronomy.pdf.

*Deuteronomy 20:5*: In verse 5, exemptions from battle for soldiers were given. Nelson's commentary stated, "The exemptions indicate God's compassion for people whose minds are somewhere else (home, vineyard, wife) or whose hearts are not with Him (fear)."[2] Wiersbe identified three types of exemptions. The first exemption was about home and "was to allow the soldier to dedicate a new house to the Lord and start living in it . . . to start living in the house with his family and enjoying it."[3] This had to do with the immediacy of war, and suggests that if the soldier couldn't focus on the battle because of what he'd left behind, it would be better for him not to be there. Eugene Merrill says, "It's a well-attested fact that fear or preoccupation in the midst of a conflict can endanger the life not only of the person afflicted by it but also the person's compatriots"[4] (Luke 9:23–27; 57–62; 2 Timothy 2:4; James 1:8).

*Deuteronomy 20:6*: Wiersbe explains the second reason for an exemption was about the harvest and allowing the soldier to return home "to harvest a vineyard whose fruit the soldier hadn't yet tasted."[5] Nelson's commentary explains, "It took as many as five years for a vineyard to begin to produce. A man who had waited for several years for the first produce from his vines was allowed to oversee the vines until they produced grapes."[6] Maybe this is a picture of God's compassion for a family— being in a short battle wasn't worth the family losing their harvest.

*Deuteronomy 20:7*: Wiersbe explains the third exemption was about the honeymoon and "was to permit the engaged soldier to go home and get married."[7] Deuteronomy 24:5 says, "When a man takes a bride, he must not go out with the army or be liable for any duty. He is free to stay at home for one year so that he can bring joy to the wife he has married." We interviewed two young men who wanted to come on the mission field with the Time to Revive organization, but both were about to get married. We turned them down because we thought it was more important, at that time, for them to get their marriages established before being on the road one week per month. This seems to point to that same idea: Get your marriage grounded before you do this.

---

[2] Earl D. Radmacher, Ronald B. Allen, and H. Wayne House, eds., *Nelson's New Illustrated Bible Commentary* (Nashville: Thomas Nelson, 1999), 255.

[3] Warren W. Wiersbe, *The Bible Exposition Commentary: Genesis–Deuteronomy* (Colorado Springs: David C. Cook, 2001), 428.

[4] Merrill in Constable, 90.

[5] Wiersbe, 428.

[6] Radmacher et al., 255.

[7] Wiersbe, 428.

*Deuteronomy 20:8–9*: This is another exemption. If the soldier was afraid or a coward, they were to go home. Constable says, "God's purpose was to use only the best soldiers, those that were confident in God's promise of victory."[8] God didn't need a big army because He was in charge. Remember what happened with Gideon? He started with 32,000 men, but 22,000 turned back (Judges 7:1–3). There were too many for God to receive glory in the victory.

*Deuteronomy 20:10–15*: When coming to each city, they must first offer peace. If they accepted the peace, they became the Israelites' slaves (vv. 10–11). If the city didn't offer peace, then the Israelites would wage war and strike down all the males (vv. 12–13). Everything besides the men—women, children, all the livestock, and whatever was in the city—was to be kept as plunder (v. 14). This was what was done in distant cities (not Canaanite cites).

*Deuteronomy 20:16–18*: When they went into Canaanite cities, they were to destroy everything (v. 16–17). This was so the Canaanites would not corrupt the Israelites with their false gods (v. 18).

*Deuteronomy 20:19–20*: When the Israelites laid siege to a city for a long time, they were not to cut down the trees because the trees could provide food. However, they could cut down trees that produced no food or were needed to build "siege works against the city . . . until it falls" (v.20).

## Closing

God was getting His people ready for war. The reality is that when we wake up, we, too, are in a battle every day. Do you realize you are in a battle?

> Ephesians 6:12–18: "For our battle is not against flesh and blood, but against the rulers, against the authorities, against the world powers of this darkness, against the spiritual forces of evil in the heavens. This is why you must take up the full armor of God, so that you may be able to resist in the evil day, and having prepared everything, to take your stand. Stand, therefore, with truth like a belt around your waist, righteousness like armor on your chest, and your feet sandaled with readiness for the gospel of peace. In every situation take the shield of faith, and with it you will be able to extinguish all the flaming arrows of the evil one. Take the helmet of salvation, and the sword of the Spirit which is God's word. Pray at all times in the Spirit with every prayer and request and stay alert in this with all perseverance and intercession for all the saints."

[8] Constable, 123.

Deuteronomy 19 spells out what refuge cities were. Deuteronomy 20 explains who was going to go to battle. The priests were to be the mediators. There are three exemptions to being able to fight in the army: home, harvest, and honeymoon.

## The Daily Word

As the Israelites prepared to enter the Promised Land, the Lord prepped them for the battles ahead. It's almost as though Moses gave them a war manual. You may never be called to fight on the front lines of a physical war. However, every day as a believer in Christ, you are in a spiritual battle against the world, your own flesh, and Satan. Moses commanded the people to listen and to not be cowardly, afraid, alarmed, or terrified.

As a believer, you are to stand firm and equip yourself with the armor of God. The Lord has victory over all, and He promises to go with you to fight your enemies! Today is your day to stand and not be afraid of your enemies. The Lord will help you through whatever you face. It's going to be a great day of victory for you in Christ Jesus!

**He is to say to them: "Listen, Israel: Today you are about to engage in battle with your enemies. Do not be cowardly. Do not be afraid, alarmed, or terrified because of them. For the Lord your God is the One who goes with you to fight for you against your enemies to give you victory." —Deuteronomy 20:3–4**

Further Scripture: Psalm 20:7; Isaiah 41:10; Ephesians 6:12–13

## Questions

1. Moses had already set up three cities of refuge on the east side of the Jordan (Deuteronomy 4:41–43). How many cities did God command to set apart this time (Deuteronomy 19:2; Joshua 20:7–8)? What was the purpose for cities of refuge (Deuteronomy 19:3–6; Numbers 35:9–28)? How do these cities of refuge point to Jesus (Psalm 46:1; Hebrews 6:18)?

2. What were the Israelites to do if the Lord enlarged their territory (Deuteronomy 19:8)? What was God's condition of getting this enlarged land? (Deuteronomy 6:5; 11:22)

3. Deuteronomy 19:16–20 is the heart of the ninth commandment (Exodus 20:16). What was the penalty for bearing false witness against someone? With all the allegations going on in our own country, some real and some not, do you think this law would be effective for preventing false allegations today?

4. God told the Israelites to not be afraid of their surrounding enemies because the Lord was with them. How can you take Deuteronomy 20:1–4 and apply it to your own circumstances? How can you apply it to sharing the gospel?

5. What did God command the Israelites to do in the towns that the Lord was giving them (Deuteronomy 20:16–17)? What was His reasoning to doing something like that? (Deuteronomy 9:5; 12:30)

6. What did the Holy Spirit highlight to you in Deuteronomy 19—20 through the reading or the teaching?

# Lesson 103: Deuteronomy 21—22

*Prophet*: Unsolved Murders, Captured Women, and Rebellious Sons

## Teaching Notes

### Intro

Yesterday in Deuteronomy 20, we learned about the Israelites' preparations for war. The army wasn't formed until the book of Numbers, but they were given the manual in advance.

### Teaching

*Deuteronomy 21:1–9*: Chapter 21 begins with explaining what to do if a murder victim is found in the land God had given them and gives practical instructions for how to handle it. Wiersbe says the sin had "defiled the land."[9] If there was blood on the land, someone would have to atone for it. If a victim was found, the judges and elders were to measure the distance to nearby cities to see who would have to take responsibility for the victim (v. 2). Unresolved issues could bring about serious problems for that land (Genesis 4:10–12; 9:5–6; Psalm 9:12; Isaiah 26:21; Hebrews 12:24).

The elders of the city nearest the victim were to get a young cow that hadn't been yoked or used (v. 3) and bring the cow down to a continually flowing stream and break its neck (v. 4). The priest was instructed to come forward and pronounce a blessing and give a ruling (v. 5). Then all the elders were to wash their hands in the stream over the young cow (v. 6). Wiersbe says that they were removing the impurity that would rest on the community and that they needed to atone for their guilt by breaking the neck and offering this cow.[10] The elders were cleansing themselves of defilement (Leviticus 18:24–25). They were instructed to declare, "Our hands did not shed this blood and our eyes did not see it," and they would be absolved of the responsibility for the bloodshed (v. 7).

---

[9] Warren W. Wiersbe, *The Bible Exposition Commentary: Genesis–Deuteronomy* (Colorado Springs: David C. Cook, 2001), 430.

[10] Wiersbe, 420.

Sin leads to death. This is what Jesus did for us. Jesus died for our sins like the cow died here (Isaiah 53:8; John 1:29; Romans 6:23; 5:12; Ephesians 5:25–26; Hebrews 9:13–14; 1 John 4:14). Jesus died for Israel.

The Israelites' prayer was for God to forgive His people and not to hold this against them (v. 8). They were also told to purge themselves from the guilt of shedding innocent blood (v. 9). The only way we can now shed ourselves of the sin we've done is to turn to Christ and the blood He shed for us.

*Deuteronomy 21:10–14*: Verses 10–14 give instructions for the fair treatment of captured women. The Israelites were told that while at war, if they saw an enemy's wife and wanted her as their own, they were to take her home, shave her head, and trim her nails (vv. 10–12). Then she was to remove her former clothes, live in the Israelite's house, and mourn for her parents for 30 days. When the 30 days were over, the Israelite could take the woman as his wife (v. 13). If the Israelite was not satisfied, he was to let her go, but could not sell her for money (v. 14). They had a way to get out of the marriage, but not by selling the wife.

*Deuteronomy 21:15–17*: Verses 15–17 spell out the rights of the firstborn children. When a man had two wives, one loved and one unloved, both with two sons, and the unloved wife's son was the firstborn, he could show no favoritism over the second son (vv. 15–16). Instead, the man had to acknowledge the firstborn by birth order and give him a double portion of his inheritance (v. 17).

*Deuteronomy 21:18–21*: The final instructions were about dealing with a rebellious son—a problem child (v. 18). If a rebellious son would not listen to his mother or father and refused to change with punishment, then his parents were to bring him to a city gate where the elders were (v.19). After telling the elders that their son was stubborn and rebellious, a glutton and a drunkard, the men of the city would stone him to death (v. 20–21). They were told to purge the evil from themselves and all of Israel. Wiersbe pointed out that the sin of one person could impact the entire nation.[11]

In the story of the prodigal son (Luke 15:11–13), the son was rebellious, took his inheritance, and left to live a wicked life. When the son came back, the father went out and embraced him (Luke 15:20). He probably should have been stoned. When Jesus gave this picture, His audience would have known the penalty the son should have faced. But with the father's embrace, the son was safe from that penalty. The Father is holding us in His arms, so we don't get the death that we deserve.

---

[11] Wiersbe, 432.

*Deuteronomy 21:22–23*: If anyone is found guilty of an offense deserving death and is executed, you must hang the body on a tree, take him down that night and bury him. Anyone hung on a tree was under God's curse. The intent was to bring fear to the Israelites for disobedience to God's law. The chapter ends with the statement that they must not defile the land God had given them as an inheritance.

## Closing

Only one person took that place for us. Jesus took on the curse, and He hung on a tree:

- Galatians 3:13: "'Christ has redeemed us from the curse of the law by becoming a curse for us, because it is written: Everyone who is hung on a tree is cursed.'" Jesus takes on the cursing so we can have the blessing.
- Act 5:30: "The God of our fathers raised up Jesus, whom you had murdered by hanging Him on a tree."
- 1 Peter 2:24: "He Himself bore our sins in His body on the tree, so that, having died to sins, we might live for righteousness; you have been healed by His wounds."

Jesus heals us by taking on the curse. Christ redeemed us. He himself bore our sins. The law always points to the Messiah.

## The Daily Word

Moses' instructions to the Israelites included the law and penalty regarding stubborn and rebellious children. In the event of children who would not listen to their parents or were drunkards and gluttons, the parents were to bring their children to the elders of the city. A *drunkard* is a person affected by alcohol to the extent of losing control of one's behavior. A *glutton* is a person with a remarkably great desire or capacity for something, whether it's work or food or drink or material items. Both a drunkard and a glutton excessively seek something other than the Lord for their satisfaction.

New Testament believers can also be stubborn and rebellious. Satan may tempt you into justifying overeating, overworking, overdrinking, or overspending to the point you no longer listen to the voice of the Lord, just like rebellious children who don't listen to the voice of their parents. Every day, the Lord says to seek Him, and you will find Him when you seek Him with all your heart. The Lord's arms are always open to welcome His sons and daughters back into His unconditional love. Today, listen to the voice of the Lord, and turn back to Jesus for your satisfaction.

They will say to the elders of his city, "This son of ours is stubborn and rebellious; he doesn't obey us. He's a glutton and a drunkard." Then all the men of his city will stone him to death. You must purge the evil from you, and all Israel will hear and be afraid. —Deuteronomy 21:20–21

Further Scripture: Psalm 81:11–13; Matthew 5:6; Luke 15:20

## Questions

1. How were the Israelites supposed to cleanse the guilt of murder from their community (Deuteronomy 21:1–9)?

2. Deuteronomy 21:15–17 mentions the honoring of the firstborn son and giving him the inheritance that was rightly his. What are some examples of God circumventing this law? Why do you think He would seemingly show favoritism (Deuteronomy 10:17; 1 Samuel 16:6; 1 Chronicles 5:1–2; Romans 2:11; 9:10)?

3. What were parents to do with a son who was rebellious? (Deuteronomy 21:18–21) There is no indication in Scripture that this ever had to be done, but what are your thoughts on such a discipline? How do you see this same language (rebellious and stubborn) being used with the Israelites? (Psalms 78:8; Jeremiah 5:23)

4. How did Jesus fulfill what was written in Deuteronomy 21:22–23? (Matthew 27:57–58; John 19:31; 2 Corinthians 5:21; Galatians 3:13)

5. In Deuteronomy 22:22, if a man committed adultery with a woman, both had to die. How did Paul describe dealing with adulterers in the Church (1 Corinthians 5:1–13; 6:9–13)? How should the church respond if those same people have repented? (2 Corinthians 2:5–11)

6. What did the Holy Spirit highlight to you in Deuteronomy 21—22 through the reading or the teaching?

# Lesson 104: Deuteronomy 23—24
## *Prophet*: Lists to Live By

## Teaching Notes

### Intro

We have several lists of different things, which were created as guardrails for the Israelites. It's going to feel like we are trudging through mud. We are going to talk about inclusion and exclusion, cleanliness of the camp, neighbors' crops, and marriage—and it all feels like legalism. But what we are after is the heart condition.

### Teaching

*Deuteronomy 23*: This chapter covers the inclusion and exclusion of members into the community, the cleanliness of the camp, how to deal with fugitive slaves, the need to avoid cult prostitution, interest on loans, the importance of keeping vows, and rules for how to treat neighbors' crops.

*Deuteronomy 24:1*: It's never easy to teach on divorce, and these rules are not easy to accept. First, if a man married and found something improper about his wife, he could write a divorce certificate. She could have had a sexual sin or menstrual irregularities that prevented them from having consistent sexual relations. In Matthew 19:3, the Pharisees asked Jesus if there could be any reason for a man to divorce his wife. In the New Testament there are only two reasons for a divorce: if the husband dies, the wife could move on (Romans 7:1–3), and adultery (Deuteronomy 22:22). Divorce was not an option. Some of the best stories have come out of spouses working it out and restoring their marriage after adultery.

If the woman became another man's wife and the second man also hates her, divorces her, and sends her away, she could not go back to the first husband because she has been defiled (vv. 2–4). Marriage can be seen as two pieces of wood glued together. If the pieces are split apart, there is no way for a clean separation, because there will always be some part of the wood left on the other. That means a part of you is still with each person you have had sexual relations with.

*Deuteronomy 24:5*: A newly married man did not have to go into the military for the first year so he can make his wife happy before leaving her.

*Deuteronomy 24:6–9*: To guard the security of families' livelihoods, the Israelites were instructed not to take a millstone as a security for debt since that was how they made their living (v. 6). If someone kidnapped one of his Israelite brothers, he must die so that death would purge the evil from the community (v. 7). If someone had an infectious skin disease, the Israelites were instructed to carefully do everything the Levitical priest instructed (v. 8). Remember what the Lord did to Miriam on the journey after the Israelites left Egypt and she was stricken with leprosy (v. 9).

*Deuteronomy 24:10–13*: The next set of instructions was to show consideration of people to whom loans were made: (1) they were not to enter the house to collect what someone asking for a loan had offered as security (v. 10); (2) they were to wait for him outside while the security was brought out to the loaner (v. 11); (3) if the person receiving the loan was poor, the person who received their garment as security could not sleep in it but must give it back each night to provide them protection against the cold (v. 12); and (4) they were not to accept the only clothes the borrower owned as security (v. 13).

*Deuteronomy 24:14–18*: Hired hands who were poor were to be paid daily (vv. 14–15). Fathers were not to be put to death for punishment of their children or the children for the punishment of their fathers (v. 16). Rather, each person must be responsible for their own sins (Exodus 20:5; Joshua 7:24–25). Sin does lead to death, but, praise God, His love comes in and takes care of the death. Justice was to be given to the foreigners, orphans, and widows (v. 17). The Israelites were to remember what it had been like while they were slaves in Egypt before God redeemed them and treat these groups accordingly (v. 18).

*Deuteronomy 24:19–22*: The Israelites were instructed to leave the sheaf for the foreigners, orphans, and widows to have (v. 19). And what was left on olive trees after knocking on the branches or the vines after picking the grapes were to be left for them as well (v. 20–21), showing God's concern for the foreigners, orphans, and widows. God reminded the Israelites again that they had once been slaves and had only been redeemed through Him. Therefore, they were to do as He instructed (v. 22).

All of these instructions deal with the heart condition of how the Israelites were to treat each other justly. Jesus brings a new perspective to these instructions. Matthew 5:17–20 says, "Don't assume that I came to destroy the Law or the Prophets. I did not come to destroy but to fulfill. For I assure you: Until heaven and earth pass away, not the smallest letter or one stroke of a letter will pass from the law until all things are accomplished. Therefore, whoever breaks one of the least of these commands and teaches people to do so will be called least in the kingdom of heaven. But, whoever practices and teaches these commands will be called great in the kingdom of heaven. For I tell you, unless your righteousness surpasses that of the scribes and Pharisees, you will never enter the kingdom of heaven."

> Matthew 5:21–48: Jesus extended God's law against murder to include anger. Likewise, Jesus extended adultery to include lust, put stricter guidelines on divorce, and restrained retaliation (vv. 21–42). Then Jesus extended God's law to love our neighbors, to also include loving our enemies (vv. 43–48). The only way we can live out these conditions is if we have a heart change that is not based on legalism.

In Matthew 23:27, Jesus said, "Woe to you, scribes and Pharisees, hypocrites! You are like whitewashed tombs, which appear beautiful on the outside, but inside are full of dead men's bones and every impurity."

In Romans 8:10, Paul wrote, "Now if Christ is in you, the body is dead because of sin, but the Spirit is life because of righteousness." You can't fake walking with legalism. Jesus wants you to work on everything inside. The only way righteousness comes out is because we put our trust in Christ and not ourselves.

## Closing

Again, we are dealing with a lot of rules. Deuteronomy 23 went over who could enter the assembly, cleanliness of the camp, fugitive slaves, prostitution, loans, keeping vows, and harvesting the crops. Then, in Deuteronomy 24 we dealt with marriage, debt, kidnapping, and skin disease. Moses emphasized taking care of the needs of the people, especially the foreigner, fatherless, and widow, because the Israelites had already received God's care in their lives.

## The Daily Word

The Lord had a plan for the Israelites to care for needs in the community. When they harvested grain from the fields, fruit off the olive trees, or grapes in the vineyard, if they forgot to gather some of the crop, they were told to leave it. These "leftovers" would go to foreigners, orphans, and widows. The Lord specifically highlighted these less fortunate groups in the community, prioritizing their care.

Open your eyes to see the foreigners, orphans, and widows around you. Who has the Lord placed in your circle for you to care for and help look after? The Lord calls you to love others as Christ has loved you. Today, ask the Lord for a plan for you to love and care for the foreigners, widows, and orphans around you.

**When you reap the harvest in your field, and you forget a sheaf in the field, do not go back to get it. It is to be left for the foreigner, the fatherless, and the widow, so that the LORD your God may bless you in all the work of your hands. —Deuteronomy 24:19**

Further Scripture: Psalm 82:3; John 13:34; James 1:27

## Questions

1. Deuteronomy 23:19–20 instructed the Israelites to not charge interest to their countrymen. Who could they charge interest to? Why this distinction? What was the outcome for complying?

2. According to Deuteronomy 23:22, if making a vow to the Lord was not required, why would people make one? Have you ever made a vow to the Lord? What motivated you?

3. The Lord allowed the Israelites to divorce (Deuteronomy 24:1), but what did Jesus tell the Pharisees in Mark 10:2–9? Do you see this as a contradiction? Why or why not?

4. Do you see a correlation between Deuteronomy 24:16 and Romans 3:23?

5. The law of Moses often outlined statutes regarding strangers, orphans, and widows (Deuteronomy 24:17–22), which included both protection and provision. Why was this so important? Have you ever identified with one of these groups?

6. What did the Holy Spirit highlight to you in Deuteronomy 23—24 through the reading or the teaching?

# Lesson 105: Deuteronomy 25—26

*Prophet*: Firstfruits, Tithe, and Covenant Summary

## Teaching Notes

### Intro

Here we are in the last book of the Pentateuch and are almost transitioning to the New Testament. We are going to move from the Pentateuch to the Gospels, and then back to the historical books of the Old Testament.

### Teaching

*Deuteronomy 25*: We have more lists of rules that include the following: when there is a dispute between men, they could be flogged up to 40 times; how to preserve the family lines when a family member died; legal weights and scales; and revenge upon the Amalekites.

*Deuteronomy 26:1–4*: When they took the land, they were required to collect the firstfruits of the land, put them in a container, and place them in the tabernacle where God dwelled. Nelson's commentary points out that God wanted the Israelites to give the firstfruits, even though they could not be sure that the rest of the harvest would ripen or be harvested as a way to show they trusted God to provide for them.[1] They were to say to the priest who was serving, "Today I acknowledge to the Lord your God that I have entered the land the Lord swore to our fathers to give us." The priest then received these offerings and placed them in the tabernacle for God. Wiersbe refers to this as a "confession of God's goodness."[2]

*Deuteronomy 8:11–20*: "Be careful that you don't forget the LORD your God by failing to keep His command—the ordinances and statutes—I am giving you today. When you eat and are full, and build beautiful houses to live in, and your

---

[1] Earl D. Radmacher, Ronald B. Allen, and H. Wayne House, eds., *Nelson's New Illustrated Bible Commentary* (Nashville: Thomas Nelson, 1999), 259.

[2] Warren W. Wiersbe, *The Bible Exposition Commentary: Genesis–Deuteronomy* (Colorado Springs: David C. Cook, 2001), 422.

herds and flocks grow large, and your silver and gold multiply, and everything else you have increases, be careful that your heart doesn't become proud and you forget the LORD your God who brought you out of the land of Egypt, out of the place of slavery. He led you through the great and terrible wilderness with its poisonous snakes and scorpions, a thirsty land where there was no water. He brought water out of the flint-like rock for you. He fed you in the wilderness with manna that your fathers had not known, in order to humble and test you, so that in the end He might cause you to prosper. You may say to yourself, 'My power and my own ability have gained this wealth for me,' but remember that the LORD your God gives you the power to gain wealth, in order to confirm His covenant, He swore to your fathers, as it is today. If you ever forget the LORD your God and go after other gods to worship and bow down to them, I testify against you today that you will perish. Like the nations the LORD is about to destroy before you, you will perish if you do not obey the LORD your God."

*Deuteronomy 26:5–10*: Jacob was a wandering Aramean and father of the 12 tribes. He went to Egypt because of the famine. They took everything they had with them—all the family and all their possessions (Genesis 46:3–7). He went with a total of 70 people. Exodus 1:7 recorded: "But the Israelites were fruitful, increased rapidly, multiplied, and became extremely numerous so that the land was filled with them." Estimates are that the 70 multiplied into 2 million people and they became a great nation. The suffering and persecution they went through in Egypt led to the people multiplying (Exodus 2:23–25). The same is true in the New Testament. Every time the church was persecuted and scattered, it multiplied in numbers. God heard the groaning and the cries of the Israelites. He brought them out of Egypt with a strong arm and signs and wonders to a land flowing with milk and honey. The firstfruits from the Promised Land were offered to God and caused the Israelites to remember all that God had done for them. They bowed down to worship God. Nelson's commentary explains that "the most common Hebrew word for worship literally means 'to cause oneself to lie prostrate.'"[3] Bowing down symbolizes worship and adoration.

*Deuteronomy 26:12–15*: Wiersbe identifies these verses as "a confession of honesty and generosity."[4] When the Israelites finished paying the tenth in the third year, they were to give it to the Levite, foreigner, fatherless, and widow—those that needed it most (v. 12). Then, they were to say that they had done this in the presence of the Lord (v. 13). They had also not eaten any of it or offered it to the dead like the Canaanites. Constable points out that this means "God's

---

[3] Radmacher et al., 260.

[4] Wiersbe, 423.

people should continue to trust Him for the fulfillment of promised blessings yet unrealized."[5]

*Deuteronomy 26:16–19*: Wiersbe identifies these verses as a "confession of obedience."[6] The Israelites were to follow these commandments with all their heart and soul (Deuteronomy 6:5—called the Shema). This was also Jesus' language in Matthew 22:34–39 (Jeremiah 31:33; Ezekiel 11:19; 36:26). Wiersbe states that the first two confessions were looking forward to the land (v. 17).[7] The next one dealt with "today" as they affirmed that God is their life, as God affirmed they were His special people (v. 18) (Exodus 19:5; Malachi 3:17). God promised to elevate them to praise, fame, and glory above all nations as a holy people to the Lord (v. 19; Psalm 81:11–14, 16).

# Closing

I want to be a blessing to the nation of Israel. It is dependent upon a heart condition of loving God and loving others.

Deuteronomy 25 is more rules and regulations. Deuteronomy 26 is mainly about giving of firstfruits and giving the tithe for the first three years, then giving it to the poor the third year. These are laws that change the heart to see people as God sees them. If these concerns are in our hearts, we won't have a problem doing them.

## The Daily Word

Moses reiterated the commands, statues, and ordinances to this second generation of Israelites. They looked back and remembered God's faithfulness and redemption. They reviewed all the details of the law. And then Moses confirmed once again to the Israelite people that they must follow the Lord their God with all their hearts and with all their souls.

You may not be part of the Israelite community, but the same truth applies to your relationship with Jesus. Pause and check your heart. If your heart doesn't love the Lord fully, then following Him will begin to feel hard and burdensome. So check your heart today. Get honest with yourself and ask, "Do I love the Lord with all my heart?" Pause and listen. The heart drives our actions. When you have your heart aligned with the Lord, everything else in life will flow freely.

---

[5] Thomas L. Constable, *Expository Notes of Dr. Thomas Constable: Deuteronomy*, 152, https://planobiblechapel.org/tcon/notes/pdf/deuteronomy.pdf.

[6] Wiersbe, 424.

[7] Wiersbe, 424.

The LORD your God is commanding you this day to follow these statutes and ordinances. You must be careful to follow them with all your heart and all your soul. —Deuteronomy 26:16

Further Scripture: Proverbs 4:23; Jeremiah 31:33; Matthew 22:37–38

## Questions

1. In Deuteronomy 25:4, the law forbade muzzling an ox while he was threshing. According to 1 Corinthians 9:9–11, what is the real purpose of this law (1 Timothy 5:18)?

2. The law forbade using differing (false) weights and measures, thus cheating people (Deuteronomy 25:13–16). Does it surprise you that the Lord concerns Himself with these kinds of details for His people? (Proverbs 11:1; 16:11; 20:10)

3. According to Deuteronomy 26:16, the Lord doesn't just want obedience from His people, but He wants them to obey with all their heart and their soul. Has your obedience always been from your heart? If not, what can you do differently to change that?

4. What did the Holy Spirit highlight to you in Deuteronomy 25—26 through the reading or the teaching?

# Lesson 106: Deuteronomy 27
## *Prophet:* Living Under the Law

## Teaching Notes

### Intro

In Deuteronomy 26, we talked about giving up the firstfruits, about giving ten percent of the harvest to the poor every third year, and about the covenantal summary. Moses was with the younger Israelites, looking over the plains of Moab, and getting ready to enter the Promised Land. Deuteronomy 27 focused on God's faithfulness in the future. In Deuteronomy 27—30, Moses explained what could be expected of God's faithfulness in the future.

### Teaching

*Deuteronomy 27:1–4:* This was time for a ceremony. Moses and the commanders of the people told the Israelites to "keep every commandment." When they crossed the Jordan River into the land of Israel, to claim the land that God had already given them—it was a done deal. They were to set up large stones and cover them with plaster or lime to create a white background[8] so "all the writing can be seen." And on this backdrop, they were to write all the words of "this law" (either Deuteronomy or the entire Pentateuch) as soon as they crossed into Israel. They were to do it immediately—don't put it off, don't wait.

The place where the Israelites entered was Mt. Ebal, located north of Shechem, in the center of the Promised Land. This is the place where the Lord created the first covenant with Abraham and Abraham first built an altar to the Lord (Genesis 12:6–7). In Deuteronomy, the Israelites were told again to put up an altar. We're bookending what God has done in Genesis and Deuteronomy.

*Deuteronomy 27:5–8:* Moses instructed them to build an altar with uncut stones and forbade them to use iron tools on them. The altar was for burnt offerings—to burn up the best. The best would be completely consumed, showing complete devotion to the Lord. With the large stones, the Israelites were remembering what God had done, and with the altar of stones they were showing God their

---

[8] John MacArthur, *The MacArthur Bible Commentary* (Nashville: Thomas Nelson, 2005), 229.

devotion. We, too, can see what God has done in the past. Now it's time to give up our burnt offerings on the altar to God. Why? So that we can see God move the way we saw Him move in our fathers and our grandfathers. This was the mentality Moses was giving to the younger generation, who had seen what God had done for their forefathers.

*Deuteronomy 27:7–10*: "There you are to sacrifice fellowship offerings, eat, and rejoice in the presence of the LORD your God." As we continue to offer ourselves to the Lord, we cannot stay in the posture of, "I'm a Christian and life just stinks." Who wants to follow that faith? Moses was saying to the people, "I want you to celebrate in joy what you have in the Lord. I want you to have life." In verse 8, Moses told them to be sure to write clearly all the words of the law on the plastered stone. The Israelites were writing things down, and they were celebrating and rejoicing as proof of their devotion to God.

In verse 9, Moses and the Levitical priests spoke to all Israel and told them to be silent and to listen. This was Moses' third sermon in Deuteronomy, given at the time of transition, and wrapping up his time of leadership. He told them, "This is the day you've become the people of God." They were now receiving what God had intended for them all along—it was being passed down to them. In verse 10, Moses told them how: "Obey the Lord your God and follow His commands and statutes I am giving you today." In verses 11–12, Moses commanded the people to obey and then named the people who would stand atop Mt. Gerizim, six of the 12 tribes of Israel—Simeon, Levi, Judah, Issachar, Joseph, and Benjamin. They were told to bless the people.

In verse 13, the other six tribes—Reuben, Gad, Asher, Zebulun, Dan, and Naphtali—were to stand atop Mt. Ebal to deliver the curse to the people. Mt. Gerizim had all the vegetation, while Mt. Ebal was barren. It makes sense that on Mt. Ebal, they would deliver the curse, and on Mt. Gerizim, they would deliver the blessing. While these two groups were voicing blessings or curses in verse 14, the Levities were to release 12 curses to every Israelite.

MacArthur describes it differently, explaining that the Levite priests, who were the voice of the people, would be standing beside the Ark of the Covenant, reading both the blessings and curses, while six tribes faced Mt. Gerizim and the other six tribes faced Mt. Ebal, possibly without either group actually being on those mountains.[9] The phrase "every Israelite" suggests that the representatives of the 12 tribes would also be present, so everyone had to be able to hear what was going on. As these curses were given, the Israelites had to agree to the conditions, crying out "So be it."[10] They agreed to it.

---

[9] MacArthur, 229.

[10] MacArthur, 230.

One of the curses (v. 15) was against those who worshipped idolatry. What does it mean to be cursed? MacArthur explains that to be bound by the curse (the opposite of the blessing) meant illness and injury came across a person.[11] Wiersbe states that curses "weren't predicting what would happen . . . but were calling upon the Lord to send the curses on His people if they turned away from Him."[12] Another curse (v. 16) was for those who dishonored their fathers and mothers. Many of these tie into the Ten Commandments. Other curses were against those who moved a neighbor's boundary marker, which was a form of stealing (v. 17); those who led a blind man astray (v. 18); those who denied justice to a foreigner, an orphan, or a widow (v. 19); those who sleep with his father's wife or participate in any form of sexual immorality (bestiality, incest, adultery) (vv. 20–23); and those who commit murder in secret or accept a bribe to kill someone (vv. 24–25). We are told to love God and love our neighbor, so to kill a neighbor goes against the core of what God has told us to be.

After each of these curses, the people would answer, "Amen," to show that they accepted the curse if they were found to be disobedient. In verse 26, those who disobeyed these laws were cursed. Why was this final curse most important? Because if they didn't obey these laws (all of Deuteronomy, maybe all of the Pentateuch), they received curses. Remember when Moses first began this sermon, he told them to write everything he was telling them to do. The Israelites couldn't keep up with all the instructions. And that's the point. Israel agreed to keep God's Law on Mt. Sinai, and right after that, they built and worshipped the golden calf. They were agreeing that they were in, but then they couldn't do it. Warren Wiersbe emphasized that it takes more than learning "a religious vocabulary, and even [memorizing] Bible verses and religious songs," to be a devoted child of God (Matthew 7:21–23).[13]

Jesus was speaking to people who could not keep up with the law. We have to be careful not to become a lip-service believer—saying amen all the time. Praise the Lord that Jesus took care of this (Galatians 3:10–12). This is exactly what Moses was saying. Read James 2:10. This is key! If we can't keep up with one law, we're guilty of all.

## Closing

All sin . . . always, always . . . leads to the ultimate curse (Romans 3:23; 6:23; Galatians 3:13). Jesus redeemed us from the curse of the law because Jesus became the curse for us. Jesus knew we couldn't keep up with the laws, so He took on

---

[11] MacArthur, 230, "Key Word."

[12] Warren W. Wiersbe, *The Bible Exposition Commentary: Genesis–Deuteronomy* (Colorado Springs: David C. Cook, 2001), 441.

[13] Wiersbe, 442.

that curse for us. Do you still hang on to that curse, or did you give it all to Jesus? Deuteronomy 27 says that if you can't live up to these rules, you are cursed. And what I love about Jesus is that He says, "Give it to me. I'll take that curse for you."

## The Daily Word

Moses instructed the Israelites to write the words of the law on stones covered with plaster after they crossed into the land God had promised them. Moses did not want the people to forget the commands of the Lord. In today's world, we don't have to write the Word of the Lord on stones covered with plaster, yet the practice of writing out Bible verses is still a wise discipline.

Do you have a favorite journal, decorative notecards, a chalkboard in your home, or a whiteboard at work? All these tools can be used to write down the Word of the Lord and point you to God's truth as you go through your day. Write a Bible verse on a notecard and put it by your computer, close to the steering wheel in the car, or on your bathroom mirror. Take time to write down a Bible verse that holds meaning to you. Then as you read the verse throughout the day, give thanks to the Lord for His truth in your life.

**Write all the words of this law on the stones after you cross to enter the land the LORD your God is giving you, a land flowing with milk and honey, as Yahweh, the God of your fathers, has promised you. —Deuteronomy 27:3**

Further Scripture: Deuteronomy 6:9; Psalm 119:105; Habakkuk 2:2

## Questions

1. In Deuteronomy 27:5, the Israelites were told to build an altar of uncut stones. Why do you think they were told that no iron tool could touch the stones? Where were they to set it up? Do you think that the altar points to Christ? Why or why not?

2. In Deuteronomy 27, how many curses were there and what were they?

3. Why do you think that one-third of the curses are based on sexual sin? What do you think this meant for the Israelites (Ephesians 5:3; Colossians 3:5; 1 Thessalonians 4:1–8)?

4. In verse 26, a person is cursed if they do not heed all the words of the law. Are we still bound by these laws? Why or why not? (Galatians 3:11b–14)

5. What did the Holy Spirit highlight to you in Deuteronomy 27 through the reading or the teaching?

# Lesson 107: Deuteronomy 28
## Prophet: Receiving God's Blessings

## Teaching Notes

### Intro

We looked at Deuteronomy 27 last time, which outlined the curses the Israelites would face if they did not obey God's Law. To all 12 curses, the Israelites replied their agreement with, "*Amen!*" Deuteronomy 27:26 states that if they broke any one of the commands, they would be guilty of breaking them all. In Deuteronomy 27—28, a kind of "reprimand sandwich" was created, with the curses in chapter 27 (the top bun), the blessings for obedience in the beginning of chapter 28 (the meat part), and then more curses at the end of the chapter (the bottom bun). Usually we think of blessing/curse/blessing, but this is opposite. We're starting in the "meat section" of Deuteronomy 28.

### Teaching

*Deuteronomy 28:1*: Verse 1 says if the Israelites follow the commands Moses gave them today (remember, "today" was the day when Moses gave them the laws and told them to write them all down, Deuteronomy 27), if they chose—and it was their choice—to follow God and not themselves, God would put them far above all other nations in the world and pour out His blessings on them. Then, Moses began to name those blessings for them. God would put them above the nations of the earth, elevate them to praise, fame, and glory, and they would be a special holy people before God (Deuteronomy 26:19). But in Deuteronomy 8:1, God said that to get to this point, the Israelites had to follow His commands. Right now, as far as Israel being top dog, we don't see this tangibly, but we know that Israel's king is going to be the King of everyone, and His name is King Jesus (Romans 11:25–27). This is what is ultimately going to happen when Jesus comes back. The only way this will happen will be when the fullness of the Gentiles turns to the Lord. The Jews will become jealous, and that will usher in the return of the Messiah. Then Israel will be lifted up higher than any other nation.

Eventually the Jews are going to become the light for everyone (Isaiah 49:6). That eventually comes through the Messiah when He ushers in the kingdom, and it comes through the Jewish people. The *Seed* in Genesis will ultimately lead to God's salvation and will be ushered in through Jesus and place Israel above all other nations. This is why the nation of Israel cannot be wiped off the earth because God has a salvation plan that comes through that country and through His people.

*Deuteronomy 28:2–4*: In this verse, all these blessings will come through obedience. We know there is a partial fulfillment of these blessings that will come. According to Joshua 21:45, "None of the good promises the LORD had made to the house of Israel failed. Everything was fulfilled." I said partial because the ushering in of the millennial reign hasn't happened yet. Because they obeyed the law, they would be blessed. Verse 3, basically, is the Beatitudes of the Old Testament. They will be blessed in the city and in the country. Verse 4 states the descendants will be blessed, and everything that they touch will be blessed.

*Deuteronomy 28:6–7*: In verse 5, "the basket and kneading bowl will be blessed." In Deuteronomy 28:17, the curse side of this verse is given. Verse 16 says they will be cursed in the city and the country. This is true over and over again. Verse 18 corresponds to verse 4. This is where the sandwich analogy is best seen—here's the way you can be blessed or here's the way you can be cursed. In verse 6, the blessing will happen in daily life, or, in verse 19, the curse will happen in daily life, depending upon what is chosen. We can't control every decision in our lives, but we can control our decisions of how we respond to those scenarios. In verse 7, enemies who attack one who was blessed will flee in seven different directions.

*Deuteronomy 28:8–10*: In verse 8, the Lord will fill up the storehouses—fill them with abundance—and bless everything the obedient followers will do. In verse 9, God will establish the obedient followers as His holy people—when they choose to be faithful, obey His commands, and walk in His ways. All people of the earth will see the faithful followers and recognize God in their lives (v. 10). Israel becomes a witness to all the other nations. They become the light for everyone else, and in the last days, they become a witnessing nation.

Revelation 7:4–8 records this event, beginning with the words, "And I heard the number of those who were sealed: 144,000 sealed from every tribe of the Israelites," and then in verse 9, "There was a vast multitude from every nation, tribe, people, and language, which no one could number, standing before the throne and before the Lamb." In verse 10 they cried out, "Salvation belongs to our God, who is seated on the throne and to the Lamb!" Guess who initiated this process? The Jewish people who served as a witness in the last days. So, at the end of Deuteronomy, the people were told to be a light, a witness to everyone, because that will carry on to the very end . . . to the last days. Scripture also says that Israel is going to be a witness during the actual time of the ushering in of the kingdom (Zechariah 8:1–12). Jerusalem will be known as the Faithful City and the mountain of the Lord will be known as the Holy Mountain (Zechariah 8:3). The reality is that Jerusalem will become the center hub, the key component of all of the kingdom of God, and everyone will see what God is doing there.

Deuteronomy 28:10 sums it up—people will see that you are called by the Lord God and will stand in awe if you walk out the commands, if you obey what God has called you to do. For me, everything always points to the bigger picture. And it's not about us; it's all about Him.

*Deuteronomy 28:11–14*: The list of blessings continues in verse 11 and includes prosperity with children, livestock, and land. Verse 12 adds the blessing of His abundant storehouse, the sky, and the rains, because God is the one who brings the rains. Interestingly, it states that followers of God will have no need to borrow but will become the bank to the world. In verse 13, followers of God will only move upward, not downward—will be made the leaders—as long as they do not turn to the right or the left, away from Him, or worship other gods (v. 14). One commentator wrote, "Obedience is what builds godly character in people." Verses 1–14 are actually a list of blessings Israel would receive: agricultural, family, financial, and military blessings. In fact, between chapters 27 and 28, there are four times more curses than blessings.

*Deuteronomy 28:15–24*: In verse 15, we see disobedience was cursed. Why would anyone choose curses instead of blessings? In verse 18, disobedience means the children will be cursed. In verse 20, "curses, confusion, and rebuke" are sent against the Israelites in everything they do because of disobedience. And the curses continue throughout the chapter. Do any of these still apply today? Some disobedience and sin can lead to consequences that we bring upon ourselves. The cool part is that Jesus can set us apart from all this.

*Deuteronomy 28:25–68:* In verses 25–26, we see that disobedience can lead to defeat in battle, and corpses will become food for birds. In verse 28, disobedience can lead to mental confusion. All of these become examples of what will happen in the Old Testament (Jeremiah 8:10; Amos 5:11; Zephaniah 1:13). When they stay in the state of disobedience, nothing seems to go right. So, Israel can be a horror or a light to the other nations in the world. In verse 64, God will scatter the people all over the earth. And they will even be taken back to Egypt but will be unwanted (v. 68). But they had a choice . . . to obey or disobey God's commands. In the American church, we're going more and more toward the path that moves away from God. Blessing or curse?

# Closing

Luke 12:48 reminds us that, for believers, "much will be required of everyone who has been given much." We've been entrusted with the gift of life, with the blessing of Jesus. We are God's holy people. We too, as Gentiles, represent God to the world. Do we want the blessings or the curses? We are to advertise His godly virtues.

1 Peter 4:17 states: "For the time has come for judgment to begin with God's household, and it begins with us, what will the outcome be for those who disobey the gospel of God?" We get to choose.

## The Daily Word

The Lord told the Israelites that if they listened to His commands and followed them carefully, He would move them upward and never downward. He said they would always be the head and never the tail. However, for this to happen, the Israelites were instructed to never turn to the right or the left nor worship other gods.

Do things in life on your right or left ever sidetrack you? The Lord longs for you to keep seeking Him. He longs for you to keep walking in relationship with Him. He doesn't want you to live with Jesus plus a few side gods—He wants you to live solely in Jesus and His grace. A relationship with Jesus is enough. He promises to meet all your needs and bless you abundantly along the way.

**The LORD will make you the head and not the tail; you will only move upward and never downward if you listen to the LORD your God's commands I am giving you today and are careful to follow them. Do not turn aside to the right or the left from all the things I am commanding you today, and do not go after other gods to worship them. —Deuteronomy 28:13–14**

Further Scripture: Joshua 1:7; Psalm 24:5–6; Proverbs 4:25–27

## Questions

1. In Deuteronomy 28:1–14, what are the blessings that the Lord gives to His children?

2. In verses 15–68, the Lord tells us what will happen (curses) because of disobedience. Read the following verses: Amos 5:11, Zephaniah 1:13 and Jeremiah 8:10. Does this follow what Deuteronomy 28 says? Are these curses still relevant today?

3.  In Deuteronomy 28:53–57, much suffering is explained. Do you believe that this was a warning for that specific time or a picture of what is to come? Why or why not?

4.  Do you think that all of the blessings and all of the curses came to pass? Why or why not? (Joshua 21:45)

5.  What did the Holy Spirit highlight to you in Deuteronomy 28 through the reading or the teaching?

# Lesson 108: Deuteronomy 29—30
*Prophet:* Choose Life

## Teaching Notes

### Intro

We're almost done with the study of Deuteronomy and talking about how we believe everything in Deuteronomy points to the Messiah. What I've been encouraged by is that many of the students are slowing down in their readings, allowing the Word of God to sink into their hearts. And that's what we're after. That, according to Deuteronomy 30, we're allowing the Holy Spirit to circumcise our hearts. Here's the outline of Deuteronomy 29. The first eight verses are basically a historical review. Deuteronomy contains a lot of repeating information. To make sure they understood everything, Moses repeated the Law to the younger generation who were about to go into the Promised Land. I think we need to do the same kind of thing in the United States—get all the younger people together and walk through the Declaration of Independence and other historical documents, because we don't know them. Moses was possibly internally nervous that the younger generation would forget these laws, so he did the historical review, and then the covenant review (vv. 9–15)—the instructions to gather the stones, to write the laws on a white background, and to make a burnt offering. They were to remember what God had done and walk it out in their lives. Finally, in Deuteronomy 29:16–29, they were given the consequences of disobedience. According to verse 20, the names of the disobedient in the Old Testament will be blotted out.

### Teaching

*Deuteronomy 30:1–3:* Verse 1 says that when the Israelites came to their senses, from wherever they had been driven, after the blessings and the curses, God would restore them back to Himself. Tom Constable states that in these first ten verses is the key of restoration.[14] Restoration can happen when we turn to the Lord, and He will have compassion on the people and gather them back to Himself. Nelson states that "God allowed Moses to foresee Israel's future apostasy and God's dispersal of the people among the nations . . . [and] he also saw Israel's

---

[14] Thomas L. Constable, *Expository Notes of Dr. Thomas Constable: Deuteronomy*, 165, https://planobiblechapel.org/tcon/notes/pdf/deuteronomy.pdf.

future repentance and return to the land," possibly in a future fulfillment.[15] Here was a prophetic word being released. In Acts 3:19–21, the picture of repentance is shown through Peter, who said: "repent and turn back, so your sins may be wiped out, that seasons of refreshing may come from the presence of the Lord, and He may send Jesus, who has been appointed for you as Messiah. Heaven must welcome Him until the times of the restoration of all things, which God spoke about by the mouth of His holy prophets from the beginning." Ultimate restoration will come from Jesus, but it will start when we repent and turn back to Him (v. 19). That period of refreshing comes through Jesus. I believe that there is a partial fulfillment of this, but not all of it. There are some prophets who talk about how the restoration will come by turning back and repenting (Isaiah 54:7–8; Ezekiel 36:33–38; Hosea 14:4–8; Joel 3:16–21).

God is beginning to show our little team our role in these verses. Sixty percent of Israel is in the Negev wilderness, and God is beginning to turn it, little by little, into the Garden of Eden. People will eventually be in awe of what God is rebuilding and restoring, and God has promised to multiply the number of Jews, like a flock. In 1948, modern Israel was established as a nation, and the scattered people are beginning to return. Old City Jerusalem now feels like you're moving through a flock of people. The Jews are already coming back to Jerusalem (Ezekiel 36:33–38). While things may seem desperate, God will heal their apostasy, and the people will return to live under His shade of rest and protection (Hosea 14:4–8). Jerusalem will be the holy city, and foreigners will never again overrun it. Egypt and Edom will become desert wasteland, but Judah will be inhabited forever. The Lord's Presence dwells in Zion and eventually nothing will ever fall again in Jerusalem (Joel 3:16–21).

*Deuteronomy 30:4*: This verse promises that God will bring His people back even from the farthest ends of the world.

The question becomes, what do we do with Israel now? Wiersbe explains the various positions of how the new Israel can be interpreted. Some people believe that the church today has become the new Israel, or the spiritual Israel, and all of God's promises will come through the church. They believe that all Old Testament prophecies and promises are being fulfilled now, through the church. Others say that these prophecies "must be taken at face value," and that "we should expect a fulfillment of them when Jesus Christ returns to establish His kingdom on earth."[16] That means that there is a pause button on some of these prophecies, for Jesus to return. Wiersbe says that "Moses seems to be speaking

---

[15] Earl D. Radmacher, Ronald B. Allen, and H. Wayne House, eds. *Nelson's New Illustrated Bible Commentary* (Nashville: Thomas Nelson, 1999), 264.

[16] Warren W. Wiersbe, *The Bible Exposition Commentary: Genesis–Deuteronomy* (Colorado Springs: David C. Cook, 2001), 445.

here to and about Israel and not some other 'people of God' in the future, such as the church."[17] I think the "people of God" are actually the people of Israel. "The church has no covenant relationship to the land of Israel for God gave that land to Abraham and his descendants (Genesis 15)."[18] God gave this land to Israel, not to us, and all the blessings and the curses were given to Israel, not to us. Much of the promises were conditional of what the people of Israel did or did not do. Why do we feel we have to blend these two worlds together? Why do we think there can be a plan for Israel and a plan for the church?

*Deuteronomy 30:5*: "The LORD your God will bring you into the land your fathers possessed, and you will take possession of it. He will cause you to prosper and multiply you more than He did your fathers." That's not a promise for the church, because we never possessed the land. Israel today does not yet have all the land that was promised to them. The Lord has a plan for His people that will cause them to flourish and multiply. Israel is the apple of God's eye.

*Deuteronomy 30:6–7*: "The LORD your God will circumcise your heart and the hearts of your descendants, and you will love Him with all your heart and all your soul so that you will live." This is a condition: "Therefore, circumcise your hearts and don't be stiff-necked any longer" (Deuteronomy 10:16). "Circumcise yourselves to the LORD; remove the foreskin of your hearts" (Jeremiah 4:4) . . . or God's wrath will break out. We must also circumcise ourselves with the Word of God so our hearts can change, and we will live.

*Deuteronomy 30:8–10*: We are instructed to keep His statutes and "return to Him with all your heart and all your soul." Why not choose life? Why not return to God and let His Word circumcise your life?

*Deuteronomy 30:19–20*: "I call heaven and earth as witnesses against you today that I have set before you life and death, blessing and curse. Choose life so that you and your descendants may live, love the LORD your God, obey Him, and remain faithful to Him. For He is your life, and He will prolong your life in the land the LORD swore to give to your fathers Abraham, Isaac, and Jacob."
  This proves that these verses are not for us. It's important not to make things speak directly to us that weren't meant to.

---

[17] Wiersbe, 445.

[18] Wiersbe, 445.

# Closing

Acts 17:28 says, "For in him, we live and move and exist, as even some of your own poets have said, 'For we are also His offspring.'" Jesus comes to give us life and life abundantly. He does not want to bring us destruction. We get to choose whether we want life or death. Choose life in Him!

## The Daily Word

Moses addressed the Israelites at a final community talk before his death and before they crossed over into the Promised Land. He told the people they had a choice and commanded them to love the Lord their God, to walk in His ways, and to keep His commands. Moses even told them this decision was not difficult or beyond their reach—it was near to them in their mouths and in their hearts. Moses understood he couldn't force the Israelites to make the decision to love the Lord, yet he made one final plea with them to choose life in the Lord God. Like a loving father with his children, Moses desperately longed for the Israelites to walk with God and not turn away to other gods.

As a believer, you made the decision for life in Christ Jesus when you received Him as your Savior. However, you will be tempted to turn and look away from Christ. Today, fix your eyes on Jesus. Remain steadfast and hold on to your faith in Christ without wavering, for the Lord has promised to be faithful.

**This command that I give you today is certainly not too difficult or beyond your reach. . . . But the message is very near you, in your mouth and in your heart, so that you may follow it. —Deuteronomy 30:11, 14**

Further Scripture: 1 Corinthians 15:58; Hebrews 10:23; Hebrews 12:2

## Questions

1. If we remember that the generation of adults which came out of Egypt would not enter the Promised Land (Numbers 14:22–23, 29) due to their unbelief (Hebrews 3:19), then what did Moses mean by his address to the Israelites in Deuteronomy 29:2–3?

2. What do you think Moses meant by a root bearing poisonous fruit or wormwood in Deuteronomy 29:18 (Jeremiah 9:15; Amos 6:12; Hebrews 13:15)?

3. Deuteronomy 30:6 talks about a circumcised heart. What is the purpose and outcome of this circumcision (Romans 2:28–29)? Who will circumcise their hearts?

4. In Romans 10:6–8, the Apostle Paul quotes Deuteronomy 30:12–14. What did Paul mean in Romans 10:8 when he referred to "the word" or "the message" as the word of faith?

5. How many times in Deuteronomy 30 are the Israelites called to love the Lord? How many times are they called to obey Him? Do you think this is significant (John 15:10; 1 John 2:5; 3:24; 2 John 1:6)?

6. What did the Holy Spirit highlight to you in Deuteronomy 29—30 through the reading or the teaching?

# Lesson 109: Deuteronomy 31
*Prophet*: Moses' Song for the People

## Teaching Notes

### Intro

We're only one day away from finishing the study of Deuteronomy and all of Moses' writings in the Pentateuch (Genesis, Exodus, Leviticus, Numbers, and Deuteronomy). The last few days have been a whole lot about blessings and curses. I say, let's just choose *life*, which is really what Deuteronomy 30 was all about. As we dig into Deuteronomy 31, we'll be talking about tangible, practical stories that we can follow. In fact, in the first eight verses, there's a change in leadership—from Moses to Joshua.

### Teaching

*Deuteronomy 31:1–2*: Verse 1 says, "Moses continued to speak these words to all Israel." His sermon continues. In verse 2, Moses stated he was 120 years old, that he was old, and that he couldn't go across the Jordan.

What do we know about Moses' life?

- The first 40 years, Moses spent in Egypt.
- The second 40 years, Moses spent in Midian taking care of sheep and being with his family.
- The last 40 years, Moses spent in the wilderness, leading the Israelites out of Egypt to the Promised Land.
- He died at 120 years, his eyesight was good, and he was full of vitality. His health and ability did not keep him from leading (Deuteronomy 34:7). His sin did.
- Moses' sin prevented him from entering the Promised Land (Deuteronomy 1:37–38).
- Moses begged God to allow him to enter the Promised Land and continue to lead the people.
- God refused and used Moses' sin to bring in new leadership (Deuteronomy 3:23–29).

*Deuteronomy 31:3–6*: Moses explained to the Israelites that Joshua would lead them across the Jordan (v. 3). And God would defeat their enemies just as He did with Sihon and Og, the kings of the Amorites, and turn them over to the Israelites (vv. 4–5). According to Joshua 1:5, God told Joshua, "No one will be able to stand against you as long as you live. I will be with you, just as I was with Moses. I will not leave you or forsake you." That word is still good today. No matter what we're facing—addiction, marriage issues, poor decisions—God will not leave us or forsake us. Therefore, in verse 6, Moses told Joshua: "Be strong and courageous; don't be terrified or afraid of them. For it is the LORD your God who goes with you; He will not leave you or forsake you." "Them" referred to the Israelites. Moses didn't want Joshua to be terrified of the people he was to lead or be afraid that Moses was not going to be there. Instead, Moses wanted Joshua to depend upon God. In Joshua 1, God commanded Joshua and the people to be strong and courageous three times (vv. 6–7, 9). Louis B. Smeedes says, "Courage is only fear soaked in prayer."[1] The only way we can walk out in courage is to pray and ask God to help us to overcome our fears as we go into a new land, because God is with us.

The people of Israel were commanded to go into the Promised Land. Matthew 28:18–20 says we've been commissioned by Jesus who has all authority, to go into all kinds of lands, local neighborhoods, big cities, and foreign countries, and baptize them in the name of the Father, the Son, and the Holy Spirit. As we do this, we're commissioned to teach and make disciples. No matter where we go, God will be there and never leave us. The phrase "end of the age" means until Jesus comes back; He'll be with us forever. When fear gets in the way, none of this works.

*Deuteronomy 31:7–8*: Moses summoned Joshua in front of all the Israelites and told him he would lead the people into the Promised Land (v. 7). Walter Lippmann says, "The final test of a leader is that he leaves behind him in other men the conviction and the will to carry on."[2] Moses had Joshua to lead after him. This is clearly a biblical model of godly leadership. Think about Jesus and the apostles. He had 12 men He poured into. What should be an encouragement to us is that one of the 12 bailed on Him. He had three whom He really poured into and some who doubted. It wasn't a perfect group. The Apostle Paul poured into Timothy and Titus. What happened in Joshua's case is that Moses stood before

---

[1] Louis B. Smedes, "An Introduction to Mission Beyond the Mission," *Theology, News, and Notes* 30:3 (October 1983), 3; quoted in Thomas L. Constable, *Expository Notes of Dr. Thomas Constable: Deuteronomy*, 171, https://planobiblechapel.org/tcon/notes/pdf/deuteronomy.pdf.

[2] Walter Lippman, Quotes, Britannica, https://www.britannica.com/quotes/biography/Walter-Lippmann.

the people and told them he was trusting Joshua with more. It was a transfer of leadership. Wiersbe says that when there is no leadership change, it's evidence of God's judgment on His people[3] (Deuteronomy 1:38; 31:14; 32:51–52; Isaiah 3:1–4). When a transfer God puts in place doesn't work, it is because of instability caused by disobedience. Joshua was ready and prepared to take over, and God's hand was upon Him. Joshua came with Moses before the people and recited all the words of Moses' song. This shows that Moses was willing to relinquish his authority to Joshua, so that Joshua could take over.

*Deuteronomy 31:9–13*: As leadership changed from Moses to Joshua, Moses instructed the priests to read the law every seven years before all the people assembled, adults and children alike. Regardless of who was in charge, the Word of God always takes precedence over anyone else. The law, the Word of God, had to remain the foundation. This must go wherever the Israelites went.

*Deuteronomy 31:14–15*: As Moses' time grew short, God told him to bring Joshua in to be commissioned. And the Lord personally showed up in a pillar of cloud at the entrance to the tent. God had shown up for Moses, and now He was showing up for Joshua's commissioning, so the people could see that God was with Joshua.

*Deuteronomy 31:16–23*: God told Moses he was about to die and that the people would be disobedient and unfaithful (v.16). God said He would grow angry with them and abandon them, and they would face troubles and afflictions. One day they would realize the troubles had come because God abandoned them (v. 17). Therefore, Moses was to write a song he could teach to the Israelites so it could be a witness about God (v.19). Moses wrote the song that day and taught it to the Israelites (v. 22). And Joshua was commissioned (v.23).

*Deuteronomy 31:24–29*: The preservation of God's word came through the song Moses wrote down. Because verse 24 states, "When Moses had finished writing down on a scroll every single word of this law," some people think this song was actually the entire Pentateuch. Moses was instructed to place the song beside the Ark of the Covenant as a witness against the Israelites (v. 26). Sadly, when Moses left them, the Israelites were obedient, but they would turn to apostasy just as God said they would (v.29).

---

[3] Warren W. Wiersbe, *The Bible Exposition Commentary: Genesis–Deuteronomy* (Colorado Springs: David C. Cook, 2001), 447.

## Closing

Moses ended his time of leadership with this song, a written legacy that would tell the Israelites of their own sins. Knowing what was to happen couldn't have been easy for Moses, but he did as God commanded, ending his time of leadership by remaining faithful and obedient to God.

## The Daily Word

As Moses began the change of command and commissioning of Joshua as the next leader, he repeated these powerful words of encouragement three times: "Be strong and courageous; don't be terrified or afraid of them. For it is the Lord your God who goes with you; He will not leave you or forsake you."

Moses and Joshua anticipated the change in their lives as they looked ahead. You too will have times of change in your life when you will face an uncertain future, and you will have a choice. You can walk with fear and trembling or you can be strong and courageous, trusting the Lord is with you and will not leave you.

Whatever you face today, may you feel strengthened by the Lord who is with you, empowering you to walk with courage. The Lord is with you and will help you face whatever the future holds. You can do this!

**Be strong and courageous; don't be terrified or afraid of them. For it is the LORD your God who goes with you; He will not leave you or forsake you. — Deuteronomy 31:6**

Further Scripture: Isaiah 43:2; Jeremiah 29:11; Psalm 32:8

## Questions

1. Who would cross the Jordan ahead of the Israelites to destroy these nations before them (Deuteronomy 31:3)? How does this symbolize Christ crossing ahead of us to destroy our enemies (John 14:3; Colossians 2:15; 1 John 3:8b)? Did you know (and do you think it's significant) that the name Joshua is a derivative of Yeshua?

2. In verses three, six and eight of Deuteronomy 31, Moses informed the Israelites that the Lord would go before them, and ahead of them, and not to be afraid. Do you struggle with fear in some area? Do you believe the Lord will not fail you or forsake you (Matthew 28:20b; Hebrews 13:5–6)?

3. What did Moses command the priests and elders of Israel to do in Deuteronomy 31:9–13? Why was this important?

4.  The Lord informed Moses that the Israelites would forsake Him and break His covenant; even with all the warnings of curses they would suffer as a result, they would reject Him. Why do you think the Israelites could not remain faithful to the Lord? Do you see this same propensity in believers today? How about in yourself?

5.  What did the Holy Spirit highlight to you in Deuteronomy 31 through the reading or the teaching?

# Lesson 110: Deuteronomy 32—34
*Prophet*: Give Back to the Jews

## Teaching Notes

### Intro

In this final lesson of Deuteronomy, I'm going to start in Deuteronomy 31:30 to give a backdrop of where we're headed. I'll give a complete summary of the whole teaching, and then focus on one text.

### Teaching

*Deuteronomy 31:30*: In verse 30, Moses was told to write a song, and he recited every word of the song to the entire assembly of Israel—about 2 million people. Moses also had another song in Exodus 15:1–18, which he wrote as a tribute for being rescued at the Red Sea, and in Numbers 21, the Israelites had sung as though they were given life-giving wells. This was Moses' funeral song, which he sung just before his death. Deborah and Barak, in Judges 5, sang a victory song after the Israelites defeated the Canaanites. The Israelite women, in 1 Samuel 18:6–7, sang a song to celebrate David's defeat of Goliath. Most of these songs were about life-giving victories they won. The Levites in 2 Chronicles 29:30 sang a song of praise and dedication for the Jerusalem Temple. Moses' song in this chapter was about Israel as a rebellious people.

*Deuteronomy 32:1–14*: God is steadfast, but no one else, especially the Israelites, were steadfast. Wiersbe says that Moses began to identify the character of God in this process.[1] Verse 4 describes God as "The Rock—His work is perfect; all His ways are entirely just. A faithful God, without prejudice, He is righteous and true." Then God's election of Israel is presented—God had a plan for Israel (vv. 8–9). Moses' song began by reminding them of God's care for them in the wilderness. God had protected them. Moses reminded them that the blessings of God were found in the land He promised them (vv. 13–14).

---

[1] Warren W. Wiersbe, *The Bible Exposition Commentary: Genesis–Deuteronomy* (Colorado Springs: David C. Cook, 2001), 449.

*Deuteronomy 32:15–21*: But in verse 15, Moses presented the neglect of God's goodness: "Then Jeshurun became fat and rebelled . . . and scorned the Rock of his salvation." "Jeshurun" is another name for Israel, and I believe the words at the end of the verse are prophetic, pointing to how the Jews would reject the Cornerstone in the New Testament. If the Israelites stayed in this position, they would reject everything God brought before them. The Israelites moved so far away from God that they even sacrificed to demons (v. 17). They were giving in to demonic worship and fallen angels. In response, God had an outpouring of His wrath and even hid His face from them (v. 20). They provoked God's jealousy with unknown gods (v. 21), so He said He would "provoke their jealousy with an inferior people; I will enrage them with a foolish nation." This is the verse we'll camp out on after the summary.

*Deuteronomy 32:28–52*: Israel showed blind stubbornness against what God had commanded (vv. 28–33), so God stripped Israel of their power (vv. 34–38). When God says He will lift His hand to "heaven and declare: As surely as I live forever, when I sharpen My flashing sword" (v. 40–42), we're given a beautiful picture of the flashing sword of Christ in Revelation. In verse 43, the nations can rejoice, because God heals—"He will purify His land and His people." Moses' song became a warning (v. 46), so the people should heed the warning. Then God told Moses to go up Mount Nebo where he would die for his own unfaithfulness. Moses would be able to look over the land of Canaan, although he would never enter it (vv.48–52).

*Deuteronomy 33*: In verses 1–5, Moses gave an overall blessing over the Israelites, and then beginning in verse 6, Moses gave a blessing to the tribes of Reuben, Judah, Levi, Benjamin, Joseph, Zebulun, Gad, Dan, Naphtali, and Asher. In verses 26–29, he instructed the Israelites to consider God in all this.

*Deuteronomy 34*: Moses was given a view of the Promised Land (vv. 1–4), and in verses 5–8, Moses died and the whole country mourned. Verses 9–12 record that Joshua was given much wisdom, but that there was no other name like Moses ever again. This was the end of the era of Moses and leadership was transferred to Joshua.

Now, back to Deuteronomy 32:21, Moses served as a prophet who pointed to another *Prophet*—Jesus. That's the story of Deuteronomy. God warned the Israelites that if they continued with their rebellion, He would be so jealous that He would use a foolish nation to make the Israelites (Jews) jealous. The group God was talking about to make the Jews jealous is us— the non-Jews, the Gentiles.

Here's why studying the Pentateuch is so important. We as believers need to know more about the Word of God than the Jews do. Why? I want them to want what we have in Christ. The entire first five books of the Bible ultimately point to Jesus . . . with the *Seed*, the *Deliverer*, the *Atonement*, the *Rock*, and the *Prophet*. These five words all point to Jesus.

The Jews are still God's chosen people. "For you are a holy people belonging to the LORD your God. The LORD your God has chosen you to be His own possession out of all the peoples on the face of the earth. The LORD was devoted to you and chose you, not because you were more numerous than all peoples, for you were the fewest of all peoples. But because the LORD loved you and kept the oath He swore to your fathers, He brought you out with a strong hand and redeemed you from the place of slavery, from the power of Pharaoh king of Egypt" (Deuteronomy 7:6–8). The Jews were God's chosen people.

Romans 1:16: "For I am not ashamed of the gospel, because it is God's power for salvation to everyone who believes, first to the Jew, and also to the Greek." The word "first" means the gospel was meant for the Jews. But through their rejection of the gospel (New Covenant), salvation came to the Gentiles. Studying the Israelites through the Pentateuch makes their rejection of Jesus Christ make sense.

Romans 11:11: "I ask, then, have they stumbled in order to fall? Absolutely not! On the contrary, by their stumbling, salvation has come to the Gentiles to make Israel jealous." Because of their stubbornness, salvation came to the Gentiles instead. Deuteronomy 32:21 prophesied this moment, when the gospel came to the Gentiles to make the Jews angry. There's a remnant of Jews who place their trust in Yeshua as their Christ. All of what happened in Deuteronomy led to salvation coming to the Gentiles. God has not rejected the Jews; He still has a plan for His chosen people.

Romans 10:19–20: "But I ask, 'Did Israel not understand?' First, Moses said: I will make you jealous of those who are not a nation; I will make you angry by a nation that lacks understanding. And Isaiah says boldly: I was found by those who were not looking for Me; I revealed Myself to those who were not asking for Me." The Gentiles weren't seeking God, but God chose to give them salvation to make the Jews jealous. For the Jews who turn to Jesus after becoming jealous, the veil is lifted and they will be regrafted into the vine, and they will bring riches into the world. Romans 11:12: "Now if their stumbling brings riches for the world, and their failure riches for the Gentiles, how much more will their full number bring!"

Romans 11:24: "For if you were cut off from your native wild olive and against nature were grafted into a cultivated olive tree, how much more will these—the natural branches—be grafted into their own olive tree?" God had intended for the Jews to accept salvation because of the fall of man and wanted to bring them back into His family. When are the Jews going to get this? As we say yes to Jesus, the Jews will want what we have. Are we living in Christ in a way that will make them jealous? We have to be different and set apart for them to see what we have. And we must be thankful for the spiritual blessing we have received since the Jews rejected it. We need to pour back into God's chosen people, the Jews. It started with God's chosen people, and it will end with God's chosen people.

Romans 15:27: "Yes, they were pleased, and indeed are indebted to them. For if the Gentiles have shared in their spiritual benefits, then they are obligated to minister to Jews in material needs." As Gentiles, we are obligated to minister to the Jews physically and tangibly with what they need.

## Closing

We are the beneficiaries of the stubbornness of the Jews and of what they went through in rebellion against God. It's our job to minister and give back to them in any way we can.

## The Daily Word

Before Moses died in the land of Moab at the age of 120, he sang a final song and stated a final blessing over the Israelites. His words were full of memories and truth about the good times, the hard times, and the days ahead Moses knew were coming for the people. The Israelites were a chosen group, saved and protected by the Lord, to bear witness of the Lord's mighty power. Moses was a man of God, a prophet like no other, who saw God face-to-face and was God's chosen leader of His people. Even though Moses foretold how the Israelites would respond to God in the days ahead, there was still a sense of "now what?" in his words. How would the Israelites really walk with God after Moses died? They had every reason to follow the Lord with all their hearts, souls, and minds. But what would they decide?

As believers, the same is true for you. How will you choose to spend today? Will you follow the Lord with all your heart? Will you walk in His ways? Will you remember His faithfulness from yesterday? Or will you make the choice to turn away and seek your own interest? Today, choose to believe the Lord loves you unconditionally and longs for you to love Him with all your heart. As you receive the truth of His love, you will have strength to walk firmly in His ways and love others.

**How happy you are, Israel! Who is like you, a people saved by the LORD? He is the shield that protects you, the sword you boast in. Your enemies will cringe before you, and you will tread on their backs. —Deuteronomy 33:29**

Further Scripture: Psalm 28:7; Psalm 143:8; Romans 16:25–27

## Questions

1. One of the ways that Israel passed down their history was through songs. God instructed Moses to help the people of Israel learn the song in Deuteronomy 32:1–43. What part of this song speaks to you the most? Praise the Lord right now with one of your favorite hymns or worship songs.

2. Who was Moses asking to listen as he began the song (Deuteronomy 32:1)? What did Moses then turn his attention to and praise the Lord for (Deuteronomy 32:3–4)?

3. Name some things that the Israelites did that provoked God's anger (Deuteronomy 32:15–19; Judges 10:6)? What was the penalty of their disobedience? What was God trying to teach them about Himself?

4. Moses blessed each tribe in Deuteronomy 33 except one. Which tribe was not mentioned (Genesis 49:5–7)? Why do you think that the tribe of Levi was blessed (Deuteronomy 33:8–11) even though they participated in the acts mentioned in the curse from Jacob (Malachi 2:5)?

5. Moses represented the law and couldn't go into the Promised Land. What was the law's intended purpose (Romans 3:19–20; Galatians 3:24)? How does Joshua symbolize Jesus (John 14:6)?

6. What did the Holy Spirit highlight to you in Deuteronomy 32—34 through the reading or the teaching?

# Contributing Authors

### Dr. Kyle Lance Martin

Kyle Lance Martin is the founder of Time to Revive, a ministry based in Dallas, Texas, whose mission is to equip the saints for the return of Christ. His heart's desire, aside from loving his wife and four kids, is to engage people with the Word of God directly in their own environment. Kyle believes when people turn to the Messiah in humility and have a willingness to walk in the Holy Spirit, they can know and experience the calling of being a disciple of Jesus Christ. Kyle received his master of biblical studies from Dallas Theological Seminary and his doctor of ministry in outreach and discipleship from Gordon-Conwell Theological Seminary.

### Laura Kim Martin

Laura Kim Martin lives in Dallas, Texas, with her husband, Kyle Lance Martin, and their four children. Together they founded the ministry Time to Revive to equip the saints for the return of Christ. Through years of trusting the Lord's faithfulness, she passionately encourages others to press on in their faith journeys.

### Pastor Gordon Henke

Gordon Henke is a pastor from northern Indiana, serving the church for 25 years. His passion is the studying of the Word. With confidence in the truth of the Word, he passionately helps people boldly share their faith.

### Pastor Tom Schiefer

Tom Schiefer is the senior pastor of Nappanee First Brethren Church in Nappanee, Indiana. Prior to accepting a call to pastoral ministry, he was a band and choir director in Ohio. In the context of these two careers, he loves to orchestrate the Word of God, and the message it contains, into harmony with people's lives.

### Pastor Fred Stayton

Fred Stayton is the lead pastor of Sonrise Church in Fort Wayne, Indiana, and has a passion for turning the hearts of fathers back to their children. Fred and his wife, Cheryl, have six children and one grandchild.

## Ryan Schrag

Ryan Schrag is the national director for Time to Revive and has a heart to "equip the saints for the return of Christ" in the United States. Prior to joining full-time ministry, he was formerly the owner/operator of a lawn care business.

## Wesley Morris

Wesley Morris is the Georgia state chairman for Time to Revive. A former construction worker turned pastor, he now trains and equips people to encounter Jesus and boldly share their faith.

## Josh Edwards

Josh Edwards is the Minnesota state chairman for Time to Revive and leads worship both nationally and internationally. For the past 20 years he has been leading worship and speaking to the body of Christ about his heart's desire to see the church united, revived, and equipped to do the work of the ministry.

## Shawn Carlson

Shawn Carlson is the executive director for Time to Revive. He has a strong desire to see people grow closer to Jesus through the study of God's Word and the carrying out of His mission.

## Matt Reynolds

Matt Reynolds is the president of Spirit & Truth, a ministry aimed at equipping believers and churches to be more empowered by the Spirit, rooted in the truth, and mobilized for the mission. After serving as a local pastor for 13 years, Matt responded to a missionary calling to pursue Spirit-filled renewal in the church.

## Larry Hopkins

Larry Hopkins is a businessman and entrepreneur in Dallas, Texas, who loves studying and discussing God's Word. He has a heart for revival, which stems from his love and desire for the Bible.

## Pastor Kyle Felke

Kyle Felke is a former pastor in northern Indiana. He grew up in a home where both parents were teachers, which instilled in him a passion for teaching. This, combined with a love for Jesus, led him to pursue a biblical education and pastor a church in northern Indiana.

# Contributing Authors

*The Pentateuch*
Kyle Lance Martin
Laura Kim Martin

*The Gospels*
Kyle Lance Martin
Laura Kim Martin
Josh Edwards
Ryan Schrag
Matt Reynolds

*The Historical Books*
Kyle Lance Martin
Laura Kim Martin
Wesley Morris
Josh Edwards
Pastor Gordon Henke
Pastor Tom Schiefer
Pastor Kyle Felke
Larry Hopkins

*Acts*
Kyle Lance Martin
Laura Kim Martin
Pastor Gordon Henke
Pastor Tom Schiefer
Wesley Morris
Shawn Carlson

*The Wisdom Books*
Kyle Lance Martin
Laura Kim Martin
Pastor Gordon Henke
Pastor Tom Schiefer
Wesley Morris
Ryan Schrag
Pastor Fred Stayton
Shawn Carlson
Josh Edwards

*Paul's Letters*
Kyle Lance Martin
Laura Kim Martin
Pastor Gordon Henke
Pastor Tom Schiefer
Wesley Morris
Shawn Carlson
Josh Edwards
Ryan Schrag

*The Major Prophets*
Kyle Lance Martin
Laura Kim Martin
Pastor Gordon Henke
Pastor Tom Schiefer
Pastor Fred Stayton
Ryan Schrag
Josh Edwards

*General Letters*
Kyle Lance Martin
Laura Kim Martin
Pastor Fred Stayton
Shawn Carlson

*The Minor Prophets*
Kyle Lance Martin
Laura Kim Martin
Josh Edwards

*Revelation*
Kyle Lance Martin
Laura Kim Martin
Pastor Gordon Henke
Pastor Tom Schiefer

Made in the USA
Monee, IL
14 October 2022

97c388b0-43d9-4a00-9658-4385ca5d1384R01